宁波
统计年鉴

Ningbo Statistical YearBook

宁波市统计局　国家统计局宁波调查队编
NINGBO MUNICIPAL STATISTICS BUREAU　STATE STATISTICAL BUREAU NINGBO INVESTIGATION TEAM

2013

中国统计出版社
China Statistics Press

图书在版编目(CIP)数据

宁波统计年鉴. 2013 / 宁波市统计局, 国家统计局
宁波调查队编. -- 北京 : 中国统计出版社, 2013.7
ISBN 978-7-5037-6852-1

Ⅰ. ①宁… Ⅱ. ①宁… ②国… Ⅲ. ①统计资料-宁
波市-2013-年鉴 Ⅳ. ①C832.553-54

中国版本图书馆 CIP 数据核字(2013)第 160407 号

宁波统计年鉴 -2013

作　　者/宁波市统计局　国家统计局宁波调查队
责任编辑/陈越月　徐霞欢　朱　惠
装帧设计/李　鹏
出版发行/中国统计出版社
通信地址/北京市西城区月坛南街 75 号　　　邮政编码/　100826
办公地址/北京市丰台区西三环南路甲 6 号　　邮政编码/　100073
电　　话/邮购(010)63376909　书店(010)68783171
网　　址/http://csp.stats.gov.cn
印　　刷/宁波市鄞州荣升印刷厂
经　　销/新华书店
开　　本/880mm×1230mm　1/16
字　　数/1013 千字
印　　张/29.60
版　　别/2013 年 7 月第 1 版
版　　次/2013 年 7 月第 1 次印刷
定　　价/328.00 元

本书附同版本 CD-ROM 一张，光盘内容以书面文字为准。

如有印装差错，由本社发行部调换。

2013 NING BO Statistical YearBook 宁波统计年鉴

编者说明

一、《宁波统计年鉴—2013》以大量统计数据，全面、系统地反映了2012年宁波经济、科技、社会各方面的发展情况，是一本信息密集的资料性年刊和工具书。本年鉴采用中英文排版方式。

二、《宁波统计年鉴—2013》在内容编排顺序上做了调整，本年鉴内容包括：

1.2012年宁波市国民经济和社会发展概况；2.综合；3.人口与劳动力；4.国民经济核算；5.财政、金融、保险、证券；6.物价指数、人民生活；7.农业；8.工业、能源消费和电力；9.固定资产投资和建筑业；10.港口、交通运输、邮电业；11.国内贸易、餐饮业；12.对外经济、旅游；13.文化、教育、卫生、体育、科学；14.市政、环保、民政、政法及其他；15.企业景气等十五个部分组成。为方便读者使用，各篇章前设有《主要统计指标》，篇末附有《主要统计指标解释》。

三、《宁波统计年鉴—2013》辑入的统计数据，以2012年年报为主，考虑到读者使用，年鉴中还列示了1978年改革开放以来历年的主要统计数据，这些统计数据已重新予以核实，凡以往发表过的统计数据与本年鉴有出入的，均以本年鉴为准。

四、《宁波统计年鉴—2013》在编辑中作如下规定，以使读者在使用时明了：

1、凡有注解均注在第一张表的下方。

2、“?”示之，表示有数据但不足计量单位中的最小数，故不再列数；凡在表内显示“空格”的，表示该项统计数据不详或无该项统计数据；显示“#”表示其中的主要项。

五、《宁波统计年鉴—2013》辑入的统计数据，对来自非政府统计部门的，注明数据来源。

六、《宁波统计年鉴》出版以来，受到社会各界的关心、支持，不少读者对于年鉴的内容和编辑工作提出了许多宝贵的意见，对此，我们深表感谢。并欢迎读者一如既往地对年鉴的不足之处给予批评指正，以进一步提高编辑水平。

2013 NING BO Statistical YearBook 宁波统计年鉴

EDITOR'S NOTE

I. Ningbo Statistical Yearbook 2013 is an annual publication which provides comprehensive and systematic data covering the economic, technological and social development in Ningbo Municipality in 2012. This yearbook uses the Chinese and English mix typesetting the way.

II. This yearbook has made the adjustment in the content arrangement order. This yearbook is comprised of 15 parts including: 1.Brief Introduction of 2012 Ningbo National Economy and Social Development; 2.General Survey; 3.Population and labor force; 4.National Economic Accounting; 5.Finance, Banking, Insurance and Securities; 6.Price Index and People´s Livelihood; 7.Agriculture; 8.Industry, Energy Consumption and Electricity; 9.Investment in Fixed Assets and Construction; 10.Port, Transportation, Post and Telecommunication; 11.Domestic Trade and Catering Trade; 12.Foreign Trade and Tourism; 13. Education, Culture, Public Health and Sports, Science and Technology; 14.Civil Facilities, Environmental Protection, Civil Affairs, Judicature and Others; 15.Prosperity Index on Enterprises. Major statistical indicators at the beginning of each chapter, Explanatory Notes on Main Statistical Indicators are provided at the end of each chapter.

III. The content of this yearbook are comprised of mainly the statistic of 2012 and statistical data of those key years after reform and opening to the outside world. The data in this yearbook have been already checked. If ever the readers find inconsistency of data here as compared with those in previous year books, please refer to this yearbook as accurate and final.

IV. This yearbook makes following stipulation in the edition, causes the reader to use is clear about. The footnotes are placed at the first page. Explanations on symbols used in this yearbook: "…"indicates that the data are not large enough to be rounded into the minimal unit; "space" indicates that the data is unknown or indicates the data not available; "#" indicates major item in a category.

V. In this yearbook, to come from the non- statistical department´s statistical data, dedicates the data origin.

VI. Here we´d like to express our sincere thanks to the readers who have provided us so many invaluable suggestions on content selection and compilation of the yearbook. Our thanks also go to those friends in all circles of society who have shown their support and care to the publication of the yearbook. We welcome any suggestions and comments from readers at large so as to help us to further improve our work of compilation.

目 录
CONTENTS

第一篇 综合 CHAPTER 1 GENERAL SURVEY

第二篇 人口与劳动力 CHAPTER 2 POPULATION AND LABOR FORCE

第三篇 国民经济核算 CHAPTER 3 NATIONAL ECONOMIC ACCOUNTING

第四篇 财政、金融、保险、证券 CHAPTER 4 FINANCE,BANKING,INSURANCE AND SECURITIES

第五篇 物价指数和人民生活 CHAPTER 5 PRICES INDEX AND PEOPLE'S LIVELIHOOD

第六篇 农 业 CHAPTER 6 AGRICULTURE

第七篇 工业、能源消费和电力 CHAPTER 7 INDUSTRY, ENERGY CONSUMPTION AND ELECTRICITY

第八篇 固定资产投资和建筑业 CHAPTER 8 INVESTMENT IN FIXED ASSETS AND CONSTRUCTION

第九篇 港口、交通、运输、邮电 CHAPTER 9 PORT,TRANSPORTATION, POST AND TELECOMMUNICATION SERVICE

第十篇 国内贸易、餐饮业 CHAPTER 10 DOMESTIC TRADE AND CATERING TRADE

第十一篇 对外经济、旅游 CHAPTER 11 FOREIGN TRADE AND TOURISM

第十二篇 文化、教育、卫生、体育、科学技术 CHAPTER 12 CULTURE,EDUCATION, PUBLIC HEALTH AND SPORTS,SCIENCE & TECHNOLOGY

第十三篇 市政、环保、民政、政法及其他 CHAPTER 13 CIVIL FACILITIES,ENVIRONMENT, CIVIL AFFAIRS,JUDICATURE AND OTHERS

第十四篇 企业景气指数 CHAPTER 14 PROSPERITY INDEX ON ENTERPRISES

2012年宁波市国民经济和社会发展统计公报

宁波市统计局　国家统计局宁波调查队

2013年2月4日

2012年，面对国内外复杂多变的宏观经济形势，全市上下克难攻坚，深入实施“六个加快”战略，牢牢把握“稳中求进，进中求好”的总基调，有效落实稳增长、调结构、惠民生各项政策措施，经济运行稳中缓升，质量效益逐步提升，创新转型有效推进，民生保障持续加大，人民生活不断改善，在建设现代化国际港口城市的征程上迈出了坚实的步伐。

一、综 合

地区生产总值。2012年全市实现地区生产总值6524.7亿元，按可比价格计算，比上年增长7.8%。其中，第一产业实现增加值270.0亿元，增长1.6%；第二产业实现增加值3516.7亿元，增长6.0%；第三产业实现增加值2738.0亿元，增长10.9%。三次产业之比为4.1∶53.9∶42.0，第三产业增加值占地区生产总值比重比上年提高1.5个百分点。按常住人口计算人均生产总值为85475元(按年平均汇率折算为13541美元)。

财政收支。2012年全市完成公共财政预算收入1536.5亿元，比上年增长7.3%，其中地方财政收入完成725.5亿元，增长10.3%，增速比上年分别下降14.9和13.5个百分点。在地方税收中，营业税、增值税、企业所得税、个人所得税分别增长20.3%、11.3%、6.7%和-6.9%。全市完成公共财政预算支出828.4亿元，增长10.4%，增速同比下降14.6个百分点。财政支出继续向民生领域倾斜，全市财政用于民生支出548.5亿元，增长13.5%，增速快于公共财政预算支出3.1个百分点，占财政支出的比重为66.2%，同比提高1.8个百分点，其中社会保障和就业支出79.0亿元，增长34.8%，增速最快；教育支出141.7亿元，占民生支出比重最高，达25.8%，增长20.4%，增速居第三位。

就业和再就业。2012年全市新增城镇就业岗位15.2万个，比上年增长2.7%，7.3万名城镇失业人员实现再就业，其中困难人员再就业2.4万人，分别增长17.4%和30.5%。全年人力资源市场提供岗位196.9万个，求职登记数109.1万人次。组织农村劳动力培训3.8万人。年末城镇登记失业率为2.55%，处于历史低位水平。

市场价格。2012年居民消费价格指数为101.7%，比上年回落3.6个百分点，比全国、全省平均水平分别低0.9和0.5个百分点，在全国36个大中城市中居末位。八大类商品和服务项目价格同比涨跌格局为“六升二降”：食品类上涨5.2%，家庭设备用品及维修服务类上涨3.3%，烟酒类上涨2.4%，居住类上涨2.1%，衣着类上涨1.7%，医疗保健和个人用品类上涨1.1%；娱乐教育文化用品及服务类下降5.0%，交通和通信类下降0.4%。全年工业生产者购进价格和出厂价格指数均为97.1%，工业品价格“进出倒挂”得以扭转。12月全市新建商品住宅销售价格同比下降7.4%，降幅居全国70个大中城市中第三位。

2012年宁波主要价格分月变化趋势

二、农业、农村

农业生产。2012年全市实现农林牧渔业总产值420.5亿元，按可比价格计算，比上年增长1.9%。其中，农业200.0亿元，下降0.3%；林业11.4亿元，下降2.4%；畜牧业65.9亿元，增长4.9%；渔业137.5亿元，增长3.7%；农林牧渔服务业5.7亿元，增长8.4%。受天气影响，粮食产量有所下降，全年粮食总产量85.7万吨，下降4.9%。席草、葡萄、杨梅等经济作物产量增长较快，分别增长15.3%、7.2%和16.0%；生猪生产平稳，完成猪肉产量15.7万吨，增长5.9%。全年新增市级农业龙头企业20家，累计已达273家，其中产值(销售额)上亿元的达91家，年末市级龙头企业已获国家农产品名牌13件、浙江省名牌65件。

新农村建设。2012 年全市共投入"百千工程"资金 11 亿元，其中各级财政投入 4.2 亿元。累计 2411 个村启动村庄整治建设，占全部行政村的 93%；建设生活污水生态处理设施村 132 个。新增全面小康村 45 个，累计达 479 个。全年在 70 个欠发达村实施村庄整治，共投入各类资金 3 亿多元，实施建设项目 836 个，拆除危旧房 31.6 万平方米，外立面改造 125.6 万平方米，村内道路硬化 36.5 万平方米，村庄绿化 25.1 万平方米，村内河道整治 4.4 万平方米。全年完成农村住房"两改"建设投资 194 亿元，开工改造建设农村住房 9.5 万户，已完工 4.6 万户，面积 633 万平方米，四年来全市累计投入农房建设项目资金 600 亿元，完成农房改造建设面积 2500 万平方米。乡村旅游快速发展，全年新增市级农家乐特色村 3 个，累计达 35 个，新增农家乐休闲旅游示范点 15 个，累计达 91 个，全年共接待游客 1719 万人次，实现营业收入 17.2 亿元，比上年分别增长 44.2%和 51.4%，解决农民就业 4.3 万人。

三、工业、建筑业

工业经济。2012 年全市实现全部工业总产值 15843.9 亿元，比上年增长 2.7%。其中规模以上工业企业实现总产值 11962.1 亿元，增长 1.3%，占全部工业总产值的比重达 77.1%。规模以上工业中产值前十位的行业共完成总产值 8710.6 亿元，占全部规模以上工业总产值的比重达 72.8%，同比提高 0.2 个百分点。其中，石油加工、炼焦及核燃料加工业完成总产值 1568.6 亿元，产值居各行业之首；汽车制造业增长 16.8%，增速居前十位行业之首。全年规模以上轻工业完成总产值 3419.3 亿元，增长 4.5%；重工业 8542.8 亿元，与上年持平。轻重工业之比由上年的 1 : 2.6 变化为 1 : 2.5。全年规模以上工业企业实现增加值 2132.5 亿元，增长 5.0%；实现利润 520.3 亿元，下降 15.2%，实现利税总额 1057.5 亿元，下降 8.3%。

工业创新转型。2012 年规模以上工业企业科技活动经费支出 156.5 亿元，比上年增长 12.5%，占主营业务收入的比重达到 1.4%，同比提高 0.2 个百分点；实现新产品产值 2415.0 亿元，增长 10.4%，快于规模以上工业总产值增速 9.1 个百分点，新产品产值率达 20.2%，同比提高 1.7 个百分点，创历史新高；规模以上高新技术产业实现工业总产值 3431.0 亿元，增长 4.0%，快于规模以上工业平均增速 2.7 个百分点。

建筑业。2012 年全市完成建筑业产值 2510.5 亿元，比上年增长 29.9%，增速位居全省第一，高出全省平均水平 14.8 个百分点。全年房屋建筑施工面积 22572.3 万平米，竣工面积 6047.8 万平米。

四、固定资产投资、城市建设

固定资产投资。2012 年全市完成固定资产投资 2901.4 亿元，比上年增长 21.6%，增速快于上年 4.0 个百分点。其中，民间投资完成 1306.8 亿元，增长 13.9%；基础设施投资完成 850.1 亿元，增长 21.9%；房地产开发投资完成 884.4 亿元，增长 17.1%。分产业看，第一产业投资完成 10.9 亿元，下降 40.5%；第二产业投资完成 822.2 亿元，增长 22.2%；第三产业投资完成 2068.3 亿元，增长 22.1%。全年工业投资完成 817.2 亿元，增长 22.3%，快于固定资产投资增速 0.7 个百分点，扭转了多年低位徘徊的局面。符合转型升级方向的项目投资领先增长，全年医药制造、汽车制造等行业工业投资分别增长 119.6%和 94.9%。

现代都市建设。中心城区功能提升渐显成效，东部新城、南部商务区、铁路宁波站(南站)综合客运枢纽等 33 个区块完成投资 871 亿元。城乡环境更新改造稳步实施，"三江六岸"滨江休闲带工程总体方案基本完成，启动段(姚江大桥到解放桥)基本建成；完成 22 个老小区整治，建筑面积 108 万平方米，投资 8133 万元；完成背街小巷综合整治 42 条，全年道路完好率达 90%以上，路灯亮灯率保持在 98%以上；实施中心城区道路清爽行动，市区两级落实保洁经费及配套资金 3.6 亿元，1195 条道路实现常态保洁，机扫率从 36.9%提高到 75.0%。综合交通网络构建日臻完善，轨道交通一号线一期工程隧道已贯通，二号线一期工程地下站已全面开工建设；南、北环快速路进行柱墩和现浇箱梁主体结构施工；年内计划打通的 21 条"断头路"已全部贯通，完成 18 个支路卡口项目；全市共新建公共停车泊位 4996 个。公共交通体系进一步优化，年内新辟、优化调整公交线路 108 条，共有

66条公交线路实行早班提前晚班延时服务；更新、投放公交车1220辆，其中天然气公交车520辆，是前两年总和的1.5倍，运力总规模超过6千标台，市区公交车中天然气公交车、空调车的比例分别达到21%和98%；更新和新增油气两用出租汽车1200辆，已有5座加气站可以向出租车提供加气服务，年末共有出租车5834辆。

五、贸易、旅游、会展

贸易业。2012年全市商品销售总额首次突破万亿大关，达10610.8亿元，比上年增长13.1%。全年完成社会消费品零售总额2329.3亿元，增长15.4%。分城乡看，城镇消费品零售额1954.9亿元，增长14.9%；乡村消费品零售额374.4亿元，增长17.7%。在限额以上企业销售的商品类值中，汽车类增长4.8%，石油及制品类增长19.7%，食品、饮料、烟酒类增长11.9%，服装、鞋帽、针纺织品类增长39.0%，金银珠宝类增长19.0%、通讯器材类增长33.3%。年末全市限额以上贸易企业达2828家，全年实现营业收入6983.2亿元，实现利润总额51.3亿元。

旅游业。2012年全市实现旅游总收入862.8亿元，比上年增长14.8%。接待入境旅游者116.2万人次，增长8.2%；旅游外汇收入7.3亿美元，增长12.1%；全年接待国内旅游者5748.3万人次，增长11.0%；国内旅游收入816.4亿元，增长15.2%。年末全市共有星级饭店170家，其中五星级19家，比上年新增1家；4A级旅游景区28处，比上年新增5处，5A级旅游景区1处。

会展业。2012年共举办各类会展活动282个，其中举办展会150个，展览总面积达179万平米。宁波国际会展中心、慈溪国际会展中心、余姚中塑国际会展中心、宁海国际会展中心四大专业场馆共举办展会活动66个，展览总面积达129万平米。规范庆典、研讨会、论坛的举办，全年县级以上举办商务性会议(论坛)77个，节庆活动55个，比上年分别减少3.7%和5.2%。

六、对外经济、合作交流

对外贸易。2012年全市完成口岸进出口总额1975.8亿美元，比上年下降1.4%。完成外贸自营进出口总额965.7亿美元，下降1.6%。其中，出口614.4亿美元，增长1.0%；进口351.3亿美元，下降5.9%。新增对外贸易经营备案登记企业2520家，累计达19763家，有进出口实绩企业12928家。私营企业完成出口305.5亿美元，增长8.8%，占全市自营出口额的比重达49.7%，同比提高3.5个百分点。机电产品出口和进口分别增长1.7%和3.6%。一般贸易出口占全市出口总额的比重为80.0%，进口占全市进口总额的比重为69.8%，同比分别提高1.4和1.7个百分点。

2007-2012年宁波自营进出口总额及增长速度

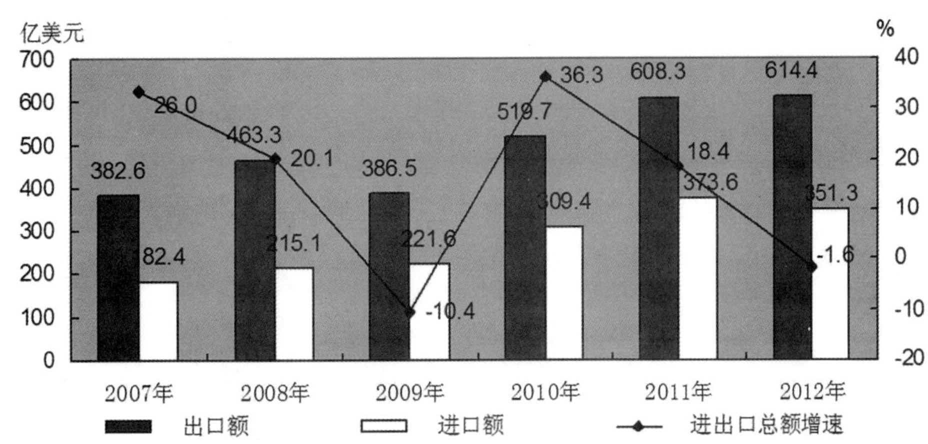

利用外资。2012年新批外商投资项目437个，合同利用外资53.1亿美元，增长5.9%，实际利用外资28.5亿美元，增长1.5%。其中制造业实际利用外资12.8亿美元，增长8.4%；批发和零售业实际利用外资5.2亿美元，增长96.1%。引进世界500强工作初见成效，法国标致、美国康德乐等先后落户甬城，使我市引进的世界500强公司达38家。目前，38家公司已在宁波投资兴办94家企业，总投资达92亿美元。

对外合作。2012年全市新批境外投资企业和机构205家，核准中方投资额13.1亿美元，比上年增长18.3%，实际中方投资额6.1亿美元。完成境外承包工程劳务合作营业额12.4亿美元，增长12.2%。

服务外包。2012年全市完成服务外包合同额114.6亿元，执行额84.6亿元，比上年分别增长33.8%和34.1%；离岸服务外包合同额5.3亿美元，执行额4.1亿美元，分别增长39.8%和46.4%。年末全市服务外包企业达723家，从业人员2.9万人。

国内合作。凝聚"宁波帮"力量，全力推进浙商回归引进和国内招商引资，组织邀请261名市外国内重要甬商回乡参加了首届世界"宁波帮"大会。2012年实际引进内资562.6亿元，比上年增长6.1%，完成省外浙商回归引进项目实际到位资金273.7亿元。立足宁波需求，持续深化区域经济合作，新增山海协作产业合作项目49个，实际到位资金11.8亿元。创新"宁波周"活动，助推加快融入上海"两个中心"建设，完成接轨上海参与长三角合作项目125个，协议总投资233亿元。援助贵州、万州、云和项目291个、资金1.06亿元。成功举办了"2012上海?宁波周"活动，以及深圳青年企业家联合会、团中央青年企业家协会代表、在沪甬商及上海现代服务业企业等"宁波行"活动。组织企业参加了第十六届"西洽会"、第二十三届"哈洽会"、第十八届"津洽会"、第十三届"西博会"等国内重要展会。

七、港口、交通

港口生产。2012年宁波港货物吞吐量完成4.53亿吨，比上年增长4.5%；完成外贸货物吞吐量2.45亿吨，增长6.5%。主要货类"二升一降"，铁矿石吞吐量8218万吨，增长14.6%；煤炭吞吐量6631万吨，增长1.1%；原油吞吐量5509万吨，下降14.9%。全年集装箱吞吐量突破1500万标箱，达1567.1万标箱，增长8.0%，稳居大陆港口第3位，世界港口第6位。集装箱航线总数达到235条，其中远洋干线120条，近洋支线63条，内支线20条，内贸线32条；月均航班约1465班，9月份创下了1693班的最高月航班记录。内支线箱量首破百万标箱，达100.6万标箱，增长83.9%。完成海铁联运箱量5.95万标箱，增长27.5%。

交通基础设施。2012年全市交通基础设施建设投资完成181.5亿元。象山港大桥及接线建成通车，标志我市"一环六射"高速公路网络正式建成，全市进入"一小时交通圈"。年末全市公路总里程达到1.07万公里，公路网密度108.6公里/百平方公里，达到中等发达国家水平，其中高速公路461.9公里，一级公路959.9公里，二级公路813.4公里，三级公路1549.7公里，四级公路6176.2公里，基本形成了以高速公路为骨架、国省道为支撑、农村公路为脉络的公路网络。铁路建设难中求进，完成投资32.5亿元，铁路宁波站改建、货运北环线和北站迁建主体工程均全面展开，杭甬客专宁波段进入联调联试阶段。国际强港建设加快推进，建成北仑港区五期集装箱码头10#和11#泊位、穿山港区中宅煤炭码头工程、镇海港区通用散货码头等万吨级以上泊位7个，新增货物吞吐能力3738万吨，集装箱吞吐能力100万标箱。

综合运输。2012年完成全社会货运量3.26亿吨，比上年增长4.4%。其中，水路货运量1.41亿吨，货物周转量1768.5亿吨公里，分别增长2.5%和4.7%；公路货运量1.66亿吨，货物周转量302.6亿吨公里，分别增长8.4%和7.5%；铁路货物发送量1924.1万吨，下降11.3%；机场货邮行吞吐量9.1万吨，增长6.4%。全社会客运量2.89亿人次，旅客周转量143.2亿人公里，分别增长4.4%和3.5%；铁路旅客发送量1118.7万人，增长1.1%；民航旅客吞吐量526.7万人次，增长5.0%。

八、银行、证券、保险

2012年全市金融业实现增加值502.4亿元，按可比价计算，比上年增长12.6%，增速比上年提高3.7个百分点，占全市服务业增加值的比重达到18.3%，对服务业增加值的贡献率为20.8%。

银行业。年末全市金融机构本外币存款余额11980.5亿元，比上年增长12.4%，其中人民币存款余额11602.3亿元，增长

11.2%;年末金融机构本外币贷款余额11961.0亿元,增长12.0%。年末全市银行业金融机构不良贷款率1.21%,比年初上升0.32个百分点,贷款质量整体保持平稳。全年银行业金融机构实现税后净利润266.5亿元,增长8.1%。年末银行业金融机构达到60家,其中政策性银行3家,大型银行5家,股份制商业银行11家,城市商业银行11家,邮储银行1家,外资银行5家,农村合作金融机构9家,新型农村金融机构12家,非银行金融机构3家。

证券业。2012年全市证券成交总额14494.9亿元,比上年下降6.9%,其中股票和基金成交9856.2亿元,下降29.0%。证券客户交易结算资金余额69.7亿元,下降12.3%。期货代理交易量4643.4万手,代理交易额41991.5亿元,分别增长113.6%和59.8%。年末证券投资者开户93.2万户,增长4.7%。年内新增期货营业部4家,年末全市共有58家证券营业部,2家证券投资咨询公司,1家期货公司和31家期货营业部。年内新增境内上市公司4家,实现IPO融资49.3亿元,境内上市公司总数达到42家。

保险业。2012年全市保险业实现保费收入164.7亿元,比上年增长10.8%,高于全国8.0%的平均增幅。其中,财产险86.2亿元,增长11.6%;人身险78.5亿元,增长10.0%。保险业累计赔款和给付64.3亿元,增长33.4%,高于全国20.0%的平均水平。其中,财产险赔付支出51.9亿元,增长38.5%,人身险赔付支出12.4亿元,增长15.4%。年末共有50家保险公司在我市设立分支机构,较上年增加4家,其中产险公司28家,寿险公司22家。保险业资产总额突破300亿,达到311.0亿元,较年初增长20.1%。

九、科技、教育、人才

科技创新。由宁波大学为主完成的“非线性应力波传播理论及应用”项目获得国家自然科学二等奖,成为我市首次获得的国家自然科学奖。全年获得省级科学技术奖26项,其中一等奖1项,二等奖2项,三等奖23项。全年专利申请量73647件,授权量59175件,比上年分别增长54.8%和58.5%,其中发明专利授权量2065件,增长27.1%。全市认定省级高新技术企业研发中心38家,省级企业工程中心12家,市级企业工程(技术)中心130家。年内新增高新技术企业189家,市级科技型企业261家,国家级创新型企业3家,省级创新型示范企业4家,省级创新型试点企业7家;新认定市级重点实验室2家,新增市级产学研技术创新联盟1家。年末全市有高新技术企业930家,市级科技型企业563家,市级企业工程(技术)中心746家,省级高新技术企业研究开发中心212家,国家认定企业技术中心8家,国家级创新型试点和创新型企业16家,省级创新型示范和试点企业52家,市级创新型试点企业156家。年末限额以上科技服务业企业258家,全年实现营业收入103.9亿元,实现利润总额19.2亿元,比上年分别增长19.5%和20.8%。

教育事业。年末全市拥有各级各类学校2064所,在校学生总数133.1万人,教职工总数10.0万人,其中专任教师约达7.6万人。全市累计义务段标准化学校达到492所,标准化学校创建率达到69.5%。学前三年幼儿纯入园率保持在99.7%以上,义务教育段入学率和巩固率分别保持在100%和99%以上,初中毕业生升入高中段的比例保持在99.1%以上,普职比为1∶1。年末全市共有全日制民办中小学(幼儿园)1072所,在校(园)生约32万人,占全市全日制中小学(幼儿园)在校(园)生数的28.4%。在甬全日制普通高校在校生14.5万人,本专科在校生比为60∶40;在甬研究生达到6700人;全市每万人在校大学生数达到252人。全年有240余家单位开展培训工作,培训项目180多个,完成培训8.1万人。完成成人“双证制”培训毕业人数8445人,农村预备劳动力职业技能培训人数2323人。

人才开发。2012年新增各类人才14.5万人,年末全市人才总量达到130万。其中,专业技术人才71.2万;高技能人才21万;硕博人才3.3万;海外留学人才超过3500人。高层次人才开发计划加快推进。新增海外高层次人才国家级“千人计划”5名、省级“千人计划”28名、市“3315计划”34名。选拔推荐国家特殊津贴人选8名,新增省151工程重点资助人选2名、第一层次人选4名、第二层次人选23名。确定首批市级领军和拔尖培养人选605名,新储备中高层次人才近4200名。产学研平台建设成效显著。新建留学人员创业园3家,实现县(市)区全覆盖。新增博士后科研工作站(流动站)17家,总数达到63家,累计招收博士后302名,全面完成博士后“135”计划。新增市级企业技术创新团队40家、省级团队4家。建立首批市级技能大师工作室11家,其中国家级1家、省级8家;建成首家高技能人才公共实训中心。

十、文化、卫生、体育

文化建设。公共文化服务更加丰富,全年各级文化部门共组织举办精品展览、公益讲座、高雅艺术演出各500多场,送电影下乡25000多场、送戏下乡2500场,为1100多艘渔船新装广播电视,行政村全部建立了"农家书屋",我市"零门槛公共文化服务打造书香宁波"专题在《新闻联播》播出。城乡文化活动更趋活跃,承办了第七届全国优秀儿童剧展演、"群星璀璨"全国群众美术书法摄影优秀作品展等多项国家级大型文化活动,成功举办首个大型城市音乐欢唱活动——"2012阿拉音乐节"、第四届全民读书月、第五届中国(宁波)农民电影节等品牌节庆活动,形成了以国家级高水平文化活动为引领、市区(县)联动的节庆文化品牌为支撑的发展模式。文化产品创作与生产再获丰收,音乐剧《告诉海》、电视剧《向东是大海》、动画电视系列剧《少年阿凡提》、纪实文学作品《主义之花》四部优秀作品荣获全国第十二届精神文明建设"五个一工程"奖。儿童剧《神奇的田螺壳》获第七届全国优秀儿童剧展演优秀剧目奖,甬剧《宁波大哥》获"中国现代戏研究会突出贡献奖"。文化产业发展势头迅猛,浙江大丰实业有限公司被文化部授予"国家文化产业示范基地",成为我国舞台机械设备领域内唯一一家获评企业。海伦钢琴股份有限公司在深交所创业板成功上市,成为我市第四家文化类上市公司。全年电影票房首次突破两亿元大关,达到2.3亿元,比上年增长28.3%,增幅位列全省第一。新增影院6家,年末共有多厅影院23家;全年引进电影112部,其中国产影片80部、国外影片32部。

卫生事业。城乡居民医疗卫生条件进一步改善,年末实有病床2.8万张,拥有卫生技术人员4.9万人,其中执业医师(含助理)1.9万人,注册护士1.8万人。按户籍人口统计,每千人床位数、卫技人员数、执业医师(含助理)数和注册护士数分别达到4.8张、8.4人、3.3人和3.1人。年末全市共设置社区卫生服务中心(卫生院)151家,建成省级规范化社区卫生服务中心(卫生院)131家,创建率达86.8%,居全省前列;建成省级示范社区卫生服务中心21家,其中国家级4家。新型农村合作医疗制度进一步巩固,参合人数为292.8万,参合率达97.7%,人均筹资水平从上年的396元增加到565元。公共卫生工作成效显著。全市甲乙类传染病报告总发病率为189.81/10万;适龄儿童免疫规划疫苗接种率99.6%,免疫预防服务质量保持全省先进水平;全年常住人口孕产妇死亡率为0,首次实现零死亡,婴儿死亡率2.96‰,5岁以下儿童死亡率4.05‰,均稳定在较低水平。无偿献血工作稳步推进。全年无偿献血70016人次,无偿献血量占临床用血比例为104.2%,继续保持我市临床用血全部来自无偿献血的目标。

体育事业。开展"体育系统直属场馆公益开放"活动,市民参与健身热情高涨,仅局属各大体育场馆已有近10万人次参与免费健身活动。全年有12个乡镇街道成功创建省体育强镇,4个街道51个社区成功创建浙江省城市体育先进街道社区。公共体育健身设施建设维护力度加大,全年更新体育健身路径586条,新建各类球场200个。群众体育活动丰富多彩,培训广播体操指导员(志愿者)500多名,举办各级各类广播体操比赛30多场次,使第九套广播体操成宁波市民健身新热点。竞技体育综合实力显著提高,征战奥运成绩取得新的突破,共有李金子、董程、汪顺、单丹娜、李玲等5名运动员参加了伦敦奥运会,获得了首枚奥运会女子拳击奖牌和2个第五名,加上输送到中国武警总队的女拳选手任灿灿,参赛人数超过了历届奥运会。另外,2012年我市运动健儿还在各级大赛中分别获得2个世界冠军、9个亚洲冠军和24个全国冠军。体育事业与体育产业协调发展,全年全市共举办了42项国家级以上赛事,11选5成功上市助推体彩销售再上新台阶,销量首次超过13亿元,超过温州,跃居全省第二。

十一、人口、居民生活、社会保障、社会组织

人口增长。年末全市户籍人口577.7万人,比上年末增长2.27‰,其中市区人口226.1万人。人口出生率8.65‰,人口死亡率6.56‰,人口自然增长率2.09‰。

居民收入。全年市区居民人均可支配收入37902元,比上年增长11.3%,扣除价格因素,实际增长9.4%;农村居民人均纯收入18475元,增长11.8%,扣除价格因素,实际增长10.0%。从收入来源看,工资性收入仍是居民收入增长的决定性因素,对城乡

居民收入增长的贡献分别达82.3%和69.3%。城乡居民收入比由2011年的2.06∶1缩小为2012年的2.05∶1，明显低于全国3.10∶1的平均水平。

社会保障体系。2012年新增基本养老、基本医疗、失业、工伤和生育保险参保人数39.9万人、21.6万人、15.6万人、16.9万人和18.4万人，年末参保人数分别达474.3万人、326.6万人、216.2万人、270.2万人和233.1万人。年末外来务工人员参加五大社会保险人数为179.4万人，全年参保人数净增22.6万人。新增城乡居民养老保险、城镇居民医疗保险参保人数10.1万人和18.1万人。本地户籍人口养老保障参保率达到83.4%。2012年企业退休人员基本养老金每月增加223元，人均每月达到2048元。医疗补助范围和标准进一步扩大，城镇职工和城镇居民政策范围内住院及特殊病种费用报销比例提高到85%和70.4%。城镇职工和居民医保市级统筹稳步推进，社会保障卡"一卡通"工程取得阶段性成果，累计发放社保卡突破200万张。

民生保障。年末全市共有城乡低保39355户59483人，支出低保资金2.29亿元。全市农村五保对象5224人，集中供养人数4990人，集中供养率为95.5%，城镇"三无"对象1380人，集中供养人数1353人，集中供养率为98.0%。养老机构年内新增床位2468张，年末全市共有养老机构220个，床位33168张。

保障性安居工程。2012年全市新开工建设保障性安居工程140.3万平方米、18858套，其中公共租赁住房56.1万平方米、10269套；竣工保障性安居工程6202套；新增发放廉租住房货币补贴3721户，超额完成省政府下达的各项住房保障目标任务。

慈善事业。2012年市县两级慈善机构募集善款4.4亿元，救助支出3.6亿元，受助的困难群众达35.5万余人次。至2012年底，全市慈善机构累计募集已达34.3亿元，累计救助支出23.4亿元，受助170.5万余人次。全年共开展各种志愿服务活动500余次，参加服务的义工6000余人次。服务时间累计达13000小时。

社会组织。年末全市共有6个区、2个县、3个县级市、78个镇、11个乡、64个街道办事处、533个社区、106个居民委员会、2567个村民委员会。

十二、生态建设、社会安全

生态建设。实施城市"禁燃区"建设和机动车排气污染防治，累计淘汰改造燃煤锅炉465台，市六区四个机动车排气检测站正式上线运行。强化饮用水源等重点水域及农村环境综合整治工作，排查各类水库127座，建立各类污染源工作台帐；建成太阳能生化减量处理设施400多座、分散式村级生活污水处理设施建设项目100多个。环境执法监管继续强化，全年共出动执法人员42748人次、检查企业21867家次，立案查处企业938家，罚款总额4208.6万元，个案处罚额度4.5万元。监测监控能力不断提升，3月25日起在全省率先按照新的环境空气质量标准发布中心城区PM2.5实时监测数据，11月16日起发布所有8个国控点位空气质量指数(AQI)。全年共完成淘汰落后产能任务企业568家，其中关停淘汰64家；淘汰落后设备4500台(套)，节能42.8万吨标煤，累计减少CO2排放107万吨、COD排放719吨、SO2排放2231吨、氨氮排放32吨、氮氧化物排放1561吨。大力开展建筑节能和可再生能源推广应用工作，全年组织实施可再生能源建筑应用示范项目15个，面积110万平方米；新增节能建筑面积1675万平方米；新增太阳能光热应用面积100万平方米，地源热泵60万平方米。2012年宁波顺利通过国家环保模范城市现场复核验收，慈溪市、鄞州区通过省级生态市(区)考核验收，宁海县通过国家级生态县技术评估。

"平安宁波"建设。2012年全市共发生各类安全生产事故3578起、死亡778人、受伤3136人、直接经济损失4315.7万元，比上年分别下降5.3%、5.2%、8.3%和8.2%，连续第八年实现安全生产主要指标同比下降。积极推进食品监管体制建设创新，依法做好食品安全监督工作，全年完成食品定量检验53715批次，为全年任务总量的127.9%。加大药械市场监管力度，全面实施新版GMP，完成辖区18家原料药、制剂生产企业日常监督检查，检查覆盖面100%。全年共查处各类违法药械保健食品广告98件，其中移送工商部门处理的67件，行政告诫31件；药械及餐饮案件立案共1112件，结案979件，移送公安8件，没收违法生产经营各类货值金额108.9万元，罚没款总计1544万元，罚没款和移送案件数均为历年之最。积极打造"无欠薪宁波"品牌，和谐劳动关系保持总体稳定，全市已筹集工资支付保证金15.0亿元、欠薪应急周转金1.5亿元，全年处理劳动违法案件3385件，责令补签劳动合同5.7万份，为3.3万名职工追回被拖欠工资2.0亿。全年共受理群众信访36503件(人)次，接待群众集体上访1431批19388人次。全年人民调解组织共调处各类民事纠纷126447件，调解成功124658件，成功率达98.6%，防止民间纠纷引起的自杀25件、32人次；防止民间纠纷转换为刑事案件135件、779人次。

注：(1)本公报所列各项数据均为初步统计数。

(2)全市生产总值、各产业增加值绝对数按当年价格计算，增长速度按可比价格计算。

(3)规模以上工业企业指年主营业务收入2000万元及以上企业。

限额以上批发、零售、住宿、餐饮企业指：

批发业：年主营业务收入2000万元及以上；

零售业：年主营业务收入500万元及以上；

住宿业：年主营业务收入200万元及以上；

餐饮业：年主营业务收入200万元及以上。

2012 Statistics Bulletin of National Economy and Social Development of Ningbo

Ningbo Municipal Statistics Bureau State Statistical Bureau
Ningbo Investigation Team

Feb. 4, 2013

In face of complex and fast-changing macro-economy home and abroad in 2012, Ningbo people strive to tide over adversity and solve problems confronted through adopting the strategy of "six accelerations" and sticking to the keynote of "advancing in stability and then bettering in advancement", in order to implement relevant policies and strategies favorable to ensuring steady growth, adjusting structure and benefiting livelihood. With such actions taken, the economy and quality & benefits in Ningbo have witnessed increase and improvement, and the innovation and transformation have advanced effectively, and people were well secured for better living standard, paving a promising path for the modernization of an international port city.

I. Comprehensive Summary

Regional GDP: The GDP in Ningbo in 2012 amounted to ¥652.47 billion, up by 7.8% compared with that of last year if calculated by comparable price, among which, the added value of primary industry was ¥27.0 billion, up by 1.6%; the added value of secondary industry was ¥351.67 billion, up by 6.0%; and the added value of tertiary industry was ¥273.8 billion, up by 10.9%. The ratio of the increase of the three industries was 4.1 : 53.9 : 42.0. The proportion of increase of the tertiary industry in the regional GDP was 1.5% higher than that of last year. The GDP per capita was ¥85,475 if calculated by permanent resident population (converted to USD 13,541 according to annual average exchange rate).

Fiscal revenue and expenditure: The public fiscal budget revenue in Ningbo in 2012 was ¥153.65 billion, up by 7.3% compared with that of last year, among which, the local fiscal revenue was ¥72.55 billion, up by 10.3%, with growths of total local fiscal revenue and increase witnessing 14.9% and 13.5% respectively lower than that of last year. For local taxation, the growths for operation tax, VAT, enterprise income tax and individual were 20.3%, 11.3%, 6.7% and -6.9% respectively. The public fiscal budget expenditure was ¥82.84 billion, up by 10.4%, with growth of 14.6% lower than the same period of last year. More fiscal expenditure has still been made to livelihood areas. The total fiscal expenditure in livelihood was ¥54.85 billion, up by 13.5%, with growth 1.8% higher than that of public fiscal budget expenditure and accounting for 66.2% of the total fiscal expenditure (1.8% higher than the same period of last year). Among the fiscal expenditure in livelihood areas, expenditure in social insurance and employment was ¥7.9 billion, up by 34.8% (the fastest growth); expenditure in education was ¥14.17 billion, taking the largest share in livelihood areas (25.8%), up by 20.4% (third fastest growth).

Employment and re-employment: Jobs newly created in urban areas and towns in Ningbo were 152,000 in 2012, up by 2.7% compared with that of last year. 73,000 laid-off workers in urban areas and towns in Ningbo were re-employed, 24,000 of which were the workers in trouble, with the growths of 17.4% and 30.5% respectively. The national HR market has provided 1.969 million jobs and 1.091 million people were registered in this market for job seeking. 38,000 rural labor forces were trained for jobs. The unemployment rate registered at the end of 2012 was 2.55%, which was historically low.

Market price: The consumer price index (CPI) in Ningbo was 101.7% in 2012, 3.6% lower than that of last year, and 0.9% and 0.5% respectively lower than those of national and provincial levels, ranking the last in 36 large and medium-sized cities in China. The rises and falls of six major goods and services items: 5.2% increase for foods, 1.7% increase for household facilities and articles, 1.1% increase for health care and personal products, 5.0% decrease for entertainment, education and cultural articles and services, 0.4% decrease for transportation and communication. Both the purchase price index and ex-factory price index for manufacturers were 97.1% in 2012, which had abated the difficult circumstances of "high purchase price but low ex-factory price" for manufactured goods. The sales price of new commercial housing was 7.4% lower in December, with the decline ranking third among 70 large and medium-sized cities in China.
2012 Fluctuation of Main Prices by Months in Ningbo

II. Agriculture and Rural Area

Agricultural production: The gross output value of farming, forestry, husbandry and fishing in Ningbo has reached ¥42.05 billion in 2012, up by 1.9% than that of last year if calculated by comparable price. Among the gross value, the farming was ¥20 billion, down by 0.3%; the forestry ¥1.14 billion, down by 2.4%; the husbandry ¥6.59 billion, up by 4.9%; the fishing ¥13.75 billion, up by 3.7%; and the service of farming forestry, husbandry and fishing ¥0.57 billion, up by 8.4%. Affected by weather, the grain output declines. The gross grain output in 2012 was 857,000 tons, down by 4.9%. Commercial crops such as mat grass, grape and red bayberry have witnessed a relatively rapid growth, respectively 15.3%, 7.2% and 16.0%. Output of live pigs was stable and the pork output amounted to 157,000 tons, up by 5.9%. The new leading agricultural enterprises at municipal level were 20 in 2012, totaling 273 by far. Among those enterprise, 91 ones had their output value (sales value) exceed ¥100 million. At the end of 2012, those enterprises have been granted with 13 national agricultural famous brands and 65 Zhejiang provincial famous brands.

New countryside construction: Ningbo has invested ¥1.1 billion in the Project of "setting up chain shops in hundreds of towns and quality-assured stores in thousands of villages" in 2012, ¥0.42 billion of which was fiscal investment at different levels. 2,411 villages (accounting 93% of total administrative villages) in total have started village renovation, and 132 villages have established biological treatment of domestic waste water. 45 new all-round well-off villages were established, totaling 479 by far. Village renovation was carried out in 70 under-developed villages in 2012, having over ¥300 million invested, 836 projects constructed, 316,000m2 old and dilapidated houses removed, 1,256,000 m2 of fa?ade renovated, 365,000 m2 of road hardening within countries conducted, 251,000 m2 of village greening carried out, and 44,000 m2 of river channel improved. ¥19.4 billion was invested in "two reconstructions" for countryside houses in 2012, including 95,000 houses starting reconstruction (46,000 houses completed, covering 6.33 million m2). Funds totally invested in countryside house construction project in Ningbo was ¥60 billion in the past four years, completing countryside house reconstruction of 25 million m2. Tourism industry in countryside has witnessed a rapid development. In 2012, there were 3 new municipal "happy farmhouses" (35 in total by far) and 15 pilot leisure tourism points of "happy farmhouses" (91 in total by far), receiving 17.19 million tourists and actual operation revenue of 1.72 billion in 2012, up by 44.2% and 51.4% respectively, and creating 43,000 for farmers.

III. Industry and Construction

Industrial economy: The total industrial output value in Ningbo amounted to ¥1584.39 billion in 2012, up by 2.75% compared with that of last year. Among which, the total industrial output value for industrial enterprise above designated size was ¥1196.21 billion, up by 1.3%, accounting for 77.1% of total industrial output value. The output value for top 10 industries above designated size was ¥871.06 billion, accounting for 72.8% of total industrial output value above designated size and achieving 0.2% of increase compared with the same period of last year. Petroleum processing, coking and nuclear fuel processing have obtained ¥156.86 billion of total industrial output value, topping all industries; vehicle industry has witnessed a growth of 16.8%, ranking first in growth among top ten industries. The gross output value of light industry in 2022 was ¥341.93 billion, up by 4.5%; and that for heavy industry was ¥854.28 billion, same as that of last year. The ratio of light and heavy industries has changed from 1: 2.6 last year to 1:2.5 in 2012. The added output value for industrial enterprises in 2012 was ¥213.25 billion, up by 5.0%; profits achieved was ¥52.03 billion, down by 15.2%; and taxation of profit achieved was ¥105.75 billion, down by 8.3%.

Industrial transformation and innovation: Expenditure in scientific and technological activities of industrial enterprises above designated size totaled¥15.65 billion in 2012, up by 12.5% compared with that of last year and accounting for 1.4% of main business revenue (0.2% higher compared with the same period of last year). The output value of new products was ¥254.1 billion, up by 10.4%, 9.1% faster in growth than that of total industrial output value above designated size. The rate of output value of new products accounted for 20.2%, 1.7%higher compared with the same period last year, hitting a record high; the high-tech industry above designed size has achieved ¥343.1 billion in total industrial output value, up by 4.0%, 2.7% faster in growth than the average growth in industry above designated size.

Construction industry: The output value of construction industry in Ningbo totaled ¥251.05 billion in 2012, up by 29.9% compared with that of last year, ranking No. 1 in terms of growth in Zhejiang Province and 14.8% higher than the average level in Zhejiang. The construction area of house in 2012 was 225,723,000m2, and the completion area was 60,478,000m2.

IV. Investment in Fixed Asset and Urban Construction

Investment in fixed asset: Investment in fixed asset in Ningbo was ¥290.14 billion in 2012, which are 21.6% and 4.0% faster respectively in terms of growth than those of the previous year. The private investment was ¥130.68 billion, up by 13.9%; investment in infrastructure was ¥85.01 billion, up by 21.9%; investment in real estate development was ¥88.44 billion, up by 17.1%. If viewed by different industries, the investment in primary industry was ¥1.09 billion, down by 40.5%; investment in secondary industry was ¥82.22 billion, up by 22.2%; and investment in tertiary industry was ¥206.83, up by 22.1%. The total industrial investment in 2012 was ¥81.72 billion, up by 22.3% and 0.7% faster in growth than that of fixed assets, abating the difficult circumstances of continuous low growth Project investment satisfying transformative innovation orientation takes a lead in growth. The industrial investments in pharmaceutical manufacture and in vehicle manufacture have witnessed the growth of 119.6% and 94.9% respectively.

Modern urban construction: The functional improvement of the central urban has achieved good results, and the investment in 33 blocks such as new eastern town, southern business district and Ningbo Railway (southern station) integrated railway hub was ¥87.1 billion. The environmental update and reconstruction was under steady progress. The leisure belt project of "three rivers and six banks" was basically completed and the initialization section (from Yaojiang River Bridge to Jiefang Road) was basically built. 22 old communities have been renovated, covering an area of 1,080,000m2 and with a total investment of ¥81,330,000. 42 lanes adjourning the main streets have been renovated. The rate of roads under good state has reached over 90% in 2012 and the illumination coverage rate of street lamps remained over 98%. The cleaning action of roads in central downtown was implemented, and clean-keeping funds and the supporting funds have amounted to ¥0.36 billion. 1,195 roads have been retained regularly clean, and machine cleaning rate has increased from 36.9% to 75.0%. The comprehensive transportation network was becoming more sophisticated. Phase I project of rail transit No. 1 channel was connected, and the construction of underground station of Phase I of rail transit No. 2 was commenced. The south and north express road were under main structure construction (stub and cast-in-situ box girder). The 21 "unconnected roads" planned to be finished in 2012 was connected and 18 items of guard and inspection spots in by-passes have been finished. 4,996 public parking points have been set up in Ningbo. The public transportation system was further improved with 108 public transportation lines newly established and optimized and 66 lines advancing morning shift and postponing night shift. 1,220 buses in total were updated and put into use, 520 of which were natural gas buses (1.5 times than the total number of the past two years). The total transportation size has reached over 6,000 standard vehicle units, and the ratio of natural gas buses and air-conditioning buses among urban buses were 21% and 98% respectively. 1,200 oil-gas-available taxies have been renewed and added, and there have been 5 gas stations available for taxies by far. And the total taxies at the end of 2012 were 5,834.

V. Trade, Tourism and Exhibition

Trade: The total sales volume of goods in Ningbo exceeded, for the first time, ¥1 trillion in 2012, amounting to ¥1.06108 trillion, up by 13.1%. If viewed by countryside and town respectively, the total volume of consumer retail sales in towns was ¥195.49 billion, up by 14.9%, and total volume of consumer retail sales in countryside was ¥37.44 billion, up by 17.7%. In goods sales volume enterprises above designated size, automobile sales have been up by 4.8%; petroleum and related products 19.7%; foods, beverage, tobacco and liquor 11.9%; clothing, shoes and hats, and needle textile 39.0%; gold, silver and jewelry 19.0%; and communication device 33.3%. The number of trade companies above designated size in Ningbo has reached 2,828 at the end of 2012. The total operation revenue was ¥698.32 billion and profits of ¥5.13 billion.

Tourism: Total revenue of tourism in Ningbo in 2012 was ¥86.28 billion, up by 14.8% compared with that of last year. The inbound tourists hit 1,162,000, up by 8.2%; foreign exchange earnings were USD 0.73 billion, up by 12.1%; domestic tourists in 2012 were 57,483,000, up by 11.0%; revenue from domestic tourists was ¥81.64 billion, up by 15.2%. There were 170 star-rated hotels in Ningbo in 2012, where 19 were five-star hotels (up by 1). There were 28 4A-class tourist attractions (up by 5) and 1 5A-class tourist attraction.

Exhibition: 282 exhibition activities of various kinds were held in 2012 in Ningbo, of which 150 were exhibitions, with a total exhibition area of 1,790,000 m2. 66 exhibition activities in total have been arranged in Ningbo International Convention and Exhibition Center, Cixi International Convention and Exhibition Center, Yuyao Zhongsu International Convention and Conference Center and Ninghai International Convention and Conference Center, with total exhibition area of 1,290,000 m2. Ceremonies, seminar and forums should be held up to standards. In 2012, 77 business conferences and 55 festival activities above county level were held, which witnesses decreases of 3.7% and 5.2% respectively.

VI. Foreign Economy and Cooperation & Exchange

Foreign trade: The total volume of export and import in Ningbo reaches USD 197.58 billion in 2012, decreased by 1.4% compared to that of last year. The total volume of self-support export was USD 96.57 billion, decreased by 1.6%. Among the above, USD 61.44 billion for export, up by 1.0%; and USD 35.13 billion for import, down by 5.9%. New enterprises for foreign trade registered were 2,250, totaling 19,763 by far, and enterprises with actual export business were 12,928. Private enterprises have completed the export volume of USD 30.55 billion, up by 8.8%, accounting for 49.7% of the total self-support export volume in Ningbo (3.5% higher compared with the same period of last year). The growth in export and import volumes of mechanical and electrical products was 1.7% and 3.6% respectively. The export volume of general trade accounted for 80.0% among the total export volume and the import volume accounted for 69.8%, respectively witnessing 1.4% and 1.7% higher compared to the same period of last year respectively.

2007-2012 Self-support Import & Export Volume and Growth in Ningbo

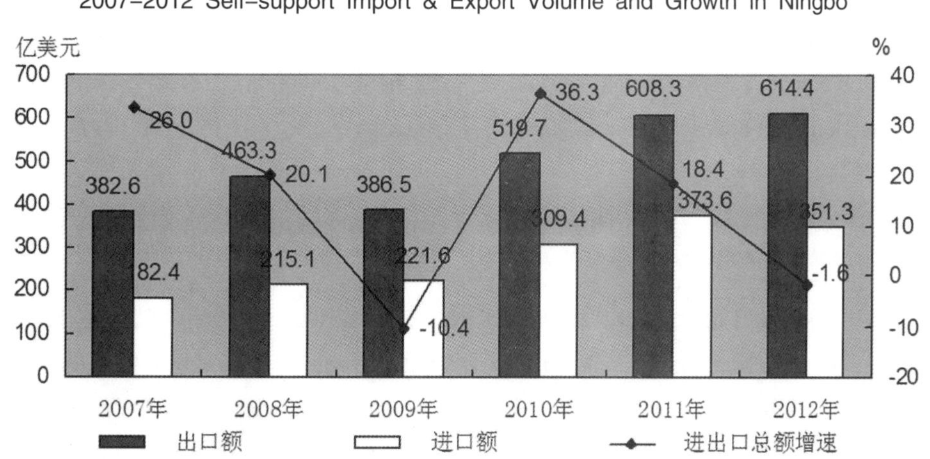

Foreign capital utilization: 423 new foreign-invested projects were approved in 2012; foreign capital utilization by contract was USD 5.31 billion, up by 5.9%; and actual utilization of foreign capital was USD 2.85 billion, up by 1.5%. Among the above, the actual utilization of foreign capital in manufacturing industry was USD 1.28 billion, up by 8.4%; and USD 0.52 billion for retail and wholesale industry, up by 96.1%. Introduction and attraction of Fortune 500 has achieved good results, with Peugeot, Cardinal Health Company and other Fortune 500 establishing businesses in Ningbo, making the number of total Fortune 500 companies become 50. At present, these 38 companies have set up 94 relevant enterprises in Ningbo, with a total investment up to USD 9.2 billion.

Foreign cooperation: 205 overseas investment enterprises and organizations were approved in Ningbo in 2012, with Chinese investment approved up to USD 1.31 billion, up by 18.3%, and the actual Chinese investment up to USD 0.61 billion. The turnover of labor cooperation for overseas contracting projects was USD 1.24 billion, up by 12.2%. Outsourcing service: the contract volume of outsourced service completed in 2012 was ¥11.46 billion and the executed volume of ¥8.46 billion, up by 33.8% and 34.1% respectively; the contract volume of offshore outsourced service was USD 0.53 billion and the executed volume of USD was 0.41 billion, up by 39.8% and 46.4% respectively. The enterprises specialized in outsourced services at the end of 2012 amounted to 723, with total employees of 29,000.

Domestic cooperation: With the cohesive strength of "Ningbo People", Ningbo endeavored to attract and promote the return of Zhejiang-born merchants and invite domestic investment. 261 Ningbo merchants with influences outside Ningbo but within China were invited to attend the first conference of "Ningbo People". The actual introduction of domestic capital in 2012 was ¥56.26 billion, up by 6.1%, and the actual paid-in capital of ¥27.37 billion from merchants outside Zhejiang Province. To continuously deepen the regional economic cooperation based on the demands of Ningbo, 49 industrial cooperation projects of Nanshan District + Zhoushan Isles, with actual paid-in capital of ¥1.18 billion. "Ningbo Week" for innovation was also advanced to accelerate the integration of "two centers" construction of Shanghai and had completed 125 connection projects with Yangtze River Delta cooperation, with total investment agreed of ¥23.3 billion. In addition, the assistance to Guizhou, Wanzhou and Yunhe covered 291 projects, with capital of ¥106 million. "2012 Shanghai -Ningbo Week" activities were successfully held and the "a visit to Ningbo" activities such as Shenzhen Young Entrepreneurs Association, representative of Yong Entrepreneurs Committee of the Central Committee of Communist Youth League, and Ningbo-born merchants in Shanghai and Shanghai enterprises engaging in modern services took place. Also, enterprises in Ningbo were organized to attend 16th "E-W Cooperation and Investment Conference", 23rd "Harbin International Trade Conference", 18th "Tianjin Trade and Investment Conference", 13th "Western China International Expo" and other important domestic exhibitions.

VII. Port and Transportation

Port production: The cargo handling capacity of Ningbo Port in 2012 was 453,000,000 tons, up by 4.5%; and the handling capacity of foreign trade goods completed was 245,000,000 tons, up by 6.5%. The rises and falls of major cargo: 82.18 million tons for iron ore, up by 14.6%; 66.31 million tons for coals, up by 1.1%; 55.09 million tons for crude oil, decreased by 14.9%. The container throughput in 2012 has exceeded 15 million TEU (15.671 million

TEU), up by 8.0%, ranking third among ports in China mainland, and sixth among the worldwide ports. The total container marine lines have totaled 235, where the ocean-going lines were 120, near marine lines were 63, domestic container feeder lines were 63, and domestic trade lines were 32. The monthly navigation times were about 1,465 and the September hit a new record of 1,693. The container number of domestic container feeder lines has exceeded 1 million TEU for the first time, amounting to 1.006 million TEU, up by 83.9%. The total containers through marine and railway amount to 59,500 TEU, up by 27.5%.

Transportation infrastructure: The investment to the transportation infrastructure in Ningbo was ¥18.15 billion in 2012. The Xiangshan Port and its bridging line have been completed, marking the overall completion of expressway network of "one ring expressway and six connection lines", which enabled Ningbo to step into "one-hour transportation circle". At the end of 2012, the total mileage of roads has reached 10,700 km, and the highway density was 108.6 km per 100 km2, equaling the level of that in moderately developed countries. The length of expressway was 461.9 km, first-class road 959.9 km, secondary road 813.4 km, tertiary road 1,549.7 km, and forth-class road 6,176.2 km, basically forming the a highway network supported by expressway, national and provincial roads and countryside roads. The railway construction was striving in difficulties with an investment of ¥3.25 billion. Construction of Ningbo Railway, replacement of north goods ring lines and north station all commence in 2012, and the Ningbo section of Hangzhou-Ningbo passenger special line was under joint-debugging. The construction of internationally-competitive port was accelerated. Construction of seven 10,000-ton berths was completed; these berths included berth 10# and Berth 11# of the container wharf in Phase V of Beilun Pork, other berths in Zhongzhai Coal wharf in Chuangshan Pork, and General wharf for bulk cargo in Zhenhai Pork. The cargo handling capacity was up by 37,380,000 tons and the capacity for containers was up by 1 million TEU.

Integrated transportation: The social cargo transportation volume in 2010 was 326,000,000 tons, up by 4.4%, where, the water cargo transportation volume was 141,000,000 tons with turnover volume of 176.85 billion tons, increased respectively by 2.5% and 4.7%; and road cargo transportation volume was 166,000,000 tons with turnover volume of 30.26 billion tons, increased respectively by 8.4% and 7.5%; railway transportation volume was 19,241,000 tons, decreased by 11.3%; airport cargo transportation volume was 91,000 tons, up by 6.4%. The total passenger volume was 0.289 billion person-time with passenger turnover volume of 14.32 billion km, increased respectively by 4.4% and 3.5%; railway passenger transportation volume was 11.187 million person-time, up by 1.1%; and the passenger transportation volume by civil aviation was 5.267 million person-time, up by 5.0%.

VIII. Banking, Securities and Insurance

The added value in financial sector in Ningbo was ¥50.24 billion in 2012, up by 12.6% if calculated by comparable price, with a growth rate 3.7% higher than that of last year, accounting to 18.3% of total added value in service sector in Ningbo and with the contribution rate of service added value of 20.8%.

Banking: The deposit balance of domestic and foreign currency in the financial institutions in Ningbo has reached ¥1,198.05 billion at the end of 2012, up by 12.4% compared with that of last year. Among which, the deposit balance was ¥1,160.23 billion, up by 11.2%; the loan balance of domestic and foreign currency in financial institutional at the end of 2012 was ¥1,196.1 billion, up by 12.0%. The non-performing loan ratio of financial institutions in Ningbo at the end of 2012 was 1.21%, up by 0.32% compared with that at the beginning of 2012, indicating that the overall quality of loan remained stable. The net profits of financial institutions in 2012 were ¥26.65 billion, up by 8.1%. The number of financial institutions at the end of 2012 has totaled 60, including 3 strategic banks, 5 large-scale banks, 11 joint-stock commercial banks, 11 city commercial banks, 1 postal savings bank, 5 foreign banks, 9 rural cooperative financial institutions, 12 new-type rural financial institutions and 3 non-bank financial institutions.

Securities: The total transaction volume of securities in Ningbo in 2012 has reached ¥1,449.49 billion, decreased by 6.9%, where, the transaction volume of share and funds was ¥985.62 billion, decreased by 29.0%. The settlement amount of securities transaction was ¥6.97 billion, decreased by 12.3%. The transaction volume of futures agent was 46.434 million and agent transaction amount of ¥4,199.15 billion, increased respectively by 113.6% and 59.8%. The new clients of securities at the end of 2012 were 932,000, up by 4.7%. The new operation offices of futures were 4 within 2012. By the end of 2012, there were 58 securities operation offices, 2 securities investment and consultation company, 1 futures company and 31 futures operation offices. The new public company within 2012 was 4, achieving IPO of ¥4.93 billion, totaling 42 public companies by far.

Insurance: The premium income of insurance industry in Ningbo in 2012 was ¥16.47 billion, up by 10.8% and 8.0% higher than the average growth in China. Among the above, ¥8.62 billion for property insurance, up by 11.6%; ¥7.85 billion for life insurance, up by 10.0%. The accumulative compensation and payment in insurance industry was ¥6.43 billion, up by 33.4% and 20.0% higher than the average level in China. Among the above, ¥5.19 billion was for property insurance, up by 38.5%; and ¥1.24 billion for life insurance, up by 15.4%. There were 50 insurance companies setting up branches in Ningbo in 2012 (including 28 property insurance companies and 22 life insurance companies), up by 4. The total assets in insurance industry have exceeded ¥30 billion, reaching ¥31.10 billion, up by 20.1% compared with that at the beginning of 2012.

IX. Science & Technology, Education and Talents

Scientific and technical innovation: The project of "Theory and application of nonlinear stress wave propagation" led by Ningbo University won the second price of national prize in nature and science, marking the first national prize in this field in Ningbo. There were 26 provincial prizes in science and technology in 2012, including 1 first prize, 2 second prizes and 23 third prizes. The number of patent application was 73,647, with 59,175 awarded, increased respectively by 54.8% and 58.5%. Among the above, 2,065 patents for invention have been awarded, up by 27.1%. 38 R&D centers of provincial high-tech technical enterprises, 12 engineering centers of provincial enterprises and 130 engineering (technical) centers of municipal enterprises were evaluated and identified by Ningbo city. The new high-tech enterprises in Ningbo was 189, with 261 municipal science enterprises, 3 national innovative enterprises, 4 provincial innovation model enterprises, and 7 provincial innovation model enterprises. 2 municipal key labs and 1 municipal industry-university-research innovation alliance were newly evaluated and identified. At the end of 2012, there were 930 high-tech enterprises, 563 municipal science enterprises, 746 engineering (technical) centers of municipal enterprises, 212 R&D centers of provincial high-tech enterprises, 8 technical centers of enterprises identified at state level, 16 national innovate pilot and innovative enterprises, 52 provincial innovative model and pilot enterprises, and 156 municipal innovative pilot enterprises at the end of 2012. There were 258 technical service enterprises above designed size at the end of 2012, achieving annual turnover revenue of ¥10.39 billion and total profits of ¥1.92 billion, increased respectively by 19.5% and 20.8%.

Education: There were 2,064 schools at different levels in Ningbo at the end of 2012, with students enrolled of 1.331 million and teaching and administrative staff of 100 thousand (including full-time teachers of about 76 thousand). The standardized schools at the stage of compulsory education totaled 492, with the standardization rate of 69.5%. The kindergarten enroll rate of three-year preschool education was kept above 99.7%; the enroll rate and consolidation rates at the stage of compulsory education were 100% and over 99%; the rate for junior students entering into senior students was kept over 99.1%, with the ordinary professional secondary schools rate of 1:1. There were 1,072 full-time non-state-run secondary and primary schools (including kindergarten) with 320,000 students at school, accounting for 28.4% of that of total full-time secondary and primary schools in Ningbo. There were 145,000 students of regular full-time higher-education institutions in Ningbo, with the ratio of undergraduates and junior college students were 60:40; the postgraduates in Ningbo were 6,700. There were 252 college students per ten thousand persons in Ningbo. There were over 240 units conducting training all the year around, with training items of over 180 covering 81,000 persons. Persons completing training of "double certificates" were 8,445 and the reserved labor forces being trained with professional skills were 2,323.

Talent cultivation: The number of talents of different industries was up by 145,000 in 2012 and the total talents in Ningbo at the end of 2012 amounted to 1.3 million, including 712,000 professional talents, 210,000 high-skilled talents, 33,000 talents with master and doctor diploma, and 3,500 students studying abroad. The high-level program of talent cultivation was active promoted. There were 5 new talents from national "Program of overseas talent introduction", 28 new talents from provincial "Program of overseas talent introduction", and 34 new talents from municipal "3315 Program". 8 persons were chosen for gaining access to special state subsidiary; 2 persons were chosen as the key financial-aid subjects by provincial "151 program", and 5 first-class persons and 23 second-class persons were also determined. 605 persons were recognized as the first leading ones and under key training at municipal level, and there were near 4,200 persons were chosen as back-up high-level talents. The construction of industry-university-research platform had fruitful yield. There were 3 new innovation parks for persons studying abroad, with these parks being located at county (urban) areas. The new scientific research stations (moving stations) for post doctors, totaling 63 by far with post doctors accumulating 302, indicating comprehensive completion of "135 Program". There were 40 new teams of technical innovation at municipal level and 4 provincial teams. 11 studios for first municipal masters (1 national one and 8 provincial ones) has been established. The first practice center of first highly skilled talents was established.

X. Culture, Health and Sports

Cultural construction: The public cultural services have been enriched and there have been 500 boutique exhibitions, 500 public lectures and 500 classic art performances, over 25,000 free-movie projections in countryside and 2,500 free-operas performed in countryside. New radio and television have been installed in over 1,100 fishing boats. A "farmhouse reading room" was established for each administrative village. The feature of "Threshold-free public cultural service for a new Ningbo with literary reputation" programmed by Ningbo was aired in CCTV News. Cultural activities in urban and rural areas tended to be more activated. In 2012, Ningbo undertook several state-level large-scale cultural activities such as the 7th National Excellent Child Play and "Shining stars" national arts and photographic exhibition for non-specialized persons. What's more, Ningbo has successively undertaken the first large urban music singing activities - "Music Festival for Ningbo People", the 4th Reading Month, and 5th China (Ningbo) Farmer Film Festival, forming a development mode led by national high-level cultural activities and backed by festival actives at municipal (county) level. Cultural works and production have also witnessed a fruitful year. The music drama "Tell the sea", TV play "Marching eastwards the sea", animated series "Young Effendi", and non-fiction literature work "Woman Warrior" have been granted with "Five tops" of 12th national spiritual cultivation. The child play "Magic freshwater snail shell" was awarded by 7th national excellent child play. "The man from Ningbo" was awarded by "Outstanding contribution of China Modern Opera Research Commission". In the tide of strong momentum of cultural industry, Zhejiang Dafeng Industrial Limited Company was granted as "Model base for national cultural industry" by Ministry of Culture, becoming the only enterprise in stage machinery area wining the prize. China Hailun Piano Company Limited was successfully listed in Shenzhen Stock Exchange, becoming the forth one in culture area in Growth Enterprise Market of China listed. The box-office sales in 2012 has firstly exceeded ¥200 million, totaling ¥230 million, up by 28.3%, with the second fastest growth in Zhejiang Province. There were 6 new cinemas and 23 multi-hall cinemas in total at the end of 2012. 112 films were introduced to the cinemas in 2012, including 80 domestic ones and 32 foreign ones.

Medical and health services: The medical treatment and public health conditions of urban and rural residents have been further improved. At the end of 2012, Ningbo owned 28,000 hospital beds, 49,000 health workers, including 19,000 medical practitioners (assistants included) and 18,000 registered nurses. According to the statistics of registered population, the number of hospital beds, health workers, medical practitioners (assistants included) and registered nurses per thousand people reached 4.8, 8.4, 3.3 and 3.1 respectively. By the end of 2012, there have been 151 community health service centers (health center) in total, 131 of which satisfied the provincial level, at a rate of 86.8%, ranking the first in Zhejiang Province. In addition, 21 demonstration community health service centers at provincial level have been established, 4 of which meet national standard. New rural co-operative medical system was further consolidated, benefiting 2,928,000 people, accounting for 97.7% of the rural population. Per capita funding level has increased from ¥396 of last year to ¥565. The works in public health have made remarkable achievements. The total reported morbidity of Class A and B infectious diseases was 189.81/100,000; the vaccine inoculation rate of children at school age was 99.6%. The immunoprophylaxis service quality stood out around the whole province. The maternal mortality rate among permanent resident population was 0 for the first time. The infant mortality rate was 2.96‰ and that of children under the age of 5 was 4.05‰, both of which stayed at low level. The work of blood donation without payment was under steady development with 70,016 person-time donation around the year. Voluntary blood donation accounted for 104.2% of blood for clinical use, maintaining our target that all blood for clinical use was from voluntary blood donation.

Sports: We have held "activities of opening stadiums directly under sports system for public use", finding that citizens were enthusiastic about participating in sports. There have been 100,000 visits to the stadiums under management of sports bureau free of charge. In 2012, there have been 12 villages, towns and sub-districts successfully horned as outstanding sports towns at provincial level, and 4 streets with 51 communities have been successfully honored as advanced sports streets & communities of Zhejiang Province. We have strengthened the maintenance of public sports facilities, updating 586 workout paths and building 200 ball fields in the whole year. The mass sports were abundant and colorful; we have more than 500 coaches (volunteers) of radio calisthenics, holding more than 30 games of all kinds of radio calisthenics competition and enabling the ninth radio calisthenics to become the new fitness hot spot of Ningbo people. Comprehensive strength in competitive sports was improved remarkably and we have made breakthroughs in Olympic Games. Li Jinzi, Dong Cheng, Wang Shun, Shan Danna and Li Ling took part in London Olympic Games, wining two women boxing medals; and two athletes ranked fifth. Plus with Ren Cancan, transferred to PAP Corps, the number of athletes participating in the Games has exceeded the previous Olympics. Moreover, our athletes won two world champions, 9 Asian champions and 24 national champions in 2012. The sports undertakings and sport industry were under harmonious development. We have held 42 games of national level or above and the sales of sports lottery tickets have witness a new breakthrough, reaching ¥1.3 billion and ranking at the second place by surpassing Wenzhou.

XI. Population, Livelihood, Social Insurance and Social Organization

Population increase: The population in Ningbo was 5.777 million in 2012, up by 2.27‰, including 2.261 million urban population. The birth rate, death rate and natural population growth rate were 8.65‰, 6.56‰ and 2.09‰ respectively.

Resident income: The disposable income per urban resident was ¥37,902 in 2012, up by 11.3% (actual growth of 9.4% if the price element counted); the net income per rural resident was ¥18,475, up by 11.8% (actual growth of 10.0% if the price element counted). From the perspective of income source, wage remained the decisive element for the income increase for residents, which contributed to the income increase for urban and rural residents at 82.3% and 69.3% respectively. The ratio of income of urban and rural residents was reduced from 2.06:1 in 2011 to 2.05:1 in 2012, which was remarkably lower than the national average level (3.10:1).

Social security system: In 2012, the newly increased number of people purchasing basic retirement insurance, basic medical insurance, unemployment insurance, work-related injury insurance and maternity insurance was 399,000, 216,000, 156,000, 169,000 and 184,000 respectively. By the end of 2012, the total numbers of people purchasing basic retirement insurance, basic medical insurance, unemployment insurance, work-related injury insurance and maternity insurance were 4,743 million, 3.266 million, 2.162 million, 2.702 million and 2.331 million respectively. By the end of 2012, the number of migrant workers purchasing five social insurances has reached 1,794,000 and the net increased number of people purchasing such insurances during the whole year has been 226,000. The newly increased number of people purchasing urban and rural resident endowment insurance and medical insurance for urban residents was 101,000 and 181,000 respectively. 83.4% of people with local registered permanent residence have bought endowment insurance. In 2012, monthly basis pension of enterprise retirees has increased to ¥2048 for each person, up by ¥233. Medical aid range and standards have been further widened and ratio for reimbursement of hospitalization expenses and special disease expenses within the policy area of urban employees and residents has risen to 85% and 70.4% respectively. Moreover, municipal integration of medical insurances of urban employees and residents was promoted stably. Social insurance card "One-card" project has obtained the staged achievements and the accumulated number of social insurance cards issued was over 2 million.

People's livelihood security: By the end of 2012, there have been 39,355 households (namely 59,483 people) which had access to the minimum living guarantee in the urban and rural areas of the city and total living guarantee funds paid were ¥229 million. There were 5,224 people gaining access to five guarantees. The number of people concentratedly provided for was 4,990 with ratio of 95.5%. There were 1380 homeless, friendless and helpless people without source of income. Among these people, 1,353 people were concentratedly provided for with ratio of 98.0%. In 2012, the number of newly increased beds of nursing institution for the aged was 2,468. By the end of 2012, there were 220 nursing institutions for the aged and 33,168 beds in the city.

Government-subsidized housing project: In 2012, the area and number of government-subsidized housing projects newly constructed in the city was 1,403,000 m2 and 18,858 sets. Among these, the area and number of public rental housing was 561,000 m2 and 10,269 sets; the number of completed government-subsidized housing projects was 6,202 sets; the number of newly increased households receiving low-rent housing monetary subsidies was 3,721. Various housing security goals and tasks specified by provincial government have been outperformed.

Charity: In 2012, city and county level charitable organizations have raised a donation of ¥440 million and paid ¥360 million for aid work. The number of people in straitened circumstances and receiving help from such charitable organizations was 355,000. By the end of 2012, the accumulated funds raised by charitable organizations in the city have reached ¥3.43 billion and accumulated funds paid for aid work have been ¥2.34 billion. The number of people in straitened circumstances and receiving help from such charitable organizations was 1.705 million. Over 500 various voluntary service activities have been conducted and more than 6,000 volunteers have participated in providing the service all the year around. The accumulated service time was 13,000 hours.

Social organization: By the end of 2012, there were 6 districts, 2 counties, 3 county-level cities, 78 towns, 11 villages, 64 sub-district offices, 533 communities, 106 neighborhood committees and 2,567 villages committees in the whole city.

XII. Ecological Construction and Social Safety

Ecological construction: City "Fuel forbidden area" construction and exhaust pollution prevention of motor vehicles was performed. 465 coal-fired boilers have been eliminated and transformed. Four motor vehicle exhaust test stations in six districts of the whole city have been put into operation officially. Comprehensive improvement of major waters, such as the source of drinking water, and rural environment was consolidated. 127 reservoirs have been subject to troubleshooting and work account of various pollution sources was established; over 400 solar energy biochemical reduction treatment facilities have been established and there were more than 100 scattered village-level domestic sewage treatment facility projects. Environmental law enforcement supervision was consolidated continuously. In 2012, 42,748 law enforcement officers were dispatched, 21,867 enterprises were inspected and 938 enterprises were investigated. Total fines have reached ¥42,086,000 and penalty limit of individual case was ¥45000. Monitoring and controlling capacity was improved continuously. Since March 25, 2012, Ningbo City took the lead in releasing PM 2.5 real-time monitored data of central urban area according to new standards of environment air quality. Since November 16, 2012, Ningbo City began to release air quality index (AQI) of all 8 national controlling points. In 2012, 568 enterprises with outdated capacity have been eliminated. Among these enterprises, 64 enterprises have been closed down and removed; 4,500 sets of outdated equipment were discarded and about 428,000 tons of standard coal was saved. The accumulated decreased discharge quantities of CO2, COD, SO2, ammonia nitrogen and nitric oxide were 1,070,000 tons, 719 tons, 2,231 tons, 32 tons and 1,561 tons respectively. Building energy conservation and renewable energy promotion and application was conducted vigorously. During the whole year, 15 renewable energy building application demonstration projects have been organized and implemented with the area of 1,100,000 m2; the area of newly increased energy-saving buildings was 16,750,000 m2; the newly increased application area of solar energy heat was 1,000,000 m2. The area of ground source heat pump was 600,000 m2. In 2012, Ningbo City has successfully passed on-site review and acceptance of national environmental protection model city. Cixi City and Yinzhou District have successfully passed the review and acceptance of provincial ecological city (or district). Ninghai County has passed the technical evaluation of state-level ecological county.

"Peaceful Ningbo" construction: In 2012, there were 3,578 work safety accidents occurred in Ningbo, which resulted in 778 deaths, 3,136 injuries and direct economic losses of ¥43,157,000. Such figures have dropped by 5.3%, 5.2%, 8.3% and 8.2% respectively when compared with those of last year. Main indicators of safety production have been lowered in the 8th consecutive year when compared with that of last year. Construction and innovation of food monitoring system was actively promoted and food safety supervision was performed well in accordance with laws and regulations. In 2012, 53,715 batches of food have been subject to quantitative inspection, accounting for 127.9% of total task load of the whole year. Control over medical instrument market was tightened and new version GMP was conducted fully. Daily supervision and inspection of 18 crude drug and preparation manufacturers within the jurisdiction was completed and the percentage of area covered by inspection was 100%. 98 illegal advertisements about medical instrument and health-care food have been investigated and punished. Among these advertisements, 67 advertisements were handed over to business sectors and administrative warning was given to advertisers of 31 advertisements; 1,112 cases about medical instrument and catering were put on record. Among these cases, 979 cases were settled and 8 cases were handed over to public security organ. ¥1.089 million goods value generated by illegal production and operation was confiscated and total amounts confiscated have reached ¥15.44 million. The amount confiscated and the number of cases handed over to public security organ has reached a record high.

"Ningbo without back salary" brand was created vigorously and harmonious labor relations have generally been kept stable. The whole city has raised the security deposit of ¥1.5 billion for wage payment and emergency revolving fund of ¥150 million for dealing with back salary. 3385 labor cases have been settled in the whole city. 57000 labor contracts have been concluded and unpaid salaries of ¥200 million have been recovered for 33,000 employees. In 2012, 36,503 letters and visits of the masses had been accepted and 1431 times (19,388 people.) of collective appeals from the masses had been received. People's compromise organizations have mediated 126,447 civil disputes during the whole year. Among these disputes, 124,658 disputes have been successfully settled through mediation with success rate of 98.6%. 25 suicides committed by 32 people because of civil disputes have been prevented; 135 civil disputes involving 779 people have been prevented from developing into criminal cases.

Note:

(1)All figures in this Bulletin are preliminary statistics.

(2)Figures in value terms on gross municipal product and value-added quoted in this Bulletin are at current prices, whereas growth rates are calculated at comparable prices.

(3)Industrial enterprises above designated size refer to those enterprises with annual main business income equal to more than ¥20 million.

Wholesale, retail, accommodation and catering enterprises above the limit refer to:

Wholesale industry: wholesale enterprises with annual main business income equal to or more than ¥20million;

Retail industry: retail enterprises with annual main business income equal to or more than ¥5 million;

Accommodation industry: enterprises with annual main business income equal to or more than ¥2 million;

Catering industry: catering enterprises with annual main business income equal to or more than ¥2 million.

NINGBO

Statistical YearBook

第一篇

综合

GENERAL SURVEY

综合
General Survey

宁波的经济发展
Economic Development of Ningbo

		2012	比上年增长(%) Increase Over Last Year
国内生产总值(亿元)	Gross Domestic Product(100 million yuan)	6582.21	7.8
第一产业	Primary Industry	268.52	1.0
第二产业	Secondary Industry	3516.84	6.0
第三产业	Tertiary Industry	2796.85	10.9
规模以上工业总产值	Gross Output Value of Above Designated Sized Industry	12155.08	0.9
固定资产投资	Investemnt in Fixed Assets	2901.42	21.6
社会消费品零售总额	Total Retail Sales of Consumer Goods	2329.26	15.4
公共财政预算收入	Public Fiscal Budget Revenue	1536.51	7.3
港口货物吞吐量(万吨)	Ports Cargo Handling Capacity(10000 tons)	45303.70	4.5
集装箱吞吐量(万标箱)	Container Handled at Ports(10000 TEU)	1567.14	8.0
自营进出口额(亿美元)	Directive Import and Export(USD 100 million)	965.73	-1.6
出口额(亿美元)	Export(USD 100 million)	614.45	1.0
实际利用外资	Amount of Foreign Capital Actually Used	28.53	1.5

宁波的一天
One Day in Ningbo

国内生产总值	Gross Domestic Product	179842	万元	10000 yuan
农业增加值	Value-added of Agriculture	7337	万元	10000 yuan
工业增加值	Value-added of Industry	86614	万元	10000 yuan
第三产业增加值	Value-added of Tertiary Industry	76417	万元	10000 yuan
固定资产投资	Investment in Fixed Assets	79274	万元	10000 yuan
社会消费品零售额	Retail Sales of Consumer Goods	63641	万元	10000 yuan
公共财政预算收入	Public Fiscal Budget Revenue	41981	万元	10000 yuan
港口货物吞吐量	Ports Cargo Handling Capacity	123.78	万吨	10000 tons
集装箱吞吐量	Container Handled at Ports	42818	标箱	TEU
自营出口额	Directive Export	16788	万美元	USD 10000
全社会用电量	Electricity Consumption	14046	万千瓦时	10000 kwh

表 1—1 行政区划和陆域面积(2012) Administrative Division and Land Area

单位:个(unit)

地区	Region	镇 Town	乡 Township	街道办事处 Subdistrict Offices	居民委员会 Neighborhood Committee	村民委员会 Villages Committee	陆域面积(平方公里) Land Area (sq. km)
全市	**Whole Municipality**	**78**	**11**	**64**	**639**	**2567**	**9816.23**
市区	**Urban Area**	**22**	**2**	**41**	**387**	**797**	**2461.76**
海曙	Haishu			8	76		29.38
江东	Jiangdong			8	74		33.75
江北	Jiangbei	1		7	57	93	208.16
北仑	Beilun	2	1	7	46	213	599.03
镇海	Zhenhai	2		4	29	60	245.90
鄞州	Yinzhou	17	1	7	105	431	1345.54
县级市	**County**	**56**	**9**	**23**	**252**	**1770**	**7354.47**
余姚	Yuyao	14	1	6	55	265	1500.80
慈溪	Cixi	15		5	78	297	1360.63
奉化	Fenghua	6		5	35	355	1267.60
象山	Xiangshan	10	5	3	44	490	1382.18
宁海	Ninghai	11	3	4	40	363	1843.26

表 1—2 各月主要气象指标(2012) Main Climate Indicators

时间 Item	平均气温(℃) Average Temperature (℃)	降水量(毫米) Precipitation (millimeters)	相对湿度(%) Relative Humidity (%)	日照时数(小时) Sunshine Hours (hours)
1月 Jan.	5.3	132.6	77.0	67.1
2月 Feb.	5.3	81.6	77.0	64.7
3月 Mar.	10.7	206.9	71.0	133.6
4月 Apr.	18.3	83.0	69.0	163.4
5月 May	21.4	225.4	73.0	145.9
6月 June	24.8	211.5	82.0	72.1
7月 July	30.1	203.1	70.0	280.0
8月 Aug.	28.8	442.8	75.0	198.6
9月 Sept.	23.3	209.2	75.0	153.3
10月 Oct.	19.4	24.0	68.0	227.9
11月 Nov.	12.2	123.6	74.0	142.9
12月 Dec.	6.9	104.2	72.0	119.6

注:本表数据来自宁波市气象局。

Note:Data in this table are obtained from Ningbo Meteorological Bureau.

表1—3 部分年份国民经济主要指标 Main Indicators of National Economy in Partial Years

指标	单位	Indicators	Unit
人口		**Population**	
年末总人口	万人	Year—end Population	10000 persons
#非农业人口	万人	Non—Agriculture Population	10000 persons
地区生产总值	**亿元**	**Gross Domestic Product**	**100 million yuan**
第一产业增加值	亿元	Added Value of Primary Industry	100 million yuan
第二产业增加值	亿元	Added Value of Secondary Industry	100 million yuan
第三产业增加值	亿元	Added Value of Tertiary Industry	100 million yuan
人均生产总值(户籍人口)	**元**	**Per Capital GDP(by Registered Population)**	**yuan**
人均生产总值(常住人口)	**元**	**Per Capital GDP(by Permanent Population)**	**yuan**
农业		**Agriculture**	
农村实有劳动力	万人	Rural Labor force	10000 persons
粮食产量	万吨	Yield of Grain Crops	10000 tons
工业		**Industry**	
全部工业增加值	亿元	Added Value of Industry	100 million yuan
运输、邮电和通信		**Transportation. Post and Telecommunications Services**	
港口货物吞吐量	万吨	Cargo Handled at Ports	10000 tons
集装箱吞吐量	万标箱	Container Handled at Ports	10000 TEU
旅客运输量	万人	Passenger Traffic	10000 persons
货物运输量	万吨	Freight Traffic	10000 tons
固定电话用户	万户	Number of Local Telephone Subscribers	10000 subscribers
移动电话用户	万户	Number of Subscribers of Mobile Telephone	10000 subscribers
全社会用电量	**亿千瓦时**	**Total Consumption of Electricity**	**100 million kwh**
#工业用电	亿千瓦时	Electricity Consumption for Industry Use	100 million kwh
生活用电	亿千瓦时	Electricity Consumption for Urban and Rural Residents	100 million kwh
固定资产投资	**亿元**	**Investment in Fixed Assets**	**100 million yuan**
#房地产开发投资	亿元	Real Estate Development	100 million yuan
财政金融		**Finance and Banking**	

注:本表价值量指标按当年价格计算,发展速度按可比价格计算。自2011年始,全社会固定资产投资更名为固定资产投资,并且调整口径。

Note:Figures in value terms are calculated at current prices,While the indices and growth rates are calculated at comparable prices. Since the begining of 2011,Total investment in fixed assets changed its name to fixed assets investment,and aperture adjustment.

1978	1990	2000	2010	2011	2012	指数(2012 为以下各年%) Index(2011As Percentage of the Following Years)			年平均增长(%) Average Annual Growth Rate(%)	
						1978	2000	2010	1978—2012	2000—2012
457.70	510.76	540.94	574.08	576.40	577.71	126.2	106.8	100.6	0.7	0.5
63.42	102.98	142.03	205.23	208.18	211.45	333.4	148.9	103.0	3.6	3.4
20.17	141.40	1144.57	5163.00	6059.24	6582.21	8546.1	397.1	118.6	14.0	12.2
6.52	29.35	94.24	219.13	255.23	268.52	464.1	156.8	104.9	4.6	3.8
9.69	80.31	635.83	2870.69	3349.53	3516.84	14839.4	398.3	116.3	15.8	12.2
3.96	31.74	414.50	2073.18	2454.48	2796.85	10659.8	449.5	123.2	14.7	13.3
437	2777	21208	90175	105333	114065	6262.7	364.7	117.7	12.9	11.4
			69368	79524	86228			115.6		
195.42	254.12	257.44	306.32	306.36	293.79	150.3	114.1	95.9	1.2	1.1
180.51	189.06	132.51	87.13	90.14	86.57	48.0	65.3	99.4	-2.1	-3.5
8.62	72.12	578.30	2586.17	3019.00	3170.07	19223.3	408.5	116.9	16.7	12.4
214	2554	11547	41217	43339	45303	21169.5	392.3	109.9	17.1	12.1
	2.21	90.20	1300.35	1451.24	1567.14		1737.4	120.5		26.9
2966	7378	22736	33911	28745	28053	945.8	123.4	82.7	6.8	1.8
1385	4763	10819	30553	31228	32616	2354.9	301.5	106.8	9.7	9.6
1.07	6.19	130.15	317.39	312.45	308.00	28785.0	236.7	97.0	18.1	7.4
		117.92	845.50	1029.46	1088.00		922.7	128.7		20.3
7.09	31.49	113.48	459.04	505.30	514.09	7250.9	453.0	112.0	13.4	13.4
4.37	23.38	84.01	354.27	388.62	384.59	8800.7	457.8	108.6	14.1	13.5
0.43	4.30	15.13	49.83	53.59	59.31	13793.8	392.0	119.0	15.6	12.1
5.02	39.28	360.75	2193.28	2385.50	2901.43			132.3		
	2.49	59.71	557.27	754.94	884.35		1481.1	158.7		25.2

表 1—3 续表 Continued

指标	单位	Indicators	Unit
财政总收入	亿元	Financial Budgetary Revenue	100 million yuan
财政支出	亿元	Financial Expenditure	100 million yuan
年末金融机构存款余额	亿元	Balance of Deposits of Financial Institutions	100 million yuan
＃城乡居民储蓄存款	亿元	Saving Deposits of Urban and Rural Residents	100 million yuan
年末金融机构贷款余额	亿元	Balance of Loans of Financial Institutions	100 million yuan
社会消费品零售总额	**亿元**	**Total Retail Sales of Consumer Goods**	**100 million yuan**
对外经济		**Foreign Trade**	
进出口总额	亿美元	Total Exports and Imports Value	USD 100 million
＃出口总额	亿美元	Total Exports Value	USD 100 million
进口总额	亿美元	Total Imports Value	USD 100 million
合同利用外资	亿美元	Foreign Investment Contracted	USD 100 million
实际利用外资	亿美元	Foreign Investments Actually Use	USD 100 million
城乡居民生活		**Living Standard**	
市区居民人均可支配收入	元	Per Capital Disposable Income of Urban Households	yuan
市区居民人均消费性支出	元	Per Capital Annual Expenditure for Consumption of Urban Households	yuan
农村居民人均纯收入	元	Per Capital Annual Net Income of Rural Housholds	yuan
农村居民人均生活消费支出	元	Per Capita Annual Living Expenditure of Rural Residents	yuan
教育		**Education**	
高等学校在校学生数	万人	Students Enrollment in Institutions of Higher Education	10000 persons
中等专业学校在校学生数	万人	Students Enrollment in Specializad Secondary Schools	10000 persons
中学在校学生数	万人	Students Enrollment in Secondary Schools	10000 persons
小学在校学生数	万人	Students Enrollment in Primary Schools	10000 persons
专任教师数	万人	Number of Full－times Teachers	10000 persons
卫生事业		**Health Care**	
卫生技术人员数	万人	Number of Medical Technical Personnel	10000 persons
＃医生	万人	Doctor	10000 persons
卫生机构床位数	张	Number of Beds in Health Institutions	bed

1978	1990	2000	2010	2011	2012	指数(2012 为以下各年%) Index(2011As Percentage of the Following Years)			年平均增长(%) Average Annual Growth Rate(%)	
						1978	2000	2010	1978—2012	2000—2012
4.97	15.89	148.01	2068.62	2271.95	2206.04	44387.0	1490.5	106.6	19.6	25.2
1.12	9.71	89.23	1452.17	1596.78	1516.16	135371.0	1699.2	104.4	23.6	26.6
4.84	90.13	1172.94	9552.03	10435.92	11602.32	239717.3	989.2	121.5	25.7	21.0
1.52	46.12	586.06	3282.26	3666.23	4175.96	274734.4	712.5	127.2	26.2	17.8
6.50	97.44	883.12	9000.62	10209.99	11300.32	173851.1	1279.6	125.6	24.5	23.7
7.07	**54.98**	**389.29**	**1704.51**	**2018.86**	**2329.26**	**32945.7**	**598.3**	**136.7**	**18.6**	**16.1**
	2.98	75.41	829.04	981.87	965.73		1280.6	116.5		23.7
	2.80	51.68	519.67	608.32	614.45		1189.0	118.2		22.9
	0.18	23.73	309.37	373.55	351.27		1480.3	113.5		25.2
	0.56	9.52	40.46	50.15	53.13		558.1	131.3		15.4
	0.22	6.22	23.23	28.09	28.53		458.6	122.8		13.5
306	1963	10921	30166	34058	37902	12386.2	347.1	125.6	15.2	10.9
299	1628	7997	19420	21779	23288	7788.7	291.2	119.9	13.7	9.3
	1254	5069	14261	16518	18475		364.5	129.5		11.4
	1166	3929	9794	11253	12699		323.2	129.7		10.3
0.10	0.49	2.59	14.08	14.44	14.54	14535.8	561.2	103.2	15.8	15.5
0.29	0.90	2.51	8.07	8.28	8.03	2768.8	319.9	99.5	10.3	10.2
27.16	19.65	27.98	32.54	30.86	29.52	108.7	105.5	90.7	0.2	0.4
59.11	42.70	42.40	46.19	47.61	47.88	81.0	112.9	103.7	—0.6	1.0
3.55	3.34	5.17	7.29	7.70	7.63	214.9	147.6	104.7	2.3	3.3
0.93	1.58	1.92	4.31	4.67	4.92	528.9	256.2	114.1	5.0	8.2
0.36	0.75	0.95	1.72	1.84	1.91	529.3	200.6	110.8	5.0	6.0
5989	11449	14535	26097	27127	28290	472.4	194.6	108.4	4.7	5.7

表 1－4 各县(市)社会经济基本情况(2012)
Main Indicators of Society and Economy by Region

指标	单位	Indicators	Unit
人口、劳动力及土地面积		**Population, Employment and Land Areas**	
年末总人口	万人	Year－end Population	10000 persons
年平均人口	万人	Annual Average Population	10000 persons
常住人口	万人	Permanent Population	10000 persons
年末总户数	万户	Total Households of Year－end	10000 households
全社会从业人员	万人	Total Employment Personnel	10000 persons
第一产业	万人	Primary Industry	10000 persons
第二产业	万人	Secondary Industry	10000 persons
第三产业	万人	Tertiary Industry	10000 persons
年末城镇集体以上从业人员数	万人	Employed Personnel in Urban Collective－owned Units and Above Level	10000 persons
第一产业	万人	Primary Industry	10000 persons
第二产业	万人	Secondary Industry	10000 persons
第三产业	万人	Tertiary Industry	10000 persons
城镇私营和个体从业人员	万人	Employed Persons Individuals and Private Enterprises in Urban Areas	10000 persons
年末城镇登记失业人员数	人	Unemployed Persons in Urban Areas at Year－end	person
行政区域土地面积	平方公里	Land Area of Districts	sq. km
#建成区面积	平方公里	Developed Areas	sq. km
综合经济		**General Economy**	
生产总值(当年价格)	万元	Gross Domestic Product(at Current Price)	10000 yuan
第一产业增加值	万元	Value－added of Primary Industry	10000 yuan
第二产业增加值	万元	Value－added of Secondary Industry	10000 yuan
#工业增加值	万元	Value－added of Industry	10000 yuan
第三产业增加值	万元	Value－added of Tertiary Industry	10000 yuan
人均生产总值(常住)	元	Per Capital GDP(by Permanent Population)	yuan
人均生产总值(户籍)	元	Per Capital GDP(by Registered Population)	yuan
生产总值增长率	%	Increase Rate of GDP Over 2011	%
地方财政收入	万元	Local Financial Revenue	10000 yuan
公共财政预算支出	万元	Public Fiscal Budget Revenue	10000 yuan
#一般性公共服务支出	万元	Expenditure for General Public Services	10000 yuan
科学技术支出	万元	Expenditure for Science and Technology Promotion	10000 yuan
教育支出	万元	Expenditure for Education	10000 yuan
文化体育与传媒支出	万元	Expenditure for Culture, Sports & Media Services	10000 yuan
医疗卫生支出	万元	Expenditure for Medical and Health	10000 yuan
节能保护支出	万元	Expenditure for Energy Saving and Environmental Protection	10000 yuan
城乡社区事务支出	万元	Expenditure for Urban and Rural Community Services	10000 yuan
交通运输支出	万元	Expenditure for Transportation	10000 yuan
社会保障和就业支出	万元	Expenditure for Social Security & Employment	10000 yuan
住房保障支出	万元	Expenditure for Housing Security	10000 yuan
农林水事务支出	万元	Expenditure for Farming, Forestry and Fishery Service	10000 yuan

全市 Total	市区 Urban District	#鄞州 Yinzhou	余姚 Yuyao	慈溪 Cixi	奉化 Fenghua	象山 Xiangshan	宁海 Ninghai
577.71	226.11	83.12	83.45	104.19	48.35	54.03	61.57
577.06	225.43	82.67	83.46	104.17	48.37	54.10	61.53
763.90	350.97	136.55	101.29	146.68	49.37	50.83	64.75
223.46	90.06	33.55	31.01	42.52	18.24	18.83	22.80
501.58	233.59	90.23	65.62	84.00	35.05	36.22	47.10
29.74		6.24	8.14	10.40	6.37	8.17	8.80
275.27	135.66	51.89	32.27	50.30	18.01	16.93	22.10
196.57	110.07	32.10	25.21	23.30	10.67	11.12	16.20
174.70	99.25	25.28	15.23	15.92	5.84	31.38	7.07
0.06	0.02	0.00	0.01	0.03	0.00	0.00	0.01
117.02	58.31	17.81	10.94	11.06	3.61	28.83	4.27
57.62	40.92	7.46	4.28	4.84	2.23	2.56	2.80
164.11	111.64	45.04	15.38	7.10	10.53	8.26	11.20
82078	64320	4940	4607	5584	2599	3435	1533
9816.23	2461.76	1345.54	1500.80	1360.63	1267.60	1382.18	1843.26
457.14	289.83		45.56	42.30	18.75	28.00	32.70
65822064	39509830	10876479	7090713	9582077	2742507	3371599	3525338
2685159	606684	384298	434637	465351	276749	537669	364069
35168381	20509249	6805554	4223347	5600405	1303059	1583874	1948447
31700695	18507170	6506999	3937687	5212212	1117435	1169696	1756495
27968524	18393897	3686627	2432729	3510321	1162699	1250056	1212822
86228	112653	79707	70052	65374	55591	66375	54483
114065	175268	131565	84970	91985	56699	62322	57291
7.8	7.5	9.3	8.8	9.4	5.4	5.7	8.3
7255003	5009336	1362224	616855	813852	243728	272793	298439
8284437	5475083	1375506	678191	866031	389930	458059	417143
1004625	643566	157887	92309	115026	47040	47640	59044
324076	217047	55221	28821	43754	11208	12000	11246
1417046	838249	252653	132919	194258	77245	88677	85698
127706	85934	21383	13042	12220	3689	5520	7301
563787	317674	86220	68636	73052	31426	33339	39660
114735	76775	41490	12882	9022	3907	5631	6518
849136	754533	112095	27028	33761	9434	14115	10265
506672	403089	69637	22109	15037	25520	15494	25423
790129	473017	122289	90298	105222	35541	34536	51515
170191	118074	22041	18236	16189	3806	6841	7045
721950	268513	110522	81226	79573	98697	137901	56040

表 1—4 续 1 Continued

指标	单位	Indicators	Unit
年末金融机构存款余额	万元	Balance of Deposits of Financial Institutions	10000 yuan
#城乡居民储蓄年末余额	万元	Saving Deposits of Urban and Rural Residents	10000 yuan
年末金融机构各项贷款余额	万元	Balance of Loans of Financial Institutions	10000 yuan
保险		**Insurance**	
保费收入	万元	Insurance Income	10000 yuan
#财产险	万元	Property Insurance	10000 yuan
人身险	万元	Life Insurance	10000 yuan
赔款、给付	万元	Insurance Paid	10000 yuan
规模以上工业企业		**Industry Enterprises Above Designated Size**	
工业企业数	个	Number of Industrial Enterprises	unit
从业人员年平均人数	万人	Annual Average Employees	10000 persons
工业总产值(当年价)	万元	Gross Output Value of Indutry (at current price)	10000 yuan
主营业务收入	万元	Prime Operating Revenue	10000 yuan
本年应交增值税	万元	Value—added Taxes Payable in This Year	10000 yuan
利润总额	万元	Total Profits	10000 yuan
交通运输、邮电通信、能源电力		**Transport, Post & Telecommunications, Energy and Electricity**	
铁路客运量	万人	Railway Passenger Traffic	10000 persons
铁路货运量	万吨	Railway Freight Traffic	10000 tons
公路客运量	万人	Highways Passenger Traffic	10000 persons
公路货运量	万吨	Highways Freight Traffic	10000 tons
水运客运量	万人	Waterways Passenger Traffic	10000 persons
水运货运量	万吨	Waterways Freight Traffic	10000 tons
民用航空客运量	万人	Civil Aviation Passenger Traffic	10000 persons
民用航空货邮运量	万吨	Civil Aviation Freight Traffic	10000 ton
民用汽车拥有量	辆	Number of Civil Motor Vehicles	unit
#私人汽车拥有量	辆	Number of Private Car	unit
公路里程	公里	Length of Highways	km
邮政业务收入	万元	Business Value of Post	10000 yuan
电信业务收入	万元	Business Value of Telecommunications	10000 yuan
本地电话用户数	万户	Number of Subscribers of Local Telephone	10000 subscribers
年末移动电话用户数	万户	Number of Mobile Telephone Subscribers at Year—end	10000 subscribers
#3G 移动电话用户	万户	User of 3G Mobile Phone	10000 subscribers
国际互联网用户数	万户	User of International Computer Network	10000 subscribers
能源消费量	万吨标准煤	Total Volume of Energy Consumptions	10000 tons SCE
全年用电量	万千瓦时	Electricity Consumption	10000 kwh
国内贸易、对外经济		**Domestic Trade, Foreign Trade**	
社会消费品零售额	万元	Total Retail Sales of Consumer Goods	10000 yuan

全市 Total	市区 Urban District	#鄞州 Yinzhou	余姚 Yuyao	慈溪 Cixi	奉化 Fenghua	象山 Xiangshan	宁海 Ninghai
116023188	79101644	15251705	10807496	15636652	3574098	3245132	3658165
41759634	24207658	6832514	5050704	7501295	1981777	1413757	1604442
113003187	75422062	13058522	10336279	13865492	4038330	4653373	4687651
1647056							
862294							
784762							
642725							
6804	3240	1618	1111	1155	437	403	458
147.06	75.58	31.59	18.76	27.94	8.76	9.14	6.88
121550760	81133945	19810205	11275033	16089841	3536980	4351251	5163711
117959823	79846596	18943357	10773592	14910131	3451265	4112333	4865906
3007829	1993970	426929	243605	376877	88988	122520	181870
5532121	3685660	1241391	510053	660388	95397	208463	372160
2237.47	1767.83		336.79		22.64		110.21
2594.34	2417.72	7.74	134.18	42.44			
27110	13880	3560	2860	3050	2520	2250	2550
16570	11160	3150	1455	1430	1105	690	730
122.79	8.98	7.99				80.00	33.61
14113	10443	862	38	10	370	2362	890
526.60	526.60	526.60					
90849.40	90849.40	90849.40					
1232485	670568	214122	162314	197443	68440	64570	69150
895247	465353	148572	123571	153290	49635	51544	51854
10661	3251	1904	1799	1551	1247	1270	1543
86097	39238	5828	11142	21396	5346	3596	5379
1160429	654720	142600	127465	186136	61969	60556	69583
308.00	161.50	47.25	38.97	50.90	20.60	20.61	15.42
1088.00	495.61	159.15	153.41	223.71	62.46	79.36	73.45
236.05	99.97		53.50	32.77	26.58	11.18	12.05
231.18	129.75	28.57	27.04	35.42	12.26	13.94	12.78
2255.20	1776.34	170.11	137.97	170.84	39.12	51.72	79.21
5140915	3012523	710681	653552	836957	247141	165369	225373
23292590	12458556	3111429	3051602	3919838	1098347	1482154	1282092

表 1—4 续 2 Continued

指标	单位	Indicators	Unit
当年新签合同项目数	个	New Signed Constract	unit
当年实际使用外资金额	万美元	Amount of Foreign Capital Actually Used	USD 10000
进口额	万美元	Total Import	USD 10000
出口额	万美元	Total Export	USD 10000
固定资产投资		**Investemnt in Fixed Assets**	
固定资产投资	万元	Investment in Fixed Assets	10000 yuan
#房地产开发投资完成额	万元	Real Estate Development	10000 yuan
#住宅	万元	Residential Buildings	10000 yuan
全年新增固定资产	万元	Newly Increase Fixed Assets in This Year	10000 yuan
商品房屋销售面积	万平方米	Floor Space of Building Sold	10000 sq. m
#住宅	万平方米	Residential Buildings	10000 sq. m
商品房屋销售额	万元	Total Actually Sales of Commercial Buildings	10000 yuan
#住宅	万元	Residential Buildings	10000 yuan
待售面积	万平方米	Floor Space of Sale Building	10000 sq. m
文教、卫生、科技		**Culture, Education, Public Health, Science**	
全日制学校数	所	Number of Full—time Schools	unit
各类学校专任教师数	人	Teachers	person
各类学校在校学生数	人	Students in School	person
从事科技活动人员数	人	Number of Technical Personnel	person
专利申请受理量	项	Number of Patent Appliactions	piece
专利申请授权量	项	Number of Patent Certified	piece
#发明专利	项	Inventions	piece
体育场馆数	个	Number of Public Stadiums and Gymnasiums	unit
剧场、影剧院数	个	Number of Cinemas and Theatres	unit
公共图书馆图书藏量	千册、件	Collection of Public Libraries	1000 copies
医院、卫生院数	个	Number of Health Institutions	unit
卫生机构床位数	张	Number of Beds in Health Institutions	bed
医生数	人	Number of Doctors	person
注册护士	人	Number of Register Nurses	person
人民生活		**People's Livelihood**	
在岗职工平均人数	万人	Number of Full Employed Staff and Workers	10000 persons
在岗职工工资总额	万元	Total Wage of Full Employed Staff and Workers	10000 yuan
城镇居民人均可支配收入	元	Per Capital Annual Disposable Income of Urban Residents	yuan
城镇居民人均消费支出	元	Per Capital Annual Expenditure for Consumption of Urban Residents	yuan
农村居民人均纯收入	元	Per Capital Annual Net Income of Rural Residents	yuan
农村居民人均消费性支出	元	Per Capital Annual Expenditure for Consumption of Rural Residents	yuan
居民消费价格指数(上年=100)	%	Consumer Price Index (Preceding Year=100)	%

全市 Total	市区 Urban District	#鄞州 Yinzhou	余姚 Yuyao	慈溪 Cixi	奉化 Fenghua	象山 Xiangshan	宁海 Ninghai
262	102	85	67	47	10	15	21
285252	202301	39111	36676	25452	5596	7575	7652
3512743	3049523	302626	184844	186754	48463	25672	17487
6144526	4121772	1006841	593911	842179	186296	195022	205346
29014258	16871766	4203661	3615419	4432783	1281439	1375848	1437003
8843514	5179366	1521651	1354376	1274158	340949	444510	250155
5156454	2752771	818352	813968	925043	217610	304727	142335
13815589	8561635	2185530	2011687	1294521	577783	780320	589643
590.22	339.91	102.12	87.27	86.35	16.95	25.25	34.48
458.74	259.52	82.24	62.18	77.17	12.69	23.82	23.36
6633948	4053116	1353978	989800	852254	196279	286534	255965
5222892	3205264	1149026	695158	726041	134430	270289	191710
239.92	162.00	24.31	28.35	7.15	5.46	10.57	26.39
2062	843	318	304	401	150	153	206
76296	36330	11139	8718	12890	4640	5359	6059
1437800	646007	191864	154561	299422	80191	90523	112764
115784	62643	20498	15003	23013	4724	3909	6492
73647	38210	22057	12869	15469	2765	1666	2668
59175	30396	18925	10819	12348	1943	1512	2157
2065	1393	472	190	303	62	41	76
41	16	8	2	12	4	3	4
48	26	12	10	4	2	3	3
7327	5522	860	455	542	195	319	293
204	84	29	22	16	30	23	29
26311	16134	3304	2508	2483	2106	1504	1576
19055	10644	2711	1923	2872	1166	1103	1347
18280	10599	2363	1941	2581	968	1022	1169
148.94	87.33	24.20	14.26	15.16	5.39	20.43	6.36
8378694	5337135	1296872	700326	751677	287003	957071	345484
38043	37902	40607	37217	37711	36293	36872	36496
22887	23288	25636	21108	25412	21566	19917	17345
18475	20164	20831	17977	20383	17675	16388	16547
12699	13687	13360	12071	13974	9434	10286	11077
101.7	101.7	101.7	103.3	103.0	101.6	102.0	101.8

表 1—4 续 3 Continued

指标	单位	Indicators	Unit
基本养老保险参保人数	人	Number of Personnel Engaged Basic Endowment Insurance	person
基本医疗保险参保人数	人	Number of Personnel Engaged Basic Medical Insurance	person
失业保险参保人数	人	Number of Personnel Engaged Unemployment Insurance	person
社会福利院床位数	张	Number of Beds in Social Welfare Institutions	bed
社区服务设施数	个	Volunm of Service Establishment in Community	unit
城镇居民最低生活保障人数	人	Number Personnel Below Minimum Standard of Living	person
社会治安		**Social Security**	
交通事故死亡人数	人	Death of Traffic Accidents	person
交通事故损失额	万元	Losses Converted into Cash of Traffic Accidents	10000 yuan
刑事案件立案数	件	Number of Criminal Cases Registered	case
犯罪人数	人	Number of People of the Crime	person
市政公用事业		**Civil Facilities,Environment Protection**	
城市维护建设资金支出	万元	Expenditure on Urban Construction and Maintenance	10000 yuan
年末实有城市道路面积	万平方米	Area of City Roads(Year—end)	10000 sq. m
排水管道总长度	公里	Length of Sewage Pipes	km
供水综合生产能力(含自备水源)	万吨/日	General Productive Capacity of Tap Water Supply	10000 tons/day
全年售水总量	万吨	Annuall Volume of Tap Water Sale	10000 tons
#居民家庭用水量	万吨	Water Consumption for Residents Use	10000 tons
用水人口	万人	Population with Access Tap Water	10000 persons
液化石油气供气总量	吨	Total Volume of Liquefied Petroleum Gas	ton
#家庭用量	吨	For Residents Use	ton
用液化气人口	万人	Population with Access Liquefied Petroleum Gas	10000 persons
年末实有公共汽(电)车营运车辆数	辆	Number of Public Transportations Vehicles under Operation	unit
全年公共汽(电)车客运总量	万人次	Number of Passengers Carried with Public Transportations Vehicles	10000 person—times
年末实有出租汽车数	辆	Operating Taxes at Year—end	unit
绿地面积	公顷	Green Areas	hectare
#公园绿地面积	公顷	Public Green Areas	hectare
建成区绿化覆盖面积	公顷	Coverage Area of Green Area in Developed Area	hectare
环境保护		**Environment Protect**	
工业废水排放量	万吨	Valume of Industrial Waste Water Discharged	10000 tons
工业二氧化硫产生量	吨	Volume of Industrial sulfur dioxide production	ton
工业二氧化硫排放量	吨	Volume of Industrial Sulphur Dioxide Emission	ton
工业烟(粉)尘去除量	吨	Volume of Dispeled Industrial Soot	ton
工业烟(粉)尘排放量	吨	Volume of Industrial Soot Emission	ton
一般工业固体废物综合利用率	%	Rate of General Industrial Solid Waste Treated and Utilized	%
污水处理厂集中处理率	%	Rate of Disposal Living Waste Water in Sewage Treatment Plant	%
生活垃圾无害化处理率	%	Rate of Living Garbage Harmless Treatment	%

全市 Total	市区 Urban District	#鄞州 Yinzhou	余姚 Yuyao	慈溪 Cixi	奉化 Fenghua	象山 Xiangshan	宁海 Ninghai
4743021	2910474	817289	544457	690155	202856	189854	205225
4304790	2835083	694845	502459	407505	231288	158329	170126
2162204	1512084	407975	174282	211211	81702	93425	89500
30945	15254	6556	3570	3702	1895	3316	3208
1105	492	60	206	325	21	53	8
10289	7189	847	908	644	697	549	302
680	279	99	122	141	49	36	53
871.10	385.08	103.76	94.79	78.06	139.72	95.50	77.95
13984	6255	1719	2035	2700	1030	883	1081
20286	8875	2401	3140	4153	1389	1220	1509
1286094	747272	24608	129516	262354	24401	105540	17011
7125	2786	337	1046	1707	422	694	469
6907	3794	265	664	1265	188	488	509
364	225	32	33	44	18	22	23
60483	39697	12615	4198	8455	3000	2664	2469
23130	14062	8412	2012	3110	1521	1124	1301
346.99	175.53	101.24	44.45	50.97	34.30	23.59	18.15
201292	138584	46286	6095	31102	6566	10450	8495
100933	44553	43275	4751	30491	5625	7910	7603
202.46	54.89	70.60	32.34	40.99	34.30	23.59	16.35
5380	4046	1354	576	217	133	191	217
60039	45109	10434	4830	2825	1455	2640	3179
5834	4101	1209	440	605	200	210	278
17107	10689	579	1722	1862	910	706	1218
3807	1853	327	448	658	337	274	237
17469	11080	1059	1950	1675	761	689	1314
20125	13166	1741	1588	1915	1219	1616	620
991959	821709	6896	6364	12659	2665	52058	96504
144356	99876	3785	4951	9179	2389	9362	18600
6062220	3450738	43790	393052	74382	4355	969331	1170363
32135	15219	2715	3942	3900	806	3514	2278
92	89	82	96	76	93	99	99
75	72		82	84	78	76	81
100.00	100.00	100.00	100.00	100.00	100.00	100.00	100.00

表1—5 部分年份经济社会结构指标 Structural Indicators of Society and Economy in Partial Years

单位：%

指标	Indicators	1995	2000	2010	2011	2012
生产总值产业结构	**Industrial Structure of GDP**					
第一产业	Primary Industry	13.5	8.2	4.2	4.2	4.1
第二产业	Secondary Industry	56.3	55.6	55.6	55.3	53.4
第三产业	Tertiary Industry	30.3	36.2	40.2	40.5	42.5
农林牧渔业产值结构	**Structure of Agricultural Gross Output Value**					
农业	Farming	54.2	48.2	49.3	48.2	47.9
林业	Forestry	3.4	3.1	2.9	2.7	2.7
牧业	Animal Husbandry	16.7	13.8	15.2	15.7	15.4
渔业	Fishery	25.7	34.9	31.1	32.1	32.6
农林牧渔服务业	Services			1.4	1.3	1.4
规模以上工业总产值比例	**Structure of Gross Industrial Output Value**					
轻工业	Light Industry		46.6	31.4	28.8	28.0
重工业	Heavy Industry		53.4	75.4	71.2	72.0
全社会固定资产投资产业结构	**Industrial Structure of Fixed Assets Investment**					
第一产业	Primary Industry	0.8	2.5	0.5	0.8	0.9
第二产业	Secondary Industry	34.8	41.1	31.8	28.0	28.3
第三产业	Tertiary Industry	64.4	56.3	67.7	71.2	70.8
自营进出口结构	**Structure of Directive Import and Export**					
出口	Exports	58.9	68.5	62.7	62.0	63.6
进口	Imports	41.1	31.5	37.3	38.0	36.4
社会消费品零售额结构	**Structure of Retail Sales of Consumer Goods**					
批发和零售贸易业	Wholesale and Retail Sale Trades	71.8	76.2	90.7	90.9	90.8
餐饮业	Catering Trade	5.5	9.7	9.3	9.1	9.2
其他	Others	22.7	14.1			
农业人口与非农业人口比例	**Structure of Population by Agriculture and Non－argiculture**					
农业人口	Agriculture	78.1	70.6	64.3	63.9	63.4
非农业人口	Non－Agriculture	21.9	29.4	35.7	36.1	36.6

表1—6 部分年份平均每天主要社会经济活动 Indicators on Average Daily Social and Economic Activities in Partial Years

指标	单位	Indicators	unit	1995	2000	2010	2011	2012
平均每天创造财富		**Daily Production**						
生产总值	万元	Gross Domestic Product	10000 yuan	16511	31358	140433	166007	179842
第一产业	万元	Primary Industry	10000 yuan	2222	2582	6004	6993	7337
第二产业	万元	Secondary Industry	10000 yuan	9287	17420	78649	91768	96088
#工业增加值	万元	Added—value of Industry	10000 yuan	8107	15844	70400	82712	86614
第三产业	万元	Tertiary Industry	10000 yuan	5001	11356	56415	67246	76417
公共财政预算收入	万元	Public Fiscal Budget Revenue	10000 yuan	1455	3922	32103	39226	41981
每天其他经济活动		**Other Daily Economic Activities**						
固定资产投资额	万元	Invesment in Fixed Assets	10000 yuan	7238	9884	60452	65356	79274
社会消费品零售总额	万元	Total Retail Sales of Consumer Goods	10000 yuan	6214	10666	46699	55311	63641
港口货物吞吐量	万吨	Cargo Throughput	10000 tons	18.78	31.64	112.92	118.74	123.78
集装箱吞吐量	标箱	Container Throughput	TEU	438	2471	35627	39760	42818
全社会用电量	万千瓦时	Total Electricity Consumption	10000 kwh	1697	3109	12577	13844	14046
#工业用电量	万千瓦时	Industrial Electricity Consumption	10000 kwh	1204	2302	9706	10647	10508
客运量	万人	Passenger Traffic	10000 persons	53.99	62.29	92.91	78.75	76.65
货运量	万吨	Freight Traffic	10000 tons	26.24	29.64	83.71	85.56	89.11
进出口总额	万美元	Total Imports and Exports	USD 10000	1056	2066	22713	26900	26386
#出口	万美元	Exports	USD 10000	621	1416	14238	16666	16788
实际利用外资	万美元	Foreign Capital Actually Used	USD 10000	109	170	637	770	779
人口变动和婚姻		**Population Changes and Marriages**						
出生	人	Births	person	163	137	134	126	137
死亡	人	Deaths	person	90	92	97	95	104
结婚	对	Marriages	couple	126	111	146	136	147
离婚	对	Divorces	couple	7	10	38	38	41

注：本表价值量指标按当年价格计算。

Note: The data in value terms in the table are calculated at current prices.

表1－7 部分年份国民经济主要指标人均水平
Main Per Capita Indicators of National Economy in Partial Years

单位：元（yuan）

指标	Indicators	1995	2000	2010	2011	2012
经济活动	**Economical Indicators**					
生产总值（户籍）	Gross Domestic Products（by Registered Population）.	12024	21208	90175	105334	114065
农业总产值	Gross Agritural Output Value	2354	2749	5931	6918	7275
固定资产投资额	Investment in Fixed Assets	5018	6685	38307	41470	50279
社会消费品零售总额	Total Retail Sales of Consumer Goods	4308	7213	29769	35096	40364
自营进出口额（美元）	Directive Exports and Imports（USD）	732	1397	14480	17069	16735
＃出口（美元）	Export（USD）	431	958	9076	10575	10648
实际利用外资（美元）	Foreign Capital Actually Used（USD）	76	115	406	488	494
公共财政预算收入	Public Fiscal Budget Revenue	1009	2653	20465	24890	26627
公共财政预算支出	Public Fiscal Budget Expenditure	672	1653	10492	13051	14356
人民生活	**People's Livelihood**					
城镇集体以上在岗职工工资	Avergae Wage of Working Staff and Workers in Urban Collective－owned Units andAbove	7361	14823	43476	49755	56257
市区居民人均可支配收入	Annual Disposable Income of Urban Residents	7275	9193	30166	34058	37902
市区居民人均消费性支出	Annual Living Expenditures of Urban Residents	5566	7912	19420	21779	23288
农村居民人均纯收入	Annual Net Income of Rural Residents	3484	4697	14261	16518	18475
农村居民生活消费支出	Annual Living Expenditure of Rural Residents	2432	3929	9794	11253	12699
城乡居民储蓄存款余额	Balance of Saving Deposits of Urban and Rural Households	3977	10859	57850	63734	72366
人均生活用电量（千瓦时）	Residential Electricity Consumption（kwh）	193	280	870	932	1028
社会事业	**Society Indicators**					
人均拥有道路面积（平方米）	Per Capita Area of Roads (sq. m)		13.85	19.65	20.44	20.53
人均公园绿地面积（平方米）	Per Capita Public Green Area (sq. m)		7.32	10.62	10.80	10.97

表1—8 部分年份社会经济发展相对指标
Relative Indicators on Social and Economic Development in Partial Yeats

指标	Indicators	1995	2000	2010	2011	2012
人口与劳动力	**Population and Labor**					
出生率(‰)	Birth Rate(‰)	11.4	9.3	8.5	8.0	8.7
死亡率(‰)	Death Rate(‰)	6.2	6.2	6.2	6.1	6.6
自然增长率(‰)	Natural Growth Rate(‰)	5.1	3.1	2.3	2.0	2.1
人口净迁移率(‰)	Migration Rate(‰)	1.7	2.3	3.4	2.4	1.4
全社会从业人员结构(%)	Structure of Total Employment Personnel (%)					
第一产业比重	Perentage of Primary Industry	32.4	31.0	6.8	6.6	5.9
第二产业比重	Perentage of Secondary Industry	46.3	43.1	55.9	55.4	54.9
第三产业比重	Perentage of Tertiary Industry	21.3	25.9	37.3	38.0	39.2
国民经济	**Domestic Economic**					
第三产业占GDP比重(%)	Perentage of Tertiary Industry as GDP (%)	30.3	36.2	40.2	40.5	42.5
固定资产投资占GDP比重(%)	Perentage of Investment in Fixed Assets as GDP (%)	43.8	31.5	42.5	39.4	44.1
社会消费品零售额占GDP比重(%)	Perentage of Total Retail Sales of Cunsumer Goods as GDP (%)	37.6	34.0	33.0	33.3	35.4
财政总收入占GDP比重(%)	Total Fiscal Revenue as Percentage of GDP (%)	8.8	12.9	40.1	37.5	33.5
进出口总额占GDP比重(%)	Total Value of Imports and Exports as Perentage of GDP (%)	53.4	54.6	108.7	104.7	92.6
出口总额占GDP比重(%)	Total Value of Exports as Perentage of GDP (%)	31.4	37.4	68.1	64.8	58.9
研究与实验发展经费占GDP比重(%)	R&D Expenditure as Percentage of GDP (%)			1.60	1.89	2.04
外资项目平均利用合同外资(万美元)	Contractual Foreign Investment on Per Project (USD 10000)	231.1	173.0	817.4	1220.1	1215.7
金融机构贷款占存款比重(%)	Loans as Percentage of Deposits in Financial Institutions (%)	85.6	75.3	96.5	100.2	99.8

注：在进出口、出口总额占GDP比重中，美元汇率按当年平均汇率计算。

Note: Total Value of Imports and Exports as Perentage of GDP, Exchange rate of USD are calculated according to in those years.

表 1—8 续表 Continued

指标	Indicators	1995	2000	2010	2011	2012
每公顷播种面积农产品产量(公斤)	Output of Farm Crops Per Hectare of Sowning Area (kg)					
粮食	Grain	5457	5369	5765	5972	5828
油料	Oil Plants	1822	2023	2438	2512	2497
蔬菜	Vegetables	28901	29662	31790	32764	32355
城乡居民收入比例	Ratio of Annual Disposable Income of Urban Resident to Rural's	2.09	2.15	2.12	2.06	2.05
社会发展	**Social Development**					
日均接待境外旅游者人数(人)	Number of Oversea Tourists Average Daily (person)	221	339	2608	2943	3175
日均旅客周转量（万人公里）	Turnover Volume of Passengers Average Daily (10000 persons—km)	1917	2192	3732	3789	3912
日均货物周转量（万吨公里）	Turnover Volume of Freight Traffic Average Daily (10000 tons—km)	3975	6486	43160	57270	56586
每万人拥有在校大学生数(人)	Students Enrollment of Higher Education Per 10000 Persons (person)	18.5	48.0	245.3	245.7	251.9
初中毕业生升学率（%）	Enrollment Rate of Junior Middle School Graduates (%)	56.8	82.4	99.0	99.1	99.1
每万人拥有移动电话数	Subscribers of Mobile Telephone Per 10000 Persons (subscriber)	89	2185	14728	17860	18833
每万人拥有医生数(人)	Number of Doctors Per 10000 Persons (Person)	16.5	17.0	30.0	31.8	33.0
每万人拥有病床数(张)	Total Beds of Per 10000 Persons(bed)	25.06	26.93	45.46	47.06	48.97
每万人拥有公共图书馆藏书量（册）	Number of Publice Libraries Collection Book Per 10000 persons (volume)	2912	3280	12786	12712	12683
每万人拥有公共交通车辆（辆）	Number of Buses Per 10000 Persons (vehicle)			6.5	7.0	8.1
每十万人拥有律师数（人）	Number of Lawyer Per 100,000 Persons (persons)	7.8	9.9	21.4	24.1	25.9
建成区绿化覆盖率（%）	Coverage Rate of Green Area in Developed Area (%)	11.00	28.44	37.52	37.82	38.21
污水处理率（%）	Percentage of Sewage Disposed (%)		35.92	82.81	84.16	85.75
计划生育率（%）	Rate of Famili Planning	99.29	99.22	95.50	96.15	93.30

表1—9 “六五”以来各计划时期社会经济主要指标 Major Social and Economic Indicators of Each Period since "Sixth Five—Year Plan" Period

单位:亿元(100 million yuan)

时期	Period	生产总值 Gross Domestic Product	其中 of Which			工业增加值 Value—added of Industry
			第一产业 Primary Industyr	第二产业 Secondary Industyr	第三产业 Tertiary Industry	
“六五”时期	"Sixth Five—Year Plan" Period	234.77	61.74	128.16	44.87	118.28
“七五”时期	"Seventh Five—Year Plan" Period	573.48	128.31	322.89	122.28	292.77
“八五”时期	"Eighth Five—Year Plan" Period	1777.40	258.70	1015.70	503.00	893.52
“九五”时期	"Ninth Five—Year Plan" Period	4777.61	450.59	2671.33	1655.69	2412.79
“十五”时期	"Tenth Five—Year Plan" Period	9040.12	564.70	4946.76	3528.66	4403.76
“十一五”时期	"11th Five—Year Plan" Period	19765.80	860.64	10912.17	7992.99	9838.51
“十二五”时期	"12th Five—Year Plan" Period	12641.45	523.75	6866.37	5251.33	6189.07
2012	2012	6582.21	268.52	3516.84	2796.85	3170.07

表1—9 续1 Continued

单位:单位:亿元(100 million yuan)

时期	Period	固定资产投资 Investment in Fixed Assets	社会消费品零售总额 Retail Sale of Consumer Goods	自营出口总额(亿美元) Value of Direct Exports (100 million USD)	公共财政预算收入 Public Fiscal Budgetary Revenue	财政支出 Fiscal Expenditure
“六五”时期	"Sixth Five—Year Plan" Period	51.68	86.81	0.04	40.23	10.83
“七五”时期	"Seventh Five—Year Plan" Period	159.35	222.77	5.88	66.07	34.75
“八五”时期	"Eighth Five—Year Plan" Period	705.73	651.23	63.86	161.00	101.10
“九五”时期	"Ninth Five—Year Plan" Period	1600.03	1596.17	168.72	475.78	328.22
“十五”时期	"Tenth Five—Year Plan" Period	4347.56	2825.19	654.04	1641.17	1007.84
“十一五”时期	"11th Five—Year Plan" Period	9026.05	6325.15	2039.70	4233.99	4264.53
“十二五”时期	"12th Five—Year Plan" Period	5286.93	4348.12	1222.77	2968.27	3112.94
2012	2012	2901.43	2329.26	614.45	1536.51	1516.16

表1—9 续表2 Continued

时期	Period	港口货物吞吐量(万吨) Cargo of Ports Throughput (10000 tons)	集装箱吞吐量(万标箱) Container Throughput (10000 TEU)	全社会用电量(亿千瓦时) Total Electricity Consumption (100 million Kwh)	粮食产量(万吨) Yield of Grain (10000 tons)	人口自然增长(人) Population NaturalIncrease (person)
“六五”时期	"Sixth Five—Year Plan" Period	2840		74.52	913.51	191824
“七五”时期	"Seventh Five—Year Plan" Period	10502	2.2	135.67	936.76	203889
“八五”时期	"Eighth Five—Year Plan" Period	25781	45.3	244.06	907.96	128862
“九五”时期	"Ninth Five—Year Plan" Period	45772	231.5	423.77	850.60	102695
“十五”时期	"Tenth Five—Year Plan" Period	96260	1505.7	955.17	446.52	49734
“十一五”时期	"11th Five—Year Plan" Period	181275	5069.1	1924.91	417.94	60064
“十二五”时期	"12th Five—Year Plan" Period	88641	3018 .4	1019.39	176.71	23378
2012	2012	45303	1567.1	514.09	86.57	12091

注:2006年粮食产量根据农普数据调整。
Note: Yield of grain crops of the year 2006 has been amended according to the last census of agriculture.

表1—10 "六五"以来各计划时期社会经济主要指标平均增长率
Growth Rate of Major Social and Economic Indicators of Each Period since "Sixth Five—Year Plan" Period

单位:%

时期	Period	生产总值 Gross Domestic Product	其中 of Which			工业增加值 Value—added of Industry
			第一产业 Primary Industyr	第二产业 Secondary Industyr	第三产业 Tertiary Industry	
"六五"时期	"Sixth Five—Year Plan" Period	17.2	8.5	21.0	17.4	21.7
"七五"时期	"Seventh Five—Year Plan" Period	8.8	0.9	10.9	8.5	11.0
"八五"时期	"Eighth Five—Year Plan" Period	21.0	7.7	23.4	23.9	28.5
"九五"时期	"Ninth Five—Year Plan" Period	13.0	3.6	13.9	14.2	14.7
"十五"时期	"Tenth Five—Year Plan" Period	13.8	3.9	14.4	14.5	14.0
"十一五"时期	"11th Five—Year Plan" Period	12.0	4.3	11.8	13.1	12.6
"十二五"时期	"12th Five—Year Plan" Period	8.9	2.4	7.8	11.0	8.1
2012	2012	7.8	1.0	6.0	10.9	6.0

表1—10续1 Continued

单位:%

时期	Period	固定资产投资 Investment in Fixed Assets	社会消费品零售总额 Retail Sale of Consumer Goods	自营出口总额 Value of Direct Exports	公共财政预算收入 Public Fiscal Budgetary Revenue	财政支出 Fiscal Expenditure
"六五"时期	"Sixth Five—Year Plan" Period	15.9	17.8		10.1	17.1
"七五"时期	"Seventh Five—Year Plan" Period	19.5	16.8	135.1	11.7	22.9
"八五"时期	"Eighth Five—Year Plan" Period	46.2	32.8	52.0	27.3	29.5
"九五"时期	"Ninth Five—Year Plan" Period	6.5	11.4	17.9	21.9	20.3
"十五"时期	"Tenth Five—Year Plan" Period	30.9	11.8	33.9	26.7	29.6
"十一五"时期	"11th Five—Year Plan" Period	10.4	17.5	18.5	20.2	34.8
"十二五"时期	"12th Five—Year Plan" Period	19.6	16.9	8.7	14.5	2.2
2012	2012	21.6	15.4	1.0	7.3	—5.1

表1—10续表2 Continued

单位:%

时期	Period	港口货物吞吐量 Cargo of Ports Throughput	集装箱吞吐量 Container Throughput	全社会用电量 Total Electricity Consumption	粮食产量 Yield of Grain	人口自然增率(‰) Natural Growth Rate
"六五"时期	"Sixth Five—Year Plan" Period	26.1		11.7	1.9	8.0
"七五"时期	"Seventh Five—Year Plan" Period	19.7		11.2	0.1	8.2
"八五"时期	"Eighth Five—Year Plan" Period	21.8	48.7	14.5	—1.8	5.1
"九五"时期	"Ninth Five—Year Plan" Period	11.0	41.3	12.9	—5.2	3.9
"十五"时期	"Tenth Five—Year Plan" Period	18.4	42.0	18.8	—9.6	1.8
"十一五"时期	"11th Five—Year Plan" Period	8.9	20.1	11.3	1.7	3.0
"十二五"时期	"12th Five—Year Plan" Period	4.8	9.8	5.8	—0.3	2.0
2012	2012	4.5	8.0	1.7	—4.0	2.1

表1－11 国民经济主要指标比上年增长(1978－2012)
Growth Rate of Major National Economic Indicators Increase Precding Year

单位:%

年份 Year	生产总值 Gross Domestic Product	#第二产业 Secondary Industry	第三产业 Tertiary Industry	工业增加值 Value－added of Industry	固定资产投资 Investment in Fixed Assets	社会消费品零售总额 Retail Sales of Consumer Goods	公共财政预算收入 Public Fiscal Budgetary Revenue
1978	22.5	33.2	6.7		54.9	15.1	22.7
1979	13.4	16.4	19.2	14.1	15.3	24.0	－1.7
1980	17.7	28.4	4.9	38.7	12.3	27.6	15.2
1981	9.3	16.4	11.4	20.3	－1.7	16.4	16.2
1982	13.7	5.5	16.1	4.0	34.1	7.4	9.3
1983	17.7	24.8	15.0	21.3	－10.3	12.2	12.9
1984	18.0	19.5	19.1	25.0	42.4	19.7	15.5
1985	28.1	41.4	25.7	40.7	65.1	34.8	－2.2
1986	9.0	8.0	16.9	7.4	21.7	20.2	12.1
1987	14.1	18.2	11.1	18.6	33.8	16.5	10.8
1988	11.1	16.2	6.8	19.2	21.6	38.3	17.7
1989	4.5	8.8	－4.6	7.2	－8.4	7.7	14.5
1990	5.7	4.0	13.6	3.7	19.8	4.1	4.0
1991	24.9	18.2	52.0	24.0	30.9	15.3	11.9
1992	17.9	26.2	15.6	29.4	48.3	25.3	11.5
1993	20.8	26.4	14.8	37.4	69.5	48.9	42.4
1994	21.1	22.6	25.1	21.4	42.8	38.2	48.8
1995	20.5	24.0	15.5	24.4	43.1	38.8	26.4
1996	17.2	18.5	17.9	18.3	17.3	14.3	24.2
1997	13.7	16.4	15.4	19.4	－3.0	11.3	13.8
1998	11.1	11.5	12.1	12.0	3.1	8.6	16.8
1999	11.0	10.7	12.7	11.2	2.9	10.3	18.7
2000	12.0	12.6	13.2	12.7	13.1	12.6	37.6
2001	12.1	13.0	12.4	12.9	30.4	6.4	32.9
2002	13.2	15.0	12.4	15.0	27.9	11.8	35.8
2003	15.6	16.9	15.9	15.7	39.0	12.7	25.8
2004	15.5	16.6	15.7	16.0	32.1	14.2	－11.3
2005	12.6	10.8	16.3	10.9	21.1	14.0	16.4
2006	13.6	12.7	16.2	13.9	12.5	16.1	20.3
2007	14.9	15.1	15.8	16.4	6.3	17.3	29.0
2008	10.1	10.0	11.0	9.9	8.2	19.6	12.0
2009	8.9	8.3	10.4	8.5	16.0	15.9	19.2
2010	12.5	13.4	12.2	14.3	9.4	19.2	21.3
2011	10.0	9.7	11.1	10.3	17.6	18.4	22.2
2012	7.8	6.0	10.9	6.0	21.6	15.4	7.3

表 1—11 续表 Continued

单位：%

年份 Year	自营进出口总额 Value of Direct Exports and Imports	#出口 Export	实际利用外资 Foreign Capital Actually Used	港口货物吞吐量 Cargo at Throughput Ports	集装箱吞吐量 Container Throughput	市区居民人均可支配收入 Per Capital Annual Disposable Income of Urban Residents
1978						
1979				10.3		11.1
1980				38.1		26.2
1981				7.1		12.1
1982				6.3		5.8
1983				30.2		4.1
1984				23.6		21.3
1985			1609.5	74.2		38.3
1986	102.0	38.8	39.3	72.8		24.9
1987	−0.9	46.5	−14.2	8.0		7.4
1988	616.4	1348.5	60.6	3.2		27.3
1989	49.2	57.1	155.2	10.3		14.8
1990	35.5	55.3	25.0	15.6		12.7
1991	92.2	70.0	22.0	32.7	63.6	11.2
1992	72.8	64.9	329.0	28.8	47.2	22.5
1993	71.0	41.4	199.7	21.8	49.1	49.0
1994	48.4	57.9	3.9	9.9	58.2	50.8
1995	53.2	29.6	11.4	17.1	28.0	21.1
1996	8.6	2.7	25.7	11.5	26.3	14.8
1997	10.1	25.9	10.5	7.6	27.2	8.6
1998	−8.6	1.0	−9.2	5.9	37.4	1.4
1999	18.9	17.3	3.4	10.9	70.3	3.3
2000	50.5	48.6	19.5	19.5	50.1	15.1
2001	17.9	20.8	40.6	11.3	34.5	9.8
2002	38.0	30.7	42.6	19.8	53.3	8.2
2003	53.3	47.9	38.5	20.4	49.1	10.1
2004	38.8	38.2	21.8	21.8	44.5	11.2
2005	28.5	33.2	9.9	19.0	30.0	9.6
2006	26.0	29.4	5.2	15.2	35.7	13.0
2007	33.8	33.0	3.1	11.5	32.3	13.4
2008	20.1	21.1	1.3	4.8	16.0	13.4
2009	−10.4	−16.6	−13.1	6.1	−3.9	9.2
2010	36.3	34.5	5.3	7.4	24.8	10.2
2011	18.4	17.1	20.9	5.1	11.6	12.9
2012	−1.6	1.0	1.5	4.5	8.0	11.3

主要统计指标解释

【行政区划】 指国家对行政区域的划分。根据宪法规定，我国的行政区域划分如下：⑴全国分为省、自治区、直辖市；⑵省、自治区分为自治州、县、自治县、市；⑶自治州分为县、自治县、市；⑷县、自治县分为乡、民族乡、镇；⑸直辖市和较大的市分为区、县；⑹国家在必要时设立的特别行政区。

【气温】 指空气的温度，我国一般以摄氏度(℃)为单位表示。气象观测的温度表是放在离地面约 1.5 米处通风良好的百叶箱里测量的，因此，通常说的气温指的是离地面 1.5 米处百叶箱中的温度。其统计计算方法为：

月平均气温是将全月各日的平均气温相加，除以该月的天数而得。

年平均气温是将 12 个月的月平均气温累加后除以 12 而得。

【相对湿度】 指空气中实际水气压与当时气温下的饱合水气压之比。其统计方法与气温相同。

【降水量】 指从天空降落到地面的液态或固态(经融化后)水，未经蒸发、渗透、流失而在地面上积聚的深度。其统计计算方法为：

月降水量是将全月各日的降水量累加而得。

年降水量是将 12 个月的月降水量累加而得。

【日照时数】 指太阳实际照射地面的时间。其统计方法与降水量相同。

【可比价格】 指计算各种总量指标所采用的扣除了价格变动因素的价格，可进行不同时期总量指标的对比。按可比价格计算总量指标有两种方法：一种是直接用产品产量乘某一年的不变价格计算；另一种是用价格指数进行缩减。

【不变价格】 指以同类产品某年的平均价格作为固定价格，用于计算各年的产品价值。按不变价格计算的产品价值消除了价格变动因素，不同时期对比可以反映生产的发展速度。新中国成立后，随着工农业产品价格水平的变化，国家统计局先后五次制定了全国统一的工业产品不变价格和农业产品不变价格。从 1952 年到 1957 年使用 1952 年工(农)业产品不变价格，从 1957 年到 1970 年使用 1957 年不变价格，从 1971 年到 1980 年使用 1970 年不变价格，从 1981 年到 1990 年使用 1980 年不变价格，从 1991 年开始使用 1990 年不变价格。

【平均增长速度】 我国计算平均增长速度有两种方法：一种是习惯上经常使用的"水平法"，又称几何平均法，是以间隔期最后一年的水平同基期水平对比来计算平均每年增长(或下降)速度；另一种是"累计法"，又称代数平均法或方程法，是以间隔期内各年水平的总和同基期水平对比来计算平均每年增长(或下降)速度。在一般正常情况下，两种方法计算的平均每年增长速度比较接近；但在经济发展不平衡、出现大起大落时，两种方法计算的结果差别较大。

本《年鉴》内所列的平均增长速度，除固定资产投资用"累计法"计算外，其余均用"水平法"计算。从某年到某年平均增长速度的年份，均不包括基期年在内。

Explanatory Notes on Main Statistical Indicators

【Administrative Division】 refers to the division of administrative areas by the state. The Constitution of the People's Republic of China stipulates that the administrative areas in China are divided as: 1) The whole country is divided into provinces, autonomous regions and municipalities directly under the central government; 2) Provinces and autonomous regions are divided into autonomous prefectures, counties, autonomous counties and cities; 3) Autonomous prefectures are divided into counties, autonomous counties and cities; 4) Counties and autonomous counties are divided into townships, nationality townships and towns; 5) Municipalities and large cities are divided into districts and counties, 6) The state shall, when necessary, establish special administrative regions.

【Temperature】 refers to the air temperature. China uses centigrade as the unit. The thermometry used for weather observation is put in a breezy shutter, which is 1. 5 meters high from the ground. Therefore, the commonly used temperature refers to the temperature in the breezy shutter 1. 5 meters away from the ground. The calculation method is as follows:

Monthly average temperature is the summation of average daily temperature of one month divided by the actual days of that particular month.

Annual average temperature is the summation of monthly average of a year divided by 12 months.

【Relative Humidity】 refers to the ratio of actual water vapor pressure to the saturation water vapor density under the current temperature. The statistical method is the same as that of temperature.

【Volume of Precipitation】 refers to the deepness of liquid state or solid state (thawed) water falling from the sky to the ground that has not been evaporated, infiltrated or run off. The calculation method is as follows:

Monthly precipitation is the summation of daily precipitation of a month.

Annual precipitation is the summation of 12 months precipitation of a year.

【Sunshine Hours】 refer to the actual hours of sun irradiating the earth. The calculation method is the same as that of the precipitation.

【Comparable Prices】 refer to prices that are used to remove the factors of price change in calculating economic aggregates, so as to facilitate comparison of aggregates over time. Two methods are used for calculating economic aggregates at comparable prices: 1. Multiplying the output of products by their constant prices of certain year; 2. Deflation of data at current prices by relevant price index.

【Constant Price】 refers to the average price of a given product in certain year, which is used for comparison of output value over time. As the output value at constant prices removes the factor of price changes, it reflects the trend of production development over time. Since 1949, with the changes in general price level, National Bureau of Statistics has issued nationally unified constant prices five times: the 1952 constant prices for 1949—1957; the 1957 constant prices for 1957—1971; the 1970 constant prices for 1971—1981; the 1980 constant prices for 1981—1990; and the 1990 constant prices have been used since 1991.

【Average Annual Growth Rate】 Two methods for calculating average annual growth rate are applied in China, one is often called "level approach", or the method of calculating geometric average, which is derived by comparing the level of the last year of the interval with that of the beginning year; the other is called "accumulative approach" or algebraic average or equation method, which is derived by the summation of the actual figure of each year in the interval divided by the figure in the base year.

Usually the results calculated by the two methods are fairly close, but they differed sharply when uneven economic development occurred with striking fluctuations in growth.

The average annual growth rates listed in this statistical yearbook are calculated by "level approach" except for the growth rate of investment in fixed assets. The base years are not listed when the years are listed for average annual growth rates.

NINGBO

Statistical YearBook

第二篇

人口与劳动力

POPULATION AND LABOR FORCE

人口和劳动力
Population and Labour Force

主要统计指标
Major Statistics Indicators

2012 年末户籍人口数	2012 Year—end Registred Populations	577.71	万人	10000 persons
其中:非农业人口	Non—agriculture	211.45	万人	10000 persons
其中:市区	Urban Districts	226.11	万人	10000 persons
2012 年出生人口	Birth Population	49998	人	persons
2012 年死亡人口	Death Population	37907	人	persons
2012 年人口自然增长率	Natural Growth Rate	2.10	‰	
2012 年人口净迁移率	Migration Rate	1.38	‰	
2012 年末人口密度	Density of Population	588	人/平方公里	person/sq. km
2012 年计划生育率	Rate of Family Planning	93.30	%	
2012 年末全社会从业人员数	Total Employmed Personnel at The Year—end	501.58	万人	10000 persons
2012 年城镇从业人员数	Number of Employed Personnel at The Year—end Above Town Level	174.22	万人	10000 persons
2012 年城镇在岗职工数	Number of Staff and Workers at Work Above Town Level	150.16	万人	10000 persons
2012 年城镇集体以上在岗职工平均工资	Average Wage of Staff and Workers at Work Above Town Level	56257	元	yuan
2012 城镇集体以上在岗职工大专以上人数	Number of Junior College and Above at Worker at Work Above Toen Level	55.16	万人	10000 persons
2012 年末城镇登记失业人员数	Number of Registered Urban Unemployment at the Year—end	82078	人	persons
2012 年末城镇登记失业率	Registered Urban Unemployed Rate	2.55	%	

表2—1 历年总户数和总人口 Households and Population Over the Years

单位:万户,万人(10000 households,10000 persons)

年份 Year	总户数 Total Households	总人口 Total Population	其中 of Which 按性别分 By Sex 男性 Male	女性 Female	按农业和非农业分 By Agriculture &Non—agriculture 农业人口 Agriculture	非农业人口 Non—agriculture
1978	123.30	457.70	234.18	223.52	394.28	63.42
1979	124.48	462.07	235.78	226.29	394.31	67.76
1980	128.57	465.99	237.98	228.01	393.13	72.86
1981	136.86	471.76	240.95	230.81	394.39	70.37
1982	140.56	478.33	244.20	234.13	396.40	81.93
1983	143.27	481.46	245.79	235.67	397.68	83.78
1984	147.57	484.18	247.26	236.92	398.64	85.54
1985	153.57	487.74	249.24	238.50	394.50	93.24
1986	158.53	491.89	251.56	240.33	394.69	97.20
1987	164.78	498.15	254.80	243.35	399.48	98.67
1988	170.92	503.06	257.19	245.89	402.81	100.25
1989	175.12	507.64	259.75	247.89	406.08	101.56
1990	176.06	510.76	260.99	249.77	407.78	102.98
1991	179.22	514.16	262.68	251.48	409.61	104.55
1992	180.89	516.72	264.09	252.63	409.90	106.82
1993	182.80	519.85	265.72	254.26	410.17	109.81
1994	184.38	522.85	267.24	255.61	410.17	112.68
1995	186.26	526.20	268.72	257.48	410.94	115.29
1996	186.82	530.08	270.30	259.78	410.57	119.51
1997	188.83	533.31	271.89	261.42	409.81	123.50
1998	190.39	535.27	272.40	262.87	404.79	130.48
1999	192.52	538.41	273.65	264.76	401.29	137.12
2000	193.99	540.94	274.50	266.44	398.91	142.03
2001	196.10	543.34	275.50	267.84	392.48	150.86
2002	198.94	546.19	276.60	269.60	383.76	162.43
2003	203.47	549.07	277.64	271.44	380.26	168.81
2004	207.01	552.69	278.84	273.85	376.50	176.19
2005	211.17	556.70	280.35	276.35	374.09	182.61
2006	215.03	560.45	281.71	278.74	371.47	188.98
2007	218.77	564.56	283.42	281.14	370.35	194.21
2008	221.48	568.09	284.84	283.25	369.60	198.49
2009	222.46	571.02	285.96	285.05	368.98	202.04
2010	222.98	574.08	287.15	286.93	368.86	205.23
2011	223.79	576.40	287.90	288.50	368.23	208.18
2012	223.46	577.71	288.30	289.41	366.26	211.45

表 2－2 历年人口自然变动情况 Population Natural Changes Over the Years

单位:人,‰(persons,‰)

年份 Year	出生 Birth		死亡 Death		自然增长 Natural Growth	
	人数 Population	出生率 Birth Rate	人数 Population	死亡率 Death Rate	人数 Population	自然增长率 Natural Growth Rate
1978	75180	15.06	26150	5.74	49030	9.32
1979	71642	15.58	27393	5.96	44249	9.62
1980	57417	12.37	27989	6.03	29428	6.34
1981	78132	16.66	28557	6.09	49575	10.57
1982	84905	17.87	28258	5.95	56647	11.92
1983	69668	14.52	30875	6.43	38793	8.09
1984	51040	10.57	28114	5.82	22926	4.75
1985	53366	10.98	29483	6.07	23883	4.91
1986	62535	12.77	28738	5.87	33797	6.90
1987	83541	16.88	30239	6.11	53302	10.77
1988	69248	13.83	30171	6.03	39077	7.80
1989	71283	14.11	30364	6.01	40919	8.10
1990	67464	13.25	30670	6.02	36794	7.23
1991	60140	11.74	29329	5.75	30811	6.01
1992	50700	10.22	30573	5.93	20127	4.29
1993	55242	10.66	29169	5.63	26073	5.03
1994	54990	10.55	30050	5.76	24940	4.78
1995	59600	11.36	32689	6.23	26911	5.13
1996	58282	11.04	30652	5.80	27630	5.24
1997	55231	10.39	31417	5.91	23814	4.48
1998	47116	8.82	32902	6.16	14214	2.66
1999	51544	9.57	31237	5.80	20307	3.77
2000	50168	9.30	33438	6.20	16730	3.10
2001	39867	7.35	30632	5.65	9235	1.70
2002	41404	7.60	32361	5.94	9043	1.66
2003	42445	7.80	35173	6.40	7272	1.30
2004	49192	8.93	36558	6.64	12634	2.29
2005	45185	8.15	33635	6.06	11550	2.08
2006	41749	7.47	31380	5.62	10369	1.86
2007	46830	8.33	33737	6.00	13093	2.33
2008	46155	8.15	33804	5.97	12351	2.18
2009	45114	7.92	34277	6.02	10837	1.90
2010	48837	8.53	35423	6.19	13414	2.34
2011	46103	8.01	34816	6.05	11287	1.96
2012	49998	8.66	37907	6.57	12091	2.10

表 2－3 历年人口迁移情况
Bacis Statistics on Migration Over the Years

单位：人，‰（person，‰）

年份 Year	迁入 inflows	其中 of Which 省内迁入 From Zhejiang	省外迁入 Form Other Province	迁出 Outflows	其中 of Which 迁往省内 Outflow to Zhejiang	迁往省外 Outflow to Other Province	净迁移率 Migration Rate
1990	43055	34763	8292	43996	35646	8350	−0.18
1991	35526	27628	7898	32260	25142	7118	0.64
1992	54895	46773	8122	49969	43721	6248	0.96
1993	51257	41921	9336	43716	36697	7019	1.45
1994	55877	46390	9487	49826	42731	7095	1.16
1995	61832	50483	11349	52873	45598	7275	1.71
1996	66392	53141	13251	55103	47097	8006	2.14
1997	64083	51097	12986	53669	45306	8363	1.96
1998	73735	59605	14130	67191	58068	9123	1.22
1999	99809	82531	17278	89491	79170	10321	1.92
2000	85277	66946	18331	73024	60774	12250	2.27
2001	112559	91837	20722	95907	82261	13646	3.07
2002	105609	77127	28482	85498	71518	13980	3.69
2003	105057	76140	28917	80102	65019	15083	4.56
2004	104523	72455	32068	74307	59665	14642	5.49
2005	93433	64157	29276	62900	48874	14026	5.50
2006	90684	60320	30364	59694	46742	12952	5.55
2007	85199	55378	29821	54649	44955	9694	5.43
2008	77022	46195	30827	52036	40749	11287	4.41
2009	69949	40163	29786	48037	37595	10442	3.85
2010	67588	40093	27495	47814	37584	10230	3.45
2011	56088	31626	24462	42543	31859	10684	2.35
2012	47704	25619	22085	39715	28056	11659	1.38

表 2－4 部分年份各县（市）人口密度
Density of Population by Region in Partial Years

单位：人/平方公里（person/sq. km）

地区	Region	2006	2007	2008	2009	2010	2011	2012
全市	**Total**	**571**	**575**	**579**	**582**	**585**	**587**	**588**
市区	Urban Districts	877	886	894	901	907	913	916
＃鄞州	Yinzhou	582	587	592	597	604	611	514
余姚	Yuyao	551	552	553	554	556	556	556
慈溪	Cixi	750	755	758	761	764	765	766
奉化	Fenghua	378	379	380	380	381	382	382
象山	Xiangshan	383	385	387	389	391	392	391
宁海	Ninghai	320	323	326	328	331	334	334

注：2006 年人口密度按最新勘界的陆域面积计算。

Note：Population density in 2006 are calculated according to surveying stable land region area most newly.

表 2—5 各县(市)、区人口、户口情况(2012 年底)
Basic Statistics on Population and Households by Region(End of 2012)

指标	单位	Indiators	Unit	全市 Total	市区 Urban District	海曙 Haishu
总户数	**户**	**Total Households**	**household**	**2234602**	**900567**	**112502**
总人口	**人**	**Total Population**	**person**	**5777125**	**2261116**	**298843**
男性	人	Male	person	2882985	1117041	146903
女性	人	Female	person	2894140	1144075	151940
非农业人口	人	Non－agriculture Population	person	2114509	1413222	298834
未落常住户口的	人	Non－registered Residence	person	1416	45	4
平均人口	**人**	**Average Population**	**person**	**5770584**	**2254247**	**299445**
出生人数	**人**	**Birth Population**	**person**	**49998**	**20262**	**2622**
男性	人	Male	person	25937	10556	1356
女性	人	Female	person	24061	9706	1266
出生率	‰	Birth Rate	‰	8.66	8.99	8.76
死亡人数	**人**	**Death Population**	**person**	**37907**	**12820**	**1487**
男性	人	Male	person	20976	7033	815
女性	人	Female	person	16931	5787	672
死亡率	‰	Death Rate	‰	6.57	5.69	4.97
本年自然增加人数	**人**	**Natural Growth Population**	**person**	**12091**	**7442**	**1135**
人口自然增长率	‰	Natural Growth Rate	‰	2.10	3.30	3.79
迁入人数	**人**	**Number of the Persons Moved in**	**person**	**47704**	**22569**	**2759**
省内迁入	人	From Zhejiang Province	person	25619	8709	1231
省外迁入	人	From Other Province	person	22085	13860	1528
迁出人数	**人**	**Number of the Persons Moved Out**	**person**	**39715**	**15052**	**2453**
迁往省内	人	To Zhejiang Province	person	28056	8123	1444
迁往省外	人	To Other Province	person	11659	6929	1009

注:本表数据来自宁波市公安局。

Note:Data in this table are obtained from Bureau of Public Security of Ningbo Municipality.

各区 by Districts									
江东 Jiangdong	江北 Jiangbei	北仑 Beilun	镇海 Zhenhai	鄞州 Yinzhou	余姚 Yuyao	慈溪 Cixi	奉化 Fenghua	象山 Xiangshan	宁海 Ninghai
106262	**100458**	**153703**	**92107**	**335535**	**310127**	**425201**	**182404**	**188281**	**228022**
279291	**241105**	**383034**	**227611**	**831232**	**834493**	**1041904**	**483548**	**540322**	**615742**
137711	118564	189500	114615	409748	413670	513540	244207	275230	319297
141580	122541	193534	112996	421484	420823	528364	239341	265092	296445
279291	158246	214948	167357	294546	188594	192089	108814	113391	98399
		1		40	183	1183		5	
278882	**240802**	**381558**	**226876**	**826686**	**834552**	**1041704**	**483743**	**541005**	**615334**
2780	**2431**	**3516**	**1428**	**7485**	**6035**	**7723**	**3490**	**5741**	**6747**
1449	1230	1840	764	3917	3079	3945	1775	2977	3605
1331	1201	1676	664	3568	2956	3778	1715	2764	3142
9.97	10.10	9.21	6.29	9.05	7.23	7.41	7.21	10.61	10.96
1430	**1442**	**2188**	**1248**	**5025**	**6421**	**7386**	**3440**	**3497**	**4343**
778	809	1228	702	2701	3582	4036	1925	1944	2456
652	633	960	546	2324	2839	3350	1515	1553	1887
5.13	5.99	5.73	5.50	6.08	7.69	7.09	7.11	6.46	7.06
1350	**989**	**1328**	**180**	**2460**	**−386**	**337**	**50**	**2244**	**2404**
4.84	4.11	3.48	0.79	2.98	−0.46	0.32	0.10	4.15	3.91
2854	**3171**	**4061**	**2461**	**7263**	**8289**	**6735**	**3336**	**2575**	**4200**
1384	1132	904	722	3336	6063	4483	2201	1357	2806
1470	2039	3157	1739	3927	2226	2252	1135	1218	1394
1694	**2899**	**2154**	**1045**	**4807**	**7284**	**5868**	**3428**	**4366**	**3717**
841	1596	787	468	2987	6108	4659	2538	3531	3097
853	1303	1367	577	1820	1176	1209	890	835	620

表2－6 部分年份各县(市)、区总户数与总人口
Householes and Population by Region in Partial Years

单位：人(person)

指标	Indicators	2009	2010	2011	2012
总户数(户)	**Total Households(Household)**	**2224625**	**2229770**	**2237911**	**2234602**
海曙区	Haishu	113416	112893	112571	112502
江东区	Jiangdong	104732	105321	105832	106262
江北区	Jiangbei	98149	99171	99999	100458
北仑区	Beilun	152988	153297	153468	153703
镇海区	Zhenhai	92201	91962	91916	92107
鄞州区	Yinzhou	326621	329992	334318	335535
余姚市	Yuyao	311421	311793	311331	310127
慈溪市	Cixi	427496	425462	427423	425201
奉化市	Fenghua	182701	183049	182987	182404
象山县	Xiangshan	190806	190604	189901	188281
宁海县	Ninghai	224094	226226	228165	228022
总人口	**Total Population**	**5710172**	**5740836**	**5764042**	**5777125**
海曙区	Haishu	304633	302384	300047	298843
江东区	Jiangdong	276341	277701	278472	279291
江北区	Jiangbei	236691	238867	240498	241105
北仑区	Beilun	373171	377206	380081	383034
镇海区	Zhenhai	224642	225227	226140	227611
鄞州区	Yinzhou	802785	812068	822140	831232
余姚市	Yuyao	832456	833837	834611	834493
慈溪市	Cixi	1035224	1038847	1041503	1041904
奉化市	Fenghua	482137	483455	483937	483548
象山县	Xiangshan	537135	540330	541688	540322
宁海县	Ninghai	604957	610914	614925	615742
男性人数	**Number of Male**	**2859646**	**2871526**	**2878994**	**2882985**
海曙区	Haishu	150503	149091	147710	146903
江东区	Jiangdong	137082	137400	137566	137711
江北区	Jiangbei	117192	117948	118508	118564
北仑区	Beilun	185672	187357	188416	189500
镇海区	Zhenhai	113593	113711	113959	114615

表 2－6 续表 Continued　　　　单位：人(person)

指标	Indicators	2009	2010	2011	2012
鄞州区	Yinzhou	396134	400771	405477	409748
余姚市	Yuyao	414701	414593	414333	413670
慈溪市	Cixi	511745	513088	513813	513540
奉化市	Fenghua	244512	244773	244708	244207
象山县	Xiangshan	274378	275805	275688	275230
宁海县	Ninghai	314134	316989	318816	319297
女性人数	**Number of Female**	**2850526**	**2869310**	**2885048**	**2894140**
海曙区	Haishu	154130	153293	152337	151940
江东区	Jiangdong	139259	140301	140906	141580
江北区	Jiangbei	119499	120919	121990	122541
北仑区	Beilun	187499	189849	191665	193534
镇海区	Zhenhai	111049	111516	112181	112996
鄞州区	Yinzhou	406651	411297	416663	421484
余姚市	Yuyao	417755	419244	420278	420823
慈溪市	Cixi	523479	525759	527690	528364
奉化市	Fenghua	237625	238682	239229	239341
象山县	Xiangshan	262757	264525	266000	265092
宁海县	Ninghai	290823	293925	296109	296445
非农业人口	**Number of Non－agriculture**	**2020381**	**2052283**	**2081751**	**2114509**
海曙区	Haishu	304573	302362	300036	298834
江东区	Jiangdong	276341	277701	278472	279291
江北区	Jiangbei	151146	153572	155843	158246
北仑区	Beilun	191911	199283	206123	214948
镇海区	Zhenhai	161257	162701	164720	167357
鄞州区	Yinzhou	258966	269344	281656	294546
余姚市	Yuyao	181755	184515	186617	188594
慈溪市	Cixi	182770	186892	189741	192089
奉化市	Fenghua	106534	107531	108168	108814
象山县	Xiangshan	111333	111861	112558	113391
宁海县	Ninghai	93795	96521	97817	98399

表 2—7 部分年份各县(市)、区人口自然变动情况
Natural Changes of Population by Region in Partial Years

单位:人(person)

指标	Indicators	2008	2009	2010	2011	2012
出生人口	**Birth**	**46155**	**45114**	**48837**	**46103**	**49998**
海曙区	Haishu	2670	2282	2397	2390	2622
江东区	Jiangdong	2598	2491	2688	2465	2780
江北区	Jiangbei	1836	1866	2035	2228	2431
北仑区	Beilun	2876	3009	3248	3125	3516
镇海区	Zhenhai	1040	1070	1105	1229	1428
鄞州区	Yinzhou	6214	6024	6306	6766	7485
余姚市	Yuyao	5379	5396	5624	5396	6035
慈溪市	Cixi	7947	7967	7797	7349	7723
奉化市	Fenghua	3453	3506	4013	3285	3490
象山县	Xiangshan	5058	4727	5497	5031	5741
宁海县	Ninghai	7084	6776	8127	6839	6747
死亡人口	**Death**	**33804**	**34277**	**35423**	**34816**	**37907**
海曙区	Haishu	1084	1131	1404	1432	1487
江东区	Jiangdong	1090	1106	1165	1123	1430
江北区	Jiangbei	1334	1219	1250	1187	1442
北仑区	Beilun	2144	2216	2098	2192	2188
镇海区	Zhenhai	1172	1051	1159	1169	1248
鄞州区	Yinzhou	4682	4692	4995	4719	5025
余姚市	Yuyao	6124	6059	6023	6233	6421
慈溪市	Cixi	6428	6670	7011	6803	7386
奉化市	Fenghua	2975	3345	3293	3129	3440
象山县	Xiangshan	3301	3269	3352	3265	3497
宁海县	Ninghai	3470	3519	3673	3564	4343

表 2—7 续表 Continued　　单位：人(person)

指标	Indicators	2008	2009	2010	2011	2012
自然增长	**Natural Growth**	**12351**	**10837**	**13414**	**11287**	**12091**
海曙区	Haishu	1586	1151	993	958	1135
江东区	Jiangdong	1508	1385	1523	1342	1350
江北区	Jiangbei	502	647	785	1041	989
北仑区	Beilun	732	793	1150	933	1328
镇海区	Zhenhai	−132	19	−54	60	180
鄞州区	Yinzhou	1532	1332	1311	2047	2460
余姚市	Yuyao	−745	−663	−399	−837	−386
慈溪市	Cixi	1519	1297	786	546	337
奉化市	Fenghua	478	161	720	156	50
象山县	Xiangshan	1757	1458	2145	1766	2244
宁海县	Ninghai	3614	3257	4454	3275	2404
自然增长率(‰)	**Natural Growth Rate(‰)**	**2.18**	**1.90**	**2.34**	**1.96**	**2.10**
海曙区	Haishu	5.18	3.77	3.27	3.18	3.79
江东区	Jiangdong	5.59	5.05	5.50	4.83	4.84
江北区	Jiangbei	2.16	2.75	3.30	4.34	4.11
北仑区	Beilun	2.01	2.14	3.07	2.46	3.48
镇海区	Zhenhai	−0.59	0.08	−0.24	0.27	0.79
鄞州区	Yinzhou	1.93	1.67	1.62	2.51	2.98
余姚市	Yuyao	−0.90	−0.80	−0.48	−1.00	−0.46
慈溪市	Cixi	1.48	1.26	0.76	0.52	0.32
奉化市	Fenghua	0.99	0.33	1.49	0.32	0.10
象山县	Xiangshan	3.29	2.72	3.98	3.26	4.15
宁海县	Ninghai	6.04	5.40	7.33	5.34	3.91

表 2—8 部分年份各县(市)、区人口迁移情况
Migration of Population by Region in Partial Years

单位:人(person)

指标	Indicators	2008	2009	2010	2011	2012
迁入人口	**Population Inflows**	**77022**	**69949**	**67588**	**56088**	**47704**
海曙区	Haishu	5231	4648	3203	2815	2759
江东区	Jiangdong	4616	4239	3384	2995	2854
江北区	Jiangbei	5631	5370	4477	3758	3171
北仑区	Beilun	6867	6489	5099	4355	4061
镇海区	Zhenhai	3074	3020	2723	2413	2461
鄞州区	Yinzhou	13106	10912	9934	8631	7263
余姚市	Yuyao	7337	10522	13589	9498	8289
慈溪市	Cixi	10178	10554	9728	7517	6735
奉化市	Fenghua	6642	4174	4222	3596	3336
象山县	Xiangshan	7829	4625	5176	5939	2575
宁海县	Ninghai	6511	5396	6053	4571	4200
其中:省内迁入	**of Which:From Zhejiang**	**46195**	**40163**	**40093**	**31626**	**25619**
海曙区	Haishu	2745	2184	1482	1259	1231
江东区	Jiangdong	2260	2018	1577	1339	1384
江北区	Jiangbei	2510	2028	1610	1267	1132
北仑区	Beilun	2007	1532	1188	1077	904
镇海区	Zhenhai	1090	912	866	732	722
鄞州区	Yinzhou	7631	5477	4682	3763	3336
余姚市	Yuyao	4736	8283	10964	7134	6063
慈溪市	Cixi	7022	7787	6947	4961	4483
奉化市	Fenghua	5098	2896	2796	2352	2201
象山县	Xiangshan	6510	3375	3851	4703	1357
宁海县	Ninghai	4586	3671	4130	3039	2806

表 2—8 续表 Continued　　　　单位：人(person)

指标	Indicators	2008	2009	2010	2011	2012
迁出人口	**Population Outflows**	**52036**	**48037**	**47814**	**42543**	**39715**
海曙区	Haishu	3688	3373	2587	2478	2453
江东区	Jiangdong	1353	1550	1668	1620	1694
江北区	Jiangbei	4789	3806	3495	3166	2899
北仑区	Beilun	2005	1896	2019	2244	2154
镇海区	Zhenhai	2335	1683	1263	1200	1045
鄞州区	Yinzhou	9296	8201	6401	5403	4807
余姚市	Yuyao	4474	8414	11648	7823	7284
慈溪市	Cixi	7309	7410	6560	5353	5868
奉化市	Fenghua	5777	3606	3564	3195	3428
象山县	Xiangshan	6397	3947	4122	6358	4366
宁海县	Ninghai	4613	4151	4487	3703	3717
其中:迁往省内	**Of Which:To Zhejiang**	**40749**	**37595**	**37584**	**31859**	**28056**
海曙区	Haishu	2798	2475	1777	1571	1444
江东区	Jiangdong	629	790	885	833	841
江北区	Jiangbei	3642	2755	2332	1840	1596
北仑区	Beilun	1105	999	933	891	787
镇海区	Zhenhai	1618	1109	702	572	468
鄞州区	Yinzhou	7832	6752	4782	3749	2987
余姚市	Yuyao	2939	7161	10522	6723	6108
慈溪市	Cixi	5800	6031	5473	4312	4659
奉化市	Fenghua	4933	2986	2825	2614	2538
象山县	Xiangshan	5684	3229	3587	5677	3531
宁海县	Ninghai	3769	3308	3766	3077	3097

表 2－9 各县(市)计划生育情况(2012)
Basic Statistics on Family Planning by Region

指标	单位	Indicators	Unit
计划生育率	%	Rate of Family Planning	%
年内出生人数	人	Number of Birth in This Year	person
#女	人	Female	person
1.一孩人数	人	One－Child	person
#计划内	人	Under Control	person
2.两孩人数	人	Two－Child	person
#计划内	人	Under Control	person
3.多孩人数	人	Over Two Child	person
#政策性	人	Policy	person
计划内出生人数	人	Number of Birth Under Control	person
计划外出生人数	人	Number of Birth Out of Control	person
1.一孩人数	人	One－Child	person
2.两孩人数	人	Two－Child	person
3.多孩人数	人	Over Two Child	person
育龄妇女人数	万人	Number of Women at Child－Bearing Age	10000 persons
已婚育龄妇女人数	万人	Number of Marriged Women at Child－Bearing Age	10000 persons
#已有一孩	万人	1st Birth	10000 persons
#已领独生证	万人	With One－Child Certificate	10000 persons
#已婚育龄妇女一孩率	%	Rate of 1st Birth of Marriged Women at Child－Bearing Age	%
#已婚育龄妇女领独生证率	%	Rate of One－Child Certificate	%
初婚妇女人数	人	Number of First Marrige for Women	10000 persons
已婚育龄妇女节育率	%	Rate of Controlling－Birth for Marriged Women at Child－Bearing Age	%
采取节育措施人数	万人	Number of Controlling－Birth Method	10000 persons
年内节育手术例数	例	Number of Controlling－Birth Surgery in This Year	case
年内取环例数	例	Number of Remove Contraceptive	case
出生率	‰	Brith Rate	‰
死亡率	‰	Death Rate	‰

注：本表数据来自宁波市计划生育委员会。

Note:Data in this table are obtained from Ningbo Family Planning Committee.

全市 Total	市区 Urban District	#鄞州 Yinzhou	余姚 Yuyao	慈溪 Cixi	奉化 Fenghua	象山 Xiangshan	宁海 Ninghai
93.30	96.64	96.14	96.93	94.28	95.44	89.75	81.65
49258	20239	7429	5739	7322	3464	5277	7217
23589	9759	3621	2802	3563	1710	2518	3237
37697	17386	6050	4483	5542	2555	3609	4122
37438	17351	6024	4471	5525	2549	3557	3985
11143	2780	1335	1231	1729	875	1610	2918
8438	2181	1104	1081	1365	749	1174	1888
418	73	44	25	51	34	58	177
83	26	14	11	13	8	5	20
45959	19558	7142	5563	6903	3306	4736	5893
3299	681	287	176	419	158	541	1324
259	35	26	12	17	6	52	137
2705	599	231	150	364	126	436	1030
335	47	30	14	38	26	53	157
151.34	58.35	22.44	22.04	26.74	12.36	15.10	16.75
116.94	45.82	17.60	16.60	20.63	9.39	11.47	13.03
88.02	37.39	14.29	12.63	14.99	7.37	7.72	7.92
45.53	22.37	8.61	6.96	8.60	3.81	2.21	1.57
75.27	81.60	81.19	76.12	72.63	78.50	67.31	60.76
38.93	48.82	48.91	41.96	41.68	40.55	19.31	12.08
36418	13816	4959	5935	7173	2376	3505	3613
89.16	88.06	89.57	90.35	90.36	91.36	88.86	88.31
104.27	40.35	15.77	15.00	18.64	8.58	10.19	11.51
38613	10465	5690	2936	5447	3451	6259	10055
10997	4256	2249	1286	1464	1034	1348	1609
8.54	8.98	8.84	6.88	7.03	7.16	9.75	11.73
6.57	5.69	6.00	7.69	7.09	7.11	6.46	7.06

表 2—10　各县(市)婚姻状况(2012)
Basic Statistics on Marrige by Region

指标	单位	Indicators	Unit	全市 Total
准予登记结婚数	对	**Registering Marrige Permitted**	**couple**	**53721**
#涉外婚姻	人	Chinese—Foreign Marrige	person	284
(1)国内公民	人	Demestic Citizen	person	142
#女性	人	Female	person	113
(2)港澳台同胞	人	Chinese of Hong Kong,Macao and Taiwan	person	45
(3)华侨	人	Overseas Chinese	person	9
(4)外国人	人	Foreigner	person	88
1.初婚人数	人	First Marriage	person	92191
2.再婚人数	人	Remarriage	person	15251
#再婚中恢复结婚	对	Resume Marriage	couple	2787
准予离婚数	对	**Divorce Approved**	**couple**	**14893**

注:本表数据由市民政局提供。

Note:Data in this table are obtained from Ningbo Municipal Bureau of Civil Affairs.

表 2—11　主要年份婚姻状况
Marriage Statistics in Main Years

年份 Year	准予登记结婚(对) Marriage Registration Permitted (Couple)	初婚(人) First Marriage (person)	再婚(人) Remarriage (person)	再婚中恢复结婚(对) Resume Marriage (Couple)	准予离婚数(对) Divorce Approved (couple)
1990	51349	96680	3312		1378
1991	46429	88283	4373	85	1508
1992	47504	91636	3372	152	1543
1993	43522	83451	3593	224	1815
1994	48029	92611	3447	209	2201
1995	45950	88406	3494	160	2501
1996	47197	89369	5025	169	2870
1997	40432	75369	5495	228	3689
1998	44559	83403	5715	466	3623
1999	39616	72299	6531	269	3881
2000	40505	74415	6125	242	3781
2001	38813	70658	6326	288	4206
2002	46931	85892	7572	371	4444
2003	42075	75735	8097	394	5538
2004	48214	86584	9518	743	7570
2005	39445	68699	9835	525	8570
2006	51725	90762	12688	736	9687
2007	41954	73877	10031	840	10232
2008	51956	90228	13684	509	11376
2009	46181	77918	14444	961	12698
2010	52508	87780	17236	1333	13754
2011	49710	83624	15796	2291	13911
2012	53721	92191	15251	2787	14893

市区 Urban District	#鄞州 Yinzhou	余姚 Yuyao	慈溪 Cixi	奉化 Fenghua	象山 Xiangshan	宁海 Ninghai
22742	**7487**	**7669**	**9241**	**3378**	**5261**	**5430**
284						
142						
113						
45						
9						
88						
39642	13932	14200	16071	5112	8438	8728
5842	1042	1138	2411	1644	2084	2132
1300	334	225	387	275	315	285
6620	**1987**	**1687**	**1849**	**1350**	**1679**	**1708**

涉外婚姻(对) Chinese－Foreign Marriage (couple)	其中:of Which				
	国内公民(人) Chinese Citizens (person)	#女性 Female	港澳台同胞(人) Cninese of HongKong,Macao,Taiwan(person)	华侨(人) Overseas Chinese (person)	外国人(人) Foreigner (person)
85	85	80	69	11	5
101	101	95	88	8	5
133	133	127	114	9	10
157	157	150	128	20	9
119	119	112	93	20	6
127	127	121	70	27	30
160	160	154	105	23	32
144	144	144	84	16	44
142	142	134	82	16	44
201	201	188	144	14	43
235	235	229	177	7	51
321	321	313	249	10	62
199	199	189	137	10	52
159	159	152	106	8	45
163	163	154	88	14	61
178	178	166	96	9	73
181	178	162	100	13	71
170	170	154	78	10	82
172	168	148	60	17	99
162	160	133	63	7	94
138	136	114	44	8	88
306	153	127	69	4	80
284	142	113	45	9	88

表 2—12 城乡劳动力资源配置情况(2012 年底)
Sources and Distribution of Urban and Rural Labor Force(End of 2012)

单位:万人(10000 persons)

项目	Item	城乡合计 Total	其中 of Which 城镇 Urban	乡村 Rural
年末人口数	**Total Population at The Year—end**	**763.90**	**433.00**	**320.90**
年末 16 岁以上全部人口数	Total Population Above 16 Ages at the Year—end	669.20	388.10	281.10
#不计入劳动力资源的人数	Non labor Force Resource	25.80	10.30	15.50
年末劳动力资源总数	**Total Labor Force Resource at The Year—end**	**643.40**	**377.80**	**265.60**
经济活动人口	**Economically Activity Population**	**509.79**	**346.54**	**163.25**
从业人员数	Number of Employmed Person	501.58	338.33	163.25
按就业身份分组	Group by Employment Identity			
城镇集体以上单位从业人员	Urban Collective—Owned Level and Above	174.22	174.22	
私营业主	Private Owner	30.91	19.87	11.04
个体户主	Self—employed Worker	35.99	16.72	19.27
私营企业和个体从业人员	Employed Persons in Private and Individual Units	233.46	127.52	105.94
乡镇企业从业人员	Employed Persons in Township Enterprises			
乡村农业劳动力	Rural Labor Force	27.00		27.00
其他	Others			
按登记注册类型分组	Group by Registered Type			
国有单位	State—Owned Units	31.18	31.18	
集体单位	Collective—Owned Units	30.23	3.23	27.00
股份合作单位	Share—holding Cooperative Units	1.63	1.63	
联营单位	Joint Ownership Units	0.13	0.13	
有限责任公司	Limited Liability Corporations	30.03	30.03	
股份有限公司	Share—holding Coporations Ltd.	36.70	36.70	
私营单位	Private Enterprises	198.80	116.36	82.44
其他	Others	1.71	1.71	
港、澳、台商投资单位	HongKong,Macao and Taiwan Funded	38.20	38.20	
外商投资单位	Foreign Funded Units	31.41	31.41	
个体	Self—employed Individual	101.56	47.45	53.81

表 2－12 续表 Continued　　单位：万人(10000 persons)

项目	Item	城乡合计 Total	其中 of Which	
			城镇 Urban	乡村 Rural
按国民经济行业分组	Group by Sector			
农、林、牧、渔业	Framing, Forestry, Animal Husbandry and Fishery	29.74	0.87	28.87
采矿业	Mining and Quarrying	0.12	0.03	0.09
制造业	Manufacuring	231.55	144.06	87.49
电力、燃气及水的生产和供应业	Electric Power, Gas and Water Production and Supply	2.03	1.96	0.07
建筑业	Construction	41.57	37.96	3.61
交通运输、仓储和邮政业	Transportation, Storage and Post	15.87	11.36	4.51
信息传输、计算机服务和软件业	Information Transmission, Computer Service and Software	4.80	4.42	0.38
批发和零售业	Wholesale and Retail Trade	89.48	62.77	26.71
住宿和餐饮业	Hotel and Catering Services	10.36	7.26	3.10
金融业	Financial Industries	7.06	6.98	0.08
房地产业	Real Estate Industries	5.14	4.36	0.78
租赁和商务服务业	Leasing and Business Service Industries	17.66	16.11	1.55
科学研究、技术服务和地质勘查业	Scientific Research, Technical Service and Geologic Prospecting	8.43	6.44	1.99
水利、环境和公共设施管理业	Water Conservancy, Environment and Public Facility Management	1.95	1.81	0.14
居民服务和其他服务业	Resident Service and Other Service Industries	10.46	7.14	3.32
教育	Education	8.54	8.49	0.05
卫生、社会保障和社会福利业	Health Care, Social Security and Social Welfare	5.72	5.68	0.04
文化、体育和娱乐业	Culture, Sports and Entertainment	2.39	1.92	0.47
公共管理和社会组织	Public Management and Social Organizations	8.71	8.71	
国际组织	International Organizations			
城镇登记失业人员数	**Number of Registered Unemployed Persons in Urban**	**8.21**	**8.21**	
非经济活动人口	**Non Economically Activity Population**	**133.61**	**31.26**	**102.35**
＃16 岁以上在上在校学生	Student Enrollment Above 16 Ages	25.80	16.30	9.50
家务劳动者	House Work Labourer	72.10	7.00	65.10

表 2－13　部分年份按就业者身份和经济类型分组的从业人员
Employees Grouped by Identity and Registered Type in Partail Years

单位:万人(10000 persons)

指标	Indicators	2010	2011	2012
从业人员数	**Number of Employmed Person**	**476.51**	**493.83**	**501.58**
按就业身份分组	**Group by Employment Identity**			
城镇集体以上单位从业人员	Urban Collective－Owned and Above	140.18	151.79	174.22
私营业主	Private Owner	25.04	28.23	30.91
个体户主	Self－employed Worker	29.51	33.04	35.99
私营企业和个体从业人员	Employed in Private and Individual Units	211.78	230.77	233.46
乡镇企业从业人员	Employed in Township Enterprises	30.00	20.00	
乡村农业劳动力	Rural Labor Force	30.00	30.00	27.00
其他	Others	10.00		
按登记注册类型分组	**Group by Registered Type**			
国有单位	State－Owned Units	30.04	31.83	31.18
集体单位	Collective－Owned Units	63.33	53.43	30.23
股份合作单位	Share－holding Cooperative Units	1.73	1.30	1.63
联营单位	Joint Ownership Units	0.15	0.13	0.13
有限责任公司	Limited Liability Corporations	20.27	22.90	30.03
股份有限公司	Share－holding Coporations Ltd.	27.55	29.15	36.70
私营单位	Private Enterprises	176.33	192.13	198.80
其他	Others	10.52	0.72	1.71
港、澳、台商投资单位	HongKong,Macao and Taiwan Funded	27.58	31.16	38.20
外商投资单位	Foreign Funded Units	29.01	31.17	31.41
个体	Self－employed Individual	90.00	99.91	101.56

表 2－14 部分年份按国民经济行业分组的从业人员数
Employees Grouped by Sectors in Partail Years

单位：万人(10000 persons)

指标	Indicators	2010	2011	2012
从业人员数	**Number of Employmed Person**	**476.51**	**493.83**	**501.58**
按国民经济行业分组	**Group by Sector**			
农、林、牧、渔业	Framing,Forestry,Animal Husbandry and Fishery	32.21	32.54	29.74
采矿业	Mining and Quarrying	0.14	0.18	0.12
制造业	Manufacuring	230.50	230.21	231.55
电力、燃气及水的生产和供应业	Electric Power,Gas and Water Production and Supply	1.88	2.27	2.03
建筑业	Construction	34.04	41.00	41.57
交通运输、仓储和邮政业	Transportation,Storage and Post	12.38	15.36	15.87
信息传输、计算机服务和软件业	Information Transmission,Computer Service and Software	4.41	4.68	4.80
批发和零售业	Wholesale and Retail Trade	78.71	88.65	89.48
住宿和餐饮业	Hotel and Catering Services	11.39	9.96	10.36
金融业	Financial Industries	5.45	6.35	7.06
房地产业	Real Estate Industries	4.47	5.08	5.14
租赁和商务服务业	Leasing and Business Service Industries	13.56	15.12	17.66
科学研究、技术服务和地质勘查业	Scientific Research,Technical Service and Geologic Prospecting	4.72	6.94	8.43
水利、环境和公共设施管理业	Water Conservancy,Environment and Public Facility Management	1.59	1.88	1.95
居民服务和其他服务业	Resident Service and Other Service Industries	19.38	10.01	10.46
教育	Education	7.49	7.91	8.54
卫生、社会保障和社会福利业	Health Care,Social Security and Social Welfare	4.86	5.44	5.72
文化、体育和娱乐业	Culture,Sports and Entertainment	2.03	2.29	2.39
公共管理和社会组织	Public Management and Social Organizations	7.30	7.96	8.71
国际组织	International Organizations			

表 2－15　全市城镇集体以上从业人员和劳动报酬情况(2012)
Employed Personnel and Remuneration Payment in Urban Collective－owned Units and Above Level

指标	Indicators
总计	**Total**
按企、事业和机关分组	**Grouped by Enterprises,Institutions and Agencies**
企业	Enterprises
事业	Institutions
机关	Agencies
按国民经济行业分组	**Grouped by Sector**
农、林、牧、渔业	Framing,Forestry,Animal Husbandry and Fishery
采矿业	Mining and Quarrying
制造业	Manufacuring
电力、燃气及水的生产和供应业	Electric Power,Gas and Water Production and Supply
建筑业	Construction
交通运输、仓储和邮政业	Transport,Storage and Post
信息传输、计算机服务和软件业	Information Transmission,Computer Service and Software
批发与零售业	Wholesale and Retail Trade
住宿与餐饮业	Hotels and Catering Trade
金融业	Financial Industries
房地产业	Real Estate Trade
租赁与商务服务业	Leasing and Business Services
科学研究、技术服务与地质勘查业	Scientific Research,Technical Service and Geologic Prospecting
水利环境和公共设施管理业	Water Conservancy,Environment and Public Facility Management
居民服务和其他服务业	Resident Service and Other Service Industries
教育	Education
卫生、社会保障和社会福利业	Health Care,Sports and Social Welfare
文化、体育和娱乐业	Culture,Sports and Entertainment
公共管理与社会组织	Public Management and Social Organizations
按经济类型分	**Group by Type of Ownership**
国有单位	State－Owned Units
城镇集体单位	Collective Owned Units
其他单位	Others Units

单位从业人员年末人数(人) Number of Employees at the Year-end (person)	其中 of Which		职工平均工资(元) Average Wage of Staff and Workers (yuan)
	女性 Female	在岗职工合计 Working Staff and Workers	
1746989	**681221**	**1501644**	**56257**
1485373	553032	1265109	50372
178058	101455	162597	86337
71063	20195	62265	99162
622	193	612	52338
54	8	48	46143
819865	398544	770579	42850
19112	4284	13481	104106
331136	24810	220473	46214
60393	15428	49171	67595
11996	5283	8773	94701
60696	34030	52170	52335
19267	9769	18616	35872
67849	38960	44477	152892
24882	7946	23086	57260
55339	9012	51745	55313
18828	5437	15885	90803
16287	6133	15839	46023
4909	1226	3970	40808
84548	53079	76680	86924
54664	37385	50580	90517
9389	4077	8537	81832
87153	25617	76922	94610
316587	130054	269474	88219
32226	15659	28780	61678
1398176	535508	1191102	48895

表 2－16　城镇集体以上从业人员文化程度情况(2012)
Educational Level of Working Staff and Workers in Urban Collective－owned Units and Above Level

指标	Indicators	单位从业人员 Working Staff and Workers
总计	**Total**	**1746989**
按企、事业和机关分组	**Grouped by Enterprises, Institutions and Agencies**	
企业	Enterprises	1485373
事业	Institutions	178058
机关	Agencies	71063
按国民经济行业分组	**Grouped by Sector**	
农、林、牧、渔业	Framing, Forestry, Animal Husbandry and Fishery	622
采矿业	Mining and Quarrying	54
制造业	Manufacuring	819865
电力、燃气及水的生产和供应业	Electric Power, Gas and Water Production and Supply	19112
建筑业	Construction	331136
交通运输、仓储和邮政业	Transport, Storage and Post	60393
信息传输、计算机服务和软件业	Information Transmission, Computer Service and Software	11996
批发与零售业	Wholesale and Retail Trade	60696
住宿与餐饮业	Hotels and Catering Trade	19267
金融业	Financial Industries	67849
房地产业	Real Estate Trade	24882
租赁与商务服务业	Leasing and Business Services	55339
科学研究、技术服务与地质勘查业	Scientific Research, Technical Service and Geologic Prospecting	18828
水利环境和公共设施管理业	Water Conservancy, Environment and Public Facility Management	16287
居民服务和其他服务业	Resident Service and Other Service Industries	4909
教育	Education	84548
卫生、社会保障和社会福利业	Health Care, Sports and Social Welfare	54664
文化、体育和娱乐业	Culture, Sports and Entertainment	9389
公共管理与社会组织	Public Management and Social Organizations	87153
按经济类型分	**Group by Type of Ownership**	
国有单位	State－Owned Units	316587
城镇集体单位	Collective Owned Units	32226
其他单位	Others Units	1398176

单位:人(person)

单位从业人员按文化程度分 Group by Educational Background of Personnel				单位从业人员人才资源 Number of Trained Personnel Resources	单位从业人员专业技术人员 Specialized Technical Personnel
大学本科及以上 Regular Collage and Higher Level	大专 Junior College	中专及高中 Specialized Secondary Schools & Senior Secondary Schools	初中及以下 Junior Secondary Schools and Below Level		
286982	**264643**	**502109**	**693255**	**1101935**	**377366**
150242	207431	466057	661643	885496	245208
94898	36731	22933	23496	145451	121602
39202	17496	10470	3895	63874	6664
100	51	145	326	246	137
4	11	28	11	43	3
52481	99760	253834	413790	448463	106494
5491	5237	4629	3755	16004	4930
21910	37271	115841	156114	244452	55116
8390	13304	20827	17872	37176	8930
4633	4452	2326	585	6873	4683
8652	13411	21048	17585	20033	5897
1011	3358	7015	7883	4871	1433
32731	17658	15044	2416	52679	38198
4550	4456	5697	10179	10834	5114
6031	5942	16862	26504	35120	7532
9558	4049	2806	2415	14899	11186
1610	1803	2212	10662	7386	2312
348	595	1216	2750	1946	244
56092	14602	6746	7108	72173	65869
24707	15188	10590	4179	50018	46107
3210	2287	1908	1984	6023	3557
45473	21208	13335	7137	72696	9624
142435	66484	54462	53206	249652	129571
7682	6448	7134	10962	21797	16026
136865	191711	440513	629087	830486	231769

表2－17 部分年份按行业分组的城镇集体以上在岗职工平均工资
Avergae Wage of Working Staff and Workers in Urban Collective－owned Units and Above Grouped by Sectors in Partial Years

单位：元(yuan)

项目	Item	2010	2011	2012
总计	**Total**	**43476**	**49755**	**56257**
按企业、事业、机关分组	**Grouped by Enterprises, Institutions and Agencies**			
企业	Enterprises	37432	44365	50372
事业	Institutions	71454	77432	86337
机关	Agencies	82743	93382	99162
按国民经济行业分组	**Grouped by Sector**			
农、林、牧、渔业	Framing, Forestry, Animal Husbandry and Fishery	45407	52700	52338
采矿业	Mining and Quarrying	19709	29580	46143
制造业	Manufacuring	31022	37517	42850
电力、燃气及水的生产和供应业	Electric Power, Gas and Water Production and Supply	84292	95079	104106
建筑业	Construction	33436	39312	46214
交通运输、仓储和邮政业	Transport, Storage and Post	61301	67080	67595
信息传输、计算机服务和软件业	Information Transmission, Computer Service and Software	85542	95633	94701
批发与零售业	Wholesale and Retail Trade	37821	49168	52335
住宿与餐饮业	Hotel and Catering Services	25341	31197	35872
金融业	Financial Industries	131085	148732	152892
房地产业	Real Estate Industries	43298	51451	57260
租赁与商务服务业	Leasing and Business Service	34334	48240	55313
科学研究、技术服务与地质勘查业	Scientific Research, Technical Service and Geologic Prospecting	68906	82877	90803
水利环境和公共设施管理业	Water Conservancy, Environment and Public Facility Management	40207	43296	46023
居民服务和其他服务业	Resident Service and Other Service	29609	33050	40808
教育	Education	76618	80484	86924
卫生、社会保障和社会福利业	Health Care, Social Security and Social Welfare	72289	79702	90517
文化、体育和娱乐业	Culture, Sports and Entertainment	65076	74244	81832
公共管理与社会组织	Public Management and Social Organizations	79972	89850	94610
按经济类型分组	**Group by Type of Ownership**			
国有单位	State－Owned Units	72632	81725	88219
城镇集体单位	Collective Owned Units	43178	50052	61678
其他单位	Others Units	35483	42493	48895

表 2－18 部分年份城镇登记失业人数和城镇登记失业率 Number of Registered Urban Unemployed and Registered Urban Unemployed Rate in Partial Years

单位：人(person)

指标	Indicators	2008	2009	2010	2011	2012
失业人员总数	Total Unemployment	140222	121246	56642	127192	102409
#新增失业人员	Newly Added Unemployment	92931	63210	64116	70550	14965
#女性	Female	46016	28667	32451	35591	7765
失业人员转就业人数	Unemployed to Reemployed	82186	62063	66657	62673	20331
#女性	Female	42584	28691	31226	31019	9115
城镇登记失业人员数	Registered Urban Unemployment	58036	59183	56642	64519	82078
#女性	Female	29240	26797	27475	30763	38891
#长期失业者	Long－term Unemployment	9287	7599	6680	6955	8577
城镇登记失业率(%)	Registered Urban Unemployed Rate(%)	3.31	3.16	3.03	3.44	2.55

注：本表至 2－21 表数据来自宁波市劳动和社会保障局。

Note：Dara from Tables 2－18 to 2－21 are obtained from Ningbo Municipal Bureau of Labor and Social Security.

表 2－19 部分年份社会保险基本情况 Basic Statistics on Social Insurance in Partial Years

单位：万人(10000 persons)

指标	Indicators	2008	2009	2010	2011	2012
企业养老保险参保人数	Number of Staff and Worker Participated in Basic Pension Insurance at the year－end	297.55	344.28	383.50	434.44	474.30
企业养老保险实际缴费人数	Number of Factial Pay Participated in Basic Pension Insurance at the year－end	206.84	216.05	241.27	261.22	277.02
基本医疗保险参保人数	Population Particaipated Medical Insurance at the year－end	223.55	251.84	281.28	304.98	326.56
失业保险参保人数	Population Particaipated Unemployment Insurance at the year－end	161.42	173.21	186.25	200.62	216.22
工伤保险参保人数	Population Particaipated Work Injury Insurance at the year－end	209.28	214.90	238.14	253.36	270.22
生育保险参保人数	Population Particaipated Maternity Insurance at the year－end	164.71	177.63	201.46	214.71	233.09
被征地人员养老保障参保人数	Number of Taken Over Land Farmers Participated in Rural Social Old－aged Security	53.86	55.69	56.78	56.61	55.85

表 2—20 各县(市)城镇登记失业人员基本情况(2012)
Basic Statistics On Unemployed Persons in Urban Areas by Region

指标	Indicators	全市 Total
总计	**Total**	**82078**
按年龄和性别分	**Group by Age and Sex**	
16—25 周岁	Between 15 to 25 Years Old	6507
#女性	Female	2840
26 岁及以上	26 Years Old and Above	75571
#女性	Female	36051
按失业时间分	**Group by Unemployment Time**	
六个月以下	Below 6 Months	73501
#女性	Female	27840
六个月以上	6 Months and Above	8577
#女性	Female	11051
按文化程度分	**Group by Education Background**	
大专及以上	Junior College Degree and Above	7500
#女性	Female	3890
中专和高中	Special Secondary school and Senior Secondary Schools Degree	31224
#女性	Female	13661
初中及以下	Junior Secondary Schools Degree and Below	43354
#女性	Female	21340

注:失业时间以办理失业登记时间开始计算。

Note: Unemployment time begins to calculate with the time of applying for unemployment registration.

表 2—21 各县(市)城镇就业和失业人员变化情况(2012 年底)
Number of Being Employed and Being Unemployed by Region (End of 2012)

指标	Indicators	全市 Total
本期失业人员总数	**Total Unemployment at the Year—end**	**167979**
上期末结转的失业人数	From the Previous Year	64519
本期增加的失业人员	Newly Added in this Year	103460
#女性	Female	49218
由就业转失业	Reemployed to Unemployed	73399
本期失业人员就业人数	**Unemployed to Reemployed at This Year**	**85901**
#女性	Female	41090
期末实有登记失业人数	**Registered Unemployment at the Year—end**	**82078**
#女性	Female	38891
长期失业者	Long—term Unemployment	8577
本期末从业人员总数	**Total Employed Persons at the Year—end**	
城镇登记失业率(%)	**Registered Urban Unemployed Rate (%)**	**2.55**

单位：人(person)

市区 Urban District	#鄞州 Yinzhou	余姚 Yuyao	慈溪 Cixi	奉化 Fenghua	象山 Xiangshan	宁海 Ninghai
64320	**4940**	**4607**	**5584**	**2599**	**3435**	**1533**
4643	115	80	8	411	544	821
2077	61	55	4	162	223	319
59677	4825	4527	5576	2188	2891	712
28821	2540	2219	2458	672	1591	290
60627	4797	3707	2822	2574	3364	407
21980	2536	1714	1270	818	1776	282
3693	143	900	2762	25	71	1126
8918	65	560	1192	16	38	327
6331	513	380	272	24	173	320
3327	287	190	122	17	81	153
24104	3581	1900	1594	1107	1517	1002
10520	1896	890	717	319	828	387
33885	846	2327	3718	1468	1745	211
17051	418	1194	1623	498	905	69

单位：人(person)

市区 Urban District	#鄞州 Yinzhou	余姚 Yuyao	慈溪 Cixi	奉化 Fenghua	象山 Xiangshan	宁海 Ninghai
124930	**12451**	**6365**	**8303**	**8176**	**6516**	**13689**
52555	3967	1818	2965	2566	2932	1683
72375	8484	4547	5338	5610	3584	12006
35144	4596	2301	2275	3059	1910	4529
57237	5935	3977	5272	4184	2729	
60610	**7511**	**1758**	**2719**	**5577**	**3081**	**12156**
31346	3937	928	1778	2551	1640	2847
64320	**4940**	**4607**	**5584**	**2599**	**3435**	**1533**
30898	2601	2274	2462	834	1814	609
3693	143	900	2762	25	71	1126
2.53		**2.28**	**2.37**	**2.95**	**3.27**	**2.75**

主要统计指标解释

【出生率(又称粗出生率)】 指在一定时期内(通常为一年)平均每千人所出生的人数的比率,一般用千分率表示。计算公式为:

出生率=年出生人数/年平均人数×1000‰

式中:出生人数指活产婴儿,即胎儿脱离母体时(不管怀孕月数),有过呼吸或其他生命现象。年平均人数指年初、年底人口数的平均数,也可用年中人口数代替。

【死亡率(又称粗死亡率)】 指在一定时期内(通常为一年)一定地区的死亡人数与同期平均人数(或期中人数)之比,一般用千分率表示。计算公式为:

死亡率=年死亡人数/年平均人数×1000‰

【人口自然增长率】 指在一定时期内(通常为一年)人口自然增加数(出生人数减死亡人数)与该时期内平均人数(或期中人数)之比,一般用千分率表示。计算公式为:

人口自然增长率=(本年出生人数-本年死亡人数)/年平均人数×1000‰=人口出生率-人口死亡率

【经济活动人口】 指在16岁以上,有劳动能力,参加或要求参加社会经济活动的人口;包括从业人员和失业人员。

【单位从业人员】 各单位的从业人员是指在各级国家机关、政党机关、社会团体及企业、事业单位中工作,并取得劳动报酬的全部人员。包括:在岗职工、再就业的离退休人员、民办教师以及在各单位中工作的外方人员和港澳台方人员、兼职人员、聘用的外单位下岗人员、借用的外单位人员和第二职业者。不包括离开本单位仍保留劳动关系的职工。

【在岗职工】 指在本单位工作并由单位支付劳动报酬的职工。包括由单位派出学习、劳务及病伤产假且仍由单位支付劳动报酬的人员。

【职工平均工资】 指企业、事业、机关单位的职工在一定时期内平均每人所得的货币工资额。它表明一定时期职工工资收入的高低程度,是反映职工工资水平的主要指标。计算公式为:

职工平均工资=报告期实际支付的全部职工工资总额/报告期全部职工平均人数

【专业技术人员】 指从事专业技术和从事专业技术管理工作的人员。统计对象为事业、企业单位中已经聘任专业技术职务从事专业技术工作的人员,以及未聘任专业技术职务,现在专业技术岗位上工作的具有中专以上学历的人员。

【城镇登记失业人员】 指有非农业户口,在一定的劳动年龄内,有劳动能力,无业而要求就业,并在当地就业服务机构进行求职登记的人员。

【城镇登记失业率】 指城镇登记失业人数同城镇从业人数与城镇登记失业人数之和的比。计算公式为:

城镇登记失业率=城镇登记失业人数/(城镇从业人数+城镇登记失业人数)×100%

Explanatory Notes on Main Statistical Indicators

【Birth Rate or (Crude Birth Rate)】 refers to the ratio of the number of births to the average population (or mid—period population) during a certain period of time (usually a year) which is often expressed in ‰. Birth rate in the chapter refers to annual birth rate. The following formula is used:

Birth Rate = Number of Births/Average Number of Population×1000‰

Number of births refers to live births i. e. the births when babies had showed any vital phenomena regardless of the length of pregnancy. Annual Average Number of Population is the average of the number of population at the beginning of the year and that at the end of the year. Sometimes it is substituted for with the mid year population.

【Death Rate (or Crude Death Rate)】 refers to the ratio of the number of deaths to the average population (or mid—period population) during a certain period of time (usually a year) which is often expressed in ‰. Death rate in the chapter refers to annual death rate. The following formula is used:

Death Rate= Number of Deaths/Annual Average Number of Population×1000‰

【Natural Growth Rate of Population】 refers to the ratio of natural increase in population (number of births minus number of deaths) in a certain period of time (usually a year) to the average population (or mid—period population) of the same period which is often expressed in ‰. The following formulas are applied:

Natural Growth of Population = (Number of Births—Number of Deaths)/Average Number of Population×1000‰

Natural Growth Rate of Population = Birth Rate—Death Rate

【Economically Active Population】 refers to the population aged 16 and over who are capable to work, are participating in or willing to participate in economic activities, including employed persons and unemployed persons.

【Employees of the Unit】 refers to the personnel who work in the government offices, political parties, social communities, enterprises and public undertakings and get paid. Including: on—the—job employees, reemployed retirees, teachers in schools run by the local people, personnel from abroad or HK, Macao, TW who work in the unit, persons on part time, laid—off personnel from other units, hands borrow ed from other units and concurrent employees. Employees who had left their units but still retain labor contracts with them are excluded.

【Full Employed Staff and Workers】 refers to the employees who work for the unit and get paid by it, including those who are leave because of illness, injuries and pregnancies.

【Average Wage of Staff and Workers】 refers to the average wage in money terms per person during a certain period of time for staff and workers in enterprises, institutions, and government agencies, which reflects the general level of wage income during a certain period of time and is calculated as follows:

Average Wage of Staff and Workers = Total Wages of Staff and Workers in Reference Period/Average Number of Staff and Workers in Reference Period.

【Specialized Technical Personnel】 refer to the professional technology and administrative personnel. Its statistical targets include personnel who had been employed and given professional posts by the enterprises and pubic under takings, and the personnel who work in the unit have degrees higher than polytechnic school, but not given professional posts.

【Registered Urban Unemployed Persons】 The registered unemployed persons in urban areas refer to the persons who are registered as permanent residents in the urban areas engaged in non—agricultural activities, aged within the range of working age, capable to labor, unemployed but desirous to be employed and have been registered at the local employment service agencies to apply for a job.

【Registered Urban Unemployment Rate】 Registered unemployment rate in urban areas refers to the ratio of the number of the registered unemployed persons to the sum of the number of employed persons and the registered unemployed persons . The formula is as follows:

Registered urban unemployment rate = number of registered urban unemployed persons÷(number of urban employed persons + number of registered urban unemployed persons) × 100%.

NINGBO

Statistical YearBook

第三篇

国民经济核算

NATIONAL ECONOMIC ACCOUNTING

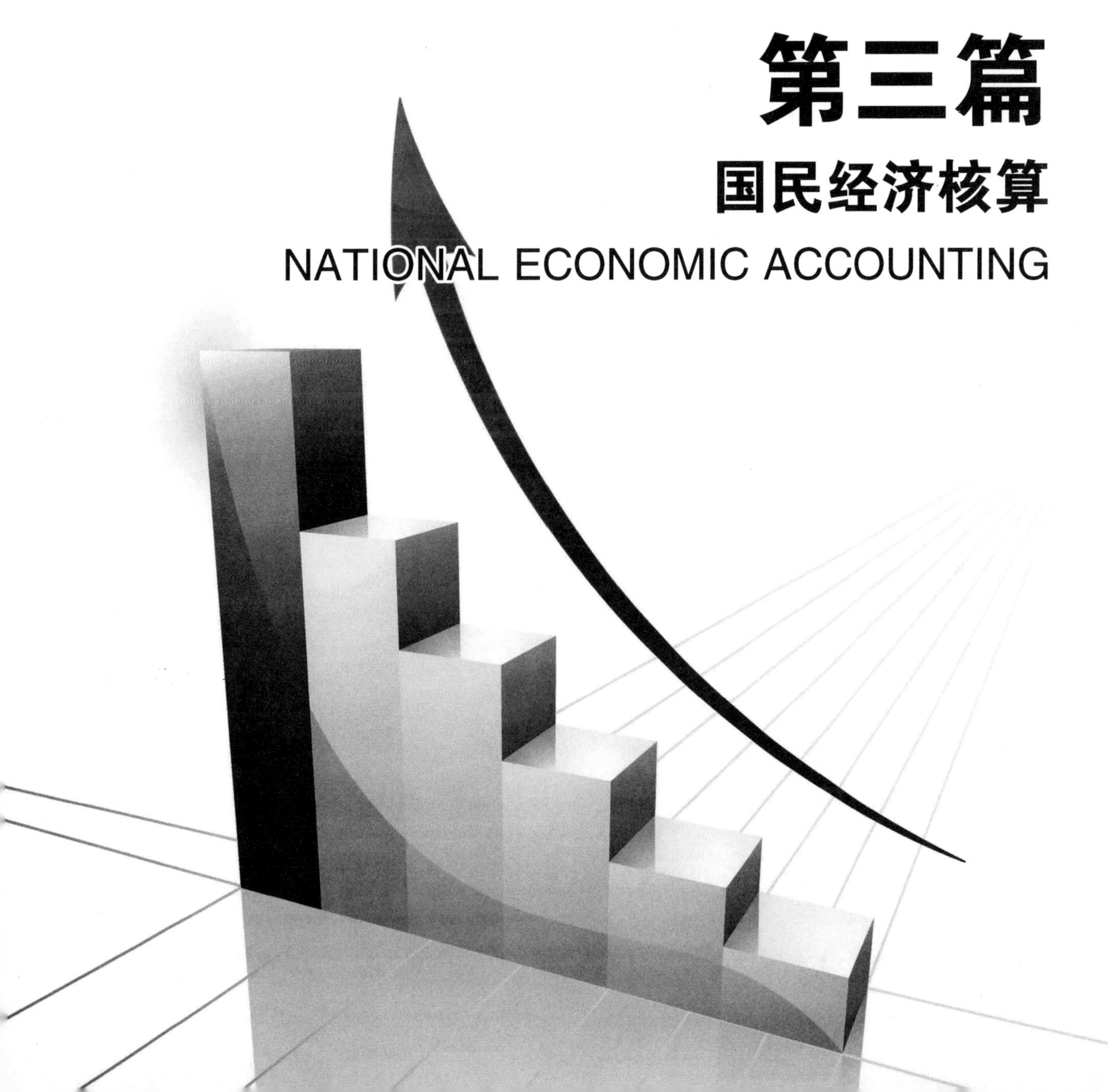

国民经济核算
National Economic Accounting

主要统计指标
Major Statistics Indicators

		总量 Total	比上年增长(%) Increase Over Last Year
宁波市生产总值(亿元)	Gross Domestic Product (100 million yuan)	6582.21	7.8
第一产业	Primary Industry	268.52	1.0
第二产业	Secondary Industry	3516.84	6.0
工业增加值	Value－added of Industry	3170.07	6.0
第三产业	Tertiary Industry	2796.85	10.9

			比上年增减(百分点) Increase Over Last Year(percent)
产业结构(%)	Structure of Gross Domestic Product		
总计	Total		
第一产业	Primary Industry	4.08	－0.13
第二产业	Secondary Industry	53.43	－1.85
第三产业	Tertiary Industry	42.49	1.98
最终消费构成(%)	Compositon of Final Consumption		
总计	Total		
居民消费	Resident Consumption	51.0	－0.2
农村居民	Rural Resident	23.8	0.5
城镇居民	Urban Resident	27.2	－0.7
政府消费	Government Consumption	49.0	0.2

表 3－1 历年生产总值 Gross Domestic Product Over the Years

单位：亿元、元(100 million yuan、yuan)

年份 Year	生产总值 Gross Domestic Product	其中 of Which				人均生产总值（按户籍人口） Per Capita GDP (by Registered Population)	人均生产总值（按常住人口） Per Capita GDP (by Permanent Population)
		第一产业 Primary Industry	第二产业 Secondary Industry	#工业 Industry	第三产业 Tertiary Industry		
1978	20.17	6.52	9.69	8.62	3.96	437	
1979	24.15	7.99	11.43	10.11	4.73	522	
1980	29.53	8.69	15.54	14.21	5.30	634	
1981	31.99	7.85	18.11	16.82	6.03	680	
1982	36.88	11.20	18.79	17.26	6.89	776	
1983	41.68	10.91	22.63	21.22	8.14	864	
1984	53.17	14.93	28.23	26.02	10.01	1096	
1985	71.05	16.85	40.40	36.96	13.80	1455	
1986	80.22	18.61	44.47	40.59	17.14	1626	
1987	95.99	22.11	53.99	48.76	19.89	1928	
1988	118.62	27.11	66.43	60.28	25.08	2356	
1989	137.25	31.13	77.69	71.02	28.43	2702	
1990	141.40	29.35	80.31	72.12	31.74	2777	
1991	169.87	32.75	98.39	88.22	38.73	3315	
1992	213.05	35.32	128.70	116.20	49.03	4516	
1993	315.11	46.09	189.12	165.61	79.90	6079	
1994	459.66	63.48	260.97	227.59	135.21	8815	
1995	602.65	81.11	338.99	295.90	182.55	12024	
1996	784.07	92.21	442.64	390.74	249.22	14846	
1997	879.10	84.53	500.06	452.24	294.51	16534	
1998	952.79	87.76	528.73	478.67	336.30	17832	
1999	1017.08	91.85	564.07	512.84	361.16	18946	
2000	1144.57	94.24	635.83	578.30	414.50	21208	
2001	1278.75	98.53	690.81	624.92	489.41	23587	
2002	1453.34	103.60	793.01	715.24	556.73	26678	
2003	1749.27	109.77	954.04	847.79	685.46	31943	
2004	2109.45	120.54	1167.44	1027.26	821.47	38292	
2005	2447.32	132.25	1341.87	1184.21	973.20	44120	36824
2006	2874.42	139.31	1580.70	1412.87	1154.41	51459	42299
2007	3418.57	150.92	1894.14	1703.20	1373.51	60774	49142
2008	3946.52	166.85	2190.78	1957.42	1588.89	69687	55616
2009	4329.30	183.53	2362.14	2110.82	1783.63	76012	60000
2010	5163.00	219.13	2870.69	2586.17	2073.18	90175	69368
2011	6059.24	255.23	3349.53	3019.00	2454.48	105333	79524
2012	6582.21	268.52	3516.84	3170.07	2796.85	114065	86228

表3—2 历年生产总值指数(以1978年为100)
Index of Gross Domestic Product Over the Years(1978=100)

年份 Year	生产总值 Gross Domestic Product	其中 of Which 第一产业 Primary Industry	第二产业 Secondary Industry	#工业 Industry	第三产业 Tertiary Industry	人均生产总值(按户籍人口) Per Capita GDP (by Registered Population)
1978	100.0	100.0	100.0	100.0	100.0	100.0
1979	113.4	106.4	116.4	114.1	119.2	113.6
1980	133.5	108.8	156.0	158.3	125.0	132.7
1981	145.9	103.1	181.6	190.5	139.2	143.6
1982	165.9	134.7	191.5	198.2	161.6	161.1
1983	195.2	143.1	239.0	240.4	185.8	187.5
1984	230.4	162.8	285.7	300.5	221.3	219.9
1985	295.1	163.6	403.9	422.8	278.2	279.8
1986	321.7	171.5	436.2	454.0	325.2	302.4
1987	367.0	177.3	515.6	538.5	361.3	341.4
1988	407.8	170.2	599.2	641.9	385.9	374.9
1989	426.1	163.6	651.9	688.1	368.1	388.0
1990	450.4	171.1	678.0	713.5	418.2	407.0
1991	562.5	188.7	801.3	884.8	635.6	479.9
1992	663.2	184.0	1011.3	1144.9	734.8	566.8
1993	801.2	203.0	1278.3	1573.1	843.5	664.9
1994	970.2	217.2	1567.2	1909.8	1055.2	803.1
1995	1169.1	247.6	1943.3	2373.8	1218.8	960.5
1996	1370.2	269.1	2302.8	2808.3	1436.9	1118.0
1997	1558.0	252.2	2680.5	3353.1	1658.2	1261.1
1998	1730.9	265.0	2988.7	3755.4	1858.9	1394.8
1999	1921.3	286.5	3308.5	4176.0	2094.9	1541.3
2000	2151.9	296.0	3725.4	4706.4	2371.5	1717.0
2001	2412.3	310.8	4209.7	5313.5	2665.5	1916.2
2002	2730.7	322.6	4841.2	6110.5	2996.1	2161.5
2003	3156.7	334.2	5659.4	7069.8	3472.4	2485.7
2004	3646.0	350.9	6598.9	8201.0	4017.6	2853.6
2005	4094.5	357.6	7311.6	9094.9	4672.5	3121.4
2006	4651.3	374.8	8230.6	10362.1	5429.9	3521.3
2007	5332.8	395.0	9474.3	12059.2	6254.1	4009.1
2008	5880.5	411.0	10394.0	13259.0	6986.9	4391.0
2009	6405.6	426.6	11251.6	14389.4	7710.4	4756.0
2010	7207.1	442.3	12762.8	16450.6	8651.3	5323.1
2011	7928.1	459.3	13999.5	18142.5	9610.4	5828.2
2012	8546.1	464.1	14839.4	19223.3	10659.8	6262.7

表 3—3　历年生产总值比上年增长
Growth Rate of Gross Domestic Product Raised Preceding Year Over the Years

单位:%

年份 Year	生产总值 Gross Domestic Product	其中 of Which 第一产业 Primary Industry	第二产业 Secondary Industry	#工业 Industry	第三产业 Tertiary Industry	人均生产总值（按户籍人口） Per Capita GDP (by Registered Population)	人均生产总值（按常住人口） Per Capita GDP (by Permanent Population)
1978	22.5	19.8	33.2		6.7	21.4	
1979	13.4	6.4	16.4	14.1	19.2	13.6	
1980	17.7	2.3	34.0	38.7	4.9	16.8	
1981	9.3	−5.2	16.4	20.3	11.4	8.2	
1982	13.7	30.6	5.5	4.0	16.1	12.2	
1983	17.7	6.2	24.8	21.3	15.0	16.4	
1984	18.0	13.8	19.5	25.0	19.1	17.3	
1985	28.1	0.5	41.4	40.7	25.7	27.2	
1986	9.0	4.8	8.0	7.4	16.9	8.1	
1987	14.1	3.4	18.2	18.6	11.1	12.9	
1988	11.1	−4.0	16.2	19.2	6.8	9.8	
1989	4.5	−3.9	8.8	7.2	−4.6	3.5	
1990	5.7	4.6	4.0	3.7	13.6	4.9	
1991	24.9	10.3	18.2	24.0	52.0	17.9	
1992	17.9	−2.5	26.2	29.4	15.6	18.1	
1993	20.8	10.3	26.4	37.4	14.8	17.3	
1994	21.1	7.0	22.6	21.4	25.1	20.8	
1995	20.5	14.0	24.0	24.4	15.5	19.6	
1996	17.2	8.7	18.5	18.3	17.9	16.4	
1997	13.7	−6.3	16.4	19.4	15.4	12.8	
1998	11.1	5.1	11.5	12.0	12.1	10.6	
1999	11.0	8.1	10.7	11.2	12.7	10.5	
2000	12.0	3.3	12.6	12.7	13.2	11.4	
2001	12.1	5.0	13.0	12.9	12.4	11.6	
2002	13.2	3.8	15.0	15.0	12.4	12.8	
2003	15.6	3.6	16.9	15.7	15.9	15.0	
2004	15.5	5.0	16.6	16.0	15.7	14.8	
2005	12.3	1.9	10.8	10.9	16.3	9.4	
2006	13.6	4.8	12.6	13.9	16.2	12.8	11.1
2007	14.7	5.4	15.1	16.4	15.2	13.9	12.0
2008	10.3	4.1	9.7	9.9	11.7	9.5	8.1
2009	8.9	3.8	8.3	8.5	10.4	8.3	7.1
2010	12.5	3.7	13.4	14.3	12.2	11.9	9.1
2011	10.0	3.8	9.7	10.3	11.1	9.5	7.5
2012	7.8	1.0	6.0	6.0	10.9	7.5	7.6

表 3—4　历年生产总值构成
Strucure of Gross Domestic Productoin Over the Years

单位:%

年份 Year	生产总值 Gross Domestic Product	其中 of Which			
		第一产业 Primary Industry	第二产业 Secondary Industry	#工业 Industry	第三产业 Tertiary Industry
1978	100.00	32.33	48.04	42.74	19.63
1979	100.00	33.08	47.33	41.86	19.59
1980	100.00	29.43	52.62	48.12	17.95
1981	100.00	24.54	56.61	52.58	18.85
1982	100.00	30.37	50.95	46.80	18.68
1983	100.00	26.18	54.29	50.91	19.53
1984	100.00	28.08	53.09	48.94	18.83
1985	100.00	23.72	56.86	52.02	19.42
1986	100.00	23.20	55.43	50.60	21.37
1987	100.00	23.03	56.25	50.80	20.72
1988	100.00	22.85	56.00	50.82	21.15
1989	100.00	22.68	56.60	51.74	20.71
1990	100.00	20.76	56.80	51.00	22.45
1991	100.00	19.28	57.92	51.93	22.80
1992	100.00	16.58	60.41	54.54	23.01
1993	100.00	14.63	60.02	52.56	25.35
1994	100.00	13.81	56.77	49.51	29.42
1995	100.00	13.46	56.25	49.10	30.29
1996	100.00	11.76	56.45	49.83	31.79
1997	100.00	9.62	56.88	51.44	33.50
1998	100.00	9.21	55.49	50.24	35.30
1999	100.00	9.03	55.46	50.42	35.51
2000	100.00	8.23	55.55	50.53	36.22
2001	100.00	7.71	54.02	48.87	38.27
2002	100.00	7.13	54.56	49.21	38.31
2003	100.00	6.28	54.54	48.47	39.18
2004	100.00	5.71	55.34	48.70	38.95
2005	100.00	5.40	54.83	48.39	39.77
2006	100.00	4.85	54.99	49.15	40.16
2007	100.00	4.41	55.41	49.82	40.18
2008	100.00	4.23	55.51	49.60	40.26
2009	100.00	4.24	54.56	48.76	41.20
2010	100.00	4.24	55.60	50.09	40.16
2011	100.00	4.21	55.28	49.82	40.51
2012	100.00	4.08	53.43	48.16	42.49

表 3-5　按产业划分的生产总值(2011—2012)
Gross Domestic Product Classified by Industries

单位:万元(10000 yuan)

指标	Indicators	2011	2012	发展速度(%) Growth Rate over 2011(%)
宁波市生产总值	**Gross Domestic Product**	**60592409**	**65822064**	**107.8**
第一产业	Primary Industry	2552270	2685159	101.0
第二产业	Secondary Industry	33495283	35168381	106.0
工业	Industry	30189965	31700695	106.0
建筑业	Constructions	3305318	3467686	106.4
第三产业	Tertiary Industry	24544856	27968524	110.9
交通运输、仓储和邮政业	Transportation, Storage and Post	2671088	2971215	107.3
信息传输、计算机服务和软件业	Information Transmission, Computer Service and Soltware Industries	795753	914560	115.3
批发和零售业	Retail and Wholesale Industries	6218905	6784344	114.2
住宿和餐饮业	Hoteling and Catering	1171355	1491370	121.7
金融业	Financial Industry	4432476	4506628	101.4
房地产业	Real Estate Industry	2653808	3697576	113.1
租赁和商务服务业	Leasehold and Busniess Service	1199598	1480442	121.9
科学研究、技术服务和地质勘查业	Scientific Research, Technology Service and Geological Prospecting	554588	661922	116.5
水利、环境和公共设施管理业	Water Conservancy, Environment and Public Facility Management	162692	190212	114.0
居民服务和其他服务业	Resident Service and Other Service Industries	621221	726544	115.6
教育	Education	1279852	1368208	103.6
卫生、社会保障和社会福利业	Health, Social Security and Welfare Industries	836787	1003991	117.5
文化、体育和娱乐业	Culture, Sports and Entertainment	281333	300217	104.6
公共管理和社会组织	Public Administration and Social Organizations	1665400	1871295	109.9

表 3－6 生产总值项目构成(1993－2012) Structure of Gross Domestic Product

单位:万元(10000 yuan)

年份	增加值 Value－Added	其中 of Which 劳动者报酬 Compensation of Employees	生产税净额 Net Taxes on Production	固定资产折旧 Depreciation of Fixed Assets	营业盈余 Operating Surplus
总计 Gross Domestic Product					
1993	3151137	1506857	499355	311430	833495
1994	4596645	2480140	699264	432964	984277
1995	6026524	3092917	953362	589020	1391225
1996	7840727	4197455	1297978	761269	1584025
1997	8791042	4760824	1466876	1000186	1563156
1998	9527859	4405743	1756795	1329018	2036303
1999	10170826	4858140	1765615	1485977	2061094
2000	11445653	5197257	1898185	1503767	2846444
2001	12787531	6129433	1872390	1619514	3166194
2002	14533421	6574217	2288833	1702915	3967456
2003	17492728	7522559	2888138	1983778	5098253
2004	21094461	8252916	3428099	2584132	6829314
2005	24473219	9538821	3773843	3121554	8039001
2006	28744210	11332844	4850566	3698732	8862068
2007	34185710	12843300	5480230	4593868	11268312
2008	39465245	16647075	6572526	5614314	10631330
2009	43293025	15876983	8602395	5178915	13634732
2010	51630017	19567241	9972959	5500116	16589701
2011	60592409	24455961	12282823	6803754	17049871
2012	65822064	28475509	13437771	8097017	15811767
第一产业 Primary Industry					
1993	460932	362995	6022	12583	79332
1994	634751	497816	11730	16599	108606
1995	811080	642492	17182	24416	126990
1996	922101	715773	17978	29039	159311
1997	845307	665351	21563	32441	125952
1998	877645	691633	15435	34769	135808
1999	918527	722231	15389	38032	142875
2000	942353	737186	14797	39345	151025
2001	985257	770231	15638	41004	158384
2002	1035968	812679	16182	43465	163642
2003	1097567	861928	10418	46163	179058
2004	1205371	1156158	10467	38746	
2005	1322475	1250993	14513	56969	
2006	1393123	1338826	－9413	63710	
2007	1509165	1473464	－33840	69541	
2008	1668464	1651964	－61244	77744	
2009	1835355	1785501	－42707	92561	
2010	2191327	2143132	－60191	108386	
2011	2552270	2498175	－70923	125018	
2012	2685159	2627034	－75549	133674	

表 3－6 续 Continued　　单位：万元(10000 yuan)

年份	增加值 Value－Added	其中 of Which 劳动者报酬 Compensation of Employees	生产税净额 Net Taxes on Production	固定资产折旧 Depreciation of Fixed Assets	营业盈余 Operating Surplus
第二产业 Secondary Industry					
1993	1891201	822727	360007	189250	519217
1994	2609752	1307376	541991	254130	506255
1995	3389919	1499859	728377	342581	819102
1996	4426403	2279485	966565	422195	758158
1997	5000559	2709675	1035314	520105	735465
1998	5287306	2080907	1265643	708150	1232606
1999	5640654	2355823	1271128	809524	1204179
2000	6358306	2462503	1378338	794615	1722850
2001	6908111	2768675	1404624	806206	1928606
2002	7930119	3381081	1752335	730237	2066466
2003	9540385	4030508	1808864	912346	2788667
2004	11674425	4360196	2305394	1266901	3741934
2005	13418692	4952203	2504702	1602800	4358987
2006	15806994	6113649	3285801	2129942	4277602
2007	18941412	7005672	3824969	2450357	5660414
2008	21907835	9744814	3606886	3451214	5104921
2009	23621397	8139761	5196507	2887974	7397155
2010	28706872	10178369	5778262	2894652	9855589
2011	33495283	12960405	7164265	3817708	9552905
2012	35168381	14852736	7641880	4253104	8420661
第三产业 Tertiary Industry					
1993	799004	321135	133326	109597	234946
1994	1352142	674948	145543	162235	369416
1995	1825525	950566	207803	222023	445133
1996	2492223	1202197	313435	310035	666556
1997	2945176	1385798	409999	447640	701739
1998	3362908	1633203	475717	586099	667889
1999	3611645	1780086	479098	638421	714040
2000	4144994	1997568	505050	669807	972569
2001	4894163	2590527	452128	772304	1079204
2002	5567334	2380457	520316	929213	1737348
2003	6854776	2630123	1068856	1025269	2130528
2004	8214665	2736562	1112238	1278485	3087380
2005	9732052	3335625	1254628	1461785	3680014
2006	11544093	3880369	1574178	1505080	4584466
2007	13735133	4364164	1689101	2073970	5607898
2008	15888946	5250297	3026884	2085356	5526409
2009	17836273	5951721	3448595	2198380	6237577
2010	20731818	7245740	4254888	2497078	6734112
2011	24544856	8997381	5189481	2861028	7496966
2012	27968524	10995739	5871440	3710239	7391106

表 3－7 部分年份按支出法计算的生产总值
Gross Domestic Product Calculated with Expenditure Approach in Partial Years

单位：亿元(100 million yuan)

指标	Indicators	2008	2009	2010	2011	2012
支出法生产总值	**Gross Domestic Product**	**3976.87**	**4334.45**	**5167.47**	**6065.97**	**6592.60**
最终消费	Final Consumption	1471.62	1658.29	1834.85	2187.58	2404.79
居民消费	Resident Consumption	852.98	938.19	980.16	1119.22	1225.32
农村居民	Rural Resident	416.28	443.37	443.36	509.42	572.33
城镇居民	Urban Resident	436.70	494.82	536.80	609.80	652.99
政府消费	Government Consumption	618.64	720.10	854.69	1068.36	1179.47
资本形成总额	Total Capital Formation	1842.13	2068.74	2523.96	2771.37	2912.88
固定资本形成总额	Fixed Capital Formation	1728.26	2004.22	2193.28	2385.51	2901.42
库存增加	Stock Increased	113.87	64.52	330.68	385.86	11.46
货物和服务净流出	Net Outflows of Goods and Services	663.12	607.42	808.66	1107.02	1274.93
流出	Outfloe	2937.59	2650.87	3518.19	4074.41	4384.94
流入	Inflows	2274.47	2043.45	2709.53	2967.39	3110.01
统计误差	Statistical Error	－30.35	－5.15	－4.47	－6.73	－10.39

表 3－8 部分年份按支出法计算的生产总值指数(以上年为 100)
Index of Gross Domestic Product Calculated with Expenditure Approach in Partial Years(Preceding Year＝100)

指标	Indicators	2008	2009	2010	2011	2012
支出法生产总值	**Gross Domestic Product**	**110.2**	**109.6**	**113.8**	**110.4**	**107.7**
最终消费	Final Consumption	117.0	113.4	106.4	113.2	108.1
居民消费	Resident Consumption	110.3	110.7	100.5	108.4	107.6
农村居民	Rural Resident	108.4	107.2	96.2	109.1	110.5
城镇居民	Urban Resident	112.1	114.0	104.3	107.9	105.3
政府消费	Government Consumption	127.7	117.1	114.1	118.7	108.6
资本形成总额	Total Capital Formation	103.7	113.0	115.6	108.4	105.2
固定资本形成总额	Fixed Capital Formation	103.0	116.7	104.2	108.1	121.7
库存增加	Stock Increased	114.2	57.0	470.2	110.2	2.9
货物和服务净流出	Net Outflows of Goods and Services	115.4	92.2	128.0	110.6	113.2
流出	Outfloe	106.8	90.8	127.6	105.9	105.8
流入	Inflows	104.5	90.4	127.5	104.5	103.1

表 3－9 部分年份按行业划分的资本形成总额
Gross Capital Formation by Sector in Partial Years

单位:亿元(100 million yuan)

指标	Indicators	2008	2009	2010	2011	2012
资本形成总额	**Gross Capital Formation**	**1842.13**	**2068.74**	**2523.96**	**2771.37**	**2912.88**
固定资本形成总额	Fixed Assets Formation	1728.26	2004.22	2193.28	2385.51	2901.42
第一产业	Primary Industry	4.11	4.80	10.42	18.39	27.02
第二产业	Secondary Industry	838.16	800.11	831.28	672.79	819.86
工业	Industry	821.93	778.95	819.50	668.36	817.24
建筑业	Construction	16.23	21.16	11.78	4.43	2.62
第三产业	Tertiary Industry	885.99	1199.30	1351.58	1694.33	2054.54
交通运输邮电通讯业	Transportation, Storage, Post and Telecommunications	224.35	300.01	297.21	336.26	351.35
批发和零售贸易、餐饮业	Wholesale, Retail Trade and Catering Services	48.48	55.28	72.58	64.24	89.52
金融保险业	Banking and Insurance	1.83	15.16	22.83	6.52	5.98
房地产业	Real Estate	403.24	455.33	533.84	919.92	1143.46
其他行业	Others	208.09	373.52	425.12	367.39	464.23
库存增加	Stock Change	113.87	64.52	330.68	385.86	11.46
第一产业	Primary Industry	0.29	0.26	0.35	0.47	0.59
第二产业	Secondary Industry	77.37	39.40	297.86	347.71	55.44
工业	Industry	62.81	33.99	290.74	338.14	43.27
建筑业	Construction	14.56	5.41	7.12	9.57	12.17
第三产业	Tertiary Industry	36.21	24.86	32.47	37.68	－44.57
交通运输邮电通讯业	Transportation, Storage, Post and Telecommunications	0.38	0.36	0.51	0.63	0.85
批发和零售贸易、餐饮业	Wholesale, Retail Trade and Catering Services	17.00	6.52	8.59	10.46	－79.89
其他行业	Others	18.83	17.98	23.37	26.59	34.47

表 3－10　最终消费情况(2011－2012)
Final Consumption

单位:亿元(100 millon yuan)

指标	Indicators	2011	2012
最终消费支出	**Final Consumption Expenditure**	**2187.58**	**2404.79**
一、居民消费支出	**Household Consumption Expenditures**	**1119.22**	**1225.32**
(一)农村居民	Rural Household	509.42	572.33
1.食品类支出	Food	184.97	199.39
2.衣着类支出	Garments	31.96	33.01
3.居住类支出	Residence	87.14	122.29
4.家庭设备、用品及服务类支出	Houshold Facilities Articles and Services	15.91	19.25
5.医疗保健类支出	Medical and Hygiencic Expenditure	38.16	32.44
6.公共医疗消费支出	Public Health	0.78	0.69
7.交通和通信类支出	Traffic and Telecommunications	47.52	50.71
8.文教娱乐用品及服务类支出	Recreation,Education and Cultural Services	49.71	53.09
9.金融中介服务虚拟支出	Imaginary Expenditure of Middle Finance Services	3.12	3.57
10.金融机构实际服务消费支出	Fact Expenditure of Finance Services	6.02	6.51
11.保险服务消费支出	Expenditure of Insurance Services	7.92	8.47
12.自有住房服务虚拟支出	Imaginary Expenditure of Freeform Resident Services	23.89	27.63
13.其它商品和服务类支出	Other Goods and Services	12.32	15.28
(二)城镇居民	Urban Household	609.80	652.99
1.食品类支出	Food	142.56	157.87
2.衣着类支出	Garments	47.43	51.68
3.居住类支出	Residence	105.81	94.89
4.家庭设备、用品及服务类支出	Houshold Facilities Articles and Services	26.79	26.29
5.医疗保健类支出	Medical and Hygiencic Expenditure	15.46	15.29
6.公共医疗消费支出	Public Health	2.76	2.73
7.交通和通信类支出	Traffic and Telecommunications	71.42	83.58
8.文教娱乐用品及服务类支出	Recreation,Education and Cultural Services	67.84	75.19
9.金融中介服务虚拟支出	Imaginary Expenditure of Middle Finance Services	3.59	4.11
10.金融机构实际服务消费支出	Fact Expenditure of Finance Services	5.59	6.17
11.保险服务消费支出	Expenditure of Insurance Services	10.61	11.42
12.自有住房服务虚拟支出	Imaginary Expenditure of Freeform Resident Services	80.69	92.53
13.实物消费支出	Reality Consumption	13.76	16.27
14.其它商品和服务类支出	Other Goods and Services	15.49	14.97
二、政府消费支出	**Government Consumption Expenditures**	**1068.36**	**1179.47**

表 3-11 部分年份居民总消费水平 Resident Consumption Level in Partial Years

单位:元/人(yuan/person)

指标	Indicators	2008	2009	2010	2011	2012
当年价居民消费水平	**Resident Consumption Level at Current Price**	**15062**	**16473**	**17119**	**19457**	**21234**
农村居民	Rural Resident	11252	12006	12018	13823	15586
城镇居民	Urban Resident	22241	24709	26361	29502	31123
可比价居民消费水平	**Resident Consumption Level at Comparable Price**	**14345**	**16572**	**16508**	**18477**	**20879**
农村居民	Rural Resident	10716	12078	11589	13127	15324
城镇居民	Urban Resident	21182	24858	25420	28017	30602
居民年平均人口(人)	**Annual Average Population(person)**	**5663237**	**5695523**	**5725504**	**5752421**	**5770584**
农村居民	Rural Resident	3699751	3692896	3689172	3685395	3672454
城镇居民	Urban Resident	1963486	2002627	2036332	2067026	2098130

表 3-12 部分年份居民消费指数(以上年为 100) Index of Resident Consumption in Partial Years(Preceding Year=100)

指标	Indicators	2008	2009	2010	2011	2012
当年价居民消费水平	**Resident Consumption Level at Current Price**	**118.4**	**109.4**	**103.9**	**113.7**	**109.1**
农村居民	Rural Resident	118.7	106.7	100.1	115.0	112.8
城镇居民	Urban Resident	117.0	111.1	106.7	111.9	105.5
可比价居民消费水平	**Resident Consumption Level at Comparable Price**	**112.7**	**110.0**	**100.2**	**107.9**	**107.3**
农村居民	Rural Resident	113.1	107.3	96.5	109.2	110.9
城镇居民	Urban Resident	111.4	111.8	102.9	106.3	103.7
居民年平均人口(人)	**Annual Average Population(person)**	**100.7**	**100.6**	**100.5**	**100.5**	**100.3**
农村居民	Rural Resident	99.7	99.8	99.9	99.9	99.6
城镇居民	Urban Resident	102.5	102.0	101.7	101.5	101.5

表 3－13　各县(市)按产业划分的生产总值(2012)
Gross Domestic Product Classified by Industries and by Region

指标	Indicators	全市 Total
地区生产总值	**Gross Domestic Product**	**65822064**
第一产业	Primary Industry	2685159
第二产业	Secondary Industry	35168381
工业	Industry	31700695
建筑业	Constructions	3467686
第三产业	Tertiary Industry	27968524
交通运输、仓储和邮政业	Transportation,Storage and Post	2971215
信息传输、计算机服务和软件业	Information Transmission,Computer Service and Soltware Industries	914560
批发和零售业	Retail and Wholesale Industries	6784344
住宿和餐饮业	Hoteling and Catering	1491370
金融业	Financial Industry	4506628
房地产业	Real Estate Industry	3697576
租赁和商务服务业	Leasehold and Busniess Service	1480442
科学研究、技术服务和地质勘查业	Scientific Research,Technology Service and Geological Prospecting	661922
水利、环境和公共设施管理业	Water Conservancy,Environment and Public Facility Management	190212
居民服务和其他服务业	Resident Service and Other Service Industries	726544
教育	Education	1368208
卫生、社会保障和社会福利业	Health,Social Security and Welfare Industries	1003991
文化、体育和娱乐业	Culture,Sports and Entertainment	300217
公共管理和社会组织	Public Administration and Social Organizations	1871295

单位:万元(10000 yuan)

市区 Urban Districts	#鄞州 Yinzhou	余姚 Yuyao	慈溪 Cixi	奉化 Fenghua	象山 Xiangshan	宁海 Ninghai
39509830	**10876479**	**7090713**	**9582077**	**2742507**	**3371599**	**3525338**
606684	384298	434637	465351	276749	537669	364069
20509249	6805554	4223347	5600405	1303059	1583874	1948447
18507170	6506999	3937687	5212212	1117435	1169696	1756495
2002079	298555	285660	388193	185624	414178	191952
18393897	3686627	2432729	3516321	1162699	1250056	1212822
2233641	160662	136556	231128	107874	130448	131568
598837	129851	71462	120397	36331	44068	43465
4093464	934635	679645	1146741	252450	294838	317206
906413	124624	126095	202577	81854	100321	74110
3236895	630505	375996	450192	146475	161876	135194
2509414	689432	318546	514183	94218	144586	116629
1180733	129985	77784	107542	26218	54429	33736
556251	59011	33617	35440	11607	13521	11486
123037	26574	18204	11282	17622	6618	13449
324541	87559	95207	164213	52331	37091	53161
799709	297359	170588	170075	69718	74867	83251
597353	107240	110134	118936	66287	52546	58735
149072	29020	30912	39367	38132	24626	18108
1084537	280170	187983	204248	161582	110221	122724

表 3－14　各县(市)生产总值结构及增长速度(2012)
Structure and Grawth Rate of Gross Domestic Product by Region

单位:%

地区	Region	生产总值 Gross Domestic Product	其中 of Which 第一产业 Primary Industry	第二产业 Secondary Industry	#工业 Industry	第三产业 Tertiary Industry
产业结构	**Structure**					
全市	Ningbo	100.0	4.1	53.4	48.2	42.5
市区	Urban Districts	100.0	1.5	51.9	46.8	46.6
#鄞州	Yinzhou	100.0	3.5	62.6	59.8	33.9
余姚	Yuyao	100.0	6.1	59.6	55.5	34.3
慈溪	Cixi	100.0	4.9	58.4	54.4	36.7
奉化	Fenghua	100.0	10.1	47.5	40.7	42.4
象山	Xiangshan	100.0	15.9	47.0	34.7	37.1
宁海	Ninghai	100.0	10.3	55.3	49.8	34.4
增长速度	**Grawth Rate**					
全市	Ningbo	7.8	1.0	6.0	6.0	10.9
市区	Urban Districts	7.5	－0.3	4.2	4.4	11.8
#鄞州	Yinzhou	9.3	2.3	10.2	9.7	8.4
余姚	Yuyao	8.8	1.9	10.2	10.1	7.4
慈溪	Cixi	9.4	1.8	8.9	8.9	11.5
奉化	Fenghua	5.4	1.8	5.5	3.6	6.0
象山	Xiangshan	5.7	0.5	7.0	4.6	6.1
宁海	Ninghai	8.3	1.5	6.7	7.0	13.2

主要统计指标解释

【国内生产总值(GDP)】 指一个国家(或地区)所有常住单位在一定时期内生产活动的最终成果。国内生产总值有三种表现形态,即价值形态、收入形态和产品形态。从价值形态看,它是所有常住单位在一定时期内生产的全部货物和服务价值超过同期中间投入的全部非固定资产货物和服务价值的差额,即所有常住单位的增加值之和;从收入形态看,它是所有常住单位在一定时期内创造并分配给常住单位和非常住单位的初次收入分配之和;从产品形态看,它是所有常住单位在一定时期内最终使用的货物和服务价值与货物和服务净出口价值之和。在实际核算中,国内生产总值有三种计算方法,即生产法、收入法和支出法。三种方法分别从不同的方面反映国内生产总值及其构成。

【三次产业】 根据社会生产活动历史发展的顺序对产业结构的划分,产品直接取自自然界的部门为第一产业;对初级产品进行再加工的部门称为第二产业;为生产和消费提供服务的部门称为第三产业。它是世界上通用的产业结构分类,但各国的划分不尽一致。我国的三次产业划分为:

第一产业:农业(包括种植业、林业、牧业、渔业、农林牧渔服务业)。

第二产业:工业(包括采掘业、制造业、电力、燃气及水的生产和供应业)和建筑业。

第三产业:除第一、第二产业以外的其他各业。

【劳动者报酬】 指劳动者因从事生产活动所获得的全部报酬。包括劳动者获得的各种形式的工资、奖金和津贴,既包括货币形式的,也包括实物形式的;还包括劳动者所享受的公费医疗和医药卫生费、上下班交通补贴和单位支付的社会保险费等。

【生产税净额】 指生产税减生产补贴后的余额。生产税指政府对生产单位生产、销售和从事经营活动以及因从事生产活动使用某些生产要素(如固定资产、土地、劳动力)所征收的各种税、附加费和规费。生产补贴与生产税相反,指政府对生产单位的单方面收入转移,因此视为负生产税,包括政策亏损补贴、粮食系统价格补贴、外贸企业出口退税收入等。

【固定资产折旧】 指一定时期内为弥补固定资产损耗按照核定的固定资产折旧率提取的固定资产折旧,或按国民经济核算统一规定的折旧率虚拟计算的固定资产折旧。它反映了固定资产在当期生产中的转移价值。各类企业和企业化管理的事业单位的固定资产折旧是指实际计提并计入成本费中的折旧费;不计提折旧的政府机关、非企业化管理的事业单位和居民住房的固定资产折旧是按照统一规定的折旧率和固定资产原值计算的虚拟折旧。原则上,固定资产折旧应按固定资产的重置价值计算,但是目前我国尚不具备对全社会固定资产进行重估价的基础,所以暂时只能采用上述办法。

【营业盈余】 指常住单位创造的增加值扣除劳动者报酬、生产税净额和固定资产折旧后的余额。它相当于企业的营业利润加上生产补贴,但要扣除从利润中开支的工资和福利等。

【支出法国内生产总值】 指一个国家(或地区)所有常住单位在一定时期内用于最终消费、资本形成总额,以及货物和服务的净出口总额,它反映本期生产的国内生产总值的使用及构成。

【最终消费】 指常住单位在一定时期内对于货物和服务的全部最终消费支出,也就是常住单位为满足物质、文化和精神生活的需要,从本国经济领土和国外购买的货物和服务的支出;不包括非常住单位在本国经济领土内的消费支出。最终消费分为居民消费和政府消费。

【资本形成总额】 指常住单位在一定时期内获得的减去处置的固定资产加存货的变动,包括固定资本形成总额和存货增加。

Explanatory Notes on Main Statistical Indicators

【Gross Domestic Product (GDP)】 refers to the final products of all resident units in a country (or a region) during a certain period of time. Gross domestic product is expressed in three different forms, i. e. value, income, and products respectively. The form of value refers to the total value of all products and services produced by all resident units during a certain period of time ,minus total value of intimidate input of materials and services of the nature of non—fixed assets or the summation of the value—added of all resident units; the form of income includes all the income created by all resident units and distributed primarily to all resident and non—resident units; the form of products refers to the value of all final goods and services for final use by all resident units plus the value of net exports of goods and services during a given period of time. In the practice of national accounting, gross domestic product is calculated with three approaches, i. e. production approach, income approach, and expenditure approach, which reflect gross domestic product and its composition from different aspects.

【Three Industries Industry】 structure has been classified according to the historical sequence of development. Primary industry refers to extraction of natural resources; secondary industry involves processing of primary products; and tertiary industry provides services of various kinds for production and consumption. The above classification is universal although it various to some extent from country to country. Industry in China comprises;

Primary Industry: agriculture (including farming, forestry, animal husbandry,fishery and services).

Secondary Industry: industry (including mining and quarrying, manufacturing, electric power,Gas and water production and supply) and construction.

Tertiary Industry: all other industries not included in primary or secondary industries.

【Laborers' Remuneration】 refers to the whole payment of various forms earned by the laborers from the productive activities they are engaged in. It includes wages, bonuses and allowances the laborers earned in monetary form and in kind. It also includes the free medical services provided to the laborers and the medicine expenses, traffic subsidies and social insurance fee paid by the laborers' working units for them.

【Net Taxes on Production】 refers to the residual of the taxes on production minus the subsidies on production. The taxes on production refers to the various taxes, extra charges and fees levied on the production units on their production, sale and business activities as well as on some factors of production, such as fixed assets, land and labor force, used in the production activities they are engaged in. In contrast to the taxes on production, the subsidies on production refer to the unilateral transfer of part of the government's revenue to the production units and is therefore regarded as negative taxes on production. They include subsidies on the loss due to implementation of government policies, price subsidies to the grain institutions, foreign trade corporations receipts from drawback, etc.

【Depreciation of Fixed Assets】 refers to the depreciation of fixed assets of a given period, drawn in accordance with the stipulated depreciation rate for the purpose of compensating the wear loss of the fixed assets or the depreciation of fixed assets calculated in a fictitious way in accordance with the stipulated unified depreciation rate in the national economic accounting system. It reflects the value of transfer of the fixed assets in the production of the current period. The depreciation of fixed assets in various enterprises and institutions managed as enterprises refers to the depreciation expenses actually drawn and calculated as part of the cost. In government agencies and institutions not managed as enterprises which do not draw the depreciation expenses, as well as for the houses of residents, the depreciation of fixed assets is the imputed depreciation, which is calculated in accordance with the stipulated unified depreciation rate. In principle, the depreciation of fixed assets should be calculated on the basis of the re—purchased value of the fixed assets. However, there is no actual condition to re—evaluate all the fixed assets in China. Therefore, the above—mentioned methods are temporarily adopted at present.

【Operating Surplus】 refers to the balance of the value added created by the resident units deducting the laborers' remuneration, net taxes on production and the depreciation of fixed assets. It is equivalent to the business profit of the enterprises plus subsidies on production, but the wages and welfare expenses paid from the profits should be deducted.

【GDP Calculated with Expenditure Approach】 refers to total expenditure on final consumption, total capital formation and net export of goods and services by resident units of a country in a certain period of time. It reflects the composition of GDP by its use.

【Final Consumption】 refers to the total expenditure of resident units on final consumption of goods and services in a certain period, namely the expenditure of the resident units for purchases of goods and services from domestic economic territory and abroad to meet the requirements of material, cultural and spiritual life. It excludes the expenditure of non—resident units on consumption in the economic territory of the country. The final consumption is classified into household consumption and government consumption.

【Total Capital Formation】 refers to the fixed assets acquired minus those disposed and the change in inventory, including the total fixed assets formation and the increase in inventory.

第四篇

财政、金融、保险、证券

FINANCE,BANKING,INSURANCE AND SECURITIES

财政、金融、保险、证券
Finance, Banking, Insurancen and Securities

主要统计指标
Major Statistics Indicators

2012 年全市财政总收入	Total Financial Revenue	2206.04	亿元	100 million yuan
比上年增长	Increase Over Last Year	－2.9	%	
2012 年全市公共财政预算收入	Public Fiscal Budget Revenue	1536.51	亿元	100 million yuan
比上年增长	Increase Over Last Year	7.3	%	
2012 年地方财政收入	Local Financial Revenue	725.50	亿元	100 million yuan
比上年增长	Increase Over Last Year	10.3	%	
2012 年财政支出	Total Financial Expenditure	1516.16	亿元	100 million yuan
比上年增长	Increase Over Last Year	－5.1	%	
2012 年公共财政预算支出	Public Fiscal Budget Expenditure	828.44	亿元	100 million yuan
比上年增长	Increase Over Last Year	10.4	%	
2012 年金融机构人民币存款余额	Deposits of Financial Institutions at Year－end	11602.32	亿元	100 million yuan
比上年增长	Increase Over Last Year	11.2	%	
2012 年城乡居民储蓄存款余额	Urban and Rural Residents SavingBalance at Year－end	4175.96	亿元	100 million yuan
比上年增长	Increase Over Last Year	13.9	%	
2012 年金融机构人民币贷款余额	Loans Balance of Financial Institutions at Year－end	11300.32	亿元	100 million yuan
比上年增长	Increase Over Last Year	10.7	%	

表4—1 历年公共财政预算收入及支出情况
The Public Fiscal Budget Revenue and Expenditure Over Years

单位:万元(10000 yuan)

年份 Year	公共财政预算收入 Public Fiscal Budget Revenue		财政支出 Financial Expenditure	
	全市 Total	市区 Urban District	全市 Total	市区 Urban District
1978	49697	29662	11176	4672
1979	48860	29536	11803	4252
1980	56290	34924	15712	6956
1981	65432	41157	14585	5812
1982	71546	44574	14689	5331
1983	80801	49130	18873	7747
1984	93318	58817	25544	12148
1985	91237	46963	34610	17449
1986	102264	50872	48978	27413
1987	113351	55227	41655	19490
1988	133395	66580	70336	38395
1989	152751	74892	89355	50141
1990	158910	75725	97133	54389
1991	177875	86733	106961	58704
1992	198354	96918	119133	62758
1993	282429	137495	180622	92931
1994	420202	244253	250553	145946
1995	531135	328458	353700	231321
1996	659529	424052	453292	306509
1997	750412	485289	549989	364757
1998	876351	572222	646089	417522
1999	1039976	679852	740516	477550
2000	1431511	937655	892345	566103
2001	1903064	1209606	1219330	759071
2002	2583984	1869395	1501556	1039828
2003	3250078	2287641	1870929	1268421
2004	4009592	2896291	2223509	1535768
2005	4664968	3294643	3263061	2323203
2006	5611702	3922945	3903046	2678424
2007	7239222	5124685	5691897	3878062
2008	8109020	5698607	7838113	5116301
2009	9662496	7109554	10690545	7038194
2010	11717470	8758532	14521735	9766602
2011	14317563	10691006	15967831	9732235
2012	15365101	11311780	15161555	9387493

表 4－2　各县(市)财政收入情况(2012)
Basic Statistics on Financial Revenue by Region

指标	Indicators	全市 Total	市区 Urban District
财政收入	**Financial Revenue**	**22060351**	**15178836**
公共财政预算收入	Public Fiscal Budget Revenue	15365101	11311780
中央财政收入	Revenue of Central Government	8110098	6302444
＃消费税	Consumption Tax	2114630	2089188
地方财政收入	Local Financial Revenue	7255003	5009336
税收收入小计	**Total Tax Revenue**	**6678405**	**4608934**
增值税	Value－added Tax	1226704	810384
＃成品油价税费改革增值税划出	Refined Oil Prices to Draw	－45893	－45893
改征增值税	VAT	1440	891
营业税	Business Tax	1952195	1347915
企业所得税	Enterprises Income Tax	1157361	908725
个人所得税	Individual Income Tax	361056	243161
城市维护建设税	Tax on Urban Construction and Maintenance	527684	401849
＃成品油价税费改革城市维护建设税划出	Refined Oil Prices to Draw	－88390	－88390
耕地占用税	Tax on the Use of Cultivated Land	88773	32271
契税	Contract Tax	383633	241621
非税收收入小计	**Total non－Tax Revenue**	**576598**	**400402**
专项收入	Special Projects Income	261817	183350
＃教育费附加	Additional Education Tax	241234	171389
＃成品油价税费改革教育费附加收入划出	Refined Oil Prices to Draw	－37939	－37939
排污费	Sewage Tax	12699	8263
行政事业性收费收入	Administrative Fees and Charges Income	113397	90966
罚没收入	Penally and Confiscatory Income	133356	72007
国有资本经营收收入	State－owned Capital Management Income	－104990	－68287
＃国有企业计划亏损补贴	Subsidies to Loss of State－owned Enterprises	－106044	－68937
基金收入	Fund Revenue	6695250	3867056
＃政府性基金收入	Government Fund Revenue	4408058	2299322
社会保险基金收入	Social Insurance Fund Revenue	2287192	1567734

单位:万元(10000 yuan)

海曙 Haishu	江东 Jiangdong	江北 Jiangbei	北仑 Beilun	镇海 Zhenhai	鄞州 Yinzhou	余姚 Yuyao	慈溪 Cixi	奉化 Fenghua	象山 Xiangshan	宁海 Ninghai
959855	**785511**	**870180**	**2008089**	**1063740**	**3439053**	**1910171**	**2423750**	**756304**	**937521**	**853769**
708983	606677	603588	1525398	750388	2373723	1128512	1460356	446040	466772	551641
222677	185119	241804	757964	339115	1011499	511657	646504	202312	193979	253202
3423	383	143	13957	-1309	4790	1155	16182	5130	48	2927
486306	421558	361784	767434	411273	1362224	616855	813852	243728	272793	298439
471230	**381985**	**356406**	**715360**	**380650**	**1240537**	**579270**	**767768**	**215063**	**243608**	**263762**
27604	19683	43914	157803	79108	191634	120993	143450	49852	44510	57515
			161	68	-1					
72	150	141	191	86	224	134	233	39	57	86
229677	189830	123331	172266	132452	340730	162349	224531	62414	82441	72545
55428	58120	53438	146197	51094	210701	66323	95563	22283	29123	35344
35473	24787	19342	35262	18653	76844	34548	41451	10949	12991	17956
23620	18967	20317	59324	29349	79064	31501	45991	16874	12884	18585
			308	130	-1					
529	9	4334	13504	1407	12488	8997	17081	7511	11772	11141
36067	27390	19620	27371	16113	113249	40642	49754	13238	19705	18673
15076	**39573**	**5378**	**52074**	**30623**	**121687**	**37585**	**46084**	**28665**	**29185**	**34677**
10104	8120	8684	27784	16538	36383	20880	25498	9329	9087	13673
10104	8120	8639	24224	12619	34351	19250	24642	7939	7445	10569
			134	56	-1					
			2700	3877	852	475	516	344	1260	1841
4690	3307	4224	9241	5085	27514	4439	2564	2430	4705	8293
2249	1676	1134	10392	6644	18268	12178	15280	7772	14375	11744
-2200	-4017	-14720	-5000	-6000	-2850	-4596	-26576		-2242	-3289
-2200	-4017	-14720	-5000	-6000	-3500	-5000	-26576		-2242	-3289
250872	178834	266592	482691	313352	1065330	781659	963394	310264	470749	302128
21187	15937	125938	267629	180918	598606	547721	799029	189201	387632	185153
229685	162897	140654	215062	132434	466724	233938	164365	121063	83117	116975

表 4－3　各县(市)财政支出情况(2012)
Basic Statistics on Financial Expenditure by Region

指标	Indicators	全市 Total	市区 Urban District
财政支出	**Financial Expenditure**	**15161555**	**9387493**
公共财政预算支出	**Public Fiscal Budget Expenditure**	**8284437**	**5475083**
一般公共服务	General Public Service	1004625	643566
公共安全	Public Safety	576880	369607
教育	Education	1417046	838249
科学技术	Science and Technology	324076	217047
文化体育与传媒	Culture,Sports and Media	127706	85934
社会保障和就业	Social Security and Reemployment	790129	473017
医疗卫生	Health Care	563787	317674
节能环保	Energy Saving and Environmental Protection	114735	76775
城乡社区服务	Community Service in Urban and Rural Areas	849136	754533
农林水事务	Affairs Such as Agriculture, Forestry, Water Conservancy,etc.	721950	268513
交通运输	Communications and Transportation	506672	403089
资源勘探电力信息等事务	Resource exploration and Power Information	496712	398127
商业服务业等事务	Business services and Other Services	271146	215512
粮油物资储备管理事务	Grain Material Reserve Management Services	10399	7349
基金支出	**Fund Expenditure**	**6877118**	**3912410**
政府性基金	Government Funds	4589925	2344675
社会保险基金	Social Insurance Funds	2287193	1567735

单位:万元(10000 yuan)

海曙 Haishu	江东 Jiangdong	江北 Jiangbei	北仑 Beilun	镇海 Zhenhai	鄞州 Yinzhou	余姚 Yuyao	慈溪 Cixi	奉化 Fenghua	象山 Xiangshan	宁海 Ninghai
534883	**511664**	**460853**	**922680**	**630398**	**2125938**	**1466746**	**1885391**	**735757**	**929214**	**756954**
223511	**255028**	**286935**	**688712**	**409511**	**1375506**	**678191**	**866031**	**389930**	**458059**	**417143**
40071	36635	53309	93261	50292	157887	92309	115026	47040	47640	59044
23998	24474	26294	37210	31284	71894	47915	75916	23878	25646	33918
45411	53266	50701	113402	72981	252653	132919	194258	77245	88677	85698
10600	15075	14087	38649	17624	55221	28821	43754	11208	12000	11246
1364	2332	3643	9019	7551	21383	13042	12220	3689	5520	7301
26917	23905	17540	36193	35322	122289	90298	105222	35541	34536	51515
14426	15321	14216	49889	31534	86220	68636	73052	31426	33339	39660
1535	525	4226	9252	4908	41490	12882	9022	3907	5631	6518
30242	48074	30231	82791	44077	112095	27028	33761	9434	14115	10265
1388	234	17932	46842	17184	110522	81226	79573	98697	137901	56040
259	131	14759	23170	20423	69637	22109	15037	25520	15494	25423
8115	3998	12929	108936	52920	126897	18089	58215	4399	9029	8853
5971	13527	6921	12913	8791	56478	11843	22661	5332	7903	7895
			687	762	74	565		12	2451	22
311372	**256636**	**173918**	**233968**	**220887**	**750432**	**788555**	**1019360**	**345827**	**471155**	**339811**
311372	256636	173918	233968	220887	750432	554617	854995	224764	388038	222836
						233938	164365	121063	83117	116975

表 4—4 历年金融机构人民币存贷款与现金收支情况
Savings Deposits and Loans Balances of Financial Institutions & Cash Revenue and Expenditures Over the Years(RMB)

单位:万元(10000 yuan)

年份 Year	存款余额 Deposits Balance	#城乡居民储蓄 Urban and Rural Savings Deposits	贷款余额 Loans Balance	现金收入 Cash Income	现金支出 Cash Expenditure	货币投放(+) 回笼(—) Currency Issues (+) or Cash Withdrawal(—)
1978	50194	14997	68843	92387	101326	8939
1979	64379	20612	78939	119923	130544	10621
1980	90536	28781	107339	159955	174339	14384
1981	107253	34418	114394	187306	198061	10755
1982	130697	46298	130617	216530	227547	11017
1983	154150	60536	146636	277321	288711	11390
1984	207363	81558	242546	356422	392814	36392
1985	266510	109853	304823	522442	562304	39862
1986	354390	149451	414921	640814	679516	38702
1987	445081	199524	522160	860563	926247	65684
1988	522116	215357	643234	1212594	1328827	116233
1989	639228	317572	765704	1344442	1415310	70868
1990	899295	461220	973946	1044032	1102545	58513
1991	1180588	605796	1227009	1321446	1401416	79970
1992	1605229	792466	1603689	1957225	2099612	142387
1993	2012813	979740	2116122	3295921	3441608	145687
1994	2972601	1468634	2671174	4949086	5199010	249924
1995	4546806	2094162	3892271	7121855	7452530	330675
1996	5981440	2846051	5240845	9312625	9789622	476997
1997	7172242	3644769	5747533	12202712	12646470	443758
1998	8552754	4596343	6700817	19733593	20136905	403312
1999	10080232	5296350	7734820	24090235	24591240	501005
2000	11729400	5860592	8831213	30467325	31088353	621028
2001	14445304	6994639	10515601	36286694	37062049	775355
2002	19062375	8623909	14794722	49240318	50379541	1139223
2003	26290346	10596339	21027772	68390220	69703625	1313405
2004	30917954	12089813	24836090	90446530	91895140	1448610
2005	37919362	14588012	29597759	100679426	102368573	1689147
2006	45734811	17520388	37274957	121414154	123296128	1881974
2007	51772379	18274856	47359146	153033733	155234259	2200526
2008	62164580	23670651	56727416	155387621	157911068	2523447
2009	80839363	28695587	74248698	143230611	145798647	2568037
2010	95520308	32822564	90006170	158421425	161613115	3191690
2011	104359176	36662324	102099855			
2012	116023188	41759634	113003187			

注:本表至 4—9 表数据来自中国人民银行宁波中心支行。2011 年现金收支统计制度取消。

Note: Data from Tables 4—4 to 4—9 are obtained from Central Subbranch of Ningbo of The People's Bank of China. Cancel the cash income and expenditure statistics system in 2011.

表 4—5 金融机构人民币信贷资金来源主要指标(2012)
Main Indicators of Credit Funds of Financial Institutions—Sources of Funds

(年末余额)单位:万元(year—end)(10000 yuan)

指标	Indicators	2012
资金来源总计	**Funds Sources**	**141299108**
一、各项存款	Total Deposits	116023188
1.单位存款	Unit Deposits	66234696
其中按产品	By Product	
活期存款	Demand Deposits	20947650
定期存款	Time Deposits	18326919
通知存款	Call Deposits	1650103
保证金存款	Margin Deposits	13685874
其中按交易对手	By Counterparty	
企业存款	Deposits by Enterprises	50059602
机关团体存款	Deposits by Government Departments & Organizations	9616290
社保基金存款	Social Security Fund Deposits	4793829
部队存款	Force Deposits	566869
住房公积金存款	Housing Provident Fund Deposits	946147
非居民存款	Nonresisdent Deposits	17534
2. 个人存款	Individual Deposits	42898879
储蓄存款	Household Savings Deposits	41759634
保证金存款	Margin Deposits	77005
结构性存款	Structured Deposits	1062240
3. 财政性存款	Fiscal Deposits	2389167
4. 临时性存款	Temporary Deposits	170664
5. 委托存款	Commissiom Deposits	374713
6. 其他存款	Other Deposits	3955069
二、金融债券	Financial Bond	1314161
三、中长期借款	Medium&Long—Term Deposits	562
四、应付及暂收款	Account Payable and Collecting of Money for the Time Being	3349231
其中:应付利息	Interest Payable	1582990
五、同业往来(来源方)	Inter—bnak Credits	333809
六、系统内资金往来(来源方)	Inter—system Credit	7898639
七、外汇买卖(来源方)	Foreign Exchange	14053969
其中:结售汇	Exchange Settlement and Sales	10977720
八、各项准备	Provisions	2253629
其中:贷款损失准备金	Loan Loss Provisions	2226462
九、所有者权益	Creditors Equity	6598762
其中:实收资本	Capital Obtained	1483749
十、其他	Others	—10526840

注:金融机构包括人民银行、政策性银行、国有商业银行、邮政储蓄银行、股份制商业银行、城市商业银行、农村合作银行、农村信用社、城市信用社、外资银行、村镇银行、信托投资公司、租赁公司、财务公司等。

Note: Financial institutions including the people's Bank of China, policy banks, state—owned commercial banks, postal savings banks, joint—stock commercial banks, city commercial banks, rural cooperative banks, rural credit cooperatives, city credit cooperatives, rural banks, foreign banks, Trust Investment Company, financial leasing companies etc.

表 4－6 金融机构人民币信贷资金运用主要指标(2012)
Main Indicators of Credit Funds of Financial Institutions－Use of Funds (RMB)

(年末余额)单位:万元(year－end)(10000 yuan)

指标	Indicators	2012
资金运用总计	**Funds Uses**	**141299108**
一、各项贷款	Total Loans	113003187
(一)境内贷款	Domestic Loans	112995066
1.短期贷款	Short－term Loans	62159592
(1)个人贷款及透支	Individual Loans and Overdrafts	12081824
其中:个人消费贷款	Individual Consumption Loans	5337322
其中:住房贷款	Housing Mortgage	51016
(2)单位普通贷款及透支	Unit Loans and Overdrafts	46445697
其中:经营贷款	Business Loans	45951375
固定资产贷款	Fixed Asset Loans	492651
(3)普通并购贷款	Ordinary Aquasition Loans	
(4)银团贷款	Syndicated Loans	113314
(5)贸易融资	Trade Loans	3518756
(6)境外筹资转贷款	Overseas Financing Transiferred Loans	
2.中长期贷款	Medium&Long－Term Loans	46964712
(1)个人贷款	Individual Loans	14076306
其中:个人消费贷款	Individual Consumption Loans	12589461
其中:住房贷款	Housing Mortgage	10759529
(2)单位普通贷款	Unit Loans	28119501
其中:经营贷款	Business Loans	3387657
固定资产贷款	Fixed Asset Loans	24731843
(3)普通并购贷款	Ordinary Aquasition Loans	129115
(4)银团贷款	Syndicated Loans	4082323
(5)贸易融资	Trade Loans	557467
(6)境外筹资转贷款	Overseas Financing Transiferred Loans	
3.融资租赁	Financial and Leasehold	530103
4.票据融资	Bill Financing	3088289
其中:贴现	Discount	3088289
5.各项垫款	Advances	252369
(二)境外贷款	Foreign Loans	8121
二、有价证券	Securities	4940400
三、股权及其他投资	Euqities and Other Investment	7347690
四、应收及预付款	Receivables and Prepayments	1105457
其中:应收利息	Interest Receivable	585494
五、同业往来(运用方)	Inter－Bank Trasactions/use	1206411
六、系统内资金往来(运用方)	Inter－systmen Trasacton/use	
七、金银占款	Gold and Silver	
八、外汇买卖(运用方)	Foreign Exchange	11452559
其中:结售汇	Exchange Settlement and Sales	8732018
九、固定资产	Fixed Asset	1542527
十、库存现金	Cashes	694975
十一、投资性房地产	Investment Real Estate	5903

表4－7 各县(市)金融机构人民币存贷款情况(2012) Savings Deposits and Loans Balances of Financial Institutions by Region(RMB)

单位:万元(10000 yuan)

地区	Region	存款余额 Deposits	其中 of Which 单位存款 Unit Deposits	企业存款 by Enterprise	个人存款 Individual Deposits	储蓄存款 Savings Deposits	贷款余额 Loans	其中 of Which 短期贷款 Short－term Loans	中长期贷款 Medium and Long－term Loans
全市	**Total**	**116023188**	**66234696**	**50059602**	**42898879**	**41759634**	**113003187**	**62159592**	**46964712**
市区	Urban Districts	79101644	47483903	35892997	25067559	24207658	75422062	36597482	35349127
#鄞州	Yinzhou	15251705	7781966	6636746	7059018	6832514	13058522	8899837	3414013
余姚	Yuyao	10807496	5579308	4402837	5167854	5050704	10336279	7070694	3135382
慈溪	Cixi	15636652	7776069	6300956	7598872	7501295	13865492	10359292	3312086
奉化	Fenghua	3574098	1565418	915553	2005460	1981777	4038330	2597351	1426602
象山	Xiangshan	3245132	1810315	1379676	1427782	1413757	4653373	2869928	1763682
宁海	Ninghai	3658165	2019683	1167583	1631352	1604442	4687651	2664846	1977833

表4－8 部分年份金融机构本外币存贷款情况 Savings Deposits and Loans Balances of Financial Institutions in Partial Years(in RMB and Foreign Currency)

单位:万元(10000 yuan)

指标	Indicators	2009	2010	2011	2012
本外币存款余额	**Total Deposits in RMB and Foreign Currency**	**82414306**	**97555158**	**106592654**	**119804984**
#人民币	RMB	80839363	95520308	104359176	116023188
外币	Foreign Currency	1574943	2034850	2233478	3781795
#本外币储蓄存款	Household Savings Deposits in RMB and Foreign Currency	29017634	33121737	36962819	42088122
本外币贷款余额	**Total Loans in RMB and Foreign Currency**	**77159070**	**94141982**	**106768424**	**119610158**
#人民币	RMB	74248698	90006170	102099855	113003187
外币	Foreign Currency	2910372	4135812	4668569	6606972

表 4－9 保险公司业务经济技术指标(2012) Economic and Technical Indicators of Insurance Companies

单位:万元(10000 yuan)

指标	Indicators	保费收入 Premiums		赔付支出 Claim and Payment	
		绝对量 Total	同比增长(%) Growth Rate(%)	绝对量 Total	同比增长(%) Growth Rate(%)
合计	**Total**	**1647056**	**10.8**	**642725**	**33.4**
财产险	Property Insurance	862294	11.6	519027	38.5
＃机动车辆保险	Motor Vehicle Insurance	622919	12.1	379219	27.2
人身险	Life Insurance	784762	10.0	123698	15.4
人身意外伤害险	Personal Accident Insurance	40161	13.4	7261	20.7
健康险	Health insurance	52088	19.8	19331	20.0
寿险	Life insurance	692513	9.2	97106	14.1
按公司类别分	**Of Which**				
财产保险公司	**Property Insurance Companies**	**892685**	**11.8**	**528175**	**38.1**
财产险	Property Insurance	862294	11.6	519027	38.5
＃机动车辆保险	Motor Vehicle Insurance	622919	12.1	379219	27.2
人身险	Life Insurance	30391	18.7	9148	19.1
人身意外伤害险	Personal Accident Insurance	18690	15.5	3762	38.5
健康险	Health insurance	11701	24.3	5386	8.5
寿险	Life insurance				
人寿保险公司	**Property Insurance Companies**	**754371**	**9.7**	**114550**	**15.1**
财产险	Property Insurance				
＃机动车辆保险	Motor Vehicle Insurance				
人身险	Life Insurance	754371	9.7	114550	15.1
人身意外伤害险	Personal Accident Insurance	21471	11.7	3500	6.1
健康险	Health insurance	40387	18.5	13945	25.1
寿险	Life insurance	692513	9.2	97106	14.1

注:本表数据来自于中国保险监督管理委员会宁波监管局。

Note:Data in this table are obtained from China Insurance Regulatory Commission Ningbo Burean.

表 4—10 部分年份保险业务情况 Conditions of Insurance Business in Partial Years

单位:亿元(100 million yuan)

指标	Indicators	2006	2007	2008	2009	2010	2011	2012
保费收入	**Premiums**	**59.14**	**72.22**	**87.11**	**107.44**	**144.06**	**148.60**	**164.71**
财产险	Property Insurance	27.27	34.43	40.34	51.08	66.20	77.29	86.23
人身险	Life Insurance	31.88	37.80	46.76	56.37	77.86	71.31	78.48
赔付支出	**Claim and Payment**	**20.18**	**26.28**	**37.90**	**36.29**	**38.14**	**48.19**	**64.27**
财产险	Property Insurance	15.62	18.08	24.54	25.44	27.45	37.47	51.91
人身险	Life Insurance	4.56	8.21	13.37	10.85	10.69	10.72	12.37

注:2011 年起,保险业采用新会计准则二号解释的新口径进行计算。

Note:From 2011,the insurance industry in accordance with the new accounting standards new dianeter calculation.

表 4—11 证券市场基本情况(2011) Basic Statistics on Securities Markets

指标	单位	Indicators	unit	绝对量 Total	比上年增长(%) Growth Rate(%)
上市公司总家数	家	Total Listed Companies (A Share and H Share)	Unit	55	10.0
#A 股上市公司	家	A Share	Unit	42	10.5
A 股上市公司总股本	亿股	Total Issued Capital of Listed Companies (A Share)	100 million shares	340.14	7.5
A 股上市公司总市值	亿元	Total Market Capitalization of Listed Companies(A Share)	100 million yuan	2034.46	7.8
境内证券市场融资额	亿元	Total Financing on Securities Markets in Mainland	100 million yuan	57.17	1.9
证券成交总额	亿元	Total Negotiable Securities Turnover	100 million yuan	14494.85	−6.9
#股票和基金	亿元	Stock and Fund	100 million yuan	9856.21	−29.0
权证	亿元	Warrant	100 million yuan		
证券客户交易结算资金余额	亿元	Total Exchange and Settlement Capital of Securities Customer	100 million yuan	69.72	−12.3
指定与托管证券市值	亿元	Securities Market Capitalization of Appointment and Trusteeship	100 million yuan	1140.69	14.9
证券投资者股票账户数	万户	Total Stock Investors	10000 accounts	93.24	4.7
证券营业部利润总额	亿元	Total Profits of Stock Exchange	100 million yuan	2.87	−44.2
期货代理交易量	万手	Agency's Trading Volume of Futures	10000 pieces	6166.41	183.7
期货代理交易额	亿元	Agent's Turnover of Futures	100 million yuan	41991.54	59.8
期货保证金余额	万元	Balance Cover Cost	10000 yuan	298125	37.5
期货投资者开户数	户	Total Future Investors	account	19137	19.3

注:本表数据来自于中国证券监督管理委员会宁波监管局。

Note:Data in this table are obtained from China Securities Regulatory Commission Ningbo Burean.

表 4—12　银行业分支机构及人员数(2012)
Branches and Personnel of the Banking Sector

单位:家,人(Unit,person)

行列名称		法人 corporation	分行(分公司) Branch	支行 Subbranch	分理处(储蓄所) Saving Branch	机构小计 Total	人员数 Employee
全市	**Total**	**27**	**33**	**1206**	**772**	**2038**	**37466**
政策性银行合计	**Policy Bank**		**3**	**8**		**11**	**363**
国家开发银行	China Development Bank		1			1	125
进出口银行	Export—Import Bank		1			1	49
农业发展银行	Agricultural Development Bank of China		1	8		9	189
大型银行合计	**State—owned Commercial Bank**		**5**	**564**	**117**	**686**	**16387**
工商银行	Industrial and Commercial Bank of China		1	162	7	170	4043
农业银行	Agricultural Bank of China		1	146	50	197	4270
中国银行	Bank of China		1	115	9	125	3365
建设银行	China Constuction Bank		1	102	51	154	3593
交通银行	Bank of Communications		1	39		40	1116
股份制商业银行合计	**Joint—stock Commercial Bank**		**11**	**137**		**148**	**5958**
中信银行	China CITIC Bank		1	18		19	786
光大银行	China Everbright Bank Co.,Ltd.		1	16		17	674
华夏银行	Huaxia Bank		1	6		7	266
广发银行	China Guangfa Bank		1	13		14	480
平安银行	Ping An Bank Co.,Ltd		1	12		13	675
招商银行	China Merchants Bank		1	18		19	753
浦东发展	Shanghai Pudong Development Bank		1	19		20	757
兴业银行	Industrial Bank Co.,Ltd.		1	12		13	507
民生银行	China Minsheng Banking Co.,Ltd.		1	16		17	612
浙商银行	China Zheshang Bank Co.,Ltd.		1	7		8	368
恒丰银行	EverGrowing Bank Co.,Ltd		1			1	80

表 4－12 续表 单位:家,人(Unit,person)

行列名称		法人 corporation	分行（分公司） Branch	支行 Subbranch	分理处（储蓄所） Saving Branch	机构小计 Total	人员数 Employee
城市商业银行合计	**City Commercial Bank**	**3**	**8**	**175**		**186**	**6520**
宁波银行（宁波地区）	Bank of Ningbo (Ningbo Area)	1		134		135	3512
宁波通商银行	Niingbo Commmerce Bank	1		1		2	213
宁波东海银行	Ningbo Donghai Bank	1		8		9	344
上海银行	Shanghai Bank		1	8		9	420
包商银行	Baoshang Bank		1	2		3	190
温州银行	Wenzhou Bank		1	3		4	164
泰隆银行	Zhejiang Tailong Commercial Bank		1	6		7	513
临商银行	Linshang Bank		1	5		6	391
杭州银行	Bank of Hangzhou		1	4		5	268
民泰银行	Zhejiang Mintai Commercial Bank		1	3		4	365
稠州银行	Zhejiang Chouzhou Commercial Bank		1	1		2	140
邮储银行	**Postal Savings Bank of China**		**1**	**148**	**159**	**308**	**2627**
农村中小金融机构	**Rural Small and Medium Financial Institutions**	**21**		**171**	**496**	**688**	**5409**
农村合作金融机构	Rural Cooperative Financial Institutions	9		163	495	667	4953
新型农村金融机构	New－type Rural Financial Institutions	12		8	1	21	456
非银行金融机构合计	**Non－bank Financial Institutions**	**2**	**1**			**3**	**14**
信托投资公司	Trust and Investment Corporation	1				1	
财务公司	Finance Company	1				1	
租赁公司	Leasing Company		1			1	14
外资银行合计	**Foreign Bank**	**1**	**4**	**3**		**8**	**188**
协和银行	Union Bank	1				1	
恒生银行(中国)	Hang Seng Bank(China)		1			1	38
汇丰银行(中国)	HSBC Bank (China)		1	1		2	49
渣打银行(中国)	Standard Chartered Bank (China)		1	2		3	76
东亚银行(中国)	The Bank of East Asia Limited		1			1	25

注:本表数据来自于中国银行业监督管理委员会宁波监管局。

Note:Data in this table are obtained from China Banking Regulatory Commission Ningbo Burean.

主要统计指标解释

【财政收入】 国家财政参与社会产品分配所取得收入，是实现国家职能的财力保证。财政收入包括的内容几经变化，目前主要包括：

(1)各项税收 包括增值税、营业税、消费税、土地增值税、城市维护建设税、资源税、城市土地使用税、印花税、固定资产投资方向调节税、个人所得税、企业所得税、关税、农牧业税和耕地占用税等。

(2)专项收入 包括征收排污费、征收城市水资源费收入，教育费附加收入等。

(3)其他收入 包括基本建设贷款归还收入、国家能源交通重点建设基金收入、国家预算调节基金等。

(4)国有企业计划亏损补贴 这项为负收入，冲减财政收入。

【财政支出】 国家财政将筹集起来的资金进行分配使用，以满足经济建设和各项事业的需要，主要包括(2007 年支出项目作过调整)：

(1)基本建设支出

(2)企业挖潜改造资金

(3)地质勘探费用

(4)科技三项费用

(5)支援农村生产支出

(6)农林水利气象等部门的事业费用

(7)工业交通商业等部门的事业费

(8)文教科学卫生事业费

(9)抚恤和社会福利救济费

(10)国防支出

(11)行政管理费

(12)价格补贴支出

【存款】 企业、机关、团体或居民根据可以收回的原则，把货币资金存入银行或其他信用机构保管并取得一定利息的一种信用活动形式。根据存款对象的不同可划分为企业存款、财政存款、机关团体存款、基本建设存款、城镇储蓄存款、农村存款等科目。它是银行信贷资金的主要来源。

【贷款】 银行或其他信用机构根据必须归还的原则，按一定利率，为企业、个人等提供资金的一种信用活动形式。我国银行贷款分为流动资金贷款、固定资产贷款、城乡个体工商户贷款以农业贷款等科目。

【承保额】 又叫保险金额。它是保险人员对被保险人负提损失补偿或约定给付的金额。它是保险合同上的最高责任额，也是计算保费的依据。

【保费】 又叫保险费。是保险人根据保险合同的有关规定，为被保险人取得因约定危险事故发生所造成的经济损失补偿(或给付)权利，付给保险人的代价。包括财产险和人身险储金收入。

【赔款】 保险事故发生后，经查证确属保险责任范围以内的保险标的损失，保险人根据保险合同的规定履行赔偿义务，给与被保险人的款项叫做赔款。赔款可以分为已决赔款和未决赔款两种。

Explanatory Notes on Main Statistical Indicators

【Government Revenue】 refers to the revenue of government finance by means of participating the distribution of the social products, which is the financial resources for ensuring the government to function. The contents of government revenue have been changed several times. Now it includes the following main items:

(1) Various tax revenue, including value added tax, business tax, consumption tax, land value added tax, tax on city maintenance and construction, resources tax, tax on the urban land, stamp tax, tax on the adjustment of orientation of investment in the fixed assets, personal income tax, tariff, tax on agriculture and animal husbandry and tax on occupation of cultivated land, etc.

(2) Special revenues, including revenue collected from imposing fee on sewage treatment, revenue collected from imposing fee on urban water resources, and extra—charges for educations, etc.

(3) Other revenues, including revenue from the re—payment of capital construction loan, the funds for the state key construction projects in energy industry and transportation, and the funds for state budget adjustment, etc.

(4) Planned subsidies for the losses of the state——owned enterprises. This is an item of negative revenue, used to eat up part of the government revenue.

【Government Expenditure】 refers to the distribution and use of the funds the government finance has raised, so as to meet the need s of economic construction and various causes. It included the following main items(The items has changed from the year of 2007):

(1) Expenditure for capital construction

(2) Innovation funds of the enterprises(3) Geological prospecting expenses

(4) Expenditures for science and technology promotion

(5) Expenditure for supporting rural production

(6) Operating Expenses of departments of farming, forestry, water conservancy and meteorology etc.

(7) Operating expenses of departments of industry, transport and commerce

(8) Operating expenses of departments of culture, education, science and public health

(9) Pension for the disabled or the families of the bereaved and relief funds for social welfare

(10) Expenditures for national defense

(11) Administrative expenses:

(12) Expenditure for price subsidies

【Deposit】 is a form a of credit by which enterprises, institutions, organizations or residents can put money into banks and other credit institutions for safekeeping and interest earning under the principle of free withdrawal. According to different depositors, deposits are divided into enterprise deposits, deposits of government agencies and institutions, capital construction deposits, urban savings deposits, rural deposits and other deposits. Deposits are major sources of the credit funds of banks.

【Loan】 is a form a of credit by which banks and other institutions provide funds at a certain interest rate to enterprise sand individuals in light of the principle of unconditional re—payment. Loans from Chinese banks include circulating capital loans, fixed assets loans, loans to urban and rural individuals engaged in industrial and commercial business and agricultural loans.

【Amount Insured】 refers to the amount of compensation for loss or agreed sum of money to be paid by the insurer to the insurant. It is the maximum amount of liabilities written in the insurance contract and is also used as a basis to calculate the premium.

【Premium】 is the fee paid by the insurant based on a proportion of the benefit he or she may get from the insurance plus the insurance value. It includes the income from the deposit of property insurance and personal insurance.

【Settled Claim】 is the compensation paid by the insurer to the insurant in accordance with the insurance contract for the loss which has been checked and found to be in the range of liability of insurance after an accident has happened to the insured property or to a person who has insured for his life. It is further divided into settled and unsettled claim.

NINGBO

Statistical YearBook

第五篇

物价指数和人民生活

PRICES INDEX AND PEOPLE´S LIVELIHOOD

物价指数和人民生活
Price Index and People's Livelihood

主要统计指标
Major Statistics Indicators

以上年价格为 100	The Price of Preceding Year is Taken as 100			
2012 年市区居民消费价格总指数	General Consumer Price Index of Urban Residents	101.7		
2012 年市区商品零售价价格指数	General Retail Price Index of Commodities in Urban Area	101.8		
2012 年全部工业品出厂价格指数	Total Industrial Products Producer Price Index	97.05		
2012 年全部原材料购进价格指数	Purchase Price Indices of Raw Mater,Fuels and Power	97.05		
2012 年市区居民人均可支配收入	Per Capital Disposable Income of Urban Resident	37902	元	yuan
2012 年市区居民人均消费支出	Per Capita Living Expenditure for Consumption of Urban Area	23288	元	yuan
2012 年农村居民人均纯收入	Per Capital Net Income of Rural Resident	18475	元	yuan
2012 年农村居民生活消费性支出	Per Capita Living Expenditures for Consumption of Rural Resident	12699	元	yuan

表 5－1 市区居民消费价格指数及商品零售价格指数（以上年价格为 100）
Consumer Price Indices and Retail Price Indices in Urban Area(Preceding Year＝100)

年份 Year	各年以上年价格为 100 （The Price of Preceding Year is Taken as 100）		
	居民消费价格总指数 General Consumer Price Index	＃服务项目 Service	商品零售价格总指数 General Retail Price Index of Commodities
1978	100.0	104.4	99.3
1985	116.6	113.6	116.9
1986	106.4	106.0	106.4
1987	110.6	105.2	111.1
1988	124.2	123.9	124.2
1989	116.7	111.6	117.1
1990	104.0	113.7	103.2
1991	106.8	111.5	106.4
1992	112.2	119.5	111.4
1993	126.0	149.5	122.8
1994	123.5	129.8	118.0
1995	119.1	129.8	112.6
1996	110.4	122.0	106.3
1997	103.9	119.5	100.8
1998	99.8	108.4	97.6
1999	100.1	117.8	97.3
2000	100.3	114.0	98.3
2001	99.3	105.4	94.8
2002	99.2	100.6	98.6
2003	101.2	101.3	101.6
2004	102.7	101.9	102.0
2005	102.0	101.7	101.1
2006	101.9	101.2	101.8
2007	103.9	100.6	103.3
2008	105.0	98.2	107.1
2009	99.4	97.7	98.8
2010	103.7	102.0	103.9
2011	105.3	101.8	105.7
2012	101.7	99.5	101.8

表 5－2 市区居民消费价格指数及商品零售价格指数(以 1952 年为 100)
Residents Consumer Price Indices and Retail Price Indices in Urban Area(1952＝100)

年份 Year	以 1952 年为 100 (1952＝100) 居民消费价格总指数 General Consumer Price Index	#服务项目 Service	商品零售价格总指数 General Retail Price Index of Commodities
1953	106.8	100.0	106.1
1957	110.7	113.6	108.8
1965	117.2	114.2	116.4
1975	116.5	105.2	116.5
1978	116.3	109.8	115.4
1980	135.4	109.8	124.6
1985	171.6	137.4	158.2
1989	292.7	211.8	272.1
1990	304.4	240.9	280.8
1991	325.1	268.5	298.7
1992	364.7	320.9	332.8
1993	459.6	479.8	408.7
1994	567.6	622.7	482.2
1995	676.0	808.3	543.0
1996	746.3	986.1	577.2
1997	775.4	1178.4	581.8
1998	773.8	1277.4	567.8
1999	774.6	1504.8	552.5
2000	776.9	1715.5	543.1
2001	771.5	1808.1	514.9
2002	765.3	1819.0	507.7
2003	774.5	1842.6	515.8
2004	795.4	1877.6	526.1
2005	811.3	1909.6	531.9
2006	826.8	1932.5	541.5
2007	859.0	1944.1	559.3
2008	901.9	1909.1	599.1
2009	896.5	1865.2	591.9
2010	929.7	1902.5	614.9
2011	979.0	1936.7	650.0
2012	995.6	1927.0	661.7

表 5－3 城市及农村居民消费价格分类指数(2012)
Residents Consumer Price Indices by Category and by Urban and Rural

(以上年价格为 100 The Price of Preceding Year is Taken as 100)

指标	Indicators	城市 Urban	农村 Rural
居民消费价格总指数	**General Consumer Price Index**	**101.7**	**102.5**
服务项目价格指数	**Price Index for Service**	**99.5**	**100.2**
一、食品	Food	105.2	107.1
1. 粮食	Grain	103.2	105.4
2. 肉禽及其制品	Meat,Poultry and Related Products	102.5	103.5
3. 蛋	Eggs	97.9	99.3
4. 水产品	Aquatic Products	109.7	111.8
5. 蔬菜	Vegetables	113.0	117.7
#鲜菜	Fresh Vegetables	115.4	120.3
6. 在外用膳食品	Eating Outside	102.5	104.2
二、烟酒	Tobacco and Liquor	102.4	101.3
三、衣着	Garments	101.7	101.7
四、家庭设备用品及维修服务	Houshold Facilities Articles and Maintenance Services	103.3	102.8
#耐用消费品	Durable Consumer Goods	102.7	102.6
五、医疗保健和个人用品	Medicine, Medical Articles and Personal Goods	101.1	100.0
#医疗保健	Medicine and medical Articles	100.9	99.3
六、交通和通信	Transportation and Communication	99.6	99.3
1. 交通	Transportation	100.0	99.7
2. 通信	Communication	98.5	98.6
七、娱乐教育文化用品及服务	Recreation. Education. Culture Articles and Services	95.0	95.4
#文娱用耐用消费品及服务	Durable Consumer Goods for Recreational Use	93.4	93.8
教育	Education	95.2	95.1
八、居住	Residence	102.1	102.9

表 5－4　市区商品零售价格分类指数(2012) Urban Retail Price Index by Category of Commodities

（以上年同期价格为 100 The Price of Preceding Years is Taken as 100）

指标	Indicators	城市 Urban
商品零售价格总指数	**General Retail Price Index**	**101.8**
一、食品	Food	105.2
1.粮食	Grain	103.2
2.油脂	Oil or Fat	104.0
3.肉禽及其制品	Meat,Poultry and Eggs	103.1
4.水产品	Aquatic Products	109.7
5.蔬菜	Vegetables	113.0
#鲜菜	Fresh Vegetables	115.4
6.在外用膳食品	Eating Outside	102.5
二、饮料、烟酒	Beverages,Tobacco and Liguor	103.7
三、服装、鞋帽	Garments,Shoes and Hats	101.8
四、纺织品	Textiles	94.8
五、家用电器及音像器材	Household Appliance and Audio－video Apparatus	99.1
六、文化办公用品	Stationery and Office Goods	99.3
七、日用品	Daily Use Articles	102.4
八、体育娱乐用品	Sports and Recreation Articles	99.4
九、交通、通信用品	Transportation and Communication Articles	96.9
十、家具	Furniture	101.6
十一、化妆品	Cosmetics	105.4
十二、金银珠宝	Gold,silvrt and Jewelry	95.6
十三、中西药品及医疗保健用品	Traditional Chinese and Western Medicines,Medical Treatment &Health Proterction Articles	100.1
十四、书报杂志及电子出版物	Book,Newspapers,Magazines and Electronic Publication	101.3
十五、燃料	Fuels	102.6
十六、建筑材料及五金电料	Building,Hardware and Electrical Equipment Materials	100.3

表 5－5 部分年份工业生产者出厂价格指数
Industrial Producers Ex－factory Price Index in Partial Years

指标	Indicators	各年以上年价格为 100 (The Price of Preceding Years is Taken as 100)				
		2008	2009	2010	2011	2012
总指数	**Combined Index**	**104.50**	**94.04**	**108.89**	**105.86**	**97.05**
轻工业	Light Industry	103.27	96.57	104.66	104.92	98.46
以农产品为原料	Using Farm Products as Raw Materials	103.56	97.15	106.04	106.93	98.39
以非农产品为原料	Using Non Farm Products as Raw Materials	103.11	96.21	103.98	103.11	98.52
重工业	Heavy Industry	105.77	91.46	113.13	106.36	96.31
采掘	Mining and Quarrying Industry	141.73	85.58	127.80	100.00	100.00
原料	Raw Material Industry	112.22	91.26	119.57	110.77	98.18
加工	Manufacturing Industry	100.67	91.62	108.00	104.19	95.41
生产资料	Production Goods	105.11	91.95	111.61	106.31	95.73
采掘	Mining and Quarrying Industry	141.73	85.58	127.80	100.00	100.0
原料	Raw Material Industry	111.03	90.61	119.94	110.08	97.36
加工	Manufacturing Industry	101.95	92.63	107.43	104.54	94.98
生活资料	Means of Subsistence	103.23	98.32	101.83	104.67	100.55
食品	Food	107.70	97.57	107.58	108.09	101.97
衣着	Garments	101.20	99.07	102.43	106.05	100.85
一般日用品	Articles for Daily Use	102.28	97.99	100.53	104.09	101.51
耐用消费品	Durable Consumer Goods	103.80	98.55	100.53	102.55	98.32

表 5－6 部分年份工业生产者购进价格指数 Purchase Price Index of Industrial Producers in Partial Years

指标	Indicators	各年以上年价格为 100 (The Price of Preceding Years is Taken as 100)				
		2008	2009	2010	2011	2012
总指数	**Combined Index**	**112.33**	**88.99**	**113.10**	**108.56**	**97.05**
燃料动力类	Fuels and Energy	130.78	83.47	124.81	113.15	100.53
黑色金属材料类	Ferrous Metals	122.97	83.49	110.95	108.10	91.46
有色金属材料及电线类	Nonferrous Metal and Electric Wire	88.71	81.72	137.74	112.68	90.48
化工原料类	Chemical Raw Materials	105.55	87.22	115.82	111.94	93.15
木材及纸浆类	Wood and Paper Pulps	102.52	95.12	122.53	101.35	95.02
建筑材料及非金属矿类	Building Materials and Nonmetal Minerals	109.42	98.46	106.97	118.75	93.65
其它工业原材料及半成品类	Other Industrial Raw and Processed Materials	112.62	95.26	101.39	102.33	98.52
农副产品类	Farm and Sideline Products	106.67	93.85	122.45	124.93	101.73
纺织原料类	Textile Raw Materials	102.19	95.55	112.08	110.02	92.57

表 5－7 住宅销售价格指数(2012) Residential Building Sales Price Index

（以上年同期价格为 100 The Price of Preceding Years is Taken as 100）

月份	Mouth	新建住宅 New Residential Buildings	新建商品住房 New Commodity Housing	按套型分 By House Size 90 平方及以下 90 Sq. m and Below	90－144 平方米 90－144 Sq. m	144 平方米以上 More than 144 Sq. m	二手住宅 Second－hand Residential Buildings	按套型分 By House Size 90 平方及以下 90 Sq. m and Below	90－144 平方米 90－144 Sq. m	144 平方米以上 More than 144 Sq. m
一月份	January	98.5	98.4	99.5	98.7	97.8	97.2	96.9	97.2	98.2
二月份	February	97.9	97.8	97.7	97.9	97.8	96.4	96.1	96.4	97.5
三月份	March	97.0	96.8	96.8	94.5	98.7	96.0	95.8	96.0	96.9
四月份	April	94.5	94.2	93.6	92.4	96.0	95.3	95.1	95.6	95.4
五月份	May	92.7	92.4	91.2	90.1	94.6	94.6	94.5	94.8	94.4
六月份	June	92.4	92.0	90.8	89.8	94.3	95.1	95.5	94.8	94.4
七月份	July	92.2	91.8	90.7	89.8	93.8	94.8	95.0	94.9	94.0
八月份	August	91.9	91.5	90.6	89.5	93.3	94.9	95.2	95.1	93.6
九月份	September	91.8	91.4	90.5	89.6	93.2	94.5	95.0	94.8	92.5
十月份	October	92.0	91.5	90.6	89.6	93.4	94.7	95.3	94.7	92.8
十一月份	November	92.5	92.1	91.5	90.4	93.7	94.8	95.2	95.3	92.2
十二月份	December	92.9	92.6	91.9	90.9	94.1	95.3	96.0	95.5	92.3

注：由于 2011 年房地产价格专业制度全方面改革，故指标分类有所变化。且只计算月度数据，没有季度和年度汇总数据。

Note: Due to the reform of the professional system of 2011 real estate prices, so the index classification are subject to change. And only monthly data, there is no summary of quarterly and annual data.

表 5－8 房地产其他价格指数(2012) Other Price Index of Real Estate

指标	Indicators	（以上年同期价格为 100 The Price of Preceding Years is Taken as 100） 一季度 1. Quarter	二季度 2. Quarter	三季度 3. Quarter	四季度 4. Quarter
住宅租赁价格指数	Real Estate Rent and Leasing Price Index	103.6	105.8	105.6	105.6
住宅物业服务价格指数	Residential property service price index	100.2	100.2	100.2	100.2
土地交易价格指数	Land Transcation Price Index	100.7	100.1	101.3	103.3

表 5－9　36 个大中城市基本情况(2012)
Basic Statistcis on Urban Households of 36 Largest Cities

城市	City	价格指数以上年价格为 100 The Price Index of Preceding Year is Taken as 100			
		人均可支配收入(元) Per Capita Disposable Income(yuan)	人均消费性支出(元) Per Capita Consumption Expenditure(yuan)	居民消费价格指数(%) General Consumer Price Index(%)	商品零售价格指数(%) General Retail Price Index(%)
36 个城市平均	**Average of 36 Cities**	**30595**	**20993**	**102.8**	**101.8**
北京	Beijing	38546	25718	103.3	100.6
天津	Tianjin	29626	20024	102.7	103.0
石家庄	Shijiazhuang	23038	13378	102.8	101.9
太原	Taiyuan	22587	13970	102.1	101.2
呼和浩特	Hohhot	30772	21361	103.1	101.5
沈阳	Shenyang	26431	20003	103.0	102.4
大连	Dalian	27539	20417	103.4	102.5
长春	Changchun	22970	17863	102.3	101.8
哈尔滨	Harbin	22477	17602	103.2	102.5
上海	Shanghai	40188	26253	102.8	101.2
南京	Nanjing	36267	23145	102.7	101.4
杭州	Hangzhou	37511	22800	102.5	101.9
宁波	Ningbo	37902	23288	101.7	101.8
合肥	Hefei	25434	18758	102.2	101.9
福州	Fuzhou	30073	20571	102.0	101.1
厦门	Xiamen	37576	24922	102.1	101.6
南昌	Nanchang	23602	16450	102.9	102.4
济南	Jinan	32570	20032	102.4	101.8

表 5－9 续表 Continued

城市	City	价格指数以上年价格为 100 The Price Index of Preceding Year is Taken as 100			
		人均可支配收入（元）Per Capita Disposable Income(yuan)	人均消费性支出（元）Per Capita Consumption Expenditure(yuan)	居民消费价格指数(%) General Consumer Price Index(%)	商品零售价格指数(%) General Retail Price Index(%)
青岛	Qingdao	32145	20391	102.7	101.7
郑州	Zhengzhou	25301	16779	102.7	102.4
武汉	Wuhan	27090	18813	102.8	102.3
长沙	Changsha	29084	18522	102.3	101.5
广州	Guangzhou	38054	30490	103.0	101.9
深圳	Shenzhen	40742	26728	102.8	102.4
南宁	Nanning	22024	14988	102.9	101.7
海口	Haikou	22296	15736	103.3	102.8
重庆	Chongqing	24539	17872	102.6	101.6
成都	Chengdu	27194	19054	103.0	101.4
贵阳	Guiyang	21796	15718	102.6	102.0
昆明	Kunming	24660	17418	103.1	102.0
拉萨	Lhasa	19545	13953	103.2	102.9
西安	Xian	23847	18016	102.8	102.3
兰州	Lanzhou	18199	14110	102.4	102.4
西宁	Xining	17634	12114	102.7	102.3
银川	Yinchuan	21901	16390	102.6	100.6
乌鲁木齐	Urumqi	18385	13785	103.4	102.9

表 5—10 各县(市)城镇居民家庭生活基本情况(2012)
Basic Living Statistics of Urban Households by Region

指标	Indicators	单位	Unit
调查户数	**Number of Households Surveyed**	**户**	**household**
人均房屋总建筑面积	Per Capita Total Living Space of Buildings	平方米	sq. m
平均每户家庭人口	**Average Household Size**	**人**	**person**
平均每户就业人数	Average Number of Employed Persons Per Household	人	person
负担系数	Persons Supported By Each Employee	人	person
全年人均总收入	**Per Capita Annual Total Income**	**元**	**yuan**
#可支配收入	Per Capita Disposable Income	元	yuan
全年人均总支出	**Per Capita Annual Total Expenditure**	**元**	**yuan**
(一)消费支出	Per Capita Annual Living Expenditure	元	yuan
#服务性消费支出	Living Expenditure for Services	元	yuan
恩格尔系数	Engel Coeffcient	%	%
1.食品	Food	元	yuan
2.衣着	Garments	元	yuan
3.家庭设备用品及服务	Houshold Facilities Articles and Services	元	yuan
4.医疗保健	Medicine and medical Articles	元	yuan
5.交通和通信	Transportation and Communication	元	yuan
6.教育文化娱乐服务	Recreation,Education and Cultural Services	元	yuan
7.居住	Residence	元	yuan
8.杂项商品和服务	Miscellaneous Commodities and Service	元	yuan
(二)财产性支出	Per Capita Expenditure for Property	元	yuan
(三)转移性支出	Per Capita Expenditure for Transfer	元	yuan
(四)社会保障支出	Per Capita Expenditure for Social Security	元	yuan
(五)购房与建房支出	Per Capita Expenditure for Houseing	元	yuan

注明:本表至5—13表为城镇居民家庭抽样调查资料。

Note:Data from Tables 5—10 to 5—13 are obtained from the sample surveys on urban households.

全市 Total	市区 Urban Districts	余姚 Yuyao	慈溪 Cixi	奉化 Fenghua	象山 Xiangshan	宁海 Ninghai
1250	**600**	**150**	**150**	**100**	**100**	**100**
34.97	32.55	36.87	41.24	36.73	35.45	49.12
2.63	**2.60**	**2.54**	**2.68**	**2.66**	**2.78**	**2.81**
1.44	1.42	1.38	1.39	1.37	1.54	1.51
1.83	1.83	1.84	1.93	1.94	1.81	1.86
42281	**42643**	**39824**	**41252**	**39341**	**38258**	**39978**
38043	37902	37217	37711	36293	36872	36496
33098	**33717**	**27780**	**33048**	**30223**	**29181**	**28518**
22887	23288	21108	25412	21566	19917	17345
5831	5728	5559	8037	5166	3651	5170
37.22	37.89	38.56	33.56	37.43	32.98	38.52
8518	8823	8140	8529	8072	6568	6682
2278	2401	2129	2415	2108	1819	1514
1128	1080	1154	1552	1033	816	878
1038	953	849	1263	2173	783	851
4536	4720	3791	4791	3672	6514	2886
3203	3235	3001	4529	2541	1989	2609
1437	1296	1197	1502	1492	1131	1482
750	781	848	831	476	297	443
417	401	308	124	634	841	658
4209	4131	3717	4429	4526	5573	4326
3686	4094	2111	3047	2638	1126	3328
1899	1803	536	37	859	1724	2862

表 5－11　市区城市住户基本情况(2012)
Basic Statistics on Urban Districts Households

指标	Indicators	单位	Unit	合计 Total
现住房总建筑面积	**Total Floor Space of Buildings**	**平方米**	**sq. m**	**32.55**
住宅配套率	**Rate of Housing Complete Unit**	**%**	**%**	**99.51**
房屋产权(合计)	**Housing Property Right (Total)**	**%**	**%**	**100.00**
租赁公房	Leasing of State－owned Housing	%	%	0.97
租赁私房	Leasing of Private Housing	%	%	4.40
原有私房	Private Housing existed	%	%	4.68
房改私房	Private Housing through Housing Reforming	%	%	23.58
商品房	Commercial Housing	%	%	66.36
其他	Other	%	%	
住宅建筑式样(合计)	**Construction Model of Building (Total)**	**%**	**%**	**100.00**
单栋住宅	Single Housing	%	%	0.51
四居室	With Four Rooms	%	%	4.61
三居室	With Three Rooms	%	%	47.40
二居室	With Two Rooms	%	%	41.88
一居室	Only One Rooms	%	%	4.27
普通楼房	Common Building	%	%	0.84
平房及其他	One－Story Housing and Other	%	%	0.49
装修状况(合计)	**Dekoration (Total)**	**%**	**%**	**100.00**
有装修	Dekorated	%	%	88.81
未装修	Non－Dekorated	%	%	11.19
饮水情况(合计)	**Drink (Total)**	**%**	**%**	**100.00**
自来水	Tap Water	%	%	89.01
矿泉水	Mineral Water	%	%	5.69

表 5—11 续表 Continued

指标	Indicators	单位	Unit	合计 Total
纯净水	Clean Water	%	%	5.30
井、河水	Well—Water, River Water	%	%	
用水情况(合计)	**Consumption of Water (Total)**	**%**	**%**	**100.00**
独用自来水	Separate Using Tap Water	%	%	100.00
公用自来水	Public Using Tap Water	%	%	
井、河水	Well and River Water	%	%	
卫生设备(合计)	**Sanitary Equipment**	**%**	**%**	**100.00**
无卫生设备	Non—sanitary Equipment	%	%	0.36
有厕所浴室	With Toilet	%	%	97.99
有厕所无浴室	Non—toilet	%	%	1.65
公用	Public Using Tap Water	%	%	
取暖设备(合计)	**Warm Equipment (Total)**	**%**	**%**	**100.00**
无取暖设备	Non—warm Equipment	%	%	3.23
空调设备	With Air—Condition	%	%	96.77
暖气	With Heating Installation	%	%	
炊用燃料使用情况(合计)	**Consumption of Fuil (Total)**	**%**	**%**	**100.00**
煤炭	Coal	%	%	
罐装液化石油气	Liquefied Petroleum By Gas Cylinders	%	%	27.10
管道液化石油气	Liquefied Petroleum By Pipeline	%	%	6.03
管道煤气	Gas By Pipeline	%	%	
管道天然气	Piped Natural Gas	%	%	66.32
柴油	Diesel Fuel	%	%	
其他燃料	Other Fuel	%	%	0.55

表5－12 市区居民家庭生活基本情况(2012)
Basic Living Statistics on Urban Districts Households

指标	Indicators	单位	Unit
调查家庭所占比重	**Weight of Surveyed Households**	**%**	**%**
人均房屋总建筑面积	Per Capita General Usable Floor Area of Housing	平方米	sq. m
平均每户家庭人口数	**Average Household Size**	**人**	**person**
＃平均每户就业人数	Average Number of Employed Persons Per Household	人	person
负担系数	Persons Supported By Each Employee	人	person
全年人均总收入	**Per Capita Annual Total Income**	**元**	**yuan**
＃可支配收入	Per Capita Disposable Income	元	yuan
全年人均总支出	**Per Capita Annual Total Expenditure**	**元**	**yuan**
㈠消费支出	Per Capita Annual Living Expenditure	元	yuan
＃服务性消费支出	Living Expenditure for Services	元	yuan
恩格尔系数	Engel Coeffcient	%	%
1.食品	Food	元	yuan
2.衣着	Garments	元	yuan
3.家庭设备用品及服务	Houshold Facilities Articles and Services	元	yuan
4.医疗保健	Medicine and medical Articles	元	yuan
5.交通和通信	Transportation and Communication	元	yuan
6.教育文化娱乐服务	Recreation,Education and Cultural Services	元	yuan
7.居住	Residence	元	yuan
8.杂项商品和服务	Miscellaneous Commodities and Service	元	yuan
㈡财产性支出	Per Capita Expenditure for Property	元	yuan
㈢转移性支出	Per Capita Expenditure for Transfer	元	yuan
㈣社会保障支出	Per Capita Expenditure for Social Security	元	yuan
㈤购房与建房支出	Per Capita Expenditure for Houseing	元	yuan

	按可支配收入分组 Group by Disposable Income				
合计 Income Total	低收入户 Low Income Households	较低收入户 Relatively Low Income Households	中间收入户 Medium Income Households	较高收入户 Medium—high Income Households	高收入户 high Households
100	**20**	**20**	**20**	**20**	**20**
32.55	24.85	29.94	31.61	38.49	39.41
2.60	**2.76**	**2.67**	**2.48**	**2.56**	**2.53**
1.42	1.43	1.46	1.20	1.49	1.54
1.83	1.93	1.83	2.07	1.72	1.64
42643	**18844**	**28193**	**36370**	**50484**	**83223**
37902	15716	24965	32884	44525	75017
33717	**15981**	**22219**	**28938**	**36906**	**67598**
23288	12132	17497	21746	26825	39966
5728	2949	4024	5220	6954	9935
37.89	52.26	47.60	41.53	36.56	27.30
8823	6341	8329	9030	9808	10911
2401	1156	1699	2083	3070	4189
1080	494	717	983	1425	1867
953	306	560	647	1663	1682
4720	1048	2397	3948	4485	12376
3235	1672	2283	2991	3703	5781
1296	939	1068	1527	1348	1649
781	175	444	537	1323	1510
401	35	214	281	320	1222
4131	935	1581	2946	4599	11192
4094	2879	2927	3044	5162	6682
1803			922		8536

表 5－13　部分年份市区每百户居民家庭主要耐用消费品拥有量
Per 100 Urban Households Annual Average Possession of Durable Consumer Goods in Partial Years

指标	Indicators	单位	Unit	2008	2009	2010	2011	2012
摩托车	Motorcycles	辆	unit	6.08	5.38	5.57	4.24	4.39
助力车	Electric Bicycles	辆	unit	46.33	46.90	52.78	53.64	57.35
家用汽车	Homeuse Car	辆	unit	17.87	22.10	25.13	33.15	37.01
洗衣机	Washing Machines	台	unit	89.83	93.78	94.54	95.54	96.24
电冰箱	Refrigerators	台	unit	95.70	97.56	99.07	100.26	100.08
彩色电视机	Color TV Sets	台	unit	170.80	174.50	184.78	193.36	197.27
家用电脑	Micro－Computers	台	unit	77.12	82.43	92.87	102.52	107.69
组合音响	Music Centers	套	set	31.08	28.86	30.64	30.38	30.44
摄像机	Video Camera	架	unit	10.21	10.21	10.30	9.19	10.00
照相机	Cameras	架	unit	49.74	49.57	53.73	52.82	55.69
钢琴	Pianos	架	unit	3.04	3.02	3.96	3.65	3.85
微波炉	Microwave Ovens	台	unit	67.39	73.63	75.12	78.80	79.61
空调器	Air－conditioners	台	unit	171.23	185.36	197.00	213.50	214.63
淋浴热水器	Shower Heaters	台	unit	95.41	97.82	100.96	102.69	103.90
消毒碗柜	Disinfecting Case	台	unit	16.64	16.70	20.05	18.69	18.23
洗碗机	Dishwasher	台	unit	2.09	1.85	1.15	0.65	0.78
健身器材	Training Equipment	套	set	6.01	5.13	6.10	5.07	6.05
普通电话	common Telephone	部	set	87.77	89.51	88.38	87.53	87.39
移动电话	Handy	部	set	177.22	182.45	194.79	202.86	211.55

表 5－14 历年城乡居民人均收支及住房情况 Per Capita Annual Income and Living Expenditures and Housing Conditions of Urban and Rural Residents Over the Years

单位：元，平方米(yuan, sq. m)

年份 Year	市区居民人均可支配收入 Per Capita Annual Disposable Income of Urban Districts Residents	市区居民人均消费性支出 Per Capita Annual Expenditure for Consumption of Urban Districts Residents	农村居民人均纯收入 Per Capita Annual Net Income of Rural Residents	农村居民人均生活消费支出 Per Capita Annual Living Expenditure of Rural Residents	市区居民人均建筑面积 Per Capita Floor Space of Urban Districts Residents	农村居民人均住房面积 Per Capita Floor Space of Rural Residents
1978	306	299				
1979	340	332				
1980	429	419	222	183		
1981	481	490	217	274		
1982	509	492	353	338		
1983	530	502	340	375	12.62	
1984	643	561	483	428	12.84	
1985	889	862	627	564	12.94	21.30
1986	1110	1057	735	673	12.92	22.80
1987	1192	1076	871	762	13.44	24.50
1988	1518	1469	1066	964	14.49	26.00
1989	1742	1543	1199	1051	15.32	27.30
1990	1963	1628	1254	1166	15.56	27.70
1991	2182	1854	1441	1221	15.93	29.90
1992	2674	2204	1624	1368	16.00	31.00
1993	3983	3139	2060	1599	16.08	30.20
1994	6008	4442	2685	2215	17.25	33.60
1995	7275	5566	3484	2432	17.41	31.30
1996	8354	6545	4267	3283	17.09	30.75
1997	9069	7189	4568	3483	17.42	39.95
1998	9193	7912	4697	3589	18.21	37.58
1999	9492	7493	4798	3591	19.40	39.78
2000	10921	7997	5069	3929	20.34	41.57
2001	11991	9463	5362	4383	21.53	43.14
2002	12970	9396	5764	4508	21.86	45.74
2003	14277	10463	6221	4194	23.22	46.86
2004	15882	11283	7018	6102	23.85	49.90
2005	17408	11758	7810	6623	24.92	50.44
2006	19674	12666	8847	7378	24.91	51.88
2007	22307	13921	10051	8062	26.09	53.24
2008	25304	16739	11450	9174	28.85	55.86
2009	27368	18203	12641	9789	29.72	55.88
2010	30166	19420	14261	9794	30.22	56.00
2011	34058	21779	16518	11253	32.88	57.22
2012	37902	23288	18475	12699	32.55	58.29

表 5－15　部分年份农村居民人均总收入和纯收入 Per Capita Annual Total Income and Net Income of Rural Households in Partial Years

单位：元(yuan)

指标	Indicators	2008	2009	2010	2011	2012
全年人均总收入	**Per Capital Annual Total Income**	**14001**	**15090**	**17160**	**18393**	**20220**
工资性收入	Wages Incomes	6816	7373	8125	9667	11023
家庭经营收入	Household Business Income	5346	5551	6790	5621	5661
农业收入	Planting	1190	1241	1384	1225	1295
林业收入	Forestry	84	90	110	119	92
牧业收入	Animal Husbandry	787	818	1090	440	240
渔业收入	Fishery	769	716	883	790	588
工业收入	Industry	618	607	899	774	1030
建筑业收入	Construction	479	575	624	701	756
交通运输邮电业收入	Transport,Post & Communications	581	601	628	471	518
批零贸易和餐饮业收入	Wholesale. Retail Sale & Catering Services	427	445	597	633	561
服务业收入	Social Service Trade	134	214	252	338	460
其他家庭经营收入	Others	229	244	323	130	121
转移性收入	Per Capital Annual Transfer Income	955	1144	1259	2216	2530
财产性收入	Per Capital Annual Property Income	884	1023	986	888	1007
全年人均纯收入	**Per Capital Annual Net Income**	**11450**	**12641**	**14261**	**16518**	**18475**
恩格尔系数(%)	**Engel Coeffcient(%)**	**40.9**	**38.7**	**41.3**	**43.6**	**41.7**

注：本表至5－20表为农村住户抽样调查资料。

Note：Data from Tables 5－15 to 5－20 are obtained from the sample surveys on rural households.

表 5－16 按收入等级分组的农村居民人均收入(2012)
Per Capita Annual Income of Rural Households Grouped by Level of Income

单位:元(yuan)

指标	Indicators	按人均纯收入等级分组 Grouped by Level of Net Income				
		低 20% 收入户 Lower Income Households (20%)	次低 20% 收入户 Low Income Households (20%)	中等 20% 收入户 Middle Income Households (20%)	次高 20% 收入户 High Income Households (20%)	高 20% 收入户 Higher Income Households (20%)
全年人均总收入	**Per Capital Annual Total Income**	**10152.32**	**15020.41**	**18953.85**	**23904.90**	**36487.11**
工资性收入	Per Capital Annual Wages Income	4143.49	8021.65	11186.10	14993.18	17776.57
在非企业组织中劳动得到	From Other Orgazination	157.13	368.18	484.86	1003.30	1623.09
在本乡地域内劳动得到收入	From Rural Area	3341.16	6938.81	9616.22	12435.15	13655.49
#在企业中劳动得到收入	From Enrerprises	2536.16	6092.29	8623.06	11623.93	12732.58
常住人口外出从业得到	From Permanent Population Outside Work	645.20	714.67	1085.01	1554.73	2497.99
家庭经营收入	Household Business Income	3197.57	4034.28	4226.70	4783.66	12976.74
农业收入	Agriculture	684.08	1016.65	1171.75	1144.39	2625.16
林业收入	Forestry	87.39	104.61	56.40	4.32	219.97
牧业收入	Animal Husbandy	352.76	21.71	286.51		586.82
渔业收入	Fishery	598.52	299.57	263.88	95.49	1828.38
工业收入	Industry	858.79	486.45	451.16	961.95	2592.75
建筑业收入	Construction	167.56	326.46	722.12	419.60	2349.66
交通运输和邮电业收入	Transport, Posts & Telecommunication	146.61	545.81	380.04	983.99	543.39
批零贸易、餐饮收入	Wholesale. Retail Sale & Catering Services	194.77	385.93	418.16	576.19	1329.03
社会服务业收入	Social Services	95.65	716.74	400.54	449.60	649.49
文教卫生业收入	Culture. Education and Health Care	5.85	126.32	51.18	88.40	244.92
其他家庭经营收入	Others	5.58	4.02	24.95	59.72	7.18
财产性收入	Per Capital Annual Property Income	253.32	485.02	743.90	1340.58	2403.54
转移性收入	Per Capital Annual Transfer Income	2557.94	2479.45	2797.16	2787.49	3330.26
全年人均纯收入	**Per Capital Annual Net Income**	**8054.00**	**13704.60**	**17951.34**	**22786.95**	**33644.96**

表 5－17　各县(市)农村住户收入与支出情况(2012)
Per Capita Annual Income and Per Capita Annual Expenditure of Rural Households by Region

指标	Indicators	全市 Total
全年人均总收入	**Per Capita Annual Total Revenue**	**20219.85**
工资性收入	Wages Income	11022.65
家庭经营收入	Income from　Households Business Operation	5660.62
财产性收入	Porperty Income	1006.91
转移性收入	Transfer Income	2529.66
全年人均总支出	**Per Capita Annual Total Expenditures**	**15582.54**
家庭经营费用支出	Expenditure for Households Business	1091.18
购置生产性固定资产支出	Purchasing Productive Fixed Assets	154.31
生产性固定资产折旧	Depreciation of Productive Fixed Assets	470.74
税费支出	Expenditure for Tax and Public Expense	2.09
生活消费支出	Living Expenditures for Consumption	12698.64
财产性支出	Prorerty Expenditure	3.58
转移性支出	Transfer Expenditure	1630.96
全年人均纯收入	**Per Capita Annual Net Income**	**18475**
工资性收入	Wages Income	11023
家庭经营纯收入	Income from Households Business Operation	4097
非经营性纯收入	Income from Non－business Operation	3355

单位:元(yuan)

市区 Urban District	余姚 Yuyao	慈溪 Cixi	奉化 Fenghua	象山 Xiangshan	宁海 Ninghai
21384.38	**19583.11**	**22894.80**	**18881.54**	**19300.83**	**18664.50**
12322.38	12183.33	11976.30	9418.60	8143.56	9336.65
3651.49	5399.55	7113.16	6697.17	9199.33	7441.60
2009.13	566.62	781.42	499.73	325.63	741.78
3401.37	1433.62	3023.91	2266.04	1632.31	1144.47
16573.56	**14836.61**	**17338.56**	**12147.99**	**13400.17**	**13858.90**
604.65	14836.61	1283.69	919.03	1832.30	1790.29
97.33	287.56	139.78	5.42	307.48	286.35
412.84	476.67	563.59	103.93	762.58	303.64
1.41	1.47	0.94	1.70	4.02	
13686.67	12070.59	13974.29	9433.91	10285.95	11077.35
9.14	4.03	0.94	0.98	1.83	5.87
2172.36	1284.04	1937.94	1780.08	968.57	699.03
20164	**17977**	**20383**	**17675**	**16388**	**16547**
12322	12183	11976	9419	8144	9336
2633	3765	5265	5672	6600	5348
5209	2029	3142	2584	1644	1863

表 5—18　部分年份农村居民人均支出情况
Per Capita Annual Expenditure of Rural Households in Partial Years

单位:元(yuan)

指标	Indicators	2008	2009	2010	2011	2012
全年人均总支出	**Per Capita Annual Total Expenditure**	**12626**	**13086**	**13266**	**13935**	**15583**
家庭经营费用支出	Expenditure for Household Business	1909	1757	2160	1288	1091
农业生产支出	Framing	306	322	337	306	282
林业生产支出	Forestry	5	7	24	29	25
牧业生产支出	Animal Husbandry	727	758	997	271	175
渔业生产支出	Fishery	412	335	433	403	134
工业生产支出	Industry	254	149	138	78	277
建筑业支出	Construction	56	36	64	69	47
交通运输邮电业支出	Transport,Post and Communications	107	105	78	62	37
批零售贸易餐饮业支出	Wholesale. Retail Sale and Catering Trade	30	17	34	22	51
服务业支出	Social Service Trade	5	10	12	43	61
其他经营支出	Others	6	18	42	5	2
生活消费支出	Living Expenditure for Consumption	9174	9789	9794	11253	12699
食品	Food	3751	3788	4049	4905	5293
衣着	Clothing	678	662	774	888	918
居住	Residence	1399	1868	1305	1404	2228
家庭设备、用品及服务	Household Facilities. Articles and Services	433	381	398	578	702
交通和通讯	Transportations and Communications	1168	1167	1407	1244	1328
文教娱乐服务	Cultural. Edcational and Recreational Services	984	1037	939	960	1026
医疗保健	Medicines and Medical Services	540	657	694	998	858
其他商品和服务	Other Commodities and Services	221	229	228	276	346
购置生产用固定资产	PurchasingProductive Fixed Assets	70	309	113	64	154
税费支出	Expenditure for Taxes and Expenses	27	9	21	2	2
财产性支出	Prorerty Expenditure	40	37	57	14	4
转移性支出	Transfer Expenditure	1406	1185	1122	1314	1631
生产用固定资产折旧	**Depreciation of Productive Fixed Assets**	**363**	**418**	**476**	**417**	**471**

表 5－19 按收入等级分组的农村居民人均支出(2012) Per Capita Annual Expenditure of Rural Households Grouped by Level of Net Income

单位:元(yuan)

指标	Indicators	按人均纯收入等级分组 Grouped by Level of Net Income				
		低 20% 收入户 Lower Income Households (20%)	次低 20% 收入户 Low Income Households (20%)	中等 20% 收入户 Middle Income Households (20%)	次高 20% 收入户 High Income Households (20%)	高 20% 收入户 Higher Income Households (20%)
全年人均总支出	Per Capita Annual Total Expenditure	**11276.27**	**10452.76**	**14933.42**	**18103.24**	**24114.67**
生活消费支出	Per Capita Annual Living Expenditure	8529.65	8641.70	12969.28	14980.55	19042.26
食品	Food	3605.77	4539.15	5407.09	6070.33	7108.55
衣着	Clothing	408.07	638.97	885.57	1190.99	1561.39
居住	Residence	1969.25	828.26	2505.43	2741.71	3286.02
家庭设备、用品及服务	Household Facilities. Articles and Services	288.28	443.48	612.07	882.04	1375.98
交通和通迅	Transportation and Communications	438.90	576.77	1433.57	1499.19	2581.79
文教娱乐用品及服务	Cultural. Educational and Recreational Articles and Services	571.76	584.55	892.23	1463.84	1722.59
医疗保健	Medicines and Medical Services	1085.50	773.86	963.09	688.35	771.92
其他商品和服务	Other Commodities and Services	162.12	256.66	270.22	444.10	634.01
家庭经营费用支出	Expenditure for Household Business	1905.81	726.46	495.95	615.77	1793.75
农业生产支出	Agriculture	255.66	168.59	225.68	305.18	481.09
林业生产支出	Forestry	15.53	22.79	61.40	3.61	18.79
牧业生产支出	Animal Husbandry	452.40	12.92	138.44	5.33	280.98
渔业生产支出	Fishery	208.92	82.29	2.68	0.69	409.01
工业生产支出	Industry	717.68	95.34	36.17	191.92	356.61
财产性支出	Prorerty Expenditure	1.34	2.84	0.01	5.45	8.94
转移性支出	Transfer Expenditure	757.62	1063.76	1454.49	2299.22	2746.11
生产费用现金支出	Productive Expenditure Pay for Cash	1986.87	742.28	509.21	812.16	2310.17
生活消费现金支出	Living Expenditure Pay for Cash	8391.46	8572.48	12896.74	14933.60	18984.42
食品	Food	3467.76	4469.92	5334.55	6023.38	7050.71
衣着	Clothing	408.07	638.97	885.57	1190.99	1561.39
居住	Residence	1969.07	828.26	2505.43	2741.71	3286.02
家庭设备、用品及服务	Household Facilities. Articles and Services	288.28	443.48	612.07	882.04	1375.98
交通和通讯	Transportation and Communications	438.90	576.77	1433.57	1499.19	2581.79
文教娱乐用品及服务	Cultural. Educational and Recreational Articles and Services	571.76	584.55	892.23	1463.84	1722.59
医疗保健	Medicines and Medical Services	1085.50	773.86	963.09	688.35	771.92
其他商品和服务	Others	162.12	256.66	270.22	444.10	634.01

表 5－20　部分年份农村居民家庭平均每百户耐用消费品拥有量
Per 100 Rual Huoseholds Annual Averger Possession of Durable Consumer Goods in Partial Years

指标	Indicators	2007	2008	2009	2010	2011	2012
洗衣机（台）	Washing Machine (unti)	63	71	73	74	71	74
电冰箱	Refrigerator	91	95	96	99	95	96
空调机	Air Conditioner	77	87	93	99	105	109
抽油烟机	Range Hoods	78	80	82	83	76	77
微波炉	Micro－wave Oven	25	27	28	30	37	38
热水器	Shower Heaters	58	61	65	67	72	74
摩托车(辆)	Motorcycle	48	49	47	48	28	27
汽车(生活用)	Homeuse Car	4	4	6	7	9	10
电话机（部）	Telephone (set)	98	98	99	98	87	86
移动电话	Mobile Phone	160	170	179	186	175	180
彩色电视机（台）	Color TV Set (unit)	168	175	180	181	172	174
摄像机	Pickup Camera	2	2	2	2	2	2
影碟机	Video CD Sets	41	43	43	43	22	22
照相机（架）	Cameras (unit)	15	16	17	17	17	18
家用计算机（台）	Micro－Computers	31	40	44	49	46	47
中高档乐器（件）	Medium and High Grade Musical Instruments	1	1	1	2	2	2

主要统计指标解释

【居民消费价格指数】 居民消费价格，是指城乡居民支付生活消费品和服务项目消费的价格，是社会产品和服务项目的最终价格。居民消费价格指数，就是反映一定时期内居民消费价格变动趋势和变动程度的相对数。利用居民消费价格指数，可以全面观察居民消费价格变动对居民生活的影响。居民消费价格指数还是反映通货膨胀程度的重要指标。

【商品零售价格指数】 商品的零售价格是商品在流通过程中的最后一个环节的价格，是工业、商业、餐饮业和其他零售企业向城乡居民、机关团体出售生活消费品和办公用品的价格。因此，商品零售价格指数是全面反映市场零售物价总水平变动趋势和程度的相对数。其目的在于掌握零售商品的价格变动状况，为国家制定经济政策、研究城乡市场流通和为国民经济核算提供科学依据。

【工业品出厂价格指数】 工业品出厂价格，是指工业企业向商业（物资）部门或商业企业、其他生产单位、个人出售的或调拨产品的价格，亦称工业生产者价格。它是工业品进入流通领域的最初价格。工业品出厂价格指数是指反映一定时期内工业品出厂价格水平变动趋势及变动程度的相对数，是国民经济核算和计算工业发展速度的一个重要参考指标。

【原材料、燃料和动力购进价格指数】 是反映工业企业作为生产投入，而从物资交易市场和能源、原材料生产企业购买原材料、燃料、动力产品时，所支付的价格水平变动趋势和程度的统计指标，是扣除工业企业物质消耗成本中价格变动影响的重要依据。

【房屋销售价格指数】 房屋销售价格是指房产所有权转移时买卖双方实际成交的价格。它包括商品房销售、旧房交易和公有住房出售三部分。房屋销售价格指数，就是反映一定时期内房屋销售价格变动趋势和变动程度的相对数。

【城镇居民家庭就业人口】 指城镇居民从事社会劳动并取得劳动报酬或经营收入的人口。就业人口包括国家统筹规划和指导由劳动部门介绍就业，自愿组织起来就业合自谋职业等方式，在国有制、集体所有制、中外合资、中外合作、外商在华独资的企事业单位或私营企业单位工作或从事个体劳动又固定性职业或临时性职业的人口。被聘用或留用的离退休人员也计入就业人口。本指标可以反映出城镇人口的就业情况，是计算就业面、负担系数的资料。

【城镇居民家庭全部收入】 指调查户中生活在一起的所有家庭成员在调查期得到的工薪收入、经营净收入、财产性收入、转移性收入的总和，不包括出售财物和借贷收入。收入的统计标准以实际发生的数额为准，无论收入是补发还是预发，只要是调查期得到的都如实计算，不作分摊。

【城镇居民家庭可支配收入】 指调查户可用于最终消费支出和其它非义务性支出以及储蓄的总和，即居民家庭可以用来自由支配的收入。它是家庭总收入扣除交纳的所得税、个人交纳的社会保障费以及调查户的记帐补贴后的收入。

【城镇居民家庭消费性支出】 指被调查的居民家庭用于满足家庭日常生活消费需要的全部支出，包括食品、衣着、家庭设备用品及服务、医疗保健、交通与通讯、娱乐教育文化服务、居住、杂项商品及服务支出等八大类。包括用于赠送的商品和劳务，不包括罚没、丢失款和缴纳的各种税款（如个人所得税、牌照税、房产税等），也不包括个体劳动者生产经营过程中发生的各项费用。

【农村住户纯收入】 是总收入扣除各项费用性支出后，归农民所有的收入。它是用于生产、非生产投资，改善物质文化生活，以及用于再分配和结余的收入。这个指标用来观察农民实际收入水平，以及农民扩大再生产和改善生活的能力。

纯收入＝总收入－家庭经营费用支出－生产用固定资产折旧－税收

【农村住户生活消费支出】 是指农村住户年内用于物质生活和精神生生活方面的支出，直接反映出农民的生活水平、研究农民消费结构的基本指标。生活消费支出包括食品、衣着、家庭设备用品及服务、医疗保险、交通与通讯、文教娱乐服务、其他商品和服务等消费支出。

【恩格尔系数】 恩格尔（E. ENGEL）是十九世纪德国的统计学家。他根据经验统计资料，对消费结构的变化提出这样一个看法：一个家庭收入越少，家庭收入中或家庭总支出中用来购买食物的支出所占的比例就越大；一个国家越穷，每个国民的平均收入或平均支出中用来购买食物的费用所占比例就越大；随着家庭收入的增加，家庭收入中或家庭支出中用来购买食物的比例将会下降。这就是恩格尔定律。恩格尔系数是根据恩格尔定律而得出的比例数。即：

恩格尔系数＝食物支出金额/总消费支出金额×100％

国际上常常用恩格尔系数来衡量一个国家和地区人民生活水平的状况。根据联合国粮农组织提出的标准，恩格尔系数在60％以上为贫困、50％－60％为温饱、40％－50％为小康、低于40％以下为富裕。

Explanatory Notes on Main Statistical Indicators

【Consumer Price Index】 refers to the consumption price for living necessities and services by people in urban and rural areas. It is the ultimate price of consumer goods and services. Thus it reflects the relative change in prices of consumer goods and services purchased by urban and rural families and can be used to observe and analyse the impact of price changes in consumer goods and services on living expenditure and actual charge in urban and rural households. The index also serves as a key norm in inflation.

【Retail Price Index】 refers to the last price of goods in the circulation. It is the price that industry, commerce, catering trade and other retail enterprises sell consumer goods and appliances to urban and rural residents, institutions and social organizations. The index thus reflects the relative change of the price in retail markets and as a result the index provides basis for the government on the policymaking, studies of market circulation in urban and rural areas, and national economy accounting.

【Ex—factory Price Index of Industrial Products】 It means that the industrial enterprises sell, allocate and transfer the products price from the commercial (or goods and material) departments or commercial enterprises, other manufactures and individuals, it is also called as industrial producers price. It is the initial price that the industrial products enter into circulate domain. The industrial products Ex—factory price index means that it reflects the ex—factory price level alteration trend and the change degree comparative figure for the industrial products within a certain period of time. It is an important reference target for the national economy accounting and calculation industry development speed as well.

【Price Index of the Purchased Materials, Fuel and Power】 refers to the statistical index of the trend and extent of the price fluctuation which industrial enterprises paid in purchasing the raw materials, fuel and power from goods exchange markets and fuel, material manufacturing enterprises for their own production needs. It is an important basis for the industrial enterprises in deducting fluctuant affections of the price from the material consumption cost.

【Price Index of Houses Selling】 houses selling price refers to the actual price paid in the deal between buyer and seller when the proprietary of houses transfers. Include commodity houses sales, second—hand houses transactions and the public—owned houses sales. The price index of house selling reflects the relative figures which indicate the trend and extent of house price fluctuations within a certain period.

【Employment Population in Urban Households】 refers to urban residents engaged in certain work and receiving payment for their labor or income from their business operation, including those who work in state—owned or collective units, joint ventures, foreign—owned units and private with permanent or temporary jobs. The self—employed individuals and re—employed retirees are also included. This indicator reflects the situation of urban employment and is the basic data for calculating employment rate and dependency ratio.

【Total Income of Urban Households】 It means the summation of the salary income, business net income, property income and transferring income obtained from all the family members lived together who were investigated during the period of investigation, it does not include property sale and the income of the debit and credit. The income statistical standard is subjected to the actual occurred amount no matter what complementary or advanced income. So long as the amount obtained during the period of investigation, it should be calculated as what it is, not be calculated by apportionment.

【Disposable Income of Urban Households】 It means that the investigated family can use final consumed expenditure and the other non—obligation expenditure as well as the saving deposit summation that is the income disposed freely by the resident family. It is the income after the paid income tax, individual paid social security fee and billing allowance of which are deducted from the family total income.

【Expenditure for Consumption of Urban Households】 refers to total expenditure of the sample households for consumption in daily life, including expenditure for various commodities and expenses for non—commodity items such as culture and service, etc., but excluding fines and confiscation, loss, tax payments (such as income tax, license tax, real estates tax, etc.)and various expenses by individual laborers for business purposes.

【Net income of Rural Households】 refers to the income owned by peasants after the deduction of various expenses from total income. It's used for productive and non—productive investment, for improvement of material and cultural life, for expenditure and balance in redistribution. This indicator is used to observe the actual income level of peasants, and the peasants' capacity of expanding reproduction and improving livelihood.

Net income = total income—expenditure of household operational expenses—depreciation of fixed assets from production—tax—payment for collective units for contracted tasks—collective reserve and apportion—subsidy from survey.

【Expenditure of Rural Households for Consumption】 refer to total expenditure of rural households on daily life, including expenses on food, clothing, housing, fuel, articles for daily use, and expenditures on daily life and services. This indicator is used to show the actual consumption level of peasants.

【Engel Coefficient】 Mr. E. Engel is a German Statistician at the nineteenth century. According to his experience for statistic information, he pointed out such an opinion for the variation of the consumption structure: the lower a family's income is, the higher ratio is for the expenditure used to buy food from the family total expenditure. The poorer the country is, the higher ratio is for the expenditure used to buy food from every civil average income or average expenditure. Along with the family income increasing, the ratio for the expenditure used to buy food from family income or family expenditure will be decreased. This is called as Engel Law. Engel coefficient is the proportion figure obtained according to the Engel Law. That is: Engel coefficient = food expenditures amount / overall consumption expenditures amount X 100 %.

Internationally, Engel coefficient is frequently used for evaluating the people's living standard in a country or area. According to the Standard by the Food and Agricultural Organization's of the United Nation, Engel coefficient above 60% deems as poverty, 50%—60% deems as subsistence level, 40%—50% deems as fairly well—off level, less than 40% deems as well—riched level.

NINGBO

Statistical YearBook

第六篇

农业

AGRICULTURE

农业
Agriculture

主要统计指标
Major Statistics Indicators

2012年农村劳动力	Rural Laborers in this Year	293.79	万人	10000 persons
比上年增长	Increase Over Last Year	－4.1	%	
2012年农业总产值	Total Output Value of Agriculture	419.81	亿元	million yuan
比上年增长	Increase Over Last Year	1.69	%	
2012年粮食总产量	Total Yield of Grain Grops	865700	吨	ton
比上年增长	Increase Over Last Year	－3.96	%	
2012年油料总产量	Yield of Oil－bearing Crops	36664	吨	ton
比上年增长	Increase Over Last Year	－3.0	%	
2012年肉类产量	Output of Meat	212430	吨	ton
比上年增长	Increase Over Last Year	1.81	%	
2012年水产品总产量	Total Aquatic Products	991531	吨	ton
比上年增长	Increase Over Last Year	0.23	%	
2012农业机械总动力	Total Power of Agricultural Machinery	3411544	千瓦	kw
比上年增长	Increase Over Last Year	1.65	%	

表 6－1 部分年份农村基本情况
Basic Statistics on Rural Areas in Partial Years

项目	Item	2009	2010	2011	2012
农村基层组织	**Rural Grass Roots Units**				
乡镇政府(个)	Township and Town Governments (unit)	89	89	89	89
#镇政府(个)	Town Governments	78	78	78	78
乡政府(个)	Township Governments	11	11	11	11
农村街道办事处(个)	Subdistrict Offices(unit)	40	40	39	40
农村居民委员会(个)	Neighbourhood Committees(unit)	13			
农村社区居委会(个)	Neighbourhood Committees of community(unit)	99	80	70	41
村民委员会(个)	Villages Committees(unit)	2595	2578	2559	2558
村民小组(万个)	Villages Groups(10000 units)	3.26	3.21	3.17	3.17
农村住户数、人口	**Rural Households and Population**				
农村住户数(万户)	Rural Households (10000 households)	181.21	180.48	180.19	174.84
#农业生产户数	Agricultural Produeing	60.95	59.6	59.07	58.44
农村居委会住户数	Neighborhoood Committees	2.04			
农村社区居委会住户数	Rural community neighborhood committees	5.74	5.64	5.66	3.99
外来住户数	Household from Other Places	37.92	40.6	40.62	38.29
农村人口(万人)	Rural Population (10000 persons)	477.89	475.78	475.77	462.97
#农村居委会住户人口数	Neighborhoood Committees	4.43			
农村社区居委会住户人口数	Neighbourhood Committees of community	14.56	13.85	14.48	10.04
外来人口数	Population from Other Places	108.18	112.18	110.34	104.73
农村社会基础设施	**Social Basic Facilities in Rural Areas**				
自来水受益村数(个)	Villages with Tap Water (unit)	2589	2577	2558	2557
通汽车村数(个)	Villages with Bus Services (unit)	2594	2577	2558	2557
通电话村数(个)	Villages with Telephone Communication (unit)	2595	2578	2559	2558
通宽带村数(个)	Villages with Broadband Access (unit)				2544
通电村数(个)	Villages with Electricity (unit)	2595	2578	2559	

注：2012 年起，年报填报通宽带村数，不再填报通电村数，以下表同。

Note: Since 2012, annuat report began to fill in the broadband village number, no longer fill electricity villiage number, the same as the following table.

表 6－2　各县(市)、区农村基本情况(2012)
Basic Statistics on Rural Areas by Region

指标	Indicators	全市 Total	市区 Urban District	海曙 Haishu
农村基层组织	**Rural Grass Roots Units**			
乡镇政府(个)	Township and Town Governments(unit)	89	24	
乡政府(个)	Township Governments	11	2	
镇政府(个)	Town Governments	78	22	
农村街道办事处(个)	Subdistrict Offices(unit)	40	18	
农村居民委员会(个)	Neighbourhood Committees(unit)			
农村社区居委会(个)	Neighbourhood Committees of Community(unit)	41	15	
村民委员会(个)	Villages Committees(unit)	2558	787	
村民小组(万个)	Villages Groups(10000 units)	3.17	0.75	
农村住户数、人口	**Households and Population**			
农村住户数(万户)	Rural Households (10000 households)	174.84	58.03	
#农业生产户数	Agricultural Produeing	58.44	12.58	
农村居委会住户数	Neighborhoood Committees			
村社区居委会住户数	Neighbourhood Committees of Community	3.99	1.45	
外来住户数	Household from Other Places	38.29	16.29	
农村人口(万人)	Rural Population (10000 persons)	462.97	142.67	
#农村居委会住户人口数	Neighborhoood Committees			
农村社区居委会住户人口数	Neighbourhood Committees of Community	10.04	3.84	
外来人口数	Population from Other Places	104.73	41.83	
农村社会基础设施	**Social Basic Facilities in Rural Areas**			
自来水受益村数(个)	Villages with Tap Water (unit)	2557	787	
通汽车村数(个)	Villages with Bus Services (unit)	2557	787	
通电话村数(个)	Villages with Telephone Communication (unit)	2558	787	
通宽带村数(个)	Villages with Broadband Access (unit)	2544	775	

各区 by Districts									
江东 Jiangdong	江北 Jiangbei	北仑 Beilun	镇海 Zhenhai	鄞州 Yinzhou	余姚 Yuyao	慈溪 Cixi	奉化 Fenghua	象山 Xiangshan	宁海 Ninghai
	1	3	2	18	15	15	6	15	14
		1		1	1			5	3
	1	2	2	17	14	15	6	10	11
	3	6	3	6	6	4	5	3	4
		6	3	6	7	10	1		8
	93	204	62	428	265	297	256	490	363
	0.09	0.16	0.11	0.39	0.40	0.71	0.46	0.42	0.43
	4.77	10.77	9.90	32.59	25.63	45.70	14.63	13.16	17.69
	0.68	3.25	1.26	7.39	12.22	10.49	7.02	6.58	9.55
	0.00	0.20	0.39	0.86	0.70	0.69	0.11	0.00	1.04
	1.25	1.35	4.89	8.79	3.33	12.18	2.95	0.83	2.70
	11.21	25.07	23.53	82.86	70.84	119.80	38.90	39.89	50.87
	0.00	0.52	0.77	2.54	1.69	1.44	0.28	0.00	2.79
	3.55	3.07	10.26	24.95	8.05	35.92	8.37	2.46	8.10
	93	204	62	428	265	297	355	490	363
	93	204	62	428	265	297	356	489	363
	93	204	62	428	265	297	356	490	363
	93	192	62	428	265	297	356	488	363

表 6－3 各县(市)、区农村劳动力资源情况(2012) Basic Statistics on Rural Laborers by Region

指标	Indicators	全市 Total	市区 Urban District	海曙 Haishu
农村劳动力资源总数	**Total Rural Laborers**	**320.31**	**95.37**	
其中:劳动年龄内的人口数	Number of Population in Working Age	288.98	86.01	
按性别分:	Grouped by Sex			
男劳动力资源数	Male	167.74	50.02	
女劳动力资源数	Female	152.57	45.35	
农村实有劳动力合计	**Rural Laborers**	**293.79**	**88.19**	
#外出劳动力	Laborers Going Outside	39.53	11.88	
#出省的劳动力	Going to Other Province	8.58	1.34	
按性别分	Grouped by Sex			
男劳动力	Male	154.43	46.31	
女劳动力	Female	139.36	41.88	
按部门分	Grouped by Sector			
农、林、牧、渔业	Farming,Forestry,Animal Husbandry & Fishery	55.31	11.15	
农业	Farming	44.35	9.68	
林业	Forestry	3.08	0.55	
牧业	Animal Husbandry	2.60	0.42	
渔业	Fishery	5.28	0.50	
工业	Industry	156.36	51.76	
建筑业	Construction	19.47	4.66	
其他行业从业人员	Other Industries	62.65	20.62	
附报:外来劳动力	**Labor from Other Places**	**143.50**	**60.26**	

单位:万人(10000 persons)

各区 by Districts									
江东 Jiangdong	江北 Jiangbei	北仑 Beilun	镇海 Zhenhai	鄞州 Yinzhou	余姚 Yuyao	慈溪 Cixi	奉化 Fenghua	象山 Xiangshan	宁海 Ninghai
	7.42	**18.52**	**16.47**	**52.96**	**46.28**	**84.40**	**30.69**	**27.65**	**35.92**
	6.60	16.89	13.61	48.91	43.44	76.42	25.52	25.46	32.13
	3.92	9.62	8.38	28.10	23.97	43.60	16.07	15.01	19.07
	3.50	8.90	8.09	24.86	22.31	40.80	14.62	12.64	16.85
	6.34	**17.13**	**15.62**	**49.10**	**43.32**	**77.88**	**26.80**	**25.24**	**32.36**
	0.72	2.69	2.06	6.41	4.62	4.67	3.21	6.72	8.43
	0.05	0.48	0.30	0.51	0.76	1.50	0.37	1.93	2.68
	3.34	8.77	8.01	26.19	22.57	40.44	13.97	13.76	17.38
	3.00	8.36	7.61	22.91	20.75	37.44	12.83	11.48	14.98
	0.57	2.89	1.31	6.38	8.52	10.26	6.93	9.60	8.85
	0.45	2.66	1.13	5.44	6.71	9.22	5.36	6.79	6.59
	0.05	0.04	0.04	0.42	0.99	0.19	0.55	0.34	0.46
	0.06	0.05	0.11	0.20	0.52	0.24	0.30	0.54	0.58
	0.01	0.14	0.03	0.32	0.30	0.61	0.72	1.93	1.22
	3.86	7.54	9.23	31.13	23.72	46.34	14.19	5.72	14.63
	0.26	1.02	1.52	1.86	3.01	4.41	1.28	3.47	2.64
	1.65	5.68	3.56	9.73	8.07	16.87	4.40	6.45	6.24
	6.00	**15.18**	**9.75**	**29.33**	**21.23**	**43.97**	**5.75**	**3.23**	**9.06**

表 6—4 历年农村劳动力按三次产业分的构成情况
Composition of Rural Labor Force by Three Industries Over the Years

单位:万人(10000 persons)

年份 Year	乡村实有劳动力 Rural Laborers	按三次产业分 Group by Three Industries					
		第一产业 Primary Industry		第二产业 Secondary Industry		第三产业 Tertiary Industry	
		人数 Population	比重% Proportion	人数 Population	比重% Proportion	人数 Population	比重% Proportion
1978	195.42						
1979	196.47						
1980	197.16						
1981	197.91						
1982	201.95						
1983	211.75						
1984	225.96						
1985	234.79	131.71	56.10	80.37	34.23	22.71	9.67
1986	240.88	130.51	54.18	85.73	35.59	24.64	10.23
1987	246.55	131.22	53.22	90.79	36.82	24.54	9.96
1988	250.35	132.86	53.07	90.64	36.21	26.85	10.72
1989	252.37	138.57	54.91	85.19	33.76	28.61	11.33
1990	254.12	142.33	56.01	81.83	32.20	29.96	11.79
1991	256.36	141.80	55.31	83.49	32.57	31.07	12.12
1992	260.65	141.29	54.21	82.79	31.76	36.57	14.03
1993	261.89	132.39	50.55	87.99	33.60	41.51	15.85
1994	263.13	126.79	48.19	89.13	33.87	47.21	17.94
1995	260.40	116.99	44.93	91.08	34.98	52.33	20.09
1996	260.37	115.02	44.18	93.06	35.74	52.29	20.08
1997	259.99	110.34	42.44	93.18	35.84	56.47	21.72
1998	259.23	109.77	42.35	91.96	35.47	57.50	22.18
1999	257.77	105.86	41.07	93.36	36.22	58.55	22.71
2000	257.44	99.83	38.78	97.90	38.03	59.71	23.19
2001	266.14	95.70	35.96	107.68	40.46	62.76	23.58
2002	270.04	92.29	34.17	114.46	42.39	63.29	23.44
2003	290.30	87.04	29.98	135.08	46.53	68.18	23.49
2004	306.15	78.32	25.58	153.53	50.15	74.30	24.27
2005	324.92	75.27	23.17	167.12	51.43	82.53	25.40
2006	320.85	69.14	21.55	170.56	53.16	81.15	25.29
2007	317.16	65.44	20.63	180.86	57.03	70.86	22.34
2008	305.56	64.14	21.00	173.42	56.75	68.00	22.25
2009	304.12	62.29	20.48	173.83	57.16	68.00	22.36
2010	306.32	59.17	19.32	177.28	57.87	69.87	22.81
2011	306.36	58.25	19.01	181.24	59.16	66.87	21.83
2012	293.79	55.31	18.83	175.83	59.85	62.65	21.32

表 6－5 历年农林牧渔业总产值 Gross Output Value of Farming, Forestry, Animal Husbandry and Fishery Over the Years

单位：亿元(100 million yuan)

年份 Year	农林牧渔业总产值 Gross Output Value	其中 Of Which				
		农业 Farming	林业 Forestry	牧业 Animal Husbandry	渔业 Fishery	服务业 Services
1978	8.83					
1979	10.93					
1980	11.70					
1981	11.07					
1982	14.79					
1983	14.81					
1984	19.68					
1985	21.89	15.40	0.83	3.53	2.13	
1986	24.31	16.85	0.93	4.26	2.27	
1987	28.99	19.47	1.13	5.71	2.68	
1988	36.23	23.41	1.28	7.53	4.01	
1989	40.98	27.37	1.52	8.31	3.78	
1990	40.68	26.94	1.30	8.30	4.14	
1991	45.86	29.35	1.74	8.42	6.35	
1992	51.47	31.51	1.57	9.59	8.80	
1993	69.89	40.29	2.40	11.75	15.45	
1994	96.40	51.60	3.00	17.26	24.54	
1995	123.95	67.22	4.18	20.71	31.84	
1996	138.65	75.77	3.92	22.85	36.11	
1997	129.44	67.19	4.22	21.65	36.38	
1998	136.36	71.92	4.09	20.53	39.82	
1999	142.82	73.04	4.34	20.16	45.28	
2000	148.37	71.57	4.59	20.45	51.76	
2001	156.43	74.31	5.14	22.21	54.77	
2002	163.31	73.65	4.92	24.25	60.49	
2003	173.75	77.42	5.03	26.03	63.10	2.17
2004	193.13	86.94	5.01	29.61	69.18	2.39
2005	207.40	91.14	5.31	32.93	75.31	2.71
2006	207.93	97.14	6.01	32.20	68.97	3.60
2007	236.96	107.22	6.77	46.27	72.67	4.02
2008	262.44	119.31	7.32	48.29	83.27	4.25
2009	286.78	134.64	8.85	47.87	90.82	4.60
2010	339.59	167.51	9.83	51.74	105.62	4.89
2010	339.59	167.51	9.83	51.74	105.62	4.89
2011	397.93	191.64	10.86	62.54	127.68	5.21
2012	419.81	201.19	11.43	64.70	136.73	5.76

注：本表按现行价格计算，2006 及 2007 年数据已根据农普数据进行调整

Note: Note: Data in this table are calculated at current prices. Data of the year 2006 & 2007 has been amended according to the last census of agriculture

表 6－6　各县(市)、区农林牧渔业总产值(2012)
Gross Output Value of Farming, Forestry, Animal Husbandry and Fishery by Region

指标	Indicators	全市 Total	市区 Urban District	海曙 Haishu
合计	**Gross Output Value**	**4198058**	**913864**	
农业产值	**Farming**	**2011924**	**620735**	
#副产品产值	By－products	7806	2077	
粮食作物	Grain	281189	74216	
谷物	Cereal	200171	65547	
豆类	Beans	36593	4835	
薯类	Tubers	44425	3834	
油料	Oil Plants	26516	2361	
棉花	Cotton	16410	136	
麻类	Fiber Crops			
甘蔗	Sugarcane	7514	1999	
药材类	Crude Drugs	25897	20163	
蔬菜	Vegetables	631964	198386	
食用菌	Edible Mushroom	722	27	
花卉园艺	Flower & Horticulture	297568	105195	
茶、桑、水果、坚果	Tea, Mulberry & Fruits	687225	185828	
其他	Others	36919	32424	
林业产值	**Forestry**	**114301**	**24793**	
人造林木生长	Artificial Forestry	11383	5437	
林产品	Forest Products	72556	8472	
竹木采运	Cut Lumbering	26069	9832	
采集野生作物	Wild Plant Collected	4293	1052	
牧业产值	**Animal Husbandry**	**646977**	**166123**	
牲畜	Livestock Raising	414026	112642	
家禽饲养	Poultry Raising	101292	21506	
活的畜禽产品	Livestock Products	96978	29364	
捕猎野兽野禽	Hunting Wild Beast and Wild Fowl	1151	121	
其他动物饲养	Other Animals Raising	33530	2490	
渔业产值	**Fishery**	**1367257**	**82292**	
海水产品	Seawater Aquatic Products	1179800	47083	
淡水产品	Freshwater Aquatic Products	187457	35209	
农林牧渔服务业	**Services**	**57599**	**19921**	

注：本表按当年价格计算。

Note: Data in this table are calculated at current prices

单位：万元(10000 yuan)

各区 by Districts									
江东 Jiangdong	江北 Jiangbei	北仑 Beilun	镇海 Zhenhai	鄞州 Yinzhou	余姚 Yuyao	慈溪 Cixi	奉化 Fenghua	象山 Xiangshan	宁海 Ninghai
6547	**90136**	**139304**	**107695**	**570182**	**671526**	**679938**	**448934**	**981162**	**502634**
	52846	**95837**	**75958**	**396094**	**435762**	**429248**	**185856**	**186206**	**154117**
	524	77	323	1153	1447	1806	590	796	1090
	8504	3163	6579	55970	65472	38683	23029	33222	46567
	8090	593	5551	51313	50952	17780	18873	25254	21765
	168	1134	690	2843	7076	18283	735	2759	2914
	246	1436	338	1814	7453	2620	3421	5209	21888
	78	279	30	1974	7714	11543	738	1781	2379
		33	2	101	5127	7909		53	3185
	91	6	192	1710	388	914	18	4009	186
		400		19763	2210	2765	47	560	152
	16050	20223	27871	134242	155346	186629	8480	53296	29827
		27			499	173	23		
	5706	45808	27064	26617	57720	24030	85599	20288	4736
	19824	25460	10790	129754	141228	154053	66198	72873	67045
	2593	438	3430	25963	58	2549	1724	124	40
	3453	**1922**	**2004**	**17414**	**30324**	**4972**	**31655**	**6883**	**15674**
	346	799	314	3978	2081	286	1257	1639	683
	2136	587	362	5387	24800	1917	24005	2772	10590
	971	535	628	7698	3340	2661	6134	268	3834
		1	700	351	103	108	259	2204	567
6547	**22455**	**27603**	**25438**	**84080**	**143426**	**95888**	**83473**	**83005**	**75062**
6547	12374	22189	11631	59901	83902	62681	56320	56769	41712
	2791	3535	5262	9918	39034	7960	7844	11456	13492
	7255	1767	6722	13620	8894	10785	18774	11772	17389
				121	26		13	986	5
	35	112	1823	520	11570	14462	522	2022	2464
	10234	**9627**	**1635**	**60796**	**56998**	**133064**	**143000**	**696417**	**255486**
	9064	7685	617	29717	6951	71573	138424	668831	246938
	1170	1942	1018	31079	50047	61491	4576	27586	8548
	1148	**4315**	**2660**	**11798**	**5016**	**16766**	**4950**	**8651**	**2295**

表6－7 部分年份农林牧渔业分项产值
Gross Output Value of Farming, Forestry, Animal Husbandry and Fishery by Branch in Partial Years

单位：万元（10000 yuan）

指标	Indicators	2008	2009	2010	2011	2012
合计	**Gross Output Value**	**2624431**	**2867805**	**3395923**	**3979320**	**4198058**
农业产值	**Farming**	**1193126**	**1346351**	**1675123**	**1916397**	**2011924**
#副产品产值	By－products	6723	6804	7127	7968	7806
粮食作物	Grain	199432	209857	241746	280624	281189
谷物	Cereal	140782	142258	167853	197813	200171
豆类	Beans	30922	30482	31790	39763	36593
薯类	Tubers	27728	37117	42103	43048	44425
油料	Oil Plants	18334	21826	23455	24580	26516
棉花	Cotton	8715	10570	17832	17253	16410
麻类	Fiber Crops	4				
甘蔗	Sugarcane	9447	9772	9392	10113	7514
药材类	Crude Drugs	14239	10116	12356	24220	25897
蔬菜	Vegetables	362714	420859	547737	607582	631964
食用菌	Edible Mushroom	764	618	556	612	722
花卉园艺	Flower & Horticulture	161991	187262	239054	274437	297568
茶、桑、果	Tea, Mulberry & Fruits	392 513	447409	559431	643140	687225
其他	Others	21930	24370	23564	33836	36919
林业产值	**Forestry**	**73231**	**88522**	**98252**	**108564**	**114301**
人造林木生长	Artificial Forestry	8309	8217	8349	11441	11383
林产品	Forest Products	42182	58721	62801	69674	72556
村及村以下竹木采伐	Cut Lumbering	22740	21584	24660	24509	26069
采集野生作物	Wild Plant Collected	3043	3692	2442	2940	4293
牧业产值	**Animal Husbandry**	**482861**	**478671**	**517412**	**625444**	**646977**
牲畜	Livestock Raising	271773	261299	293829	385045	414026
家禽饲养	Poultry Raising	83426	85012	90666	104780	101292
活的畜禽产品	Livestock Products	86544	89915	94687	102513	96978
捕猎野兽野禽	Hunting Wild Beast and Wild Fowl	1646	748	592	552	1151
其他动物饲养	Other Animals Raising	39472	4697	37638	32554	33530
渔业产值	**Fishery**	**832683**	**908243**	**1056250**	**1276779**	**1367257**
海水产品	Seawater Aquatic Products	716093	785820	901585	1095365	1179800
淡水产品	Freshwater Aquatic Products	116590	122423	154665	181414	187457
农林牧渔服务业	**Services**	**42530**	**46018**	**48886**	**52136**	**57599**

注：本表按当年价格计算整。

Note: Data in this table are calculated at current prices.

表 6－8 各地农林牧渔业中间消耗(2012) Intermediate Consumption of Farming, Forestry, Animal Husbandry and Fishery by Region

单位:万元(10000 yuan)

地区	Region	中间消耗 Intermediate Consumption	其中 of Which 农业 Farming	林业 Forestry	牧业 Animal Husbandry	渔业 Fishery	服务业 Services
全市	**Total**	**1512899**	**519199**	**38474**	**368211**	**564982**	**22033**
市区	Urban Area	307180	172523	4902	81192	41562	7001
海曙	Haishu						
江东	Jiangdong	2095			2095		
江北	Jiangbei	30096	12654	963	11304	4698	477
北仑	Beilun	46237	18000	542	18908	7552	1235
镇海	Zhenhai	42868	27002	1230	12731	981	924
鄞州	Yinzhou	185884	114867	2167	36154	28331	4365
县市	Rural Area						
余姚	Yuyao	236889	102150	9198	108887	14684	1970
慈溪	Cixi	214587	114371	2569	48752	42190	6705
奉化	Fenghua	172185	41308	14952	37097	76848	1980
象山	Xiangshan	443493	48254	3618	44453	343709	3459
宁海	Ninghai	138565	40593	3235	47830	45989	918

表 6—9 农林牧渔业增加值(2012)
Value Added of Farming, Forestry, Animal Husbandry and Fishery

单位:万元(10000 yuan)

指标	Indicators	总产值 Gross Output Value	其中 of Which 中间消耗 Depreciation	其中 of Which 增加值 Value—added	增加值率(%) Value—adding Rate
总计	**Total**	**4198058**	**1512899**	**2685159**	**63.96**
农业	Farming	2011924	519199	1492725	74.19
林业	Forestry	114301	38474	75827	66.34
牧业	Animal Husbandry	646977	368211	278766	43.09
渔业	Fishery	1367257	564982	802275	58.68
服务业	Services	57599	22033	35566	61.75

表 6—10 各县(市)农林牧渔业增加值(2012)
Value Added of Farming, Forestry, Animal Husbandry and Fishery by Region

单位:万元(10000 yuan)

地区	Region	增加值 Value—added	其中 of Which 农业 Farming	林业 Forestry	牧业 Animal Husbandry	渔业 Fishery	服务业 Services
全市	**Total**	**2685159**	**1492725**	**75827**	**278766**	**802275**	**35566**
市区	Urban Area	606684	448212	19891	84931	40730	12920
余姚	Yuyao	434637	333612	21126	34539	42314	3046
慈溪	Cixi	465351	314877	2403	47136	90874	10061
奉化	Fenghua	276749	144548	16703	46376	66152	2970
象山	Xiangshan	537669	137952	3265	38552	352708	5192
宁海	Ninghai	364069	113524	12439	27232	209497	1377

表 6－11 历年主要农作物播种面积及产量
Sown Areas and Yield of Major Farm Crops Over the Years

单位：面积：千公顷 Sown：1000 hectares
产量：万吨 Yield：10000 tons

年份 Year	农作物播种面积 Sown Area	其中 of Which							
		粮食 Grain		棉花 Cotton		油料 Oil Plants		蔬菜 Vegetables	
		面积 Area	产量 Yield	面积 Area	产量 Yield	面积 Area	产量 Yield	面积 Area	产量 Yield
1978	638.43	422.61	180.51						
1979	638.61	420.13	196.36						
1980	625.37	413.95	171.60						
1981	622.19	396.91	153.88						
1982	626.41	402.19	191.11						
1983	624.95	410.17	166.30	51.88	4.79	40.21	5.97		
1984	616.76	410.39	213.70	51.36	6.98	32.96	5.99		
1985	612.90	380.39	188.52	48.13	3.91	44.45	7.99	34.57	143.97
1986	596.50	361.81	188.65	41.39	3.66	48.70	8.41	36.09	158.75
1987	595.54	372.05	185.23	34.27	2.95	45.09	7.77	42.89	166.61
1988	580.01	369.58	189.98	34.65	1.80	46.70	8.47	41.01	161.74
1989	579.97	360.69	183.84	31.30	2.07	49.44	7.55	47.79	151.00
1990	591.03	368.77	189.06	34.55	3.34	52.51	9.50	48.79	135.64
1991	587.53	372.02	205.63	33.84	3.84	52.08	9.19	44.58	135.36
1992	572.68	357.66	181.62	33.03	2.59	49.15	8.62	46.82	126.89
1993	522.02	317.08	175.44	27.37	2.36	32.28	6.13	52.73	152.20
1994	504.73	308.04	172.51	26.93	2.07	30.17	4.84	56.37	162.65
1995	512.08	316.57	172.76	27.59	2.48	40.29	7.34	50.04	144.62
1996	519.48	318.99	190.30	27.14	2.73	40.37	8.00	54.20	164.26
1997	502.21	316.44	173.73	24.19	1.53	35.27	6.81	51.86	158.10
1998	510.73	317.76	180.39	25.81	2.69	34.21	5.05	58.01	174.67
1999	504.82	308.98	173.67	14.75	1.59	36.16	7.37	69.73	207.62
2000	445.90	246.79	132.51	9.69	1.05	32.58	6.59	82.16	243.70
2001	406.64	200.16	112.17	10.20	1.18	27.28	5.59	99.25	299.22
2002	386.85	172.34	94.89	6.85	0.80	24.51	4.76	104.71	291.67
2003	348.64	136.73	75.61	6.55	0.76	19.98	4.21	98.86	275.04
2004	338.09	145.12	83.73	6.53	0.74	17.67	4.04	91.80	286.76
2005	332.53	145.27	80.12	6.77	0.72	17.71	4.01	93.36	274.86
2006	317.17	141.01	81.30	6.21	0.73	14.91	3.62	88.75	264.73
2007	314.67	134.98	74.77	6.11	0.69	14.47	3.52	94.03	266.00
2008	330.07	153.80	88.42	6.45	0.75	14.21	3.55	89.49	272.92
2009	321.72	148.14	86.32	6.53	0.75	17.52	4.33	86.76	274.42
2010	318.56	151.14	87.13	6.73	0.77	16.82	4.10	83.59	265.73
2011	314.28	150.95	90.14	6.48	0.82	15.05	3.78	82.13	269.09
2012	309.45	148.53	86.57	5.98	0.71	14.70	3.67	80.73	261.20

注：2006 年数据已根据农普数据进行调整。从 2008 年年报开始，马铃薯作为粮食，不算蔬菜

Note：Data of the year 2006 has been amended according to the last census of agriculture. Potato is classified as food，not vegetable from 2008.

表 6－12 各县(市)、区农作物播种面积和产量(2012)
Total Sown Area and Yield of Major Farm Crops by Region

指标	Indicators	全市 Total	市区 Urban District	海曙 Haishu
农作物播种面积总计	**Sown Area of Farm Crops**	**309450**	**83538**	
粮食作物播种面积	**Sown Area of Grain**	**148532**	**38371**	
总产量	**Total Yield of Grain**	**865700**	**256721**	
谷物面积	Sown Area of Cereal	104150	32456	
总产量	Yield of Cereal	704561	230941	
稻谷面积	Sown Area of Rice	85701	29706	
总产量	Yield of Rice	629778	218329	
＃早稻面积	Sown Area of Early Rice	16073	7075	
总产量	Yield of Early Rice	104249	45331	
晚稻及单季稻	Sown Area of Late Rice & Single Season Rice	69628	22631	
总产量	Yield of Late Rice & Single Season Rice	525529	172998	
小麦面积	Sown Area of Wheat	9026	1262	
总产量	Yield of Wheat	30063	4344	
大麦面积	Sown Area of Barley	866	162	
总产量	Yield of Barley	2389	544	
豆类面积	Sown Area of Beans	30873	3361	
总产量	Yield of Beans	91309	12568	
蕃薯面积	Sown Area of Tubers	13509	2554	
总产量	Yield of Tubers	69830	13212	
油料播种面积	**Sown Area of Oil Plants**	**14702**	**1277**	
总产量	**Yield of Oil Plants**	**36664**	**4058**	
油菜籽面积	Sown Area of Rapeseeds	10348	639	
总产量	Yield of Rapeseeds	23038	1389	
花生面积	Sown Area of Peanuts	3632	607	
总产量	Yield of Peanuts	12285	2614	
芝麻面积	Sown Area of Sesame	722	31	

单位:公顷,吨(hectare ton)

各区 by Districts									
江东 Jiangdong	江北 Jiangbei	北仑 Beilun	镇海 Zhenhai	鄞州 Yinzhou	余姚 Yuyao	慈溪 Cixi	奉化 Fenghua	象山 Xiangshan	宁海 Ninghai
	8260	**7560**	**9906**	**57812**	**63001**	**80381**	**22246**	**31198**	**29086**
	4461	**1791**	**4004**	**28115**	**32818**	**28886**	**11457**	**17461**	**19539**
	32075	**6701**	**25033**	**192912**	**209193**	**121876**	**72040**	**104541**	**101329**
	4125	448	3139	24744	27129	11082	9687	10966	12830
	30749	2306	21971	175915	184508	64246	66541	78778	79547
	3981	216	2918	22591	22289	5361	9027	9898	9420
	30090	1447	20805	165987	162171	40391	64347	75254	69286
	954	44	901	5176	6585	195	1040	992	186
	6258	257	5605	33211	43213	1234	6600	6622	1249
	3027	172	2017	17415	15704	5166	7987	8906	9234
	23832	1190	15200	132776	118958	39157	57747	68632	68037
	16	1	39	1206	2847	1855	251	376	2435
	52	4	89	4199	10522	6319	849	1175	6854
	53	2		107	19	430	32	169	54
	173	5	9	357	72	969	104	545	155
	151	825	601	1784	3933	16578	775	2993	3233
	543	2193	1888	7944	15188	48924	1677	6792	6160
	185	518	264	1587	1756	1226	995	3502	3476
	783	2202	1174	9053	9497	8706	3822	18971	15622
	109	**133**	**39**	**996**	**3220**	**7046**	**407**	**1195**	**1557**
	176	**452**	**98**	**3332**	**8462**	**17199**	**841**	**3098**	**3006**
	109	78	33	419	2776	5102	157	694	980
	176	179	75	959	6596	12080	237	1101	1635
		47	6	554	372	1441	239	467	506
		263	23	2328	1707	4160	586	1944	1274
		8		23	72	503	11	34	71

表 6－12 续表 Continued

指标	Indicators	全市 Total	市区 Urban District	海曙 Haishu
总产量	Yield of Sesame	1341	55	
棉花(皮棉)播种面积	Sown Area of Cotton	5984	71	
棉花(皮棉)总产量	Yield of Cotton	7133	77	
麻类播种面积	Sown Area of Fiber Crops			
麻类总产量	Yield of Fiber Crops			
甘蔗播种面积	Sown Area of Sugarcane	726	243	
甘蔗总产量	Yield of Sugarcane	43257	16023	
药材类播种面积	Sown Area of Medicinal Material	1468	701	
药材类总产量	Yield of Medicinal Material	6260	3000	
蔬菜类播种面积	Sown Area of Vegetables	80728	20304	
蔬菜类总产量	Yield of Vegetables	2611971	631748	
食用菌产量	Edible Mushroom	886	31	
果用瓜播种面积	**Sown Area of Melon as Fruits**	**19946**	**5889**	
总产量	**Yield of Melon as Fruits**	**585974**	**208490**	
西瓜播种面积	Sown Area of Watermelon	14172	4601	
总产量	Yield of Watermelon	463247	175521	
草莓面积	Sown Area of Strawberry	1440	330	
总产量	Yield of Strawberry	25719	7904	
花卉苗木播种面积	**Sown Area of Flowers and Plants Nursery Stock**	**22671**	**8106**	
花卉面积	Sown Area of Flowers	9519	3869	
苗木面积	Sown Area of Plants Nursery Stock	12701	4156	
盆栽类园艺(万盆)	Potted Horticulture(10000 units)	237	197	
其他农作物播种面积	**Sown Area of Other Farm Crops**	**14693**	**8576**	
绿肥面积	Sown Area of Green Manure	3418	1759	
席草面积	Sown Area of Rush	5440	4633	
总产量	Yield of Rush	50580	44567	

单位:公顷,吨(hectare ton)

各区 by Districts									
江东 Jiangdong	江北 Jiangbei	北仑 Beilun	镇海 Zhenhai	鄞州 Yinzhou	余姚 Yuyao	慈溪 Cixi	奉化 Fenghua	象山 Xiangshan	宁海 Ninghai
		10		45	159	959	18	53	97
		20	4	47	1451	3366		53	1043
		23	4	50	1740	3868		41	1407
	13	1	17	212	70	139	6	227	41
	860	36	873	14254	4800	8843	189	12131	1271
	1	4		696	150	552	17	40	8
		8		2992	582	2417	25	199	37
	2099	1858	3274	13073	17110	27545	2524	8963	4282
	65031	47173	85442	434102	824993	803622	47385	187083	117140
		31			652	173	30		
	392	**479**	**766**	**4252**	**1999**	**7473**	**826**	**1972**	**1787**
	11004	**12112**	**19231**	**166143**	**77303**	**170534**	**20554**	**46577**	**62516**
	326	332	461	3482	1415	4911	513	1342	1390
	9038	8819	12787	144877	57104	128759	15177	34984	51702
	18	11	139	162	139	522	248	128	73
	627	239	3421	3617	2825	6688	4345	2471	1486
	939	**3241**	**1389**	**2537**	**4834**	**2749**	**5391**	**907**	**684**
	189	2338	339	1003	3758	700	826	306	60
	736	901	1009	1510	1019	1977	4327	599	623
	77	17	71	31	26	4	8	2	1
	246	**33**	**413**	**7884**	**1349**	**2625**	**1618**	**380**	**145**
	188	10	172	1389	523	44	735	222	135
				4633	28		779		
				44567	213		5701		

表 6－13　各县(市)、区农业机械拥有量(2012 年末)
Possession of Agricultural Machinery by Region (End of 2012)

指标	单位	Indicators	Unit	全市 Total	市区 Urban District	海曙 Haishu
农业机械总动力	千瓦	Total Power of AgriculturalMachinery	kw	3411544	699868	118
耕作机械		Cultivation Machinery				
耕作机械动力合计	台	Mechanical Power of Cultivation	unit	25876	9252	
	千瓦		kw	297741	90984	44
大中型拖拉机	台	Large and Medium Sized Tractors	unti	2598	584	
	千瓦		kw	93869	19634	
农用小型拖拉机	台	Mini－tractors for Agriculture	unit	17569	4748	2
	千瓦		kw	163531	47012	18
收获机械		Harvest Machinery				
收获机械动力合计	台	Mechanical Power of Harvesting	unit	7593	999	7
	千瓦		kw	106844	29952	25
联合收割机	台	Combine Harvesters	unit	3018	893	1
	千瓦		kw	89487	25776	15
谷物烘干机	台	Cereal Dryer	unit	564	214	
植保机械		Plant Protection Machinery				
植保机械动力合计	台	Mechanical Power of Plant Protection	unit	42755	2517	
	千瓦		kw	66983	4403	
机动喷雾(粉)器	架	Motorized Sprayer	unit	38807	2357	
	千瓦		kw	59998	3868	
排灌机械		Drainage & Irrigation Machinery				
排灌机械动力	台	Mechanical Power of Drainage and Irrigation	unit	76609	17383	2
	千瓦		kw	288868	75627	28
农用水泵	台	Water Pump for Agricultural Use	unit			
农副产品加工机械		Processing Machinery of Agricultural Products				
农副产品加工机械动力合计	台	Mechanical Power of Farm Sideline Products Manufacturing	unit	17749	4338	1
	千瓦		kw	133467	30591	10
运输机械		Transport Machinery				
运输机械动力	台	Mechanical Power of Transportation	unit	37780	6615	
	千瓦		kw	721395	141761	
农用运输车	辆	Vehicles for Agricultural Use	unit	16639	2058	
	千瓦		kw	304554	57927	
运输型拖拉机	辆	Transport Tractors	unit	18448	4192	
	千瓦		kw	351762	72426	
其他农用机械		Other Mechanical				
其他农业机械动力合计	台	Other Mechanical Power	unit	33240	13071	10
	千瓦		kw	335220	121932	3

注：本表数据来自宁波市农业机械服务总站。

Note：Date in this table are obtained from Agricultural Machinery General Servise Station of Ningbo.

各区 by Districts									
江东 Jiangdong	江北 Jiangbei	北仑 Beilun	镇海 Zhenhai	鄞州 Yinzhou	余姚 Yuyao	慈溪 Cixi	奉化 Fenghua	象山 Xiangshan	宁海 Ninghai
318	54017	188341	67502	389572	627534	470617	436325	881281	295919
	665	2594	779	5214	5140	5120	3196	1497	1671
	8273	18629	7653	56385	69741	60744	33587	23988	18697
	175	71	43	295	813	525	203	330	143
	4010	2269	1643	11712	30042	19135	7232	11257	6578
	250	848	287	3361	3809	4095	2679	1107	1131
	2215	8535	2349	33895	34789	36158	25122	10205	10245
	204	126	125	537	970	2088	348	2992	196
	3655	1670	4479	20123	27486	13920	7452	17768	10266
	195	85	125	487	923	318	342	362	180
	3655	1516	4479	16111	25608	9531	7207	11459	9906
	22	13	36	143	163	30	42	53	62
	383	884	259	991	10837	17858	323	6038	5182
	716	955	649	2083	15253	26020	908	10266	10133
	383	882	259	833	8801	17664	323	4492	5170
	716	952	649	1551	13084	25241	908	6866	10031
	1370	5599	1553	8859	22809	9290	9042	13870	4215
	11964	19982	6932	36721	92317	42573	34046	32428	11877
	286	461	180	3410	6254	2708	1751	1173	1525
	3313	5259	1217	20792	40749	19097	15978	12706	14346
23	242	2005	497	3848	9715	8267	3280	3682	6221
318	4712	33473	8136	95122	154872	129663	88022	91541	115536
		819		1239	5658	5002	1322	227	2372
		13240		44687	79701	75159	46988	7752	37027
23	242	1110	497	2320	3800	3147	1931	2063	3315
318	4712	18242	8124	41030	70408	47834	40914	47250	72930
	714	730	319	11298	5130	4892	3602	5003	1542
	1985	22302	1336	96306	80023	64856	21968	25449	20992

表 6－14　各县(市)、区灌溉和水利情况(2012)
Irrigation and Water Conservancy Facilities of Farmland by Region

指标	单位	Indicators	Unit	全市 Total	市区 Urban District	海曙 Haishu
水库年末累计	座	Total Number of Reservoirs at the Year－end	set	411	99	
总库容量	万立方米	Total Capacity of Reservoirs at the Year－end	10000 cu. m	181660	52073	
#大型水库	座	Large－sized Reservoirs	set	6	2	
总库容	万立方米	Capacity	10000 cu. m	78705	23181	
中型水库	座	Medium－sized Reservoirs	set	25	6	
总库容	万立方米	Capacity	10000 cu. m	67505	18350	
小型水库	座	Small－sized Reservoirs	set	380	91	
总库容	万立方米	Capacity	10000 cu. m	35450	10542	
灌溉面积总计	千公顷	Total Irrigated Area	1000 hectares	210.27	61.09	0.04
有效灌溉面积	千公顷	Effective Irrigated Area	1000 hectares	191.45	57.09	0.04
有效实灌面积	千公顷	Effective Fact Irrigated Area	1000 hectares	178.89	56.53	0.04
旱涝保收面积	千公顷	Farmland Area of Stable Yields Despite Drought or Excessive Rain	1000 hectares	151.80	38.82	0.04
机电排灌面积	千公顷	Mechanical and Electrical Irrigated Area	1000 hectares	176.13	55.15	0.04
水土流失治理面积	千公顷	Area of Soil Erosion under Control	1000 hectares	147.43	29.50	
水闸座数	座	Sluice	set	1061	266	
堤防长度	公里	Total Length of Dikes	km	1853.60	375.92	12.00
机电井眼数	眼	Motor－electric－pumped Well	unit	291		
固定机电排灌站处数	处	Number of Project of Water－taking and Drainage Pumping Station	unit	10098	1497	6
装机容量	千千瓦	Installed Capacity	1000 kw	129.97	25.49	0.06
水利工程年实际供水量	亿立方米	Annually Water Supply of Water Conservancy	100 million cu. m	213351	68094	
#农业供水	亿立方米	Water Supply for Agriculture	100 million cu. m	65079	15331	50
工业供水	亿立方米	Water Supply for Industry	100 million cu. m	62430	35220	
城镇生活用水	亿立方米	Water Supply for Urban life	100 million cu. m	52807	12383	

注：本表数据来自宁波市水利局。

Note：Data in this tables are obtained from Ningbo Municipal Bureau of Water Conservancy.

各区 by Districts									
江东 Jiangdong	江北 Jiangbei	北仑 Beilun	镇海 Zhenhai	鄞州 Yinzhou	余姚 Yuyao	慈溪 Cixi	奉化 Fenghua	象山 Xiangshan	宁海 Ninghai
	5	32	6	56	58	23	92	74	65
	2168	4738	4598	40569	26949	13070	31747	15224	42597
				2	1		2		1
				23181	12354		26330		16840
		1	1	4	3	4		6	6
		1650	2300	14400	9345	7334		9722	22754
	5	31	5	50	54	19	90	68	58
	2168	3088	2298	2988	5250	5736	5417	5502	3003
	7.11	11.46	9.55	32.93	38.58	42.33	26.40	21.50	20.37
	6.45	10.02	8.67	31.91	36.73	41.20	25.70	17.28	13.45
	6.45	10.02	8.67	31.35	36.73	41.20	13.70	17.28	13.45
	3.15	6.98	5.60	23.05	26.67	37.67	22.00	16.80	9.81
	6.00	10.02	8.22	30.87	35.94	41.20	13.34	19.04	11.46
		9.08	0.77	19.65	54.53	5.73	49.70	3.87	4.10
	78	23	55	110	77	27	134	405	152
	40.49	146.45	41.21	135.77	481.09	72.35	201.77	197.00	525.47
								15	276
	417	165	214	695	4086	870	1409	936	1300
	5.90	1.11	11.58	6.84	49.76	11.37	11.32	13.56	18.47
	670	7860	4875	54689	40110	23059	15733	20185	46120
	600	1600	1305	11776	17100	10280	7878	6900	7590
	36	4360	2500	28324	8700	5788	2162	4920	5640
	34	1400	750	10199	4010	1603	1836	7865	25110

表6—15 各县(市)、区林业生产情况(2012)
Basic Statistics on Forestry by Region

指标	Indicators	全市 Total	海曙 Haishu	江北 Jiangbei
营林情况（公顷）	**Afforestation (hectare)**			
造林面积合计(公顷)	Total Afforestation Area(hectare)	2990		159
按方式分	By Way of Afforestation			
当年人工造林面积	Area of Afforest artificially in this Year	2990		159
按用途分	By Use of Afforestation			
经济林	Economic Forest	910		
防护林	Shelter Forest	1935		159
迹地更新面积	Area of Forest Updating	396		
封山育林面积	Area of Afforestation in Enclosed Mountain	95123		3061
零星(四旁)植树（万株）	Planting Trees Piecemeal(10000 trees)	163		3
育苗面积(公顷)	Area of Growing Seedings(hectare)	200793		374
未成林抚育作业面积	Unpaired Forest Tending Operations Area	4286		
成林抚育面积	Area of Grown Forest Cultivated	7641		267
其中:中、幼龄林抚育面积	In, Young Forest Tending Area	7355		267
低产林改造面积	Area of Transform Low Yield Forest	326		
抚育改造出材量（立方米）	Output of Transform and Foster (Cubic Meter)			
主要林产品产量(吨)	**Output of Major Forest Products (ton)**			
笋罐头	Bamboo Can			
板栗	Chestnut	996		
竹笋干	Dried Bamboo Shoots	15847		385
竹壳	Shell of Bamboo	250		
白果	Gingko	210		
毛料	Bamboo			
人造板原料	Artificial Plank			

注:本表数据来自宁波市林业局。

Note:Data in this tables are obtained from Ningbo Municipal Bureau of Forestry.

各县(市)、区 by Region								
北 仑 Beilun	镇海 Zhenhai	大榭 Daxie	鄞州 Yinzhou	余姚 Yuyao	慈溪 Cixi	奉化 Fenghua	象山 Xiangshan	宁海 Ninghai
80	149	5	704	410	512	275	420	276
80	149	5	704	410	512	275	420	276
			42	30	290	204	159	185
80	149		662	380	222	71	167	45
12		7	38	30	10	87	80	102
667			18569	1666		40350	30000	270
5	1		10	20	20.0	13.0	50	40
4085	233		1971	3750	2306	7066	730	67
180		121		85			1500	2400
790	35	96	2000	1606	233	2067	133	280
600	35		2000	1606	233	2067	133	280
		16		46		103	161	
13			115	600		228	40	
179	120		1190	3875	985	5632	501	2920
							250	
			60			150		

表 6－16　各县(市)、区茶叶和水果生产情况(2012)
Basic Statistics on Tea and Fruits Production by Region

指标	Indicators	全市 Total	市区 Urban District	海曙 Haishu	江东 Jiangdong
茶叶生产	**Tea**				
茶园总面积(公顷)	**Tea Field Area(hectare)**	**11986**	**3008**		
本年新增	New－added in This Year	69	22		
本年采摘	Pluck in This Year	9740	2376		
茶叶总产量(吨)	**Output of Tea (ton)**	**16604**	**6073**		
春茶	Spring Tea	9086	2967		
夏茶	Summer Tea	4935	1892		
秋茶	Autumn Tea	2583	1214		
水果生产	**Fruits**				
果园面积合计(公顷)	**Area of Orchards(hectare)**	**48145**	**6885**		
柑桔园	Citrus	11604	1768		
梨园	Pears	2873	758		
桃园	Peaches	4504	410		
杨梅园	Red Bayberry	17524	1430		
枇杷园	Loquat	2099	45		
柿子园	Persimmon	287	63		
葡萄园	Grapery	5252	1645		
弥猴桃园	Kiwi Fruit	390	24		
其他果园	Others	3612	742		
水果总产量(吨)	**Output of Fruits (ton)**	**1262397**	**342107**		
柑桔	Citrus	245945	44664		
柑	Mandarin Orange	17491	7863		
桔	Mandarin	226260	35936		
橙	Orange	1215	218		
柚	Shaddock	979	647		
梨	Pears	73773	24150		
桃子	Peaches	65047	5970		
杨梅	Red Bayberry	125803	12407		
枇杷	Loquat	5594	379		
柿子	Persimmon	2902	849		
葡萄	Grapes	133509	36770		
弥猴桃	Kiwi Fruit	1594	124		
果用瓜	Melon Used as Fruits	585974	208490		
其他	Others	22256	8304		

各区 by Districts								
江北 Jiangbei	北仑 Beilun	镇海 Zhenhai	鄞州 Yinzhou	余姚 Yuyao	慈溪 Cixi	奉化 Fenghua	象山 Xiangshan	宁海 Ninghai
244	**495**	**83**	**2186**	**3997**	**260**	**881**	**1172**	**2668**
2	4	1	15	11	5	18		13
226	407	75	1668	3926	250	586	761	1841
94	**492**	**170**	**5317**	**4745**	**146**	**1277**	**1510**	**2853**
51	355	50	2511	2628	140	684	689	1978
37	98	50	1707	1480	2	377	579	605
6	39	70	1099	637	4	216	242	270
1317	**1334**	**972**	**3262**	**7974**	**8244**	**4491**	**12487**	**8064**
112	578	289	789	96	247	642	6229	2622
323	65	31	339	766	505	50	297	497
35	66	12	297	225	325	2636	331	577
240	324	161	705	5001	4277	634	3938	2244
2	4	5	34	4	43	11	1072	924
6	18	2	37	102	29	15	34	44
559	221	278	587	767	2294	156	313	77
11	3		10	42	28	40	21	235
29	55	194	464	971	496	307	252	844
36285	**37538**	**30261**	**238023**	**184886**	**301069**	**83580**	**194922**	**155833**
2886	14069	3079	24630	2406	5850	11135	113585	68305
168	1179	280	6236	392	3321	41	5758	116
2633	12766	2240	18297	1687	2522	10799	107166	68150
85	39		94		7	292	659	39
	85	559	3	327		3	2	
11459	1224	994	10473	24618	14767	645	5124	4469
511	661	159	4639	4321	8096	39797	2314	4549
1443	4286	915	5763	39821	40267	5006	16257	12045
6	49	38	286	5	513	117	3483	1097
68	221	40	520	1206	343	143	261	100
8674	4843	5098	18155	31016	56318	2440	6177	788
9	30		85	59	254	104	110	943
11004	12112	19231	166143	77303	170534	20554	46577	62516
225	43	707	7329	4131	4127	3639	1034	1021

表 6－17 各县(市)、区畜牧业生产情况(2012)
Basic Statistics on Animal Husbandry By Region

指标	Indicators	全市 Total	市区 Urban District	海曙 Haishu
生猪（万只）	**Hogs (10000 heads)**			
年末存栏头数(含未断奶小猪)	Being Raised at Year－end	117.52	26.59	
＃能繁殖的母猪	Reproducable	11.31	2.54	
年内肥猪出栏头数	Slaughtered Fattened Hogs	182.62	51.97	
全年饲养量	Number of Hogs Raised	300.14	78.56	
牛(头)	**Cattles & Buffaloes(head)**			
年末存栏头数	Being Raised at Year－end	18253	5583	
＃良种及改良种乳牛	Milch Cows of Fine Breed and Improved Varieties	7719	4171	
年内出栏头数	Slaughtered Cattles & Buffaloes of the Year	8965	2279	
羊(万只)	**Sheep & Goat(10000 heads)**			
年末存栏只数	Being Raised at Year－end	9.06	0.97	
年内出栏只数	Slaughtered Sheep & Goat of the Year	9.28	1.19	
家禽（万只）	**Poultry(10000 heads)**			
年末存栏只数	Being Raised at Year－end	1410.07	314.10	
年内出栏只数	Slaughtered Poultry of the Year	2994.65	776.95	
兔（万只）	**Rabbits (10000 heads)**			
年末存栏只数	Being Raised at Year－end	47.18	9.43	
年内出栏只数	Slaughtered Rabbits	80.61	21.35	
养蜂年末箱数(箱)	**Number of Beehives(box)**	**94277**	**3041**	
畜禽产品产量（吨）	**Output of Livestock Production(ton)**			
肉类产量	Output of Meat	212430	53399	
猪肉	Pork	157209	40837	
牛肉	Beef	1560	376	
羊肉	Mutton	1658	215	
兔肉	Rabbits Meat	1422	386	
禽肉	Poultry Meat	50373	11585	
其他	Others	208		
禽蛋产量	Poultry Eggs	86602	25475	
蜂蜜产量	Honey	8007	239	
蜂皇浆产量(公斤)	Royal Jelly(kg)	290024	11939	
牛奶产量（吨）	Milk (ton)	26822	16391	
兔毛产量	Rabbit Wool	131	4	

各区 by Districts									
江东 Jiangdong	江北 Jiangbei	北仑 Beilun	镇海 Zhenhai	鄞州 Yinzhou	余姚 Yuyao	慈溪 Cixi	奉化 Fenghua	象山 Xiangshan	宁海 Ninghai
1.02	4.75	2.41	2.29	16.12	21.94	22.48	17.31	13.97	15.23
0.12	0.54	0.19	0.09	1.60	2.13	2.00	1.75	1.34	1.55
2.86	5.67	10.63	4.94	27.87	33.18	35.02	22.80	19.86	19.79
3.88	10.42	13.04	7.23	43.99	55.12	57.50	40.11	33.83	35.02
	2384	261	505	2433	2350	978	2026	965	6351
	2304	1	308	1558	1725	612	371		840
	451	376	513	939	431	233	2975	749	2298
	0.05	0.17	0.12	0.63	1.84	2.13	1.19	1.82	1.11
	0.04	0.22	0.31	0.62	2.05	2.33	1.04	1.87	0.80
	65.29	26.32	85.01	137.48	300.83	184.14	175.59	168.82	266.59
	128.38	87.66	297.00	263.91	847.95	320.80	295.97	218.91	534.07
	2.11	1.32	5.41	0.59	17.70	18.68	0.18	1.12	0.07
	1.43	1.67	17.74	0.51	26.40	25.69	1.04	6.06	0.07
	150	**397**	**860**	**1634**	**9473**	**51863**	**4241**	**7273**	**18386**
2558	6755	10684	8161	25241	50506	35507	25217	23636	24165
2558	4627	8925	4124	20603	29195	28290	20528	19615	18744
	69	65	87	155	136	42	486	158	362
	11	46	48	110	473	368	158	328	116
	36	42	295	13	493	429	21	92	1
	2012	1606	3607	4360	20055	6353	4024	3414	4942
					154	25		29	
	5109	1798	6890	11678	8184	9966	17511	10964	14502
	2	12	86	139	938	5262	209	281	1078
	600	2593	1039	7707	30045	199644	11548	16015	20833
	9815		696	5880	3025	2018	2662		2726
			2	2	45	81		1	

表 6－18　各县(市)、区水产品产量及养殖面积(2012)
Output and Area of Artificially Cultured of Aquatic Production by Region

指标	Indicators	全市 Total	市区		
			海曙 Haishu	江东 Jiangdong	江北 Jiangbei
水产品总产量	**Total Aquatic Products**	**991531**			**9418**
海水产品产量	**Seawater Aquatic Products**	**903552**			**8049**
按生产性质分	By Production Character				
海洋捕捞	Catching in Ocean	599481			2100
鱼类	Fish	468596			2100
甲壳类	Shrimps. Prawns and Crabs	69149			
贝类	Shell－Fish	9225			
其他类	Others	10154			
海水养殖	Seawater Aquiculture	276914			
鱼类	Fish	10695			
甲壳类	Shrimps. Prawns and Crabs	42511			
贝类	Shell－Fish	213530			
其他类	Others	2846			
远洋渔业	Pelagic Fishery	27157			5949
淡水产品产量	**Freshwater Aquatic Products**	**87979**			**1369**
按生产性质分	By Production Character				
淡水捕捞	Catching in Freshwater	10389			473
淡水养殖	Freshwater Aquiculture	77590			896
按类别分	By Category				
鱼类	Fish	52175			1221
虾蟹类	Shrimps. Prawns and Crabs	28884			83
贝类	Shell－Fish	1889			14
其他类	Others	5031			51
海水养殖面积(公顷)	**Seawater Aquiculture Area(ha)**	**35899**			
淡水养殖面积(公顷)	**Freshwater Aquiculture Area(ha)**	**23968**			**486**

注:本表数据来自宁波市海洋渔业局。

Data in this tables are obtained from Ningbo Municipal Bureau of Ocean and Fishery.

单位：吨(ton)

Urban Districts			余姚 Yuyao	慈溪 Cixi	奉化 Fenghua	象山 Xiangshan	宁海 Ninghai
北仑 Beilun	镇海 Zhenhai	鄞州 Yinzhou					
4217	**904**	**18821**	**31679**	**50590**	**136334**	**582441**	**146404**
3130	**297**	**7538**	**1949**	**25733**	**132982**	**572145**	**141006**
2125	297	2786	1753	4711	125613	449863	10093
1444	223	1254	641	1185	108028	350453	3128
671	14	179	541	754	3095	60656	3239
6	8		439	2580	721	2306	3165
	52	1263	59	192	7576	1012	
1005		4752	196	21022	7369	111657	130913
			53	1469	1742	5448	1983
277		2049	143	7064	1666	15065	16247
728		2560		11970	2547	83077	112648
				96	144	2606	
						10625	
1087	**607**	**11283**	**29730**	**24857**	**3352**	**10296**	**5398**
470	115	3876	2364	2136	719		236
617	492	7407	27366	22721	2633	10296	5162
920	585	8787	21162	12253	2230	2342	2675
114	14	1166	4181	11957	878	7461	3030
53	5	507	765	413	106		26
	3	823	3622	234	138	160	
454		**1020**	**30**	**6721**	**1651**	**10833**	**15190**
414	**851**	**4289**	**5507**	**5958**	**1677**	**2700**	**2086**

表 6－19 各县(市)、区农村能源和农业物资消耗情况(2012)
Consumption of Energy and Agriculture Materials in Rural Areas by Region

指标	Indicators	全市 Total	市区 Urban District	海曙 Haishu
农村用电量 (万千瓦小时)	**Electricity Consumed for Rural (10000 kwh)**	**1738039**	**584582**	
农用化肥施用量	**Agricultural Consumption of Chemical Fertilizers**			
按实物量计算	Calculated by Fact Use	363999	110409	
氮肥	Nitrogenous Fertilizer	171512	43956	
磷肥	Phosphate Fertilizer	74673	26446	
钾肥	Potash Fertilizer	29122	14749	
复合肥	Compound Fertilizer	88692	25258	
按折纯法计算	Calculated by Pure Consumption	111774	28398	
氮肥	Nitrogenous Fertilizer	52998	9730	
磷肥	Phosphate Fertilizer	16034	5036	
钾肥	Potash Fertilizer	8702	3881	
复合肥	Compound Fertilizer	34040	9751	
农用塑料薄膜使用量	**Plastic Film Use for Agriculture**	**10634**	**2309**	
#地膜使用量	Use of Plastic Film	5007	1276	
地膜覆盖面积 (公顷)	Overcast Area of Plastic Film (hectate)	24305	8751	
农用柴油	**Consumption of Diesel Oil**	**344022**	**12331**	
农药使用量	**Consumption of Pesticide**	**7492**	**1822**	

单位:吨(ton)

各区 by Districts									
江东 Jiangdong	江北 Jiangbei	北仑 Beilun	镇海 Zhenhai	鄞州 Yinzhou	余姚 Yuyao	慈溪 Cixi	奉化 Fenghua	象山 Xiangshan	宁海 Ninghai
23	**15513**	**35810**	**77116**	**456120**	**243328**	**655674**	**112041**	**51011**	**91403**
	22469	5875	3003	79062	42315	95579	56933	31320	27443
	8583	1839	985	32549	24812	36745	31119	19450	15430
	4893	1287	825	19441	3365	24626	10076	5775	4385
	2517	100	507	11625	517	8625	3773	1130	328
	6476	2649	686	15447	13621	25583	11965	4965	7300
	4970	2416	974	20038	12685	25906	20648	12998	11139
	1910	700	285	6835	5705	10288	12626	8169	6480
	947	450	140	3499	605	4925	1814	2079	1575
	689	42	243	2907	130	3019	943	565	164
	1424	1224	306	6797	6245	7674	5265	2185	2920
	344	**120**	**305**	**1540**	**274**	**5257**	**534**	**1240**	**1020**
	138	40	86	1012	82	2275	274	850	250
	954	180	559	7058	542	8234	1885	2660	2233
9	**274**	**5716**	**2386**	**3946**	**8808**	**8733**	**104351**	**205085**	**4714**
	142	**145**	**482**	**1053**	**2174**	**997**	**541**	**950**	**1008**

主要统计指标解释

【农林牧渔业总产值】 指以货币表现的农、林、牧、渔业全部产品的总量。它反映一定时期内农业生产总规模和总成果。

农林牧渔业的统计范围是：

⑴ 农业 包括种植业和其他农业。

⑵ 林业 包括林木的载培(不包括茶园、桑园和果园的栽培、管理和收获等活动)、林产品的采集和村及村以下合作经济和农户的竹木采伐。

⑶ 牧业 包括除渔业养殖以外的一切动物饲养和放牧以及野生动物的捕猎和饲养。

⑷ 渔业 包括水生动物和海藻类植物的养殖和捕捞。

农林牧渔业总产值的计算方法通常是按农林牧渔产品及其副产品的产量分别乘以各自单位产品价格求得，少数生产周期长，当年没有产品或产品产量不易统计，则采用间接方法匡算其产值，然后将四业产品产值相加即为农林牧渔业总产值。

1957 年以前的农业总产值包括了厩肥和农名自给性手工业(如农民自制衣服、鞋、袜，自己从事粮食加工等)。1958 年以后的农业总产值，林业中增加了村以及村以下的竹木采伐产值；牧业取消了厩肥产值；副业中取消了农民自给性手工业产值，增加了村以及村以下的工业产值；渔业中增加了海洋捕捞产品产值。1980 年及以后的农业总产值，在副业中增加了农民家庭兼营工业商品部分的产值。从 1984 年起村以及村以下半工业产值划归工业。从 1993 年起，取消副业，将野生动物的捕猎划入牧业。2010 年起野生植物采集从农业划入林业，坚果从林业划入农业。

【粮食产量】 指全社会的产量。包括国有经济经营的、集体统一经营的和农民家庭经营的粮食产量，还包括工矿企业办的农场和其他生产单位的产量。粮食除包括稻、小麦、玉米、高粱、谷子及其他杂粮外，还包括薯类和豆类。其产量计算方法，豆类按去豆荚后的干豆计算；薯类(番薯和马铃薯，不包括芋头和木薯) 1963 年以前按每 4 公斤鲜薯折 1 公斤粮食计算，从 1964 年开始及以后改为按 5 公斤鲜薯折 1 公斤粮食计算。其他粮食一律按脱粒后的原粮计算。2008 年起马铃薯从蔬菜中划出 5 折 1 后作为粮食统计。

【油料产量】 指全部油料作物的生产量。包括花生、油菜籽、芝麻、向日葵籽、胡麻籽(亚麻籽)和其他油料。不包括大豆，也不包括木本油料和野生油料。花生以带壳干花生计算。

【水产品产量】 指人工养殖的水产品和天然生长的水产品的捕捞量。包括海水的鱼类、虾蟹类、贝类和藻类以及内陆水域的鱼类、虾蟹类和贝类，不包括淡水生植物。

【猪、牛、羊肉产量】 指当年出栏并已屠宰后除去头蹄下水后带骨肉(即胴体重)的重量。

【农作物播种面积】 指实际播种或移植有农作物的面积。凡是实际种植有农作物的面积，不论种植在耕地上还是种植在非耕地上，均包括在农作物播种面积中，同时还包括因遭灾而重新改种和补种的农作物面积。

【农用化肥施用量】 指本年内实际用于农业生产的化肥数量。包括氮肥、磷肥、钾肥和复合肥。化肥施用量要求按折纯量计算数量。折纯法化肥施用量是把氮肥、磷肥和钾肥分别按含氮、含五氧化二磷、含氧化钾的百分之一百成份折算后的数量。复合肥按其所含主要成分折算。

【农业机械总动力】 指主要用于农、林、牧、渔业的各种动力机械的动力总和。包括耕作机械、排灌机械、收获机械、农产品加工机械、运输机械、植物保护机械、牧业机械、林业机械、渔业机械和其他农业机械[内燃机按引擎马力折成瓦(特)计算，电动机按功率折成瓦(特)计算]。不包括专门用于乡、镇、村、组办工业、基本建设、非农业运输、科学试验和教学等非农业生产方面用的动力机械与作业机械。

Explanatory Notes on Main Statistical Indicators

【Gross Output Value of Farming, Forestry, Animal Husbandry and Fishery】 refers to the total volume of products of farming, forestry, animal husbandry and fishery in value terms, which reflects the total scale and total result of agricultural production during a given period of time.

The statistical coverage of farming, forestry, animal husbandry and fishery is as follows:

(1) Farming includes cultivation of farm crops and other agricultural activities.

(2) Forestry refers to planting trees of various kinds (excluding tea plantations, mulberry fields and orchards), gathering of the forest products, and cutting and felling of bamboo and trees by villages and other cooperative organizations under villages.

(3) Animal Husbandry refers to raising and grazing of all animals except fishery and aquaculture, and hunting and raising of wild animals.

(4) Fishery refers to cultivation and catching of fish and other aquatic animals and cultivation and collection of seaweed and other aquatic plants.

Gross output value of farming, forestry, animal husbandry and fishery is obtained by first multiplying the output of each product by its price, resulting in the output of each single item. For a small number of products, animal output of which is not available or difficult to get due to the long production/growing process involved, the output value is estimated through an indirect approach. The sum of output value of all products of farming, forestry, animal husbandry and fishery is then equal to their gross output value.

Prior to 1957, China's gross agricultural output value included barnyard manure and handicraft products for self—consumption (clothes, shoes, stockings, and initial grain processing undertaken by peasants). Since 1958, cutting and felling of bamboo and trees by villages and other cooperative organizations under villages have been included in forestry. ; value of barnyard manure has been excluded from animal husbandry; self—consumed handicrafts have been excluded from sideline occupations, while the output value of industries run by villages and cooperative organizations under village has been included in sideline occupations and the out put value of fish catches by motor fishing boats has been added to fishery. Since 1980, the value of handicraft products made for sale by individual in the households has been added to sideline occupations. Since 1984, industries run by villages and cooperatives organizations under villagers have been included in the sector of industry. Since 1993, the subdivision of sideline occupations has been canceled, and the hunting of wild animals has been classified into animal husbandry, Since 1993, the subdivision of sideline occupations has been canceled, and the hunting of wild animals has been classified into animal husbandry. Since 2010, collection of wild plants has been classified from agriculture into forestry, nuts from forestry into agriculture..

【Grain Yield】 refers to the yield in the whole country including grains produced by state farms, collective units, industrial enterprises and mines. Grain includes rice, wheat, corn, sorghum, millet and other miscellaneous grains as well as tubers and beans. Output of beans refers to dry beans without pods. The output of tubers (potatoes, do not including taros and cassava) was converted into that of grain at the ratio 4:1,I. e. Four kilograms of fresh tubers was equivalent to one kilogram of grain up to 1963. Since 1964 the ratio for conversion has been 5:1. Output of all other grains refers to husked grain. Since 2008, potato has been classified from vegetables into food crops at the ratio 5:1.

【Yield of Oil—bearing Crops】 refers to the total yield of oil bearing crops of various kinds, including peanuts, (dry, in shell) rapeseeds, sesame, sunflower seeds, flax seeds, and other oil bearing crops. Soybeans, oil bearing woody plants, and wild oil—bearing crops are not included.

【Output of Aquatic Products】 refers to catches of both artificially cultured and naturally grown aquatic products, including fish, shrimps, crabs and shellfish in sea and inland water as well as seaweed. Freshwater plants are not included.

【Output of Pork, Beef, and Mutton】 refers to the meat of slaughtered hogs, cattle, sheep and goats with head, feet, and offal taken away.

【Sown Area of Crops】 refers to area of land sown or transplanted with crops regardless of being in cultivated area or non cultivated area. Area of land re sown due to natural disasters is also included, every sown hectare is calculated.

【Consumption of Chemical Fertilizers in Agriculture】 refers to the quantity of chemical fertilizers applied in agriculture in the year, including nitrogenous fertilizer, phosphate fertilizer ,potash fertilizer and compound fertilizer. The consumption of chemical fertilizers is required in calculation to convert the gross weight into weight containing 100% effective component(e. g. 100% nitrogen content in nitrogenous fertilizer, 100% phosphorous pentoxide contents in phosphate fertilizer, 100% potassium oxide contents in potash fertilizer). Compound fertilizer is converted with its major component.

【Total Power of Farm Machinery】 refers to total mechanical power of machinery used in farming, forestry, animal husbandry, and fishery, including ploughing, irrigation and drainage, harvesting, transport, plant protection, stock breeding, forestry and fishery. The power of internal combustion engines is required to convert horsepower into watts and the power of electric motors is required to be converted into watts. Machinery employed for non agricultural purposes, such as the machines used in township run and village run industry, construction, non agricultural transport, scientific experiments and teaching, is excluded.

NINGBO

Statistical YearBook

第七篇

工业、能源消费和电力

INDUSTRY, ENERGY CONSUMPTION AND ELECTRICITY

工业、能源消费和电力
Industry, Energy Consumption and Electricity

主要统计指标
Major Statistics Indicators

2012年规模以上工业企业数	Number of Industrial Enterprises Above The Set Scale	6804	家	unit
比上年增长	Increase Over Last Year	2.8	%	
2012年规模以上工业总产值	Output Value of Industrial Enterprises Above The Set Scale	121550760	万元	10000 yuan
比上年增长	Increase Over Last Year	0.9	%	
2012年规模以上工业销售产值	Gross Industrial Products Sales of Industrial Enterprises Above The Set Scale	117880641	万元	10000 yuan
比上年增长	Increase Over Last Year	0.0	%	
2012年规模以上工业实现利税	Total Profits and Taxes of Industrial Enterprises Above The Set Scale	11128603	万元	10000 yuan
比上年增长	Increase Over Last Year	−6.7	%	
2012年规模以上工业实现利润	Total Profits of Industrial Enterprises Above The Set Scale	5532121	万元	10000 yuan
比上年增长	Increase Over Last Year	−12.4	%	
2012年规模以上应交增值税	Value−added Taxes Payable of Industrial Enterprises Above The Set Scale	3007829	万元	10000 yuan
比上年增长	Increase Over Last Year	0.9	%	

表 7-1 部分年份规模以上工业企业单位数
Number of Industrial Enterprises Designated Size in Partial Years

单位:个(unit)

指标	Indicators	2008	2009	2010	2011	2012
工业企业单位数	**Number of Industrial Enterprises**	**12120**	**12059**	**12492**	**6616**	**6804**
按轻重工业分	**By Light and Heavy Industry**					
轻工业	Light Industry	5302	5313	5392	2792	2801
重工业	Heavy Industry	6818	6746	7100	3824	4003
按注册登记类型分	**By Registered Type**					
国有企业	State-owned Enterprises	34	36	36	32	36
集体企业	Collective-owned Enterprises	110	90	80	26	23
股份合作企业	Share Cooperative Enterprises	169	152	59	18	25
联营企业	Joint-owned	5	7	6	2	1
有限责任公司	Limited Liability Corporations	1015	915	886	540	546
股份有限公司	Share-holding Corporations Ltd.	158	140	140	101	109
私营企业	Private Enterprises	7397	7643	8325	3715	3958
港、澳、台商投资公司	Hongkong,Macao and Taiwan Funded	1577	1536	1529	1163	1118
外商投资企业公司	Enterprises with Foreign Investment	1588	1490	1431	1019	983
在总计中:亏损企业	Of the Total:Loss Making Enterprises	2201	1836	1377	826	1034
在总计中:国有及国有控股	Of the Total:State-owned and State-holding	101	103	99	91	97
按规模分	**By Enterprises Size**					
大型企业	Large-Sized	31	28	35	108	107
中型企业	Medium-Sized	959	900	1014	1086	1005
小型企业	Small-Sized	11130	11131	11443	5352	5539

注:2011 年起,规模以上工业企业为年主营业务收入 2000 万元及以上的企业,下表同。

Note:From 2011,Industrial enterprises above designated size are those with annual revenue from principal business over 20 million yuan. The others table are the same.

表 7－2 部分年份规模以上工业企业总产值
Gross Output Value of Industrial Enterprises Above Designated Size in Partial Years

单位:万元(10000 yuan)

指标	Indicators	2008	2009	2010	2011	2012
工业总产值	**Gross Industrial Output Value**	**87463573**	**82728469**	**108535474**	**120447699**	**121550760**
按轻重工业分	**By Light and Heavy Industry**					
轻工业	Light Industry	28147769	27927737	34112854	34683454	34049449
重工业	Heavy Industry	59315804	54800732	74422621	85764245	87501311
按注册登记类型分	**By Registered Type**					
国有企业	State－owned Enterprises	5384198	5803085	7193904	8013730	8547018
集体企业	Collective－owned Enterprises	248770	175097	193152	170815	111059
股份合作企业	Share Cooperative Enterprises	634747	597211	163059	106743	137049
联营企业	Joint－owned	17993	20919	20762	11779	9128
有限责任公司	Limited Liability Corporations	9907107	8161975	11145328	12189111	12142989
股份有限公司	Share－holding Corporations Ltd.	11698043	9730314	13630949	17468406	17252477
私营企业	Private Enterprises	22167160	23084430	31749621	31028632	32872411
港、澳、台商投资公司	Hongkong,Macao and Taiwan Funded	17862727	18902072	24131396	29448789	28862744
外商投资企业公司	Enterprises with Foreign Investment	19100597	15881040	20307304	22009694	21553507
在总计中:亏损企业	Of the Total:Loss Making Enterprises	24725212	9972888	5055244	10908447	13314051
在总计中:国有及国有控股	Of the Total:State－owned and State－holding	19386936	18245477	24426588	31162756	30369003
按规模分	**By Enterprises Size**					
大型企业	Large－Sized	18268566	14772479	21449940	38131433	40247278
中型企业	Medium－Sized	31190497	30988021	40851033	39522112	36402444
小型企业	Small－Sized	38004509	36967970	46234502	42444047	43739373

注:工业总产值按现行价格计算。

Note:Gross industrial output value are calculated at current prices.

表 7－3 部分年份规模以上工业企业销售产值 Sales Value of Industrial Enterprises Above Designated Size in Partial Years

单位:万元(10000 yuan)

指标	Indicators	2008	2009	2010	2011	2012
工业销售产值	**Gross Industrial Products Sales**	**84916407**	**80492735**	**105629245**	**117898629**	**117880641**
按轻重工业分	**By Light and Heavy Industry**					
轻工业	Light Industry	27164405	27109132	33032063	33639832	33104213
重工业	Heavy Industry	57752002	53383603	72597182	84258797	84776428
按注册登记类型分	**By Registered Type**					
国有企业	State－owned Enterprises	5387102	58800116	7189224	8017179	8536128
集体企业	Collective－owned Enterprises	244297	171398	187285	165908	111743
股份合作企业	Share Cooperative Enterprises	621003	582031	160539	102713	131655
联营企业	Joint－owned	17848	20767	20716	11688	9125
有限责任公司	Limited Liability Corporations	9527744	7895091	10887393	11969274	11928565
股份有限公司	Share－holding Corporations Ltd.	11565407	9687753	13387235	17376222	16889319
私营企业	Private Enterprises	21498582	22234379	30779754	29950680	31394168
港、澳、台商投资公司	Hongkong,Macao and Taiwan Funded	17099786	18275721	23226285	28642232	28044561
外商投资企业公司	Enterprises with Foreign Investment	18520462	15462333	19790814	21662734	20772067
在总计中:亏损企业	Of the Total:Loss Making Enterprises	24169447	9717038	4896009	10657194	13013311
在总计中:国有及国有控股	Of the Total:State－owned and State－holding	19119592	18054011	24149681	31299012	30125079
按规模分	**By Enterprises Size**					
大型企业	Large－Sized	17712614	14575048	20807766	37600731	38897059
中型企业	Medium－Sized	30287582	29984116	39727953	38561314	35321924
小型企业	Small－Sized	36916211	35933571	45093526	41391137	42512942

注:工业销售产值按现行价格计算。

Note:Sales value of industrial products are calculated at current prices.

表 7－4　规模以下工业企业及个体工业单位主要经济指标(2012) Main Economic Indicators of Industrial Enterprises Below Designated Size and Private and Individuals

指标	单位	Indicators	Unit	总计 Total
总计		**Total**		
企业(单位)数	个	Number of Enterprises(unit)	unit	117426
期末从业人员	人	Total Employees at Year－end	person	1539373
工业总产值	万元	Gross Industrial Output Value	10000 yuan	35551071
资产总计	万元	Total Asset	10000 yuan	27476363
企业主要经济指标		**Main Economic Indicators of Enterprises**		
企业数	个	Number of Enterprises(unit)	unit	41555
期末从业人员	人	Total Employees at Year－end	person	911498
工业总产值	万元	Gross Industrial Output Value	10000 yuan	21096005
主营业务收入	万元	Prime Operating Revenue	10000 yuan	20887134
#出口产品销售收入	万元	Export Sales Revenue	10000 yuan	4016785
主营业务成本	万元	Operating Costs	10000 yuan	17953504
税金总额	万元	Total Taxes	10000 yuan	1091024
#所得税	万元	Income Taxes	10000 yuan	189441
营业利润	万元	Business Profits	10000 yuan	1036287
应付职工薪酬	万元	Employee Compensation Payable	10000 yuan	2653859
本年折旧	万元	Depreciation	10000 yuan	702108
资产总计	万元	Total Asset	10000 yuan	21420947
负债合计	万元	Total Liabilities	10000 yuan	11553302
固定资产原值	万元	Actual Value of Fixed Assets	10000 yuan	8227381
固定资产净值	万元	Net Fixed Assets	10000 yuan	5382694
应收帐款	万元	Accounts Receivable	10000 yuan	3980118
利息支出	万元	Interest Expense	10000 yuan	339578
#银行借款利息	万元	Interest on Bank Borrowings	10000 yuan	319432
民间借款利息	万元	Civil Borrowing Interest	10000 yuan	20146
期末剩余订单额	万元	Final Remaining Orders	10000 yuan	1092005
生产能力(设备)利用率	%	Capacity Utilization	%	79.53
个体工业主要经济指标		**Main Economic Indicators of Individuals**		
单位数	个	Number of Units	unit	75871
期末从业人员	人	Total Employees at Year－end	person	627875
营业收入	万元	Operating Revenue	10000 yuan	14455065
生产支出	万元	Production Expenditure	10000 yuan	10744744
应付职工薪酬	万元	Employee Compensation Payable	10000 yuan	1843641
资产总计	万元	Total Asset	10000 yuan	6055416

表 7-5 历年工业企业主要经济指标
Main Economic Indicators of Industrial Enterprises Over the Years

单位：亿元 万人(100 million yuan, 10000 persons)

年份 Year	总产值(当年价) Gross Industrial Output Value (current prices)	固定资产原值 Original Value of Fixed Assets	固定资产净值 Net Value of Fixed Assets	主营业务收入 Prime Operating Revenue	利税总额 Total Profits and Taxes	利润总额 Total Profits	全部从业人员年平均人数 Annual Average Employees
1978	15.79	7.07			4.29	2.59	
1979	18.11	8.25	6.28	18.71	4.73	2.86	
1980	23.73	9.59	7.35	24.89	6.17	3.93	
1981	29.67	11.38	8.76	30.05	6.94	4.26	
1982	29.99	13.53	10.49	32.36	7.99	4.86	
1983	35.23	15.84	12.17	38.98	9.07	5.57	
1984	50.93	21.09	16.67	54.57	11.30	6.53	
1985	68.63	32.55	26.43	76.16	14.62	7.65	65.48
1986	81.96	38.43	30.49	86.67	15.86	7.94	68.69
1987	102.16	52.61	41.79	110.96	18.54	9.92	71.29
1988	132.17	62.81	48.85	147.85	23.24	12.00	72.06
1989	159.41	74.80	56.60	162.81	23.64	11.47	69.05
1990	200.00	89.31	64.39	167.35	20.99	8.21	67.71
1991	261.62	107.17	79.45	218.15	25.27	11.79	72.02
1992	341.42	128.57	95.03	282.90	31.65	14.82	73.15
1993	491.07	192.06	147.38	430.65	45.15	22.68	73.94
1994	642.18	276.98	225.18	480.46	53.56	26.06	71.53
1995	837.80	357.05	281.28	664.70	62.61	29.46	66.08
1996	843.48	407.73	312.70	722.15	66.57	28.63	64.60
1997	842.62	496.05	374.92	747.51	78.60	33.32	55.88
1998	940.59	567.09	423.50	835.24	88.00	37.52	50.78
1999	1062.29	668.71	490.07	985.32	118.65	61.21	52.38
2000	1427.70	829.69	601.93	1350.52	163.26	88.11	58.42
2001	1629.66	926.49	648.50	1538.70	213.72	115.95	66.90
2002	2000.16	1058.90	727.01	1945.02	267.09	152.34	77.22
2003	2630.29	1251.24	854.79	2604.90	322.01	189.30	91.96
2004	3815.04	1602.75	1113.37	3660.69	417.63	241.31	128.94
2005	4890.97	1926.51	1337.30	4698.16	446.13	262.36	140.82
2006	6187.91	2469.35	1755.66	5930.59	525.65	312.63	159.64
2007	7789.01	2886.87	2013.56	7456.24	639.83	387.31	174.24
2008	8746.36	3422.49	2363.23	8283.18	489.32	221.25	178.59
2009	8272.85	3908.81	2633.33	7824.88	867.35	462.11	168.67
2010	10853.55	4431.40	2920.36	10396.63	1160.55	657.77	181.09
2011	12044.77	4543.83		11803.24	1193.21	631.66	152.25
2012	12155.08	4792.65		11795.98	1112.86	553.21	147.06

注：1997年以前为乡及乡以上独立核算工业企业。1998年及以后为规模以上工业企业。

Note: Data in this table refer to all industrial enterprises with annual revenue from principal business over 5 million yuan, before 1997 to enterprises with independent accounting at townships and above level.

表 7-6　全市及各县(市)、区规模以上工业企业总产值(现行价格、2012)
Gross Output Value of Industrial Enterprises Above Designated Size by Region (at Current Price)

指标	Indicators	全市 Toal	市区 Urban District	海曙 Haishu
工业总产值	**Gross Industrial Output Value**	**121550760**	**81133945**	**3302908**
按轻重工业分	**Grouped by Light and Heavy Industry**			
轻工业	Light Industry	34049449	18132831	257172
重工业	Heavy Industry	87501311	63001113	3045735
按注册登记类型分	**Grouped by Registered Type**			
国有企业	State－owned Enterprises	8547018	5404435	2933758
集体企业	Collective－owned Enterpriese	111059	59477	10195
股份合作企业	Share Cooperative Enterprises	137049	75316	
联营企业	Joint Owned Enterprises	9128	9128	
有限责任公司	Limited Liability Corporations	12142989	9044875	214822
股份有限公司	Share－holding Corporations Ltd.	17252477	15147526	21030
私营企业	Private Enterprises	32872411	12741034	24047
港澳台商投资企业	Hong Kong. Macao & Taiwan Funded	28862744	21785497	91750
外商投资企业	Foreign Funded Enterprises	21553507	16825322	7305
在总计中:亏损企业	Of the Total:Loss Making Enterprises	13314051	9697922	12866
在总计中:国有及国有控股	Of the Total:State－owned and State－holding	30369003	26890591	2933758
按规模分	**Grouped by Enterprises Size**			
大型企业	Large－Sized	40247278	33049287	2910345
中型企业	Medium－Sized	36402444	21784977	217815
小型企业	Small－Sized	43739373	25381251	169361
按工业行业分	**Grouped by Sector**			
黑色金属矿采选业	Ferrous Metals Mining and Dressing			
非金属矿采选业	Non－metallic Mining Industry	2600	2600	
农副食品加工业	Farm and Sideline Products Processing	1542863	704391	
食品制造业	Food Manufacturing	806733	236032	21817
酒、饮料和精制茶制造业	Wine, Beverages and Refined Tea Manufacturing	302647	177746	10635
烟草制品业	Tobacco Manufacturing	1197910	1197910	
纺织业	Textile Industry	3592043	2401782	69140
纺织服装、服饰业	Clothing, Apparel Industry	5904017	4361552	66004

单位:万元(10000 yuan)

各区 by Districts					余姚 Yuyao	慈溪 Cixi	奉化 Fenghua	象山 Xiangshan	宁海 Ninghai
江东 Jiangdong	江北 Jiangbei	北仑 Beilun	镇海 Zhenhai	鄞州 Yinzhou					
1990747	**3909288**	**18409603**	**22077352**	**19810205**	**11275033**	**16089841**	**3536980**	**4351251**	**5163711**
1405240	639941	3752813	1694512	9637079	4078814	7093185	1250908	1515349	1978361
585507	3269347	14656790	20382840	10173126	7196219	8996655	2286072	2835901	3185350
1312650	29279	531413	72496	524839	573999	555996	148717	668189	1195683
		4308	17263	27711	23294	16551	5386		6350
10232	37371	6324	3370	10290		38974		20752	2008
				9128					
82998	1084961	2843267	1454825	2118249	831502	1383345	148496	322912	411860
2351	807881	158322	12639548	1325355	800775	679829	28353	414527	181467
147436	968512	927593	2595688	7669035	5032766	8968559	1797271	1874964	2457818
421601	493175	8823142	2609703	5747903	2563336	2642892	975936	447457	447625
13479	488110	5115234	2684459	2375492	1449361	1786946	432822	598157	460900
84397	452166	4407704	2071734	1109418	755802	1425591	364110	439855	630771
1312650	94733	3951601	14172407	604949	686638	562468	160185	752792	1316329
1304868	802012	5467524	12917965	3817377	1360706	3233520	688447	337096	1578222
419569	1686435	5971626	3610377	6102066	3858200	6039932	1009554	2158679	1551102
257994	1414753	6932105	5081500	9543650	5939526	6748031	1811981	1830013	2028571
				2600					
3640	34547	399356	3309	154404	306329	170564	69186	280052	12341
	46471	63679	39791	53991	394319	20677	39920	57370	58415
	3876	108168	12470	42597	44625		37036	17653	25588
1197910									
	166098	689570	484139	970145	406003	524842	45592	125013	88811
69171	63770	1131409	68573	2911591	36807	131864	491218	795265	87311

表 7－6 续表 Continued

指标	Indicators	全市 Toal	市区 Urban District	海曙 Haishu
皮革、毛皮、羽毛及其制品和制鞋业	Leather, Fur, Feather and Its Products and Footwear Industry	130099	71954	
木材加工及木、竹、藤、棕、草制品业	Timber Processing, Bamboo, Rattan, Cane Palm, and Straw Products	159035	94763	
家具制造业	Furniture Manufacturing	724544	416321	
造纸及纸制品业	Paper－making and Paper Products Manufacturing	1688271	1142986	
印刷和记录媒介复制业	Printing and Record Duplicating	634497	530472	5669
文教、工美、体育和娱乐用品制造业	Culture, Art, Sports and Recreation Supplies Manufacturing	2254277	1175154	
石油加工、炼焦和核燃料加工业	Petroleum Processing. Coking & Nuclear Fuel Processing	15207781	15196637	
化学原料和化学制品制造业	Raw Chemical Materials and Chemical Products	12688180	11154026	
医药制造业	Medicines Manufacturing	502382	356068	7342
化学纤维制造业	Chemical Fiber Manufacturing	1732548	231616	
橡胶和塑料制品业	Rubber and Plastic Products Industry	3481399	1641391	7802
非金属矿物制品业	Nonmetal Mineral Products	1887257	1059562	
黑色金属冶炼和压延加工业	Smelting and Pressing of Ferrous Metals	5589887	4020814	341
有色金属冶炼和压延加工业	Smelting and Pressing of Nonferrous Metals	5227581	2916604	3443
金属制品业	Metal Products Manufacturing	3621538	2155540	3869
通用设备制造业	General Purpose Equipment Manufacturing	6785764	3712307	11107
专用设备制造业	Special Purpose Equipment Manufacturing	3376023	2151868	6892
汽车制造业	Automobile Manufacturing	5902229	3528778	21056
铁路、船舶、航空航天和其他运输设备制造业	Railroad, Marine, Aviation and Other Transport Equipment Manufacturing	1678644	602429	
电气机械和器材制造业	Electric Equipment and Machinery Manufacturing	14185855	5180337	69601
计算机、通信和其他电子设备制造业	Computer, Communications and Other Electronic Equipment Manufacturing	8635925	7224046	62825
仪器仪表制造业	Instrument Manufacturing	1694974	714253	6654
其他制造业	Other Manufacturing	484230	171655	
废弃资源综合利用业	Waste Comprehensive Utilization of Resources Industry	986543	966574	
金属制品、机械和设备修理业	Metal Products, Machinery and Equipment Repair Industry	60797	14007	
电力、热力的生产和供应业	Production and Supply Electric Power and Thermal Power	8491271	5354213	2809261
燃气生产和供应业	Production and Supply Gas	159250	134358	119451
水的生产和供应业	Production and Supply Tap Water	231166	133201	

单位:万元(10000 yuan)

各区 by Districts					余姚 Yuyao	慈溪 Cixi	奉化 Fenghua	象山 Xiangshan	宁海 Ninghai
江东 Jiangdong	江北 Jiangbei	北仑 Beilun	镇海 Zhenhai	鄞州 Yinzhou					
2180		7139	22173	35501	12250	19800	15772		10324
			2833	91930	26871	19740	17662		
1503	51964	75721	5899	273083	217441	51900	9283	13513	16087
2262	4861	531503	45326	551666	119469	258174	41477	43437	82729
2232	9336	53783	5878	450483	55734	27955	18029		2307
3416	84920	295107	51651	707743	110325	270097	45507	11845	641350
		27342	12529140	10182			6755	4389	
	120269	5031478	3372010	660615	463059	885610	73667	29986	81832
	15551	48027	93750	184062	15078	49994	53083	13297	14864
		69579	141055	20982	170330	1266372	17787	43229	3215
5660	108881	275222	202610	998912	733092	604708	139061	79023	284125
	165446	246945	125315	490159	343189	183072	46229	133469	121736
11142	81072	2585911	387460	687697	541077	618648	274398	86391	48561
44366	1450667	125811	520798	641834	799136	1132338	176970	17782	184752
28243	138799	460457	270875	996547	521209	538655	158651	34145	213338
30437	207475	644951	1000084	1599568	676668	1175964	457563	356811	406451
36319	107777	1129396	310999	490574	604854	213399	34611	191247	180044
11255	294925	1409045	109635	1456293	221587	1030696	111802	594722	414643
7782		364248	83740	88552	36963	357023	462607	196962	22660
24220	419549	681507	483803	2646498	2695107	4681184	292406	516623	820198
398934	148327	479578	280666	1364857	587712	555520	173156	16259	79232
	147886	39090	9404	466264	460019	452686	34700		33316
	29687		39992	95583	57653	204090	29707		21124
		5453	907958	53162		15460		4510	
3116			10892				2872	35064	8853
		1419428	445065	598874	587859	575098	154214	643479	1176409
		10701		4206	5360	19532			
106958	7135		10060	9048	24912	34180	6062	9715	23097

表 7—7 全市及各县(市)、区规模以上工业企业销售产值(2012)
Sales Value of Industrial Enterprises Above Designated Size by Region

指标	Indicators	全市 Toal	市区 Urban District	海曙 Haishu
工业销售产值	**Gross Industrial Products Sales**	**117880641**	**79629068**	**3289472**
按轻重工业分	**Grouped by Light and Heavy Industry**			
轻工业	Light Industry	33104213	17987838	244928
重工业	Heavy Industry	84776428	61641230	3044544
按注册登记类型分	**Grouped by Registered Type**			
国有企业	State—owned Enterprises	8536128	5393545	2933758
集体企业	Collective—owned Enterpriese	111743	58509	10712
股份合作企业	Share Cooperative Enterprises	131655	75115	
联营企业	Joint Owned Enterprises	9125	9125	
有限责任公司	Limited Liability Corporations	11928565	8952060	206019
股份有限公司	Share—holding Corporations Ltd.	16889319	14891589	18874
私营企业	Private Enterprises	31394168	12352713	23599
港澳台商投资企业	Hong Kong,Macao & Taiwan Funded	28044561	21522089	89363
外商投资企业	Foreign Funded Enterprises	20772067	16332094	7147
在总计中:亏损企业	Of the Total:Loss Making Enterprises	13013311	9567491	12596
在总计中:国有及国有控股	Of the Total:State—owned and State—holding	30125079	26660146	2933758
按规模分	**Grouped by Enterprises Size**			
大型企业	Large—Sized	38897059	32097238	2899462
中型企业	Medium—Sized	35321924	21589760	218294
小型企业	Small—Sized	42512942	25033923	166539
按工业行业分	**Grouped by Sector**			
黑色金属矿采选业	Ferrous Metals Mining and Dressing	11094	11094	
非金属矿采选业	Non—metallic Mining Industry	2200	2200	
农副食品加工业	Farm and Sideline Products Processing	1525889	743965	
食品制造业	Food Manufacturing	741303	217769	21781
酒、饮料和精制茶制造业	Wine, Beverages and Refined Tea Manufacturing	298524	174415	9158
烟草制品业	Tobacco Manufacturing	1190021	1190021	
纺织业	Textile Industry	3565545	2420314	57087
纺织服装、服饰业	Clothing, Apparel Industry	5699778	4207363	66157

单位:万元(10000 yuan)

各区 by Districts					余姚 Yuyao	慈溪 Cixi	奉化 Fenghua	象山 Xiangshan	宁海 Ninghai
江东 Jiangdong	江北 Jiangbei	北仑 Beilun	镇海 Zhenhai	鄞州 Yinzhou					
1979282	**3906397**	**18315762**	**21818991**	**19300569**	**10819371**	**15100371**	**3226056**	**4135862**	**4969914**
1394262	618799	3823597	1708982	9448341	3932912	6643404	1193009	1474203	1872848
585020	3287598	14492165	20110010	9852228	6886459	8456968	2033047	2661659	3097066
1304926	29163	534103	66646	524949	573999	555996	148717	668189	1195683
		4308	16980	26509	22411	19017	5532		6275
9675	38061	6475	3345	10044		34564		19975	2000
				9125					
79593	1094500	2813016	1428259	2091344	807026	1324973	142301	307533	394671
3192	806738	155495	12452721	1271704	774152	642274	25321	388167	167817
144117	943977	907311	2524267	7413451	4819880	8399808	1708280	1772565	2340922
424341	493327	8706344	2630922	5623617	2459537	2463068	778223	402901	418742
13439	500631	5188711	2695852	2327622	1362365	1643882	417682	572239	443804
80878	431042	4409545	2044860	1080176	739626	1346644	354881	411759	592909
1304926	98487	3926880	13965532	602041	681536	562225	160084	747490	1313598
1296979	801964	5345606	12786866	3735549	1313334	3130572	486462	303362	1566090
420782	1703779	6004686	3564640	5875924	3673035	5572702	966619	2059319	1460489
253151	1394644	6927425	5000899	9350754	5721150	6329674	1744239	1746321	1937636
		11094							
				2200					
3644	32431	432339	3054	149488	292586	152574	65357	259094	12315
	45914	62256	39318	38683	370533	18700	36502	50082	47717
	3876	105331	13550	42501	44591		36548	17485	25484
1190021									
	157676	687731	529713	966206	397252	491614	42700	129681	83984
67383	63541	1087374	67171	2804392	36561	124805	467670	779117	84262

表 7－7 续表 Continued

指标	Indicators	全市 Toal	市区 Urban District	海曙 Haishu
皮革、毛皮、羽毛及其制品和制鞋业	Leather, Fur, Feather and Its Products and Footwear Industry	127137	70942	
木材加工及木、竹、藤、棕、草制品业	Timber Processing, Bamboo, Rattan, Cane Palm, and Straw Products	155307	93390	
家具制造业	Furniture Manufacturing	686804	397312	
造纸及纸制品业	Paper－making and Paper Products Manufacturing	1728459	1208005	
印刷和记录媒介复制业	Printing and Record Duplicating	614684	511755	5609
文教、工美、体育和娱乐用品制造业	Culture, Art, Sports and Recreation Supplies Manufacturing	2213575	1175121	
石油加工、炼焦和核燃料加工业	Petroleum Processing, Coking & Nuclear Fuel Processing	15059499	15049536	
化学原料和化学制品制造业	Raw Chemical Materials and Chemical Products	12535511	11072976	
医药制造业	Medicines Manufacturing	487554	351817	7342
化学纤维制造业	Chemical Fiber Manufacturing	1572594	212407	
橡胶和塑料制品业	Rubber and Plastic Products Industry	3382890	1631791	8170
非金属矿物制品业	Nonmetal Mineral Products	1854644	1037826	
黑色金属冶炼和压延加工业	Smelting and Pressing of Ferrous Metals	5429335	3940677	131
有色金属冶炼和压延加工业	Smelting and Pressing of Nonferrous Metals	5073020	2891681	3443
金属制品业	Metal Products Manufacturing	3494421	2101917	3910
通用设备制造业	General Purpose Equipment Manufacturing	6527493	3632244	11786
专用设备制造业	Special Purpose Equipment Manufacturing	3245333	2088140	6444
汽车制造业	Automobile Manufacturing	5721172	3466038	21299
铁路、船舶、航空航天和其他运输设备制造业	Railroad, Marine, Aviation and Other Transport Equipment Manufacturing	1390043	564266	
电气机械和器材制造业	Electric Equipment and Machinery Manufacturing	13670259	5153787	70777
计算机、通信和其他电子设备制造业	Computer, Communications and Other Electronic Equipment Manufacturing	7886065	6577051	61009
仪器仪表制造业	Instrument Manufacturing	1633966	694458	6654
其他制造业	Other Manufacturing	470284	168354	
废弃资源综合利用业	Waste Comprehensive Utilization of Resources Industry	970356	951919	
金属制品、机械和设备修理业	Metal Products, Machinery and Equipment Repair Industry	60451	13796	
电力、热力的生产和供应业	Production and Supply Electric Power and Thermal Power	8468212	5337155	2809261
燃气生产和供应业	Production and Supply Gas	159242	134358	119451
水的生产和供应业	Production and Supply Tap Water	227979	133209	

单位:万元(10000 yuan)

各区 by Districts					余姚 Yuyao	慈溪 Cixi	奉化 Fenghua	象山 Xiangshan	宁海 Ninghai
江东 Jiangdong	江北 Jiangbei	北仑 Beilun	镇海 Zhenhai	鄞州 Yinzhou					
1929		8182	21836	34035	11413	19263	15400		10120
			2833	90557	25269	19249	17399		
1503	50208	73538	5533	258379	203165	47882	8534	14145	15766
2179	4252	599419	45194	549620	115820	242959	41879	41904	77892
2227	9291	53394	5873	432269	54751	27658	18213		2307
3367	79276	326056	50380	684445	109751	256506	42092	11013	619092
		26987	12342952	10132			6230	3733	
	115050	5026948	3342148	646499	438402	846988	72527	28980	75637
	14899	48491	89809	183800	13424	46440	49145	13270	13459
		63151	128427	20829	164313	1133863	16416	42359	3235
5406	110598	286583	202193	975756	714271	563059	129095	76792	267882
	168033	247239	111926	482296	338874	175460	45516	134074	122895
9719	80810	2557519	375957	667699	534657	571869	257602	80448	44083
44285	1466582	125355	504803	617802	745821	1065198	178002	17088	175231
30392	137221	443494	264567	972941	502062	501322	153763	32894	202462
30981	203782	631786	985256	1548259	645039	1078947	440266	339418	391580
34459	106761	1053349	337414	480484	573851	195295	32497	185489	170061
11328	309155	1390586	107226	1404691	209717	1001364	105121	537213	401720
7947		333790	80712	86596	34302	336393	275021	157981	22081
24272	412597	691707	464418	2655173	2584956	4402295	281141	475751	772328
398379	154567	468211	287178	1283614	546802	507527	165825	16246	72615
	144152	38346	9266	453954	444876	430301	33519		30812
	28592		40124	93344	53285	199852	29062		19731
		5379	893749	52792		14431		4006	
2904			10892				2738	35064	8853
		1419428	445453	597882	582757	574855	154214	642822	1176409
		10701		4206	5360	19524			
106958	7135		10068	9048	24912	34180	6062	9715	19901

表 7—8　全市规模以上工业企业主要经济指标(2012)
Main Economic Indicators of Industrial Enterprises Above Designated Size

指标	Indicators	企业个数(个) Number of Enterprises (unit)	#亏损企业 Loss Making
总计	**Total**	**6804**	**1034**
按轻重工业分	**Grouped by Light and Heavy Industry**		
轻工业	Light Industry	2801	473
重工业	Heavy Industry	4003	561
按注册登记类型分	**Grouped by Registered Type**		
国有企业	State—owned Enterprises	36	3
集体企业	Collective—owned Enterpriese	23	3
股份合作企业	Share Cooperative Enterprises	25	3
联营企业	Joint Owned Enterprises	1	
有限责任公司	Limited Liability Corporations	546	80
股份有限公司	Share—holding Corporations Ltd.	109	11
私营企业	Private Enterprises	3958	492
港澳台商投资企业	Hong Kong, Macao & Taiwan Funded	1118	236
外商投资企业	Foreign Funded Enterprises	983	206
在总计中:亏损企业	Of the Total: Loss Making Enterprises	1034	1034
在总计中:国有及国有控股	Of the Total: State—owned and State—holding	97	14
按规模分	**Grouped by Enterprises Size**		
大型企业	Large—Sized	107	8
中型企业	Medium—Sized	1005	126
小型企业	Small—Sized	5539	859
按工业行业分	**Grouped by Sector**		
黑色金属矿采选业	Ferrous Metals Mining and Dressing	1	1
非金属矿采选业	Non—metallic Mining Industry	1	
农副食品加工业	Farm and Sideline Products Processing	85	14
食品制造业	Food Manufacturing	46	5
酒、饮料和精制茶制造业	Wine, Beverages and Refined Tea Manufacturing	21	4
烟草制品业	Tobacco Manufacturing	1	
纺织业	Textile Industry	289	57
纺织服装、服饰业	Clothing, Apparel Industry	575	106

单位：万元(10000 yuan)

工业总产值(现价) Gross Industrial Output Value (Current Prices)	工业销售产值 Value of Industrial Products Sales	#出口交货值 Value of Export Products	资产合计 Total Asset	流动资产小计 Current Assets	固定资产小计 Total Fixed Assets	固定资产原价 Original Value of Fixed Assets
121550760	**117880641**	**26216535**	**106434700**	**63776216**	**31430321**	**47926527**
34049449	33104213	13254512	35962583	23523381	8007508	12354156
87501311	84776428	12962023	70472117	40252835	23422813	35572371
8547018	8536128	197481	7338212	2129664	4756465	7639254
111059	111743	1196	122698	91233	20944	38102
137049	131655	33093	122781	86972	25845	50952
9128	9125	338	2068	1940	128	554
12142989	11928565	1454710	12613660	6518603	4527297	7104620
17252477	16889319	725763	10406525	5400604	3577124	4947058
32872411	31394168	8438696	30034821	20228124	6379014	9103695
28862744	28044561	7198079	27392006	17777259	6657187	10089492
21553507	20772067	8128885	18360991	11505834	5483297	8945872
13314051	13013311	2640235	17238922	9845346	5853272	8288350
30369003	30125079	355546	18685538	6280869	11108951	17685543
40247278	38897059	6939883	29357660	15348288	10778829	16347361
36402444	35321924	9265061	32159397	19943290	8393911	12937318
43739373	42512942	9879850	43337464	27660034	11777579	17688144
	11094		222007	218131	2744	6273
2600	2200		1891	351	1540	1985
1542863	1525889	366123	1424989	886266	301869	458675
806733	741303	379966	709136	435372	216654	255238
302647	298524	96126	406844	209433	132735	228193
1197910	1190021	25462	1103606	775139	182359	321924
3592043	3565545	870449	3963749	2583844	970915	1727266
5904017	5699778	2938667	5803290	4206109	1027187	1591849

表 7—8 续 1 Continued

指标	Indicators	企业个数（个）Number of Enterprises (unit)	#亏损企业 Loss Making
皮革、毛皮、羽毛及其制品和制鞋业	Leather, Fur, Feather and Its Products and Footwear Industry	31	4
木材加工及木、竹、藤、棕、草制品业	Timber Processing, Bamboo, Rattan, Cane Palm, and Straw Products	29	2
家具制造业	Furniture Manufacturing	97	23
造纸及纸制品业	Paper—making and Paper Products Manufacturing	104	19
印刷和记录媒介复制业	Printing and Record Duplicating	65	11
文教、工美、体育和娱乐用品制造业	Culture, Art, Sports and Recreation Supplies Manufacturing	197	33
石油加工、炼焦和核燃料加工业	Petroleum Processing, Coking & Nuclear Fuel Processing	12	1
化学原料和化学制品制造业	Raw Chemical Materials and Chemical Products	216	38
医药制造业	Medicines Manufacturing	36	8
化学纤维制造业	Chemical Fiber Manufacturing	68	17
橡胶和塑料制品业	Rubber and Plastic Products Industry	456	61
非金属矿物制品业	Nonmetal Mineral Products	173	20
黑色金属冶炼和压延加工业	Smelting and Pressing of Ferrous Metals	229	42
有色金属冶炼和压延加工业	Smelting and Pressing of Nonferrous Metals	179	37
金属制品业	Metal Products Manufacturing	477	65
通用设备制造业	General Purpose Equipment Manufacturing	839	110
专用设备制造业	Special Purpose Equipment Manufacturing	345	47
汽车制造业	Automobile Manufacturing	401	38
铁路、船舶、航空航天和其他运输设备制造业	Railroad, Marine, Aviation and Other Transport Equipment Manufacturing	103	17
电气机械和器材制造业	Electric Equipment and Machinery Manufacturing	1062	133
计算机、通信和其他电子设备制造业	Computer, Communications and Other Electronic Equipment Manufacturing	324	46
仪器仪表制造业	Instrument Manufacturing	144	9
其他制造业	Other Manufacturing	64	13
废弃资源综合利用业	Waste Comprehensive Utilization of Resources Industry	63	42
金属制品、机械和设备修理业	Metal Products, Machinery and Equipment Repair Industry	6	
电力、热力的生产和供应业	Production and Supply Electric Power and Thermal Power	41	4
燃气生产和供应业	Production and Supply Gas	5	
水的生产和供应业	Production and Supply Tap Water	19	7

单位:万元(10000 yuan)

工业总产值(现价) Gross Industrial Output Value (Current Prices)	工业销售产值 Value of Industrial Products Sales	#出口交货值 Value of Export Products	资产合计 Total Asset	流动资产小计 Current Assets	固定资产小计 Total Fixed Assets	固定资产原价 Original Value of Fixed Assets
130099	127137	62408	145687	105557	30138	47294
159035	155307	94215	133246	92612	29542	50634
724544	686804	418086	841037	583007	185818	252292
1688271	1728459	322613	3180368	1777550	848579	1526242
634497	614684	197010	795540	506153	196228	300829
2254277	2213575	1077529	2014688	1307307	433971	641742
15207781	15059499	6279	4653161	2161410	2421082	3477323
12688180	12535511	854213	10567171	5379224	4219931	5726137
502382	487554	83854	529782	303774	146207	180745
1732548	1572594	139638	1653652	1222559	326807	512136
3481399	3382890	1267891	3404795	2199940	743774	1144771
1887257	1854644	88281	2069524	1348413	486449	765572
5589887	5429335	333351	4782299	2284565	2148672	3178362
5227581	5073020	269819	2820498	1939064	527298	732433
3621538	3494421	1654896	3248760	2233867	710322	1046158
6785764	6527493	2204729	7086201	4712019	1653545	2522299
3376023	3245333	862020	3959375	2687649	924156	1357111
5902229	5721172	933858	6479115	4076897	1265717	1802107
1678644	1390043	775275	2037493	1284257	554605	754202
14185855	13670259	5318169	14275765	9559908	2743122	3635131
8635925	7886065	3892798	6090694	4357043	1251397	2314466
1694974	1633966	394235	2236031	1479978	336083	504381
484230	470284	288575	450563	314010	87034	141063
986543	970356		382282	355957	16883	26120
60797	60451		124877	75883	41792	54993
8491271	8468212		6775459	1255356	5312988	9333546
159250	159242		487608	302636	129972	163440
231166	227979		1573517	554976	822206	1143597

表 7—8 续 2 Continued

指标	Indicators	本年折旧 Depreciation in This Year	负债小计 Total Liabilities
总计	**Total**	**3094874**	**66017051**
按轻重工业分	**Grouped by Light and Heavy Industry**		
轻工业	Light Industry	773457	23098235
重工业	Heavy Industry	2321417	42918815
按注册登记类型分	Grouped by Registered Type		
国有企业	State—owned Enterprises	468607	4257149
集体企业	Collective—owned Enterpriese	2003	76808
股份合作企业	Share Cooperative Enterprises	3816	80266
联营企业	Joint Owned Enterprises	54	665
有限责任公司	Limited Liability Corporations	416051	8427955
股份有限公司	Share—holding Corporations Ltd.	305957	5338136
私营企业	Private Enterprises	664986	21686719
港澳台商投资企业	Hong Kong,Macao & Taiwan Funded	620760	15724874
外商投资企业	Foreign Funded Enterprises	612012	10410158
在总计中:亏损企业	Of the Total:Loss Making Enterprises	506510	13241548
在总计中:国有及国有控股	Of the Total:State—owned and State—holding	1040726	11116052
按规模分	**Grouped by Enterprises Size**		
大型企业	Large—Sized	1051960	16899585
中型企业	Medium—Sized	823114	19976579
小型企业	Small—Sized	1177706	28217233
按工业行业分	**Grouped by Sector**		
黑色金属矿采选业	Ferrous Metals Mining and Dressing	421	170898
非金属矿采选业	Non—metallic Mining Industry	175	2036
农副食品加工业	Farm and Sideline Products Processing	26113	892698
食品制造业	Food Manufacturing	10505	445091
酒、饮料和精制茶制造业	Wine, Beverages and Refined Tea Manufacturing	11181	316465
烟草制品业	Tobacco Manufacturing	23451	191864
纺织业	Textile Industry	112170	2106385
纺织服装、服饰业	Clothing, Apparel Industry	93449	3510622

单位:万元(10000 yuan)

所有者权益 Creditors' Equity	实收资本 Paid－in Capital	主营业务收入 Prime Operating Revenue	主营业务成本 Operating Costs	销售费用 Sales Expenses	主营业务税金及附加 Tax and Extra Charge	管理费用 Administrative Expenses	财务费用 Finance Charge
40255941	21763062	117959823	101644982	2252981	2588652	5363924	1791067
12730095	6108600	32783993	27165274	1049989	896758	1926089	680848
27525845	15654462	85175830	74479709	1202992	1691895	3437835	1110219
3081063	1182680	8519678	6580890	60509	795849	174176	120844
45887	14239	115421	95273	1654	623	11023	1625
42515	18640	128517	105123	3506	690	10949	2574
1403	1051	9125	7998	14	342	209	1
4163567	2419286	12152022	10476319	203846	48148	540538	217707
5068389	2931313	16844499	14520288	149287	1185749	414268	111976
8289977	3616132	31232407	26859743	755375	111863	1873323	686653
11592023	6172934	28175084	24378148	655859	388809	1372889	387876
7944500	5398480	20721449	18578069	421167	56104	961754	261563
3953886	4591067	13268352	12647493	259046	28418	647640	393678
7569486	5333007	30197662	25483862	119638	2289817	525188	257885
12448075	6335561	38866742	32865397	629415	2013468	1186252	306539
12179587	6235725	35220438	30603262	711686	417944	1746900	584520
15109805	8872541	42708800	37157001	900738	152035	2374462	870017
51109	6298	12542	10599	49	85	1089	2624
－145	50	2818	982		105	610	96
531003	210707	1541623	1415686	37482	3699	50015	28991
264045	97947	760390	620308	25860	2168	26439	20034
90379	129973	297084	237376	24279	15776	16947	6145
911741	34160	1211049	225680	40531	765928	55035	－3373
1857363	843846	3486833	3011436	58979	15581	194963	57536
2221220	886582	5639148	4703911	244451	25617	334081	67822

表 7—8 续 3 Continued

指标	Indicators	本年折旧 Depreciation in this Year	负债小计 Total Liabilities
皮革、毛皮、羽毛及其制品和制鞋业	Leather, Fur, Feather and Its Products and Footwear Industry	3010	107102
木材加工及木、竹、藤、棕、草制品业	Timber Processing, Bamboo, Rattan, Cane Palm, and Straw Products	2797	82093
家具制造业	Furniture Manufacturing	14387	656104
造纸及纸制品业	Paper—making and Paper Products Manufacturing	73189	1999201
印刷和记录媒介复制业	Printing and Record Duplicating	20933	441060
文教、工美、体育和娱乐用品制造业	Culture, Art, Sports and Recreation Supplies Manufacturing	40496	1246328
石油加工、炼焦和核燃料加工业	Petroleum Processing, Coking & Nuclear Fuel Processing	209209	2493274
化学原料和化学制品制造业	Raw Chemical Materials and Chemical Products	373324	6339158
医药制造业	Medicines Manufacturing	10432	253173
化学纤维制造业	Chemical Fiber Manufacturing	42561	1372594
橡胶和塑料制品业	Rubber and Plastic Products Industry	85461	2278415
非金属矿物制品业	Nonmetal Mineral Products	56118	1440979
黑色金属冶炼和压延加工业	Smelting and Pressing of Ferrous Metals	191258	3727315
有色金属冶炼和压延加工业	Smelting and Pressing of Nonferrous Metals	62167	1731550
金属制品业	Metal Products Manufacturing	72320	2118927
通用设备制造业	General Purpose Equipment Manufacturing	179842	4318729
专用设备制造业	Special Purpose Equipment Manufacturing	94828	2062352
汽车制造业	Automobile Manufacturing	135737	3598018
铁路、船舶、航空航天和其他运输设备制造业	Railroad, Marine, Aviation and Other Transport Equipment Manufacturing	42906	1492056
电气机械和器材制造业	Electric Equipment and Machinery Manufacturing	248417	9563580
计算机、通信和其他电子设备制造业	Computer, Communications and Other Electronic Equipment Manufacturing	195978	3667770
仪器仪表制造业	Instrument Manufacturing	35600	1078645
其他制造业	Other Manufacturing	10369	338773
废弃资源综合利用业	Waste Comprehensive Utilization of Resources Industry	2745	368229
金属制品、机械和设备修理业	Metal Products, Machinery and Equipment Repair Industry	2374	66671
电力、热力的生产和供应业	Production and Supply Electric Power and Thermal Power	541916	4191965
燃气生产和供应业	Production and Supply Gas	8374	269006
水的生产和供应业	Production and Supply Tap Water	60661	1077922

单位:万元(10000 yuan)

所有者权益 Creditors' Equity	实收资本 Paid-in Capital	主营业务收入 Prime Operating Revenue	主营业务成本 Operating Costs	销售费用 Sales Expenses	主营业务税金及附加 Tax and Extra Charge	管理费用 Administrative Expenses	财务费用 Finance Charge
35585	17457	126040	107668	3480	642	9094	3280
49744	21158	155400	131640	3940	818	6596	3672
184932	158232	687988	584887	24554	2766	52873	21977
1181106	967735	1502547	1268946	53730	3702	80779	67747
354480	72159	587746	506470	9859	2143	41031	11354
768140	366938	2199189	1851630	79941	8755	144298	38634
2159887	2084254	15093136	13166227	19532	1469198	139149	26600
4227637	2719692	12632576	11543957	160800	21790	353872	183340
276080	134858	526255	387017	34521	2363	45052	9877
281058	300787	1616211	1517523	13480	1363	35827	62554
1123138	492789	3485272	2944973	105284	12256	222044	70350
618077	351921	1848626	1596086	51021	9731	82103	37483
1053938	1371564	5569725	5237924	33157	10043	195806	97270
1088714	521449	5023009	4724152	31755	7451	144089	56477
1117056	541904	3497396	2996798	87817	15020	226823	68082
2768136	1188559	6492137	5296901	191896	28549	506352	125055
1895832	768534	3272725	2565872	146079	17302	301842	48951
2877872	1277564	5653363	4583308	128726	23148	422818	77194
545622	374177	1436614	1269706	14619	6527	89491	37325
4659985	1917373	13641986	11648436	411708	46227	898600	273942
2423126	1299837	7949521	7159165	109880	18908	340801	72614
1157386	357535	1629706	1250578	61239	8542	150177	23275
111747	86264	472595	405074	15671	2033	33150	9340
14053	65437	985206	975219	4545	655	18026	5365
58207	49150	60186	48096	1395	768	6219	-83
2583495	1494495	8488785	7357551	9437	37188	112606	150953
218601	170362	155335	139458	1775	241	4181	173
495595	381315	219065	153748	11511	1567	21048	28393

表 7—8 续 4 Continued

指标	Indicators	营业利润 Business Profits	利润总额 Total Profits	#应交所得税 Income Tax Payable
总计	**Total**	**5038691**	**5532121**	**1121135**
按轻重工业分	**Grouped by Light and Heavy Industry**			
轻工业	Light Industry	1435074	1595685	306079
重工业	Heavy Industry	3603617	3936437	815057
按注册登记类型分	**Grouped by Registered Type**			
国有企业	State—owned Enterprises	627558	661407	134476
集体企业	Collective—owned Enterpriese	5554	5690	1585
股份合作企业	Share Cooperative Enterprises	5267	5673	1160
联营企业	Joint Owned Enterprises	562	553	138
有限责任公司	Limited Liability Corporations	781978	905936	243716
股份有限公司	Share—holding Corporations Ltd.	622555	675566	115510
私营企业	Private Enterprises	1156311	1257667	250399
港澳台商投资企业	Hong Kong,Macao & Taiwan Funded	1302807	1430298	241764
外商投资企业	Foreign Funded Enterprises	524470	577618	130703
在总计中:亏损企业	Of the Total:Loss Making Enterprises	—707742	—692635	77554
在总计中:国有及国有控股	Of the Total:State—owned and State—holding	1403020	1479652	390692
按规模分	**Grouped by Enterprises Size**			
大型企业	Large—Sized	1960201	2157106	453969
中型企业	Medium—Sized	1410581	1550427	293989
小型企业	Small—Sized	1618501	1773964	365672
按工业行业分	**Grouped by Sector**			
黑色金属矿采选业	Ferrous Metals Mining and Dressing	—1903	—1903	
非金属矿采选业	Non—metallic Mining Industry	18	8	2
农副食品加工业	Farm and Sideline Products Processing	9639	28442	7726
食品制造业	Food Manufacturing	73583	75906	13422
酒、饮料和精制茶制造业	Wine, Beverages and Refined Tea Manufacturing	—1570	—1321	854
烟草制品业	Tobacco Manufacturing	125318	122231	30558
纺织业	Textile Industry	158233	185870	34633
纺织服装、服饰业	Clothing, Apparel Industry	385043	389035	73119

单位:万元(10000 yuan)

亏损企业亏损总额 Total Loss	利税总额 Total Profits and Taxes	本年应付职工薪酬 Employee Compensation Payable the Year	本年应交增值税 Value－added Taxes Payable the Year	本年进项税额 Withholdings on VAT the Year	本年销项税额 Substituted Money on VAT the Year	全部从业人员年平均人数(人) Annual Average Employees (person)
692635	**11128603**	**6379515**	**3007829**	**14508554**	**15528189**	**1470578**
207718	3378954	2653512	886512	3973536	3742308	689011
484917	7749649	3726003	2121318	10535018	11785880	781567
5809	1869710	184969	412454	671325	1430041	17916
590	11233	13732	4921	13654	18037	2984
1981	10082	13877	3719	14997	15442	3646
	1212	387	317	1234	1551	131
98300	1282993	591560	328909	1604131	1748283	113659
28963	2255727	327724	394413	2468880	2754465	51719
182175	2119612	2424809	750082	3980511	3922839	643569
173013	2643117	1573754	824011	3527801	3663093	358858
201804	921810	1240574	288088	2219876	1969443	276537
692635	－479233	792553	184985	2044008	1823505	198028
75372	4983045	503106	1213576	3506051	4941143	43353
71453	5152644	1345831	982070	4477964	5363750	257940
167479	2961222	2194627	992850	4447306	4495837	509554
436175	2918303	2762452	992304	5466367	5521054	695722
1903	－1665	255	153	3526	3679	57
	915	243	802		802	59
20946	60212	55761	28071	165108	149304	15996
774	89431	44376	11357	84134	75344	12556
7519	27520	16291	13066	39956	39718	3717
	1052676	16296	164517	142285	305095	1035
29471	297948	272971	96497	428645	456222	69300
20102	565624	692938	150972	658821	614723	183398

表 7—8 续 5 Continued

指标	Indicators	营业利润 Business Profits	利润总额 Total Profits	#应交所得税 Income Tax Payable
皮革、毛皮、羽毛及其制品和制鞋业	Leather, Fur, Feather and Its Products and Footwear Industry	491	1122	722
木材加工及木、竹、藤、棕、草制品业	Timber Processing, Bamboo, Rattan, Cane Palm, and Straw Products	9016	9295	1364
家具制造业	Furniture Manufacturing	13045	13883	3071
造纸及纸制品业	Paper—making and Paper Products Manufacturing	49269	54426	10049
印刷和记录媒介复制业	Printing and Record Duplicating	36827	43220	9406
文教、工美、体育和娱乐用品制造业	Culture, Art, Sports and Recreation Supplies Manufacturing	106012	109704	21782
石油加工、炼焦和核燃料加工业	Petroleum Processing, Coking & Nuclear Fuel Processing	299454	333411	71571
化学原料和化学制品制造业	Raw Chemical Materials and Chemical Products	423218	458787	96261
医药制造业	Medicines Manufacturing	48340	50264	8134
化学纤维制造业	Chemical Fiber Manufacturing	—5739	—1218	4316
橡胶和塑料制品业	Rubber and Plastic Products Industry	154393	167097	30183
非金属矿物制品业	Nonmetal Mineral Products	78247	93841	20861
黑色金属冶炼和压延加工业	Smelting and Pressing of Ferrous Metals	13581	18617	96606
有色金属冶炼和压延加工业	Smelting and Pressing of Nonferrous Metals	96596	116206	17349
金属制品业	Metal Products Manufacturing	153834	160502	34511
通用设备制造业	General Purpose Equipment Manufacturing	384709	419053	73586
专用设备制造业	Special Purpose Equipment Manufacturing	245804	263541	40751
汽车制造业	Automobile Manufacturing	489662	562782	87265
铁路、船舶、航空航天和其他运输设备制造业	Railroad, Marine, Aviation and Other Transport Equipment Manufacturing	34146	34462	6171
电气机械和器材制造业	Electric Equipment and Machinery Manufacturing	544708	628982	96717
计算机、通信和其他电子设备制造业	Computer, Communications and Other Electronic Equipment Manufacturing	294851	314491	52239
仪器仪表制造业	Instrument Manufacturing	142472	161911	25139
其他制造业	Other Manufacturing	8393	7788	2846
废弃资源综合利用业	Waste Comprehensive Utilization of Resources Industry	—18029	—16568	—464
金属制品、机械和设备修理业	Metal Products, Machinery and Equipment Repair Industry	3833	4017	835
电力、热力的生产和供应业	Production and Supply Electric Power and Thermal Power	664041	675366	143694
燃气生产和供应业	Production and Supply Gas	13746	13981	3012
水的生产和供应业	Production and Supply Tap Water	5411	34890	2847

单位:万元(10000 yuan)

亏损企业亏损总额 Total Loss	利税总额 Total Profits and Taxes	本年应付职工薪酬 Employee Compensation Payable the Year	本年应交增值税 Value-added Taxes Payable the Year	本年进项税额 Withholdings on VAT the Year	本年销项税额 Substituted Money on VAT the Year	全部从业人员年平均人数(人) Annual Average Employees (person)
2083	5181	18379	3418	13397	12577	5562
125	13409	11637	3296	15393	12769	3246
6812	28840	78038	12192	73197	48293	19408
6209	89556	78220	31427	217172	235468	18681
877	61159	43973	15796	50135	63297	11465
11315	161930	204823	43471	228463	169756	53957
1248	2417062	126181	614453	1938571	2546849	7583
164259	672556	228171	191979	1980621	1972217	32921
2608	69014	35341	16387	54739	65108	6244
28996	20735	45387	20591	255420	263901	11690
21204	256930	274872	77577	464700	424429	74270
9186	186332	91660	82760	121569	190768	20151
96451	97276	189003	68616	804347	831931	38468
10035	177238	123950	53581	800209	828113	26333
14088	253626	301570	78103	404400	327783	76325
33242	622490	577533	174888	822033	839997	140415
21284	381368	288356	100525	399878	417078	61294
10154	741165	442677	155234	797964	854488	89469
12783	60414	122656	19425	137062	105966	27888
84684	967705	1038569	292496	1781174	1468067	261299
29783	419304	489268	85905	562122	483766	119326
4559	226096	145245	55644	193554	220468	34319
4599	20936	60580	11115	51951	39926	15604
22041	-12403	26567	3510	162017	160353	6998
	6987	12379	2203	1487	3653	1692
5185	1026328	195857	313773	629028	1260785	15187
	16076	10402	1854	21614	23557	879
8114	48632	19094	12175	3863	11942	3786

表 7－9 各县(市)、区规模以上工业企业主要财务指标(2012)
Main Financial Indicators of Industrial Enterprises Above Designated Size by Region

指标	Indicators	全市 Toal	市区 Urban District	海曙 Haishu
企业单位数(个)	Number of Enterprises(unit)	6804	3240	34
#亏损企业	Deficits Enterprises	1034	585	4
工业总产值(现价)	Gross Industrial Output Value(Current Prices)	121550760	81133945	3302908
工业销售产值	Value of Industrial Products Sales	117880641	79629068	3289472
#出口交货值	Value of Export Products	26216535	14935589	138481
资产合计	Total Asset	106434700	64479643	1853929
流动资产小计	Current Assets	63776216	37273508	533762
固定资产小计	Total Fixed Assets	31430321	20554966	1153926
本年折旧	Depreciation in this year	3094874	2056528	172661
负债合计	Total Liabilities	66017051	37051977	1483588
流动负债小计	Current Liabilities	59019651	32317308	455638
所有者权益合计	Total Owner' Equity	40255941	27304732	370340
#实收资本	Paid－in Capital	21763062	15650572	114008
主营业务收入	Prime Operating Revenue	117959823	79846596	3331674
主营业务成本	Operating Costs	101644982	69233058	2987741
主营业务税金及附加	Tax and Extra Charge	2588652	2442030	10446
销售费用	Sales Expenses	2252981	1347648	27397
管理费用	Administrative Expenses	5363924	3153009	36945
#税金	Tax	251073	133276	925
财务费用	Finance charge	1791067	836632	8483
#利息支出	Interest Exchange	1981588	964835	10492
营业利润	Business Profits	5038691	3375441	122964
利润总额	Total Profits	5532121	3685660	147133
应交所得税	Income Tax Payable	1121135	762231	5849
亏损企业亏损总额	Total Loss	692635	501832	246
利税总额	Total Profits and Taxes	11128603	8121659	223070
本年应付职工薪酬	Employee Compensation Payable in this Year	6379515	3554474	76617
本年应交增值税	Value－added Taxes Payable in this Year	3007829	1993970	65490
本年进项税额	Withholdings on VAT in this Year	14508554	9729114	95936
本年销项税额	Substituted Money on VAT in this Year	15528189	10929496	531089
全部从业人员年平均人数(人)	Annual Average Employees(person)	1470578	755759	13015

单位:万元(10000 yuan)

各区 by Districts					余姚 Yuyao	慈溪 Cixi	奉化 Fenghua	象山 Xiangshan	宁海 Ninghai
江东 Jiangdong	江北 Jiangbei	北仑 Beilun	镇海 Zhenhai	鄞州 Yinzhou					
59	273	534	545	1618	1111	1155	437	403	458
15	66	119	175	164	104	121	64	74	86
1990747	3909288	18409603	22077352	19810205	11275033	16089841	3536980	4351251	5163711
1979282	3906397	18315762	21818991	19300569	10819371	15100371	3226056	4135862	4969914
266097	738124	3205569	1696457	5687420	3337310	4230430	1180587	1151474	1381144
2440875	3600927	19342653	12515545	17042302	10954797	15480565	3568571	5814293	6136831
1363724	2157076	10569320	6924872	11166782	7535628	10030321	2312770	3299844	3324146
628488	917718	7254387	4728529	3605224	2481555	3311169	1009362	1849695	2223574
64191	83894	641988	443397	381688	243469	395674	93402	133960	171842
914052	2018110	10304880	7559193	10052689	7760215	10776264	2576077	3812310	4040208
656697	1782343	9110576	6834254	9342067	7176977	10144615	2509747	3411951	3459053
1526823	1582818	9037773	4956536	6869514	3157996	4703821	992494	2001983	2094914
360655	789127	6164196	3703711	2741122	1546791	2084593	540431	993327	947348
1995003	3904358	18240270	22226147	18943357	10773592	14910131	3451265	4112333	4865906
884908	3397038	16241559	19669461	15982666	9239785	12832029	2964564	3478374	3897174
770763	13445	59767	1198253	74173	38443	43728	19347	17224	27881
62120	80769	314058	183768	565416	237384	361152	76723	100248	129828
108154	231972	696633	548081	1251229	618904	847101	234040	201551	309319
4031	9190	36242	24192	41243	42709	41297	10513	8810	14468
15364	53029	232829	185527	251891	251695	331389	84442	134043	152865
20880	57583	284825	205423	286557	265650	355320	84265	139516	172003
232387	149506	812246	504642	1183703	454342	563377	85121	193270	367141
269112	172553	901228	528215	1241391	510053	660388	95397	208463	372160
39342	32931	264243	131643	203626	81936	121843	23432	44263	87430
3015	25959	187573	138816	43596	41047	58294	15457	25134	50870
1220754	265078	1341185	2170981	1742493	792102	1080992	203732	348206	581911
68205	256692	880900	594877	1282611	719870	1107766	339731	290161	367513
180879	79080	380191	444513	426929	243605	376877	88988	122520	181870
304328	587517	2564727	3213106	2220213	1310411	1976012	380635	530998	581383
439419	593363	2555687	3489864	2321707	1209356	1895725	368846	538576	586191
11815	56052	170462	104520	315892	187615	279410	87629	68795	91370

表 7—10 各县(市)、区国有控股工业企业主要财务指标(2012)
Main Financial Indicators of State Holding Shares Industrial Enterprises by Region

指标	Indicators	全市 Toal	市区 Urban District	海曙 Haishu
企业单位数(个)	Number of Enterprises(unit)	97	66	4
#亏损企业	Deficits Enterprises	14	10	
工业总产值(现价)	Gross Industrial Output Value(Current Prices)	30369003	26890591	2933758
工业销售产值	Value of Industrial Products Sales	30125079	26660146	2933758
#出口交货值	Value of Export Products	355546	330947	
资产合计	Total Asset	18685538	14339965	1318126
流动资产小计	Total Current Assets	6280869	5009040	166502
固定资产原价	Original Value of Fixed Assets	17685543	13692435	1988949
#累计折旧	Accumulative Depreciation	7738294	6440248	1183692
负债合计	Total Liabilities	11116052	8340611	1211239
流动负债小计	Current Liabilities	8038988	6199143	195917
所有者权益合计	Total Owners' Equity	7569486	5999354	106887
#实收资本	Paid—in Capital	5333007	4494838	43439
主营业务收入	Prime Operating Revenue	30197662	26706140	2931444
主营业务成本	Operating Costs	25483862	22567418	2661549
主营业务税金及附加	Tax and Extra Charge	2289817	2269230	8198
销售费用	Sales Expenses	119638	97041	3744
管理费用	Administrative Expenses	525188	427138	4806
财务费用	Finance Charge	257885	141132	32
营业利润	Business Profits	1403020	1073089	97754
利润总额	Total Profits	1479652	1142917	99694
亏损企业亏损总额	Total Loss	75372	72600	
本年应付职工薪酬	Employee Compensation Payable in this Year	503106	398343	37266
本年应交增值税	Value—added Taxes Payable in this Year	1213576	1049173	53379
本年进项税额	Withholdings on VAT in this Year	3506051	3066311	44579
本年销项税额	Substituted Money on VAT in this Year	4941143	4355128	474701
全部从业人员年平均人数(人)	Annual Average Employees(person)	43353	31352	4023

单位:万元(10000 yuan)

各区 by Districts					余姚 Yuyao	慈溪 Cixi	奉化 Fenghua	象山 Xiangshan	宁海 Ninghai
江东 Jiangdong	江北 Jiangbei	北仑 Beilun	镇海 Zhenhai	鄞州 Yinzhou					
3	5	14	21	9	9	3	4	7	8
	1	3	4	1	2	1		1	
1312650	94733	3951601	14172407	604949	686638	562468	160185	752792	1316329
1304926	98487	3926880	13965532	602041	681536	562225	160084	747490	1313598
25462	3476	275454	24547	338			4493	20106	
1671896	195211	3828052	5385008	217375	819831	392767	129395	1086831	1916749
837812	70232	1124385	2091672	39256	383241	125011	52913	249604	461061
938706	140398	4810979	4560990	242069	503800	338365	142635	1171465	1836842
386454	34808	2415983	2069729	80211	190582	120739	68243	427855	490627
530405	150319	2569775	2786095	76381	527648	193106	66089	752347	1236252
321541	56421	2235777	2532091	65984	351673	87265	53803	559433	787672
1141490	44892	1258277	2598913	140994	292183	199661	63306	334485	680497
248104	48463	1425332	2425036	29082	149391	21738	25472	246700	394868
1315338	98514	3962596	13986250	552599	683798	563919	162571	766465	1314769
307697	76519	3586372	12226912	515159	625790	530034	151995	649937	958689
766727	672	12735	1175014	1800	2906	1615	836	4118	11112
44761	3420	12898	22143	627	4808	2720	2027	3784	9259
62574	12442	100069	175777	4766	15767	21723	4292	8255	48013
8858	5318	59653	48605	1774	16066	5613	1607	32016	61451
124503	716	199751	368057	9946	25625	3591	1878	65849	232988
150042	2223	207675	368641	10382	30541	4693	1852	66507	233143
	5089	63912	3142	401	2390	339		43	
25620	10207	87182	182952	12498	19442	8202	9549	27291	40278
170444	5123	106499	320852	13754	24846	16676	7311	35620	79951
142856	10926	515260	2030659	11111	95148	84465	20674	93006	146448
311035	16282	580142	2349836	13799	116899	98201	27981	117412	225521
2799	1401	6793	11832	1364	2500	1809	684	3277	3731

表 7－11 各县(市)、区规模以上私营工业企业主要财务指标(2012)
Main Financial Indicators of Private Industrial Enterprises Above Designated Size by Region

指标	Indicators	全市 Toal	市区 Urban District	海曙 Haishu
企业单位数(个)	Number of Enterprises(unit)	3958	1614	7
#亏损企业	Deficits Enterprises	492	234	1
工业总产值(现价)	Gross Industrial Output Value(Current Prices)	32872411	12741034	24047
工业销售产值	Value of Industrial Products Sales	31394168	12352713	23599
#出口交货值	Value of Export Products	8438696	2910567	2217
资产合计	Total Asset	30034821	10800481	29461
流动资产小计	Total Current Assets	20228124	7260078	17626
固定资产原价	Original Value of Fixed Assets	9103695	3451663	13250
#累计折旧	Accumulative Depreciation	3262384	1227463	2897
负债合计	Total Liabilities	21686719	7307368	25338
流动负债小计	Current Liabilities	20617442	6915250	24114
所有者权益合计	Total Owners' Equity	8289977	3453470	4122
#实收资本	Paid－in Capital	3616132	1429115	1032
主营业务收入	Prime Operating Revenue	31232407	12498575	24114
主营业务成本	Operating Costs	26859743	10801324	21002
主营业务税金及附加	Tax and Extra Charge	111863	47338	69
销售费用	Sales Expenses	755375	264557	358
管理费用	Administrative Expenses	1873323	789020	1902
财务费用	Finance Charge	686653	212206	289
营业利润	Business Profits	1156311	501501	771
利润总额	Total Profits	1257667	550975	978
亏损企业亏损总额	Total Loss	182175	88950	100
本年应付职工薪酬	Employee Compensation Payable in this Year	2424809	916091	2515
本年应交增值税	Value－added Taxes Payable in this Year	750082	272042	505
本年进项税额	Withholdings on VAT in this Year	3980511	1643801	3518
本年销项税额	Substituted Money on VAT in this Year	3922839	1674399	3740
全部从业人员年平均人数(人)	Annual Average Employees(person)	643569	236598	734

单位:万元(10000 yuan)

各区 by Districts					余姚 Yuyao	慈溪 Cixi	奉化 Fenghua	象山 Xiangshan	宁海 Ninghai
江东 Jiangdong	江北 Jiangbei	北仑 Beilun	镇海 Zhenhai	鄞州 Yinzhou					
29	142	148	248	992	665	774	322	277	306
10	35	23	80	78	49	63	44	53	49
147436	968512	927593	2595688	7669035	5032766	8968559	1797271	1874964	2457818
144117	943977	907311	2524267	7413451	4819880	8399808	1708280	1772565	2340922
27731	202541	157405	431353	2024811	1316840	2530818	434016	628967	617488
153634	1111349	1015807	2079178	5774971	4498145	8348920	1725228	2141281	2520767
128947	647674	720211	1483449	3869561	3178775	5474369	1133687	1447287	1733928
27422	436677	349056	652035	1804895	1338532	2444770	596088	576912	695731
11678	142765	126391	227525	650584	461900	926237	203817	176304	266664
110976	695565	622309	1602931	3791846	3396800	6383396	1260611	1468735	1869810
110571	632596	595430	1532438	3625807	3241153	6043950	1219674	1412457	1784959
42659	415784	393497	476247	1946503	1083225	1965443	464618	672546	650674
20595	159083	261113	268030	630824	434342	916453	245183	344729	246310
145562	948200	923924	2688432	7379046	4764186	8242581	1699458	1751594	2276013
128646	766616	787793	2482124	6281821	4104626	7128228	1436626	1498728	1890212
549	4296	4554	6605	29839	16493	22903	7781	7013	10335
4003	31126	25727	41831	150678	105491	220338	44403	42693	77894
10157	83823	65738	124434	474961	263541	441001	124922	100276	154563
2606	20533	19123	46138	111948	111085	198546	47930	52146	64741
−8	48797	22619	−5543	429899	190353	270550	42735	56566	94606
8179	54745	25913	391	442903	205218	287835	50467	65129	98043
1313	6145	5880	54133	14377	14736	27349	9856	17449	23836
13920	97308	94540	153248	520461	326285	642527	202336	131776	205794
2132	28773	25395	39217	167870	103412	206881	52146	48370	67230
19287	120643	118069	400482	909632	585882	1078501	208016	214175	250136
18818	125319	122717	381040	953807	566754	992903	220977	223299	244507
3493	23970	22721	38562	138401	89242	169946	55503	36569	55711

表7－12　各县(市)、区规模以上大中型工业企业主要财务指标(2012)
Main Financial Indicators of Large and Medium Size Industrial Enterprises Above Designated Size by Region

指标	Indicators	全市 Toal	市区 Urban District	海曙 Haishu
企业单位数(个)	Number of Enterprises(unit)	1112	533	9
#亏损企业	Deficits Enterprises	134	66	
工业总产值(现价)	Gross Industrial Output Value(Current Prices)	76649722	54834264	3128160
工业销售产值	Value of Industrial Products Sales	74218982	53686998	3117756
#出口交货值	Value of Export Products	16204944	9765010	90914
资产合计	Total Asset	61517058	38648955	1564892
流动资产小计	Total Current Assets	35291578	21743241	343493
固定资产原价	Original Value of Fixed Assets	29284679	20278819	2022815
#累计折旧	Accumulative Depreciation	11955168	8840782	1191081
负债合计	Total Liabilities	36876164	21739273	1378964
流动负债小计	Current Liabilities	32553150	18754273	359474
所有者权益合计	Total Owners' Equity	24627662	16896505	185929
#实收资本	Paid－in Capital	12571286	9358880	75131
主营业务收入	Prime Operating Revenue	74087179	53535718	3156467
主营业务成本	Operating Costs	63468659	46099530	2844784
主营业务税金及附加	Tax and Extra Charge	2431413	2348807	9248
销售费用	Sales Expenses	1341101	841898	18172
管理费用	Administrative Expenses	2933153	1767425	22479
财务费用	Finance Charge	891060	406041	8433
营业利润	Business Profits	3370782	2316752	103121
利润总额	Total Profits	3707534	2523855	125727
亏损企业亏损总额	Total Loss	238932	166410	
本年应付职工薪酬	Employee Compensation Payable in this Year	3540457	2079678	61806
本年应交增值税	Value－added Taxes Payable in this Year	1974920	1414876	59927
本年进项税额	Withholdings on VAT in this Year	8925270	6326573	73688
本年销项税额	Substituted money on VAT in this Year	9859587	7400077	508391
全部从业人员年平均人数(人)	Annual Average Employees(person)	767494	419122	9822

单位:万元(10000 yuan)

各区 by Districts					余姚 Yuyao	慈溪 Cixi	奉化 Fenghua	象山 Xiangshan	宁海 Ninghai
江东 Jiangdong	江北 Jiangbei	北仑 Beilun	镇海 Zhenhai	鄞州 Yinzhou					
9	48	110	78	229	154	232	71	53	69
1	5	19	11	15	14	33	9	6	6
1724437	2488447	11439150	16528342	9919442	5218907	9273453	1698000	2495775	3129324
1717761	2505744	11350292	16351506	9611474	4986370	8703274	1453081	2362681	3026578
212763	403774	2199764	940303	3032593	1622388	2758785	707581	608101	743079
1844707	1806842	11443175	7788283	8857584	4626416	8805081	1900522	3581402	3954682
990970	1106894	6180140	4207742	5582537	3146280	5497088	1192697	1820143	1892129
974727	614288	6599237	4543201	3061924	1561778	2717521	795456	1700673	2230433
405183	209489	2660629	2036708	1306909	597783	1035593	253713	584016	643283
626354	854868	6243800	4251208	5094213	3095136	5788710	1429012	2281803	2542231
416223	806338	5366817	4088915	4730800	2966733	5421367	1398420	1965032	2047326
1218353	951975	5199375	3537075	3753194	1531280	3016371	471510	1299600	1412397
261533	383334	3441787	2625947	1454107	723392	1136791	228198	566103	557923
1726556	2484267	11210016	16550569	9275905	4976610	8583663	1691432	2311649	2988107
654154	2197657	10025728	14471112	7716743	4310398	7330911	1450387	1927217	2350215
769425	7074	35149	1182801	36642	16582	25815	11779	9790	18639
54238	38597	176310	102011	385416	99893	229579	36814	59491	73427
81427	122097	424846	291609	641139	277509	515288	112117	98216	162598
8734	20099	125964	83240	110074	98839	169315	41439	79696	95730
166576	112389	500144	465468	613053	204120	356576	47009	144209	302117
192823	129120	557499	473648	646378	248383	428963	50118	152011	304203
656	1480	100896	24887	13007	10573	24769	7126	9875	20178
45711	138297	586755	313912	638730	315823	646398	156675	150179	191704
174262	39131	200348	348574	200542	102624	228176	35635	74670	118939
268683	416875	1655089	2381682	1084612	639583	1133324	159631	311479	354680
404088	419948	1617802	2663397	1093070	568229	1072271	138271	318290	362449
6592	27030	112720	47706	148952	77118	157957	39299	31429	42569

表 7－13 各县(市)、区规模以上外商和港澳台投资工业企业主要财务指标(2012) Main Financial Indicators of Foreign Funded and Hongkong, Macao, Taiwan Funded Industrial Enterprises Above Designated Size by Region

指标	Indicators	全市 Toal	市区 Urban District	
				海曙 Haishu
企业单位数(个)	Number of Enterprises(unit)	2101	1228	10
#亏损企业	Deficits Enterprises	442	286	1
工业总产值(现价)	Gross Industrial Output Value(Current Prices)	50416251	38610819	99055
工业销售产值	Value of Industrial Products Sales	48816628	37854183	96510
#出口交货值	Value of Export Products	15326964	10600500	61516
资产合计	Total Asset	45752997	33239072	59219
流动资产小计	Total Current Assets	29283094	20605659	48292
固定资产原价	Original Value of Fixed Assets	19035363	15027210	20717
#累计折旧	Accumulative Depreciation	7534201	5977548	11707
负债合计	Total Liabilities	26135032	17974372	29139
流动负债小计	Current Liabilities	23756345	16014843	29050
所有者权益合计	Total Owners' Equity	19536523	15203550	30080
#实收资本	Paid－in Capital	11571414	9088259	17028
主营业务收入	Prime Operating Revenue	48896533	37730205	97270
主营业务成本	Operating Costs	42956218	33458171	82129
主营业务税金及附加	Tax and Extra Charge	444913	403024	889
销售费用	Sales Expenses	1077026	801535	2426
管理费用	Administrative Expenses	2334644	1590910	7761
财务费用	Finance Charge	649438	392759	709
营业利润	Business Profits	1827276	1436645	3492
利润总额	Total Profits	2007916	1567878	3977
亏损企业亏损总额	Total Loss	374817	304299	115
本年应付职工薪酬	Employee Compensation Payable in this Year	2814328	1897768	13626
本年应交增值税	Value－added Taxes Payable in this Year	1112099	869782	3454
本年进项税额	Withholdings on VAT in this Year	5747677	4361577	12382
本年销项税额	Substituted money on VAT in this Year	5632536	4471611	13333
全部从业人员年平均人数(人)	Annual Average Employees(person)	635395	410074	3097

单位:万元(10000 yuan)

各区 by Districts					余姚 Yuyao	慈溪 Cixi	奉化 Fenghua	象山 Xiangshan	宁海 Ninghai
江东 Jiangdong	江北 Jiangbei	北仑 Beilun	镇海 Zhenhai	鄞州 Yinzhou					
15	91	341	206	469	327	261	87	88	110
4	22	90	75	66	48	48	14	18	28
435080	981284	13938376	5294162	8123395	4012697	4429838	1408758	1045614	908525
437780	993957	13895054	5326774	7951239	3821902	4106951	1195906	975140	862546
175434	387192	2818308	1148609	2937159	1704791	1389128	700871	409466	522208
233513	1192802	14688093	4158086	7600512	4015486	4743822	1514143	1303343	937131
190888	762874	8704927	2485134	4991975	2913129	3215358	981976	910041	656932
53844	391943	7273381	1948083	2804611	1279646	1377800	706741	343371	300596
25564	129022	2707304	762270	1239213	539318	517734	243890	138378	117334
135019	648122	7134598	2352859	4366266	2708032	2939197	1072349	835870	605213
131385	606655	6313667	1915157	4004653	2493921	2821158	1061317	769202	595905
98493	544680	7553495	1805411	3172912	1288989	1804226	441794	467473	330492
29575	273063	4741367	1040417	1567722	803091	938913	260727	278824	201601
438698	1008814	13800170	5399017	7659744	3822865	4086070	1427674	1002595	827125
368970	823328	12313851	4884142	6324741	3270708	3482172	1236975	838869	669323
2729	4781	41391	14788	31627	11377	12189	10098	4187	4038
9978	27808	265727	96578	311857	89273	100773	26397	31008	28041
21919	82191	558361	206243	547218	245318	273675	92776	63824	68142
259	11692	145213	75639	102469	77449	93055	29636	31351	25189
43383	70676	582711	136663	530077	143651	140037	39555	37966	29422
44597	78114	657799	145272	528411	164201	163836	41473	40791	29737
1513	5519	116541	72587	22524	23123	27802	5144	7466	6984
17430	93172	685123	213558	574048	286012	337131	109114	98248	86056
6069	20253	243716	76798	159895	77194	90954	24098	26444	23627
129257	113405	2003098	763022	890497	478597	545853	128831	138002	94817
98222	99189	1921204	749496	861550	373369	501113	96740	116454	73249
3336	20910	135861	42777	136680	74416	79741	26413	21754	22997

表 7－14　部分年份工业主要产品产量 Output of Major Industrial Products in Partial Years

主要工业产品	单位	Major Industrial Products	Unit	2009	2010	2011	2012
大米	万吨	Rice	10000 tons	8.24	9.56	8.36	8.19
配合饲料	万吨	Formulated Feed	10000 tons	23.87	21.47	25.41	25.51
食用植物油	万吨	Edible Vegetable Oil	10000 tons	28.25	25.48	25.78	16.88
水产加工品	万吨	Processed Aquatic Products	10000 tons	21.11	26.60	39.84	27.76
罐头	万吨	Canned Food	10000 tons	19.50	19.92	16.43	15.00
味精	万吨	Monosodium Glutamate	10000 tons	1.19	1.11		
啤酒	千万升	Beer	ten million liters	28.19	45.79	48.39	48.82
软饮料	万吨	Soft Beverage	10000 tons	27.60	25.77	17.03	6.94
瓶(罐)装饮用水	万吨	Bottled Drinking Water	10000 tons	9.87	8.50		
精制茶	万吨	Refine Tea	10000 tons	5.74	5.36	5.14	2.64
卷烟	亿支	Cigarette	100 million	322.74	359.28	372.49	394.92
纱	万吨	Yarn	10000 tons	22.27	26.30	29.86	44.82
布	万米	Cloth	10000 m	38943	44946	38045	35380
印染布	万米	Printing and Dyeing Cloth	10000 m	69586	77592	90652	57673
帘子布	万吨	Curtain Cloth	10000 tons	4.60	3.99	3.37	2.67
绒线(毛线)	吨	Knitting Wool	ton	1738	2310	6488	5381
呢绒	万米	Wool Fabric	10000 m	4289	4347	2143	3284
服装	万件	Garment	10000 units	142790	155067	111977	113948
梭织服装	万件	Shuttle Woven Garment	10000 units	19757	19842	15792	15141
# 西服及西服套装	万件	Western－style Clothes	10000 units	3558	2764	2291	1693
衬衫	万件	Shirt	10000 units	8880	8696	6029	6378
羽绒服装	万件	Eiderdown Garment	10000 units	266.03	312.57	622.74	26.76
针织服装	万件	Knitting Garment	10000 units	123033	135224	96185	98807
机制纸及纸板	万吨	Paper－making and Paperboard	10000 tons	172.37	182.38	208.23	221.81
纸制品	万吨	Paper Products	10000 tons	94.47	118.67	86.91	84.21
原油加工量	万吨	Crude Oil Processed	10000 tons	1917.35	2084.66	2717.43	2506.12
汽油	万吨	Gasoline	10000 tons	304.18	283.03	295.53	264.08
煤油	万吨	Kerosene	10000 tons	146.08	154.56	162.89	156.23
柴油	万吨	DieselOil	10000 tons	735.38	750.62	742.00	679.24
石油沥青	万吨	Asphalt	10000 tons	214.24	281.58	277.43	263.53
液化石油气	万吨	Liquefied Petroleum Gas	10000 tons	106.42	109.47	110.37	96.40
硫酸(折 100%)	万吨	Sulphuric Acid(100%)	10000 tons	9.16	9.16	10.27	9.65
盐酸(含量 31%以上)	万吨	Hydrochloric Acid (above31%percent)	10000 tons	15.61	15.15	16.90	8.98
烧碱(折 100%)	万吨	CausticSoda(100%)	10000 tons	33.88	34.28	46.10	55.37
合成氨	万吨	SyntheticAmmonia	10000 tons	18.30	6.01	4.04	7.24
农用化肥(折纯)	万吨	ChemicalFertilizers	10000 tons	16.30	6.11	1.17	1.28

7—14 续表 Continued

主要工业产品	单位	Major Industrial Products	Unit	2009	2010	2011	2012
氮肥(折含 N100%)	万吨	NitrogenousFertilizer(100%)	10000 tons	16.30	6.11	1.17	1.28
尿素	万吨	Urea	10000 tons	14.96	4.87		
化学农药	吨	ChemicalPesticide	ton	4093.43	5865.14	4912.54	2796.50
纯苯	万吨	PureBenzene	10000 tons	16.70	29.07	41.05	37.92
建筑涂料	吨	BuildingDope	ton	2586.36	2711.58		
染料	吨	Dye	ton	9017.71	11092.40		
塑料树脂及共聚物	万吨	Plastic Resinand Copolyment	10000 tons	268.71	333.10	369.13	315.56
化学原料药	吨	Chemical Raw Medicine	ton	2157	2094	2648	2105
塑料制品	万吨	Plastic Products	10000 tons	94.07	112.41	88.77	92.00
水泥	万吨	Cement	10000 tons	944.13	1092.62	1303.81	1289.44
粗钢	万吨	Rural Steel	10000 tons	318.31	433.05	471.37	456.77
成品钢材	万吨	Rolled—steel Final Products	10000 tons	539.35	662.04	762.50	830.16
铜	万吨	Copper	10000 tons	0.09	4.19	5.61	6.79
铜加工材	万吨	Copper Material	10000 tons	54.41	64.30	51.67	61.51
铝材	万吨	Aluminium	10000 tons	22.60	29.89	25.57	18.89
液压元件	万件	Hydraulic Pressure Elements	10000 units	3242.36	5947.99	6363.74	7000.93
气动元件	万件	Pneumatic Element	10000 units	4210.28	6375.25	7311.24	6857.91
粉末冶金制品	万吨	Powder Metallurgy Products	10000 tons	2.66	3.41	3.30	3.35
大中型拖拉机	台	Lager and Medium—sized Tractor	unit	28777	36616	45990	28262
汽车	辆	Motor Vechicle	unit	106487	145660	170754	128942
轿车	辆	Car	unit	106452	145593	170754	128942
摩托车	万辆	Motorcycles	10000 units	8.82	10.40	7.67	9.12
自行车	万辆	Bicycles	10000 units	360.18	343.64	403.39	371.76
民用钢质船舶	载重吨	Civil Steel Ship	DWT	863317	897467	1032565	650674
交流电动机	万千瓦	Alternating Current Motor	10000 kw	212.65	276.32	103.64	80.69
变压器	万千伏安	Transformer	10000 kev	1436.49	1613.23	1829.46	1797.18
电力电缆	万公里	Power Cable	10000 km	13.68	26.38	33.00	126.50
自动化仪表系统	万套	Instrument and Meter for Automation	10000 units	609.81	72.60		
原电池(折一号电池)	万只	Primary Cellsand Batterices	10000 units	376593	441809	459965	437644
家用洗衣机	万台	Household Washing Machine	10000 units	1259.41	1360.46	1337.46	1483.26
吸尘器	万台	Dust Catcher	10000 units	1094.78	1027.39	1282.17	1109.28
电风扇	万台	Electric Fan	10000 units	479.94	541.18	595.76	632.10
房间空气调节器	万台	Home Air Conditioner	10000 units	241.59	418.53	380.56	414.03
排油烟机	万台	Range Hoods	10000 units	107.01	109.39	62.81	145.98
移动电话机	万部	Mobile Phone	10000 units	383.22	393.97	233.14	253.12
光学仪器	万台	Optical Instrument	10000 units	212.42	273.24	280.48	336.85
发电量	亿千瓦小时	Generating Capacity	100 million kwh	692.13	844.59	952.48	887.22

表 7－15 各县(市)、区规模以上工业企业主要经济效益指标(2012) Main Indicators on Ecnomic Benefit of Industrial Enterprises Above Designated Size by Region

指标	单位	Indicators	Unit	全市 Toal	市区 Urban District
产销率	%	Proportion of Products Sold	%	96.98	98.15
资产负债率	%	Assets Liability Ratio	%	62.03	57.46
成本费用利润率	%	Ratio of Profits to Industrial Cost	%	4.98	4.94
每百元固定资产原值实现利税	元	Pre－tax Profits Per 100 Yuan Original Value of Fixed Assets	yuan	23.22	24.92
每百元主营业务收入实现利税	元	Pre－tax Profits Per 100 Yuan Main Business	yuan	9.43	10.17
流动比率	%	Ratio of Circulating Funds to Current Liabilities	%	1.08	1.15
速动比率	%	Ratio of Quickassets to Current Liabilities	%	0.83	0.86
企业亏损面	%	Ratio of Number of Deficit Enterprises to Total Enterprises Number	%	15.20	18.06
亏损率	%	Losing Rate	%	11.13	11.98
出口交货值占工业销售产值比重	%	Ratio of Exports Products Value to Industrial Sales Value	%	22.24	18.76
利润总额占利税比重	%	Ratio of Total Profits to Total Pre－tax	%	49.71	45.38
存货周转次数	次	Number of Times of Turnover of Inventories	times	6.76	7.43

各区 by Districts						余姚 Yuyao	慈溪 Cixi	奉化 Fenghua	象山 Xiangshan	宁海 Ninghai
海曙 Haishu	江东 Jiangdong	江北 Jiangbei	北仑 Beilun	镇海 Zhenhai	鄞州 Yinzhou					
99.59	99.42	99.93	99.49	98.83	97.43	95.96	93.85	91.21	95.05	96.25
80.02	37.45	56.04	53.28	60.40	58.99	70.84	69.61	72.19	65.57	65.84
4.81	25.14	4.59	5.15	2.57	6.88	4.93	4.60	2.84	5.33	8.29
10.69	114.11	21.31	11.32	30.97	30.64	21.98	22.25	13.79	14.45	19.47
6.70	61.19	6.79	7.35	9.77	9.20	7.35	7.25	5.90	8.47	11.96
1.17	2.08	1.21	1.16	1.01	1.20	1.05	0.99	0.92	0.97	0.96
1.01	1.25	0.86	0.90	0.68	0.94	0.85	0.77	0.74	0.73	0.76
11.76	25.42	24.18	22.28	32.11	10.14	9.36	10.48	14.65	18.36	18.78
0.17	1.11	13.08	17.23	20.81	3.39	7.45	8.11	13.94	10.76	12.03
4.21	13.44	18.90	17.50	7.78	29.47	30.85	28.02	36.60	27.84	27.79
65.96	22.04	65.10	67.20	24.33	71.24	64.39	61.09	46.82	59.87	63.95
41.24	1.64	5.42	6.91	8.60	6.74	6.32	5.67	6.41	4.24	5.55

表 7－16 各县(市)、区规模以上工业企业综合能耗及产值能耗(2012) Comprehensive Energy Consumption of Industrial Enterprises Above Designated Size by Region

指标	Indicators	全市 Toal	市区 Urban District
综合能耗(吨标准煤)	**Final Energy Consumption(Ton of SCE)**	**31031654**	**21503662**
黑色金属矿采选业	Ferrous Metals Mining and Dressing	23	23
农副食品加工业	Farm and Sideline Products Processing	104388	72633
食品制造业	Food Manufacturing	102572	13795
酒、饮料和精制茶制造业	Wine, Beverages and Refined Tea Manufacturing	32483	16892
烟草制品业	Tobacco Manufacturing	11920	11920
纺织业	Textile Industry	644770	385508
纺织服装、服饰业	Clothing, Apparel Industry	148298	94849
皮革、毛皮、羽毛及其制品和制鞋业	Leather, Fur, Feather and Its Products and Footwear Industry	6831	4144
木材加工及木、竹、藤、棕、草制品业	Timber Processing, Bamboo, Rattan, Cane Palm, and Straw Products	12370	6442
家具制造业	Furniture Manufacturing	17079	10907
造纸及纸制品业	Paper－making and Paper Products Manufacturing	816747	707163
印刷和记录媒介复制业	Printing and Record Duplicating	14751	10223
文教、工美、体育和娱乐用品制造业	Culture, Art, Sports and Recreation Supplies Manufacturing	52766	26333
石油加工、炼焦和核燃料加工业	Petroleum Processing, Coking & Nuclear Fuel Processing	6361280	6359748
化学原料和化学制品制造业	Raw Chemical Materials and Chemical Products	2470538	2353867
医药制造业	Medicines Manufacturing	31421	21074
化学纤维制造业	Chemical Fiber Manufacturing	322707	112087
橡胶和塑料制品业	Rubber and Plastic Products Industry	180166	81597
非金属矿物制品业	Nonmetal Mineral Products	366350	149684
黑色金属冶炼和压延加工业	Smelting and Pressing of Ferrous Metals	3009670	2813717
有色金属冶炼和压延加工业	Smelting and Pressing of Nonferrous Metals	235758	128628
金属制品业	Metal Products Manufacturing	192638	110398
通用设备制造业	General Purpose Equipment Manufacturing	225070	110273
专用设备制造业	Special Purpose Equipment Manufacturing	83211	51614
汽车制造业	Automobile Manufacturing	197420	131760
铁路、船舶、航空航天和其他运输设备制造业	Railroad, Marine, Aviation and Other Transport Equipment Manufacturing	65801	34067
电气机械和器材制造业	Electric Equipment and Machinery Manufacturing	278421	80574
计算机、通信和其他电子设备制造业	Computer, Communications and Other Electronic Equipment Manufacturing	118959	99122
仪器仪表制造业	Instrument Manufacturing	28825	8549
其他制造业	Other Manufacturing	20102	5299
废弃资源综合利用业	Waste Comprehensive Utilization of Resources Industry	5926	5034
金属制品、机械和设备修理业	Metal Products, Machinery and Equipment Repair Industry	272	44
电力、热力的生产和供应业	Production and Supply Electric Power and Thermal Power	14858714	7478227
燃气生产和供应业	Production and Supply Gas	400	232
水的生产和供应业	Production and Supply Tap Water	13007	7236

各区 by Districts						余姚 Yuyao	慈溪 Cixi	奉化 Fenghua	象山 Xiangshan	宁海 Ninghai
海曙 Haishu	江东 Jiangdong	江北 Jiangbei	北仑 Beilun	镇海 Zhenhai	鄞州 Yinzhou					
84737	**27604**	**155086**	**9969056**	**8776530**	**1156466**	**1070227**	**913605**	**207935**	**2645023**	**4691202**
			23							
	1071	2699	53685	79	7150	8674	9471	4994	7590	1026
384		2350	3482	3932	3237	74441	4120	3230	3876	3110
1205		3	4895	3429	7360	730		7772	271	6818
	11920									
205		5354	230293	52361	85405	96173	84968	5162	66296	6663
1436	840	1172	30633	1283	59086	988	2616	18070	23693	8082
	185		842	1257	1496	318	590	247		1532
				33	6409	724	2644	2444		116
	40	1121	2507	115	6857	3723	1313	61	376	699
	117	153	379354	11934	314334	12106	54026	6796	12641	24015
376	25	257	2612		6812	3187	348	792		201
	83	2919	9131	1776	11672	3840	9210	1006	605	11772
			68067	6119012	383			1485	47	
		3479	524730	929175	24882	12016	85506	5084	2376	11689
40		133	2341	13296	4049	487	5095	2396	1281	1088
			41570	69699	817	49792	156785	1521	2503	19
514	158	5364	34390	13559	25330	41389	34347	6325	2969	13539
		9961	36794	47664	39611	137284	17885	6251	18840	36406
2	269	25171	2600406	43988	127061	78363	55992	48451	6409	6738
67	1618	50152	8686	29868	26713	37951	45327	8931	122	14799
188	160	9157	24137	32238	37362	31172	25602	10126	1565	13775
111	449	4321	17842	51809	33144	23599	54739	16103	4649	15707
157	649	1863	29614	7679	10725	15082	6113	979	4238	5185
481	180	15133	42139	4860	56190	8998	25882	3047	13240	14493
	304		19354	3448	5529	1069	10828	14204	5036	597
1830	465	5431	10066	8371	40854	54428	109945	7443	6773	19258
433	3356	4292	15300	5622	29732	5294	9734	1895	280	2634
31		2364	524	151	4508	13653	4037	1323		1263
		1326	54	586	3279	2113	9215	3202		273
			1240	3415	379	77	789		26	
	37			7				227		1
77047			5774345	1315323	176019	351179	83504	18300	2458229	4469275
231							168			
	5679	912		564	81	1377	2805	70	1090	429

表 7—16 续表 Continued

指标	Indicators	全市 Toal	市区 Urban District
产值能耗(吨标煤/万元)	**Energy Consumption of Output Value(Ton of SCE/10000 yuan)**	**0.2596**	**0.2682**
黑色金属矿采选业	Ferrous Metals Mining and Dressing		
农副食品加工业	Farm and Sideline Products Processing	0.0678	0.0968
食品制造业	Food Manufacturing	0.1253	0.0588
酒、饮料和精制茶制造业	Wine, Beverages and Refined Tea Manufacturing	0.1443	0.1678
烟草制品业	Tobacco Manufacturing	0.0100	0.0100
纺织业	Textile Industry	0.1868	0.1635
纺织服装、服饰业	Clothing, Apparel Industry	0.0254	0.0219
皮革、毛皮、羽毛及其制品和制鞋业	Leather, Fur, Feather and Its Products and Footwear Industry	0.0404	0.0369
木材加工及木、竹、藤、棕、草制品业	Timber Processing,Bamboo,Rattan,Cane Palm,and Straw Products	0.0857	0.0693
家具制造业	Furniture Manufacturing	0.0246	0.0262
造纸及纸制品业	Paper—making and Paper Products Manufacturing	0.4899	0.6182
印刷和记录媒介复制业	Printing and Record Duplicating	0.0239	0.0195
文教、工美、体育和娱乐用品制造业	Culture, Art, Sports and Recreation Supplies Manufacturing	0.0270	0.0231
石油加工、炼焦和核燃料加工业	Petroleum Processing,Coking & Nuclear Fuel Processing	0.4055	0.4057
化学原料和化学制品制造业	Raw Chemical Materials and Chemical Products	0.2148	0.2241
医药制造业	Medicines Manufacturing	0.0649	0.0617
化学纤维制造业	Chemical Fiber Manufacturing	0.1469	0.4839
橡胶和塑料制品业	Rubber and Plastic Products Industry	0.0523	0.0518
非金属矿物制品业	Nonmetal Mineral Products	0.1886	0.1607
黑色金属冶炼和压延加工业	Smelting and Pressing of Ferrous Metals	0.5370	0.6928
有色金属冶炼和压延加工业	Smelting and Pressing of Nonferrous Metals	0.0453	0.0433
金属制品业	Metal Products Manufacturing	0.0539	0.0522
通用设备制造业	General Purpose Equipment Manufacturing	0.0317	0.0303
专用设备制造业	Special Purpose Equipment Manufacturing	0.0257	0.0239
汽车制造业	Automobile Manufacturing	0.0339	0.0382
铁路、船舶、航空航天和其他运输设备制造业	Railroad,Marine, Aviation and Other Transport Equipment Manufacturing	0.0387	0.0541
电气机械和器材制造业	Electric Equipment and Machinery Manufacturing	0.0205	0.0162
计算机、通信和其他电子设备制造业	Computer, Communications and Other Electronic Equipment Manufacturing	0.0145	0.0140
仪器仪表制造业	Instrument Manufacturing	0.0185	0.0125
其他制造业	Other Manufacturing	0.0402	0.0321
废弃资源综合利用业	Waste Comprehensive Utilization of Resources Industry	0.0059	0.0052
金属制品、机械和设备修理业	Metal Products, Machinery and Equipment Repair Industry	0.0106	0.0031
电力、热力的生产和供应业	Production and Supply Electric Power and Thermal Power	1.7507	1.3980
燃气生产和供应业	Production and Supply Gas	0.0029	0.0019
水的生产和供应业	Production and Supply Tap Water	0.0583	0.0577

各区 by Districts						余姚 Yuyao	慈溪 Cixi	奉化 Fenghua	象山 Xiangshan	宁海 Ninghai
海曙 Haishu	江东 Jiangdong	江北 Jiangbei	北仑 Beilun	镇海 Zhenhai	鄞州 Yinzhou					
0.0256	**0.0134**	**0.0409**	**0.5458**	**0.4005**	**0.0599**	**0.0971**	**0.0584**	**0.0610**	**0.6234**	**0.9311**
	0.2942	0.0594	0.1096	0.0239	0.0471	0.0283	0.0646	0.0750	0.0293	0.1027
0.0176		0.0506	0.0547	0.0958	0.0629	0.1888	0.0990	0.0871	0.0743	0.0532
0.1133		0.0008	0.1575	0.2750	0.1728	0.0171		0.2098	0.0154	0.2528
	0.0100									
0.0030		0.0313	0.3373	0.1093	0.0915	0.2392	0.1884	0.1201	0.5930	0.0790
0.0218	0.0126	0.0174	0.0268	0.0166	0.0206	0.0230	0.0199	0.0380	0.0304	0.1011
	0.0849		0.0227	0.0398	0.0411	0.0226	0.0310	0.0184		0.1484
				0.0116	0.0712	0.0292	0.2724	0.1589		0.0753
	0.0266	0.0201	0.0415	0.0195	0.0240	0.0185	0.0295	0.0103	0.0343	0.0435
	0.0513	0.0759	0.7038	0.2789	0.5710	0.1076	0.2148	0.1610	0.3031	0.3195
0.0663	0.0112	0.0277	0.0510	0.0000	0.0151	0.0552	0.0177	0.0524		0.0871
	0.0243	0.0331	0.0316	0.0333	0.0173	0.0344	0.0278	0.0216	0.0483	0.0378
			0.1373	0.4884	0.0376			0.2198	0.0107	
		0.0317	0.1160	0.2790	0.0418	0.0754	0.1276	0.0782	0.0822	0.1617
0.0056		0.0108	0.0600	0.1418	0.0224	0.0323	0.1019	0.0481	0.0983	0.0732
			0.5975	0.4941	0.0389	0.1072	0.1093	0.0775	0.0579	0.0057
0.0659	0.0220	0.0514	0.1132	0.0941	0.0262	0.0603	0.0488	0.0512	0.0396	0.0477
		0.0616	0.1555	0.4612	0.0982	0.4195	0.0469	0.1550	0.1338	0.2998
0.0059	0.0222	0.2542	0.9936	0.1139	0.1871	0.1476	0.0948	0.1729	0.0719	0.1301
0.0148	0.0365	0.0345	0.0647	0.0578	0.0377	0.0482	0.0428	0.0448	0.0115	0.0844
0.0486	0.0054	0.0667	0.0538	0.1205	0.0394	0.0557	0.0509	0.0586	0.0659	0.0692
0.0101	0.0047	0.0221	0.0308	0.0527	0.0212	0.0350	0.0438	0.0377	0.0127	0.0215
0.0228	0.0179	0.0165	0.0267	0.0250	0.0204	0.0313	0.0300	0.0275	0.0224	0.0309
0.0228	0.0160	0.0533	0.0312	0.0499	0.0394	0.0274	0.0265	0.0280	0.0224	0.0390
	0.0391		0.0517	0.0379	0.0551	0.0308	0.0301	0.0307	0.0266	0.0263
0.0179	0.0187	0.0173	0.0167	0.0177	0.0156	0.0201	0.0252	0.0312	0.0132	0.0239
0.0112	0.0085	0.0280	0.0290	0.0208	0.0243	0.0122	0.0236	0.0124	0.0172	0.0296
0.0047		0.0175	0.0134	0.0161	0.0097	0.0305	0.0112	0.0381		0.0375
		0.0490	0.0151	0.0147	0.0348	0.0410	0.0384	0.1078		0.0198
			0.2280	0.0037	0.0071	0.0479	0.0394		0.0058	
	0.0119			0.0006				0.0790		0.0001
0.0274			4.0699	2.9438	0.2969	0.5974	0.1452	0.1187	3.7935	3.8112
0.0019							0.0086			
	0.0531	0.1278		0.1125	0.0130	0.0553	0.0821	0.0115	0.1122	0.0186

表 7－17 各县(市)、区千吨以上工业综合能源消费量(2012)
Comprehensive Energy Consumption of Industrial Enterprises Above One Thousand Tons

指标	Indicators	全市 Toal	市区 Urban District
综合能源消费量总计(吨标准煤)	**Final energy comprehensive consumption per million (Tons of standard coal)**	**29543449**	**20721950**
黑色金属矿采选业	Ferrous Metals Mining and Dressing		
农副食品加工业	Farm and Sideline Products Processing	87642	65237
食品制造业	Food Manufacturing	57377	7776
酒、饮料和精制茶制造业	Wine, Beverages and Refined Tea Manufacturing	29026	15394
烟草制品业	Tobacco Manufacturing	11920	11920
纺织业	Textile Industry	419200	193127
纺织服装、服饰业	Clothing, Apparel Industry	69029	41970
皮革、毛皮、羽毛及其制品和制鞋业	Leather, Fur, Feather and Its Products and Footwear Industry	1031	
木材加工及木、竹、藤、棕、草制品业	Timber Processing, Bamboo, Rattan, Cane Palm, and Straw Products	6704	1878
家具制造业	Furniture Manufacturing	3339	3339
造纸及纸制品业	Paper－making and Paper Products Manufacturing	787684	695956
印刷和记录媒介复制业	Printing and Record Duplicating	4855	3669
文教、工美、体育和娱乐用品制造业	Culture, Art, Sports and Recreation Supplies Manufacturing	13187	7197
石油加工、炼焦和核燃料加工业	Petroleum Processing. Coking & Nuclear Fuel Processing	6358592	6358592
化学原料和化学制品制造业	Raw Chemical Materials and Chemical Products	2410103	2304264
医药制造业	Medicines Manufacturing	24250	16759
化学纤维制造业	Chemical Fiber Manufacturing	305610	111270
橡胶和塑料制品业	Rubber and Plastic Products Industry	85338	50189
非金属矿物制品业	Nonmetal Mineral Products	319405	124683
黑色金属冶炼和压延加工业	Smelting and Pressing of Ferrous Metals	2938232	2778345
有色金属冶炼和压延加工业	Smelting and Pressing of Nonferrous Metals	187993	110987
金属制品业	Metal Products Manufacturing	119322	74913
通用设备制造业	General Purpose Equipment Manufacturing	84434	39458
专用设备制造业	Special Purpose Equipment Manufacturing	19015	16758
汽车制造业	Automobile Manufacturing	120244	86836
铁路、船舶、航空航天和其他运输设备制造业	Railroad, Marine, Aviation and Other Transport Equipment Manufacturing	43224	26171
电气机械和器材制造业	Electric Equipment and Machinery Manufacturing	93625	32639
计算机、通信和其他电子设备制造业	Computer, Communications and Other Electronic Equipment Manufacturing	70819	63846
仪器仪表制造业	Instrument Manufacturing	6137	1151
其他制造业	Other Manufacturing	7955	2285
废弃资源综合利用业	Waste Comprehensive Utilization of Resources Industry	1240	1240
金属制品、机械和设备修理业	Metal Products, Machinery and Equipment Repair Industry		
电力、热力的生产和供应业	Production and Supply Electric Power and Thermal Power	14848876	7468422
燃气生产和供应业	Production and Supply Gas		
水的生产和供应业	Production and Supply Tap Water	8041	5679

各区 by Districts						余姚 Yuyao	慈溪 Cixi	奉化 Fenghua	象山 Xiangshan	宁海 Ninghai
海曙 Haishu	江东 Jiangdong	江北 Jiangbei	北仑 Beilun	镇海 Zhenhai	鄞州 Yinzhou					
78637	**20139**	**107547**	**9672881**	**8664214**	**878521**	**849431**	**655852**	**115715**	**2597992**	**4602509**
		2251	53131		1905	5229	9043	3788	4345	
		1508	3482	1960	826	39906	4041	183	2429	3042
570			4675	3429	6719			7772		5860
	11920									
		1220	57911	49764	73970	90911	63738	1937	65237	4250
			17970		24000			2182	17087	7790
										1031
					1878		2621	2205		
					3339					
			377973	6811	311171	9290	45271	4183	11067	21917
			1932		1738	1186				
			1746		5451		3749			2241
			67833	6118870						
		1502	521629	898111	15899	9938	82238	3020	1374	9269
			1248	12601	2910		5095	2396		
			41570	69699		48873	142896	757	1814	
		1058	28351	8082	11576	13512	17799	1159	1070	1609
		5051	32506	47118	24629	133449	8520	1217	16544	34992
		20656	2596389	42142	102831	68180	49042	32194	4280	6191
	991	49598	2271	25647	21624	34152	29395	5591		7868
		7720	15300	27032	20588	16705	15852	6362		5490
			4300	31027	4133	8519	21141	6249	1142	7925
			15373	1385		997			1260	
		12063	31066	1319	33035	3913	14305	1101	7867	6222
			18012	959	3673		1379	12996	2678	
1050		2403	3836		16739	6593	46438		1568	6387
	1549	2517	8561	2936	10435	1914	3909			1150
					1151	4986				
					2286		3546	2124		
			1240							
77017			5764577	1315321	176013	351179	83471	18300	2458229	4469275
	5679						2362			

表 7－18 各县(市)、区千吨以上工业万元产值综合能耗(2012) Comprehensive Energy Consumption of Industrial Enterprises Above One Thousand Tons

指标	Indicators	全市 Toal	市区 Urban District
万元产值综合能耗总计(吨标准煤)	**Final energy comprehensive consumption per million (Tons of standard coal)**	**0.4030**	**0.3721**
黑色金属矿采选业	Ferrous Metals Mining and Dressing		
农副食品加工业	Farm and Sideline Products Processing	0.0903	0.1164
食品制造业	Food Manufacturing	0.1369	0.0801
酒、饮料和精制茶制造业	Wine, Beverages and Refined Tea Manufacturing	0.2298	0.2313
烟草制品业	Tobacco Manufacturing	0.0100	0.0100
纺织业	Textile Industry	0.2424	0.1742
纺织服装、服饰业	Clothing, Apparel Industry	0.0351	0.0257
皮革、毛皮、羽毛及其制品和制鞋业	Leather, Fur, Feather and Its Products and Footwear Industry	0.1254	
木材加工及木、竹、藤、棕、草制品业	Timber Processing,Bamboo,Rattan,Cane Palm,and Straw Products	0.3340	0.2756
家具制造业	Furniture Manufacturing	0.0467	0.0467
造纸及纸制品业	Paper－making and Paper Products Manufacturing	0.5906	0.6703
印刷和记录媒介复制业	Printing and Record Duplicating	0.0286	0.0241
文教、工美、体育和娱乐用品制造业	Culture, Art, Sports and Recreation Supplies Manufacturing	0.0391	0.0459
石油加工、炼焦和核燃料加工业	Petroleum Processing,Coking & Nuclear Fuel Processing	0.4081	0.4081
化学原料和化学制品制造业	Raw Chemical Materials and Chemical Products	0.2292	0.2348
医药制造业	Medicines Manufacturing	0.1315	0.1981
化学纤维制造业	Chemical Fiber Manufacturing	0.1530	0.5283
橡胶和塑料制品业	Rubber and Plastic Products Industry	0.0724	0.0749
非金属矿物制品业	Nonmetal Mineral Products	0.2660	0.2415
黑色金属冶炼和压延加工业	Smelting and Pressing of Ferrous Metals	0.6223	0.7820
有色金属冶炼和压延加工业	Smelting and Pressing of Nonferrous Metals	0.0491	0.0460
金属制品业	Metal Products Manufacturing	0.0958	0.0816
通用设备制造业	General Purpose Equipment Manufacturing	0.0560	0.0759
专用设备制造业	Special Purpose Equipment Manufacturing	0.0276	0.0255
汽车制造业	Automobile Manufacturing	0.0450	0.0604
铁路、船舶、航空航天和其他运输设备制造业	Railroad,Marine, Aviation and Other Transport Equipment Manufacturing	0.0463	0.0670
电气机械和器材制造业	Electric Equipment and Machinery Manufacturing	0.0238	0.0177
计算机、通信和其他电子设备制造业	Computer, Communications and Other Electronic Equipment Manufacturing	0.0122	0.0119
仪器仪表制造业	Instrument Manufacturing	0.0212	0.0059
其他制造业	Other Manufacturing	0.0540	0.0503
废弃资源综合利用业	Waste Comprehensive Utilization of Resources Industry	0.2280	0.2280
金属制品、机械和设备修理业	Metal Products, Machinery and Equipment Repair Industry		
电力、热力的生产和供应业	Production and Supply Electric Power and Thermal Power	1.7716	1.4225
燃气生产和供应业	Production and Supply Gas		
水的生产和供应业	Production and Supply Tap Water	0.0585	0.0531

各区 by Districts						余姚 Yuyao	慈溪 Cixi	奉化 Fenghua	象山 Xiangshan	宁海 Ninghai
海曙 Haishu	江东 Jiangdong	江北 Jiangbei	北仑 Beilun	镇海 Zhenhai	鄞州 Yinzhou					
0.0276	**0.0127**	**0.0549**	**0.6943**	**0.4703**	**0.1238**	**0.1909**	**0.0894**	**0.0867**	**1.3580**	**1.7752**
		0.1570	0.1109		0.1681	0.0244	0.1152	0.1099	0.0523	
		0.1170	0.0547	0.1175	0.2145	0.2027	0.1162	0.0231	0.0820	0.0574
0.0847			0.2247	0.2750	0.2530			0.2098		0.2577
	0.0100									
		0.1175	0.2547	0.1175	0.1696	0.3271	0.3051	0.2890	0.7319	0.1131
			0.0218		0.0297			0.0172	0.1258	0.1108
										0.1254
					0.2756		0.3912	0.3362		
					0.0467					
			0.7409	0.2749	0.6181	0.1614	0.3122	0.3562	0.4595	0.3849
			0.2758		0.0120	0.0680				
			0.0267		0.0598		0.0324			0.0344
			0.1449	0.4887						
		0.1775	0.1169	0.2819	0.0600	0.1069	0.1540	0.0836	0.1075	0.3526
			0.1989	0.1968	0.2035		0.1019	0.0481		
			0.5975	0.4941		0.1063	0.1111	0.4092	0.0470	
		0.0468	0.1773	0.1512	0.0279	0.1010	0.0566	0.0785	0.0380	0.0900
		0.0894	0.1821	0.5795	0.1357	0.5553	0.0361	0.2021	0.1442	0.3997
		0.2460	1.0481	0.1515	0.2021	0.1659	0.0970	0.1653	0.1769	0.1891
	0.0551	0.0344	0.5621	0.0572	0.0539	0.0502	0.0491	0.0698		0.1391
		0.1760	0.0648	0.1946	0.0612	0.1881	0.0823	0.3758		0.1849
			0.1125	0.0765	0.0544	0.0585	0.0674	0.0759	0.0326	0.0192
			0.0263	0.0186		0.0664			0.0745	
		0.1001	0.0337	0.4210	0.0946	0.0312	0.0273	0.0247	0.0208	0.0379
			0.0535	0.2610	0.1123		0.0589	0.0310	0.0265	
0.0178		0.0263	0.0337		0.0131	0.0197	0.0340		0.0101	0.0265
	0.0060	0.0493	0.0295	0.0233	0.0341	0.0070	0.0388			0.0304
					0.0059	0.0523				
					0.0503		0.0360	0.6201		
			0.2280							
0.0277			4.1732	3.1361	0.3004	0.5974	0.1468	0.1187	3.7935	3.8112
	0.0531						0.0776			

表 7－19 按工业行业分组的主要能源消费量(2012)
Comprehensive Energy Consumption by Industrial Sector

指标	Indicators	能源合计 吨标准煤 Total Ton of SCE	原煤 Raw Coal	焦炭 Coke
按工业行业分	**Grouped by Sector**	**84333093**	**40014267**	**1842504**
黑色金属矿采选业	Ferrous Metals Mining and Dressing	35		
农副食品加工业	Farm and Sideline Products Processing	106421	30898	
食品制造业	Food Manufacturing	104356	19563	
酒、饮料和精制茶制造业	Wine, Beverages and Refined Tea Manufacturing	32818	22683	
烟草制品业	Tobacco Manufacturing	12479		
纺织业	Textile Industry	662026	302038	
纺织服装、服饰业	Clothing, Apparel Industry	156717	68973	12
皮革、毛皮、羽毛及其制品和制鞋业	Leather, Fur, Feather and Its Products and Footwear Industry	7285	3517	
木材加工及木、竹、藤、棕、草制品业	Timber Processing, Bamboo, Rattan, Cane Palm, and Straw Products	12646	10642	
家具制造业	Furniture Manufacturing	18883	1772	113
造纸及纸制品业	Paper－making and Paper Products Manufacturing	961403	1068333	
印刷和记录媒介复制业	Printing and Record Duplicating	16349	4930	78
文教、工美、体育和娱乐用品制造业	Culture, Art, Sports and Recreation Supplies Manufacturing	56746	8156	361
石油加工、炼焦和核燃料加工业	Petroleum Processing, Coking & Nuclear Fuel Processing	44558227	1990396	
化学原料和化学制品制造业	Raw Chemical Materials and Chemical Products	2484022	708944	
医药制造业	Medicines Manufacturing	32336	8027	
化学纤维制造业	Chemical Fiber Manufacturing	325871	119015	
橡胶和塑料制品业	Rubber and Plastic Products Industry	186922	24562	
非金属矿物制品业	Nonmetal Mineral Products	389373	223727	851
黑色金属冶炼和压延加工业	Smelting and Pressing of Ferrous Metals	5693573	822982	1830020
有色金属冶炼和压延加工业	Smelting and Pressing of Nonferrous Metals	240236	67236	1770
金属制品业	Metal Products Manufacturing	200691	43149	1073
通用设备制造业	General Purpose Equipment Manufacturing	241087	19210	935
专用设备制造业	Special Purpose Equipment Manufacturing	89269	4321	317
汽车制造业	Automobile Manufacturing	205452	10056	976
铁路、船舶、航空航天和其他运输设备制造业	Railroad, Marine, Aviation and Other Transport Equipment Manufacturing	77559	3962	174
电气机械和器材制造业	Electric Equipment and Machinery Manufacturing	303376	17849	5202
计算机、通信和其他电子设备制造业	Computer, Communications and Other Electronic Equipment Manufacturing	134563	5400	422
仪器仪表制造业	Instrument Manufacturing	31525	1135	203
其他制造业	Other Manufacturing	21506	675	
废弃资源综合利用业	Waste Comprehensive Utilization of Resources Industry	6500	26	
金属制品、机械和设备修理业	Metal Products, Machinery and Equipment Repair Industry	308		
电力、热力的生产和供应业	Production and Supply Electric Power and Thermal Power	26948614	34402092	
燃气生产和供应业	Production and Supply Gas	713		
水的生产和供应业	Production and Supply Tap Water	13207		

单位：吨(ton)

原油 Crude Oil	汽油 Gasoline	煤油 Kerosene	柴油 Diesel Oil	燃料油 Fuel Oil	液化石油气 LPG	其他油制品 Other Petroleum Products	热力 百万千焦 Heat million kilo-joule	电力 万千瓦时 Electricity 10000 kwh
25061182	**66147**	**8313**	**151203**	**323872**	**357340**	**3622282**	**48009314**	**3270306**
	7							19
	570		1666	1838	148	2	1460135	20766
	527		770	10	48		409515	19129
	138		208				272339	4940
	44		2172				155726	2757
	2005		2438	16	1433	33	6724710	139699
	5307		5172	58	32	16	1193502	40079
	313		198		9	71	15434	2760
	222	145	386					2895
	816	1	1191		361	3	4523	9693
	995	15	4767	519	1		1416016	145877
	890	4	664		343		5227	7610
	1846	7	2193	1134	731	166	94923	29848
25061182	52		3747	234415	301078	3588556	1362325	280028
	3559	67	7376	54957	22818	4	27931273	484455
	369		412	120	25		481703	6629
	351		735	487	3	267	3134004	94040
	4101	266	3838	948	438	668	341313	103128
	1145	165	32371	7996	1703	21467	171970	82078
	1376	14	4399	28	14194	91	450219	357978
	1030	179	6513	16365	2044	366	76366	108141
	3787	329	7782	382	3197	558	740219	90118
	9242	6251	11577	557	1180	4104	17589	141407
	4999	64	5850	536	205	1184	30315	47671
	4311	204	7621	1728	101	558	229824	98686
	1029	168	9131	1090	2085	1377	153192	34824
	9831	189	14895	13	2650	2306	116559	190427
	2852	46	4263	126	199	350	311452	85612
	1363	158	1520	11	44	84		20594
	562		1248		2081	4	59983	10225
	290	10	2205		184	48	394	1987
	30		7					206
	1866	31	3744	538	3	1	648567	595232
	74		110					361
	247		31		3			10407

表 7－20 各县(市)、区规模以上工业企业等价综合能源消费量(2012)
Equivalent Comprehensive Energy Consumption of Industrial Enterprises Above Designated Size by Region

指标	Indicators	全市 Toal	市区 Urban District	海曙 Haishu
综合能源消费量总计(吨标准煤)	**Final energy comprehensive consumption per million (Tons of standard coal)**	**22552065**	**17763448**	**211871**
黑色金属矿采选业	Ferrous Metals Mining and Dressing	71	71	
农副食品加工业	Farm and Sideline Products Processing	146519	94968	
食品制造业	Food Manufacturing	141294	20914	530
酒、饮料和精制茶制造业	Wine, Beverages and Refined Tea Manufacturing	42356	22653	1379
烟草制品业	Tobacco Manufacturing	17803	17803	
纺织业	Textile Industry	919354	539839	446
纺织服装、服饰业	Clothing, Apparel Industry	234110	155257	2504
皮革、毛皮、羽毛及其制品和制鞋业	Leather, Fur, Feather and Its Products and Footwear Industry	12614	8096	
木材加工及木、竹、藤、棕、草制品业	Timber Processing, Bamboo, Rattan, Cane Palm, and Straw Products	18236	9705	
家具制造业	Furniture Manufacturing	37601	23911	
造纸及纸制品业	Paper－making and Paper Products Manufacturing	895151	750215	
印刷和记录媒介复制业	Printing and Record Duplicating	31045	23027	644
文教、工美、体育和娱乐用品制造业	Culture, Art, Sports and Recreation Supplies Manufacturing	114381	55524	
石油加工、炼焦和核燃料加工业	Petroleum Processing, Coking & Nuclear Fuel Processing	6380203	6378575	
化学原料和化学制品制造业	Raw Chemical Materials and Chemical Products	3399359	3225480	
医药制造业	Medicines Manufacturing	45136	29312	86
化学纤维制造业	Chemical Fiber Manufacturing	507463	130801	
橡胶和塑料制品业	Rubber and Plastic Products Industry	386062	165503	1335
非金属矿物制品业	Nonmetal Mineral Products	523563	202580	
黑色金属冶炼和压延加工业	Smelting and Pressing of Ferrous Metals	3516423	3135474	5
有色金属冶炼和压延加工业	Smelting and Pressing of Nonferrous Metals	449057	250917	176
金属制品业	Metal Products Manufacturing	374708	216103	494
通用设备制造业	General Purpose Equipment Manufacturing	514142	254557	303
专用设备制造业	Special Purpose Equipment Manufacturing	181320	110344	293
汽车制造业	Automobile Manufacturing	396015	248971	1236
铁路、船舶、航空航天和其他运输设备制造业	Railroad, Marine, Aviation and Other Transport Equipment Manufacturing	144803	69277	
电气机械和器材制造业	Electric Equipment and Machinery Manufacturing	671090	189579	4522
计算机、通信和其他电子设备制造业	Computer, Communications and Other Electronic Equipment Manufacturing	299880	249533	1089
仪器仪表制造业	Instrument Manufacturing	71292	20705	71
其他制造业	Other Manufacturing	41250	12632	
废弃资源综合利用业	Waste Comprehensive Utilization of Resources Industry	10337	7980	
金属制品、机械和设备修理业	Metal Products, Machinery and Equipment Repair Industry	707	146	
电力、热力的生产和供应业	Production and Supply Electric Power and Thermal Power	1994003	1123491	195583
燃气生产和供应业	Production and Supply Gas	1411	1176	1176
水的生产和供应业	Production and Supply Tap Water	33303	18330	

各区 by Districts					余姚 Yuyao	慈溪 Cixi	奉化 Fenghua	象山 Xiangshan	宁海 Ninghai
江东 Jiangdong	江北 Jiangbei	北仑 Beilun	镇海 Zhenhai	鄞州 Yinzhou					
51963	**297951**	**5549561**	**8203537**	**1701072**	**1379659**	**1708442**	**391233**	**517225**	**792058**
		71							
1246	3584	68177	210	11817	13948	14932	7110	14212	1349
	3622	4695	6665	4624	99706	7714	4175	4839	3947
	7	6977	4537	9753	964		9947	364	8428
17803									
	12190	305770	76690	129739	135872	137170	8741	80681	17050
1453	2894	44708	2903	99929	2731	5670	24518	36214	9720
456		2069	2462	2553	602	1120	591		2206
			96	9609	1646	3716	2968		202
70	2935	5099	288	15066	8356	3292	143	759	1140
169	269	393837	16241	338190	15622	71598	9306	17081	31330
100	688	4217		16995	5416	975	1326		302
213	6170	20207	3624	23474	9029	22365	2485	1572	23406
		89673	6107210	494			1570	58	
	6404	811305	1186127	44889	19526	127506	7623	3567	15656
	374	3487	16680	6647	1256	7387	3603	1744	1835
		47304	81886	1611	84582	281582	3946	6503	49
425	11520	66615	25348	55062	95529	73705	14945	7182	29197
	14601	61754	55896	49345	178924	31893	8952	40766	60449
529	36295	2729495	105850	228156	164845	102506	93441	10273	9884
2172	102151	14362	50099	63165	68521	90342	18129	322	20827
406	16755	46732	55892	79073	56430	51994	21950	2828	25403
886	9836	39507	120424	77191	54402	124413	37157	9338	34274
994	5015	60945	15641	25651	31158	15904	2110	8924	12881
435	27294	82951	10326	105471	20503	57298	7315	29233	32694
681		38740	5371	13584	2277	24854	37132	10451	812
1218	12987	23323	20589	94121	127879	280429	14294	15630	43279
8272	11122	38107	13418	66803	13162	26475	5033	687	4989
	5554	1019	388	11152	33866	11303	3382		2037
	3336	147	1131	7854	5237	18187	4663		532
		1524	5587	869	212	2079		66	
127			18				557		4
		536743	210481	107970	123866	104430	33913	211232	397071
						235			
14307	2347		1462	214	3591	7369	210	2701	1104

表 7－21 全市规模以上工业企业能源购、消、存情况(2012)
Purchases, Sales and Inventory of Energy of Industrial Enterprises Above the Set Scale

指标	单位	Indicators	Unit	年初库存 Stock (Year－head)	购进量 Purchases 实物量 Material Amount	购进量 Purchases 金额(千元) Value (1000 yuan)	消费量合计 Consumption
原煤	吨	Raw Coal	ton	2187549	39808270	27849991	40014267
洗精煤	吨	Clendooal	ton	167034	1451234	2501397	1483402
煤制品	吨	Coal Products	ton	3579	336484	233608	337801
焦炭	吨	Coke	ton	56153	759117	1738269	1842504
天然气(气态)	万立方米	Natural Gas (Gas)	10000 Cubic Meters		137766	3526699	137766
液化天然气(液态)	吨	Liquefied Natural Gas (Liquid)	ton	244	1550	14284	1512
原油	吨	Crude Oil	ton	771430	25069144	143256704	25061182
汽油	吨	Gasoline	ton	376	66226	562739	66147
煤油	吨	Kerosene	ton	388	8166	66001	8313
柴油	吨	Diesel Oil	ton	6155	148110	1139813	151203
燃料油	吨	Fuel Oil	ton	14131	125557	527813	323872
液化石油气	吨	Liquefied Petroleum Gas	ton	969	57498	395703	357340
炼厂干气	吨	Refinery Dry Gas	ton		1426	6136	1130330
石油焦	吨	Petroleum Coke	ton	39	13667	15033	642988
其他石油制品	吨	Other Petroleum Products	ton	26234	1222329	5434627	3622282
热力	百万千焦	Heat	million kilo－joule		47432403	3315613	48009314
电力	万千瓦时	Electricity	10000 kwh		2395724	18524249	3270306
余热余压	百万千焦	Residual Heat and Pressure	million kilo－joule		38163	2318	10227565
能源合计	吨标准煤	Total	Ton of SCE				84333093

工业生产消费 Consumptiop of Industrial Production	非工业生产消费 Consumptiop of Non－Industrial Production	年末库存 Stock (Year－end)	能源转出量 Energy Producing	能源投入 Energy Input	火力发电 Generation of Electric Power by Thermal Power	供热 Heat Supply	炼油投入 Input of Oil Refining
40006621	7646	2044349		36101305	32679130	3378837	
1483402		134865		1386438			
337450	351	2262					
1842480	24	59641	1089927				
137370	396			115042	113271	1771	
1512		282		369	332	37	
25061182		770060		25061182			25061182
27793	38354	461	2640804	3	3		
8257	57	239	1562266				
121737	29466	6117	6792420	610	610		
323823	49	9094	850928	233215		642	232573
355250	2091	1170	963964	296049			296049
1130330			1130655	158383		571	157812
642988		2945	1060043	466654	361535	105119	
3621904	378	28092	8912240	908215			908215
47443030	566284		65861581	363438	363438		
3237289	33018		8846347				
10227565				3561004	3561004		
84159094	173999		51928729	67382161	25736198	2499514	37798376

表 7－22　全市及各县(市)全社会用电量(2012)
Total Electricity Consumption by Region

指标	Indicators	全市 Total	为上年(%) The Preceding Year=100(%)
总计	**Total**	**5140915**	**101.74**
全行业用电量	**Electricity Consumption for Non－Living Electricity**	**4547780**	**100.68**
农林牧渔业	Farming, Forestry, Animal Husbandry, Fishery	28724	106.12
＃排灌	Irrigation and Drainage	8140	105.97
①农业	Farming	7051	91.21
②林业	Forestry	387	95.07
③畜牧业	Animal Husbandary	4598	116.42
④渔业	Fishery	5611	118.83
⑤其他	Others	11077	107.98
工业	Industry	3845918	98.96
轻工业	Light Industry	1242699	98.58
重工业	Heavy Industry	2603219	99.15
建筑业	Construction	79121	106.59
交通运输、仓储和邮政业	Transportation, Storage and Post	63923	107.58
交通运输	Transportation	52169	108.52
仓储业	Warehousing Industry	9947	106.59
邮政	Post	1808	89.81
信息传输、计算机服务和软件业	Information Transmission, Computer Service and Software	26512	109.15
商业、住宿和饮食业	Trade, Hotel and Catering Trade	214529	107.71
金融、房地产、商务及居民服务业	Financial, Real Estate, Business and Resident Service	112912	116.13
公共事业及管理组织	Public Service and Management Organizations	176141	117.77
城乡居民生活用电量	**Electricity Consumption for Urban and Rural Residents**	**593135**	**110.68**
城市	Urban Residents	301647	110.94
乡村	Rural Residents	291489	110.41

单位：万千瓦时(10000 kwh)

市区 Urban District	#鄞州 Yinzhou	余姚 Yuyao	慈溪 Cixi	奉化 Fenghua	象山 Xiangshan	宁海 Ninghai
3012523	**710681**	**653552**	**836957**	**247141**	**165369**	**225373**
2715545	**608474**	**583039**	**727215**	**210194**	**129076**	**182710**
12300	6365	4135	3682	1794	3886	2927
2518	1359	1979	512	653	1848	631
4488	2186	264	929	442	576	350
124	53	21	54	57	23	107
1297	459	1276	857	388	377	403
1764	793	458	1024	180	959	1226
4627	2874	2116	818	727	1950	840
2260968	506064	516986	638513	179424	93998	156030
597039	179524	195699	305645	42487	42150	59679
1663928	326540	321287	332868	136937	51848	96351
48660	12385	9121	11726	2995	4081	2539
51689	3562	4845	917	4596	816	1059
41206	2516	4517	643	4386	594	823
9435	611	141	126	152	46	47
1047	435	188	149	58	177	189
16222	4506	2658	2989	1708	1259	1676
134394	26862	22211	24215	9601	13399	10710
87280	22214	6231	11947	2932	2475	2047
104033	26517	16851	33227	7145	9163	5722
296978	**102207**	**70513**	**109741**	**36946**	**36293**	**42663**
198175	48134	21866	30839	15728	18439	16599
98803	54072	48647	78902	21218	17854	26064

表 7－23 历年全社会用电量
Total Electricity Consumption Over Years

年份 Year	总计 Total	比上年增长 Growth Rate over Preceding Year(%)	全行业用电		
			总计 Total	农业 Agriculture	工业 Industry
1978	70905				43704
1979	89023	25.6			56404
1980	106695	19.9			66886
1981	119606	12.1			72878
1982	129011	7.9			78879
1983	147338	14.2			91251
1984	164071	11.4			93618
1985	185167	12.9			98512
1986	223048	20.5			123033
1987	253457	13.6			140978
1988	279914	10.4			148756
1989	285460	2.0			218247
1990	314858	10.3	271855	16657	233766
1991	365090	16.0	315484	17682	273333
1992	421441	15.4	363939	18601	316558
1993	482578	14.5	416063	18680	359972
1994	552044	14.4	467366	20325	400080
1995	619447	12.2	517935	21262	439498
1996	670281	8.2	551953	22039	457688
1997	718416	7.2	595479	21339	496127
1998	799300	11.3	667837	20470	560624
1999	914936	14.5	778181	21063	664623
2000	1134811	24.0	983475	25777	840125
2001	1266535	11.6	1107317	30111	943788
2002	1520751	20.1	1333570	26115	1146566
2003	1890027	24.3	1651392	22305	1416625
2004	2189528	15.8	1967731	20410	1703126
2005	2684887	22.6	2421555	19142	2110735
2006	3135530	16.8	2833457	17176	2490873
2007	3671231	17.1	3321752	19856	2934498
2008	3849407	4.9	3453560	20562	3027597
2009	4002520	4.0	3577500	21990	3101523
2010	4590431	14.7	4092098	24240	3542660
2011	5053017	10.1	4517125	27067	3886156
2012	5140915	1.7	4547780	28724	3845918

单位:万千瓦时(10000 kwh)

Production Consumption				生活用电 Living Consumption		
其中 of Which					其中 of Which	
轻工业 Light Industry	重工业 Heavy Industry	建筑业 Construction	第三产业 Tertiary Industry	总计 Total	城市 Urban	农村 Rural
				4325		
				4835		
				5355		
				6315		
				6734		
				7500		
				9313		
				12603		
				17662		
				22881		
				29510		
				33088		
103301	130465	3770	21432	43003	11926	31077
122714	150619	3179	24469	49606	13406	36200
146272	170286	3898	28780	57502	15499	42003
171383	188589	5870	37412	66515	18972	47543
186145	213935	8016	46961	84678	26002	58677
209890	229608	9855	57175	101512	31626	69886
209606	248082	13586	72226	118328	40536	77792
240220	255907	12132	78013	122937	43257	79680
262246	298378	10589	86743	131463	48670	82793
305906	358717	9745	92495	136755	50740	86015
394760	445365	12559	117573	151336	59557	91779
402840	540948	14234	133418	159218	65054	94164
483275	663292	15523	160889	187188	74294	112886
574100	842525	21672	212462	238635	95616	143019
647516	1055610	31570	244195	221797	105639	116158
775922	1334813	34520	257158	263332	135827	127505
897750	1593123	36255	289154	302073	152348	149725
1013214	1921284	42460	324937	349479	174873	174606
1016912	2010684	44590	360812	395847	198536	197311
1045023	2056500	52322	401664	425020	216319	208701
1182101	2360559	62833	462365	498333	249932	248401
1260629	2625527	74231	529671	535891	271889	264003
1242699	2603219	79121	594017	593135	301647	291489

表 7－24　2012 年主营业务收入前 20 位的工业企业
The Top 20 Enterprises on Annual Revenue from Principal Business in 2012

序号 No.	企业名称 Name of Enterprises	注册类型 Registered Type
1	中国石油化工股份有限公司镇海炼化分公司 Sinopec Zhenhai Refining & Chemical Co. ,Ltd.	股份有限公司 Share－holding Corporations Ltd.
2	中海石油宁波大榭石化有限公司 CNOOC Petrochemical Ningbo Daxie Co. ,Ltd.	与港澳台商合资经营 Equity Joint Ventures with HongKong,Macao & Taiwan
3	宁波奇美电子有限公司 Chi Mei Optoelectronics(Ningbo) Co. ,Ltd.	外资企业 Enterprises with Foreign Investment
4	浙江逸盛石化有限公司 Zhejiang Yisheng Petrochemical Co. ,Ltd.	与港澳台商合资经营 Equity Joint Ventures with HongKong,Macao & Taiwan
5	宁波钢铁有限公司 Ningbo Steel Co. ,Ltd.	其他有限责任公司 Other Limited Liability Corporations
6	宁波卷烟厂 Ningbo Cigarette Factory	国有企业 State－owned Enterprises
7	宁波乐金甬兴化工有限公司 Ningbo LG Yongxing Chemical Industry Co. ,Ltd.	中外合资经营 Chinese－foreign Equity Joint Ventures Enterprises
8	浙江国华浙能发电有限公司 Zhejiang Guohua Zheneng Power Generation Co. ,Ltd.	国有企业 State－owned Enterprises
9	宁波万华聚氨酯有限公司 Ningbo Wanhua Polyurethanes Co. ,Ltd.	其他有限责任公司 Other Limited Liability Corporations
10	宁波宝新不锈钢有限公司 Ningbo Baoxin Stainless Steel Co. ,Ltd.	中外合资经营 Chinese－foreign Equity Joint Ventures Enterprises
11	宁波镇海炼化利安德化学有限公司 Ningbo ZRCC Lyondell Chemical Co. ,Ltd.	与港澳台商合作经营 Co－operative Business Operation with HongKong, Macao & Taiwan
12	宁波申洲针织有限公司 Ningbo Shenzhou Weaving Co. ,Ltd.	港澳台商独资 HongKong,Macao & Taiwan Funded Sole
13	宁波奥克斯空调有限公司 Ningbo Aux Air－condition Co. ,Ltd.	其他有限责任公司 Other Limited Liability Corporations
14	台化兴业(宁波)有限公司 Taihua Xingye (Ningbo) Co. ,Ltd.	外资企业 Enterprises with Foreign Investment
15	浙江吉润汽车有限公司 Zhejiang Girun Automobile Co. ,Ltd.	与港澳台商合资经营 Equity Joint Ventures with HongKong,Macao & Taiwan
16	宁波金田铜业(集团)股份有限公司 Ningbo Jintian Copper Group Co,. Ltd.	股份有限公司 Share－holding Corporations Ltd.
17	宁波奇美光电有限公司 Ningbo Chi Mei Photoelectricity Co. ,Ltd.	外资企业 Enterprises with Foreign Investment
18	浙江大唐乌沙山发电有限责任公司 Zhejiang Datang Wusha Power Generation Co. ,Ltd.	国有企业 State－owned Enterprises
19	慈溪市供电局 Cixi Electric Power Supply Bureau	国有企业 State－owned Enterprises
20	国电浙江北仑第三发电有限公司 Zhejiang Beilun Third Electric Power Co. ,Ltd.	其他有限责任公司 Other Limited Liability Corporations

主要统计指标解释

【工业总产值】 是以货币形式表现的,工业企业在一定时期内生产的工业最终产品或提供工业性劳务活动的总价值量。它是反映一定时期内工业生产总规模和总水平的指标。

工业总产值包括:本期生产的成品价值、对外加工费收入和在制品半成品期末期初差额价值三部分。

【工业销售产值】 是以货币形式表现的,工业企业在一定时期内销售的本企业生产的工业产品或提供工业性劳务活动的价值总量。它是反映一定时期内工业企业产品销售总规模和总水平的重要指标。

【工业增加值】 是指工业企业在报告期内以货币形式表现的工业生产活动的最终成果,是企业全部生产活动的总成果扣除了在生产过程中消耗或转换的物质产品和劳务价值后的余额,是企业生产过程中新增加的价值。

【固定资产原价】 固定资产原值指企业在建造、购置、安装、改建、扩建、技术改造某项固定资产时所支出的全部货币总额。它一般包括买价、包装费、运杂费和安装费等。

【流动资产】 流动资产是指可以在一年或者超过一年的一个生产周期内变现或者耗用的资产,包括现金及各种存款、短期投资、应收及预付货款、存货等。

【主营业务收入】 指企业在销售商品(不一定是本企业生产)、提供劳务及让渡资产使用权等日常活动中所产生的收入

【主营业务成本】 指企业在销售商品、提供劳务及让渡资产使用权等日常活动而发生的实际成本。

【主营业务税金及附加】 指企业日常活动应负担的税金及附加,包括营业税、消费税、城市维护建设税、资源税、土地增值税和教育费附加等。

【利润总额】 指企业在生产经营过程中各种收入扣除各种耗费后的盈余,反映企业在报告期内实现的亏盈总额,包括营业利润、补贴收入、投资净收益和营业外收支净额。

【利税总额】 指企业利润总额、主营业务税金及附加和本年应交增值税之和。

【资产总计】 指企业拥有或控制的能以货币计量的经济资源,包括各种财产、债权和其他权利。资产按其流动性(即资产的变现能力和支付能力)划分为:流动资产、长期投资、固定资产、无形资产、递延资产和其他资产。

【负债合计】 指企业所承担的能以货币计量,将以资产或劳务偿付的债务,偿还形式包括货币、资产或提供劳务。负债一般按偿还期长短分为流动负债和长期负债。

【所有者权益】 指企业投资人对企业净资产的所有权。企业净资产等于企业全部资产减去全部负债后的余额,其中包括投资者对企业的最初投入,以及资本公积金、盈余公积金和未分配利润,对股份制企业即为股东权益。

【实收资本】 指投资者按照企业章程,或合同、协议的约定,实际投入企业的资本。企业实收资本按照投资主体划分为国家资本、集体资本、法人资本、个人资本、港澳台资本和外商资本六种。根据"资产负债表"中的"实收资本"项填列。实收资本中如有以外币形式投入的资本,需折合成人民币形式填写。

【综合能源消费量】 指一定时期、一定地域内工业企业在工业生产活动中实际消费的各种能源的总和净值。计算综合能源消费量时,需要先将使用的各种能源折算成标准燃料后再进行计算。

Explanatory Notes on Main Statistical Indicators

【Gross Industrial Output Value】 is in a form of currency. Total value of end—products or industrial services activities industrial enterprises provide in the period. It reflects the total achievements and overall scale of industrial production during a given period.

It includes the value of the finished products in a given period, the value of industrial services rendered to other units and the changes in the value of the semi finished products and products in process between the beginning and closing of the period.

【Industrial Sales Output Value】 is in a form of currency. Is the total volume of industrial products sold in value terms of an industrial enterprise and Industrial services activities, which reflects the total achievements and overall sales scale of industrial production during a given period.

【Value Added of Industry】 refers to the final results of industrial production in money terms during the reporting period. Is the total business results of all production activities deducted consumption in the production process and converted the value of material goods and services. Is the production process to increase the value of new.

【Original Value of Fixed Assets】 refers to the original value of all fixed assets owned by industrial enterprises, calculated at the cost paid at the time of purchase, installation, reconstruction, expansion, and technical innovation and transformation of the said assets, which includes expenses on purchase, package, transportation, and installation, etc.

【Liquid Assets】 is assets that can be turned into cash or consumed in more than one year or in a year, including cash and deposits, short—term investments, accounts receivable and prepaid inventories.

【Main Business Income】 refers to the enterprises in selling products (not necessarily in this enterprises'production), providing services and transferring assets, daily activities such as the right to the revenue that generated.

【Main Business Cost】 refers to the actual incurred costs the enterprises sell products, provide services, transfer assets, and other daily activities.

【Main Business Taxes and Surcharges】 refers to taxes and surcharges in the enterprises'daily production activities, including sales tax, consumption tax, urban maintenance and construction tax, resource tax, land tax and education surcharge, etc.

【Total Profits】 refers to the Surplus an enterprise products in the process of production and business activities after deducting all cost, reflecting the company's profit and loss during the reporting period, including operating profit, subsidy income, net investment income and the net non—operating income and expenditure.

【Total Profits and Taxes】 refer to total corporate profits taxes, business taxes and surcharges, and the sum of VAT of this year.

【Total Assets】 refer to all assets which are owned or controlled by enterprises, including circulating assets, long—term investment, fixed assets, intangible assets and deferred assets, other long—term assets, and defertaxes, etc. The summation of above items is equal to total assets shown in the balance sheets of the enterprises. (1) Circulating assets (working capital) refer to assets which can be cashed in or spent or consumed in an operating cycle of one year or over one year, including cash, all kinds of deposits, short term investment, receivables, advance payment, stock,etc. (2) Fixed assets refer to the net value of fixed assets, clearance of fixed assets, project under construction, fixed assets losses in suspense. These are corporations' fund holdings. (3) Intangible assets refer to the assets without material form used by enterprises over a long time, such as patents, non—patent technologies, trade marks, copyright, land use right, business reputation, etc

【Total Liabilities】 refer to the debts that enterprises are responsible for repayment, including liquid liabilities, long term liabilities and deferred taxes, etc. Total liabilities correspond to the summation item of liabilities shown in the balance sheets of the enterprises. Liabilities include short term loans and long—term loans.

【Creditors' Equity】 refers to equity investment in an enterprise net assets of the enterprise ownership. Net assets equal total assets minus total liabilities of business the balance, including the investor's initial investment in the enterprise, and capital reserve, surplus reserve and undistributed profits of the joint—stock company is the shareholders' equity.

【Paid—in capital】 refers to the investors in accordance with corporate charter, or contract, to the agreement, the actual capital invested enterprises. Business investment in paid—in capital in accordance with the main division of the state capital, collective capital, corporate capital, personal capital, Hong Kong, Macao, Taiwan capital and foreign capital six. Filled according to the " paid—up capital" items in the "balance sheet". Paid—up capital in any foreign currency in the form of capital investment required to fill out the form converted into RMB.

【Comprehensive Energy Consumption】 in a certain period, certain areas of industrial enterprises in the industrial production activities in the actual consumption of energy is the sum of net. Calculation of comprehensive energy consumption, need to be used in a variety of energy conversion to standard fuel after calculation.

NINGBO

Statistical YearBook

第八篇

固定资产投资和建筑业

INVESTMENT IN FIXED ASSETS AND CONSTRUCTION

固定资产投资和建筑业
Investment Fixed Assets and Construction

主要统计指标
Major Statistics Indicators

2012 年固定资产投资额	Value of Investment Fixed Assets	2901.42	亿元	10000 yuan
比上年增长	Increase Over Last Year	21.6	%	
2012 年房地产开发投资额	Value of Investment in Real Estate Development	884.35	亿元	10000 yuan
比上年增长	Increase Over Last Year	17.1	%	
2012 年房屋竣工面积	Floor Space of Building Completed	8399073	平方米	sq. m
比上年增长	Increase Over Last Year	−0.3	%	
2012 年商品房销售面积	Floor Space of Commercial Building Sold	5902173	平方米	sq. m
比上年增长	Increase Over Last Year	12.1	%	
2012 年商品房实际销售额	Sales Volume of Commercial Buildings	6633948	万元	10000 yuan
比上年增长	Increase Over Last Year	14.2	%	
2012 年商品房待售面积	Floor Space of Sale Building	2399152	平方米	sq. m
比上年增长	Increase Over Last Year	49.6	%	
2012 年建筑业总产值	Gross Output Value of Construction	25091179	万元	10000 yuan
比上年增长	Increase Over Last Year	29.8	%	

表 8—1 历年固定资产投资情况 Invesment in Fixed Assets Over The Years

单位：亿元(100 million yuan)

年份 Year	总计 Total	其中 of Which 限额以上项目投资 Above Designated Size	房地产开发投资 Real Estate Development	城镇限额以下投资 Below Designated Size in Town	农村非农户限额以下投资 Non－peasant Households & Below Designated Size in Rural Area	农户投资 Peasant Households in Rural Area
1978	5.02					
1979	5.79					
1980	6.50					
1981	6.39					
1982	8.57					
1983	7.69					1.77
1984	10.95					3.28
1985	18.08					4.72
1986	22.01					5.79
1987	29.46					8.19
1988	35.81					10.75
1989	32.79					9.02
1990	39.28		2.49			9.33
1991	51.42		3.00			11.07
1992	76.25		7.36			11.95
1993	129.27		25.44			13.44
1994	184.60		50.46			22.92
1995	264.19		71.59			32.80
1996	309.97		65.90			31.39
1997	300.57		51.92			28.60
1998	309.81		43.87			25.36
1999	318.93		46.54			24.72
2000	360.75		59.71			23.73
2001	470.28		87.08			20.22
2002	601.27		125.97			23.60
2003	835.90	556.66	184.26	5.08	67.43	22.47
2004	1103.81	782.38	244.26	4.08	52.83	20.26
2005	1336.30	1009.05	259.50	8.11	38.07	21.57
2006	1502.77	1099.42	313.58	6.92	39.32	43.53
2007	1597.54	1153.65	332.89	16.91	48.38	45.71
2008	1728.24	1303.11	307.75	14.29	42.86	60.18
2009	2004.22	1485.93	374.51	17.00	63.24	63.52
2010	2193.28	1477.72	557.27	16.87	66.73	74.69
2011	2385.50	1630.56	754.94			
2012	2901.43	2017.07	884.35			

注：本表数据依据新统计口径进行调整。限额以上为计划总投资 500 万元及以上。自 2011 年始，全社会固定资产投资口径调整，不再包含城镇限额以下投资、农村非农户限额以下投资和农户投资。全社会固定资产投资更名为固定资产投资。以下表同。

Note: The data in this table have been adjusted in accordance with the new standard. Above designed size project are that the total investment of plan are 5 million yuan and above. Since the beginning of 2011, fixed assets investment of the whole society caliber adjustment, no longer contains the town below the limit of investment, rural area below the limit of investment and investment of rural households. Fixed assets investment of the whole society changed its name to fixed assets investment. The same as in the following table

表 8－2 各县(市)固定资产投资完成情况(2012)
Investment in Fixed Assets by Region

指标	Indicators	全市 Total
固定资产投资完成额(按经营地)	**Total(By Place of Business)**	**29014258**
固定资产投资完成额(按建设地)	**Total(By Place of Building)**	**29014258**
限额以上项目投资	**Investment in Fixed Assets Above Designed Size**	**20170744**
按国民经济行业分	By Sector	
农林牧渔业	Framing,Forestry,Animal Husbandry and Fishery	270188
采矿业	Mining and Quarrying	8666
制造业	Manufacuring	7260648
电力、燃气及水的生产和供应业	Electric Power,Gas and Water Production and Supply	903132
建筑业	Construction	26236
批发和零售业	Wholesale and Retail Trade	484290
交通运输、仓储和邮政业	Transportation,Storage and Post	3513512
住宿和餐饮业	Hotel and Catering Services	410920
信息传输、软件和信息技术服务业	Information Transmission ,Software and Information Technology Services	49984
金融业	Financial Industries	59775
房地产业	Real Estate Industries	2591080
租赁和商务服务业	Leasing and Business Service Industries	208674
科学研究和技术服务业	Scientific Research and Technical Services	90546
水利、环境和公共设施管理业	Water Conservancy,Environment and Public Facility Management	3228504
居民服务、修理和其他服务业	Residents Service,Repair and Other Services	30275
教育	Education	326541
卫生和社会工作	Health and Social Work	199951
文化、体育和娱乐业	Culture,Sports and Entertainment	303374
公共管理、社会保障和社会组织	Public Management,Social Security and Social Organization	204448
房地产开发投资完成额(按经营地)	**Real Estate Development(By Place of Business)**	**8843514**
#住宅	Residential Buildings	5156454
房地产开发投资完成额(按建设地)	**Real Estate Development(By Place of Building)**	**8843514**
#住宅	Residential Buildings	5156454
城镇项目投资	**Investment in Fixed Assets in Town**	**14592260**
农村非农户投资	**Investment about Rural non Farm Households**	**5578484**

注:本表按 2011 年修订的国民经济行业标准统计。

Note:Statistics in this table are classified as the national economic category that was modified in 2011.

单位:万元(10000 yuan)

市区 Urban Disctict	#鄞州 Yinzhou	余姚 Yuyao	慈溪 Cixi	奉化 Fenghua	象山 Xiangshan	宁海 Ninghai
16891686	**4149156**	**3612961**	**4404777**	**1319786**	**1371748**	**1413300**
16871766	**4203661**	**3615419**	**4432783**	**1281439**	**1375848**	**1437003**
11692400	**2682010**	**2261043**	**3158625**	**940490**	**931338**	**1186848**
29413	10960	15958	79207	74720	46078	24812
6310	6310			2356		
3537031	1156709	1185897	1766187	186321	239286	345926
625036	87109	95216	17887	23017	68989	72987
23040	14617	590			2606	
287281	73614	28502	61092	25958	62770	18687
2840602	318078	211588	59647	165012	115232	121431
219395	49792	63689	35495	11140	59879	21322
34374					7530	8080
51135		5790			2850	
1487458	500859	143803	584557	154601	27406	193255
43182	11448	25684	600	30724	32227	76257
45785	2350	29125	2200	4950	4300	4186
1851947	289542	350883	412426	227340	179207	206701
15121	4282	9079		3505	2150	420
192140	76125	40009	37806	8695	14880	33011
119716	36324	6298	49153		11269	13515
198788	34658	10236	48688	11525	17347	16790
84646	9233	38696	3680	10626	37332	29468
5199286	**1467146**	**1351918**	**1246152**	**379296**	**440410**	**226452**
2765422	771301	811718	902894	248738	300867	126815
5179366	**1521651**	**1354376**	**1274158**	**340949**	**444510**	**250155**
2752771	818352	813968	925043	217610	304727	142335
9503388	**1354520**	**1130938**	**1993839**	**705333**	**485628**	**773134**
2189012	**1327490**	**1130105**	**1164786**	**235157**	**445710**	**413714**

表 8-3 部分年份分产业固定资产投资完成额
Fixed Assets Investment by Industry in Partial Years

单位：万元(10000 yuan)

指标	Indicators	2008	2009	2010	2011	2012
总计	**Total**	**17282413**	**20042179**	**21932830**	**23855072**	**29014258**
第一产业	Primary Industry	67924	143785	113543	183918	270188
第二产业	Secondary Industry	7555536	7767319	6975776	6683611	8198682
第三产业	Tertiary Industry	9658953	27665713	14843511	16987543	20545388
限额以上项目投资	**Investment in Fixed Assets Above Designed Size**	**13031105**	**14859345**	**14777197**	**16305624**	**20170744**
第一产业	Primary Industry	60309	129961	104237	183918	270188
第二产业	Secondary Industry	7143702	7166679	6312915	6683611	8198682
第三产业	Tertiary Industry	5827094	7562705	8360045	9438095	11701874
城镇限额以下投资	**Investment in Fixed Assets Below Designed Size in Town**	**142862**	**170049**	**168730**		
第一产业	Primary Industry	495	3818	294		
第二产业	Secondary Industry	79228	100696	103551		
第三产业	Tertiary Industry	63139	65535	64885		
农村非农户限额以下投资	**Investment in Fixed Assets about Non-peasant Households & Below Designed Size in Rural Area**	**428563**	**632431**	**667306**		
第一产业	Primary Industry	7120	10006	9012		
第二产业	Secondary Industry	332206	499944	559310		
第三产业	Tertiary Industry	89237	122481	98984		
房地产开发	**Real Estate Development**	**3077538**	**3745119**	**5572683**	**7549448**	**8843514**
#住宅建设	Residential Buildings	1939969	2376419	3231195	4168184	5156454
农村私人固定资产投资	**Private Investment in Rural Areas**	**601807**	**635235**	**746914**		

表 8-4 部分年份城镇以上新增固定资产及房屋建筑面积 Newly Increase Fixed Assets and Floor Space of Buildings Above City and Town Level in Partial Years

单位:万元,万平方米(10000 yuan,10000 sq. m)

年份	本年新增固定资产额 Newly Increase Fixed Assets in This Year	房屋施工面积 Floor Space of Buliding Under Construction	#住宅 Residential Buildings	房屋竣工面积 Floor Space of Buildings Completed	#住宅 Residential Buildings
1990	179769	308.76	137.73	180.48	77.30
1991	289108	362.09	175.07	182.28	88.11
1992	253780	518.29	254.60	209.38	91.38
1993	516881	906.08	501.36	383.28	224.91
1994	908056	1205.39	615.30	528.40	285.92
1995	1007217	1386.64	760.99	515.02	312.26
1996	1433274	1395.46	681.71	579.60	332.59
1997	1758309	1264.97	543.00	442.76	232.08
1998	1685871	1156.62	467.16	506.87	232.26
1999	1915400	1050.10	519.91	499.65	233.31
2000	2464806	1208.39	681.38	446.70	227.64
2001	2776661	1626.01	886.08	622.64	341.45
2002	2382537	2342.77	1132.48	745.33	365.88
2003	3292041	3401.43	1744.41	971.64	550.62
2004	3603854	4062.61	2225.05	996.97	546.09
2005	5708349	4600.43	2225.51	1562.32	680.51
2006	7321849	4542.09	2186.55	1427.87	671.66
2007	7166189	5715.13	2190.54	1452.22	535.06
2008	7523565	6505.64	2447.55	1746.09	712.79
2009	11797353	6741.74	2352.59	1669.41	500.54
2010	9781355	7679.59	2741.93	1486.97	470.94
2011	12296942	9792.22	3532.76	2232.56	672.49
2012	10643686	10925.24	4037.87	2025.64	615.75

表 8－5　城镇以上固定资产投资完成情况(2012)
Investment in Fixed Assets of City and Town Level and Above

指标	Indicators	计划总投资 Total Investment of Project	累计完成投资 Accumulative Finish Total Investment
总计	**Total**	**53339541**	**33757190**
按登记类型	**By Registered Type**		
内资	Domestic－investment Enterprises	45109595	28435468
国有	State－owned	28928457	18274784
港澳台投资	Hongkong,Macao and Taiwan Funded	3156092	1713520
外资	Foreign Funded Enterprises	5063375	3598528
按隶属关系	**By Subordination**		
中央	Central	2438469	1972409
地方	Local	50901072	31784781
按建筑性质	**By type of Construction**		
＃新建	New Construction	31080768	19701691
扩建	Expansion	14161596	8361466
改建	Reconstruction	3622137	2424342
按国民经济行业分组	**By Sector**		
农林牧渔业	Framing,Forestry,Animal Husbandry and Fishery	901592	524489
采矿业	Mining and Quarrying		
制造业	Manufacuring	14163376	8566577
电力、燃气及水的生产和供应业	Electric Power,Gas and Water Production and Supply	2388311	1498828
建筑业	Construction	42690	30649
批发和零售业	Wholesale and Retail Trade	1348602	558564
交通运输、仓储和邮政业	Transportation,Storage and Post	13956149	10411556
住宿和餐饮业	Hotel and Catering Services	1082958	890406
信息传输、软件和信息技术服务业	Information Transmission,Software and Information Technology Services	115674	85208
金融业	Financial Industries	448200	171474
房地产业	Real Estate Industries	6170004	3671055
租赁和商务服务业	Leasing and Business Service Industries	351713	182182
科学研究和技术服务业	Scientific Research and Technical Services	217197	118936
水利、环境和公共设施管理业	Water Conservancy,Environment and Public Facility Management	9355093	5229967
居民服务、修理和其他服务业	Residents Service,Repair and Other Services	28033	18892
教育	Education	685370	475164
卫生和社会工作	Health and Social Work	584145	254180
文化、体育和娱乐业	Culture,Sports and Entertainment	818892	494507
公共管理、社会保障和社会组织	Public Management,Social Security and Social Organization	681542	574556

注：本表按2011年修订的国民经济行业标准统计。

Note：Statistics in this table are classified as the national economic category that was modified in 2011.

单位:万元(10000 yuan)

本年完成投资 Investment Completed of the Year	按构成分 by Composition					本年新增固定资产 Newly Increased Fixed Assets of the Year	本年房屋施工面积(平方米) Floor Space Under Construction (sq. m)	本年房屋竣工面积(平方米) Floor Space Completed (sq. m)
	建筑工程 Construction	安装工程 Installation	设备工器具购置 Purchase of Equipment and Instruments	其他费用 Others	#土地购置费 Purchase of Land			
14592260	**8244176**	**877726**	**2215934**	**3254424**	**1704633**	**7457549**	**48447279**	**11857285**
13030486	7509131	738334	1767482	3015539	1529851	6639209	37252072	10129424
7536985	5070203	314218	249539	1903025	809281	3995157	14841499	2511894
775985	382896	74076	185507	133506	108826	310097	4580903	976088
776115	344913	65292	262709	103201	63780	501395	6586590	731497
570359	222290	140713	128602	78754	675	259002	189325	58421
14021901	8021886	737013	2087332	3175670	1703958	7198547	48257954	11798864
7532996	4882687	401645	462195	1786469	933981	3293004	26273754	5170685
3975993	2102140	268783	574720	1030350	558557	1859374	13982090	3457504
1073554	689508	58114	64912	261020	141669	713722	883300	327572
193602	176736	860	994	15012		91619	24222	8214
4031272	1658645	334137	1515738	522752	313917	2305804	23204515	7284218
719550	242485	222056	164612	90397	8207	277507	247994	67168
16287	9112		2015	5160	3600	10457	92319	17064
314798	169527	12509	5968	126794	112219	191340	1636484	692358
3039902	1967842	58899	428988	584173	122997	2070343	1892954	415882
323577	134673	63912	51851	73141	9258	206581	1103152	260811
47141	18732	6831	10508	11070	10338	13569	135819	
54280	34964	13832	500	4984		35976	426765	39265
1829192	1288544	55873	14994	469781	355915	401142	12956632	1342468
114837	68779	8343	5100	32615	28004	48604	639123	191342
82716	55918	4609	1817	20372	16122	15097	458909	85232
2964206	1737216	44243	1948	1180799	663192	1141928	1112957	72205
16893	9146	60	850	6837	5303	8106	51955	28584
240201	194852	11933	780	32636	13002	192973	1673599	622055
172359	140782	4893	2821	23863	10652	67376	921616	116454
241315	210495	7811	4584	18425	7723	45456	641532	76256
190132	125728	26925	1866	35613	24184	333671	1226732	537709

表 8－6 各县(市)城镇以上固定资产投资主要指标(2012)
Main Indicators of Investment in Fixed Assets of City and Town Level and Above by Region

指标	Indicators	全市 Total
计划总投资	**Total Investment of Plan**	**53339541**
本年完成投资	**Finished Investment of This Year**	**14592260**
按经济注册类型分	**By Registration Status**	
国有经济	State－Owned Units	7536985
集体经济	Collective－owned Units	197593
其他有限责任公司	Share－holding Corporation Units	2001386
股份有限公司	Other Limited Liability Corporations	312382
港澳台投资经济	HongKong,Macao and Taiwan Funded	775985
外商投资经济	Foreign Funded	776115
按隶属关系分	**By Administrative Relationship**	
中央	Central	570359
省	Province	98111
省辖市	Municipalities	2806848
县(市)、区	Counties and Districts	4884449
其他	Others	6232493
按建设性质分	**By Type of Construction**	
新建	New Construction	7532996
扩建	Expansion	3975993
改建	Reconstruction	1073554
按构成分	**By Use of Funds**	
建筑工程	Construction	8244176
安装工程	Installation	877726
设备工器具购置	Purchase of Equipment and Instruments	2215934
其他费用	Others	3254424
按国民经济行业分	**By Sector**	
农林牧渔业	Framing,Forestry,Animal Husbandry and Fishery	193602
采矿业	Mining and Quarrying	
制造业	Manufacuring	4031272
电力、燃气及水的生产和供应业	Electric Power,Gas and Water Production and Supply	719550

注:①本表按 2011 年修订的国民经济行业标准统计。②从 2012 年开始国家预算内资金改为国家预算资金,以下表同。

①Statistics in this table are classified as the national economic category that was modified in 2011. ②The state on budget funds have been change into state budget funds since 2012,same as the following tables.

单位:万元(10000 yuan)

市区 Urban District	#鄞州 Yinzhou	余姚 Yuyao	慈溪 Cixi	奉化 Fenghua	象山 Xiangshan	宁海 Ninghai
37116677	**5039783**	**3543714**	**5780994**	**2189217**	**2023391**	**2685548**
9503388	**1354520**	**1130938**	**1993839**	**705333**	**485628**	**773134**
5080939	476601	572481	497020	460832	294002	631711
159747	157693	295	8865	28686		
1234696	183709	32322	572132	25593	69376	67267
213382	47329	47539	49293	1362	806	
519936	66851	85737	145780	17619		6913
669835	116559	31866	48477	5781	8939	11217
563859	11996				6500	
98111	6842					
2760172	5000	1500	32983	12193		
2496897	443923	578430	444158	390662	308930	665372
3584349	886759	551008	1516698	302478	170198	107762
4985459	558338	351761	1399974	320912	344431	130459
2438031	287332	474825	176286	280204	12483	594164
693664	159937	141476	63650	59055	77591	38118
4825229	732519	727366	1332297	525415	343833	490036
625338	68385	53531	100731	39713	9696	48717
1681715	222015	82923	338382	54194	31926	26794
2371106	331601	267118	222429	86011	100173	207587
15080		3755	70248	61968	22333	20218
2551127	494684	416930	846085	126465	11493	79172
574080	77488	56010	14974	19331	5473	49682

表 8－6 续表 Continued

指标	Indicators	全市 Total
建筑业	Construction	16287
批发和零售业	Wholesale and Retail Trade	314798
交通运输、仓储和邮政业	Transportation,Storage and Post	3039902
住宿和餐饮业	Hotel and Catering Services	323577
信息传输、软件和信息技术服务业	Information Transmission,Software and Information Technology Services	47141
金融业	Financial Industries	54280
房地产业	Real Estate Industries	1829192
租赁和商务服务业	Leasing and Business Service Industries	114837
科学研究和技术服务业	The Scientific Research and Technical Services	82716
水利、环境和公共设施管理业	Water Conservancy,Environment and Public Facility Management	2964206
居民服务、修理和其他服务业	Residents Service,Repair and Other Services	16893
教育	Education	240201
卫生和社会工作	Health and Social Work	172359
文化、体育和娱乐业	Culture,Sports and Entertainment	241315
公共管理、社会保障和社会组织	Public Management,Social Security and Social Organization	190132
本年新增固定资产	**Newly Increased Fixed Assets in This Year**	**7457549**
按资金来源分	**By Source of Funds**	
#国家预算资金	State Budget	1292692
国内贷款	Domestic Loans	2838994
利用外资	Foreign Investment	542222
自筹资金	Fund Raising	8942861
房屋建筑面积(平方米)	**Floor Space of Buildings (sq. m)**	
施工面积	Floor Space of Buildings Under Construction	48447279
#住宅	Residential Buildings	6757960
竣工面积	Floor Space of Buildings Completed	11857285
#住宅	Residential Buildings	851369
本年竣工房屋价值(万元)	Value of Building Completed(10000 yuan)	2442217
#住宅	Residential Buildings	224766

单位:万元(10000 yuan)

市区 Urban District	#鄞州 Yinzhou	余姚 Yuyao	慈溪 Cixi	奉化 Fenghua	象山 Xiangshan	宁海 Ninghai
15481	8495				806	
182502	67724	6427	49700	21058	43861	11250
2546844	48225	125626	9561	147963	91557	118351
187381	48106	29660	33932	9990	52546	10068
31531					7530	8080
49930		1500			2850	
1009661	247689	87757	485956	64463		181355
37075	11448	14901		29619	25077	8165
37955	2350	29125	2200	4950	4300	4186
1743362	251347	307973	372595	198035	148846	193395
10838	3480	2550		3505		
169052	53679	5727	15988	4385	12448	32601
101054	20213	4903	41972		10915	13515
162020	16589	1550	46948	6990	8779	15028
78415	3003	36544	3680	6611	36814	28068
4938090	**733251**	**764197**	**766957**	**399516**	**299689**	**289100**
1020391	106330	8422	96191	31412	87340	48936
2387475	177244	92665	29303	137759	53313	138479
534557	26040	3045	1505	1750		1365
4909918	991586	945730	1797314	515926	287364	486609
24960003	6260623	4077712	11325167	2347460	1756540	3980397
4698160	1469277	581756	372293	310097	90128	705526
5636266	1520487	1363585	3294408	647568	303461	611997
449511	108298	48988	158659	149628	28214	16369
1553409	238451	228338	323487	118968	79750	138265
139136	22104	10757	28294	37331	7612	1636

表 8－7 全市房地产企业开发投资情况(2012) Develop and Investment of Enterprises for Real Estate Development

指标	Indicators	总计 Total	按控股情况分 国有 State－owned	集体 Colloective－owned
计划总投资	**Total Investment of Plan**	**36048683**	**5489672**	**615438**
本年完成投资	**Investment Made of the Year**	**8843514**	**1424787**	**135363**
土地购置费	Purchase of Land	2580774	315278	20000
配套工程投资	Ancillary Works	107389	11245	3123
按构成分	**By Composition**			
建筑工程	Construction	4824582	863596	97135
安装工程	Installation	546193	109899	9057
设备工器具购置	Purchase of Equipment and Instruments	137845	12674	4163
其他费用	Others	3334894	438618	25008
按工程用途分	**By Purpose**			
住宅	Residential Buildings	5156454	757626	95416
办公楼	Office Buildings	667089	196175	7346
商业营业用房	Buildings for Commercial Business	1100395	94203	11570
其他	Others	1919576	376783	21031
本年新增固定资产	Newly Increased Fixed Assets in the Year	3186137	353595	26583
待开发土地面积(平方米)	Land Space Needed Development (sq. m)	2038537	503339	9989
本年购置土地面积(平方米)	Land Space Purchased in the Year (sq. m)	573332	42733	
本年土地成交价款	Actual Land Price of the Year	276864	934	

单位：平方米，万元(sq. m,10000 yuan)

By Holding Status			按隶属关系分 By Administrative Relationship				
私人 Private	港澳台商 Hongkong, Macao&Taiwan Funded	外商 Foreign Funds	一级 Firstl Class	二级 Secend Class	三级 Third Class	四级 Fourth Class	其他 Others
22761114	**2724198**	**2165005**	**3440098**	**3654620**	**12033292**	**1890539**	**15030134**
5443651	**686691**	**525008**	**620005**	**930638**	**2984581**	**514188**	**3794102**
1719539	190186	160591	186356	340416	599485	138258	1316259
67983	23229	1098	8007	12163	49234	5646	32339
2857654	349586	239340	311220	475142	1888985	310321	1838914
343337	69349	12303	17828	38792	210441	25605	253527
71979	27334	15634	4661	2410	47287	2423	81064
2170681	240422	257731	286296	414294	837868	175839	1620597
3146446	416870	285316	357853	667031	1741592	323817	2066161
378455	16482	47116	16249	25449	294370	15296	315725
739555	111287	73364	76349	52529	351235	62947	557335
1179195	142052	119212	169554	185629	597384	112128	854881
1810507	398316	215782	446573	380660	1363019	39494	956391
1005330	325872	194007	123972	180166	375194	155203	1204002
465202	65397		25373	50139	166883	182135	148802
261775	14155		69841	4616	37999	78727	85681

表 8－8 全市房地产企业房屋施工及竣工情况(2012)
Buildings Construction and The Completed of Enterprises for Real Estate Development

指标	Indicators	总计 Total	按控股情况分 国有 State－owned	集体 Colloective－owned
房屋施工面积	**Floor Space of Buildings Under Consrtuction**	**60805078**	**10234499**	**1428233**
1.住宅	Residential Buildings	33620766	5971242	1038941
2.办公楼	Office Buildings	5125364	989245	39814
3.商业营业用房	Buildings for Commercial Business	7387441	708860	86145
4.其他	Others	14671507	2565152	263333
本年新开工房屋施工面积	**Floor Space of Newly Started of The Year**	**14705107**	**3417180**	**70064**
1.住宅	Residential Buildings	8303184	2087681	54163
2.办公楼	Office Buildings	903777	173185	1591
3.商业营业用房	Buildings for Commercial Business	1438536	146921	
4.其他	Others	4059610	1009393	14310
房屋竣工面积	**Floor Space of Buildings Completed**	**8399073**	**1146176**	**158187**
#不可销售面积	Floor Space for Connot	1966495	326982	29810
1.住宅	Residential Buildings	5306090	809054	119326
2.办公楼	Office Buildings	452242	46740	1359
3.商业营业用房	Buildings for Commercial Business	956427	65030	9134
4.其他	Others	1684314	225352	28368
商品住宅竣工套数(套)	**Completed Residencial House (flat)**	**43486**	**7060**	**1140**
竣工房屋价值	**Value of Buildings Completed(10000 yuan)**	**2660963**	**324152**	**25516**
1.住宅	Residential Buildings	1619531	213873	18459
2.办公楼	Office Buildings	212122	22837	292
3.商业营业用房	Buildings for Commercial Business	370995	18123	1694
4.其他	Others	458315	69319	5071
出租房屋面积	**Floor Space of Lease House**	**645422**	**92733**	**4050**
1.住宅	Residential Buildings	3106		
2.办公楼	Office Buildings	85902	29553	
3.商业营业用房	Buildings for Commercial Business	543655	63180	4050
4.其他	Others	12759		
待售面积	**Floor Space of Vacant Building**	**2399152**	**421283**	**14657**
1.住宅	Residential Buildings	774651	175738	9128
2.办公楼	Office Buildings	313636	61885	
3.商业营业用房	Buildings for Commercial Business	733693	82557	2565
4.其他	Others	577172	101103	2964

单位：平方米，万元(sq. m,10000 yuan)

By Holding Status			按隶属关系分 By Administrative Relationship				
私人 Private	港澳台商 Hongkong, Macao&Taiwan Funded	外商 Foreign Funds	一级 Firstl Class	二级 Secend Class	三级 Third Class	四级 Fourth Class	其他 Others
36719814	**4224602**	**3491549**	**5084622**	**6615437**	**22532703**	**3227472**	**23344844**
20160460	2252424	1552086	3523279	4282230	12405836	2044066	11365355
2998068	316674	438510	104214	270000	2390611	95776	2264763
4530600	593210	544549	265060	469478	2717049	331068	3604786
9030686	1062294	956404	1192069	1593729	5019207	756562	6109940
8280594	**1398547**	**1072370**	**751938**	**1217611**	**5251197**	**811280**	**6673081**
4468589	848521	704359	434530	803278	3210641	465191	3389544
536957	125418	3375	78383	1216	358854	8647	456677
1074944	19560	111305	20763	103858	249402	128787	935726
2200104	405048	253331	218262	309259	1432300	208655	1891134
5085470	**825939**	**392516**	**1341735**	**1312935**	**3119282**	**149516**	**2475605**
1298914	163551	45535	335538	344819	768095	35802	482241
3116740	578091	300020	975665	910176	1878915	112547	1428787
277838	69724		325	36575	281611	74	133657
635162	36324	15622	35543	80699	408169	14188	417828
1055730	141800	76874	330202	285485	550587	22707	495333
24796	**5513**	**1756**	**8029**	**8699**	**14753**	**985**	**11020**
1555854	**262714**	**145894**	**405233**	**333656**	**1053767**	**33253**	**835054**
971131	181952	115221	295920	226030	570670	24674	502237
111540	20872		64	10972	142202	20	58864
212612	11679	5090	10074	20828	183754	3050	153289
260571	48211	25583	99175	75826	157141	5509	120664
506000	**36396**	**6243**	**24924**	**139731**	**416999**	**7159**	**56609**
3106				3106			
36644	19705				63461		22441
466050	10375		24924	136625	353338	916	27852
200	6316	6243			200	6243	6316
1542115	**216750**	**13855**	**317339**	**348449**	**962766**	**54995**	**715603**
521226	52197	8690	162019	79034	266764	27205	239629
181258	56659		7526	67132	160494	165	78319
430636	76738	2920	41773	91011	329973	12554	258382
408995	31156	2245	106021	111272	205535	15071	139273

表 8－9 全市房地产企业房屋销售情况(2012) Building Sale Situation of Enterprises for Real Estate Development

指标	Indicators	总计 Total	按控股情况分 国有 State－owned	集体 Colloective－owned
商品房销售面积	**Floor Space of Building Sold**	**5902173**	**728712**	**118291**
1.住宅	Residential Buildings	4587421	580667	109614
2.办公楼	Office Buildings	455251	72825	
3.商业营业用房	Buildings for Commercial Business	553096	41722	1751
4.其他	Others	306405	33498	6926
现房销售面积	Floor Space of Completed Building	668098	88416	2249
1.住宅	Residential Buildings	350666	63520	1874
2.办公楼	Office Buildings	59994	12491	
3.商业营业用房	Buildings for Commercial Business	144178	5746	
4.其他	Others	113260	6659	375
期房销售面积	Floor Space of Forward Delivery Building	5234075	640296	116042
1.住宅	Residential Buildings	4236755	517147	107740
2.办公楼	Office Buildings	395257	60334	
3.商业营业用房	Buildings for Commercial Business	408918	35976	1751
4.其他	Others	193145	26839	6551
商品房销售额	**Sales Volume of Commercial Buildings**	**6633948**	**762029**	**94810**
1.住宅	Residential Buildings	5222892	617217	86296
2.办公楼	Office Buildings	429654	69526	
3.商业营业用房	Buildings for Commercial Business	838365	56729	2821
4.其他	Others	143037	18557	5693
现房销售额	Sales Volume of Completed Building	629681	98959	2851
1.住宅	Residential Buildings	345339	68365	2684
2.办公楼	Office Buildings	58183	22228	
3.商业营业用房	Buildings for Commercial Business	182165	4236	
4.其他	Others	43994	4130	167
期房销售额	Sales Volume of Forward Delivery Building	6004267	663070	91959
1.住宅	Residential Buildings	4877553	548852	83612
2.办公楼	Office Buildings	371471	47298	
3.商业营业用房	Buildings for Commercial Business	656200	52493	2821
4.其他	Others	99043	14427	5526

单位:平方米,万元(sq. m,10000 yuan)

By Holding Status			按隶属关系分 By Administrative Relationship				
私人 Private	港澳台商 Hongkong, Macao&Taiwan Funded	外商 Foreign Funds	一级 Firstl Class	二级 Secend Class	三级 Third Class	四级 Fourth Class	其他 Others
3827313	**654073**	**129415**	**505378**	**828215**	**2059078**	**391608**	**2117894**
2825657	569174	94676	425731	706004	1534106	343971	1577609
323665	14020	15893	10186	47924	189585	2680	204876
473364	24592	8079	36442	30862	200607	19595	265590
204627	46287	10767	33019	43425	134780	25362	69819
418965	142197	7385	102000	41668	310922	24676	188832
199558	81851	468	48434	21350	161080	13595	106207
43996	1986		10186	2274	29384	74	18076
120629	16384		22175	6270	61648	5245	48840
54782	41976	6917	21205	11774	58810	5762	15709
3408348	511876	122030	403378	786547	1748156	366932	1929062
2626099	487323	94208	377297	684654	1373026	330376	1471402
279669	12034	15893		45650	160201	2606	186800
352735	8208	8079	14267	24592	138959	14350	216750
149845	4311	3850	11814	31651	75970	19600	54110
4587933	**707382**	**145862**	**732863**	**914743**	**1959043**	**354653**	**2672646**
3482019	638622	97681	654411	807371	1441802	318702	2000606
296247	16900	21144	5130	43886	181881	1257	197500
714765	35229	21992	57237	45533	286291	23372	425932
94902	16631	5045	16085	17953	49069	11322	48608
399058	113978	3625	106222	35172	260789	10789	216709
186857	80204	1139	65411	21327	136521	7459	114621
31116	1715		5130	2204	35978	28	14843
157347	19507		26344	7971	69298	2215	76337
23738	12552	2486	9337	3670	18992	1087	10908
4188875	593404	142237	626641	879571	1698254	343864	2455937
3295162	558418	96542	589000	786044	1305281	311243	1885985
265131	15185	21144		41682	145903	1229	182657
557418	15722	21992	30893	37562	216993	21157	349595
71164	4079	2559	6748	14283	30077	10235	37700

表 8－10 全市房地产企业经营情况(2012)
Main Economy Indicators of Real Estate Development

指标	Indicators	总计 Total	按控股情况分	
			国有 State－owned	集体 Colloective－owned
本年资金来源合计	**Total Capital Source in This Year**	**9767583**	**1428271**	**150656**
上年末结余资金	Balance at End of Previous Year	1166418	65125	2971
本年资金来源小计	Subtotal Capital of This Year	8601165	1363146	147685
1. 国内贷款	Domestic Loans	2190805	455871	35192
2. 利用外资	Foreign Investment	34364		
3. 自筹资金	Self－Financed Capital	3938384	680504	82819
4. 其他资金来源	Others	2437612	226771	29674
本年各项应付款合计	Total Account Payable This Year	1419726	183423	1458
年末资产负债情况	**Assets and Liabilities of Year－end**			
资产总计	Total Assets	876126970	94319746	388205631
＃本年固定资产折旧	Depreciation of Fixed Assets in This Year	1033054	69850	6683
负债总计	Total Liabilities	555556286	68217167	187661117
所有者权益合计	Creditors' Equity	320570684	26102579	200544514
实收资本合计	Total Capital Hold	85356086	7727627	2791570
损益情况	**Expenditureznd Income**			
主营业务收入	Prime Operating Revenue	63513242	8298445	933646
土地转让收入	Land Transferred	3000778	50691	
商品房屋销售收入	Commercial Buildings Sold	56660408	7813018	920519
房屋出租收入	Buildings Leased	1439127	109675	5106
其他收入	Others	2412929	325061	8021
主营业务成本	Prime Operating Costs	40677418	4117473	692740
主营业务税金及附加	Sales Taxes and Extra Charges	7430185	1439963	81100
主营业务利润	Prime Operating Profits	13347862	2593082	143649
销售费用	Sales Expenses	2057777	147927	16157
管理费用	Manage Expenses	3897964	443937	53922
财务费用	Finance Expenses	1761653	498958	31370
营业利润	Business Profits	10105551	1931526	61135
利润总额	Total Profits	10972122	2029798	61607
应付职工薪酬	Employee Compensation Payable	1419147	215205	26542

单位:万元(10000 yuan)

By Holding Status			按隶属关系分 By Administrative Relationship				
私人 Private	港澳台商 Hongkong, Macao&Taiwan Funded	外商 Foreign Funds	一级 Firstl Class	二级 Secend Class	三级 Third Class	四级 Fourth Class	其他 Others
6022420	**926639**	**570484**	**675094**	**895314**	**3267030**	**611569**	**4318576**
541735	141813	188758	27221	37018	245696	54119	802364
5480685	784826	381726	647873	858296	3021334	557450	3516212
1258283	240285	143478	142751	274707	693349	98314	981684
	2468	31896				2468	31896
2405981	269338	151545	294164	427682	1413525	311727	1491286
1816421	272735	54807	210958	155907	914460	144941	1011346
733557	79104	79757	15430	99326	716270	137163	451537
307013285	36398124	21218157	63540873	60233704	545825213	21199423	185327757
854591	38291	14981	54332	182197	534991	44238	217296
242216773	21852465	13281745	46368521	48309508	308681873	17693801	134502583
64796512	14545659	7936412	17172352	11924196	237143340	3505622	50825174
49335462	14070531	6742659	8689683	5685110	24578517	3506229	42896547
42850886	4674126	664250	6685167	7602416	28620889	1805520	18799250
107484				46951	2854453	48683	50691
39537801	4588288	643876	6644143	7164958	23572965	1692848	17585494
1174975	71957	20294	30018	185782	464863	25083	733381
2030626	13881	80	11006	204725	1728608	38906	429684
28473633	3260427	387915	3268146	4973621	18114645	1311389	13009617
4464699	503561	190912	1118801	848604	3745803	160772	1556205
8456889	701047	−22033	2180138	1585901	6060816	223098	3297909
1455665	209091	107456	118082	194290	699625	110261	935519
2866264	272786	135906	349333	606927	1309192	201204	1431308
1218863	−2645	27019	59334	450001	561778	34791	655749
6466346	442291	−166846	3014659	1108378	4803538	−89037	1268013
7231352	431801	−139051	3193547	1286302	5325327	−94638	1261584
884776	127897	77400	162221	182287	488947	93004	492688

表 8－11　各县(市)、区房地产企业开发投资情况(2012)
Develop and Investment of Enterprises for Real Estate Development

指标名称	Indicators	全市 Total	市区 Urban Disctict
计划总投资	**Total Investment of Plan**	**36048683**	**22238337**
本年完成投资	**Investment Made of the Year**	**8843514**	**5199286**
土地购置费	Purchase of Land	2580774	1459370
配套工程投资	Ancillary Works	107389	78971
按构成分	**By Composition**		
建筑工程	Construction	4824582	2831146
安装工程	Installation	546193	381272
设备工器具购置	Purchase of Equipment and Instruments	137845	94564
其他费用	Others	3334894	1892304
按工程用途分	**By Purpose**		
住宅	Residential Buildings	5156454	2765422
办公楼	Office Buildings	667089	592407
商业营业用房	Buildings for Commercial Business	1100395	600188
其他	Others	1919576	1241269
本年新增固定资产	Newly Increased Fixed Assets in the Year	3186137	2550155
待开发土地面积	Land Space Needed Development (sq. m)	2038537	1484121
本年购置土地面积	Land Space Purchased in the Year (sq. m)	573332	106489
本年土地成交价款	Actual Land Price of the Year	276864	85654
本年资金来源合计	**Total Funding Sources**	**9767583**	**5887088**
上年末结余资金	At the End of the Balance of Funds	1166418	967916
本年资金来源小计	Total Fund Source of the Year	8601165	4919172
1. 国内贷款	1. Domestic Loans	2190805	1274212
2. 利用外资	2. Use of Foreign Capital	34364	31896
3. 自筹资金	3. Self－Financing	3938384	2029550
4. 其他资金来源	4. Other Sources	2437612	1583514
本年各项应付款合计	**The Total Payment of the Year**	**1419726**	**544122**

注：本表房地产开发投资按建设地统计，表 8－12、8－13 同。

Note: Real Estate development investment is recorded by region in this table, as well as table 8－12. 8－13

单位：平方米，万元(sq. m，10000 yuan)

海曙区 Haishu	江东区 Jiangdong	江北区 Jiangbei	北仑区 Beilun	镇海区 Zhenhai	鄞州区 Yinzhou	余姚 Yuyao	慈溪 Cixi	奉化 Fenghua	象山 Xiangshan	宁海 Ninghai
2156730	**3095111**	**2376621**	**4048303**	**3498706**	**5704001**	**4499598**	**4982991**	**1756262**	**1564215**	**1007280**
347286	**607577**	**472306**	**1162698**	**849021**	**1467146**	**1351918**	**1246152**	**379296**	**440410**	**226452**
92350	235756	146277	331631	249430	320085	581098	208201	125691	136065	70349
7985	3910	10094	25182	21489	4045	15196	5800	2843	3329	1250
187436	276039	225640	615400	466318	902958	574078	847703	215034	245623	110998
25894	21581	45041	78975	88352	104405	62650	40994	18042	16437	26798
9015	6576	24655	29743	3715	12892	37302	4271	118	1420	170
124941	303381	176970	438580	290636	446891	677888	353184	146102	176930	88486
134491	252376	255342	710555	497044	771301	811718	902894	248738	300867	126815
75231	83572	46333	57163	115023	163410	9201	31598	1796	20347	11740
52422	99313	35529	136143	82291	161462	264940	125243	54438	34282	21304
85142	172316	135102	258837	154663	370973	266059	186417	74324	84914	66593
361258	125971	499928	362915	225382	811031	285385	10507	49795	231892	58403
111545	54665	284326	459048	52985	521552	320429	61688	70666	82602	19031
14170			28177	42733	21409	62705		223872	180266	
66316			5468	934	12936	9562		103451	78197	
391821	**818637**	**540884**	**1195100**	**1038932**	**1524556**	**391098**	**241244**	**1435301**	**1344248**	**468604**
9351	431910	213077	119879	31398	75226	43222	13210	23641	68308	50121
382470	386727	327807	1075221	1007534	1449330	347876	228034	1411660	1275940	418483
20744	181185	79115	291141	207314	443074	34209	78515	466427	240037	97405
		31664		232				2468		
185319	78696	163921	556266	468677	451524	236543	126257	582464	770298	193272
176407	126846	53107	227814	331311	554732	77124	23262	360301	265605	127806
65094	**55687**	**3605**	**95148**	**44021**	**230174**	**85878**	**29571**	**159307**	**552805**	**48043**

表 8－12　各县(市)、区房地产企业房屋施工及竣工情况(2012)
Buildings Construction and The Completed of Enterprises for Real Estate Development

指标名称	Indicators	全市 Total	市区 Urban Disctict
房屋施工面积	**Floor Space of Buildings Under Consrtuction**	**60805078**	**36676485**
1.住宅	Residential Buildings	33620766	18667983
2.办公楼	Office Buildings	5125364	4538567
3.商业营业用房	Buildings for Commercial Business	7387441	4157907
4.其他	Others	14671507	9312028
本年新开工房屋施工面积	**Floor Space of Newly Started of the Year**	**14705107**	**7147068**
1.住宅	Residential Buildings	8303184	3678300
2.办公楼	Office Buildings	903777	873460
3.商业营业用房	Buildings for Commercial Business	1438536	512965
4.其他	Others	4059610	2082343
房屋竣工面积	**Floor Space of Buildings Completed**	**8399073**	**6619638**
#不可销售面积	Floor Space for Connot	1966495	1783416
1.住宅	Residential Buildings	5306090	4123946
2.办公楼	Office Buildings	452242	429498
3.商业营业用房	Buildings for Commercial Business	956427	632695
4.其他	Others	1684314	1433499
商品住宅竣工套数(套)	**Completed Residencial House (flat)**	**43486**	**34967**
竣工房屋价值(万元)	**Value of Buildings Completed(10000 yuan)**	**2660963**	**2182583**
1.住宅	Residential Buildings	1619531	1317082
2.办公楼	Office Buildings	212122	202637
3.商业营业用房	Buildings for Commercial Business	370995	267687
4.其他	Others	458315	395177
出租房屋面积	**Floor Space of Lease House**	**645422**	**619373**
1.住宅	Residential Buildings	3106	3106
2.办公楼	Office Buildings	85902	76046
3.商业营业用房	Buildings for Commercial Business	543655	527662
4.其他	Others	12759	12559
空置面积	**Floor Space of Vacant Building**	**2399152**	**1735861**
1.住宅	Residential Buildings	774651	511335
2.办公楼	Office Buildings	313636	265491
3.商业营业用房	Buildings for Commercial Business	733693	506504
4.其他	Others	577172	452531

单位:平方米,万元(sq. m,10000 yuan)

海曙区 Haishu	江东区 Jiangdong	江北区 Jiangbei	北仑区 Beilun	镇海区 Zhenhai	鄞州区 Yinzhou	余姚 Yuyao	慈溪 Cixi	奉化 Fenghua	象山 Xiangshan	宁海 Ninghai
2772945	**3738743**	**2934662**	**8607950**	**6308861**	**9709465**	**7351138**	**8829675**	**3297691**	**2884193**	**1765896**
1323038	1156048	1543324	4822933	3686498	4737260	4192001	5440797	2277823	1917966	1124196
485819	664281	318004	899215	538118	1206347	43662	385137	172	80895	76931
335231	676910	262841	906968	763800	1089557	1410546	1158062	365207	190201	105518
628857	1241504	810493	1978834	1320445	2676301	1704929	1845679	654489	695131	459251
564975	**633385**	**696331**	**2639965**	**1039856**	**1473441**	**3300098**	**1467775**	**1043880**	**1229309**	**516977**
214679	313997	268708	1661543	645745	544104	1811082	974042	685372	804252	350136
163127	84305	141245	181511	12721	281117	27511	804	98	1904	
59644	29806	71357	130143	106773	93734	566639	101198	86538	117308	53888
127525	205277	215021	666768	274617	554486	894866	391731	271872	305845	112953
678560	**369937**	**994894**	**940035**	**703863**	**2386097**	**959608**	**28699**	**121929**	**491289**	**177910**
197707	177787	321826	300157	163748	512934	103898	8366	8130	58431	4254
251568	250605	567433	720853	369136	1575874	579110	17093	89992	380475	115474
139737		73908	84718	18401	112734	7121		74	15549	
162738	10235	61255	49748	167078	151937	246591	2136	19317	37963	17725
124517	109097	292298	84716	149248	545552	126786	9470	12546	57302	44711
2116	**2343**	**4119**	**6398**	**3746**	**13079**	**5066**	**132**	**874**	**1700**	**747**
313640	**116897**	**462163**	**220256**	**201355**	**704707**	**254471**	**8500**	**27519**	**129544**	**58346**
67451	79239	325370	167202	97312	465765	137792	5100	20192	101410	37955
97813		36856	24250	5329	38389	4864		20	4601	
113687	3186	26855	13126	59612	43205	81558	600	5166	10408	5576
34689	34472	73082	15678	39102	157348	30257	2800	2141	13125	14815
36338	**201748**	**5227**	**16969**		**321934**	**26049**				
	3106									
7041	39112	526	2210		7009	9856				
29297	153214	4701	8516		314925	15993				
	6316		6243			200				
315517	**416557**	**261514**	**251665**	**197361**	**219514**	**283465**	**71462**	**35734**	**105661**	**166969**
48192	98722	154410	83664	29360	91148	96405	16058	26797	75653	48403
44980	109674	8351	51909	6892	37086	14156	165		3824	30000
148793	105667	31932	64223	96961	43513	131775	25587	7710	21977	40140
73552	102494	66821	51869	64148	47767	41129	29652	1227	4207	48426

表8-13 各县(市)、区房地产企业房屋销售情况(2012)
Building Sale Situation of Enterprises for Real Estate Development

指标名称	Indicators	宁波市 Total	市区 Urban Disctict
商品房销售面积	**Floor Space of Building Sold**	**5902173**	**3438537**
1.住宅	Residential Buildings	4587421	2632366
2.办公楼	Office Buildings	455251	374679
3.商业营业用房	Buildings for Commercial Business	553096	278588
4.其他	Others	306405	152904
现房销售面积	Floor Space of Completed Building	668098	503988
1.住宅	Residential Buildings	350666	198817
2.办公楼	Office Buildings	59994	52799
3.商业营业用房	Buildings for Commercial Business	144178	79061
4.其他	Others	113260	103398
期房销售面积	Floor Space of Forward Delivery Building	5234075	2934549
1.住宅	Residential Buildings	4236755	2363636
2.办公楼	Office Buildings	395257	321880
3.商业营业用房	Buildings for Commercial Business	408918	199527
4.其他	Others	193145	49506
商品房销售额	**Sales Volume of Commercial Buildings**	**6633948**	**4134397**
1.住宅	Residential Buildings	5222892	3284646
2.办公楼	Office Buildings	429654	354792
3.商业营业用房	Buildings for Commercial Business	838365	426700
4.其他	Others	143037	68259
现房销售额	Sales Volume of Completed Building	629681	465471
1.住宅	Residential Buildings	345339	275725
2.办公楼	Office Buildings	58183	54046
3.商业营业用房	Buildings for Commercial Business	182165	98870
4.其他	Others	43994	36830
期房销售额	Sales Volume of Forward Delivery Building	6004267	3668926
1.住宅	Residential Buildings	4877553	3008921
2.办公楼	Office Buildings	371471	300746
3.商业营业用房	Buildings for Commercial Business	656200	327830
4.其他	Others	99043	31429

单位:平方米,万元(sq. m,10000 yuan)

海曙区 Haishu	江东区 Jiangdong	江北区 Jiangbei	北仑区 Beilun	镇海区 Zhenhai	鄞州区 Yinzhou	余姚 Yuyao	慈溪 Cixi	奉化 Fenghua	象山 Xiangshan	宁海 Ninghai
369732	**229265**	**162957**	**762759**	**574275**	**960824**	**871951**	**832963**	**211583**	**242966**	**304173**
232051	154372	115897	539737	484742	772547	621049	742145	165648	228616	197597
89917	46539	17540	47732	58319	93588	7121	28213	74	4912	40252
22878	18054	18278	116911	19669	68849	191484	31904	37128	6878	7114
24886	10300	11242	58379	11545	25840	52297	30701	8733	2560	59210
42262	73252	47545	168098	54013	97236	86581	3871	15732	11621	46305
20678	53685	32600	77961	1111	1685	10116	44054	16669	33604	47406
2163	14954	2600	15685	391	10843	7121		74		
4843	1809	2294	24919	15170	23961	54852	356	6954	1390	1565
14578	2804	10051	49533	4848	15026	7939	300	822	115	686
327470	156013	115412	594661	520262	863588	785370	829092	195851	231345	257868
211373	100687	83297	461776	451138	725141	604380	738930	157766	218500	153543
87754	31585	14940	32047	57928	82745		28213		4912	40252
18035	16245	15984	91992	4499	44888	136632	31548	30174	5488	5549
10308	7496	1191	8846	6697	10814	44358	30401	7911	2445	58524
513029	**377090**	**313373**	**700506**	**539139**	**1302724**	**989498**	**802596**	**207015**	**274207**	**226235**
376675	247655	232486	512752	476899	1100607	694860	677268	144274	257962	163882
79828	67640	30581	31325	36376	87570	4109	24581	28	5892	40252
43805	56090	43366	136858	21116	100180	255106	76878	59894	8856	10931
12721	5705	6940	19571	4748	14367	35423	23869	2819	1497	11170
45530	83243	65410	111250	36731	101636	102617	2061	7600	12074	39858
25539	49344	51615	61389	23143	60245	15720	1741	3500	9545	39108
4100	25388	3386	10569	301	5815	4109		28		
9179	6942	4766	25860	11854	29812	76605	178	3696	2430	386
6712	1569	5643	13432	1433	5764	6183	142	376	99	364
467499	293847	247963	589256	502408	1201088	886881	800535	199415	262133	186377
351136	198311	180871	451363	453756	1040362	679140	675527	140774	248417	124774
75728	42252	27195	20756	36075	81755		24581		5892	40252
34626	49148	38600	110998	9262	70368	178501	76700	56198	6426	10545
6009	4136	1297	6139	3315	8603	29240	23727	2443	1398	10806

表 8－14 各县(市)农村非农户固定资产投资主要指标(2012)
Main Indicators of Investment in Fixed Assets of Non－peasant Households in Rural Area by Region

指标	Indicators	全市 Total
本年完成投资	**Finished Investment of This Year**	**5578484**
按国民经济行业分	**By Sector**	
农林牧渔业	Framing, Forestry, Animal Husbandry and Fishery	76586
采矿业	Mining and Quarrying	8666
制造业	Manufacuring	3229376
电力、燃气及水的生产和供应业	Electric Power, Gas and Water Production and Supply	183582
建筑业	Construction	9949
批发和零售业	Wholesale and Retail Trade	169492
交通运输、仓储和邮政业	Transportation, Storage and Post	473610
住宿和餐饮业	Hotel and Catering Services	87343
信息传输、软件和信息技术服务业	Information Transmission, Software and Information Technology Services	2843
金融业	Financial Industries	5495
房地产业	Real Estate Industries	761888
租赁和商务服务业	Leasing and Business Service Industries	93837
科学研究和技术服务业	The Scientific Research and Technical Services	7830
水利、环境和公共设施管理业	Water Conservancy, Environment and Public Facility Management	264298
居民服务、修理和其他服务业	Residents Service, Repair and Other Services	13382
教育	Education	86340
卫生和社会工作	Health and Social Work	27590
文化、体育和娱乐业	Culture, Sports and Entertainment	62059
公共管理、社会保障和社会组织	Public Management, Social Security and Social Organization	14316

注：本表按 2011 年修订的国民经济行业标准统计。

Note: Statistics in this table are classified as the national economic category that was modified in 2011.

单位:万元(10000 yuan)

市区 Urban Disctict	#鄞州 Yinzhou	余姚 Yuyao	慈溪 Cixi	奉化 Fenghua	象山 Xiangshan	宁海 Ninghai
2189012	**1327490**	**1130105**	**1164786**	**235157**	**445710**	**413714**
14333	10960	12203	8959	12752	23745	4594
6310	6310			2356		
985904	662025	768967	920102	59856	227793	266754
50956	9621	39206	2913	3686	63516	23305
7559	6122	590			1800	
104779	5890	22075	11392	4900	18909	7437
293758	269853	85962	50086	17049	23675	3080
32014	1686	34029	1563	1150	7333	11254
2843						
1205		4290				
477797	253170	56046	98601	90138	27406	11900
6107		10783	600	1105	7150	68092
7830						
108585	38195	42910	39831	29305	30361	13306
4283	802	6529			2150	420
23088	22446	34282	21818	4310	2432	410
18662	16111	1395	7181		354	
36768	18069	8686	1740	4535	8568	1762
6231	6230	2152		4015	518	1400

表 8－15 部分年份城镇以上固定资产投资主要指标
Main Indicators of Investment in Fixed Assets of City and Town Level and Above in Partial Years

单位：万元(10000 yuan)

指标	Indicators	2008	2009	2010	2011	2012
计划总投资	**Total Investment of Plan**	**37009529**	**43943918**	**44888914**	**47604813**	**53339541**
累计完成投资	**Accumulative Finished Investment**	**22266713**	**28390303**	**28253456**	**29262704**	**33757190**
本年完成投资	**Finished Investment of This Year**	**9772019**	**11740560**	**11182943**	**12129369**	**14592260**
按经济注册类型分	**By Registration Status**					
国有经济	State－Owned Units	4689771	5425442	5804442	6119819	7536985
集体经济	Collective－owned Units	66404	68312	95167	123743	197593
股份有限公司	Share－holdingCorporation Units	558705	1290064	362382	1372970	2001386
其他有限责任公司	Other Limited Liability Corporations	704268	1097525	1037261	332185	312382
外商投资经济	Foreign Investment	1393090	970546	991368	593015	775985
港澳台投资经济	HongKong,Macao and Taiwan Funded	758070	683459	492546	1098615	776115
其他经济	Others	1601711	2205212	2399777		
按隶属关系分	**By Administrative Relationship**					
中央	Central Government	958530			504730	570359
省	Province	592995			91767	98111
省辖市	Municipalities	1808175			2679433	2806848
县(市)、区	Counties and Districts	2442753			3456025	4884449
其他	Others	4231489			5397414	6232493
按建设性质分	**By Type of Construction**					
新建	New Construction	4212338	6004342	5532359	6171252	7532996
扩建	Expansion	3457329	3148747	2783093	3419622	3975993
改建	Reconstruction	707684	853728	1005946	763358	1073554
其他	Others	1394668	1733743	1861545		
按构成分	**By Use of Funds**					
建筑工程	Construction	4466645	5635210	6031102	6828481	8244176
安装工程	Installation	868752	1116482	753456	845852	877726
设备工器具购置	Purchase of Equipment and Instruments	2386819	2522294	2077616	1928683	2215934
其他费用	Others	2049803	2466574	2320769	2526353	3254424
按资金来源分	**By Source of Funds**					
#国家预算资金	State Budget	568209	569611	593052	733398	1292692
国内贷款	Domestic Loans	1887390	1980857	2574096	2572961	2838994
利用外资	Foreign Investment	893704	536241	556315	556010	542222
自筹资金	Self－Financed Capital	6023507	8275184	6684896	7382210	8942861

表 8－16　部分年份建筑业生产经营及主要财务指标
Basic Statistics and Main Financial Indicators of Construction Enterprises in Partial Years

单位：万元(10000 yuan)

指标	Indicators	2009	2010	2011	2012
企业个数(家)	**Number of Enterprises (unit)**	**729**	**753**	**844**	**922**
建筑业总产值	**Gross Output Value of Construction**	**10777257**	**14250727**	**19333581**	**25091179**
1.建筑工程	Construction	9273217	12423675	17219536	22149575
2.安装工程	Installation	1229644	1430114	1585508	2205438
3.其他	Building Repair and Maintenance	274396	396938	528536	736167
竣工产值	Output Value of Buildings Completed	7944470	9609406	10890263	13418936
房屋建筑施工面积(万平方米)	Floor Space of Buildings Under Construction (10000 sq. m)	11206	14288582	18161	22343
房屋建筑竣工面积(万平方米)	Floor Space of Buildings Completed (10000 sq. m)	4176	4586	5180	6058
年末自有机械设备总台数(台)	Number of Machinery and Equipment (year－end) (set)	95805	115541	111675	113171
年末自有机械设备总功率(万千瓦)	Total Power of Machinery and Equipment (10000kw)	140.34	161.66	200.62	203.23
年末自有机械设备净值	Net Value of Machinery and Equipment	441925	481635	5804214	660815
计算劳动生产率的年平均人数(万人)	Average Employed Persons by Calculatied Labor Productivity (10000 persons)	59.62	72.10	76.96	89.04
年末资产负债	**Asset and Liabilities at Year－end**				
流动资产	Circulating Assets	6169311	7853800	9910592	1243742
固定资产小计	Fixed Assets	885558	1008050	1138322	1326727
固定资产原价	Original Value of Fixed Assets	1091707	1252919	1556294	1786162
本年折旧	Depreciation in This Year	66909	119301	91618	136199
资产总计	Total Assets	7773221	9721438	12127310	15082502
流动负债	Liquid Liabilities	4670538	6028401	7538632	9396904
长期负债	Long－term Liabilities	258031	233647		
所有者权益	Creditors' Equity	2844652	3459391	4184209	5191820
损益及分配	**Expenditure, Income and Distribution**				
工程结算收入	Revenue of Project Settlement Accounts	9227498	11922883	14577208	17996050
工程结算成本	Costs of Project Settlement Accounts	8254431	10620358	12957730	15973781
工程结算税金及附加	Taxes and Extra Charges on Project Settlement Accounts	294548	382964	463273	588015
工程结算利润	Profits of Project Settlement Accounts	652538	886895	1116603	1386848
工资、福利费	**Wages and Welfare Expenses**				
本年应付工资总额	Total Wages Payable in this Year	1360470	1 899023		
本年应付福利费总额	Total Welfare Expenses Payable in this Year	75809	86161		
建筑业增加值	**Value－added of Construction**	**2190722**	**3035482**		

表 8－17　建筑业企业生产情况(2012) Basic Statistics on Production of Construction Enterprises

指标	Indicators	企业个数（家） Number of Enterprises (unit)	建筑业总产值 Gross Output Value of Construction	在外省完成的产值 Output Value of Other Province
总计	**Total**	**922**	**25091179**	**9857864**
按登记注册类型分组	**By Registered Type**			
内资企业	Domestic Funded Enterprises	917	25037970	9857864
国有企业	State－owned Enterprises	14	170262	2576
集体企业	Collective－oened Enterprises	8	43464	
股份合作企业	Share－holding Cooperative Enterprises	3	231133	36312
有限责任公司	Limited Liability Corporations	74	2609557	762886
股份有限公司	Share－holding Corporations Ltd.	14	6490656	4886057
私营企业	Private Enterprises	804	15492899	4170033
港、澳、台商投资企业	HongKong，Macro and Taiwan Funded	2	40329	
外商投资企业	Enterprises with Foreign Investment	3	12880	
按建筑业行业分组	**By Sector**			
房屋和土木工程建筑业	Building and Civil Engineering	533	23040955	9536553
房屋工程建筑	Building	301	17209790	7152753
土木工程建筑	Civil Engineering	232	5831165	2383800
建筑安装业	Construction Installation	141	924740	198434
建筑装饰业	Construction Decoration	203	784814	46624
其他建筑业	Other Construction	12	41169	817
按控股情况分	**By Holding Status**			
国有控股	State－holding	37	1956774	566873
集体控股	Collective－holding	22	512466	36312
私人控股	Private－holding	860	22596179	9248038
港澳台控股	Hong Kong，Macao and Taiwan Holdings			
外商控股	Foreign－holding			
按企业资质等级分组	**By Qualification Criteria**			
施工总承包	Construc General Contractor	472	22653904	9319283
特级	Special Class	6	5734052	3478765
一级	First Class	78	10938863	4705386
二级	Second Class	132	3892084	977435
三级	Third Class	256	2088905	157696
专业承包	Special General Contractor	450	2437275	538582
一级	First Class	50	1329172	381474
二级	Second Class	112	578843	103143
三级	Third Class	288	529261	53964

单位：万元(10000 yuan)

建筑业总产值按构成分			承包工程完成产值 Gross Output Value of Contract Project			竣工产值 Output Value of Buildings Completed
1.建筑工程 Construction	2.安装工程 Installation	3.其他 Others	1.直接从建设单位承揽工程 Contract Project from Construction Unit Directly	其中 of Which 自行完成 Finish by Oneself	2.从建设单位以外承揽工程 Contract Project Outside Construction Unit	
22149575	**2205438**	**736167**	**24451746**	**24140792**	**950387**	**13418936**
22104532	2199345	734094	24399407	24088453	949517	13402958
142319	12045	15897	157049	157049	13213	93981
23735	19728		42981	42981	483	43714
231133			231116	231116	17	49804
2103460	391265	114833	2637876	2525881	83677	1305554
5560579	693887	236190	6490454	6341535	149121	3545141
14043306	1082419	367174	14839932	14789892	703007	8364764
38256		2073	40329	40329		4598
6787	6093		12009	12009	870	11379
21142574	1312155	586227	22514678	22285361	755594	12391621
15981124	885232	343435	16936180	16755049	454742	9159940
5161450	426923	242792	5578498	5530313	300852	3231681
158272	668020	98448	860097	781297	143443	475334
632981	121617	30216	769377	766719	18096	424331
38425	2745		39313	39133	2037	39589
1695654	161577	99543	1939182	1892025	64749	877117
272004	222942	17520	576370	511983	483	311376
20171482	1806589	618108	21919180	21719769	876410	12206023
20781755	1270835	601315	22298653	22049898	604006	11991866
5087778	474563	171711	5734052	5659146	74906	2911433
10317400	449974	171489	10826457	10677798	261065	5672084
3592000	123399	176685	3731270	3711151	180933	2089044
1784576	222898	81430	2006874	2001803	87102	1319305
1367820	934603	134852	2153093	2090893	346382	1427070
784003	459332	85837	1141218	1110856	218315	629271
330355	228816	19672	542216	518306	60537	435392
253462	246455	29343	469660	461731	67530	362406

表 8—17 续表 Continued

指标	Indicators	房屋建筑施工面积（平方米）Floor Space Under Construction (sq. m)	其中 of Which #本年新开工 Newly Operating Projects in this Year	#投标承包面积 Floor Space of Biding System
总计	**Total**	**223432495**	**81466053**	**157375671**
按登记注册类型分组	**By Registered Type**			
内资企业	Domestic Funded Enterprises	223229829	81290117	157375671
国有企业	State—owned Enterprises			
集体企业	Collective—oened Enterprises			
股份合作企业	Share—holding Cooperative Enterprises	1441889	496116	1441887
有限责任公司	Limited Liability Corporations	8381199	2703062	6211679
股份有限公司	Share—holding Corporations Ltd.	73119660	17883639	55744423
私营企业	Private Enterprises	140287081	60207300	93977682
港、澳、台商投资企业	HongKong, Macro and Taiwan Funded			
外商投资企业	Enterprises with Foreign Investment	202666	175936	
按建筑业行业分组	**By Sector**			
房屋和土木工程建筑业	Building and Civil Engineering	222659781	81068676	157157135
房屋工程建筑	Building	211986332	77091265	148746651
土木工程建筑	Civil Engineering	10673449	3977411	8410484
建筑安装业	Construction Installation	439908	191818	171026
建筑装饰业	Construction Decoration	48004	48004	
其他建筑业	Other Construction	825		
按控股情况分	**By Holding Status**			
国有控股	State—holding	5295106	1217503	5125339
集体控股	Collective—holding	1461889	496116	1441887
私人控股	Private—holding	216283178	79411885	150808445
港澳台控股	Hongkong, Macao & Taiwan—holding			
外商控股	Foreign—holding			
按企业资质等级分组	**By Qualification Criteria**			
施工总承包	Construc General Contractor	215395939	76519199	155764850
特级	Special Grade	70132053	15404896	53869194
一级	First Grade	91606663	36738471	76503977
二级	Second Grade	38539572	15546839	18294924
三级	Third Grade	15117651	8828993	7096755
专业承包	Special General Contractor	8036556	4946854	1610821
一级	First Grade	4861114	2675579	1072090
二级	Second Grade	2670427	2015551	358198
三级	Third Grade	505015	255724	180533

房屋建筑竣工面积(平方米) Floor Space Completed (sq. m)	竣工房屋价值 Value of Completed Building	年末自有机械设备总台数(台) Number of Machinery and Equipment (year－end)(set)	年末自有机械设备总功率(千瓦) Total Power of Machinery and Equipment (kw)	年末自有机械设备净值(万元) Net Value of Machinery and Equipment (10000yuan)	年末人数(人) Employed Persons at Year－end (person)	计算劳动生产率的年平均人员(人) Average Employed Persons by Calculatied Labor Productivity (person)
60576468	**9066596**	**113171**	**2032332**	**660815**	**955891**	**890493**
60459046	9062369	113046	2023044	656302	954578	889381
		721	26549	3220	7244	6549
		190	2646	971	1608	724
300859	46765	2449	10383	3401	7235	6861
3076120	682124	14919	262577	143316	42423	49540
16103979	3031501	12352	282159	77285	250834	221383
40978088	5301979	82415	1438730	428110	645234	604324
		12	8520	4083	922	731
117422	4227	113	768	430	391	381
60364552	9041386	92397	1804659	604812	871987	816259
56821161	8409418	68353	1053072	269589	711745	627949
3543391	631968	24044	751587	335223	160242	188310
203314	24337	10846	135143	31674	31998	31686
		7952	48280	8469	38589	31056
		249	2789	1017	2143	1230
726891	508694	7908	143228	119172	20762	25702
100060	47015	6345	50026	12586	13029	16375
28430407	8497220	98492	1833892	527232	921488	847657
55928015	8804687	89287	1735396	545877	861317	802741
13602178	2864659	8328	124177	21196	206464	180152
25136246	4004737	39992	739889	296452	378907	361957
11030788	1315103	25072	422802	129256	176132	172264
6158803	620188	15895	448528	98973	99814	88368
4648453	261908	23884	296936	114938	94574	87752
2401228	143696	8850	107562	33259	49286	45447
1980126	90618	8033	75087	26575	25809	23344
267099	27594	7001	114287	55104	19479	18961

表 8－18　建筑业企业财务情况(2012)
Main Financial Indicators of Construction Enterprises

指标	Indicators	年末资产负债		
		资产合计 Total Assets	流动资产合计 Circulating Assets	固定资产合计 Fixed Assets
总计	**Total**	**15082502**	**12437423**	**1326727**
按登记注册类型分组	**By Registered Type**			
内资企业	Domestic Funded Enterprises	15022353	12385339	1321860
国有企业	State－owned Enterprises	426205	394679	8936
集体企业	Collective－oened Enterprises	48106	42786	2357
股份合作企业	Share－holding Cooperative Enterprises	49329	42791	4598
有限责任公司	Limited Liability Corporations	2348665	1869967	269504
股份有限公司	Share－holding Corporations Ltd.	3224768	2728927	159251
私营企业	Private Enterprises	8925281	7306189	877215
港、澳、台商投资企业	HongKong,Macro and Taiwan Funded	46485	39330	4306
外商投资企业	Enterprises with Foreign Investment	13664	12753	560
按建筑业行业分组	**By Sector**			
房屋和土木工程建筑业	Building and Civil Engineering	12969006	10686591	1136479
房屋工程建筑	Building	8480987	7144052	573498
土木工程建筑	Civil Engineering	4488019	3542539	562981
建筑安装业	Construction Installation	1165419	955877	114585
建筑装饰业	Construction Decoration	661307	572982	45661
其他建筑业	Other Construction	41732	37785	3861
按控股情况分	**By Holding Status**			
国有控股	State－holding	2099406	1748366	200953
集体控股	Collective－holding	437391	385326	33736
私人控股	Private－holding	12510588	10276420	1085415
港澳台控股	Hong Kong, Macao and Taiwan Holdings			
外商控股	Foreign－holding			
按企业资质等级分组	**By Qualification Criteria**			
施工总承包	Construc General Contractor	12770406	10615816	1048663
特级	Special Class	2762473	2398099	69779
一级	First Class	5795755	4814554	475502
二级	Second Class	2410263	1931661	274484
三级	Third Class	1801915	1471503	228898
专业承包	Special General Contractor	2312096	1821606	278063
一级	First Class	944517	751116	82793
二级	Second Class	601894	474978	76477
三级	Third Class	765685	595512	118793

单位:万元(10000 yuan)

Total Assets and Liabilities at Year-end			损益及分配 Expenditure,Income and Distribution		
#本年折旧 Depreciation in this year	负债合计 Current Liabilities	所有者权益 Creditors' Equity	工程结算收入 Revenue of Project Settlement Accounts	工程结算成本 Costs of Project Settlement Accounts	工程结算税金及附加 Taxes and Extra Charges on Project Settlement Accounts
136199	**9886856**	**5191820**	**17996050**	**15973781**	**588015**
117094	9837775	5180752	17941969	15925724	586136
604	347759	78445	156932	140190	4022
419	32907	13901	48443	35624	1616
321	19985	29345	140762	129469	4629
24370	1717032	629105	2257592	2010697	63918
12108	2318490	906279	3684812	3367439	117267
79272	5401602	3523678	11653429	10242305	394685
18992	39491	6995	42463	38755	1448
113	9590	4074	11618	9303	431
114308	8464659	4504347	16171347	14425783	536560
47278	5501486	2979501	11562929	10411900	386195
67031	2963173	1524846	4608418	4013883	150366
12593	798649	362944	857974	729418	19425
5903	443813	217494	659432	556966	22008
597	26222	15511	42851	32363	1310
36693	1588868	510537	1698152	1527821	46566
3481	334029	99537	467747	408431	13931
95398	7937036	4573552	15807757	14019613	527077
86458	8288650	4480459	15889283	14196072	527065
6217	1992368	770106	3719522	3429068	119912
42461	3734592	2061164	7334881	6543040	239066
19601	1451720	958543	3076624	2703672	104836
18179	1109971	690646	1758255	1520292	63250
49741	1598206	711362	2106767	1777709	60950
26759	675809	268708	1083922	950152	28805
7716	383202	218692	505513	419782	15029
15266	539195	223962	517332	407776	17116

表 8—18 续表 Continued

		损益及分配	
		工程结算利润 Profits of Project Settlement Accounts	其他业务利润 Other Profits from Business
总　　计	**Total**	**1386848**	**21464**
按登记注册类型分组	**By Registered Type**		
内资企业	Domestic Funded Enterprises	1382704	21473
国有企业	State—owned Enterprises	12633	1172
集体企业	Collective—oened Enterprises	11166	356
股份合作企业	Share—holding Cooperative Enterprises	6664	235
有限责任公司	Limited Liability Corporations	178310	10580
股份有限公司	Share—holding Corporations Ltd.	198315	4472
私营企业	Private Enterprises	975615	4658
港、澳、台商投资企业	HongKong,Macro and Taiwan Funded	2260	—10
外商投资企业	Enterprises with Foreign Investment	1884	1
按建筑业行业中类分组	**By Sector**		
房屋和土木工程建筑业	Building and Civil Engineering	1172333	15521
房屋工程建筑	Building	49648	3786
土木工程建筑	Civil Engineering	422685	11736
建筑安装业	Construction Installation	105105	2798
建筑装饰业	Construction Decoration	76155	1722
其他建筑业	Other Construction	8451	1015
按控股情况分	**By Holding Status**		
国有控股	State—holding	121147	2484
集体控股	Collective—holding	44800	8172
私人控股	Private—holding	1217046	10708
港澳台控股	Hong Kong, Macao and Taiwan Holdings		
外商控股	Foreign—holding		
按企业资质等级分组	**By Qualification Criteria**		
施工总承包	Construc General Contractor	1137130	14646
特级	Special Grade	170248	—1135
一级	First Grade	545588	5095
二级	Second Grade	260783	8818
三级	Third Grade	160512	1869
专业承包	Special General Contractor	249718	6818
一级	First Grade	101111	3007
二级	Second Grade	65171	1428
三级	Third Grade	83437	2382

单位:万元(10000 yuan)

Expenditure, Incomeand Distribution				应付职工薪酬 Employee Compensation Payable
管理费用 Management Expense	财务费用 Financial Expense	营业利润 Operating Profits	利润总额 Total Profits	
446852	147981	768643	791965	3744536
8385	−504	3795	4545	21586
2951	−101	8717	8828	6742
2571	−245	4740	4849	40892
87671	10580	94569	98769	386583
50067	34505	132352	138572	1056059
295207	103746	524470	536402	2232675
1460	310	480	630	2526
1211	245	430	390	3345
343112	129172	674574	697037	
184096	90959	442417	454914	2693759
159016	38213	232157	242123	728902
59563	8976	40098	41110	166355
36195	7264	33772	33442	117013
2592	116	6758	7024	6462
61775	4649	56666	60263	279280
26452	−1074	30046	31196	91168
359086	144229	681830	700508	3377535
326740	117035	666189	686407	3388827
51043	17999	114760	114865	983433
144260	65629	297350	322365	1488992
70508	24199	163711	158310	594024
60929	9208	90368	90867	322377
122783	31502	103364	106578	361580
43487	16825	43353	43208	195427
31827	7826	26982	28813	88001
47469	6851	33028	34557	78152

表 8－19 新增生产能力或效益(2012) Newly Increase Production Capacity or Benefit

指标	单位	Indicators	Unit	本年新增 Added at this Year
粗钢	万吨/年	Crude Steels	10000 tons/year	3.6
钢材	万吨/年	Steels	10000 tons/year	75.1
其中:电解锌	吨/年	Electrolytic Zinc	tones/year	15000
铝加工材	吨/年	Alumina	tones/year	70000
铜加工材	吨/年	Copper	tones/year	275010.06
风力发电	万千瓦	Wind Power	10000 kw	3
输电线路长度(11万伏及以上)	公里	Length of Transmission Lines (110,000 Volts and Above)	kilometer	659.42
水泥	万吨/年	Cement	10000 tons/year	130
平板玻璃	万重量箱/年	Plate Grass	10000 weightboxes/year	1.8
塑料树脂及共聚物	吨/年	Plastic Resin and Copolymer	tons/year	32500
轮胎外胎	万条/年	Tire	10000 units/year	20
轿车制造	辆/年	Car	units/year	50000
化学纤维	吨/年	Chemical Fiber	tons/year	347900
#合成纤维	吨/年	#Synthetic Fiber	tons/year	1200
粘胶纤维	吨/年	Viscose Fiber	tons/year	8000
棉纺锭	锭	Cotton Spindles	Spindles	170000
白酒	万吨/年	White Spirit	10000 tons/year	0.01
其他酒	万吨/年	Other Wine	10000 tons/year	10.8
家用电冰箱	万台/年	Household Refrigerators	10000 units/year	151
家用洗衣机	万台/年	Household Washing Machines	10000 units/year	40
房间空气调节器	万台/年	Room Air Conditioners	10000 units/year	50
新建公路	公里	New Highway	kilometer	163.79
#一级公路	公里	First Standard Road	kilometer	45.15
二级公路	公里	Second Standard Road	kilometer	36.88
改建公路	公里	Road Reconstruction	kilometer	269.29
#一级公路	公里	First Standard Road	kilometer	25.36
二级公路	公里	Second Standard Road	kilometer	12
新建独立公路桥梁	延长米	New Highway Bridge	meter	26.3
新建独立公路桥梁	座	New Highway Bridge	units	1
新建独立公路隧道	延长米	New Highway Tunnel	meter	1385
新建独立公路隧道	处	New Highway Tunnel	units	1
新(扩)建公路客、货运站	个	New (Expanding) Existing Road Passenger and Freight Station	units	2
新(扩)建公路客、货运站	平方米	New (Expanding) Existing Road Passenger and Freight Station	square meters	36307
城市自来水供水能力	万吨/日	Tap Water Supply Capacity	10000 tons/day	1
城市污水处理能力	万吨/日	Urban Sewage Treatment Capacity	10000 tons/day	18.31

表 8－20 本年完成建筑业总产值前 20 位企业(2012) The Top 20 Enterprises of Completed Total Output Value for Construction Industry

企业名称 Name of Enterprises	资质等级 Grade of Natural Endowments
龙元建设集团股份有限公司 Longyuan Construction Group Co. ,Ltd.	房屋建筑工程施工总承包特级 Whole Contract To Project of Building Construction by Special Grade
华丰建设股份有限公司 Ningbo Huafeng Construction Group Co. ,Ltd.	房屋建筑工程施工总承包特级 Whole Contract To Project of Building Construction by Special Grade
宏润建设集团股份有限公司 Hongrun Construction Group Co. ,Ltd.	市政工程施工总承包壹级 Whole Contract To Municipal Engineering Construction by First Grade
宁波建工集团有限公司 Ningbo Construction And Industry Group Co. , Ltd.	房屋建筑工程施工总承包特级 Whole Contract To Project of Building Construction by Special Grade
浙江省二建建设集团有限公司 Zhejiang No. 2 Construction Group Co. ,Ltd.	房屋建筑工程施工总承包特级 Whole Contract To Project of Building Construction by Special Grade
中达建设集团股份有限公司 Zhongda Construction Group Co. ,Ltd.	房屋建筑工程施工总承包特级 Whole Contract To Project of Building Construction by Special Grade
浙江欣捷建设有限公司 Zhe Jiang Xinjie Construction Co. ,Ltd.	房屋建筑工程施工总承包壹级 Whole Contract To Project of Building Construction by First Grade
浙江建安实业集团股份有限公司 Zhejiang Jian'an Industry Group Ltd.	房屋建筑工程施工总承包壹级 Whole Contract To Project of Building Construction by First Grade
宁波市建设集团股份有限公司 Ningbo Construction Group Co. ,Ltd.	房屋建筑工程施工总承包壹级 Whole Contract To Project of Building Construction by First Grade
华锦建设股份有限公司 Huajing Construction Co. ,Ltd.	房屋建筑工程施工总承包壹级 Whole Contract To Project of Building Construction by First Grade
浙江天元建设(集团)股份有限公司 Zhejiang Tianyuan (Group) Co. ,Ltd.	房屋建筑工程施工总承包壹级 Whole Contract To Project of Building Construction by First Grade
中交上航局航道建设有限公司 SDC Waterway Construction Co. ,Ltd.	港口与航道工程施工总承包壹级 Whole Constract To Port and Waterway Construction by First Grade
大荣建设有限公司 Darong Construction Engineering Co. ,Ltd.	房屋建筑工程施工总承包壹级 Whole Contract To Project of Building Construction by First Grade
海达建设集团有限公司 Haida Construction Group Co. ,Ltd.	房屋建筑工程施工总承包壹级 Whole Contract To Project of Building Construction by First Grade
华恒建设集团有限公司 Huaheng Construction Group Co. ,Ltd.	房屋建筑工程施工总承包壹级 Whole Contract To Project of Building Construction by First Grade
博宏恒基集团有限公司 Bohohk Group Co. ,Ltd	房屋建筑工程施工总承包壹级 Whole Contract To Project of Building Construction by First Grade
浙江沈氏建设有限公司 Zhejiang Shen Construction Co. ,Ltd.	房屋建筑工程施工总承包壹级 Whole Contract To Project of Building Construction by First Grade
宁波住宅建设集团股份有限公司 Ningbo Residential Construction Group Co. ,Ltd.	房屋建筑工程施工总承包壹级 Whole Contract To Project of Building Construction by First Grade
宁波市政工程建设集团有限公司 Ningbo Municipal Engineering Construction Group Co. ,Ltd.	市政工程施工总承包壹级 Whole Contract To Municipal Engineering Construction by First Grade
浙江新中源建设有限公司 Zhejiang New Zhongyuan Construction Co. ,Ltd.	房屋建筑工程施工总承包壹级 Whole Contract To Project of Building Construction by First Grade

表8－21　1、2级资质等级房地产开发经营企业(2012)
Enterprises for Real Estate Developing & Managing with Certificate in First, Second Grade of Natural Endowments

企业名称	Name of Enterprises	资质等级 Grade of Natural Endowments
宁波房地产股份有限公司	Ningbo Real Estate Co. ,Ltd.	1
宁波永和建设开发股份有限公司	Ningbo Yonghe Construction Development Co. ,Ltd.	1
宁波中房置业股份有限公司	Ningbo Zhongfang Real Estate Co. ,Ltd.	1
仑江集团有限公司	Lun Jiang Group Co. ,Ltd.	1
镇海石化工程有限责任公司	Zhenhai Petrochemical Engineering Co. ,Ltd.	1
宁波东方建设开发有限公司	Ningbo Dongfang Construction Development Co. ,Ltd.	1
宁波市五环房地产开发有限公司	Ningbo Wuhuan Estate Co. ,Ltd.	1
宁波市甬佳房地产开发有限公司	Ningbo Yongjia Real Estate Developing Co. ,Ltd.	1
宁波市交通房地产有限公司	Ningbo Jiaotong Real Estate Co. ,Ltd.	1
宁波华泰股份有限公司	Ningbo Huatai Co. ,Ltd.	1
雅戈尔置业控股有限公司	Youngor (Ningbo) Real Estate Co. ,Ltd.	1
宁波银亿房地产开发有限公司	Ningbo Yingyi Real Estate Developing Co. ,Ltd.	1
宁波宁兴房地产开发集团有限公司	Ningbo Ningxing Real Estate Developing Co. ,Ltd.	1
宁波和锦房地产开发有限公司	Ningbo HejinReal Estate Development Co. ,Ltd.	1
宁波舜大房地产开发有限公司	Ningbo Shunda Real Estate Developing Co. ,Ltd.	1
荣安集团股份有限公司	Rongan Group Co. ,Ltd.	1
宁波联合建设开发有限公司	Ningbo Lianhe Construction Developing Co. ,Ltd.	1
宁波奥克斯置业有限公司	Ningbo Aux Ltd.	1
余姚市房地产开发经营有限公司	Yuyao Real Estate Developing Co. ,Ltd.	1
宁波市镇海新城南区开发建设投资有限公司	Ningbo Zhenhai New South District Construction Investment Development Co. ,Ltd.	1
宁波开投置业有限公司	Ningbo Kaituo Properties Co. ,Ltd.	2
浙江广天建昌房地产股份有限公司	Zhejiang Guangtian Jianchang Real Estate Co. ,Ltd.	2
宁波信达中建置业有限公司	Ningbo Xinda Zhongjian Real Estate Co. ,Ltd.	2
宁波华丰建设房产有限责任公司	Ningbo Huafeng Construction Real Estate Ltd.	2
宁波经济技术开发区房地产总公司	Ningbo Economic and Technological Development Zone Real Estate Corporation	2
宁波市江东东城房屋开发公司	Ningbo Jiangdong Dongcheng House Development Ltd.	2
宁波市北仑区房地产建设开发有限公司	Ningbo Beilun Real Estate Construction Development Corp.	2
宁波新隆房地产股份有限公司	Ningbo Xinlong Real Estate Co. ,Ltd.	2
宁波甬城房地产有限公司	Ningbo Yongcheng Real Estate Co. ,Ltd.	2
宁波富豪房地产开发有限公司	Ningbo Fuhao Real Estate Developing Co. ,Ltd.	2
宁波华龙投资建设开发有限公司	Niingbo Hualong Investment Construction and Development Co. ,Ltd.	2
慈溪市住宅经营有限责任公司	Cixi House Managing Corp.	2
浙江兴润置业投资有限公司	Zhejiang Xingrun Real Estate Co. ,Ltd.	2
宁波滕头房地产开发有限公司	Ningbo Tengtou Real Estate Development Co. ,Ltd.	2
象山房地产开发有限公司	Xiangshan Real Estate Developing Co. ,Ltd.	2
象山县地产房产开发总公司	Xiangshan Real Estate Developing Corporation	2
宁波富邦房地产开发有限公司	Ningbo Fontune Real Estate Development Co. ,Ltd.	2
中信大榭房地产公司	CITIC Daxie Real Estate Company	2
宁波市镇海区住房发展投资有限公司	Ningbo Zhenhai House Developing & Investment Co,. Ltd.	2
象山金森房地产发展有限公司	Xiangshan Jinmiao Real Estate Development Co. ,Ltd.	2
宁波太平洋土地建设有限公司	Ningbo Pacific Land Construction Co. ,Ltd.	2
宁波市拓展房地产开发有限公司	Ningbo Tuozhan Real Estate Developing Co. ,Ltd.	2
慈溪新城房地产发展有限公司	Cixi Xincheng Real Estate Development Co. ,Ltd.	2

表 8—21 续表 Continued

企业名称	Name of Enterprises	资质等级 Grade of Natural Endowments
浙江太平洋房产开发有限公司	Zhejiang Pacific Real Estate Developing Co. ,Ltd.	2
宁波金峰房地产开发有限公司慈溪分公司	Ningbo Cixi Jinfeng Branch Real Estate Development Co. ,Ltd.	2
宁波维科置业有限公司	Ningbo Veken Real Estate Co. ,Ltd.	2
余姚市赛格特经济技术开发有限公司	Yuyao Saigete Economic & Technology Developing Co. ,Ltd.	2
浙江山水房地产开发有限公司	Zhejiang landscape Real Estate Development Co. ,Ltd.	2
宁波振兴房地产开发有限公司	Ningbo Revitalization Real Estate Co. ,Ltd.	2
宁波舜龙房地产开发有限公司	Ningbo Sunlong Real Estate Development Co. ,Ltd.	2
奉化市城市建设投资有限公司	Fenghua City Constuction Co. ,Ltd.	2
宁波市镇海茗园房地产开发有限公司	Ningbo Zhenhai Mingyuan Real Estate Co. ,Ltd.	2
余姚市东方房产有限公司	Yuyao Dongfang Real Estate Co. ,Ltd.	2
宁波市镇海华鑫房地产开发有限公司	Ningbo Zhenhai Huaxin Real Estate Developing Co. ,Ltd.	2
慈溪市大通房地产开发有限公司	Cixi Datong Real Estate Developing Co. ,Ltd.	2
宁波宁盛置业有限公司	Ningbo Ningsheng Real Estate Co. ,Ltd.	2
余姚市万里房地产开发有限公司	Yuyao Wanli Real Estate Developing Co. ,Ltd.	2
宁波中宇房地产有限公司	Ningbo Zhongyu Real Estate Co. ,Ltd.	2
慈溪市飞龙房地产开发有限公司	Cix Feilong Real Estate Developing Co. ,Ltd.	2
慈溪市环驰房地产开发有限公司	Cixi Huanchi Real Estate Developing Ltd.	2
慈溪中星房地产开发有限公司	Cixi Zhongxing Real Estate Developing Ltd.	2
宁波市恒和房地产开发有限公司	Ningbo Henghe Real Estate Development Co. ,Ltd.	2
宁波金沃房地产开发有限公司	Ningbo Jinwo Real Estate Development Co. ,Ltd.	2
宁波新恒德置业有限公司	Ningbo Xinhengde Ltd.	2
象山县万象房屋开发有限公司	Xiangshan Wanxiang Real Estate Developing Ltd.	2
宁波万基房地产开发有限公司	Ningbo Wanji Real Estate Developing Ltd.	2
余姚市久丰房地产开发有限公司	Yuyao Jiufeng Real Estate Developing Ltd.	2
宁海县和兴房地产开发有限公司	Ninghai Hexing Real Estate Developing Ltd.	2
象山华丰房地产有限责任公司	Xiangshan Huafeng Real Estate Co. ,Ltd.	2
宁波大丰房地产开发有限责任公司	Ningbo Dafeng Real Estate Co. ,Ltd.	2
宁波香格房地产开发有限公司	Ningbo Xiangge Real Estate Co. ,Ltd.	2
象山宏润房地产有限公司	Xiangshan Hongrong Real Estate Co. ,Ltd.	2
浙江华茂置业发展有限公司	Zhejiang Huanmao Real Estate Development Co. ,Ltd.	2
宁波市北仑华信置业有限公司	Ningbo Beilun Huaxin Properties Ltd.	2
宁波美华实业有限公司	Ningbo Meihua Industrial Co. ,Ltd.	2
宁波百隆房地产有限公司	Ningbo Bailong Real Estate Co. ,Ltd.	2
宁波申洲置业有限公司	Ningbo Shenzhou Properties Ltd.	2
宁波康园房地产开发有限公司	Ningbo Kangyuan Real Estate Development Co. ,Ltd.	2
宁波华垠房地产开发有限公司	Ningbo Huayin Real Estate Development Co. ,Ltd.	2
宁波前程房地产有限公司	Ningbo Future Real Estate Co. ,Ltd.	2
宁波金峰房地产开发有限公司	Ningbo Jinfeng Real Estate Development Co. ,Ltd.	2
宁波得力房地产有限公司	Ningbo Deli Real Estate Co. ,Ltd.	2
余姚市舜泉房地产开发有限公司	Yuyao Shunquan Real Estate Developing Co. ,Ltd.	2
宁波沧海控股集团有限公司	Ningbo Sea Holding Group Co. ,Ltd.	2
宁波和协拓展置业有限公司	Ningbo Hexie Real Estate Development Co. ,Ltd.	2
慈溪市城市发展有限公司房地产分公司	Cixi City Developing Ltd.	2

主要统计指标解释

【全社会固定资产投资】 固定资产投资是社会固定资产再生产的主要手段。通过建造和购置固定资产的活动，国民经济不断采用先进技术装备，建立新兴部门，进一步调整经济结构和生产力的地区分布，增强经济实力，为改善人民物质文化生活创造物质条件。这对我国的社会主义现代化建设具有重要意义。

固定资产投资额是以货币表现的建造和购置固定资产活动的工作量，它是反映固定资产投资规模、速度、比例关系和使用方向的综合性指标。全社会固定资产投资按经济类型可分为国有、集体、个体、联营、股份制、外商、港澳台商、其他等。按照管理渠道，全社会固定资产投资总额分为基本建设、更新改造、房地产开发投资和其他固定资产投资四个部分。

【房地产开发投资】 指房地产开发公司、商品房建设公司及其他房地产开发法人单位和附属于其他法人单位实际从事房地产开发或经营的活动单位统一开发的包括统代建、拆迁还建的住宅、厂房、仓库、饭店、宾馆、度假村、写字楼、办公楼等房屋建筑物和配套的服务设施，土地开发工程（如道路、给水、排水、供电、供热、通讯、平整场地等基础设施工程）的投资；不包括单纯的土地交易活动。

【农村非农户投资】 农村非农户建造和购置固定资产投资计划固定资本形成总额在500万元以上的项目，农村非农户包括以下二大类：

第一类为企业单位，分成(1)集体企业，包括集体直接经营及集体所有租赁给个人的企业；(2)股份合作企业；(3)联营企业；(4)有限责任公司(5)股份有限公司；(6)私营企业(7)与港澳台商合资、合作企业；(8)中外合资、合作企业；(9)其他企业。

联营和合资企业按其是否由农村集体与个人相对控股或绝对控股，或由农村集体、个人实际管理来确定是否纳入农村固定资产投资统计范围，其投资额按实际发生额全额统计；个体工商户外雇从业人员8人以上（含8人）的按企业统计。

第二类为乡镇行政事业单位及社会群众团体。

【新增固定资产】指通过投资活动所形成的新的固定资产价值。包括已经建成投入生产或交付使用的工程价值和达到固定资产标准的设备、工具、器具的价值及有关应摊入的费用。它是以价值形式表示的固定资产投资成果的综合性指标，可以综合反映不同时期、不同部门、不同地区的固定资产投资成果。

【新增生产能力（或工程效益）】指通过固定资产投资活动而增加的设计能力或工程效益，它是用实物形态表示的固定资产投资的成果。新增生产能力的计算，是以能独立发挥生产能力或工程效益的单项工程（或项目）为对象。当单项工程（或项目）建成，经有关部门鉴定合格，正式移交投入生产，即可计算新增生产能力。

新增生产能力或工程效益有以下几种表现形式：

⑴以建设项目或单项工程建成后的年产能力表示，如煤炭开采、石油开采等。

⑵以建设项目或单项工程建成后处理原料的能力表示，如选矿工程的年处理矿石能力、洗煤厂年洗原煤能力等。

⑶以新增的主要设备数量或容量表示，如棉纺锭锭数、发电机组容量等。

⑷以建筑物容积、容量、面积或长度表示，如水库容量、铁路公路里程等。

新增生产能力的数量一般按设计能力计算。设计能力是指设计文件中规定的在正常情况下能够达到的生产能力，而不论投产后的实际产量如何。以设备数量、建筑物容积、面积、长度等表示的新增生产能力或工程效益，则按建成的实际数量计算。

【建筑业统计单位】 指从事房屋、构筑物建造和设备安装活动的法人企业。建筑业法人企业应同时具备的条件是：①依法成立，有自己的名称、组织机构和场所，能够承担民事责任；②独立拥有和使用资产，承担负债，有权与其他单位签订合同；③独立核算盈亏，能够编制资产负债表。

【建筑业总产值（即自行完成施工产值）】 指建筑业企业或附属施工单位自行完成的按工程进度计算的建筑安装生产总值。施工产值包括：

①建筑工程产值：指列入建筑工程预算内的各种工程价值。

②设备安装工程产值：指设备安装工程价值。

③房屋、构筑物修理产值：指房屋、构筑物修理所完成的价值，但不包括被修理房屋、构筑物本身的价值和生产设备的修理价值。

④非标准设备制造产值：指加工制造没有定型的、非标准的生产设备的加工费和原材料价值，不论是现场还是附属加工厂为本单位承建工程制造的非标准设备的价值，都应计算产值。

【房屋建筑施工面积】 指报告期内施工的全部房屋建筑面积。包括本期新开工的面积、上期跨入本期继续施工的房屋面积、上期停缓建在本期恢复施工的房屋面积、本期竣工的房屋面积及本期施工后又停缓建的房屋面积。

【房屋建筑竣工面积】 指在报告期内房屋建筑按照设计要求已全部完工，达到住人和使用条件，经验收鉴定合格，正式移交使用单位的建筑面积。

【自有机械设备年末总台数】 指归本企业(或单位)所有,属于本企业固定资产的生产性机械设备年末总台数。包括施工机械、生产设备、运输设备以及其他设备。

【自有机械设备年末总功率】 指本企业(或单位)自有施工机械、生产设备、运输设备以及其他设备等列为在册固定资产的生产性机械设备年末总功率,按设定能力或查定能力计算。包括机械本身的动力和为该机械服务的单独动力设备,如电动机等。计算单位用千瓦,动力换算可按 1 马力=0.735 千瓦折合成千瓦数。电焊机、变压器、锅炉不计算动力。

【工程结算收入】 指企业(或单位)按工程的分部分项自行完成的建筑产品价值并已与甲方在报告期内办理结算手续的工程价款收入,以及向甲方收取的除工程价款以外的按规定列作营业收入的各种款项,如临时设施费、劳动保险费、施工机械调迁费等以及向甲方收取的各种索赔款。

【工程结算利润】 指已结算工程实现的利润。如为亏损以"-"号表示。其计算公式为:

工程结算利润=工程结算收入-工程结算成本-工程结算税金及附加

Explanatory Notes on Main Statistical Indicators

【Total Investment in Fixed Assets in the Whole Country】 Investment in fixed assets is the essential means for social reproduction of fixed assets. By means of construction and purchase of fixed assets, more advanced technologies and equipment are adopted in the national economy, and new sectors are established, which promote the adjustment of economic structure and the regional distribution of productive forces and enhance the economic strengths so as to provide the material conditions for improving people's livelihood. This is significant for speeding up the drive of socialist modernization in China.

Amount of investment in fixed assets refers to the volume of activities in construction and purchases of fixed assets in monetary terms. It is a comprehensive indicator which shows the size, pace, proportional relations and use orientation of the investment in fixed assets. Total investment in fixed assets in the whole country includes, by registration type of ownership, the investment by the state—owned units, collective units, individuals, joint ownership units, share—holding units, as well as investment by businessmen from foreign countries and from Hong Kong, Macao and Taiwan, and by other units. According to China 's current management system, the investment in fixed assets in the whole country is classified into the following four parts: investment in capital construction, investment in innovation, investment in real estates development and other investment in fixed assets.

【Investment in Real Estate Development】 It includes the investment by the real estate development companies, commercial buildings construction companies and other real estate development units of various types of ownership in the construction of house buildings, such as residential buildings, factory buildings, warehouses, hotels, guesthouses, holiday villages, office buildings, and the complementary service facilities and land development projects, such as roads, water supply, water drainage, power supply, heating, telecommunications, land leveling and other projects of infrastructure. It excludes the activities in simple land transactions.

【Individual Investment in Rural Areas】 The individual investment in the rural areas includes the investment in house construction and purchase of productive fixed assets by the individuals in the rural areas.

【non—agricultural investment in rural areas】 refers to the project which the estimated total investment amount of its fixed assets built or bought by the non—agriculture units in rural areas is over 5 million yuan. The non—agricultural units include two kinds as below:

I. enterprises. 1. Collective Co. (including companies both directly managed by collective leadership and rent to the private), 2. Stock—hoiding cooperation, 3. Joint Ownership Enterprises, 4. Limited liability Corporations, 5. Share—holding corporations Ltd. , 6. Private enterprises, 7. Joint ventures or Cooperative Operation with Hong kong, Macao and Taiwan, 8. Foreign joint ventures or Cooperative Operation Enterprises, 9. other Enterprises

whether the associated companies and the joint ventures should be considered as the rural fixed assets depends on whether they are actually possessed or managed by rural communities or privates. Their investment amounts refer to the capital which had been actually invested into the enterprises. Private businesses which employ 8 or more workers should be considered as enterprises in statistics

II. public undertakings and public communities in rural areas.

【Newly Increased Fixed Assets】 refer to the newly increased value of fixed assets through investment, including the value of projects completed and put into production, the value of equipment, tools, and vessels considered as fixed assets, as well as the relevant expenses as investment in fixed assets . This is a comprehensive indicator of investment in fixed assets, reflecting the achievements of investment in fixed assets in different periods, different sect ors, and different regions.

【Newly Increased Production Capacity】 refers to the increase of designed capacity and project efficiency through investment in fixed assets, which reflects the accomplishment of investment in fixed assets in kind. The calculation of newly increased production capacity is based on individual project which operates independently and efficiently. When an individual project is completed and checked and accepted and put into production, it is counted as newly increased production capacity.

The newly increased production capacity and project efficiency are usually expressed in one of the following forms:

(1)annual production capacity, such as extraction of coal and petroleum;

(2)raw material processing capacity, such as ore dressing capacity of ore dressing projects, the dressing capacity of a coal washery;

(3)number or capacity of major equipment increased, such as the number of cotton spindles increased and the capacity of generating sets increased;

(4)physical measures of construction, such as volume, capacity, area, and length, for instance, the capacity of reservoirs, the length of railways or highways.

Newly increased production capacity in terms of quantity is calculated in designed capacity in general, which refers to the production capacity of a project under normal conditions designed in construction documents regardless of the actual output.

【Statistical units in construction industries】 refers to the legal enterprises which build architectures or install equipments. The legal enterprises should meet all the demands as follows, 1. being formed legally with own name, organizational structure and working place. Can fully bear civil responsibilities. 2. possessing and using its own assets independently, which means it should be able to incur liabilities and has right to make contracts with other enterprises. 3. should be an independent accounting unit which can draw balance sheet.

【Gross Output Value of Construction(Output Value of Projects Under Construction)】 refers to total of construction products, expressed in money terms,completed by construction and installation enterprises during a given period of time. It includes:

(1)Output value of construction projects, that is the value of projects covered by the project budgets;

(2)Output value of installation projects, that is the value of the installation of equipment,(excluding the value of the equipment to be installed);

(3)Output value of repair of buildings and structures, that is the value created through the repairs of buildings or structures, but does not include the value of buildings or structures being repaired and the value of the repair of production equipment;

(4)Output value of manufactured non—standard equipment, that is the value of no-standard production equipment(including raw materials and manufacturing cost)made for the construction project, and the equipment manufactured by subsidiary workshops.

【Floor Space under Construction】 refers to total floor space of all buildings under construction during the reference period, including floor space of newly started buildings during the reference period, floor space of construction extended from the previous period to the current period, floor space of construction suspended during the previous period and resumed in the current period, floor space of construction completed in the current period, and floor space of construction started and then suspended in the current period.

【Floor Space of Buildings Completed】 refers to the floor space of buildings completed in the reference period, which have come up to the designed standards and have been put into use.

【Total Number of Machinery and Equipment Owned by the Construction Enterprises】 refers to the number of machines and equipment owned by the enterprises (or units, and listed as the fixed assets of the enterprises(or units) by the end of the year, including machinery and equipment for construction, production and transportation.

【Total Power of Machinery and Equipment Owned by the Construction Enterprises】 refer to the total power of machinery and equipment owned by the enterprises(or units), and listed as the fixed assets of the enterprises (or units) by the end of the year, including machinery and equipment for construction, production and transportation. The power of the machinery is calculated on basis of the designed or verified capacity, covering the power of the machinery/equipment and the separate power equipment serving the machinery/equipment (such as electric motors), but excluding welders, transformers and boilers. The unit use for the calculation of power is kilowatt, with horsepower converted to kilowatt by 1horsepower=0. 735 kilowatt.

【Income from Settlement of Projects】 refers to the income received by the construction enterprise/unit from the completed portion of the project through settlement procedures with the contracted during the reference period, and other charges to the contracted as operational costs, such as facility fee, labor insurance premium, moving cost of construction unit, as well as various types of claims to the contracted.

【Profit from Settlement of Projects】 refers to profit realized through settled projects. It is calculated with the following formula:

Profit from Settlement of Projects=Income from Settlement of projects—Settled Cost—Settled Taxes and Other Cost.

NINGBO

Statistical YearBook

第九篇

港口、交通、运输、邮电

PORT,TRANSPORTATION,

POST AND TELECOMMUNICATION SERVICE

港口、交通、运输、邮电
Port, Transportations, Post and Telecommunications

主要统计指标
Major Statistics Indicators

2012 年全社会客运量	Total Passenger Traffic	28053	万人	10000 persons
比上年增长	Increase Over Last Year	1.40	%	
2012 年全社会货运量	Total Freight Traffic	32616	万吨	10000 tons
比上年增长	Increase Over Last Year	4.44	%	
2012 年港口货物吞吐量	Cargo Handled at Ports	45303	万吨	10000 tons
比上年增长	Increase Over Last Year	4.53	%	
2012 年集装箱吞吐量	Container Handled at Ports	1567	万标箱	10000 TEU
比上年增长	Increase Over Last Year	7.99	%	
2012 移动电话用户	Number of Mobile Telephone Subscribers	1088.00	万户	10000 subcribers
比上年增长	Increase Over Last Year	5.7	%	
2012 年固定电话用户	Number of Local Telephone Subscribers	308.00	万户	10000 subcribers
比上年增长	Increase Over Last Year	−1.4	%	

表 9－1 历年港口、交通、邮电基本情况
Basic Statistics on Port,Transportation and Telecommunications Over the Years

年份 Year	港口货物吞吐量 （万吨） Cargo at Throughput Ports （10000 tons）	集装箱吞吐量 （万标箱） Container Throughput （10000 TEU）	货运量 （万吨） Freight Traffic （10000 tons）	客运量 （万人） Passenger Traffic （10000 persons）	固定电话用户 （万户） Number of Local Telephone Subscribers （10000 subscribers）
1978	214		1385	2966	1.07
1979	236		1430	3369	1.19
1980	326		1562	4156	1.36
1981	349		1496	4654	1.53
1982	371		1617	5192	1.71
1983	483		1641	5652	1.86
1984	597		1810	6026	2.22
1985	1040		2015	6527	2.60
1986	1797		3204	7373	2.91
1987	1940		3745	7473	3.55
1988	2002		5408	7277	4.64
1989	2209		4570	7686	5.37
1990	2554	2.2	4763	7378	6.19
1991	3390	3.6	5070	8757	8.05
1992	4367	5.3	6492	9773	12.22
1993	5321	7.9	7583	11224	18.59
1994	5850	12.5	8711	17776	27.86
1995	6853	16.0	9577	19705	41.78
1996	7638	20.2	10460	21152	53.33
1997	8220	25.7	10547	21719	67.75
1998	8707	35.3	10317	21736	83.74
1999	9660	60.1	10344	22211	104.13
2000	11547	90.2	10819	22736	130.15
2001	12852	121.3	11283	23225	163.21
2002	15398	185.9	12429	23752	203.58
2003	18543	277.2	13919	24938	242.00
2004	22586	400.5	16026	27291	296.72
2005	26881	520.8	17664	28412	339.41
2006	30969	706.8	22238	29146	345.08
2007	34519	935.0	24363	30693	334.98
2008	36185	1084.6	27508	32250	338.24
2009	38385	1042.3	29028	33791	301.41
2010	41217	1300.4	30553	33911	317.39
2011	43339	1451.2	31228	28745	312.45
2012	45303	1567.1	32616	28053	308.00

表 9—2　港口吞吐情况(2012)
Basic Statistics On Cargo at Ports Throughput

单位:万吨(10000 tons)

指标	Indicators	吞吐量 Capacity		其中 of Which			
				出口量 Export		进口量 Import	
		总计 Total	外贸 Foreign Trade	合计 Total	外贸 Foreign Trade	合计 Total	外贸 Foreign Trade
货物吞吐量	**Cargo at Throughput Ports**	**45303**	**24533**	**17112**	**8788**	**28191**	**15745**
#转口货物	Cargo of Transfer	9905	4634	4953	9	4953	4625
货物分类	**Type of Cargo**						
煤炭及制品	Coal And Its Products	6631	676	511		6120	676
石油及制品	Petroleum And Its Products	7445	4288	2127	158	5318	4129
金属矿石	Metal Ores	8348	4913	3399		4948	4913
钢铁	Steel and Iron	928	141	133	36	796	105
矿建材料	Mineral Building Materials	1901		437		1464	
水泥	Cement	581		66		516	
木材	Timber	24	11			24	11
非金属矿石	Nonmetal Ores	362	5	12	5	350	
化肥及农药	Chemical Fertilizers and Pesticides	5	1	1	1	4	
盐	Salt	115	69			115	69
粮食	Grain	199	136	14		186	136
机械设备	Machinery Equipment	2	1			2	1
化工原料及制品	Industrial Chemicals And Its Products	1319	846	169	6	1151	840
轻工、医药	Products of Leight Industry and Medicine	55	2	4		51	2
农林牧渔业产品	Products of Farming, Forestry, Animal Husbandry And Fishery	15	4	4		11	4
其他	Others	17373	13440	10235	8581	7137	4859
旅客吞吐量(万人次)	**Number of Passenger In—And Out (10000 person. times)**	**197.12**		**100.92**		**96.20**	

表 9－3　港口国际集装箱吞吐量(2012)
International Container Throughput at Ports

航线	Shipping Lines	箱数(箱) Number of Container	重量(吨)Weigh(ton)	
			合计 Total	货重 Weigh of Cargo
总计	**Total**	**15671426**	**156926102**	**124444157**
国际航线合计	International Lines	13362341	124712776	97113426
非洲合计	Africa	609975	5584515	4324492
亚洲合计	Asia	5812761	58366569	46295847
欧洲合计	Europe	3145127	28260828	21797017
北美洲合计	North America	2605698	22703860	17401679
南美洲合计	South America	607766	4852203	3571651
大洋洲及太平洋岛屿合计	Oceania	359044	3010874	2244895
世界其他	Others	221971	1933927	1477845
内支线合计	Total of Domestic Sub－Line	1005534	12323424	10232350
天津	Tianjin	1049	23433	21332
大连	Dalian	17333	334563	299583
上海	Shanghai	10616	144095	121523
江苏	Jiangsu			
浙江	Zhejiang			
福建	Fujian			
山东	Shandong			
中国其他	Others	74679	959332	803971
国内航线合计	Total of Domestic Lines	1303551	19889902	17098381

表 9－4 历年客运量
Passenger Traffic Over the Years

单位:万人(10000 persons)

年份 Year	合计 Total	其中 of Which			
		铁路 Railway	公路 Highway	水路 Waterway	航空 Civil Aviation
1978	2966	105	2311	550	
1979	3369	122	2692	555	
1980	4156	317	3241	598	
1981	4654	351	3714	598	
1982	5192	366	4277	549	
1983	5652	411	4737	504	
1984	6026	480	5073	473	
1985	6527	502	5575	450	
1986	7373	482	6472	418	1.2
1987	7473	497	6536	438	2
1988	7277	536	6339	399	3.1
1989	7686	527	6790	366	3.2
1990	7378	462	6611	299	6
1991	8757	445	8006	295	11
1992	9773	414	9076	268	14
1993	11224	435	10523	245	21
1994	17776	486	16993	265	32
1995	19705	506	18870	283	45
1996	21152	405	20432	262	53
1997	21719	342	21101	222	55
1998	21736	300	21199	182	55
1999	22211	278	21734	146	53
2000	22736	288	22255	133	59.7
2001	23225	349	22700	115	61
2002	23752	393	23160	135	64
2003	24938	438	24320	115	65
2004	27291	567	26510	119	95
2005	28412	607	27570	113	122
2006	29146	745	28120	121	160
2007	30693	842	29541	130	180
2008	32250	1770	30130	152	198
2009	33791	1700	31545	142	403
2010	33911	1012	32340	107	452
2011	28745	2186	25960	97	501
2012	28053	1119	26285	123	527

表 9－5 历年货运量
Freight Traffic Over the Years

单位:万吨(10000 tons)

年份 Year	合计 Total	其中 of Which 铁路 Railway	公路 Highway	水路 Waterway	航空(吨) Civil Aviation(ton)	管道 Pipeline
1978	1385	45	625	715		
1979	1430	67	681	682		
1980	1562	167	709	686		
1981	1496	170	714	612		
1982	1617	186	788	643		
1983	1641	217	810	614		
1984	1810	234	883	693		
1985	2015	284	955	776		
1986	3204	310	1910	984	237	
1987	3745	337	2576	832	371	
1988	5408	380	4196	832	567	
1989	4570	398	3443	729	500	
1990	4763	355	3800	608	800	
1991	5070	302	4143	625	1600	
1992	6492	429	5328	710	2200	25
1993	7583	428	6255	868	3262	32
1994	8711	455	7113	1112	4000	31
1995	9577	527	7843	1173	4900	34
1996	10460	573	8509	1233	5200	44
1997	10547	551	8642	1314	5400	41
1998	9952	569	8195	1143	6900	44
1999	10344	609	8154	1534	9000	46
2000	10819	682	8219	1829	11000	88
2001	11283	725	8300	2156	10000	101
2002	12429	980	8630	2716	12500	102
2003	13919	1158	9070	3568	13812	122
2004	16026	1210	9890	4734	18725	190
2005	17664	1207	10480	5619	23450	356
2006	22238	1238	11725	7349	23505	1924
2007	24363	1274	12889	8706	23608	1492
2008	27508	2171	13550	9993	24549	1792
2009	29028	2377	15594	11050	68700	1774
2010	30553	2060	16220	12265	81200	2109
2011	34385	2960	15280	13771	90000	2366
2012	32616	1924	16570	14113	90800	2443

表 9－6 历年全社会旅客周转量和货物周转量 Total Turnover Volume of Passengers and Turnover Volume of Freight Traffic Over the Years

单位：万人公里，万吨公里（10000 tons－km，10000 persons－km）

年份 Year	旅客周转量 Turnover Volume of Passengers			货物周转量 Turnover Volume of Freight Traffic			
	总计 Total	其中 of Which		总计 Total	其中 of Which		
		公路 Highway	水路 Waterway		公路 Highway	水路 Waterway	管道 Pipeline
1985	147863	135273	12590	132890	34369	98521	
1986	176321	163351	12970	219594	86541	133053	
1987	182877	168280	14597	294320	130907	163413	
1988	191911	176853	15058	271187	89321	181865	
1989	193779	180061	13718	319319	135845	183474	
1990	202868	190057	12811	308099	134299	173800	
1991	229727	215573	14154	438528	187032	251496	
1992	270125	258068	12057	608363	242989	365157	217
1993	324919	314471	10448	777570	262057	515229	284
1994	623257	610761	12496	1243892	448457	795435	
1995	699514	685120	14394	1450892	495929	954674	289
1996	735912	721653	14259	1742582	523495	1218722	365
1997	755941	740381	15560	1853782	533382	1320018	382
1998	752757	741848	10909	1887113	491380	1395325	408
1999	771393	764287	7106	2311376	481555	1829381	440
2000	800193	794858	5335	2367484	482518	1884241	723
2001	822326	818704	3622	2727939	492170	2231435	4335
2002	870546	867830	2716	3342614	521700	2844927	5517
2003	921901	919900	2001	4559749	553005	4002654	4090
2004	992957	990870	2087	5545297	608310	4932308	4679
2005	1042307	1040410	1897	7478890	644800	6806210	27880
2006	1060134	1058100	2034	10361127	719114	8696860	945153
2007	1213443	1211162	2281	11298162	812007	9775967	710188
2008	1235559	1232691	2868	12470705	856713	10745112	868880
2009	1245586	1242710	2876	13216223	1351300	10999544	865379
2010	1362007	1360600	1407	15753422	2465250	13288172	997675
2011	1383064	1382100	963	20903442	2815110	16884961	1203371
2012	1431814	1430930	884	20710458	3025860	17684598	1232617

表 9—7　公路运输工具拥有量(2012)
Number of Means of Transportation Through Highway

指标	单位	Indicators	Unit	营业性 Business 合计 Total	营业性 Business 个体 Individual
总计	**辆**	**Total**	**unit**	**85966**	**41504**
汽车	辆	Automobile	unit	85966	41504
载客汽车	辆	Buses And Cars	unit	4487	
	客位		seat	129880	
＃大型	辆	Large－Sized	unit	1724	
	客位		seat	77702	
中型	辆	Middle－Sized	unit	2589	
	客位		seat	51117	
载货汽车	辆	Trucks	unit	81479	41504
	吨位		ton	709542	112746
①普通载货汽车	辆	Ordinary Trucks	unit	66188	41302
	吨位		ton	282312	109696
＃大型	辆	Large－Space	unit	15053	3956
	吨位		ton	217741	54439
重型	辆	Heavy	unit	11024	3956
	吨位		ton	194072	54439
中型	辆	Middle	unit	1638	822
	吨位		ton	5756	2886
②专用载货汽车	辆	Trucks for Special Purpose	unit	15291	202
	吨位		ton	427230	3050
＃集装箱车	辆	Container Trucks	unit	11791	2
	TEU		TEU	24018	4

表 9－8 水路运输工具拥有量(2012)
Number of Means of Transportation Through Waterway

指标	单位	Indicators	Unit	总计 Total	其中 of Which 内河 Freshwater	沿海 Coastal	远洋 Ocean
总计	**艘**	**Total**	**unit**	**694**	**54**	**632**	**8**
机动船	**艘**	**Motor Vessels**	**unit**	**687**	**54**	**625**	**8**
净载重量	吨位	Dead Weight	ton	5657395	7609	5293108	356678
载客量	客位	Passenger Capacity	seat	5060	3188	1872	
标准箱位	TEU	Standard Container Space	TEU	5875		4669	1206
功率	千瓦	Power	kw	1161602	6895	1096944	57763
机动船按类别分		**Group by Type on Motor Vessels**					
客船	艘	Passenger Ships	unit	41	30	11	
载客量	客位	Passenger Capacity	seat	2549	1688	861	
功率	千瓦	Power	kw	8057	3202	4855	
客货船	艘	Passenger－cargo Vessels	unit	14	3	11	
净载重量	吨位	Dead Weight	ton				
载客量	客位	Passenger Capacity	seat	2511	1500	1011	
功率	千瓦	Power	kw	4488	506	3982	
货船	艘	Cargo Ships	unit	630	21	601	8
净载重量	吨位	Dead Weight	ton	5657395	7609	5293108	356678
标准箱位	TEU	Standard Container Space	TEU	5875		4669	1206
功率	千瓦	Power	kw	1147602	3187	1086652	57763
#①油船	艘	Tanker	unit	115		115	
净载重量	吨位	Dead Weight	ton	393293		393293	
功率	千瓦	Power	kw	128480		128480	
②集装箱船	艘	Container Ships	unit	13		10	3
净载重量	吨位	Dead Weight	ton	93579		70730	22849
标准箱位	TEU	Standard Container Space	TEU	5875		4669	1206
功率	千瓦	Power	kw	44342		31629	12713
拖船	艘	Tugboats	unit	2		2	
功率	千瓦	Power	kw	1455		1455	
驳船	艘	Barges	unit	7		7	
净载重量	吨位	Dead Weight	ton	13374		13374	

表 9—9 部分年份运输线路里程长度 Length of Transportation Routes in Partial Years

单位:公里(km)

指标	Indicators	2008	2009	2010	2011	2012
公路总里程	**Overal Length For Highway**	**9572**	**9884**	**9884**	**10439**	**10661**
按技术等级分:	**Divided by Grade**					
①等级公路	Highway Grade	8940	9272	9272	9881	10102
高速公路	Express Way	366	370	370	416	463
一级公路	Highway Grade 1	712	769	769	945	960
二级公路	Highway Grade 2	818	876	876	784	813
三级公路	Highway Grade 3	1464	1492	1492	1551	1550
四级公路	Highway Grade 4	5409	5597	5764	6026	6173
准四级公路	Near Highway Grade 4	171	167		159	143
②等外公路	Highway Without Grade	632	612	612	559	559
按路面等级分	**Divided by Road Surface**					
高级路面	High Grade Road Surface	8548	8985	8985	9736	10003
次高级路面	Sub—High Grade Road Surface	505	453	453	395	380
中级路面	Medium Grade Road Surface	519	446	446	309	278
低级路面	Lower Grade Road Surface					
按行政等级分	**Divided by Adminitrative Level**					
国道	State Way	448	453	453	497	497
省道	Province Way	718	718	718	724	771
县道	County Way	2607	2671	2671	2819	2844
乡道	Township Way	2131	2137	2137	2186	2188
专用道	Special Use Way	61	84	84	56	56
村道公路里程	Village Way	3607	3821	3821	4158	4306
内河通航里程	**Length of Navigable Inland Waterways**	**927**	**927**	**927**	**927**	**927**

表 9—10 历年电信业主要指标
Main Indicators of Telecommunications Services Over the Years

年份 Year	固定电话用户（万户） Number of Local Telephone Subscribers (10000 subcribers)	#农话 Rural Telephone Subscribers	移动电话（万户） Number of Subscribers of Mobile Telephone (10000 subscribers)	国际互联网用户（户） User of International Computer Network (user)
1978	1.07	0.49		
1979	1.19	0.53		
1980	1.36	0.58		
1981	1.53	0.64		
1982	1.71	0.70		
1983	1.86	0.76		
1984	2.22	0.89		
1985	2.60	1.05		
1986	2.91	1.14		
1987	3.55	1.35		
1988	4.64	1.68		
1989	5.37	1.92		
1990	6.19	2.15		
1991	8.05	2.88		
1992	12.22	4.92	0.14	
1993	18.59	7.49	0.80	
1994	27.86	11.60	1.92	
1995	41.78	17.80	4.71	
1996	53.33	23.10	9.05	
1997	67.75	31.14	16.44	
1998	83.74	41.40	25.72	4248
1999	104.13	54.39	56.75	37334
2000	130.15	72.69	117.92	70928
2001	163.21	90.13	195.65	93208
2002	203.58	91.52	256.86	104293
2003	242.00	107.20	379.31	835674
2004	296.72	94.79	421.00	1040127
2005	339.41		467.10	1705300
2006	345.08		514.70	908123
2007	334.98		757.70	1737851
2008	338.24		821.58	1027689
2009	301.41		866.87	1360000
2010	317.39		845.50	1720000
2011	312.45		1029.46	1900000
2012	308.00		1088.00	2360500

注：2006 年起，国际互联网用户统计口径有变化。

Note: From 2006, international Internet user's statistical method will change.

表 9－11　部分年份邮政业务情况
Basic Statistics on Post Services in Partial Years

指标	单位	Indicators	unit	2009	2010	2011	2012
邮政局、所数	处	Number of Post Offices	unit	327	318	279	280
#在农村的	处	Rural Area	unit	241	235	193	193
邮路总长度(单程)	公里	Lengh of Postal Routes	km	21656	4496	5019	5071
农村投递路线	公里	Rural Delivery Routwes	km	26029	27682	27977	27062
邮政业务总量	万元	Business volume of Post Services	10000 yuan	96592	93257	88746	76125
函件	万件	Number of Letters	10000 pcs	14275.00	12960.00	12520.80	11842.25
#国际函件	万件	International Letters	10000 pcs	13.00	20.00	43.20	131.91
国内函件	万件	Domestic Letters	10000 pcs	14262.00	12940.00	12477.60	4915.03
集邮业务	万枚	Philately	10000 pcs	1910.00	2090.00	2281.00	2260.46
报纸期发份数	万份	Newspaper Issued	10000 copies	80.71	76.5	91.33	91.84
杂志期发份数	万份	Magazine Issued	10000 copies	61.54	59.3	62.09	57.59
订销报纸累计份数	万份	Number of Newspaper Circulation	10000 copies	22081.00	24532.00	25881.00	28653.80
订销杂志累计份数	万份	Number of Magazine Circulation	10000 copies	1112.00	595.00	656.00	702.80

表 9－12 各县(市)邮政业务基本情况(2012)
Basic Statistics on Post Services by Region

指标	单位	Indicators	unit	全市 Total	市区 Urban Districts	余姚 Yuyao	慈溪 Cixi
邮政局、所数	处	Number of Post Offices	unit	280	126	43	34
#在农村的	处	Rural Area	unit	193	78	29	26
邮路总长度(单程)	公里	Lengh of Postal Routes	km	5071	3064	486	632
农村投递路线	公里	Rural Delivery Routwes	km	27062	9341	5266	5673
邮政业务总量	万元	Business volume of Post Services	10000 yuan	76125	38264	9197	16332
函件	万件	Number of Letters	10000 pcs	11842.25	7355.13	968.55	1950.79
国际函件	万件	International Letters	10000 pcs	131.91	103.61	0.73	19.61
国内函件	万件	Domestic Letters	10000 pcs	4915.03	3626.49	363.85	407.86
集邮业务	万枚	Philately	10000 pcs	2260	1982	42	23
报纸期发份数	万份	Newspaper Issued	10000 copies	92	43	12	19
杂志期发份数	万份	Magazine Issued	10000 copies	58	32	4	9
订销报纸累计份数	万份	Number of Newspaper Circulation	10000 copies	28654	14241	4109	5230
订销杂志累计份数	万份	Number of Magazine Circulation	10000 copies	703	395	66	100

表 9－12 续表 Continued

指标	单位	Indicators	unit	奉化 Fenghua	象山 Xiangshan	宁海 Ninghai
邮政局、所数	处	Number of Post Offices	unit	28	16	33
#在农村的	处	Rural Area	unit	18	13	29
邮路总长度(单程)	公里	Lengh of Postal Routes	km	318	214	357
农村投递路线	公里	Rural Delivery Routwes	km	2684	2494	1604
邮政业务总量	万元	Business volume of Post Services	10000 yuan	4902	4457	2973
函件	万件	Number of Letters	10000 pcs	620.74	578.29	368.76
国际函件	万件	International Letters	10000 pcs	4.28	0.33	3.35
国内函件	万件	Domestic Letters	10000 pcs	277.14	70.38	169.32
集邮业务	万枚	Philately	10000 pcs	51	124	38
报纸期发份数	万份	Newspaper Issued	10000 copies	7	6	6
杂志期发份数	万份	Magazine Issued	10000 copies	3	3	7
订销报纸累计份数	万份	Number of Newspaper Circulation	10000 copies	1769	1672	1632
订销杂志累计份数	万份	Number of Magazine Circulation	10000 copies	39	55	48

主要统计指标解释

【公路里程】 指在一定时期内实际达到《公路工程技术标 JTJ01－88》规定的等级公路，并经公路主管部门正式验收交付使用的公路里程数。其计算单位为：公里。它包括大中城市的郊区公路以及通过小城镇街道部分的公路里程，也包括桥梁、渡口的长度，但不包括大中城市的街道、厂矿、林区生产用道和农业生产用道的里程。两条或多条公路共同经由同一路段，只计算一次，不得重复计算里程长度。公路里程是反映公路建设发展规模的重要指标，也是计算运输网密度等指标的基础资料。

【货(客)运量】 指在一定时期内，各种运输工具实际运送的货物(旅客)数量。是反映运输业为国民经济和人民生活服务的数量指标，也是制定和检查运输生产计划，研究运输发展规模和速度的重要指标。货运按吨计算，客运按人计算。货物不论运输距离长短，货物类别，均按实际重量统计；旅客不论行程远近或票价多少，均按一人一次作为客运量统计。半价票、小孩票也按一人统计。

【货物(旅客)周转量】 指在一定时期内，由各种运输工具运送的货物(旅客)数量与其相应运输距离的乘积之总和，是反映运输业生产总成果的重要指标，也是编制和检查运输生产计划，计算运输效率、劳动生产率以及核算运输单位成本的主要基础资料。通常以吨公里和人公里为计算单位。计算货物周转量通常按发出站与到达站之间的最短距离，也就是计费距离计算。

【港口货物吞吐量】 指由水运进出港区范围，并经过装卸的货物数量，包括邮件及办理托运手续的行李、包裹以及补给运输船舶的燃、物料和淡水。其计量单位为吨。货物吞吐量的货种分类及其主要流向流量，反映了港口在国内外物资交流和对外贸易运输中的地位和作用。吞吐量可以分为进口、出口，又可以分为国内贸易和对外贸易。

【邮电业务总量】 指以货币表现的邮电部门用于传递信息和提供其他邮电服务的总数量。它综合反映了一定时期邮电工作的总成果，是研究邮电业务量构成和发展趋势的重要指标。根据邮电管理体制不同，分为中央国营业务总量和地方国营业务总量。它用各种邮电分类业务量，如函件件数、电报份数、长话张数、市内电话和农村电话的年均户数、订销报刊累计份数等，分别乘以相应的平均单价(不变价)，加总后再加上出租电路和设备的收入、代用户维护电话交换机和线路等设备的收入、其他业务收入求得。

Explanatory Notes on Main Statistical Indicators

【Length of Highways】 refers to the length of highways which are built in conformity with the grades specified by the highway engineering standard formulated by the Ministry of Communications, and have been formally checked and accepted by the departments of highways and put into use. The length of highways includes that of the suburb highways at large and medium-sized cities, highways passing through streets at small cities and towns, and also the length of bridges and ferries. It does not include the length of streets in big and medium-sized cities and highways built for the production purpose at factories, mines, forest areas and agricultural areas, If two or more highways go the same section of the way, the length of the section is only calculated for once and no duplication is allowed. The length of highways is an important indicator to show the development of the highway construction and to provide essential information to calculate the transport network density.

【Freight(Passenger) Traffic】 refers to the volume of freight (passenger) transported with various means. Freight transport is calculated in to ns and passenger traffic is calculated in the number of persons. Despite the type of freight and traveling distance, the freight transport is calculated by the principle that one person can be counted only once in one travel. The passenger who travel with a half price ticket or a child ticket is also calculated as one person. The freight (passenger) traffic provides a quantitative measure to show how the transport industry serves the national economy and people, and is also an important indicator for planning the transport industry and for studying the development scale and speed of the transport industry.

【Freight Ton—kilometers(Passenger—kilometers)】 refers to the sum of the products of the volume of transported cargo(passengers) multiplying by the transport distance, usually using ton-kilometer and passenger-kilometer as units for measurement. Normally, the shortest distance between the departure station and the destination station(i. e. , the payable distance) is the basis to calculate the freight ton—kilometers. This is an important indicator to show the total results of the transport industry, to prepare and examine the transport plan and to measure the efficiency, the labor productivity and the unit cost of transport.

【Volume of Freight Handled】 refers to the volume of cargo passing in and out the harbor area of the major coastal ports and having been loaded and unloaded. The volume includes that of the coastal matters, registered luggage and fuels, materials and fresh water as supplies of the ships. The volume of freight dandled maybe classified as import, export, or as domestic trade and foreign trade. The volume of freight handled by type of cargo and by main flow direction reflects he position and function of the ports in the inflow of Chinese and foreign commodities and in the transportation of foreign trade.

【Business Volume of Post and Telecommunications】 refers to the total amount of the information delivered and other post and telecommunications services provided by the post and telecommunications departments for the customers. It is derived by first multiplying the business volume of different types, such as number of letters, telegrams, long distance calls, city and rural telephone subscribers and accumulated number of newspapers and journals subscribed and sold, etc. by their respective average unit price (fixed price) and then adding these products together: plus the income from maintenance of telephone exchanges and lines, and the income from other business operations. The business volume of post and telecommunications indicates the total achievements made by the post and telecommunications department during a given period of time in a comprehensive way, and is an important indicator to study the composition and development of the post and telecommunications business.

NINGBO
Statistical YearBook

第十篇
国内贸易、餐饮业
DOMESTIC TRADE AND CATERING TRADE

国内贸易、餐饮
Domestic Trade and Catering Trade

主要统计指标
Major Statistics Indicators

				总计 Total	比上年增长(%) Increase Over Last Year(%)
2012年社会消费品零售总额	万元	Total Retail Sales of Consumer Goods	10000 yuan	23292590	15.4
#批发零售贸易业	万元	Wholesale and Retail Sale	10000 yuan	21159838	15.4
住宿及餐饮业	万元	Hoteling and Catering Trade	10000 yuan	2132752	15.6
限额以上批发业主要指标		Main Indicators of Wholesales Trade Above Designated Size			
企业数	个	Number of Enterprises	unit	1923	5.83
从业人员数	人	Number of Employees	person	71478	17.1
销售总额	万元	Total Sales Value	10000 yuan	80876252	26.1
资产总计	万元	Total Assets	10000 yuan	23453905	15.6
利润总额	万元	Total Profits	10000 yuan	568246	−13.2
限额以上零售业主要指标		Main Indicators of Retail Trade Above Designated Size			
企业数	个	Number of Enterprises	unit	597	6.4
从业人员数	人	Number of Employees	person	63504	−1.5
销售总额	万元	Total Sales Value	10000 yuan	10402677	3.5
资产总计	万元	Total Assets	10000 yuan	4589809	9.3
利润总额	万元	Total Profits	10000 yuan	52359	−69.9
2012年住宿餐饮业从业人员数	人	Number of Employees in Catering Trade and Hoteling	person	54314	0.7
2012年个体工商户数	户	Number of Individual Industry and Commerce	Households	359951	9.0
2012年私营企业数	个	Number of Private Enterprises	unit	154285	8.6

表 10－1 历年社会消费品零售总额
Total Retail Sales of Consumer Goods Over the Years

单位：万元(10000 yuan)

年份 Year	全市 Total	其中 of Which	
		市区 Urban District	县(市)合计 Total County
1978	70663	26175	44488
1979	87628	32386	55242
1980	111793	40368	71425
1981	130182	47157	83025
1982	139809	50056	89753
1983	156913	55343	101570
1984	187876	66573	121303
1985	253306	99210	154096
1986	304587	117850	186737
1987	354706	133444	221262
1988	490453	191994	298459
1989	528158	215768	312390
1990	549750	232255	317495
1991	633841	273167	360674
1992	794007	335769	458238
1993	1182147	522124	660023
1994	1634110	666060	968050
1995	2268195	919410	1348785
1996	2591764	1011445	1580319
1997	2885811	1154527	1731284
1998	3133608	1211018	1922590
1999	3457632	1321484	2136148
2000	3892920	1459537	2433383
2001	4141801		
2002	4628655		
2003	5215347		
2004	6667809		
2005	7621595	3625494	3996101
2006	8879552	4209769	4669783
2007	10450094	4922829	5527266
2008	12532605	5869060	6663545
2009	14344121	7633573	6710548
2010	17045103	6962526	10082577
2011	20188617	10891450	9297167
2012	23292590	12458556	10834033

表 10－2　部分年份分行业社会消费品零售总额
Total Retail Sales of Consumer Goods by Sector in Partial Years

单位：万元(10000 yuan)

年份 Year	社会消费品零售总额 Total Retail Sales of Consumer Goods	＃ 市的零售额 City	按行业分 Grouped by Sector 批发和零售贸易业 Wholesale and Retail Sale Trades	住宿及餐饮业 Hoteling and Catering Trade	其他 Others
1990	549750				
1991	633841				
1992	794007				
1993	1182147				
1994	1634110				
1995	2268195	1320420	1628556	125442	514198
1996	2591764	1555917	1929652	159592	502520
1997	2885811	1703928	2104330	199683	581798
1998	3133608	1792796	2356047	187135	590426
1999	3457632	2018154	2599967	276889	580776
2000	3892920	2247696	2965818	378127	548975
2001	4141801	2401013	3124797	442042	574962
2002	4628655	2737749	3442080	570221	616354
2003	5215347	3084765	4434412	672047	108888
2004	6667809	3947129	5845803	771788	50218
2005	7621595	4696200	6667717	917878	36000
2006	8879552	5470496	7862357	1012258	4937
2007	10450094	6428170	9289383	1158312	2400
2008	12532605	7839658	11124980	1405045	2580
2009	14344121	9207400	12776963	1564398	2760
2010	17045103	12737090	15461677	1583426	
2011	20188617	13674900	18343579	1845038	
2012	23292590	19549110	21159838	2132752	

注：①2004 年以前，住宿及餐饮业统计数据仅包含餐饮业。②2005－2008 年零售额数据根据第二次经济普查结果做出调整。③2010 年零售额的计算方法根据报表制度有所调整。

Note：①Hoteing and catering trade statistics only include the catering trade, before 2004. ②2005－2008 Retail sales data of the year 2005－2008 according had been adjusted to the results of the second economic census. ③Calculation of retail sales in 2010 had been adjusted according to the reporting system.

表 10－3　零售业零售业态(2012)
Status of Retail Sale

指标	Indicators	法人单位数(个) Number of Corporation (unit)	销售合计(万元) Total Sale (10000 yuan)	其中 of Witch 批发 Wholesale	零售 Retail
零售企业合计	**Total Retail Sale Enterprise**	**596**	**10402677**	**1138802**	**9263875**
按经营方式分：	**Grouped by Management Method**				
独立店	Sole Shop	523	7240207	589201	6651006
连锁商店总店	Chain General Shop	26	1621689	204003	1417686
连锁商店分店	Chain Shop	20	1213464	313149	900315
其他	Others	27	327317	32450	294867
按零售业态分：	**Grouped by Retail Sale Line**				
百货商店	Department Store	32	960728	145268	815460
超级市场	Super Market	38	1595061	186419	1408642
专业(专卖)店	Special (Special Sale) Shop	507	7729434	796707	6932727
其他	Others	19	117454	10408	107046

表 10－4 部分年份批发零售贸易及住宿餐饮业总额
Total Sales of Wholesale,Retail Sale and Hotel Catering Trade in Partial Years

单位:万元(10000 yuan)

指标	Indicators	2008	2009	2010	2011	2012
批发零售贸易业合计	**Wholesale and Retail Trade**					
销售总额	**Total Sale Value**	**66728994**	**54330930**	**75065955**	**93937682**	**106107789**
批发额	Wholesale	55494016	41413925	59901950	76303606	85747965
零售额	Retail Sale	11234978	12917005	15164006	17634076	20359824
1. 限额以上	Above Designated Size					
批发额	WholeSale	35383420	30095749	48594953	64989031	70289363
零售额	Retail Sale	5195227	6491536	8536179	10545544	10969875
2. 限额以下	Under Designated Size					
批发额	Wholesale	20110596	11318176	11306997	11314575	15458602
零售额	Retail Sale	6039751	6425469	6627827	7088532	9389949
住宿餐饮业合计	**Hotel and Catering Service**					
营业总收入	**Total Service Income**	**1622649**	**1787002**	**1998337**	**2516281**	**3089844**
#零售额	Retail Sale	1317767	1564398	1583426	1723695	1956446
1. 限额以上	Above Designated Size					
营业总收入	Total Service Income	560588	708616	882009	1068003	1109732
#零售额	Retail Sale	360079	486012	608977	757017	806779
2. 限额以下	Under Designated Size					
营业总收入	Total Service Income	1062061	1078386	1116328	1448278	1980112
#零售额	Retail Sale	957688	1078386	974449	966678	1149668

注:销售额及营业额均仅含产业单位数据。

Note:Total sales and turnover include data of industrial units.

表10－5 限额以上批发贸易业单位数和从业人员数(2012)
Number of Units and Employees of Wholesale Trade Above Designated Size

单位:个、人(unit,person)

指标	Indicators	法人企业数 Number of Corporations	从业人数 Number of Employees
批发业合计	**Wholesale Trade**	**1923**	**71478**
#国有及国有控股	State－owned and State－holding	55	4994
按注册类型分	**Grouped by Registration Type**		
内资企业	Domestic Funded Enterprises	1871	66397
国有企业	State－Owned Enterprises	17	1325
集体企业	Collective－Owned Enterprises	5	70
股份合作企业	Share Cooperative Enterprises	1	20
联营企业	Joint－owned Enterprises	2	13
有限责任公司	Limited Liability Corporations	266	14986
股份有限公司	Share－holding Corporations Ltd.	21	2615
私营企业	Private Enterprises	1556	47236
港、澳、台商投资企业	Hongkong,Macao and Taiwan Funded	27	3953
外商投资企业	Foreign Funded	25	1128
按行业分	**Grouped by Sector**		
农畜产品批发	Agricultural and Livestock Products	11	645
食品、饮料及烟草制品批发	Food,Beverages and Tobaccos	90	5204
#烟草制品批发	Tobacco	2	321
纺织、服装及日用品批发	Textile,Garments and Daily Consumer Articles	420	30082
#服装批发	Garments	137	8851
文化、体育用品及器材批发	Culture,Sports Appliances and Equipments	76	3181
医药及医疗器材批发	Medicines and Medical Appliance	38	2738
矿产品、建材及化工产品批发	Mineral Products,Building Materials,Chemical Products	941	17254
#石油及制品批发	Petroleum and Related Products	118	3742
金属及金属矿批发	Metal and Metallic Ore	377	5520
机械设备、五金交电及电子产品批发	Machine Equipments,Hardware,Electric Appliances,Electronic Equipment	265	10634
#汽车、摩托车及零配件批发	Motor Vehicles,Motorcycles and Parts	45	1199
家用电器批发	Household Appliances	13	696
其他批发	Others	82	1740

表 10－6 限额以上零售贸易业单位数和从业人员数(2012) Number of Units and Employees of Retail Trade Above Designated Size

单位:个、人(unit,person)

指标	Indicators	法人企业数 Number of Corporations	从业人数 Number of Employees
零售业总计	**Total**	**597**	**63484**
#国有及国有控股	State－owned and State－holding	57	4993
按注册类型分	**Grouped by Registration Type**		
内资企业	Domestic Funded Enterprises	564	51735
国有企业	State－Owned Enterprises	20	1174
集体企业	Collective－Owned Enterprises	14	346
股份合作企业	Share Cooperative Enterprises	1	23
联营企业	Joint－owned Enterprises	11	146
有限责任公司	Limited Liability Corporations	114	11917
股份有限公司	Share－holding Corporations Ltd.	8	9166
私营企业	Private Enterprises	390	28750
港、澳、台商投资企业	Hongkong,Macao and Taiwan Funded	17	2978
外商投资企业	Foreign Funded	15	8771
按行业分	**Grouped by Sector**		
综合零售	Comprehensive Retail	66	28628
百货零售	General Merchandise	29	6053
超级市场零售	Super Market	31	21870
食品、饮料及烟草制品专门零售	Food,Beverages and Tobaccos	15	983
纺织、服装及日用品专门零售	Textile,Garments and Articles for Daily Use	37	4098
#服装零售	Garments	20	3015
文化、体育用品及器材专门零售	Culture,Sports Appliances and Equipments	39	2148
#图书零售	Books	13	1003
医药及医疗器材专门零售	Medicines and Medical Appliance	25	3068
汽车、摩托车、燃料及零配件专门零售	Automobile,Motorcycles,Fuels and Parts	314	18835
#汽车零售	Motor Vehicles	218	15383
家用电器及电子产品专门零售	Household Appliances and Electronic Products	67	4857
#家用电器零售	Household Appliances	34	3234
通信设备零售	Communication Equipment	8	684
五金、家具及室内装修材料专门零售	Hardware,Furniture and Decoration Materials	12	322
无店铺及其他零售	Non－shop and Others	22	545

表 10－7 限额以上批发贸易业购进、销售、库存总额(2012)
Total Purchases, Sale and Inventory of Wholesale Trade Above Designated Size

指标	Indicators	购进总额 Total Purchases	进口 Imports
批发业	**Wholesale Trade**	**64931382**	**9631910**
＃国有及国有控股	State－owned and State－holding	6266677	470856
按注册类型分	**Grouped by Registration Type**		
内资企业	Domestic Funded Enterprises	62255221	8622128
国有企业	State－Owned Enterprises	2130988	38111
集体企业	Collective－Owned Enterprises	132292	51272
股份合作企业	Share Cooperative Enterprises	10018	
联营企业	Joint－owned Enterprises	168583	237
有限责任公司	Limited Liability Corporations	20295834	1435980
股份有限公司	Share－holding Corporations Ltd.	4209257	2462578
私营企业	Private Enterprises	35293027	4633951
港、澳、台商投资企业	Hongkong, Macao and Taiwan Funded	1625794	192419
外商投资企业	Foreign Funded	1050367	817363
按行业分	**Grouped by Sector**		
农畜产品批发	Wholesale of Agricultural and Livestock Products	97679	14597
食品、饮料及烟草制品批发	Wholesale of Food, Beverages and Tobaccos	2534150	52368
＃烟草制品批发	Tobacco	958598	
纺织、服装及日用品批发	Wholesale of Textile, Garments and Daily Consumer Articles	8611315	1026004
＃服装批发	Garments	2608766	128668
文化、体育用品及器材批发	Wholesale of Culture, Sports Appliances and Equipments	1027984	75218
医药及医疗器材批发	Wholesale of Medicines and Medical Appliance	1000689	208936
矿产品、建材及化工产品批发	Mineral Products, Building Materials and Chemical Products	45667209	7480385
＃石油及制品批发	Petroleum and Related Products	6695360	213048
金属及金属矿批发	Metal and Metallic Ore	18742164	3331767
机械设备、五金交电及电子产品批发	Machine Equipments, Hardware, Electric Appliances, Electronic Equipment	4837606	345520
＃汽车、摩托车及零配件批发	Motor Vehicles, Motorcycles and Parts	497547	31767
家用电器批发	Household Appliances	355503	2011
其他批发	Others	1154752	428884

单位:万元(10000 yuan)

销售总额 Total Sales	其中 of Which			年末库存总额 Inventory (year—end)
	批发 Wholesale	出口 Exports	零售 Retail Sale	
70473576	**69067682**	**12581708**	**1405893**	**2813418**
8217241	7820878	625385	396364	337304
67305906	66098118	12285779	1207789	2602725
2531911	2440386	88562	91525	109703
127182	120989	50655	6193	10230
10018	10018			
168562	168562	47610		11416
21122924	20887628	3799085	235296	765938
6702451	6475040	585011	227412	142087
36627650	35980654	7714856	646996	1563271
1966629	1828919	128180	137710	176092
1201040	1140645	167749	60395	34601
99318	97912		1406	28612
2962240	2855425	284231	106815	133679
1321954	1321719		235	3790
9411211	9196103	5980761	215109	468462
2852980	2732876	1888658	120104	252831
1127250	1075892	410533	51358	50958
1203941	1006495	9650	197446	95101
49508259	48786565	2454693	721694	1776974
8494026	8013504	66839	480522	160425
19280098	19211307	618729	68791	886270
4950270	4850018	3045718	100251	193333
526627	494036	293577	32590	12216
333011	321633	223519	11378	6770
1211087	1199273	396122	11814	66299

表 10－8 限额以上零售贸易业购进、销售、库存总额(2012) Total Purchases,Sale and Inventory of Retail Trade Above Designated Size

指标	Indicators	购进总额 Total Purchases	进口 Imports
零售业合计	**Retail Trade**	**9906672**	**583804**
＃国有及国有控股	State－owned and State－holding	1742588	51002
按注册类型分	**Grouped by Registration Type**		
内资企业	Domestic Funded Enterprises	7799289	410326
国有企业	State－Owned Enterprises	168287	51002
集体企业	Collective－Owned Enterprises	84902	157
股份合作企业	Share Cooperative Enterprises	6823	
联营企业	Joint－owned Enterprises	68144	
有限责任公司	Limited Liability Corporations	1878429	113368
股份有限公司	Share－holding Corporations Ltd.	1120475	
私营企业	Private Enterprises	4430092	245800
港、澳、台商投资企业	Hongkong,Macao and Taiwan Funded	742018	38196
外商投资企业	Foreign Funded	1364994	135282
按行业分	**Grouped by Sector**		
综合零售	General Retail	2335368	
百货零售	General Merchandise	864905	
超级市场零售	Super Market	1438512	
食品、饮料及烟草制品专门零售	Retail of Food,Beverages and Tobaccos	66545	
纺织、服装及日用品专门零售	Retail of Textile,Garments and Daily Use Articles	233594	2215
＃服装零售	Garments	144024	875
文化、体育用品及器材专门零售	Retail of Culture,Sports Appliances and Equipments	184705	
＃图书零售	Books	53647	
医药及医疗器材专门零售	Retail of Medicines and Medical Appliance	630241	
汽车、摩托车、燃料及零配件专门零售	Retail of Motor Vehicles,Motorcycles,Fuels and Parts	5803501	577034
＃汽车零售	Motor Vehicles	4517305	574272
家用电器及电子产品专门零售	Retail of Household Appliances and Electronic Products	560540	3847
＃家用电器零售	Household Appliances	387066	
通信设备零售	Communication Equipment	44867	
五金、家具及室内装修材料专门零售	Retail of Hardware,Furniture and Decoration Materials	19726	708
无店铺及其他零售	Non－shop and Other Retail	72453	

单位:万元(10000 yuan)

销售总额 Total Sales	其中:of Which 批发 Wholesale	出口 Exports	零售 Retail Sale	年末库存总额 Inventory (year—end)
10403047	**1138802**	**5421**	**9264245**	**972566**
1819927	464479		1355448	81017
8209611	754504	5421	7455107	834566
178456	3287		175169	26836
91741	17620		74121	6402
7086			7086	496
71453	3789		67664	521
1982838	74042	3749	1908797	189285
1211258	317137		894121	93076
4623303	332211	1672	4291092	511387
800158	62289		737870	64972
1392908	322010		1070898	73028
2535904	333419		2202485	190967
949498	141178		808320	39771
1554883	185523		1369360	149221
73599	16585		57014	10839
282854	20424	1672	262430	98433
184097	6144		177953	70508
209519	18587		190932	65446
60372	2418		57954	18063
663738	90524		573214	68322
5949629	518841	3749	5430788	474348
4611999	191062		4420938	450130
588404	123268		465136	53357
397590	38941		358650	39520
47555	8338		39217	3652
21487	4737		16750	4057
77914	12417		65496	6796

表 10—9 限额以上批发贸易业主要财务指标(2012)
Main Financial Indicators of Wholesale Trade Above Designated Size

指标	Indicators	年末资产负债		
		流动资产合计 Current Funds	#存货 Inventories	固定资产原价 Original Value of Fixed Assets
批发业合计	**Wholesale Trade**	**21099349**	**2559996**	**1194829**
#国有及国有控股	State—owned and State—holding	2105188	381954	254175
按注册类型分	**Grouped by Registration Type**			
内资企业	Domestic Funded Enterprises	19873192	2462708	1137867
国有企业	State—Owned Enterprises	780594	134378	99219
集体企业	Collective—Owned Enterprises	31319	10205	317
股份合作企业	Share Cooperative Enterprises	1088		196
联营企业	Joint—owned Enterprises	416740	6301	187
有限责任公司	Limited Liability Corporations	6020058	728508	286939
股份有限公司	Share—holding Corporations Ltd.	1128626	172902	126469
私营企业	Private Enterprises	11491061	1410203	624255
港、澳、台商投资企业	Hongkong,Macao and Taiwan Funded	512208	61646	33637
外商投资企业	Foreign Funded	713949	35642	23325
按行业分	**Grouped by Sector**			
农畜产品批发	Agricultural and Livestock Products	57380	32653	21011
食品、饮料及烟草制品批发	Food,Beverages and Tobaccos	1179540	158277	150617
#烟草制品批发	Tobacco	541161	30258	70192
纺织、服装及日用品批发	Textile,Garments and Daily Consumer Articles	3415927	357765	234238
#服装批发	Garments	1095495	141093	94461
文化、体育用品及器材批发	Culture,Sports Appliances and Equipments	362681	46096	31250
医药及医疗器材批发	Medicines and Medical Appliance	445180	87269	37537
矿产品、建材及化工产品批发	Mineral Products,Building Materials,Chemical Products	13374167	1619946	542484
#石油及制品批发	Petroleum and Related Products	1526558	174431	183257
金属及金属矿批发	Metal and Metallic Ore	5455316	788092	178175
机械设备、五金交电及电子产品批发	Machine Equipments,Hardware,Electric Appliances,Electronic Equipment	1831474	180818	134090
#汽车、摩托车及零配件批发	Motor Vehicles,Motorcycles and Parts	7286790	968910	312265
家用电器批发	Household Appliances	93610	11629	8275
其他批发	Others	305218	70531	33898

单位:万元(10000 yuan)

Total Assets and Liabilities at the Year—end				损益与分配 Profit,Loss and Distribution	
本年折旧 Depreciation in this year	资产合计 Total Asset	负债合计 Total Liabilities	所有者权益 Creditors' Equity	主营业务收入 Major Business Revenue	主营业务成本 Major Business Costs
80581	**23453906**	**19551009**	**3902897**	**64345198**	**61723612**
12925	2601520	1535463	1066058	7070937	6552791
76901	22072264	18668936	3403328	61476791	59140051
5241	926221	331915	594305	2258784	1937289
25	32088	25748	6340	117873	113694
2	1221	692	529	8562	8188
33	418522	417268	1254	154333	152891
16549	6684814	5647872	1036942	19222921	18682015
7865	1429844	1103668	326176	5948668	5759063
47171	12575607	11138538	1437069	33751382	32473248
2389	633533	395021	238512	1671589	1523170
1291	748108	487051	261057	1196818	1060391
325	78034	56677	21357	94649	90844
9153	1391813	661855	729958	2333555	1950237
4265	601674	45003	556671	1129874	821372
16575	3855906	3282748	573158	9091058	8451263
6840	1313800	1089579	224221	2708203	2485549
2364	427142	331908	95235	1059957	992914
2499	504173	385139	119035	1059113	923960
38235	14623904	12705409	1918495	44649870	43563600
10121	1937538	1490602	446936	7440916	7272492
11932	5824925	5093618	731307	17700592	17227014
8897	2050806	1705185	345621	4829285	4578746
20829	7875731	6798803	1076928	22529877	21805760
742	106494	74648	31846	494811	463798
1808	379879	299778	80101	883544	844218

表 10－9 续表 Continued

指标	Indicators	损益与分配	
		主营业务税金及附加 Tax and Extra Charge	管理费用 Management Cost
批发业合计	**Wholesale Trade**	**105438**	**563562**
＃国有及国有控股	State－owned and State－holding	73920	91234
按注册类型分	**Grouped by Registration Type**		
内资企业	Domestic Funded Enterprises	103565	524641
国有企业	State－Owned Enterprises	69807	43919
集体企业	Collective－Owned Enterprises	34	611
股份合作企业	Share Cooperative Enterprises	8	80
联营企业	Joint－owned Enterprises	24	147
有限责任公司	Limited Liability Corporations	8343	125115
股份有限公司	Share－holding Corporations Ltd.	3006	30501
私营企业	Private Enterprises	22292	323922
港、澳、台商投资企业	Hongkong,Macao and Taiwan Funded	1549	28985
外商投资企业	Foreign Funded	325	9936
按行业分	**Grouped by Sector**		
农畜产品批发	Agricultural and Livestock Products	15	3373
食品、饮料及烟草制品批发	Food,Beverages and Tobaccos	71459	72714
＃烟草制品批发	Tobacco	69389	38365
纺织、服装及日用品批发	Textile,Garments and Daily Consumer Articles	7730	149271
＃服装批发	Garments	2232	57109
文化、体育用品及器材批发	Culture,Sports Appliances and Equipments	618	19479
医药及医疗器材批发	Medicines and Medical Appliance	3741	31131
矿产品、建材及化工产品批发	Mineral Products,Building Materials, Chemical Products	18391	193810
＃石油及制品批发	Petroleum and Related Products	4049	36268
金属及金属矿批发	Metal and Metallic Ore	6552	63442
机械设备、五金交电及电子产品批发	Machine Equipments,Hardware,Electric Appliances,Electronic Equipment	1855	79392
＃汽车、摩托车及零配件批发	Motor Vehicles,Motorcycles and Parts	8407	142834
家用电器批发	Household Appliances	246	8241
其他批发	Others	1590	8270

单位:万元(10000 yuan)

Profit,Loss and Distribution			工资福利与税金 Wages,Welfare and Tax in this Year	
财务费用 Financial Expenses	营业利润 Business Profits	利润总额 Total Profits	本年应付职工薪酬总额 Total Employee Compensation Payable	本年应交增值税总额 Total Value-added Taxes Payable
324803	**442469**	**568246**	**474829**	**348534**
778	270744	310703	85182	76045
317945	296736	420484	441529	327608
-10987	192794	198043	41624	57355
642	69	496	449	302
14	29	29	264	65
3623	-3587	-3561	61	202
71462	41240	102835	116288	67223
11421	73704	82865	34996	15087
241798	-7538	39740	247601	186922
5115	33128	35938	27055	19305
1743	112605	111824	6245	1621
1580	-4560	483	3603	58
-4626	206704	238638	60316	59871
-14254	203082	202759	33842	54035
44528	31082	55812	163178	71095
20920	35456	41062	53240	12970
4154	11068	12352	16398	3310
3683	21928	37844	16313	28581
242022	146306	179783	140288	132385
15287	50493	52939	34696	22151
120153	107152	113913	45191	51821
17902	27592	38117	65905	19991
138055	134744	152029	111096	71812
2455	6177	6923	5536	1633
14312	2810	5301	4515	31576

表 10－10　限额以上零售贸易业主要财务指标(2012)
Main Financial Indicators of Retail Trade Above Designated Size

指标	Indicators	年末资产负债		
		流动资产合计 Current Funds	#存货 Inventories	固定资产原价 Original Value of Fixed Assets
零售业总计	**Total**	**3237509**	**821173**	**959720**
#国有及国有控股	State－owned and State－holding	325883	60355	94118
按注册类型分	**Grouped by Registration Type**			
内资企业	Domestic Funded Enterprises	2923054	716279	696917
国有企业	State－Owned Enterprises	103012	17809	21492
集体企业	Collective－Owned Enterprises	15322	6305	3816
股份合作企业	Share Cooperative Enterprises	2385	423	457
联营企业	Joint－owned Enterprises	3541	495	5387
有限责任公司	Limited Liability Corporations	672275	167997	161094
股份有限公司	Share－holding Corporations Ltd.	457639	40154	126017
私营企业	Private Enterprises	1638444	457705	377088
港、澳、台商投资企业	Hongkong,Macao and Taiwan Funded	170894	48613	124014
外商投资企业	Foreign Funded	143561	56282	138789
按行业分	**Grouped by Sector**			
综合零售	Comprehensive Retail	970402	120282	558476
#百货零售	General Merchandise	430484	31419	251236
超级市场零售	Super Market	532380	86962	304217
食品、饮料及烟草制品专门零售	Food,Beverages and Tobaccos	53486	12400	11788
纺织、服装及日用品专门零售	Textile,Garments and Articles for Daily Use	189980	98104	12533
文化、体育用品及器材专门零售	Culture,Sports Appliances and Equipments	115877	45022	25170
医药及医疗器材专门零售	Medicines and Medical Appliance	203662	53171	23702
汽车、摩托车、燃料及零配件专门零售	Automobile,Motorcycles,Fuels and Parts	1397365	407363	291550
#汽车零售	Motor Vehicles	1298523	392938	257449
家用电器及电子产品专门零售	Household Appliances and Electronic Products	229903	55118	23323
五金、家具及室内装修材料专门零售	Hardware,Furniture and Decoration Materials	11767	4011	5398
无店铺及其他零售	Non－shop and Others	65068	25701	7780
按经营方式分组	**Grouped by Management Method**			
#独立商店	Sole Shop	18399275	2243793	1025305
连锁商店总店	Chain General Shop	13431	2952	860
连锁商店分店	Chain Shop	128736	49618	76377
按零售业态分组	**Grouped by Retail Sale Line**			
#百货商店	Department Store	439551	34483	251304
超级市场	Super Market	439551	34483	251304
专业店	Special Shop	1324016	354460	227838
专卖店	Special Sale Shop	848619	305149	162138
便利店	Convenience Shop	15100	3256	2696

单位:万元(10000 yuan)

Total Assets and Liabilities at the Year－end				损益与分配 Profit,Loss and Distribution	
本年折旧 Depreciation in this year	资产合计 Total Asset	负债合计 Total Liabilities	所有者权益 Creditors' Equity	主营业务收入 Major Business Revenue	主营业务成本 Major Business Costs
60562	**4589810**	**3440595**	**1149215**	**8451111**	**7695457**
3789	558390	284149	274240	936515	862157
43169	3943793	2962152	981641	7213149	6578890
1220	126671	96549	30123	163084	147039
345	19214	10252	8961	81200	76579
48	2595	2281	314	6360	5883
283	8542	2302	6241	67801	64653
10037	878882	668546	210336	1686215	1543520
5358	727601	338086	389515	1071462	962184
25560	2144387	1809778	334608	4094606	3737666
7139	323857	241916	81941	714039	651762
10254	322160	236528	85633	523923	464805
28092	1729390	1173116	556274	2150128	1874254
8144	848725	536123	312601	726411	615154
19781	871468	628171	243297	1396227	1236103
672	63168	45920	17248	66029	58197
924	222224	180380	41844	263237	177121
1471	140374	104856	35518	170871	141724
1345	231545	165326	66219	574435	529555
25912	1854734	1482154	372581	4621245	4384651
23711	1681973	1390563	291410	4109034	3898797
1594	258083	215057	43027	510054	443250
82	17149	18037	－889	20707	18005
471	73143	55749	17394	74405	68700
69101	20319631	16909145	3410486	52235286	50039056
27	15672	14629	1042	20945	19350
4094	284857	185221	99635	1769283	1682121
8157	857120	545027	312093	737330	624656
8157	857120	545027	312093	737330	624656
15543	1664184	1247810	416374	3542363	3260635
16348	1089061	926727	162334	2641800	2471805
210	17433	13677	3757	38496	33102

表 10－10 续表 Continued

指标	Indicators	损益与分配	
		主营业务税金及附加 Tax and Extra Charge	管理费用 Management Cost
零售业总计	**Total**	**23922**	**239221**
＃国有及国有控股	State－owned and State－holding	3076	22688
按注册类型分	**Grouped by Registration Type**		
内资企业	Domestic Funded Enterprises	18859	202416
国有企业	State－Owned Enterprises	340	5552
集体企业	Collective－Owned Enterprises	105	1428
股份合作企业	Share Cooperative Enterprises	8	37
联营企业	Joint－owned Enterprises	59	183
有限责任公司	Limited Liability Corporations	5006	48309
股份有限公司	Share－holding Corporations Ltd.	4431	21454
私营企业	Private Enterprises	8839	124906
港、澳、台商投资企业	Hongkong,Macao and Taiwan Funded	2443	23896
外商投资企业	Foreign Funded	2620	12909
按行业分	**Grouped by Sector**		
综合零售	Comprehensive Retail	12165	90519
＃百货零售	General Merchandise	6149	52865
超级市场零售	Super Market	5914	35158
食品、饮料及烟草制品专门零售	Food,Beverages and Tobaccos	187	3317
纺织、服装及日用品专门零售	Textile,Garments and Articles for Daily Use	1160	16868
文化、体育用品及器材专门零售	Culture,Sports Appliances and Equipments	2180	9762
医药及医疗器材专门零售	Medicines and Medical Appliance	840	12857
汽车、摩托车、燃料及零配件专门零售	Automobile,Motorcycles,Fuels and Parts	5782	87276
＃汽车零售	Motor Vehicles	4972	82505
家用电器及电子产品专门零售	Household Appliances and Electronic Products	1376	15586
五金、家具及室内装修材料专门零售	Hardware,Furniture and Decoration Materials	48	964
无店铺及其他零售	Non－shop and Others	185	2074
按经营方式分组	Grouped by Management Method		
＃独立商店	Sole Shop	97888	471528
连锁商店总店	Chain General Shop		219
连锁商店分店	Chain Shop	1635	10927
按零售业态分组	Grouped by Retail Sale Line		
＃百货商店	Department Store	6235	53750
超级市场	Super Market	6235	53750
专业店	Special Shop	6719	81616
专卖店	Special Sale Shop	4708	58643
便利店	Convenience Shop	112	2041

单位:万元(10000 yuan)

Profit,Loss and Distribution			工资福利与税金 Wages,Welfare and Tax in this Year	
财务费用 Financial Expenses	营业利润 Business Profits	利润总额 Total Profits	本年应付 职工薪酬总额 Total Employee Compensation Payable	本年应交 增值税总额 Total Value—added Taxes Payable
75866	**28035**	**52360**	**291027**	**104087**
2237	20644	24444	26548	8761
67845	37292	59382	239132	90346
—364	—155	1399	8175	1824
78	613	789	1771	730
151	62	62	98	72
17	1500	1497	717	485
13706	3127	8586	59335	23472
2735	42029	47135	39694	14039
51502	—6997	2798	128531	49597
7276	—2086	—1200	20881	8433
745	—7172	—5822	31014	5308
16135	28520	41979	117168	32559
14563	17676	26120	34499	15741
1420	11341	16139	80339	16376
355	—77	1989	3679	1211
1866	2554	9799	21711	10205
578	—1995	—767	13727	3701
4362	10091	11277	16457	6797
45919	—15522	—16834	92015	41428
44848	—25502	—27092	83692	38146
5915	3794	4297	23179	7322
560	—722	—650	1145	230
178	1392	1270	1946	635
282702	392865	477314	389840	276536
421	—10	—10	279	
—1692	49465	49163	19978	12807
14693	16384	24880	34644	15894
14693	16384	24880	34644	15894
28086	24299	32985	102171	42557
29076	—22418	—20687	63597	27788
67	—717	—175	3542	510

表 10—11 限额以上批发零售贸易业主要商品分类销售额(2012) Sales of Wholesale and Retail Trade Above Designated Size by Category of Commodities

单位:万元(10000 yuan)

类别	Category	合计	批发 Wholesale	零售 Retail
食品、饮料、烟酒类	Food, Beverage, Tabacco and Liquor	4140030	2955188	1184842
#粮油类	Grain and Oil	2226868	1296753	930115
饮料类	Beverage	291170	150029	141141
烟酒类	Tabacco and Liquor	1621992	1508406	113587
服装鞋帽、针、纺织品类	Garments, Shoes, Hats Knitwear and Textile	5217268	4166656	1050612
#服装类	Garments	3257621	2438646	818975
鞋帽类	Shoes, Hats	443763	312613	131150
针、纺织品类	Knitwear and Textile	1515885	1415397	100488
化妆品类	Cosmetics	146830	59318	87513
金银珠宝类	Jewelry	335170	122113	213057
日用品类	Articles for Daily Use	2932423	2678636	253787
五金、电料类	Hardware and Electrical Appliances	1193839	1168496	25342
体育、娱乐用品类	Recreation and Sports Articles	133414	117027	16387
书报杂志类	Books and Newspapers	63482	819	62662
电子出版物及音像制品类	Electronic Publications and Audio—video Products	3912		3912
家用电器和音像器材类	Household Appliances and Audio—video Equipments	1872906	1413513	459394
中西药品类	Medicines	1319774	621937	697838
文化办公用品类	Culture and Office Articles	1253856	1082336	171520
家具类	Furnitures	304571	189987	114584
通讯器材类	Telecommunication Appliances	434491	315666	118826
煤炭及制品类	Coal and Coal Products	4204226	4181225	23001
木材及制品类	Timber and Timber Products	197744	197744	
石油及制品类	Petroleum and Products	9991895	8561266	1430629
化工材料及制品类	Chemical Materials and Products	14926313	14926313	
金属材料类	Metal Materials	18587744	18587744	
建筑及装潢材料类	Materials for Construction and Decoration	464058	392997	71061
机电产品及设备类	Mechanical and Electrical Equipments	1854123	1852850	1273
汽车类	Automobile	5214993	677414	4537579
种子饲料类	Seeds and Forage	30836	30836	
棉麻土畜类	Cotton and Flax Products	94410	94410	

表 10－12　住宿餐饮业单位数和从业人员数(2012)
Number of Units and Employees of Catering Trade and Hotel

单位：个、人(unit,person)

指标	Indicators	法人企业数 Number of Corporations	从业人数 Number of Employees
总计	**Total**	**456**	**54314**
住宿业	**Hotel**	**187**	**26798**
＃国有及国有控股	State－owned and State－holding	18	3282
按登记注册类型分组	Grouped by Registration Type		
内资企业	Domestic Funded Enterprises	173	23168
国有企业	State－Owned Enterprises	10	2037
集体企业	Collective－Owned Enterprises	7	760
股份合作企业	Share Cooperative Enterprises		
有限责任公司	Limited Liability Corporations	26	5298
股份有限公司	Share－holding Corporations Ltd.	5	1647
私营企业	Private Enterprises	125	13426
港、澳、台商投资企业	Hongkong,Macao and Taiwan Funded	7	2428
外商投资企业	Foreign Funded	7	1202
按行业分	Grouped by Sector		
旅游饭店	Tour Hotel	122	22281
一般旅馆	Common Hotel	63	4424
餐饮业	**Catering Trade**	**269**	**27516**
＃国有及国有控股	State－owned and State－holding	3	235
按登记注册类型分组	Grouped by Registration Type		
内资企业	Domestic Funded Enterprises	261	26576
国有企业	State－Owned Enterprises	2	135
集体企业	Collective－Owned Enterprises	1	152
股份合作企业	Share Cooperative Enterprises		
有限责任公司	Limited Liability Corporations	23	2753
股份有限公司	Share－holding Corporations Ltd.	2	333
私营企业	Private Enterprises	233	23203
港、澳、台商投资企业	Hongkong,Macao and Taiwan Funded	8	940
外商投资企业	Foreign Funded		
按行业分	Grouped by Sector		
正餐服务业	Dinner Services	250	25786
快餐服务业	Snack Services	11	1140
饮料及冷饮服务业	Beverage Services		
其他餐饮服务业	Others		

表10－13　星级住宿业和限额以上餐饮业经营情况(2012)
Main Operation Indicators of Catering Trade and Star－rated Hotel

指标	Indicators	营业额 Business Revenue	其中 客房收入 Room Rate Revenue	其中 餐费收入 Catering Revenue
总计	**Total**	**882043**	**218703**	**575205**
住宿业	**Hotel**	**498891**	**184395**	**256726**
＃国有及国有控股	State－owned and State－holding	52348	16094	29251
按登记注册类型分组	Grouped by Registration Type			
内资企业	Domestic Funded Enterprises	402280	153000	201536
国有企业	State－Owned Enterprises	29910	10197	17059
集体企业	Collective－Owned Enterprises	9856	2987	6076
股份合作企业	Share Cooperative Enterprises			
有限责任公司	Limited Liability Corporations	97409	34798	47244
股份有限公司	Share－holding Corporations Ltd.	33951	11788	16421
私营企业	Private Enterprises	231155	93229	114736
港、澳、台商投资企业	Hongkong,Macao and Taiwan Funded	77642	22719	45751
外商投资企业	Foreign Funded	18970	8677	9439
按行业分	Grouped by Sector			
旅游饭店	Tour Hotel	434013	143263	237678
一般旅馆	Common Hotel	63766	40382	18852
餐饮业	**Catering Trade**	**383152**	**34308**	**318479**
＃国有及国有控股	State－owned and State－holding	5305	192	5112
按登记注册类型分组	Grouped by Registration Type			
内资企业	Domestic Funded Enterprises	362208	31844	309458
国有企业	State－Owned Enterprises	2384	192	2191
集体企业	Collective－Owned Enterprises	1763	759	911
股份合作企业	Share Cooperative Enterprises			
有限责任公司	Limited Liability Corporations	52667	9229	37583
股份有限公司	Share－holding Corporations Ltd.	4461	814	3575
私营企业	Private Enterprises	300934	20849	265197
港、澳、台商投资企业	Hongkong,Macao and Taiwan Funded	20944	2464	9022
外商投资企业	Foreign Funded			
按行业分	Grouped by Sector			
正餐服务业	Dinner Services	346271	34308	293998
快餐服务业	Snack Services	25199		16253
饮料及冷饮服务业	Beverage Services			
其他餐饮服务业	Others			

单位:万元

of Which		年末餐饮营业面积（平方米） Business Area of Catering in the Year－end (sq. m)	年末拥有床位数（个） Hold Beds in the Year－end (bed)	年末拥有餐位数（位） Hold Seat of Catering in the Year－end (unit)
商品销售收入 Commodity Sales Revenue	其他收入 Others			
13651	**74484**	**935070**	**83262**	**199042**
5473	**52297**	**379659**	**74338**	**82699**
234	6769	30334	4297	9038
3817	43927	298949	69813	72064
110	2544	15071	2759	5088
6	787	13133	1277	2800
699	14668	61032	7196	15064
1170	4571	11989	2513	4756
1833	21356	197724	56068	44356
1599	7573	27754	2663	4851
57	797	52956	1862	5784
5122	47949	311247	54892	69809
351	4181	67112	19065	12612
8178	**22187**	**555411**	**8924**	**116343**
	1	740	86	450
7999	12907	534797	8539	113108
	1	740	86	450
56	36	1700	188	360
3916	1939	50574	1367	12958
	71	6365	210	1526
4027	10861	475418	6688	97814
179	9280	20614	385	3235
4775	13189	534033	8924	108185
	8946	17783		7268

表 10－14 部分年份限额以上批发零售贸易业主要财务指标 Main Financial Indicators of Wholesale and Retail Trade Above Designated Size of Partial Years

单位：亿元(100 million yuan)

指标	Indicators	2008	2009	2010	2011	2012
主营业务收入	Prime Operating Revenue	3698.1	3261.5	5170.2	6758.0	7279.6
主营业务成本	Operating Costs	3515.8	3065.8	4891.9	6429.2	6941.9
主营业务税金及附加	Tax and Extra Charge	3.4	6.8	10.8	12.0	12.9
其他业务利润	Profits from Other Business	14.0	12.6	17.7	19.2	17.7
管理费用	Management Cost	45.2	46.2	59.3	72.3	80.3
财务费用	Financial Expenses	16.5	12.9	21.6	34.7	40.1
利润总额	Total Profits	41.6	58.3	69.5	82.9	62.1
资产总计	Total Assets	1225.1	1370.8	1879.3	2449.2	2804.4
#流动资产	Current Assets	1017.2	1151.0	1617.4	2140.6	2433.7
#存货	Inventory	155.5	190.6	274.3	342.2	338.1
负债合计	Total Liabilities	952.5	1061.9	1497.7	1987.6	2299.2
所有者权益合计	Total Owner's Equities	272.6	308.8	381.6	461.6	505.2
应付职工薪酬	Employee Compensation Payable				63.8	76.6
本年(主营业务)应付工资总额	Total Payable Salaries Involved in Major Business	25.8	30.8	40.3		
本年(主营业务)应付福利费总额	Total Payable Welfare Involved in Major Business	1.2	1.2	1.9		

注：2011年起，本年(主营业务)应付工资总额指标改为本年(主营业务)应付职工薪酬总额，取消本年(主营业务)应付福利费总额。
Note: From 2011, total payable employee compensation (major business) in the year replacement total payable salaries (major business) in the year, cancel total payable walfare (major business) in the year.

表 10－15 部分年份星级住宿业及限额以上餐饮业主要财务指标 Main Financial Indicators of Catering Trade Above Designated Size and Star－rated Hotel in Partial Years

单位：亿元(100 million yuan)

指标	Indicators	2008	2009	2010	2011	2012
主营业务收入	Prime Operating Revenue	55.8	53.3	73.7	83.1	86.7
主营业务成本	Operating Costs	23.5	21.9	30.1	35.0	35.7
营业费用	Business Expenses	16.5	16.5	21.5	23.7	27.3
主营业务税金及附加	Tax and Associate Charge	3.1	2.9	4.1	4.6	4.7
管理费用	Management Cost	12.0	13.1	16.8	18.8	19.9
#税金	Taxes	0.4	0.4	0.8	0.7	0.7
财务费用	Financial Expenses	2.5	2.2	3.5	4.8	5.2
利润总额	Total Profits		－1.0	－0.5	－2.0	－3.8
资产总计	Total Assets	100.5	118.7	149.3	182.1	186.9
#流动资产	Current Assets	31.6	36.9	54.7	72.3	76.7
负债合计	Total Liabilities	73.3	85.9	112.5	142.9	151.7
所有者权益合计	Total Owner's Equities	27.2	32.8	36.9	39.1	35.2
应付职工薪酬	Employee Compensation Payable				16.2	18.8
本年(主营业务)应付工资总额	Total Payable Salaries Involved in Major Business	8.3	8.5	11.5		
本年(主营业务)应付福利费总额	Total Payable Welfare Involved in Major Business	0.4	0.4	0.6		

注：2011年起，本年(主营业务)应付工资总额指标改为本年(主营业务)应付职工薪酬总额，取消本年(主营业务)应付福利费总额。
Note: From 2011, total payable employee compensation (major business) in the year replacement total payable salaries (major business) in the year, cancel total payable walfare (major business) in the year.

表 10－16 亿元以上商品交易市场成交情况(2012) Basic Statistics of Commodity Exchange Market with Total Sale Over 100 million Yuan

单位:万元(10000 yuan)

指标	Indicators	摊位个数(个) Number of Stalls (unit)	总成交额 Transaction Volume
总计	**Total**	**70300**	**25169825**
食品、饮料、烟酒类	Food, Beverage, Tabacco and Liquor	38106	5141628
食品类	Foodstuff	37252	4915880
#粮油类	Grain and Oil	1100	432628
肉禽蛋类	Meat. Poultry and Egg	3048	711933
水产品类	Aquatic Product	21863	1800687
蔬菜类	Garden Stuff	8499	1247203
干鲜果品类	Dry Fruit and Fresh Fruit	1960	571975
饮料类	Beverage	269	95351
烟酒类	Tabacco and Liquor	585	130397
服装鞋帽、针、纺织品类	Garments, Shoes, Hats Knitwear and Textile	8113	1430006
服装类	Garments	4847	751337
鞋帽类	Shoes, Hats	1171	325017
针、纺织品类	Knitwear and Textile	2095	353652
化妆品类	Cosmetics	162	33337
日用品类	Articles for Daily Use	2875	390164
五金、电料类	Hardware and Electrical Appliances	2351	321959
体育、娱乐用品类	Recreation and Sports Articles	89	3106
书报杂志类	Books and Newspapers	5	14
电子出版物及音像制品类	Electronic Publications and Audio－video Products		
家用电器和音像器材类	Houschold Appliances and Audio－video Equipments	201	32796
中西药品类	Medicines		
文化办公用品类	Culture and Office Articles	1495	200775
家具类	Furnitures	1756	264995
通讯器材类	Telecommunication Appliances		
煤炭及制品类	Coal and Products	68	1766701
木材及制品类	Timber and Timber Products	805	175040
石油及制品类	Petroleum and Products	26	916253
化工材料及制品类	Chemical Materials and Products	3246	6611508
金属材料类	Metal Materials	3743	5332509
建筑及装潢材料类	Materials for Construction and Decoration	3279	954727
机电产品及设备类	Mechanical and Electrical Equipments	145	47542
汽车类	Automobile	1114	491407
种子饲料类	Seed and Feedstuff	156	44189
棉麻类	Cotton and Flax Products		
其他类	Others	2445	1008062

表 10－17 个体工商业情况(2012)
Basic Statistics of Individual Industry and Commerce

指标	Indicators	全市期末实有 Total at the End of this Year	其中 of Which	
			本期开业 Openning for this Term	城镇 Districts
户数(户)	**Number of Households(unit)**	**359951**	**63329**	**167180**
农、林、牧、渔业	Farming. Forestry. Animal Husbandry and Fishery	3399	542	900
采矿业	Mining and Quarrying Industry	78	3	22
制造业	Manufacturing Industry	75677	11521	18249
电力、燃气及水的生产和供应业	Electric Power, Gas and Water Production and Supply	27	2	7
建筑业	Construction	1953	267	899
交通运输业、仓储和邮政业	Transportation and Warehousing	29912	6300	13708
信息传输、计算机服务和软件业	Information Transmission, Computer Service and Software Industries	314	58	184
批发和零售业	Wholesale and Retail Trade	195379	35031	102709
住宿和餐饮业	Hotel and Catering Trade	17780	3022	9590
房地产业	Real Estate Industries	1118	199	872
租赁和商务服务业	Leasing and Business Service Industries	3934	937	2791
居民服务和其它服务业	Resident Service and Other Service Industries	26865	4784	15199
卫生、社会保障和社会福利业	Health Care, Social Security and Social Welfare	447	49	313
文化、体育和娱乐业	Culture, Sports and Entertainment	1747	422	920
其它行业	Others	1321	192	817
从业人员(人)	Emplyment Personnel(person)	725610	122156	340429
农、林、牧、渔业	Farming. Forestry. Animal Husbandry and Fishery	10218	1842	2902
采矿业	Mining and Quarrying Industry	374	17	97
制造业	Manufacturing Industry	243113	34018	68684
电力、燃气及水的生产和供应业	Electric Power, Gas and Water Production and Supply	50	7	12
建筑业	Construction	6851	1036	3305
交通运输业、仓储和邮政业	Transportation and Warehousing	35143	6891	16487
信息传输、计算机服务和软件业	Information Transmission, Computer Service and Software Industries	504	100	323

表 10－17 续表 Continued

指标	Indicators	全市期末实有 Total at The End of This Year	其中 of Which	
			本期开业 Openning for This Term	城镇 Districts
批发和零售业	Wholesale and Retail Trade	306666	53040	171024
住宿和餐饮业	Hotel and Catering Trade	49271	9897	30734
房地产业	Real Estate Industries	1985	412	1573
租赁和商务服务业	Leasing and Business Service Industries	7381	1915	5301
居民服务和其它服务业	Resident Service and Other Service Industries	55402	11078	34652
卫生、社会保障和社会福利业	Health Care,Social Security and Social Welfare	971	134	690
文化、体育和娱乐业	Culture,Sports and Entertainment	5099	1284	2887
其它行业	Others	2582	485	1758
注册资金(万元)	Registered Capital (10000 Yuan)	1998978	492506	991012
农、林、牧、渔业	Farming. Forestry. Animal Husbandry and Fishery	117791	31127	36124
采矿业	Mining and Quarrying Industry	2876	190	594
制造业	Manufacturing Industry	611168	108376	162757
电力、燃气及水的生产和供应业	Electric Power,Gas and Water Production and Supply	219	20	32
建筑业	Construction	23409	2652	9408
交通运输业、仓储和邮政业	Transportation and Warehousing	165902	32252	74895
信息传输、计算机服务和软件业	Information Transmission, Computer Service and Software Industries	1232	312	741
批发和零售业	Wholesale and Retail Trade	714558	225815	459421
住宿和餐饮业	Hotel and Catering Trade	172534	44714	117883
房地产业	Real Estate Industries	3851	1231	3080
租赁和商务服务业	Leasing and Business Service Industries	26095	8166	17918
居民服务和其它服务业	Resident Service and Other Service Industries	114252	27565	74948
卫生、社会保障和社会福利业	Health Care,Social Security and Social Welfare	10845	1279	7266
文化、体育和娱乐业	Culture,Sports and Entertainment	27545	7332	21029
其它行业	Others	6701	1475	4916

表 10－18 私营企业基本情况(2012)
Basic Statistics on Private Enterprises

指标	Indicators	全市期末实有 Total at the End of this Year	其中 of Which	
			本期开业 Openning for this Term	城镇 Districts
户数(户)	**Number of Households(unit)**	**154285**	**20974**	**91486**
农、林、牧、渔业	Farming. Forestry. Animal Husbandry and Fishery	1346	180	439
采矿业	Mining and Quarrying Industry	94	5	25
制造业	Manufacturing Industry	66834	5344	26617
电力、燃气及水的生产和供应业	Electric Power, Gas and Water Production and Supply	125	11	45
建筑业	Construction	6389	1056	4477
交通运输业、仓储和邮政业	Transportation and Warehousing	4097	503	2888
信息传输、计算机服务和软件业	Information Transmission, Computer Service and Software Industries	3063	471	2500
批发和零售业	Wholesale and Retail Trade	45274	7626	34258
住宿和餐饮业	Hotel and Catering Trade	1683	238	1254
房地产业	Real Estate Industries	2479	267	1660
租赁和商务服务业	Leasing and Business Service Industries	11730	2747	9357
居民服务和其它服务业	Resident Service and Other Service Industries	2729	424	2016
卫生、社会保障和社会福利业	Health Care, Social Security and Social Welfare	166	21	110
文化、体育和娱乐业	Culture, Sports and Entertainment	991	240	791
其它行业	Others	12243	2375	8369
从业人员(人)	Emplyment Personnel(person)	1748958	174468	1014855
农、林、牧、渔业	Farming. Forestry. Animal Husbandry and Fishery	10536	1308	3267
采矿业	Mining and Quarrying Industry	1054	36	281
制造业	Manufacturing Industry	1063261	48585	495188
电力、燃气及水的生产和供应业	Electric Power, Gas and Water Production and Supply	1110	96	519
建筑业	Construction	63362	8446	35119
交通运输业、仓储和邮政业	Transportation and Warehousing	29481	4186	21030
信息传输、计算机服务和软件业	Information Transmission, Computer Service and Software Industries	29297	3740	26232

注：本表数据来自于宁波市工商行政管理局。
Note: Data in this table are obtained from Ningbo Administration for Industry & Commerce.

表 10－18 续表 Continued

指标	Indicators	全市期末实有 Total at the End of this Year	其中 of Which 本期开业 Openning for this Term	其中 of Which 城镇 Districts
批发和零售业	Wholcsale and Retail Trade	370523	61690	302476
住宿和餐饮业	Hotel and Catering Trade	13981	2013	10283
房地产业	Real Estate Industries	18745	2124	12053
租赁和商务服务业	Leasing and Business Service Industries	70954	21410	55119
居民服务和其它服务业	Resident Service and Other Service Industries	17131	3491	12530
卫生、社会保障和社会福利业	Health Care,Social Security and Social Welfare	1292	133	862
文化、体育和娱乐业	Culture,Sports and Entertainment	5690	2155	4345
其它行业	Others	90031	19303	59657
注册资金(万元)	Registered Capital (10000 Yuan)	40420521	7219867	29122906
农、林、牧、渔业	Farming,Forestry,Animal Husbandry and Fishery	220369	29972	86167
采矿业	Mining and Quarrying Industry	16697	805	7248
制造业	Manufacturing Industry	10866923	600114	5028365
电力、燃气及水的生产和供应业	Electric Power,Gas and Water Production and Supply	80628	7300	52738
建筑业	Construction	2807073	184835	2182340
交通运输业、仓储和邮政业	Transportation and Warehousing	1313446	117574	1085739
信息传输、计算机服务和软件业	Information Transmission, Computer Service and Software Industries	367345	71251	321568
批发和零售业	Wholesale and Retail Trade	7132981	896826	5917338
住宿和餐饮业	Hotel and Catering Trade	230813	11632	164554
房地产业	Real Estate Industries	4329447	242071	3146118
租赁和商务服务业	Leasing and Business Service Industries	10166190	4583104	9088087
居民服务和其它服务业	Resident Service and Other Service Industries	204986	16447	168794
卫生、社会保障和社会福利业	Health Care,Social Security and Social Welfare	16685	740	14090
文化、体育和娱乐业	Culture,Sports and Entertainment	143440	28692	125601
其它行业	Others	11182392	912646	8026395

表 10－19 限额以上服务业企业主要经济指标
Main Economic Indicators of Service enterprises Above Designated Size

指标	Indicators	企业数 Number of Enterprises	#亏损企业 Loss－making Enterprises	从业人员数 Number of Employees	资产总计 Total Asset
总计	**Total**	**5785**	**1807**	**653751**	**263821543**
#国有控股企业	State－holding Enterprises	552	109	139386	185221315
按注册类型分	**Grouped by Registration Type**				
内资企业	Domestic Funded Enterprises	5524	1732	596870	214460840
国有企业	State－Owned Enterprises	232	41	50163	24626791
集体企业	Collective－Owned Enterprises	99	19	6721	1198137
股份合作企业	Share Cooperative Enterprises	17	1	4201	6739630
联营企业	Limited Liability Corporations	18	3	1006	521325
有限责任公司	Share－holding Corporations Ltd.	827	231	124716	35105653
股份有限公司	Private Enterprises	178	52	60461	117628626
私营企业	Private enterprises	4117	1377	348124	28529968
其他企业	Other enterprises	36	8	1478	110710
港澳台商投资企业	Hongkong,Macao and Taiwan Funded	140	36	31684	8465319
外商投资企业	Foreign－invested enterprises	121	39	25197	40895385
按行业分	**Grouped by Sector**				
批发和零售业	Wholesale and retail trade	2521	862	137301	28043715
交通运输、仓储和邮政业	Transport, storage and postal service	951	293	92362	12039861
住宿和餐饮业	Accommodation and catering industry	458	220	53422	1869042
信息传输、计算机服务和软件业	Information transmission, computer services and software industry	159	59	15985	2620339
金融业	Financial sector	217	51	59592	189885789
房地产业	Real Estate industry	183	54	41611	1780740
租赁和商务服务业	Rental and business services sector	634	137	200831	24313090
科学研究、技术服务与地质勘查业	Scientific research, technical services and geological prospecting industry	251	23	22509	1172369
水利、环境和公共设施管理业	Irrigation works,environment and public facilities management	78	28	7796	1253175
居民服务和其他服务业	Resident and other services	186	45	9465	198325
教育	Education	48	7	3547	71751
卫生和社会福利业	Hygiene and social welfare	33	15	3117	140088
文化、体育与娱乐业	Civilization, sports and entertainment industry	66	13	6213	433260
公共管理、社会保障与社会组织	Public management,, The social security and social organization				

注：房地产业不包括房地产开发经营，限上服务企业包含了批发和零售业、住宿和餐饮业。

Note: Real Estate excludes Real estate development and management, Wholesale, retail, accommodation and catering are included above designated size.

单位：个、万元(unit,10000 yuan)

负债合计 Total Liabilities	所有者权益合计 Crediters' Equity	营业收入 Business Revernue	营业成本 Business Costs	营业税金及附加 Tax and Extra Charge	三项费用 Three Costs	应付职工薪酬 Employee Compensation Payable	营业利润 Business Profits	利润总额 Total Profits
232206791	**31614753**	**104367470**	**91305428**	**1045417**	**7880854**	**4289903**	**5258716**	**5782994**
171010822	14210493	25910683	19842309	650880	2467397	1606387	3525215	3746838
191503649	22957191	95701130	85062964	901894	6731228	3816937	3942895	4432092
20830197	3796594	5270669	3989800	156928	506750	455061	723384	843070
905934	292204	479236	386335	5242	58418	42392	65994	69175
6087628	652003	438247	205993	12228	116253	79838	115627	121129
482604	38721	240650	219575	1533	15853	8167	4433	5114
26933107	8172546	26077345	24188211	99697	1454593	829613	507170	693570
113071566	4557059	17390994	13602747	424626	1633827	804045	2281885	2315789
23123262	5406706	45729506	42418468	200523	2934683	1589646	232888	372881
69352	41358	74483	51835	1116	10851	8173	11512	11364
3073717	5391602	3854509	2810311	50914	536721	238517	569006	593278
37629425	3265960	4811830	3432153	92610	612906	234450	746816	757624
22991604	5052111	73108062	69572116	133789	2991191	765855	470503	620606
7274823	4765038	8170066	6869951	127488	693221	665052	520093	689819
1516562	352480	881670	361055	47296	524308	188413	−49317	−38361
550255	2070084	1519786	680736	42343	397896	141907	391680	410428
182730105	7155684	15450675	10094041	567077	2048190	1024887	3305626	3306006
1124648	656093	379400	210248	19594	137644	147176	13491	26064
14182255	10130835	3036147	2385776	56453	652572	955571	396730	510656
574538	597831	1091148	675396	32915	202832	228083	185447	198195
952175	301001	188693	126227	4144	64112	40786	−5004	−1847
115720	82604	216991	166722	2646	38747	37734	8876	15467
30713	41038	71181	36494	3075	20109	22838	11498	11583
59384	80704	81646	32290	501	44033	18730	4823	6373
104011	329249	172006	94376	8097	66000	52870	4271	28005

表 10－20　批发业销售收入前 20 位企业(2012)
The Top 20 Enterprises of Wholesales Trade at Sales Revenue

排名 No.	企业名称	Name of Corporation	所在区域	Location
1	宁波恒逸贸易有限公司	Ningbo Hengyi Trading Co. ,Ltd.	北仑区	Beilun
2	浙江前程石化股份有限公司	Zhejiang Future Petrochemical Co. ,Ltd.	北仑区	Jiangdong
3	宁波神化化学品经营有限责任公司	Ningbo Sunhu Chem Products Co. ,Ltd.	江东区	Beilun
4	中基宁波集团股份有限公司	China－Base Ningbo Foreign Trade Co. ,Ltd.	鄞州区	Yinzhou
5	中国石油化工股份有限公司浙江宁波石油分公司	Ningbo Branch of Sinopec	海曙区	Haishu
6	远大物产集团有限公司	Grand Group Corporation	江东区	Jiangdong
7	浙江省烟草公司宁波市公司	Ningbo branch of Zhejiang Tobacco	江东区	Jiangdong
8	宁波沙洲贸易有限公司	Ningbo Shazhou Trading Co. ,Ltd.	北仑区	Beilun
9	远大石化有限公司	Ningbo Yuanda Petrochemical Co. ,Ltd.	北仑区	Beilun
10	宁波杉杉物产有限公司	Ningbo Shanshan Resources Co. ,Ltd.	鄞州区	Yinzhou
11	宁波萍钢贸易有限公司	Ningbo Pinggang Trading Co. ,Ltd.	北仑区	Beilun
12	中国石油化工股份有限公司化工销售华东分公司宁波经营部	Ningbo Sales Department, East China Chemical Sales Branch, Sino Petrochenmical Co. ,Ltd.	北仑区	Beilun
13	浙江坤巍贸易有限公司	Zhe Jiang Kunwei Trading Co. ,Ltd.	北仑区	Beilun
14	宁波保税区首德贸易有限公司	Ningbo bonded area Shoude Trade Co. ,Ltd.	北仑区	Beilun
15	宁波经济技术开发区北仑电力燃料有限公司	Ningbo Economic and Technological Development Zone, Beilun Electric Power Fuel Co. ,Ltd.	北仑区	Beilun
16	中航国际钢铁贸易有限公司	AVIC international steel trade Co. ,Ltd.	北仑区	Beilun
17	宁波君安物产有限公司	Ningbo Junan Resources Co. ,Ltd.	江东区	Jiangbei
18	国电宁波燃料有限公司	Ningbo Guodian Fuel Co. ,Ltd.	北仑区	Beilun
19	宁波科元石化有限公司	Ningbo Keyuan Petrochemical Co. ,Ltd.	北仑区	Beilun
20	宁波美的材料供应有限公司	Ningbo Meidi Materials Supply Co. ,Ltd.	北仑区	Beilun

表 10－21　零售业销售收入前 20 位企业(2012)
The Top 20 Enterprises of Retail Trade at Sales Revenue

排名 No.	企业名称	Name of Corporation	所在区域	Location
1	中石化碧辟(浙江)石油有限公司宁波分公司	BP Sinopec (Zhejiang) Petroleum Co.,Ltd. Ningbo Branch	海曙区	Haishu
2	三江购物俱乐部股份有限公司	Ningbo Sanjiang Shopping Mall Co.,Ltd.	海曙区	Haishu
3	宁波医药股份有限公司	Ningbo Pharmaceutical Co.,Ltd.	海曙区	Haishu
4	浙江华润慈客隆超市有限公司	Zhejiang Cikelong Shopping Mall Ltd.	慈溪市	Cixi
5	浙江华联商厦有限公司	Zhejiang Hualian Trade Co.,Ltd.	余姚市	Yuyao
6	宁波丰颐汽车销售有限公司	Ningbo Feng Yi Automobile Sales Co.,Ltd.	鄞州区	Yinzhou
7	宁波欧尚超市有限公司	Ningbo Auchan Supermarket Co.,Ltd.	海曙区	Haishu
8	宁波润达汽车销售服务有限公司	Ningbo Runda Auto Sale & Service Co.,Ltd.	江北区	Jiangbei
9	宁波宝恒汽车销售服务有限公司	Ningbo Baoheng Auto Sale & Service Co.,Ltd.	鄞州区	Yinzhou
10	宁波市北仑加贝购物俱乐部(普通合伙)	Ningbo beilun Jiabei Shopping Mall	北仑区	Beilun
11	宁波中基汽车销售服务有限公司	Ningbo Zhongji Car Sales Services Co.,Ltd.	鄞州区	Yinzhou
12	宁波之星汽车维修服务有限公司	Ningbo Star Auto Services Co.,Ltd.	鄞州区	Yinzhou
13	宁波捷骏汽车销售服务有限公司	Ningbo Junjie Auto Sales & Service Co.,Ltd.	江东区	Jiangdong
14	浙江慈吉之星汽车有限公司	Zhejiang Chee of the stars Automobile Co., Ltd.	慈溪市	Cixi
15	浙江大生医药有限公司	Zhejiang Tai Sang Medicine Co.,Ltd.	北仑区	Beilun
16	宁波宝信汽车销售服务有限公司	Ningbo Baoxin Auto Sales & Service Co.,Ltd.	江北区	Jiangbei
17	慈溪市驰奥汽车销售有限公司	Cixi Chiao Automobile Sales Co.,Ltd.	慈溪市	Cixi
18	银泰百货宁波海曙有限公司	Intime Department Store Co.,Ltd. Ningbo Haishu	海曙区	Haishu
19	宁波浙国美电器有限公司	Ningbo Gome Electrical Appliances Co.,Ltd.	海曙区	Haishu
20	宁波宁兴新宇汽车销售服务有限公司	Ningbo Ningxing Xinyu Auto Sales & Service Co.,Ltd.	镇海区	Zhenhai

表10－22 星级住宿业营业收入前20位企业(2012)
The Top 20 Enterprises of Hotelat Business Revenue

排名 No.	企业名称	Name of Corporation	所在区域	Location
1	香格里拉大酒店(宁波)有限公司	Shangri－La Hotel (Ningbo) Co. ,Ltd.	江东区	Jiangdong
2	宁波华侨饭店有限公司	Ningbo Howard Johnson Hotel Co. ,Ltd.	海曙区	Haishu
3	宁波东港波特曼大酒店有限公司	Portman Plaza Hotel Ningbo	江东区	Jiangdong
4	宁波南苑集团股份有限公司	Ningbo Nanyuan Group Co. ,Ltd.	海曙区	Haishu
5	宁波太平洋大酒店有限公司	Ningbo Pacific Hotel Co. ,Ltd.	余姚市	Yuyao
6	宁波开元名都大酒店有限公司	Ningbo Kaiyuan Mingdu Grand Hotel Co. ,Ltd.	鄞州区	Yinzhou
7	慈溪市杭州湾大酒店有限公司	Cixi Hangzhou Gulf Hotel Co. ,Ltd.	慈溪市	Cixi
8	宁波市凯洲实业有限公司	Ningbo Kai Zhou Industrial Co. ,Ltd.	海曙区	Haishu
9	宁波开元大酒店有限公司	Ningbo Kaiyuan Hotel Co. ,Ltd.	江东区	Jiangdong
10	余姚宾馆有限责任公司	Yuyao Hotel Co. ,Ltd.	余姚市	Yuyao
11	宁波九龙湖开元华城度假村有限公司	Ningbo Kaiyuan Huacity Jiulong Lake Co. ,Ltd.	镇海区	Zhenhai
12	宁波万达置业有限公司万达索菲特大饭店	Sofitel Wanda Ningbo Wanda Hotel Properties Co. ,Ltd.	鄞州区	Yinzhou
13	慈溪市金色港湾旅业有限公司	Cixi Golden Harbour Tourism Co. ,Ltd.	慈溪市	Cixi
14	宁波新晶都酒店有限公司	Holiyacht Crystal Hotel	江东区	Jiangdong
15	慈溪国际大酒店有限公司	Cixi International Hotel Co. ,Ltd.	慈溪市	Cixi
16	宁波凯利大酒店有限公司	Ningbo Kaili Hotel Co. ,Ltd.	江北区	Jiangbei
17	余姚钱塘河姆渡宾馆有限公司	Quintessence Hemudu Hotel	余姚市	Yuyao
18	宁波金港大酒店有限公司	Ningbo Jinggang Hotel Co. ,Ltd.	江北区	Jiangbei
19	宁波南苑商务旅店连锁股份有限公司	Ningbo Nanyuan Business Hotel Chain Co. ,Ltd.	鄞州区	Yinzhou
20	宁波远洲大酒店有限公司	Smile And Natural Hotel Ningbo	江北区	Jiangbei

表 10－23　餐饮业营业收入前 20 位企业(2012)
The Top 20 Enterprises of Catering Trade at Business Revenue

排名 No.	企业名称	Name of Corporation	所在区域	Location
1	宁波南苑环球酒店管理有限公司	Nanyuan International Hotel Management Co. ,Ltd.	鄞州区	Yinzhou
2	宁波市来必堡餐饮管理有限公司	Ningbo Laibi Fort Restaurant Management Co. ,Ltd.	海曙区	Haishu
3	宁波怡骥供应链管理有限公司	Ningbo Yi Ji Supply Chain Management Co. ,Ltd.	北仑区	Beilun
4	浙江向阳渔港集团股份有限公司	Zhejiang Xiangyang Port Group Co. ,Ltd.	江东区	Jiangdong
5	余姚中塑石浦大酒店有限公司	Yuyao Zhongsu Shipu Restaurant Co. ,Ltd.	余姚市	Yuyao
6	余姚阳明温泉山庄实业有限公司	Yuyao Yangming Hot Spring Resort	余姚市	Yuyao
7	宁波东方明珠娱乐有限公司	Ningbo Oriental Pearl Amusement Co. ,Ltd.	江东区	Jiangdong
8	宁波石浦酒店管理发展有限公司	Ningbo Shipu Restaurant Management Development Co. ,Ltd.	鄞州区	Yinzhou
9	宁海金海开元名都大酒店有限公司	Ninghai Jinhai Hotel Management Co. ,Ltd.	宁海县	Ninghai
10	宁波恒元大酒店有限公司	Ningbo Hengyuan Hotel Co. ,Ltd.	慈溪市	Cixi
11	宁波市江东天港禧悦酒店管理有限公司	Ningbo Jiangdong Sky Harbor Jubilee Paradise Hotel Management Co. ,Ltd.	江东区	Jiangdong
12	宁波银苑大酒店有限公司	Ningbo Yinyuan Restaurant Co. ,Ltd.	鄞州区	Yinzhou
13	宁波市江东彩虹坊大酒店	Ningbo Caihongfang Restaurant	江东区	Jiangdong
14	余姚雍和宫大酒店有限公司	Yuyao Yonghogong Restaurant Co. ,Ltd.	余姚市	Yuyao
15	浙江竹林人家餐饮有限公司	Zhejiang Bamboo Country Food Co. ,Ltd.	海曙区	Haishu
16	宁波豪味达营养配餐服务有限公司	Ningbo Hao Taste Nutrition Catering Services Co. ,Ltd.	鄞州区	Yinzhou
17	宁海县旌表义门农家乐旅游有限公司	Ninghai Wujia Family Courtyard	宁海县	Ninghai
18	宁波汉唐餐饮管理有限公司	Ningbo Hantang Restaurant Management Co. ,Ltd.	海曙区	Haishu
19	宁波浙海大酒店有限公司	Zhe Hai Grand Hotel	鄞州区	Yinzhou
20	余姚市凤凰城文化娱乐餐饮有限公司	Yuyao Phoenix City Culture and Entertainment Catering Co. Ltd.	余姚市	Yuyao

表 10－24　年成交额前 20 位的交易市场(2012)
The Top 20 Commodity Exchange Market with Transaction Volume

排名 No.	企业名称	Name of Corporation	所在区域	Location
1	余姚市中国塑料城	China Plastic Exchange Market (Yuyao)	余姚市	Yuyao
2	宁波市镇海煤炭交易市场有限公司	Ningbo Zhenhai Coal Exchange Co. ,Ltd.	镇海区	Zhenhai
3	宁波镇海液体化工产品交易市场	Ningbo Zhenhai Liquid Chemical Products Market	镇海区	Zhenhai
4	宁波市镇海厚恒物资城	Ningbo Zhenhai Houheng Material City	镇海区	Zhenhai
5	宁波镇海大宗生产资料交易中心	Ningbo Zhenhai Mass Production Trading Center	镇海区	Zhenhai
6	宁波华东物资城	East China Material Market of Ningbo	江东区	Jiangdong
7	浙江长三角石油化工发展有限公司	Zhejiang Changsanjiao Petroleum Chemical Industry Co. ,Ltd.	慈溪市	Cixi
8	慈溪市农副产品批发市场	Cixi Wholesale Market of Farm & Sideline Products	慈溪市	Cixi
9	余姚市模板市场	Yuyao MasterPlate Market	余姚市	Yuyao
10	余姚市农副产品批发市场	Yuyao Wholesale Market of Farm & Sideline Products	余姚市	Yuyao
11	宁波轻纺城	Ningbo Light Textile Market	鄞州区	Yinzhou
12	慈溪市工业品批发市场	Cixi Wholesale Market of Industrial Products	慈溪市	Cixi
13	宁波市江北甬江物资城服务有限公司	Ningbo Steel Cyberport	江北区	Jiangbei
14	宁波鄞州新时代钢材市场	Ningbo Yinzhou New Times Steel Market	鄞州区	Yinzhou
15	宁波华东物资城王家弄市场	Wangjia Long Market of East China Material Market	鄞州区	Yinzhou
16	宁波市江东水产批发市场	Ningbo Jiangdong aquatic products wholesale market	江东区	Jiangdong
17	浙江水产城象山渔贸发展有限公司	Zhejiang Aquatic City Xiangshan Fishing Trade Development Co. ,Ltd.	象山县	Xiangshan
18	慈溪市周巷副食品批发市场	Cixi Zhouxiang Wholesale Market of Subsidiary Food	慈溪市	Cixi
19	宁波万国商城	Ningbo Wanguo Commodity Market	鄞州区	Yinzhou
20	慈溪市胜山服装布料市场	Cixi Shenshan Garment and Cloth Market	慈溪市	Cixi

主要统计指标解释

【社会消费品零售额】 指各种经济类型的批发零售贸易业、餐饮业、制造业和其他行业对城乡居民和社会集团的消费品零售额。这个指标反映通过各种商品流通渠道向居民和社会集团供应的生活消费品来满足他们生活需要，是研究人民生活，社会消费品购买力、货币流通等问题的重要指标。社会消费品零售额包括：(1)售给城乡居民作为生活用的商品和修建房屋用的建筑材料；(2)售给社会集团的各种办公用品和公用消费品(3)售给 机关、团体、学校、部队、企业、事业单位的职工食堂和旅店(招待所)附设专门供本店旅客食用，不对外营业的食堂的各种食品、燃料；企业、单位和国营农场直接售给本单位职工和职工食堂的自已生产的产品；(4)售给部队干部、战士生活用的粮食、副食品、衣着品、日用品、燃料；(5)售给来华的外国人、华侨、港澳(台)同胞的消费品；(6)居民自费购买的中、西药品、中药材及医疗用品；(7)报社、出版社直接售给居民和社会集团的报纸、图书、杂志、集邮公司出售的新、旧纪念邮票、特种邮票、首日封、集邮册、集邮工具等；(8)旧货寄售商店自购、自销部分的商品；(9)煤气公司、液化石油气站售给居民和社会集团的煤气灶具和罐装液化石油气；(10)农民售给非农业居民和社会集团的商品。不包括售给国民经济各部门企业、事业单位(包括国有经济的农场) 生产经营用的各种原材料、燃料、设备、工具等和售给批发零售贸易业、餐饮业作为转卖用的商品、旧货寄售商店受托寄售卖出的商品、服务业的营业收入、邮局出售邮票的收入、自来水、电力、煤气生产(供应)单位的产品供应收入，也不包括农民之间的商品销售。

【限额以上批发企业】 指年销售额在2000万元及以上，并且年末从业人员在20人及以上的批发贸易企业。

【限额以上零售企业】 指年销售额在500万元及以上，并且年末从业人员在60人及以上的零售企业。

【限额以上餐饮企业】 指年销售额在200万元及以上，并且年末从业人员在40人及以上的餐饮企业。

【批发零售贸易业商品购、销、存总额】 指以各种经济类型的批发、零售贸易业(不包括个体)为总体的商品购、销、存。

【商品购进总额】 指从本企业(单位)以外的单位和个人购进(包括从国外直接进口)作为转卖或加工后转卖的商品。这个指标反映批发零售贸易业从国内、国外市场上购进商品的总量。商品购进总额包括：(1)从工农业生产者购进的商品；(2)从出版社、报社的出版发行部门购进的图书、杂志和报纸；(3)从各种经济类型的批发零售贸易企业(单位)购进的商品；(4)从其他单位购进的商品，如从机关、团体、企业单位购进的剩余物资，从餐饮业、服务业购进的商品，从海关、市场管理部门购进的缉私和没收的商品，从居民收购的废旧商品等；(5)从国(境)外直接进口的商品。不包括企业(单位)为自身经营用，和未通过买卖行为而收入的商品以及销售退回、商品升溢等。

【商品销售总额】 指对本企业(单位)以外的单位和个人出售(包括对国(境)外直接出口)的商品。这个指标反映批发零售贸易业在国内市场上销售商品以及出口商品的总量。商品销售总额包括：(1)售给城乡居民和社会集团消费用的商品；(2)售给工业、农业、建筑业、运输邮电业、批发零售贸易业、餐饮业、服务业等作为生产、经营使用的商品；(3)售给批发零售贸易业作为转卖或加工后转卖的商品；(4)对国(境)外直接出口的商品。不包括：出售本企业(单位)自用的废旧包装用品，未通过买卖行为付出的商品，经本单位介绍，由买卖双方直接结算，本单位只收取手续费的业务，购货退出的商品以及商品损耗和损失等。

Explanatory Notes on Main Statistical Indicators

【Total Retail Sales of Consumer Goods】 refer to the sum of retail sales of consumer goods by the establishments in wholesale trade, retail sale trade, catering trade, manufacturing industry and other industries of different types of ownership, to urban and rural residents and social groups. This indicator is used to show the supply of consumer goods through various channels to households and institutions to meet their demands, and is therefore very important for the study of the issues on people's livelihood, on the purchasing power of consumer goods and on the circulation of money. The retail sales of consumer goods include: (1)commodities sold to urban and rural residents for residential use and building materials sold to them for the construction or repair of houses;(2)food and fuels sold to canteens of institutions, enterprises, schools, military units and to canteens of hotels and hostels that only serve their guests, and commodities produced by enterprises, institutions or state farms and sold directly to their employees or their canteens; (3)grain and non—staple food, clothing, daily articles and fuels sold to military personnel; (4)consumer goods sold to foreigners, overseas Chinese, and Chinese compatriots from Taiwan, Hong Kong and Macao during their stay in the mainland of China; (5)Chinese an d western medicines, herbs and medical facilities purchased by residents; (6) newspapers, books and magazines directly sold to residents and social groups by publishers, new and old commemorative stamps, special stamps, first day covers, stamp albums and other stamp collection articles sold by stamp companies; (7)consumer goods purchased and then sold by second—hand shops; (8)stoves and other heating facilities and liquified gas sold by gas companies to households and institutions; (9)commodities sold by farmers to non—agricultural residents and social groups. Excluded under this heading are: raw materials, fuels, equipment, tools sold to enterprises, institutions and state farms for production purpose; commodities sold to trade establishments for re—selling; commissioned sales at second—hand shops; operational income of urban public utilities; stamps sold at post offices; income of water, power, gas production and supply establishments from the supply of their products; and sales of commodities among farmers.

【Enterprises of Over—norm Wholesale Volume】 refers to wholesale trade enterprises that register an annual sales volume of over 20 million yuan RMB and a total year-end staff of more than 20.

【Enterprises of Over—norm Retail Sales Volume】 refers to those that register an annual sales volume of over 5 million yuan RMB and a total year—end staff of more than 60.

【Catering Enterprises of Over—norm Sales Volume】 refers to those that register an annual sales volume of over 2 million yuan RMB and a total year—end staff of more than 40.

【Purchase, Sales and Stock of Commodities by Wholesale and Retail Trade】 refer to the purchase, sales and stock of commodities by wholesale and retail establishments of different ownership(excluding individual sellers).

【Total Purchases of Commodities】 refer to the purchases of commodities by the establishments from other establishments or individuals (including direct import from abroad) for the purpose of re—selling, either with or without further processing of the commodities purchased. This indicator is used to show the total value of purchases of commodities by wholesale and retail establishments from domestic and overseas markets. The total purchases include: (1) agricultural and industrial products purchased from producers; (2)books, magazines and newspapers purchased from distribution departments of the publishers; (3) commodities purchased from wholesale and retail establishments; (4)commodities purchased from other units, such as surplus materials purchased from government agencies, enterprises or institutions, commodities purchased from catering and service establishments, confiscated goods purchased from customs authorities or market management agencies, second—hand goods and wastes purchased from residents; and (5)commodities directly imported from abroad. Excluded are commodities purchased by establishments(units)for use in their own business operation, commodities obtained without buying or selling procedures, rejected commodities, etc.

【Total Sales of Commodities】 refer to selling of commodities by the establishments to other establishments and individuals(including direct export) . This indicator is used to show the total value of sales of commodities at domestic markets and export. The total sales include: (1)commodities sold to urban and rural residents and social groups for their consumption; (2)commodities so ld to establishments in industry, agriculture, construction, transportation, post and telecommunications, wholesale and retail trades, catering trade and public utility for their production and operation; (3)commodities sold to wholesale an d retail establishments for re—selling, with or without further processing; and (4)commodities for direct export to other countries. Excluded are selling of waste packaging materials used by the establishments(units) themselves, commodities transferred without buying or selling procedures, commission income from brokerage in transactions whose settlement is directly handled by buyers and sellers , rejected commodities in the purchase, loss in commodities, etc.

NINGBO

Statistical YearBook

第十一篇

对外经济、旅游

FOREIGN TRADE AND TOURISM

对外经济、旅游
Foreign Trade and Tourism

主要统计指标
Major Statistics Indicators

2012 年自营进出口总额	Total Direct Import and Export	9657269	万美元	USD 10000
比上年增长	Increase Over Last Year	－1.6	%	
2012 年自营出口总额	Total Exports	6144526	万美元	USD 10000
比上年增长	Increase Over Last Year	1.0	%	
2012 年自营进口总额	Total Imports	3512743	万美元	USD 10000
比上年增长	Increase Over Last Year	－5.9	%	
2012 年新签合同数	Number of Projects of Signed Contracts	437	个	unit
比上年增长	Increase Over Last Year	6.3	%	
2012 年实际利用外资金额	Value of Foreign Captial Actually Used	285252	万美元	USD 10000
比上年增长	Increase Over Last Year	1.5	%	
2012 年接待境外旅游者人数	Number of Received Oversea Tourists	1162088	人	person
比上年增长	Increase Over Last Year	8.2	%	
2012 年旅游创汇收入	Foreign Exchange Earnings	73428	万美元	USD 10000
比上年增长	Increase Over Last Year	12.2	%	
2012 年国内旅游总收入	Earning From Domestic Tourism	816.4	亿元	100 million yuan
比上年增长	Increase Over Last Year	15.2	%	

表 11－1 历年对外经济贸易基本情况 Basic Statistics on Foreign Economy and Trade Over the Years

单位：万美元(USD 10000)

年份 Year	外商直接投资情况 Foreign Direct Investments			自营进出口 Direct Import and Export		口岸进出口 Import and Export of Port	
	新批项目数（个） Number of Projects(unit)	合同利用外资 Foreign Capital Signed Agreements	实际利用外资 Foreign Capital Actually Used	进出口 Total	#出口 Exports	进出口 Total	#出口 Exports
1980	1	5	5				
1981							
1982						14917	10963
1983						17683	12173
1984	8	850	21			26336	16102
1985	11	682	359	1029	389	45474	23521
1986	7	447	500	2079	540	54690	34432
1987	13	4341	429	2061	791	52493	29999
1988	62	4002	689	14766	11458	78717	39155
1989	64	6295	1758	22024	18005	110175	53615
1990	89	5624	2197	29840	27962	125527	63253
1991	184	17460	2680	57339	47532	219638	87101
1992	636	156725	11497	99072	78389	260387	101699
1993	1015	107152	34455	169434	110824	328871	120138
1994	680	77149	35812	251462	174992	375919	168340
1995	496	114630	39909	385335	226825	521501	232789
1996	322	87838	50162	418573	233003	586140	252248
1997	260	45849	55408	460896	293332	663807	311848
1998	281	51198	50329	421237	296386	610109	339904
1999	364	65660	52035	500898	347721	774194	411200
2000	550	95151	62186	754065	516781	1372547	703357
2001	806	195519	87446	889202	624500	1613794	869768
2002	1017	320024	124696	1227343	816304	2145755	1232723
2003	1209	344382	172727	1880962	1207398	3394193	1888206
2004	1081	413633	210322	2611222	1668967	5157576	2664100
2005	873	421015	231079	3349427	2223256	6749471	3614462
2006	1034	442746	243018	4221188	2877052	8649306	4958297
2007	854	450107	250518	5649909	3825509	11176033	6744103
2008	528	412339	253789	6784036	4632638	14018503	8371436
2009	403	342362	220541	6081252	3865068	11692277	7317493
2010	495	404608	232336	8290424	5196745	16134445	10052342
2011	411	501463	280929	9818682	6083159	20044269	12375307
2012	437	531276	285252	9657269	6144526	19757789	12419370

注：2003 年起，利用外资统计口径有变动。

Note: From 2003, the Statstistical Standard which will utilize the foreign capitals have changed.

表 11—2　按企业性质分的进出口总值(2012)
Total Value of Imports and Exports by Registered Type of Enterprises

单位:万美元(USD 10000)

企业性质	Grouped by Registered Type	进出口 Imports and Exports		其中 of Which 出口 Exports		其中 of Which 进口 Imports	
		贸易额 Value	增长率(%) Rate of Increase	贸易额 Value	增长率(%) Rate of Increase	贸易额 Value	增长率(%) Rate of Increase
合计	**Total**	**9657269**	**−1.6**	**6144526**	**1.0**	**3512743**	**−5.9**
国营企业	State—Owned Enterprises	847941	−8.6	570964	−6.4	276978	−12.8
三资企业	Foreign Funded Enterprises	3822009	−2.9	2154451	−1.5	1667559	−4.7
#外合作企业	Cooperative Operation Enterprises	35485	12.6	22837	−0.3	12649	46.9
外合资企业	Joint Venture Enterprises	1492769	−8.7	908490	−8.4	584279	−9.1
外商独资企业	Foreign—funded Sole Enterprises	2293755	1.0	1223124	4.3	1070631	−2.5
集体企业	Collective Owned Enterprises	668901	−24.5	365132	−23.3	303769	−26.0
私营企业	Private Enterprises	4309532	6.2	3046078	8.7	1263454	0.8
个体工商户	Individual Enterprises	8182	8.6	7303	41.6	879	−63.0
其他企业	Others	703	260.8	598	380.6	105	49.1

注:本表至 11—5 表数据来自宁波海关。

Note:Data from Tables 11—2 to 11—5 are obtained from Ningbo Customs.

表 11—3　按贸易方式分的进出口总值(2012)
Total Value of Imports and Exports by Trade Property

单位:万美元(USD 10000)

企业性质	Grouped by Registered Type	进出口 Imports and Exports		其中 of Which 出口 Exports		其中 of Which 进口 Imports	
		贸易额 Value	增长率(%) Rate of Increase	贸易额 Value	增长率(%) Rate of Increase	贸易额 Value	增长率(%) Rate of Increase
总额	**Total**	**9657269**	**−1.6**	**6144526**	**1.0**	**3512743**	**−5.9**
一般贸易	General Trade	7363864	0.6	4912698	2.8	2451166	−3.6
进料加工贸易	Processing by Supplied Material	1577396	−4.2	989934	−5.5	587462	−1.8
来料加工装配贸易	Processing by Import Material	218090	−7.3	121613	−0.1	96477	−15.1
外商投资企业作为投资进口的设备、物品	Imports of Foreign — invested Enterprises As Investment in Equipment&Goods	22411	13.2			22411	13.2
保税仓库进出境货物	Import & Export Commodities in Protective Tariff Zone	300779	4.8	95752	17.2	205027	−0.1
保税区仓储转口货物	Transit Goods in Protective Tariff Zone	166668	−44.3	21900	−56.6	144768	−41.8
其他	Others	5966	26.7	2629	95.1	3336	−0.7

表 11－4　分洲别及主要国家(地区)的进出口总值(2012)
Total Value of Exports and Imports by Continent and Country

单位:万美元(USD 10000)

地区 Region	进出口 Imports and Exports		其中 of Which 出口 Exports		其中 of Which 进口 Imports	
	贸易额 Value	增长率(%) Rate of Increase	贸易额 Value	增长率(%) Rate of Increase	贸易额 Value	增长率(%) Rate of Increase
合计 Total	**9657269**	**−1.6**	**6144526**	**1.0**	**3512743**	**−5.9**
亚洲 Asia	4028317	−0.1	1889581	1.6	2138736	−1.5
＃东盟 The Aaaociation of Southeast Asian Nations	778379	7.1	405527	10.7	372851	3.4
中国香港 Hongkong, China	226448	7.1	209333	7.1	17115	6.6
日本 Japan	729921	−5.361784		−4.5	368137	−6.0
韩国 Republic of Korea	492938	0.9	183341	−3.0	309597	3.4
中国台湾 Taiwan, China	806607	4.6	85712	13.6	720895	3.6
非洲 Africa	383516	0.1	315709	6.0	67807	−20.4
欧洲 Europe	2295008	−8.9	1851381	−7.9	443627	−13.1
＃欧盟 European Free Trade Association	1911695	−8.3	1561309	−9.3	350386	−4.0
南美洲 South America	863475	−1.6	565966	6.0	297509	−13.4
北美洲 North America	1681639	3.8	1320751	10.8	360887	−15.8
＃美国 USA	1504596	5.9	1202961	11.9	301635	−12.8
大洋洲 Oceania	405258	5.6	201138	6.9	204120	4.4

表 11－5 部分年份按各大洲分的进出口分类表
Total of Exports and Imports by Continent in Partial Years

单位：万美元(USD 10000)

指标	Indicators	2007	2008	2009	2010	2011
进出口总额	**Total Value**	**6784036**	**6081275**	**8290424**	**9818682**	**9657269**
亚洲	Asia	2900362	2591883	3351962	4032006	4028317
非洲	Africa	248809	230491	299694	383281	383516
欧洲	Europe	1873776	1596394	2211169	2521035	2295008
＃欧盟	European Union	1632139	1366552	1881681	2086243	1911695
南美洲	South America	485951	457860	716580	877477	863475
北美洲	North America	1058284	970730	1362281	1620770	1681639
大洋洲	Oceania	216813	233907	348612	384033	405258
出口	**Export**	**4632638**	**3865073**	**5196745**	**6083159**	**6144526**
亚洲	Asia	1453079	1265819	1561718	1860362	1889581
非洲	Africa	222903	194823	239464	298086	315709
欧洲	Europe	1624414	1263197	1755764	2009977	1851381
＃欧盟	European Union	1440792	1145332	1560351	1721005	1561309
南美洲	South America	334182	264997	419562	534138	565966
北美洲	North America	854627	746262	1034205	1192375	1320751
大洋洲	Oceania	143433	129975	186032	188220	201138
进口	**Import**	**2151399**	**2216202**	**3093679**	**3735523**	**3512743**
亚洲	Asia	1447282	1326064	1790244	2171644	2138736
非洲	Africa	25906	35668	60230	85195	67807
欧洲	Europe	249362	333197	455404	511058	443627
＃欧盟	European Union	191348	221220	321330	365238	350386
南美洲	South America	151770	192864	297019	343339	297509
北美洲	North America	203657	224468	328076	428396	360887
大洋洲	Oceania	73380	103932	162580	195813	204120

表 11-6 按投资方式分的利用外资基本情况(2012)
Utilization of Foreign Capital by Investment Way

单位:万美元(USD 10000)

指标	Indicators	项目数(个) Projects (unit)	合同利用外资 Foreign Capital Contracted	实际利用外资 Foreign Capital Actually Used
总计	**Total**	**437**	**531276**	**285252**
对外借款	**Foreign Loans**			
外国政府贷款	Foreign Government Loans			
国际金融组织贷款	Loans from International Financial Organization			
外国银行商业贷款	Commercial Loans from Foreign Banks			
其他	Others			
外商直接投资	**Foreign Direct Investment**	**437**	**531276**	**285252**
合资经营	Joint Venture Enterprises	136	79038	70949
合作经营	Cooperative Operation Enterprises	1	345	560
独资企业	Foreign－funded Sole Enterprises	298	443435	208879
外商投资股份制	Share－system Enterprises	2	8458	4864
外商其他投资	**Other Foreign Investment**			

注:本表至11－9表数据来自宁波市对外贸易经济合作局。

Note:Data from Tables 11－6 to 11－9 are obtained from Ningbo Municipal Bureau of Foreign Trade & Economic Cooperation.

表 11-7 部分年份按投资方式分的利用外资基本情况
Utilization of Foreign Capital by Investment Way in Partial Years

单位:万美元 (USD 10000)

指标	Indicators	2008	2009	2010	2011	2012
合同利用外资	**Foreign Capital Contracted**	**412339**	**342362**	**404608**	**501463**	**531276**
对外借款	Foreign Loans					
外商直接投资	Foreign Direct Investment	412339	342362	404608	501463	531276
合资经营	Joint Venture Enterprises	71096	29327	87743	129624	79038
合作经营	Cooperative Operation Enterprises	2945	5133	3674	2573	345
独资企业	Foreign－funded Sole Enterprises	328335	307297	308159	367406	443435
实际利用外资	**Actual Used Foreign Capital**	**253789**	**220541**	**232336**	**280929**	**285252**
对外借款	Foreign Loans					
外商直接投资	Foreign Direct Investment	253789	220541	232336	280929	285252
合资经营	Joint Venture Enterprises	58188	50987	80959	61695	70949
合作经营	Cooperative Operation Enterprises	5970	20	29	664	560
独资企业	Foreign－funded Sole Enterprises	188974	159241	150768	215230	208879

表 11－8 部分年份按行业分外商直接投资情况
Foreign Direct Investments by Sectors in Partial Years

指标	Indicators
总计	**Total**
农、林、牧、渔业	Farming, Forestry, Animal Housbandry and Fishery
#农业	Farming
制造业	Manufacturing
#纺织业	Textile Industry
纺织服装、鞋、帽制造业	Textile Clothing. Shoes. Cap Manufacturing
文教体育用品制造业	Cultural. Educational and Sports Goods Manufacturing
化学原料及化学制品制造业	Raw Chemical Materials and Chemical Products
塑料制品业	Plastic Products
金属制品业	Metal Products
通用设备制造业	General Equipment Manufacturing
专用设备制造业	Special Equipment Manufacturing
交通运输设备制造业	Transport Equipment Manufacturing
电气机械及器材制造业	Electric Equipment and Machinery Manufacturing
通信设备、计算机及其他电子设备制造业	Communication Equipment. Computer and Other Electronic Equipment Manufacturing
仪器仪表及文化、办公用机械制造业	Instruments. Meters. Cultural and Office Machinery
电力、燃气及水的生产和供应业	Electricity, Gas and Water Production and Supply
建筑业	Construction
交通运输、仓储和邮政业	Transport, Storage and Post
批发和零售贸易业	Wholesale and Retail Sale Trade
餐饮业	Catering Service
房地产业	Real Estate Management
居民服务和其他服务业	Resident Services and Other Services Industries
其他行业	Other Sectors

注：2003 年始利用外资数据按新口径调整。
Note: Utilization of foreign capitals data in 2003 are adjusted according to the Statistical Standard.

单位:万美元(USD 1000)

新批项目数(个) Number of Newly Projects(unit)			合同利用外资 Foreign Capital Signed Agreements			实际利用外资 Foreign Investment Actually Used		
2010	2011	2012	2010	2011	2012	2010	2011	2012
495	411	437	404608	501463	531276	232336	280929	285252
6	2	4	6965	2533	127	232336	8699	171
1	1	4	524	134	73	144	3445	171
219	201	208	252133	321371	315277	160378	117915	127785
4	2	1	5175	2606	−1606	2493	2553	2046
8	6	7	6425	19690	7968	11295	10381	7149
8	2	1	4484	3424	2783	1438	1195	1145
4	6	8	13427	31517	30511	39008	16365	25140
13	10	16	12753	7339	17063	6113	6030	6160
18	7	17	13300	12425	21207	7614	5432	5886
24	28	31	26509	39406	50142	12901	12019	12595
22	18	15	12976	17863	6833	7134	4487	3915
20	33	32	35689	41681	39833	20873	14904	12218
47	34	31	60332	41613	47935	19313	10128	5221
26	31	19	35890	46745	40094	15505	14229	10654
	5	6	821	6006	8977	808	3111	4579
1		4	1428	72	3353	2122	1307	1786
2	2	5	2787	410	13294	180		1993
4	3	3	4125	1238	4077	2624	1767	2759
184	145	144	53151	56491	70049	9653	26638	52233
4	5	4	88	1485	−51	546	279	31
12	8	8	37840	86574	82198	41097	90198	68947
5		1	2150	43	4	81	1200	
4		1	2140		4	71		

表 11－9 部分年份按国别(地区)分的外商直接投资情况
Foreign Direct Investment by Country and Territory in Partial Years

国别、地区	Country, Region	新批项目数(个) New Projects(unit)		
		2010	2011	2012
总计	**Total**	**495**	**411**	**437**
香港	Hongkong, China	232	183	151
台湾省	Taiwan, China	38	33	44
日本	Japan	16	20	17
韩国	Korea Rep	13	6	12
印度尼西亚	Indonesia	3	1	2
新加坡	Singapore	4	12	13
文莱	Brunei		2	1
马来西亚	Malaysia	4	3	5
泰国	Thailand			
阿拉伯联合酋长国	United Arab Emirates			1
毛里求斯	Mauritius	3	1	1
英国	United Kingdom	11	4	6
德国	Germany	6	17	15
法国	France	4	7	6
意大利	Italy	9	15	7
荷兰	Netherlands	3	4	7
比利时	Belgium	2	1	1
西班牙	Spain	5	5	2
瑞典	Sweden	6	3	6
瑞士	Switzerland		2	1
俄罗斯	Russia	2	1	2
巴哈马	The Bahamas			
巴西	Brazil	1	2	1
开曼群岛	Cayman Islands		4	3
乌拉圭	Uruguay			
英属维尔京群岛	British Virgin Islands	9	9	19
加拿大	Canada	10	2	9
美国	United States	32	29	35
澳大利亚	Australia	15	10	14
库克群岛	The Cook Islands			
新西兰	New Zealand	2	3	6
萨摩亚	Samoa	10	8	7

注:2003年始利用外资数据按新口径调整。

Note: Utilization of foreign capitals data in 2003 are adjusted according to the Statistical Standard.

单位：万美元（USD 10000）

合同利用外资 Foreign Investment Contracted			实际利用外资 Actual Utilization of Foreign Capital		
2010	2011	2012	2010	2011	2012
404608	**501463**	**531276**	**232336**	**280929**	**285252**
306668	340526	317369	135875	181274	187026
18227	8913	37923	4696	1705	1719
6996	7163	6089	7818	7698	5166
2019	5516	4195	8198	8339	2090
19	598	109	680	748	15
-1817	7233	20440	1721	4185	8148
-9	2853	-359	250		225
1067	68	171	140	207	94
-133		15		7	
63	-209	5	38	11	9
1624	-3251	-427	803	3008	341
7035	4564	5965	958	809	745
821	7254	3682	235	869	878
3065	1772	10006	1025	291	1420
1819	8491	1343	1311	777	173
3640	3096	205	3206	602	2966
-792	83	78	121	194	41
2927	3638	187	506	172	152
696	160	145	699	75	224
	-1528	2487	2411	521	2140
13	-612	8		3	
			37		
100	995	80		313	249
2955	16185	7729	20700	9817	5984
12055	9485	36884	18869	29004	22165
4785	-149	4174	137	102	723
463	16158	5599	3127	2895	4219
2192	821	7730	2056	707	928
77	696	3509	1053	116	114
7045	13763	27024	11964	3622	10532

表 11－10 部分年份旅游业简况
Basic Statistic on Tourism in Partial Years

指标		Indicators	Unit	2010	2011	2012
旅行社合计	（家）	International Travel Agencies	(unit)	279	332	364
＃出境旅行社	（家）	Outbound Travel Agencies	(unit)	10	13	18
国内入境旅行社	（家）	Domestic Inbound Travel Agencies	(unit)	223	246	267
旅游星级饭店	（家）	Star－rated Hotel	(unit)	198	190	170
国内旅游总人数	（万人次）	Number of Domestic Tourists	(10000 person－times)	4624	5181	5748
旅游总收入	（亿元）	Income of Tourism	(100 million yuan)	650.8	751.3	862.8
＃旅游创汇	（万美元）	Foreign Exchange Earnings	(USD 10000)	59066	65472	73428
国内旅游总收入	（亿元）	Domestic Tourism Receipts	(100 million yuan)	610.70	708.74	816.4

注：本表至 11－12 表数据来自宁波市旅游局。

Note：Dara from Tables 11－10 to 11－12 are obtained from Ningbo Municipal Bureau of Tourism.

表 11－11 部分年份国际旅游情况
Basic Statistic on International Tourism in Partial Years

指标	单位	Indicators	Unit	2010	2011	2012
接待过夜境外旅游者人数	**（人）**	**Number of Oversea Tourists Staying Overnight**	**(person)**	**951680**	**1074157**	**1162088**
外国人		Foreigner		538932	608899	631033
台湾同胞		Compatriots from Taiwan，China		202022	239832	282622
香港同胞		Compatriots from Hongkong，China		158299	170708	186801
澳门同胞		Compatriots from Macao，China		52427	54718	61632
接待过夜境外旅游者人天数	**（人天）**	**Person－days of Oversea Tourists Staying Overnight**	**(person－day)**	**2781981**	**3097184**	**3275117**
外国人		Foreigner		1743007	1862334	1883598
台湾同胞		Compatriots from Taiwan，China		491909	613188	705084
香港同胞		Compatriots from Hongkong，China		404202	454784	515853
澳门同胞		Compatriots from Macao，China		142863	166878	170582

表 11－12　部分年份接待外国旅游者人数(按国别分)
Number of Foreign Tourists by Country in Partial Years

单位:人(person)

国家(地区)	Country	2008	2009	2010	2011	2012
总计	**Total**	**477198**	**464598**	**538932**	**608899**	**631033**
亚洲	Asia	238025	226121	252894	264007	270656
#日本	Japna	96680	87695	96111	99371	80214
韩国	Korea Rep	57698	50542	56309	55243	56171
印度尼西亚	Indonesia	9771	9755	12161	11589	10555
马来西亚	Malaysia	12083	11354	14066	15383	14496
新加坡	Singapore	13903	15360	17817	18965	18751
泰国	Thailand	6970	6949	9250	12000	14210
印度	India	10428	11348	12579	15516	18003
欧洲	Europe	110019	115376	135517	164423	163241
#英国	United Kingdom	16553	16854	20245	27227	29019
法国	France	15254	15960	18481	21243	23166
德国	Germany	17900	16789	19574	26126	23524
意大利	Italy	11374	11207	14237	16236	14691
俄罗斯	Russia	9836	12889	16705	19771	7698
美洲	America	77751	74388	92254	113920	125750
#美国	United States	50618	49515	62230	80571	73084
加拿大	Canada	13212	12810	15870	19460	22416
大洋洲	Oceania	28788	27438	32746	37696	41096
#澳大利亚	Australia	16603	15215	18311	23033	24515
非洲	Africa	8258	8491	10372	11835	18431
其他	Others	14357	12784	15180	17018	11881

表 11－13　宁波市前十名出口企业(2012)
The Top 10 Enterprises For Export in Ningbo

序号 No	企业名称	Name of Corporation	所在区域	Location
1	宁波奇美电子有限公司	Ningbo Chi Mei Optoelectronics Co. ,Ltd.	保税区	Baoshui
2	宁波申洲针织有限公司	Ningbo Shenzhou Shitong Weaving Group Co. ,Ltd.	北仑区	Beilun
3	宁波市慈溪进出口股份有限公司	Ningbo Cixi Import & Export Co. ,Ltd.	慈溪市	Cixi
4	中基宁波集团股份有限公司	China－Base Ningbo Foreign Trade Co. ,Ltd.	鄞州区	Yinzhou
5	三星重工业(宁波)有限公司	SAMSUNG Heavy Industries(Ningbo) Co. ,Ltd.	北仑区	Beilun
6	浙江新景进出口有限公司	Zhejiang Xinjing Import & Export Co. ,Ltd.	江东区	Jiangdong
7	宁波中燃船舶燃料有限公司	Ningbo CHIMBUSCO Marine Bunker Co. ,Ltd.	镇海区	Zhenhai
8	宁波菱茂光电有限公司	Ningbo linmoug Optronics Co. ,Ltd.	北仑区	Beilun
9	中化宁波(集团)有限公司	Sinochem Ningbo Ltd.	海曙区	Haishu
10	宁波海田控股集团有限公司	Ningbo Haitian International Co. ,Ltd.	江东区	Jiangdong

表 11－14　宁波市前十名进口企业(2012)
The Top 10 Enterprises For Import in Ningbo

序号 No	企业名称	Name of Corporation	所在区域	Location
1	宁波奇美电子有限公司	Ningbo Chi Mei Optoelectronics Co. ,Ltd.	保税区	Baoshui
2	浙江逸盛石化有限公司	Zhejiang Yisheng Pertochemical Co. ,Ltd.	北仑区	Beilun
3	中基宁波集团股份有限公司	China－Base Ningbo Foreign Trade Co. ,Ltd.	鄞州区	Yinzhou
4	宁波萍钢贸易有限公司	Ningbo Pinggang Trade Co. ,Ltd.	北仑区	Beilun
5	宁波金田铜业(集团)股份有限公司	Ningbo Jintian Copper Group Co. ,Ltd.	江北区	Jiangbei
6	宁波钢铁有限公司	Ningbo Steel Company Limited	北仑区	Beilun
7	宁波神化化学品经营有限责任公司	Ningbo Sunhu Chem Products Co. ,Ltd.	江东区	Jiangdong
8	台化兴业(宁波)有限公司	Taiwan Industrial (Ningbo) Limited company	北仑区	Beilun
9	金光食品(宁波)有限公司	Jinguang Food(Ningbo) Co. ,Ltd.	北仑区	Beilun
10	中信金属宁波能源有限公司	CITIC Metal Ningbo Energy Co. ,Ltd.	北仑区	Beilun

主要统计指标解释

【进出口总额】 海关进出口总额是指实际进出我国国境的货物总金额。包括对外贸易实际进出口货物，来料加工装配进出口货物，国家间、联合国及国际组织无偿援助物资和赠送品，华侨、港澳台同胞和外籍华人捐赠品，租赁期满归承租人所有的租赁货物，进料加工进出口货物，边境地方贸易及边境地区小额贸易进出口货物(边民互市贸易除外)，中外合资经营企业、中外合作经营企业、外商独资经营企业进出口货物和公用物品，到、离岸价格在规定限额以上的进出口货样和广告品(无商业价值、无使用价值和免费提供出口的除外)，从保税仓库提取在中国境内销售的进口货物以及其他进出口货物。进出口总额用以观察一个国家在对外贸易方面的总规模。我国规定出口货物按离岸价格计算，进口货物按到岸价格计算。

【利用外资】 指我国各级政府、部门、企业和其他经济组织通过对外借款、吸收外商直接投资以及用其他方式筹措的境外现汇、设备、技术等。

【外商直接投资】 是指外国企业和经济组织或个人(包括华侨、港澳台胞以及 我国在境外注册的企业)按我国有关政策、法规，用现汇、实物、技术等在我国境内开办外 商独资企业、与我国境内的企业或经济组织共同举办中外合资经营企业、合作经营企业或作 合作开发资源的投资(包括外商投资收益的再投资)以及经政府有关部门批准的项目投资总 额内，企业从境外借入的资金。

【外商其他投资】 指除对外借款和外商直接投资以外的各种利用外资的形式。包括企业在境内外股票市场公开发行的以外币计价的股票(目前主要是在香港证券市场发行的 H 股和在境内证券市场发行的 B 股)发行价总额，国际租赁进口设备的应付款，补充贸易中外商提供的进口设备、技术、物料的价款，加工装配贸易中外商提供的进口设备、物料的价款。

【旅游人数】 包括入境国际旅游者人数、出境居民人数和国内旅游者人数。

⑴入境国际旅游者人数：指来中国参观、访问、旅行、探亲、访友、休养、考察、参加会议和从事经济、科技、文化、教育、宗教等活动的外国人、港澳和台湾同胞的人数。不包括外国在我国的常驻机构，如使领馆、通讯社、企业办事处的工作人员；来我国常住的外国专家、留学生以及在岸逗留不过夜人员。

⑵出境居民人数：指大陆居民因公务活动或私人事务短期出境的人数。公务活动出境居民人数包括在国际交通工具上的中国服务员工，因私出境居民人数不包括在国际交通工具上的中国服务员工。

⑶国内旅游者人数：指我国大陆居民和在我国常住 1 年以上的外国人、港澳台同胞离开常住地在境内其他地方的旅游设施内至少停留一夜，最长不超过 6 个月的人数。

【国际旅游(外汇)收入】 指入境旅游的外国人、华侨、港澳台同胞在中国大陆旅游过程中发生的一切旅游支出，对国家来说就是国际旅游(外汇)收入。

Explanatory Notes on Main Statistical Indicators

【Total Imports and Exports】 refer to the value of commodities imported into and exported from the boundary of China. They include the actual imports and exports through foreign trade, imported and exported goods under the processing and assembling trades and materials, supplies and gifts as aid given gratis between government and by the United Nations and other international organizations, and contributions denoted by overseas Chinese, compatriots in Hong Kong, Macao and Taiwan and Chinese with foreign citizenship, leasing commodities owned by tenants at the expiration of leasing period, the imported and exported commodities processed with imported materials, commodities trading, imported and exported small value trading goods in border areas (excluding mutual change goods), the imported and exported commodities and articles for public use of the Sino—foreign joint ventures, Sino—foreign cooperative enterprises and ventures exclusively with foreign own investment. They also included import and export of samples and advertising goods for those CIF or FOB value are beyond the permitted ceiling (excluding goods of no trading or no use value and free commodities for export), imported goods sold in China from bonded warehouse and other imported and exported goods. The indicator of total imports and exports at customs can be used to observe the total size of external trade in a country. In accordance with the stipulation of the Chinese government, imports are calculated at CIF, while exports are calculated at FOB.

FOB refer to Free on Board. CIF refer to Cost Insurance and Freight.

【Utilization of Foreign Capital】 refers to remittance, equipment and technology financed from abroad, by loans, foreign direct investment and other forms undertaken by the Chinese governments at all levels, by various departments, enterprises and other economic units.

【Direct Investment by Foreign Entrepreneurs】 refers to the investments inside China by foreign enterprises and economic organizations or individuals (including overseas Chinese, compatriots from Hong Kong and Macao, and Chinese enterprises registered abroad), following the relevant policies and laws of China, for the establishment of ventures exclusively with foreign own investment, Sino—foreign joint ventures and cooperative enterprises or for cooperative exploration of resources with enterprises or economic organizations in China. It includes the re—investment of the foreign entrepreneurs with the profits gained from the investment and the funds that enterprises borrow from abroad in the total investment of projects which are approved by the relevant department of the government.

【Other Overseas Investments】 refer to all kinds of investments except the foreign loan and the FDI. They include: the total value(in foreign currency) of the stocks of one enterprises distributed publicly both at home and abroad(now mainly refer to H. shares at HK bond market, and B. shares at China mainland bond market); the rent charges of the foreign equipments; the total value of Technology, raw material and foreign equipment provided by foreign investors in supplemental trades, and value of foreign raw material, equipment in the trade of assemble machining.

【tourists number】 is a sum of overseas tourists, local residents going abroad and domestic tourists.

overseas tourists number. Which refers to the number of foreigners and residents from Hongkong, Macao and Taiwan who come to China to go sightseeing, travel, visit relatives and friends, spend holidays, inspect, attend conferences and to do activities in economics, science, education, religious etc. Personnel as below are not taken into calculation, office workers in Chinese standing bodies at abroad, such as in embassies, news agencies, oversea offices of companies. Foreign experts and students living in China and foreigners who enter China only for voyage transferring are also not calculated.

number of local residents going abroad. Which refers to the number of mainland China residents who go abroad either for official business or for private affairs. Number of Chinese workers who serve in the international transportation vehicles are included in those who exit for official business, but not in those for private affairs.

domestic tourists. Which refers to the number of people who leave their living places to stay in the tourism facilities for at least one night but no more than 6 months, including mainland China residents, foreigners, residents from HK, Macao and TW who lived in China for more than one year.

【Foreign Exchange Earnings from International Tourism】 refer to the total expenditures of the foreigners, overseas Chinese, compatriots from HongKong, Macao and Taiwan in the process of their tourism in the mainland of China. Their expenditures mentioned above are foreign exchange earnings to China.

第十二篇

文化、教育、卫生、体育、科学技术

CULTURE,EDUCATION, PUBLIC HEALTH AND SPORTS,SCIENCE & TECHNOLOGY

文化、教育、卫生、体育、科学技术
Culture, Education, Public Health, Sports and Science & Technology

主要统计指标
Major Statistics Indicators

2012 年群艺馆、文化馆	Number of Mass Art Center and Cultural Center	12	个	unit
2012 年公共图书馆	Number of Public Libraries	12	个	unit
2012 年电影观众人次	Number of Spectator	860.7	万人次	10000 person－times
2012 年各类学校数	Number of Various School	2216	所	unit
2012 年各类学校招生人数	Number of New Students Enrollment of Various Schools	278379	人	person
2012 年各类学校在校学生数	Number of Students Enrollment of Various Schools	1437800	人	person
2012 年各类学校毕业人数	Number of Graduates by Various Schools	361832	人	person
2012 年专任教师数	Number of Full－time Teacher	76296	人	person
2012 年高等学校在校生人数	Number of Students Enrollmentin Institutions of Higher Education	145358	人	person
2012 年医疗机构床位数	Number of Beds in Health Institutions	28290	张	bed
2012 年卫生技术人员数	Number of Medical Technical Personnel	49188	人	person
2012 年医生数	Number of Doctors	19055	人	person
2012 年参赛获奖数	Number of Obtain Awards by Athletic Competition	593	枚	unit
2012 年有线电视用户数	Number of User Terminal for Cable TV Station	227.9	万户	10000 users

表 12－1 部分年份文化事业单位、机构、人员及活动情况
Basic Statistics on Cultural Institutions and Personnel in Partial Years

指标	单位	Indicators	Unit	2008	2009	2010	2011	2012
艺术表演团体	个	**Art Performance Troupes**	**unit**	**6**	**6**	**5**	**5**	**5**
机构人员数	人	Persons of Institutions	persons	403	408	410	518	518
国内演出场次	场次	Internal Performances	times	1214	1126	970	1200	1180
国内观众人次	千人	Internal Spectator	1000 persons times	3433	1217	1207	1111	1111
艺术表演场所	所	**Art Performance Places**	**unit**	**6**	**4**	**7**	**7**	**6**
机构人员数	人	Persons of Institutions	persons	91	42	82	78	77
演出场次	场次	Performances	times	1822	719	1430	1690	2300
观众人次	千人	Spectator	1000 persons times	408	188	316	312	689
公共图书馆	个	**Public Libraries**	**unit**	**12**	**12**	**13**	**13**	**12**
机构人员数	人	Persons of Institutions	persons	294	287	343	345	345
总藏量	万册	Total Collections	10000 volumes	610	633	734	733	733
古籍	千册	Ancient Books	1000 volumes	17	170	113	166	166
图书	万册	Books	10000 volumes	351	374	483	458	448
群艺馆、文化馆	个	**Mass Art Center and Cultural Center**	**unit**	**12**	**12**	**12**	**12**	**12**
机构人员数	人	Persons of Institutions	persons	262	293	318	311	311
文化站	个	**Cultural Center**	**unit**	**147**	**148**	**148**	**149**	**149**
机构人员数	人	Persons of Institutions	persons	331	425	447	449	449
文物单位		**Historical Relic Protection Units**						
文物保护管理机构	个	Historical Relic Protection Institutions	unit	13	13	13	13	13
国家级文保单位	个	Historical Relic Protection Units of State Level	unit	22	22	22	22	
博物馆、纪念馆	个	Museums, Memorial Hall	unit	15	7	7	7	6
文物商店	个	Historical Relic	unit	1	1	1	1	1
电影放映单位		**Film Projecting Units**						
放映管理机构	个	Projecting Management Institutions	unit	9	11	11	7	11
电影院	个	Movie House	unit	16	31	15	23	33
放映队	个	Projecting Teams	unit	176	73	167	120	117
电影放映场次	万场	Projecting Performance	10000 times	10.30	9.50	14.60	16.90	2.89
电影观众人次	万人次	Spectator	10000 persons times	1900.00	1634.20	1490.00	1112.97	860.70

注：本表至 12－4 表数据来自宁波市文化广电新闻出版局。
Note: Data from Tables 12－1 to 12－4 are obtained from Ningbo Bureau of Culture Radio & TV, Press and Publication.

表 12—2 各县(市)文化事业单位、机构、人员及活动情况(2012) Basic Statistics of Cultural Institutions and Personnel by Region

指标	单位	Indicators	Unit	全市 Total
艺术表演团体	**个**	**Art Performance Troupes**	**unit**	**5**
机构人员数	人	Persons of Institutions	persons	518
国内演出场次	场次	Internal Performances	times	1180
国内观众人次	千人	Internal Spectator	1000 persons times	1111
艺术表演场所	**所**	**Art Performance Places**	**unit**	**6**
机构人员数	人	Persons of Institutions	persons	77
演出场次	场次	Performances	times	2300
观众人次	千人	Spectator	1000 persons times	689
公共图书馆	**个**	**Public Libraries**	**unit**	**12**
机构人员数	人	Persons of Institutions	persons	345
总藏量	万册	Total Collections	10000 volumes	733
古籍	千册	Ancient Books	1000 volumes	166
图书	万册	Books	10000 volumes	448
群艺馆、文化馆	**个**	**Mass Art Center and Cultural Center**	**unit**	**12**
机构人员数	人	Persons of Institutions	persons	311
文化站	**个**	**Cultural Center**	**unit**	**149**
机构人员数	人	Persons of Institutions	persons	449
文物单位		**Historical Relic Protection Units**		
文物保护管理机构	个	Historical Relic Protection Institutions	unit	13
国家级文保单位	个	Historical Relic Protection Units of State Level	unit	
博物馆、纪念馆	个	Museums, Memorial Hall	unit	6
文物商店	个	Historical Relic	unit	1
电影放映单位		**Film Projecting Units**		
放映管理机构	个	Projecting Management Institutions	unit	11
电影院	个	Movie House	unit	33
放映队	个	Projecting Teams	unit	117
电影放映场次	万场	Projecting Performance	10000 times	2.89
电影观众人次	万人次	Spectator	10000 persons times	860.70

市区 Urban District	#鄞州 Yinzhou	余姚市 Yuyao	慈溪市 Cixi	奉化市 Fenghua	象山县 Xiangshan	宁海县 Ninghai
2	**1**	**1**				**1**
303	56	97				62
390	190	400				200
417	164	320				210
3					**1**	**1**
31					20	3
680					780	120
229					41	61
1	**1**	**1**	**1**	**1**	**1**	**1**
96	23	27	58	17	29	26
368	86	46	54	20	32	29
99	0	36	7	0	1	23
128	85	38	42	17	27	23
1	**1**	**1**	**1**	**1**	**1**	**1**
68	25	25	24	30	18	22
	23	**21**	**20**	**11**	**18**	**18**
	81	46	79	24	41	42
2	1	1	1	1	1	1
2		1	1			
1						
6	1	1	1	1	1	1
18	5	4	4	2	2	3
37	20	13	18	10	23	16
0.98	0.65	0.38	0.48	0.35	0.25	0.45
340.30	228.30	114.00	148.00	87.50	37.50	133.40

表 12－3 各县（市）广播电视基本情况（2012）
Basic Statisits on Broadcasting and Television by Region

指标	单位	Indicators	Unit	全市 Total
广播电视机构		**Broadcasting and Television Institutions**		
电台	座	Broadcasting Station	set	1
电视台	座	Broadcasting and Relaying Stations	set	10
广播电视站	个	TV and Transfer Stations	set	111
全年播出公共节目时间		**Full－year Broadcasting & TV Hours**		
广播播音时间	小时	Broadcasting Hours	hour	95936
＃制作节目播出时间	小时	Time of Self－Producting Programs	hour	76905
电视播出时间	小时	Hours Through TV Broadcasting	hour	91210
＃制作节目播出时间	小时	Time of Self－Producting Programs	hour	31949
公共电视套数	**套**	**TV Channel**	**set**	**14**
公共广播套数	**套**	**Public Broadcasting Band**	**set**	**14**
发送功率		**Transfer Power**		
中波功率	千瓦	Middle－Wave Power	kw	41
调频功率	千瓦	Frequency Modulation Power	kw	85.0
电视功率	千瓦	TV Power	kw	33.60
有线电视用户数	**万户**	**Number of User Terminal of Cable TV Station**	**10000 users**	**227.9**

表 12－4 部分年份广播电视基本情况
Basic Statisits on Broadcasting and Television in Partial Years

指标	单位	Indicators	Unit	2010	2011	2012
广播电视机构		**Broadcasting and Television Institutions**				
电台	座	Broadcasting Station	set	9	9	1
电视台	座	Broadcasting and Relaying Stations	set	9	9	10
广播电视站	个	TV and Transfer Stations	set	103	104	111
全年播出公共节目时间		**Full－year Broadcasting & TV Hours**				
广播播音时间	小时	Broadcasting Hours	hour	91827	91728	95936
＃制作节目播出时间	小时	Time of Self－Producting Programs	hour	74226	71645	76905
电视播出时间	小时	Hours Through TV Broadcasting	hour	87606	85973	91210
＃制作节目播出时间	小时	Time of Self－Producting Programs	hour	23587	21446	31949
公共电视套数	**套**	**TV Channel**	**set**	**13**	**13**	**14**
公共广播套数	**套**	**Public Broadcasting Band**	**set**	**13**	**13**	**14**
有线电视用户数	**万户**	**Number of User Terminal of Cable TV Station**	**10000 users**	**205.40**	**218.70**	**227.873**

市区 Urban District	#鄞州 Yinzhou	余姚 Yuyao	慈溪 Cixi	奉化 Fenghua	象山 Xiangshan	宁海 Ninghai
1						
5	1	1	1	1	1	1
43	20	19	19	9	13	8
62800	5859	8120	6387	6401	6205	6023
52260	4917	7149	4647	4302	3800	4747
56509	5121	5840	8760	6570	6961	6570
16749	1301	2000	5777	2600	1970	2853
9	**1**	**1**	**1**	**1**	**1**	**1**
9	**1**	**1**	**1**	**1**	**1**	**1**
41						
72.0	0.6	3.1	0.2	5.0	0.6	2.2
24.80	2.00	2.60	3.00	0.30	0.60	0.00
116.7	**44.5**	**27.6**	**33.8**	**15.1**	**15.0**	**19.7**

表 12－5 部分年份学生入、升学率 Percentage for Enrollment and Graduation of Students

单位：%

指标	Indicators	2008	2009	2010	2011	2012
小学学龄儿童入学率	Enrollment Rate for Children of School Age	100.00	100.00	100.00	100.00	100.00
小学毕业升学率	Graduation Rate for Pupils	100.00	100.00	100.00	100.00	100.00
初中毕业升学率	Graduation Rate for Students of Secondary School	98.66	98.70	98.97	99.09	99.09
升入普通高中	Rate of Enrolling Senior School	49.13	49.34	49.49	49.88	50.13
升入职业高中	Rate of Enrolling Vacational Senior School	38.03	49.36	49.49	49.21	48.96
升入中专技校	Rate of Entrolling Technical Secondary School	6.50				
高等教育毛入学率	Gross Enrollment Rate of Higher Education	48.00	49.00	50.00	55.00	

表 12－6　各县(市)各类学校数(2012)
Number of Various Schools by Region

项目	Item	全市 Total	市区 Urban District
各类学校数	**Number of Various School**		
(一)全日制学校	**Number of Full－time School**	**2062**	**843**
高等学校	Regular Institutions of Higher Education	14	9
#大专	Junior Colleges	7	4
初中	Regular Secondary Schools	219	85
高中	Senior Secondary Schools	80	38
职业中学	Vocational Secondary Schools	55	21
普通小学	Primary Schools	476	194
特殊教育学校	Special Education Schools	10	5
幼儿园	Kindergarten	1208	491
(二)成人学校数	**Number of School for Adult Education**	**154**	**34**
成人高校数	Number of Higher Education for Adult	2	2
成人中学	Secondary Education for Adult	152	32

注：本表至12－8表数据来自宁波市教育局。高等学校中包省属学校。

Note：Data from Tables 12－6 to 12－8 are obtained from Ningbo Municipal Bureau of Education. Regular institutions of higher education including the provincial school.

单位:所(unit)

#鄞州 Yinzhou	余姚市 Yuyao	慈溪市 Cixi	奉化市 Fenghua	象山县 Xiangshan	宁海县 Ninghai
318	**304**	**401**	**150**	**153**	**206**
29	43	35	17	21	18
13	10	14	5	6	7
8	9	7	5	7	6
87	82	88	29	29	54
1	1	1	1	1	1
180	159	256	93	89	120
22	**19**	**20**	**22**	**2**	**57**
22	19	20	22	2	57

表 12—7　各县(市)各类学校学生情况(2012)
Basic Statistics on Student of Various Schools by Region

项目	Item	全市 Total	市区 Urban District
各类学校招生人数	**New Students Enrollment of Various Schools**	**278379**	**140671**
研究生	Postgraduates	1287	1258
普通高校	Institutions of Higher Education	44001	31391
#大专	Junior Colleges	19197	13498
初中	Regular Secondary Schools	67233	29272
高中	Senior Secondary Schools	31427	13322
职业中学	Secondary Vacational Schools	25569	10886
普通小学	Primary Schools	85933	37379
特殊教育学校	Special Education Schools	93	50
成人高校	Higher Education for Adult	22836	17113
各类学校在校学生数	**Students Enrollment of Various Schools**	**1437800**	**646007**
研究生	Postgraduates	3428	3399
普通高校	Institutions of Higher Education	145358	103730
#大专	Junior Colleges	55068	39268
初中	Regular Secondary Schools	193919	85082
高中	Senior Secondary Schools	101284	41768
职业中学	Secondary Vacational Schools	80294	34846
普通小学	Primary Schools	478816	207655
特殊教育学校	Special Education Schools	853	462
成人高校	Higher Education for Adult	51606	38931
成人中学	Secondary Education for Adult	106518	2590
幼儿院在院人数	Persons of Kindergarten	275724	127544
各类学校毕业人数	**Graduates by Various Schools**	**361832**	**128661**
研究生	Postgraduates	925	925
普通高校	Institutions of Higher Education	38226	26561
#大专	Junior Colleges	19143	13603
初中	Regular Secondary Schools	62979	26116
高中	Senior Secondary Schools	36259	15093
职业中学	Secondary Vacational Schools	26908	11706
普通小学	Primary Schools	73173	30583
特殊教育学校	Special Education Schools	95	37
成人高校	Higher Education for Adult	19583	15265
成人中学	Secondary Education for Adult	103684	2375

单位：人(person)

#鄞州 Yinzhou	余姚市 Yuyao	慈溪市 Cixi	奉化市 Fenghua	象山县 Xiangshan	宁海县 Ninghai
34685	**29752**	**37981**	**15239**	**15793**	**20581**
10624	9726	11207	4872	5316	6840
4415	4314	6369	2293	2344	2785
4568	3456	4368	2273	1824	2762
15067	12245	16019	5795	6307	8188
11	11	18	6	2	6
191864	**154561**	**299422**	**80191**	**90523**	**112764**
30764	28523	32503	14523	14776	18512
14317	13908	21048	7489	7628	9443
14336	10717	14195	6744	5994	7798
80627	67648	90003	32884	34214	46412
140	109	134	29	65	54
1668	1585	90735	1632	6046	3930
50012	32071	50804	16890	21800	26615
32017	**31169**	**125613**	**16923**	**21318**	**22165**
9143	9583	11692	5055	4877	5656
5338	5224	7209	2621	2502	3610
5074	4008	4256	2304	2174	2460
10834	10898	13288	5295	5755	7354
8	32	18	8		
1620	1424	89150	1640	6010	3085

表 12－8　各县(市)各类学校教职工情况(2012)
Basic Statistics on Teachers and Staff of Various Schools by Region

项目	Item	全市 Total	市区 Urban District
各类学校教职工人数	**Number of Teachers and Staff of Various Schools**	**99531**	**52157**
高等学校	Regular Institutions of Higher Education	11090	11090
＃大专	Junior Colleges	3481	1901
普通中学	Regular Secondary Schools	25428	11452
职业中学	Secondary Vacational Schools	6334	2684
普通小学	Primary Schools	25354	11103
特殊教育学校	Special Education Schools	265	150
成人高校	Higher Education for Adult	637	637
成人中学	Secondary Education for Adult	838	252
幼儿园	Kindergarten	29585	14789
各类学校专任教师人数	**Number of Full－time Teachers of Various Schools**	**76296**	**36330**
普通高校	Institutions of Higher Education	7374	5074
＃大专	Junior Colleges	2320	1306
初中	Regular Secondary Schools	14784	6421
高中	Senior Secondary Schools	8237	3683
职业中学	Secondary Vacational Schools	5519	2295
普通小学	Primary Schools	23139	10364
特殊教育学校	Special Education Schools	223	127
成人高校	Higher Education for Adult	455	455
＃电大	Radio and TV Universities	341	341
成人中学	Secondary Education for Adult	621	162
幼儿园	Kindergarten	15944	7749
各类学校兼任教师人数	**Number of Part－time Teachers of Various Schools**	**2572**	**1023**
普通中学	Regular Secondary Schools	129	112
职业中学	Secondary Vacational Schools	486	272
普通小学	Primary Schools	20	20
成人高校	Higher Education for Adult	478	478
成人中学	Secondary Education for Adult	1459	141

单位：人(person)

#鄞州 Yinzhou	余姚市 Yuyao	慈溪市 Cixi	奉化市 Fenghua	象山县 Xiangshan	宁海县 Ninghai
14144	**12091**	**16153**	**5421**	**7057**	**7490**
3340	4047	4624	1789	2325	2029
1129	831	1281	479	547	512
3977	3897	4686	1608	1887	2173
31	31	34	12	14	24
197	158	192	136	21	79
5470	3127	5336	1397	2263	2673
11139	**8718**	**12890**	**4640**	**5359**	**6059**
2053	2030	2796	1107	1215	1215
1245	1007	1559	601	651	736
1019	742	1129	417	468	468
3670	3037	4396	1571	1714	2057
30	27	28	12	13	16
116	96	155	118	14	76
3006	1779	2827	814	1284	1491
193	**118**	**1002**	**170**	**63**	**196**
98	10			7	
12	46	72	18	32	46
20					
63	62	930	152	24	150

表12—9 历年教职工数和在校学生数 Number of Teachers and Staff and Students Enrollment Over the Years

单位:万人(10000 persons)

年份 Year	在校教职工 Teachers and Staff	#教师 Teachers	在校学生 Students Enrollment 大学生 Higher Education	中学生 Secondary Schools	小学生 Primary Schools
1978	4.15	3.55	0.10	27.16	59.11
1979	4.01	3.53	0.21	23.04	57.85
1980	4.28	3.48	0.25	20.99	56.39
1981	4.13	3.23	0.20	19.36	52.02
1982	3.31	2.75	0.15	18.77	46.67
1983	3.72	3.06	0.16	19.48	41.71
1984	3.73	3.00	0.21	21.42	38.50
1985	3.94	3.16	0.27	23.47	36.43
1986	4.09	3.28	0.34	24.35	36.90
1987	4.21	3.34	0.39	23.48	36.41
1988	4.32	3.47	0.45	20.34	38.69
1989	4.45	3.56	0.49	18.75	41.84
1990	4.24	3.34	0.49	19.65	42.70
1991	4.34	3.39	0.48	22.01	41.62
1992	4.37	3.47	0.53	24.39	40.16
1993	4.59	3.61	0.66	25.03	40.40
1994	4.75	3.76	0.83	26.76	41.92
1995	5.00	4.01	0.98	28.93	41.29
1996	5.12	4.17	1.04	30.07	41.80
1997	5.27	4.32	1.15	29.93	43.14
1998	5.44	4.40	1.25	29.00	43.91
1999	6.16	4.81	1.68	25.12	43.36
2000	6.59	5.17	2.59	27.98	42.40
2001	6.86	5.12	4.34	29.60	42.24
2002	7.05	5.27	6.21	30.86	44.55
2003	7.46	5.61	7.99	30.99	45.26
2004	7.85	5.92	9.60	32.09	47.61
2005	8.59	6.46	11.12	40.25	47.60
2006	8.68	6.55	12.13	40.95	47.38
2007	9.09	6.84	12.76	41.12	47.15
2008	9.27	7.04	13.04	41.70	46.80
2009	9.13	7.42	13.75	41.42	45.03
2010	9.61	7.29	14.08	40.61	46.19
2011	9.82	7.70	14.14	39.13	47.61
2012	9.95	7.63	14.54	37.55	47.88

注:在校教职工包括幼儿园。

Note: The number of teachers and staff include kinder—gardens

表 12-10 部分年份教育事业基本情况
Basic Statistics on Education in Partial Years

单位：人(person)

指标	Indicators	2007	2008	2009	2010	2011	2012
学校数(所)	**Number of Schools(unit)**						
高等学校	Institutions of Higher Education	15	15	15	14	14	14
中等专业学校	Specialized Secondary Schools	9	8				
普通中学	Regular Secondary Schools	317	310	306	301	299	299
职业中学	Vocational Secondary Schools	38	38	57	56	57	55
小学	Primary Schools	621	564	536	513	490	476
专任教师	**Number of Full-time Teachers**						
高等学校	Institutions of Higher Education	6634	6829	6933	7146	9086	7374
中等专业学校	Specialized Secondary Schools	1074	1022				
普通中学	Regular Secondary Schools	21497	22345	22718	22961	22897	23021
职业中学	Vocational Secondary Schools	2791	3146	4734	4955	5283	5519
小学	Primary Schools	20556	20864	21184	21577	22265	23139
招生数	**New Student Enrollment**						
高等学校	Institutions of Higher Education	40508	43574	42644	42806	43735	44001
中等专业学校	Specialized Secondary Schools	1919	2135				
普通中学	Regular Secondary Schools	113928	116235	110570	107982	99456	98660
职业中学	Vocational Secondary Schools	25683	25039	30058	27781	28469	25569
小学	Primary Schools	74348	79383	74952	84725	87239	85933
在校学生数	**Student Enrollment**						
高等学校	Institutions of Higher Education	127596	130440	137495	140818	144424	145358
中等专业学校	Specialized Secondary Schools	7557	6324				
普通中学	Regular Secondary Schools	335436	343449	332945	325407	308563	295203
职业中学	Vocational Secondary Schools	75747	73530	81293	80724	82783	80294
小学	Primary Schools	471510	467988	450322	461931	476085	478816
毕业生数	**Number of Graduates**						
高等学校	Institutions of Higher Education	32976	36268	37118	37733	38022	38226
中等专业学校	Specialized Secondary Schools	4040	3177				
普通中学	Regular Secondary Schools	103260	101063	110130	105199	104584	99238
职业中学	Vocational Secondary Schools	24163	25865	26406	24835	24270	26908
小学	Primary Schools	83227	87163	79440	76536	69412	73173

表12－11 部分年份平均每一专任教师负担的学生数 The Ratio of Student Enrollment and Full－time Teachers in Partial Years

单位：人(person)

年份 Year	高等学校 Institutions of Higher Education	中等专业学校 Specialized Scendary Schools	普通中学 Regular Secondary Schools	职业中学 Vocational Secondary Schools	小学 Primary Schools
1994	8.9	15.9	19.9	16.1	25.7
1995	9.1	18.0	20.0	16.2	24.6
1996	9.7	23.5	19.7	14.6	24.2
1997	10.7	21.7	18.3	16.6	24.2
1998	11.3	22.4	17.4	17.2	24.7
1999	12.8	22.3	16.9	16.6	24.5
2000	11.3	24.1	17.7	16.2	23.9
2001	15.7	30.5	17.8	16.5	23.7
2002	17.6	26.1	17.8	17.5	24.4
2003	18.9	24.1	17.0	27.9	24.5
2004	17.0	20.4	16.6	26.5	24.7
2005	18.5	15.9	16.0	29.6	23.9
2006	18.7	9.4	16.0	28.0	23.5
2007	19.2	7.0	15.6	27.1	22.9
2008	19.1	6.2	15.4	23.4	22.4
2009	19.8		14.7	17.2	21.3
2010	19.7		14.2	16.3	21.4
2011	15.6		13.5	15.7	21.4
2012	19.7		12.8	14.6	20.7

表12－12 部分年份平均每万人口在校学生数 Student Enrollment Per 10000 Populations in Partial Years

单位：人(person)

年份 Year	大学生 University and College Students	中专学生 Specialized Scendary Schools Students	中学学生 Regular Secondary Schools Students	职业中学生 Vocational Secondary Schools Students	小学生 Primary Schools Schools
1994	15.8	30.5	458.0	53.4	801.1
1995	18.5	37.3	488.8	60.5	784.2
1996	19.7	47.5	511.7	57.6	791.4
1997	21.7	43.7	493.1	69.8	811.4
1998	23.3	47.7	463.0	79.7	821.9
1999	31.3	50.8	467.9	82.2	807.6
2000	48.0	46.5	518.4	81.6	785.6
2001	80.1	41.8	545.9	83.3	779.1
2002	113.9	35.3	566.5	93.5	817.8
2003	145.9	34.4	565.8	119.0	826.4
2004	174.3	32.3	582.5	134.6	864.2
2005	199.3	26.1	582.3	143.4	858.2
2006	215.2	17.8	595.6	137.6	848.1
2007	226.0	13.4	594.2	134.2	835.2
2008	229.6	11.1	604.6	129.4	823.8
2009	240.8		583.1	142.4	788.6
2010	245.3		566.8	140.6	804.6
2011	245.7		536.4	143.9	827.6
2012	251.9		650.7	139.1	829.8

表 12－13　历年卫生事业主要指标
Basic Statistics on Health Care Over the Years

年份 Year	卫生机构数（个） Number of Health Institutions (unit)	#医院 Hospitals	卫生机构床位（张） Number of Beds in Health Institutions (bed)	#医院 Hospitals	卫生技术人员（万人） Number of Medical technical (10000 persons)	#医生 Doctors
1978	949	400	5989	5549	0.93	0.36
1979	1013	398	6618	5871	0.99	0.36
1980	1032	397	6948	6368	1.06	0.38
1981	1077	394	7537	7015	1.13	0.44
1982	1100	400	8130	7230	1.19	0.48
1983	1107	396	8372	7525	1.24	0.50
1984	1117	396	8823	7954	1.28	0.53
1985	1123	311	9067	8250	1.30	0.54
1986	1181	320	9436	8605	1.34	0.56
1987	1199	327	9922	9057	1.41	0.60
1988	1259	330	10447	9629	1.46	0.73
1989	1293	331	11073	10067	1.53	0.74
1990	1301	344	11449	10522	1.58	0.75
1991	1313	345	11731	10816	1.66	0.76
1992	1270	303	12175	11259	1.69	0.78
1993	1262	300	12529	11633	1.70	0.80
1994	1257	345	12976	12090	1.76	0.84
1995	1257	345	13193	12316	1.74	0.87
1996	1123	297	13012	12299	1.78	0.88
1997	1678	296	13654	8849	1.83	0.92
1998	1407	296	13689	9481	1.86	0.91
1999	961	54	13795	9364	1.89	0.93
2000	929	56	14535	9968	1.92	0.95
2001	921	57	14393	10246	1.96	0.97
2002	1263	58	14653	10292	2.01	0.99
2003	1297	55	15279	10654	2.15	1.06
2004	1555	58	17053	12119	2.51	1.14
2005	1667	265	18458	17856	2.91	1.32
2006	1854	268	19711	19339	3.25	1.46
2007	2270	255	21000	20306	3.53	1.54
2008	2276	257	22155	21523	3.69	1.51
2009	2359	243	23475	22299	4.00	1.62
2010	2377	230	26097	24762	4.31	1.72
2011	4221	106	27127	23046	4.67	1.84
2012	4035	108	28290	24296	4.92	1.91

表 12－14 各县(市)卫生事业单位机构情况(2012)
Basic Statistics on Health Care Institutions by Region

指标	Indicators	全市 Total
卫生事业机构数	**Number of Health Care Intitiutions**	**4035**
1.医院合计	Total Hospitals	108
综合医院	Comprehensive Hospitals	57
中医医院	Hospitals of Chinese Medicine	11
中西医结合医院	Combined Chinese and Western Medicine Hospital	2
专科医院	Specialized Hospitals	38
口腔医院	Oral and Dental Hospitals	4
眼科医院	Ophthalmology Hospitals	3
妇产(科)医院	Obstetrics and Gynecology Hospitals	4
精神病医院	Mental Hospitals	1
传染病医院	Infectious Disease Hospitals	6
皮肤病医院	Dermatology Hospital	1
骨科医院	Orthopedist Hospitals	4
康复医院	Healing Hospitals	3
其他专科医院	Others Specialized Hospitals	12
2.社区卫生服务中心(站)	Community Sanitation Service Sites	847
社区卫生服务中心	Community Health Center	73
社区卫生服务站	Community Health Service Station	774
3.卫生院	Local Hospitals	96
乡镇卫生院	Town and Township Local Hospitals	96
中心卫生院	Center Locale Hospitals	30
乡卫生院	Towhship Locale Hospitals	66
4.村卫生室	Village Health Room	1871
5.门诊部合计	Clinics	105
6.诊所、卫生所、医务室	Special Clinics	945
7.急救中心(站)	First－aid Centre(Stations)	5
8.采供血机构	Blood Collecting and Supplying Organization	1
9.妇幼保健院(所、站)	Maternity and Child Care Centers or Stations	11
10.专科疾病防治院(所、站)	Specialized Prevention and Treatment Centers or Stations	4
11.疾病预防控制中心	Center for Disease Control and Prevention	12
12.卫生监督所(中心)	Health Supervision Centers(Center)	12
13.医学科学研究机构	Research Institution of Medicine	3
14.医学在职培训机构	Medical Institution of On－the－job Training	5
15.其他卫生机构	Others Health Care Institutions	10

注:本表至 12－17 表数据来之宁波市卫生局。

Note:Data from Tables 12－14 to 12－17 are obtained from Ningbo Municipal Bureau of Health.

单位：个(unit)

市区 Urban District	#鄞州 Yinzhou	余姚 Yuyao	慈溪 Cixi	奉化 Fenghua	象山 Xiangshan	宁海 Ninghai
1624	**594**	**531**	**704**	**468**	**253**	**455**
66	11	7	16	8	6	5
32	6	5	11	4	3	2
5		1	1	1	2	1
2	1					
27	4	1	4	3	1	2
4	1					
2			1			
2			2			
1						
2		1	1	1	1	
1						
1				1		2
2	1			1		
12	2					
324	72	101	355	38		29
43	7	6	22	1		1
281	65	95	333	37		28
18	18	15		22	17	24
18	18	15		22	17	24
7	7	6		4	7	6
11	11	9		18	10	18
616	335	265	233	289	189	279
68	10	8	27		1	1
496	141	130	66	107	35	111
2	1	1	1			1
1						
6	1	1	1	1	1	1
3	2		1			
7	1	1	1	1	1	1
7	1	1	1	1	1	1
3						
1		1	1		1	1
6	1		1	1	1	1

表 12－15 各县(市)卫生事业人员、床位情况(2012)
Number of Health Care Personnel and Beds by Region

指标	Indicators	全市 Total
从业人员总计(人)	**Total Employment(person)**	**58863**
卫生技术人员	Medical Technical Personnel	49188
医生数	Number of Doctors	19055
执业医师	Medical Practitioner	16328
执业助理医师	Assistant Medical Practitioner	2727
注册护士	Register Nurse	18280
药师(士)	Pharmacists	3240
技师(士)	Laboratory Technicians	2604
检验师	Laboratory Examiner	1992
其他	Others	6009
见习医师	Trainee Doctors	2305
其他技术人员	Other Technical Personnel	1814
管理人员	Manager	2049
工勤技能人员	Logistics Workers	4330
每千人拥有卫生技术人员	Number of Medical Technical Personnel Per 1000 Persons	8.51
每千人拥有医生	Number of Doctors Per 1000 Persons	3.30
每千人拥有注册护士	Number of R. N. Per 1000 Persons	3.16
卫生事业床位数(张)	**Number of Beds (bed)**	**28290**
医院床位	Beds of Hospitals	24296
社区卫生服务中心床位	Beds of Health Service Center of Communities	1360
卫生院床位	Beds of Local Hospitals	2015
妇幼保健院(所、站)床位	Beds of Maternity and Child Care Centers	529
专科疾病防治院(所、站)床位	Beds of Specialized Prevention Stations	50
每千人拥有总床位	Total Beds of Per 1000 Persons	4.90
每千人拥有医院卫生院床位	Beds of Hospitals and Local Hospitals Per 1000 Persons	4.79

市区 Urban District	#鄞州 Yinzhou	余姚 Yuyao	慈溪 Cixi	奉化 Fenghua	象山 Xiangshan	宁海 Ninghai
33138	**8180**	**5991**	**8710**	**3452**	**3198**	**4374**
27828	6832	4945	7390	2722	2708	3595
10644	2711	1923	2872	1166	1103	1347
9536	2271	1600	2219	990	907	1076
1108	440	323	653	176	196	271
10599	2363	1941	2581	968	1022	1169
1800	490	344	483	187	199	227
1544	376	224	403	115	141	177
1177	304	179	297	91	115	133
3241	892	513	1051	286	243	675
1067	322	249	392	165	130	302
929	228	146	333	180	75	151
1464	275	126	245	68	61	85
2529	739	448	608	234	170	341
12.31	8.22	5.93	7.09	5.63	5.01	5.84
4.71	3.26	2.30	2.76	2.41	2.04	2.19
4.69	2.84	2.33	2.48	2.00	1.89	1.90
16802	**3422**	**2568**	**3419**	**2156**	**1524**	**1821**
15564	2734	2153	2483	1970	1246	880
631	98	60	669			
570	570	355		136	258	696
17			217	50		245
			50			
7.43	4.12	3.08	3.28	4.46	2.82	2.96
7.41	4.09	3.08	3.03	4.36	2.78	2.56

表 12－16 各级医院工作情况(2012)
Medical Treatment of Various Hospitals

指标	Indicators	门诊人次合计(万人次) Out－Patients (10000 person－times)
全市总计	**Total**	**7888**
1. 医院合计	Total Hospitals	3485
综合医院	Comprehensive Hospitals	2453
省辖市属医院	Urban Hospitals Administered by Province	563
#市第一医院	The No. 1 Hospital of Ningbo	178
市第二医院	The No. 2 Hospital of Ningbo	138
市第三医院	The No. 3 Hospital of Ningbo	103
市李惠利医院	Li Huili Hospital of Ningbo	127
市华慈医院	Hua Ci Hospital of Ningbo	17
中医医院	Hospitals of Chinese Medicine	549
#市中医院	Hospital of Chinese Medicine of Ningbo	102
中西医结合医院	Combined Chinese and Western Medicine Hospital	19
专科医院	Specialized Hospitals	464
口腔医院	Oral and Dental Hospitals	33
眼科医院	Ophthalmology Hospitals	46
妇产(科)医院	Obstetrics and Gynecology Hospitals	184
#市妇儿医院	Hospital for Maternity and Child of Ningbo	179
精神病医院	Mental Hospitals	73
#市康宁医院	Kangning Hospital of Ningbo	14
骨科医院	Orthopedist Hospitals	82
2. 社区卫生服务中心	Health Service Center of Communities	1883
3. 卫生院	Local Hospitals	1455
4. 门诊部	Policlinic	427
5. 村卫生室	Village Health Room	126
6. 诊所、卫生所、医务室	Clinic	310
7. 妇幼保健院(所、站)	Maternity and Child Care Centers or Stations	171
8. 专科疾病防治院(所、站)	Specialized Prevention and Treatment Centers or Stations	26

本年入院人数 (万人) Inpatients in this Year (10000 persons)	平均住院日 (天) Average Day In－patients (day)	本年出院人数 (万人) Discharged Patient in this Year (10000 persons)	期末实有病床数 (张) Factual Beds at the Year－end (bed)	平均开放病床数 (张) Average Openning Bed (bed)	病床使用率 (%) Occupancy of Hospital Beds (%)
82.7	**10.7**	**82.60**	**28290**	**27715**	**86.00**
75.4	10.9	75.20	24296	23856	92.00
58.9	9.9	58.80	17493	17134	92.90
18.5	10.4	18.50	5353	5336	99.10
4.8	11.0	4.80	1497	1480	98.10
5.5	11.1	5.50	1761	1761	95.10
3.2	9.8	3.20	835	835	103.90
5.0	9.6	5.00	1260	1260	102.70
5.7	12.0	5.60	2134	2103	88.30
1.3	16.0	1.30	600	600	97.40
0.2	9.2	0.20	120	120	32.30
10.7	15.7	10.70	4549	4499	91.80
			15	15	
0.7	6.4	0.70	192	192	70.40
4.6	8.1	4.60	1012	1012	99.90
4.6	8.0	4.60	952	952	105.10
0.8	98.6	0.80	1622	1574	98.00
0.3	55.8	0.30	520	520	102.60
3.5	10.7	3.50	1010	1010	103.00
1.8	13.1	1.80	1360	1279	51.80
2.9	9.7	2.90	2015	2004	39.10
			40		
2.6	6.1	2.60	529	526	80.30
			50	50	

表12－17 居民病伤死亡原因(2012) Main 10 Diseases of Death in Urban Residents

指标	Indicators	死亡人数(人) 合计 Total
宁波市总计	**Total in Ningbo**	**37163**
十种死因合计	Main 10 Causes of Death	34849
1.恶性肿瘤	Malignant Tumour	11805
2.脑血管病	Cerebral Vascular Disease	6548
3.呼吸系病	Respiratory Disease	6400
4.心脏病	Cardiopathy	3408
5.损伤和中毒	Trauma and Toxicosis	3375
6.消化系统疾病	Digestive Disease	952
7.内分泌等疾病	Internal System Disease	877
8.神经系统疾病	Nervous system diseases	607
9.传染病(不包括呼吸道结核)	Infectious Disease(Respiratory Tuberculosis not Included)	465
10.精神障碍	Mental Disorder	412
市区总计	**Total in Urban Destricts**	**13398**
十种死因合计	Main 10 Causes of Death	12614
1.恶性肿瘤	Malignant Tumour	4448
2.脑血管病	Cerebral Vascular Disease	2368
3.呼吸系病	Respiratory Disease	2091
4.心脏病	Heart Disease	1190
5.损伤和中毒	Injury and Poisoning	1136
6.内分泌等疾病	Internal System Disease	455
7.消化系统疾病	Digestive Disease	346
8.神经系统疾病	Nervous system diseases	210
9.泌尿系疾病	Urologic Diseases	196
10.传染病(不包括呼吸道结核)	Infectious Disease(Respiratory Tuberculosis not Included)	174

Number of Death (person)		死因构成 (%) Composition of Death(%)	死亡专率(/10 万) Death Rate (per 0.1 million persons)		
男 Male	女 Female		合计 Total	男 Male	女 Female
20712	**16451**	**100.00**	**644.01**	**718.92**	**569.32**
19654	15195	93.77	603.91	682.20	525.85
7829	3976	31.77	204.57	271.75	137.60
3372	3176	17.62	113.47	117.04	109.91
3287	3113	17.22	110.91	114.09	107.73
1760	1648	9.17	59.06	61.09	57.03
1795	1580	9.08	58.49	62.30	54.68
527	425	2.56	16.50	18.29	14.71
367	510	2.36	15.20	12.74	17.65
282	325	1.63	10.52	9.79	11.25
268	197	1.25	8.06	9.30	6.82
167	245	1.11	7.14	5.80	8.48
7405	**5993**	**100.00**	**594.34**	**664.52**	**525.74**
7069	5545	94.15	559.57	634.37	486.44
2945	1503	33.20	197.32	264.28	131.85
1209	1159	17.67	105.05	108.49	101.67
1060	1031	15.61	92.76	95.12	90.45
625	565	8.88	52.79	56.09	49.57
555	581	8.48	50.39	49.81	50.97
193	262	3.40	20.18	17.32	22.98
183	163	2.58	15.35	16.42	14.30
94	116	1.57	9.32	8.44	10.18
106	90	1.46	8.69	9.51	7.90
99	75	1.30	7.72	8.88	6.58

表 12—18 部分年份全市体育工作情况
Basic Statistics on Physical Culture Schools and Sports in Partial Years

指标	单位	Indicators	Uuit	2009	2010	2011	2012
各类体校情况		**Various Physical Culture and Sports School**					
体育运动学校数	个	Physical Education and Sports School	unit	1	1	1	1
在校学生数	人	Student Enrollment	person	712	770	720	810
专职教练员	人	Full—time Coaches	person	42	45	60	47
业余体校个数	个	Sparetime Sports Schools	unit	5	5	5	5
#重点业余体校	个	Emphatic Sparetime Sports School	unit	5	5	5	5
业余体校在校学生数	人	Student Enrollment in Sparetime Sports Schools	person	832	830	840	910
业余体校送入优秀运动队	人	Number of Persons from Sparetime Sports School Enrolling Excelent Sports Team	person	36	88	36	39
业余体校考入高等院校	人	Number of Persons Admitted to Institutions Higher Education from Sparetime Sports School	person	42	40	50	50
传统项目布局情况		**Distribution on Traditional Events**					
分布学校数	个	Number of Distributing Schools	unit	128	108	131	136
#中学	个	Secondary Schools	unit	40	20	37	21
小学	个	Primary Schools	unit	88	88	94	125
市区新增健身设施	套	New built Health—care Facilities in Urban Districts	set	229	202		
传统项目活动情况		Statistics on Traditional Events					
参加活动学生人数	人	Number of Participants in Student	person	12800	8600	19200	9620
参加田径学生	人	Track and Field	person	6200	4100	8000	4500
参加游泳学生	人	Swimming	person	800	1000	2000	1100
参加射击学生	人	Shoot	person	120	200	1000	220
参加蓝球学生	人	Basketball	person	600	500	2000	600
参加排球学生	人	Volleyball	person	300	300	1600	400
参加足球学生	人	Football	person	2000	500	1600	1200
参加乒乓排球学生	人	Pingpong	person	1000	1000	2000	800
参加羽毛球学生	人	Badminton	person	980	1000	1000	800
游泳池情况(体育系统)		**Swimming Pool Managed by Physical Department**					
游泳池个数	个	Number of Swimming Pools	unit	11	5	11	6
#室内游泳池	个	Indoor	unit	10	4	10	4
游泳池活动场次	场次	Number of Running Swimming Pool	times	11000	10020	13000	11000
#室内游泳池	场次	Indoor	times	9800	9500	10500	9500
参赛获奖数	**枚**	**Number of Obtain Awards by Athletic Competition**	**unit**	**935**	**651**	**963**	**593**
#省级及以上金牌	枚	Gold Medals Won in Province Level Competitions	unit	374	230	383	173
#省级及以上银牌	枚	Silver Medals Won in Province Level Competitions	unit	308.0	180.5	315	180
#省级及以上铜牌	枚	Bronze Medals Won in Province Level Competitions	unit	253.0	240.5	265	240

表 12—19 部分年份科协系统活动情况
Basic Statistics on Science and Technology Associations in Partial Years

指标	Indicators	2010	2011	2012
基本情况	**Basic Situation**			
科协机构数(个)	Insitutions of Science and Technology(unit)	89	90	91
科学家与工程师(人)	Scientist and Engineer (person)			
活动情况	**Activity Situation**			
学术交流会参加人数(人)	Participants of Academic Seminar(person)			
#论文数(篇)	Papers Presented (paper)			
科普讲座次数(次)	Number of S&T Popularization Lectures (times)	1918	1317	5252
科普讲座参加人数(人)	Participants of S&T Popularization Lectures(person)			
科普展览次数(次)	Number of S&T① Popularization Exhibitions (times)	406	437	548
科普展览参观人数(人)	Participants of S&T Popularization Exhibitions(person)			
科技培训班参加人数(人)	Particapants of Scinece—technology Training(person)			
科技咨询服务完成合同数(个)	Science—technology Consultative Contracts Completed (kind)	457	439	730
#实现金额 (万元)	Revenue for Fulfillment of Contract (10000 yuan)			

注:本表和 12—21 表数据来自宁波市科协。

Note:a)Data in Tables 12—19 and 12—21 are obtained from Ningbo Associations for Science and Technology.

①S&T is a short form that means Scientific and Technological. The other table are the same.

表 12—20 部分年份市级以上科技成果鉴定、获奖、专利授权情况
Basic Statistics on Verification, Award—Winning and Patent Right of Above Municipal Level in Partial Years

单位:个(unit)

指标	Indicators	2008	2009	2010	2011	2012
科技成果登记	Scientific and Technological Enrollment of Results				428	457
科学技术奖	Scientific and Technological Awards	103	104	120	106	107
国家级	State Leve	1	6	4	1	1
省级	Province Level	26	22	24	26	26
市级	Municipal Level	76	76	92	79	80
授权专利数	Number of Patent Applications Approved	9882	15824	25971	37342	59175
#发明	Inventions	505	802	1209	1625	2065
实用新型	Utility Models	4525	5943	11230	12966	21407
外观设计	Designs	4852	9078	13532	22751	35703

注:本表和 12—22 表数据来自宁波市科技局。

Note:Data in Tables 12—20 and 12—22 are obtained from Ningbo Municipal Bureau of Science and Technology.

表 12－21　科协系统情况(2012)
Basic Statistics on Science and Technology Associations

指标	单位	Indicators	Unit	市科协 S&T Associations of Ningbo Municipal	县(市)区科协 S&T Associations by Region	市级学(协)会 S&T Associations for Municipal Level
1. 科协系统基本情况		**Basic Situation**				
科协机构数	个	Institutions of Science and Technology	unit	1	11	79
直属单位	个	Organizations Attached to the Institutions	unit	3	3	
团体会员(学会、协会、研究会)	个	Group members (Academy, the Association, the Research Council)	unit	79	211	3694
企事业科协	个	Enterprise and Non－profit Organizations Institutions of S&T	unit	19	124	
2. 科学普及活动		**Activity for Popular Science**				
举办科普讲座	次	Number of S&T Popularization Lectures	times	313	853	4086
举办科普展览	次	Number of S&T Popularization Exhibitions	times	1	194	353
发放科普资料(图板)	份	Number of S&T Popularization Release (Drawing Board)	copy	1000	620800	901223
举办实用技术培训	次	Number of Practical Technology Training	times	53055	156887	
3. 青少年科技教育		**Teenagers S&T Education**				
举办青少年科技竞赛	次	Number of Teenagers' S&T Competition	times	4	105	5
举办青少年科技夏(冬)令营	次	Number of Teenagers' S&T Summer (Winter) Camp	times	7	13	4
举办青少年科技培训	人次	Number of Teenagers' S&T Training	person－time	5	201	
4. 科普基础设施建设		**Infrastructure of Popular Science**				
科技馆(科普活动中心)	个	S&T Museum (Activity Center of Popular Science)	unit		8	
科普教育(示范)基地	个	S&T Education (Model) Base	unit	57	14	
科普画廊	个	Gallery of Popular Science	unit		3075	
5. 学术交流		**Academic Activities**				
举办学术交流活动	次	Number of Academic Exchange Activities	unit	43	125	282
编著科技图书	种	Number of Editor S&T Books	kind	4	10	90
接待或派往境外科技团组	个	Receive or Sent Foreign S&T Group	unit	3	2	48
6. 科技活动和社会服务		**S&T Activities and Social services**				
开展"讲、比"活动企业数	个	Enterprise Number of S&T Competition Acitivities	unit	116	159	
"金桥工程"项目数	个	Number of "Golden Bridge project"	unit	24	26	
完成技术咨询合同数	个	Number of Technical Consultative Contracts Completed	unit	55	326	349
反映科技工作者建议	条	Number of S&T Workers' Proposal	piece	4	41	13
举办农函大培训班	人次	Number of Part－time Agricultural Training	person－time	10000	16727	

表 12—22 各县(市)市级以上科技成果鉴定、获奖、专利情况(2012) Basic Statistics on Verification, Award—Winning and Patent Right of Above Municipal Level by Region

单位:个(unit)

指标	Indicators	全市 Total	市区 Urban District	#鄞州 Yinzhou	余姚 Yuyao
科技成果登记	Scientific and Technological Enrollment of Results	457	377	37	12
科学技术奖	Science and Technology Awards	107	86	15	7
国家级	State Level	1	1		
省级	Province Level	26	22	3	3
市级	Municipal Level	80	63	12	4
授权专利数	Number of Patent Applications Approved	59175	60396	18925	10819
发明	Inventions	2065	1393	472	190
实用新型	Utility Models	21407	12693	6400	1668
外观设计	Designs	35703	16310	12053	8961

表 12—22 续表 Continued

单位:个(unit)

指标	Indicators	慈溪 Cixi	奉化 Fenghua	宁海 Ninghai	象山 Xiangshan
科技成果登记	Scientific and Technological Enrollment of Results	39	10	13	6
科学技术奖	Science and Technology Awards	5	1	2	6
国家级	State Level				
省级	Province Level				1
市级	Municipal Level	5	1	2	5
授权专利数	Number of Patent Applications Approved	12348	1943	1512	2157
发明	Inventions	303	62	41	76
实用新型	Utility Models	3961	1389	940	756
外观设计	Designs	8084	492	531	1325

注:国家级科学技术奖包括参与完成项目。

Note: Science and Technology Aowrds at State Levelincluded Participating.

表 12－23 各县(市)计量标准质监情况(2012)
Basic Statistics On Standard Measuring and Quality Supervising by Region

指标	单位	Indicators	Unit
计量验收情况		**Measuring Implements Test**	
已开展强制检定数	项	Measurement Implement Tested Compulsively	kind
开展强制检定种数	种	The Kind of Measurement Implement Tested Compulsively	piecekind
强制检定实际检出数	件	Actual Quantity Checked by Compulsively Examined Out	piece
计量仪器实际检出数	件	Actual Quantity Checked by Messurement Implement Tested	
质监情况		**Quality Supervision**	
国家监督抽查批次	批次	Batch of supervises and Check by Country	batch. time
#合格批次	批次	Regular Batch	batch. time
批次合格率	%	Ratio of Regular by Batch	%
省定期监督抽查企业数	个	Number of Enterpriese of Periodic Supervises and Check by Province	unit
省定期监督抽查批次	批次	Batch of Periodic supervises and Check by Province	batch. time
#合格批次	批次	Regular Batch	batch. time
批次合格率	%	Ratio of Regular by Batch	%
宁波市质量指数	%	Index of Product Quality about NingBo	%

注：本表数据来自宁波市质量技术监督局。

Note：Data in this table are obtained from Administration of Quality and Technology Supervision of Ningbo Municipality.

全市 Total	市区 Urban District	#鄞州 Yinzhou	余姚市 Yuyao	慈溪市 Cixi	奉化市 Fenghua	象山县 Xiangshan	宁海县 Ninghai
45	45	18	11	13	10	10	11
77	77	26	22	23	18	16	18
970672	582663	97193	82980	74741	85830	75421	69037
1163704	706656	134964	102116	107830	95030	77949	74123
270	91	51	31	127	7		14
241	83	47	24	116	7		11
0.89	0.91	0.92	0.77	0.91	1.00		0.79
2037	899	481	291	543	172	55	77
2489	1092	607	317	715	215	65	85
2334	1034	572	304	658	198	61	79
93.77	94.69	94.23	95.90	92.03	92.09	93.85	92.94
97.30	98.50	96.30	97.60	97.10	98.70	97.40	93.60

主要统计指标解释

【艺术表演团体】 指从事戏曲、音乐、舞蹈、杂技等专业艺术表演，有独立帐户，实行单独核算的团体。不包括半工半艺、半农半艺和民间职业剧团。

【艺术表演观众人数(人次)】 指售票、包场演出或民族地区免费演出的艺术表演观众人次数。不包括彩排审查和内部观摩演出的观众人次数。

【电影放映单位】 指具有放映机器设备、固定或不固定的放映场所与专职或兼职的放映技术人员，经有关部门登记批准，经常为一定的观众对象放映电影的机构。包括经批准对外开放进行营业，并与电影发行放映管理机构分帐的专用放映单位和军委系统租片单位。

【普通高等学校】 指按照国家规定的设置标准和审批程序批准举办，通过国家统一招生考试，招收高中毕业生为主要培养对象，实施高等教育的全日制大学、独立设置的学院和高等专科学校、短期职业大学。

【成人高等学校】 指按照国家有关规定审批，招收通过全国成人高教统一招生考试的具有高中毕业或同等学历的在职从业人员利用脱产、半脱产、业余或函授等多种形式对其实施高等学历教育，培养高等教育专科或本科毕业水平的专门人才，修业年限、课程设置和总学时数均按高等学历教育要求付诸实施的学校。包括广播电视大学、职工高等学校、农民高等学校、管理干部学院、教育学院、独立设置的函授学院等。

【小学学龄儿童入学率】 指调查范围内已入小学学习的学龄儿童占校内外学龄儿童总数(包括弱智儿童在内，但不包括盲聋哑儿童)的比重。计算公式为：

$$\text{小学学龄儿童入学率}=\frac{\text{已入学的小学学龄儿童数}}{\text{校内外小学学龄儿童总数}}\times 100\%$$

【医院】 指名称为医院，设有固定床位能收容病人住院并能为病人提供医疗、护理服务的医疗机构。包括县及县以上医院、农村乡卫生院、其他医院三部分。按所属性质分为卫生部门、工业及其他部门，集体经济单位三类。其中县及县以上医院按业务性质分为综合医院和专科医院。

【卫生技术人员】 指卫生事业机构支付工资的全部固定职工和合同制职工中现任职务为卫生技术工作的专业人员。具体包括中医师、西医师、中西医结合高级医师、护师、中药师、西药师、检验师、其他技师、中医士、西医士、护士、助产士、中药剂士、西药剂士、检验士、其他技士、其他中医、护理员、中药剂员、西药剂员、检验员，其他初级卫生技术人员。

【医生】 指经卫生部门审查合格，从事医疗工作的专业人员。分为中医医生和西医医生。包括卫生技术人员中的中医师、西医师、中西结合高级医师、中医士、西医士和其他中医。

【专利申请数】 指当年单位向专利管理机关提出专利申请并被受理的件数。

Explanatory Notes on Main Statistical Indicators

【Art Troupe】 refers to the troupe which is engaged in drama, opera, music, dance, acrobatics or other art performance, opens independent accounts with banks and has self—supporting accounting system; excluding the troupes which h are engaged partly in industrial or agricultural activities, partly in art performance and the professional troupes organized by the people.

【Number of Sectors at Art Performance】 refers to the number of attendants at commercial shows completely booked shows or free shows given in minority national areas, and does not include the number of spectators at rehearsals for examination and initial shows for study.

【Film Projection Units】 refer to units with film projection equipment, full or part time projectionists, permanent or nonpermanent places, approved by related administrative departments to show films regularly for certain groups of audience, including those film projection units which have been approved to give commercial shows and run business with independent accounting system as well as those film-renting units of the military system.

【Regular Institutions of Higher Learning】 refer to educational establishments set up according to the government evaluation and approval procedures, enrolling graduates from senior secondary schools and providing higher education courses and training for senior professionals. They include full—time universities, colleges, high professional schools and short—term professional universities.

【Institutions of Higher Learning for Adults】 refer to educational establishments, set up in line with relevant rules approved by the government, enrolling staff and workers with senior secondary school or equivalent education, and providing higher education courses in many forms of full—time, part—time, spare—time, or correspondence for adults. Professionals thus trained receive a qualification equivalent to graduates studying regular courses at regular universities, colleges and professional colleges. Institutions of higher learning for adults include Radio and TV universities, schools of high education for staff and workers and peasants, colleges for management cadres, pedagogical colleges, independent correspondence colleges.

【Enrollment Rate of Primary School—age Children】 refers to the proportion of school—age children enrolled at schools to the total number of school—age both in and outside schools (including retarded children, but excluding blind, deaf and mute children). The formula is:

Enrollment Rate of Primary School—age Children=Total Primary School—age Children at Schools×100%

Total Primary School—age Children at and Outside Schools

【Hospitals】 refer to medical institutions named as "hospital" with permanent hospital beds, which are able to take in patients and provide them with medical and nursing services. Hospitals are classified into three categories : hospitals at or above the county—level, hospitals of rural townships, and other hospitals. According to their ownership, hospitals can be classified into three categories: hospitals under the public health departments, hospitals under industrial and other departments and collective—owned hospitals. Hospitals at or above county level are divided into comprehensive and specialized hospitals.

【Medical Technical Personnel】 refers to all permanent medical staff and workers employed by medical institutions, including doctors of Chinese and Western medicine, senior doctors who integrate traditional Chinese therapeutics with Western therapeutics in practice, senior nurses, pharmacists of Chinese and Western medicine, laboratory specialists, other specialists, paramedics of Chinese and Western medicine, nurses, midwives, druggists in Chinese and Western medicine, laboratory technicians, other technicians, other practitioners of Chinese medicine, nursing attendants, pharmacological workers of Chinese and Western medicine, laboratory workers, and other primary medical personnel.

【Doctors】 refer to qualified professional medical workers approved to practice by public health departments. They are classified into doctors of Chinese medicine, doctors of Western medicine, senior doctors who integrate traditional Chinese therapeutics with Western therapeutics in practice, paramedics of Chinese medicine and Western medicine, and other specialists of Chinese medicine.

【Applied Number of Patents】 refers to the number of patent applied by a unit to the patent office and then accepted in a reporting year.

NINGBO

Statistical YearBook

第十三篇

市政、环保、民政、政法及其他

CIVIL FACILITIES,ENVIRONMENT, CIVIL AFFAIRS,JUDICATURE AND OTHERS

市政、环保、民政、政法及其他
Civil Facilities, Environment, Social Welfare, Judicature and Others

主要统计指标
Major Statistics Indicators

2012 年人均日生活用水量	Per Capita Daily Consunption of Tap water for Resiential Use	239.49	升	liter
2012 年人均拥有道路面积	Per Capita Area of Paved Roads	20.53	平方米	sq. m
2012 年人均公园绿地面积	Per Capita Public Green Areas	10.97	平方米	sq. m
2012 年建成区绿化覆盖率	Coverage Rate of Green Area in Developed Area	38.01	%	
2012 年废水排放总量	Total Volume of Waste Water Discharged	55579.41	万吨	10000 tons
2012 年工业废气排放量	Volume of Industrial Waste Gas Emission	5910.30	亿标立米	100 million cu. m
2012 年环境噪声达标面积	Standardization Areas of Environment Noise	260.21	平方公里	sq. km
2012 年收养性福利单位床位数	Number of Beds in Socail Welfare－Units for Adopting	30945	张	bed
2012 年社会救济总人数	Number of Persons Receiving Relief	59483	人	person
2012 年末实有社团机构数	Factual Number of Social Organizations at The Year－end	2159	个	unit
2012 年基层工会数	Number of Trade Unions at Basic－Level	25109	个	unit
2012 年律师人数	Number of Lawyers	1495	人	person
2012 年办理公证事项	Number of Notarized Documents	60899	件	case
2012 年调解纠纷总件数	Number of Mediating Disputes	126447	件	case
2012 年交通事故数	Number of Traffic Accident	3082	件	case
2012 年档案馆数	Number of Archives	12	个	unit

表 13－1 部分年份市政公用事业基本情况
Basic Statistics on Municipal Public Utilities in Partial Years

指标	单位	Indicators	Unit	2009	2010	2011	2012
供水及供气		**Water Supply and Gas Supply**					
年供水总量	万吨	Annuall Volume of Tap Water Supply	10000 tons	59923	65740	68617	70122
#居民家庭用水量	万吨	Water Consumption for Residents Use	10000 tons	23660	20928	22439	23130
人均日生活用水量	升	Per Capita Daily Consumption of Tap Water for Residential Use	liter	258.72	232.56	240.31	239.49
用水普及率	%	Percentage of Population with Access to Tap Water	%	100.00	100.00	100.00	100.00
液化石油气供气总量	万吨	Total Volume of Liquefied Petroleum Gas	10000 tons	29.40	28.50	21.66	20.13
#家庭用量	万吨	For Residents Use	10000 tons	12.74	12.17	10.37	10.09
用液化气人口	万人	Population with Access Liquefied Petroleum Gas	10000 persons	219.30	205.79	193.81	202.46
燃气普及率	%	Percentage of Population with Access to Gas	%	100.00	100.00	100.00	100.00
市政设施		**Municipal Infra－strucutre**					
年末城市实有道路面积	万平方米	Area of Paved Roads(Year－end)	10000 sq. m	5802.5	6445.3	6930.5	7124.6
人均拥有道路面积	平方米	Per Capita Area of Paved Roads	sq. m	18.21	19.65	20.44	20.53
排水管道长度	公里	Length of Sewage Pipes	km	5750	6265	6574.8	6907.4
排水管道密度	公里/平方公里	Density of Sewage Pipes	km/sq. km	16.28	14.47	14.60	15.11
公共交通		**Public Traffic**					
年末实有公交营运车辆	标台	Number of Public Transportations Vehicles under Operation	unit	4833	4842	5302.5	6143.9
每万人拥有公共交通车辆	标台	Number of Public Transportations Vehicles Per 10000 Persons	unit	6.70	6.50	6.96	8.08
年末实有出租汽车数	辆	Operating Taxes at Year－end	unit	5001	5442	5551	5834
城市绿化		**Afforestation in Cities**					
园林绿地面积	公顷	Green Areas in Parks and Gardens	hectare	13963	15780	16666	17107
#公园绿地面积	公顷	Public Green Areas	hectare	3225	3483	3662	3807
人均公园绿地面积	平方米	Per Capita Public Green Areas	sq. m	10.12	10.62	10.80	10.97
建成区绿地率	%	Rate of Green Area in Developed Area	%	33.97	33.94	34.27	34.76
建成区绿化覆盖率	%	Coverage Rate of Green Area in Developed Area	%	37.45	37.52	37.82	38.21
环境卫生		**Environmental Sanitation**					
污水处理率	%	Percentage of Sewage Disposed	%	81.27	82.81	84.16	85.75
生活垃圾无害化处理率	%	Innocuous Disposal Rate of Living Garbage	%	100.00	100.00	100.00	100.00

注:2009年开始,排水管道密度为建成区排水管道密度。

Note:Densitly of sewage pipes from 2009 refered to builting area.

表 13－2 各县(市)城市市政、公用事业情况(2012)
Basic Statistics on Civil Facilities and Public Utilities by Region

指标	单位	Indicators	Unit
城市面积		**City Areas**	
建成区面积	平方公里	Developed Areas	sq. km
城市建设用地面积	平方公里	land Areas of the Urban Construction	sq. km
居住用地面积	平方公里	For Residential Building Uses	sq. km
公共设施面积	平方公里	For Public Utilities Uses	sq. km
工业用地面积	平方公里	For Industry Uses	sq. km
供水及供气		**Water Supply and Gas Supply**	
年供水总量	万吨	Annuall Volume of Tap Water Supply	10000 tons
＃居民家庭用水量	万吨	Water Consumption for Residents Use	10000 tons
人均日生活用水量	升	Per Capita Daily Consumption of Tap Water for Residential Use	liter
用水普及率	%	Percentage of Population with Access to Tap Water	%
液化石油气供气总量	吨	Total Volume of Liquefied Petroleum Gas	ton
＃家庭用量	吨	For Residents Use	ton
用液化气人口	万人	Population with Access Liquefied Petroleum Gas	10000 persons
燃气普及率	%	Percentage of Population with Access to Gas	%
市政设施		**Municipal Infra－strucutre**	
年末城市实有道路面积	万平方米	Area of Paved Roads(Year－end)	10000 sq. m
人均拥有道路面积	平方米	Per Capita Area of Paved Roads	sq. m
排水管道长度	公里	Length of Sewage Pipes	km
建成区排水管道密度	公里/平方公里	Density of Drainpipes	km/sq. km
公共交通		**Public Traffic**	
年末实有公交营运车辆	标台	Number of Public Transportations Vehicles under Operation	unit
每万人拥有公共交通车辆	标台	Number of Public Transportations Vehicles Per 10000 Persons	unit
年末实有出租汽车数	辆	Operating Taxes at Year－end	unit
城市绿化		**Afforestation in Cities**	
园林绿地面积	公顷	Green Areas in Parks and Gardens	hectare
＃公园绿地面积	公顷	Public Green Areas	hectare
人均公园绿地面积	平方米	Per Capita Public Green Areas	sq. m
建成区绿化覆盖面积	公顷	Coverage Area of Green Area in Developed Area	hectare
建成区绿地率	%	Rate of Green Area in Developed Area	%
建成区绿化覆盖率	%	Coverage Rate of Green Area in Developed Area	%
环境卫生		**Environmental Sanitation**	
污水处理率	%	Percentage of Sewage Disposed	%
生活垃圾无害化处理率	%	Innocuous Disposal Rate of Living Garbage	%

注:本表数据来自宁波市城乡建委。

Note:Data in this table are obtained from Ningbo Municipal Construction Committee.

全市 Total	市区 Urban District	余姚市 Yuyao	慈溪市 Cixi	奉化市 Fenghua	象山县 Xiangshan	宁海 Ninghai
457.14	289.83	45.56	42.30	18.75	28.00	32.70
524.79	336.88	45.56	40.25	32.15	33.74	36.21
133.97	72.64	11.60	19.16	10.00	9.57	11.00
32.66	15.76	0.87	4.41	2.97	3.92	4.73
175.98	126.63	17.85	8.87	10.77	0.62	11.24
70122	46325	4414	9380	3353	3498	3152
23130	14062	2012	3110	1521	1124	1301
239.49	300.35	142.97	216.28	157.27	154.61	218.12
100.00	100.00	100.00	100.00	100.00	100.00	100.00
201292.11	138584.00	6094.60	31102.00	6566.40	10450.11	8495.00
100932.94	44552.51	4751.00	30491.00	5625.00	7910.38	7603.00
202.46	54.89	32.34	40.99	34.30	23.59	16.35
100.00	100.00	100.00	100.00	100.00	100.00	100.00
7125	2786	1046	1707	422	694	469
20.53	15.87	23.54	33.49	12.29	29.43	25.85
6907	3794	664	1265	188	488	509
15.11	13.09	14.57	29.91	10.02	17.44	15.56
6144	4849	546	218	120	159	206
8.08	13.90	5.70	3.80	2.40	2.90	3.50
5834	4101	440	605	200	210	278
17107	10689	1722	1862	910	706	1218
3807	1853	448	658	337	274	237
10.97	10.56	10.08	12.91	9.83	11.62	13.06
17469	11080	1950	1675	761	689	1314
34.76	34.89	37.80	35.98	37.28	22.07	37.25
38.21	38.23	42.80	39.60	40.59	24.61	40.18
85.75	88.14	81.65	84.10	77.52	75.98	80.65
100.00	100.00	100.00	100.00	100.00	100.00	100.00

表 13－3　各县(市)环境保护基本情况(2012)
Basic Statistics on Environment Protection, Enviroment Sanitation by Region

指标	单位	Indicators	Unit
废水排放总量	**万吨**	**Volume of Waste Water Discharged**	**10000 tons**
工业废水排放总量	万吨	Industrial Waste Water Discharged	10000 tons
生活污水排放量	万吨	Discharged Amount of Living Sewage	10000 tons
化学需氧量(COD)排放量	**吨**	**Discharged Amount of Chemical oxygen demand (COD)**	**tons**
工业废水中化学需氧排放量	吨	Discharged Amount of COD in Industrial Waste Water	tons
工业用水总量	万吨	Water Consumption for Industrial Use	10000 tons
工业重复用水率	%	Rate of Water Utilized Repeatedly in Industry	%
废水治理设施数	套	Number of Administration Facility of Waste Water	unit
工业废气排放量	**亿标立米**	**Industrial Waste Gas Emission**	**100 million cu. m**
工业二氧化硫排放量	吨	Industrial Sulphur Dioxide Emission	ton
工业氮氧化物(NOx)排放量	吨	Industrial Nitrogen Oxide (NOx) Emissions	ton
工业烟尘排放量	吨	Soot Emission	ton
一般工业固体废物产生量	**万吨**	**Volume of Industrial Solid Wastes Produced**	**10000 tons**
一般工业固体废物综合利用量	万吨	Volume of General Industrial Solid Waste Utilized	10000 tons
一般工业固体废物处理量	万吨	Volume of General Industial Solid Waste Treated	10000 tons
一般工业固体废物倾倒丢弃量	吨	Volume of General Industrial Solid Wastes Dumped Discarded	ton
工业固体废物综合利用率	%	Rate of Industrial Solid Waste Utilized	%
工业固体废物处置利用率	%	Rate of Industrial Solid Waste Treated and Utilized	%
工业污染处理本年施工项目数	个	Number of Projects Treating Industrial Pollution	unit
建设项目"三同时"环保投资额	万元	Investment Amount of Construction Project " Three Simultaneous " of Environment Protection	10000 yuan
环境噪声达标面积	平方公里	Standardization Areas of Environment Noise	sq. km

注：本表数据来自宁波市环境保护局。工业"三废"统计范围为重点调查工业企业与非重点调查单位测算之和。

Note：a) Data in this table are obtained from Ningbo Environment Protection Bureau. b) Statistical Information of Waste Water, Waste Gas and Waste Residue Collected is calculated data that investigate industrial enterprise especially and non－investigate unit especially

全市 Total	市区 Urban Districts	#鄞州 Yinzhou	余姚 Yuyao	慈溪 Cixi	奉化 Fenghua	象山 Xiangshan	宁海 Ninghai
56347.76	**31688.91**	**7992.20**	**6141.41**	**9094.00**	**2846.63**	**3499.36**	**3077.45**
20124.65	13166.13	1741.41	1587.52	1915.41	1219.28	1616.09	620.22
36223.11	18522.78	6250.79	4553.89	7178.59	1627.35	1883.27	2457.23
68380.10	**29351.48**	**10498.45**	**9692.14**	**11371.11**	**4678.47**	**6366.20**	**5849.59**
20066.08	10784.62	1891.69	3343.30	2380.16	1106.40	1740.80	710.80
1032226.49	997760.42	6101.62	2643.76	6834.45	1811.49	13338.81	9837.56
54.79	54.32	61.50	2.95	60.82	17.96	80.00	85.05
929	479	111	49	145	113	79	64
6217.88	**3923.40**	**98.32**	**270.00**	**193.18**	**16.33**	**764.36**	**1050.62**
144356	99876	3785	4951	9179	2389	9362	18600
235814	146759	1980	5441	3341	529	31996	47748
26159	13771	1989	3412	3088	570	3279	2039
1246.63	**870.98**	**17.41**	**15.27**	**30.88**	**8.93**	**132.63**	**187.94**
1147.00	781.88	15.05	14.97	23.81	8.73	131.46	186.14
93.24	82.71	2.48	0.30	7.07	0.20	1.16	1.79
0.02	0.02	0.00	0.00	0.00	0.00	0.00	0.00
91.59	89.38	82.02	95.83	75.56	92.77	99.06	98.96
99.43	99.19	100.00	100.00	99.98	100.00	100.00	100.00
49.00	25.00		12.00	2.00		9.00	1.00
238519.80	89221.80	3349.00	13695.30	38796.80	0.00	4308.90	3996.50
260.21	151.82	17.93	24.35	31.05	9.09	23.90	20.00

表 13－4 各县(市)社会团体机构情况(2012)
Basic Statistics on Social Organizations and Unions by Region

指标	Indicators	全市 Total
上年准予登记社团机构数	Number of Social Organizations Authorized in Last Year	2037
年末实有社团机构数	Factual Number of Social Organizations at the Year－end	2159
年末实有民办非企业数	Factual Number of Civilian－run Non－enterprises at the Year－end	3091

注:本表至 13－8 表数据来自宁波市民政局。

Note:Data from Tables 13－4 to 13－8 are obtained from Ningbo Municipal Bureau of Civil Affairs.

表 13－5 各县(市)社会福利、优抚、救济工作情况(2012)
Basic Statistics on Social Welfare,Subsidy and Commiseration by Region

指标	单位	Indicators	Unit
收养人数	**人**	**Number of Adopted Persons**	**person**
优待情况		Favoured Treatment	
安置军转干部、士兵	人	Setting Military Cadres or Soldiers Transferred to Civilian Work	person
优待军属户数	户	Service men's Families	household
优待总金额	万元	Total Amount of Give Special Treatment	10000 yuan
抚恤、补助情况		**Special Pensions,Allowances and Relief**	
年末享受定补人数	人	Number of Persons Receiving Periodical Subsidies at the Year－end	person
#在乡复员军人	人	Rural Demobilized Soldiers	person
#在乡退伍军人	人	Rural Veteransn	person
伤残人员	人	Number of Wounded or Disabled Health	person
年末定期抚恤人数	人	Number of Persons Receiving Periodical Commiseration	person
#烈士家属	人	Members of Revolutionary Martyr's Family	person

单位:个(unit)

市区 Urban District	#鄞州 Yinzhou	余姚 Yuyao	慈溪 Cixi	奉化 Fenghua	象山 Xiangshan	宁海 Ninghai
1143	165	181	239	158	161	155
1192	172	196	280	158	168	165
1387	357	356	604	175	178	391

全市 Total	市区 Urban District	#鄞州 Yinzhou	余姚 Yuyao	慈溪 Cixi	奉化 Fenghua	象山 Xiangshan	宁海 Ninghai
354	**77**	**8**	**36**	**79**	**45**	**59**	**58**
2629	912	406	424	517	254	224	298
4955	1669	670	843	907	506	428	602
7201.6	2916.2	1344.3	1250.4	1058.1	640.7	545.1	791.1
20984	6455	3198	2498	3994	2269	2243	3525
3152	1128	620	401	691	317	348	267
2048	413	375	128	355	299	334	519
2417	973	293	335	472	234	181	222
741	301	93	109	132	65	58	76
344	122	53	68	48	22	37	47

表 13－6 民政部门收养性福利优抚事业情况(2012)
Basic Statistics on Adopting, Welfare & Special Pensions by Civil Administration Department

指标	单位	Indicators	Unit	全市 Total	其中 of Which #市区 Urban District	光荣院 Homes for Disabled Veterans
收养性福利单位数	**个**	**Number of Adopting Socail Welfare Units**	**unit**	**18**	**12**	**2**
全部职工人数	**人**	**Total Numeber Staff and Workers**	**person**	**465**	**353**	**17**
#女性	人	Female	person	314	236	7
年末固定资产原值	**万元**	**Original Value of Fixed Assets at the Year－end**	**10000 yuan**	**10189**	**9045**	**95**
各院病床数	**张**	**Number of Beds in Each Hospital**	**bed**	**5300**	**4055**	**66**
年末在院人数	**人**	**In－patients at the Year－end**	**person**	**2982**	**2280**	**31**
#优抚人员	人	Adopting Persons for Enjoying Favoured Treatment	person	58	44	31
"三无"对象人员	人	Non Depending on, Non Ability to Labor and Non Income	person	749	611	
自费人员	人	Persons on Self－expense	person	2175	1625	
#老年人	人	Old People	person	1944	1360	31
青壮年人员	人	Young People	person	649	634	
少年儿童	人	Juvenile and Child	person	389	286	

表 13－6 续表 Continued

指标	单位	Indicators	Unit	其中 of Which 社会福利院 Social Welfare Homes	儿童福利院 Welfare Homes for Children	精神病福利院 Welfare Homes for Mental Patients
收养性福利单位数	**个**	**Number of Adopting Socail Welfare Units**	**unit**	**14**	**1**	**1**
全部职工人数	**人**	**Total Numeber Staff and Workers**	**person**	**392**	**24**	**32**
#女性	人	Female	person	274	19	14
年末固定资产原值	**万元**	**Original Value of Fixed Assets at the Year－end**	**10000 yuan**	**7147**	**938**	**2009**
各院病床数	**张**	**Number of Beds in Each Hospital**	**bed**	**4574**	**300**	**360**
年末在院人数	**人**	**In－patients at the Year－end**	**person**	**2291**	**300**	**360**
#优抚人员	人	Adopting Persons for Enjoying Favoured Treatment	person	27		
"三无"对象人员	人	Non Depending on, Non Ability to Labor and Non Income	person	410	245	94
自费人员	人	Persons on Self－expense	person	1854	55	266
#老年人	人	Old People	person	1791		122
青壮年人员	人	Young People	person	372	46	231
少年儿童	人	Juvenile and Child	person	128	254	7

表 13－7 城乡居民最低生活保障情况(2012) Basic Statistics on Receiving Lowest Cost－of－living in Urban and Rural Area

地区	Region	社会救济总人数(人) Number of Persons Receiving Relief (person)	城镇低保人数(人) Number of ①RLCU (person)	城镇低保家庭数(户) Households of RLCU ① (household)	城镇低保资金支出(万元) Expenditure for RLCU (10000 yuan)	农村低保人数(人) Number of RLCR② and Receiving Relief (person)	农村低保家庭数(户) Households of RLCR② (household)	农村救济资金支出(万元) Expenditure for RLCR② (10000 yuan)
宁波市	**Total**	**59483**	**10289**	**7015**	**5456.30**	**49194**	**32340**	**18010**
市区	Urban District	14137	7189	4832	4029.00	6948	4069	3642
#鄞州区	Yinzhou	5635	847	522	463.70	4788	2586	2522
余姚市	Yuyao	9891	908	670	430.70	8983	5162	2272
慈溪市	Cixi	9530	644	451	288.60	8886	5762	3543
奉化市	Fenghua	7882	697	478	353.10	7185	5386	3288
象山县	Xiangshan	9328	549	376	242.40	8779	5606	2800
宁海县	Ninghai	8715	302	208	112.50	8413	6355	2465

注:①RLCU 是城镇低保的缩写。
②RLCR 是农村低保的缩写
Note:①RLCU is the short form that means Receiving Lowest Cost－of－living in Urban Area.
②RLCR is the short form that means Receiving Lowest Cost－of－living in Rural Area.

表 13－8 社会收容遣送情况(2012) Basic Statistics on Accepted and Relief

	遣送站情况 Repatriated Units			本年救助(人次) Relief Person in this Year (person－times)
	站数(个) Number of Units (unit)	年末职工人数(人) Number of Staff and Workers (person)	年末固定资产原值(万元) Original Value of Fixed Assets (10000 yuan)	
全市总计 Total	8	67	2129.10	5327

表 13－9 各县(市)妇联工会组织及活动情况(2012)
Basic Statistics on Women Federation and Trade Unions by Region

指标	单位	Indicators	Unit
妇联组织机构		**Women's Federation**	
市、县(市)区妇联	个	Women's Federation in Municipal,County and Urban District	unit
镇、乡(街道)妇联	个	Women's Federation in Township,Town (Subdistrict)	unit
基层妇代会	个	Basic－Level Women Congress	unit
机关事业单位妇委会	个	Women Commission of Agencies and Institutions	unit
团体会员	个	Group Member	unit
人员状况		**Cadre of Women's Federation**	
市、县(市)区级干部	人	Level of Municipal,County and Urban District	person
镇、乡(街道)级干部	人	Cadre in Township,Town(Subdistrict)	person
妇联工作情况		**Works of Women's Federation**	
双学双比及巾帼建功活动		Activity of Double Study And Double Compare, And Women Making Contribution	
参赛数	万人	Number of Participants	10000 persons
＃女农民技术人员	人	Female Peasant Technician	person
先进女能手	人	Female Advanced Expert	person
巾帼建功先进个人	人	Advanced Women by Making Contribution	person
工会基本情况		**Trade Unions**	
1.基层工会数	个	Number of Trade Unions at Basic－Level	unit
2.工会专职干部人数	人	Number of Full－Time Cadres of Trade Unions	person
3.建立工会单位全部职工	人	Total Staff And Workers of Establishing Trade Unions	person
＃女职工	人	Female Staff And Workers	person
工会会员	人	Member of Trade Unions	person
＃女会员	人	Female Member	person
4.本年度职工提出合理化建议	件	Advanced Rationalization Proposals	case
本年度已实施合理化建议	件	Implement Rationalization Proposals	case
本年度已实施合理化建议产生的效益	万元	Economic Benefit Created by Rationalization Proposals	10000 yuan

注:本表数据来自宁波市总工会和宁波市妇联。

Note:Date in this table are obtained from Ningbo Federation of Trade Unions and Ningbo Women's Federation .

全市 Total	市区 Urban District	#鄞州 Yinzhou	余姚 Yuyao	慈溪 Cixi	奉化 Fenghua	象山 Xiangshan	宁海 Ninghai
12	7	1	1	1	1	1	1
149	61	23	22	19	11	18	18
8840	4013	1482	300	1057	2592	515	363
502	275	46	26	66	45	65	25
45	22	8	5	12	1	3	2
107	65	8	10	9	9	8	6
206	109	50	22	19	11	27	18
50.6	4.8	1.0	2.5	12.0	10.1	18.2	3.0
256	121	121	65	48			22
146	8	5	36	15	5	10	72
160	27	12	4	23	17	3	86
25109	13975	4537	3148	3175	1758	1496	1557
2450	1649	243	196	271	31	156	147
3395348	1856197	592830	448224	463281	217373	218771	191502
1491850	816479	269451	224316	203727	98683	63245	85400
3286990	1798956	568797	426765	457652	208186	210021	185410
1457323	797606	259990	217631	201605	95586	61573	83231
90565	79150	2345	4745	4947		793	930
47233	41832	775	2417	2098		538	348
56570	40129	2930	7938	4330		3453	720

表 13－10 各县(市)、区公务员及参照公务员管理的群团机关工作人员情况(2012) Basic Statistics on Civil Servant and Employee Refer to Civil Servant in Government Organ by Region

单位:人(person)

指标	Indicators	合计 Total	其中:女 of which: Female	按行政级别分 By Administrations Level 省部级 Province Level	地厅司局级 Department/ Bureau Level	县处级 County Level	乡科级 Section Chief	科员及以下 Section and Below
全市	**Total**	**33207**	**8595**	**2**	**298**	**7097**	**19458**	**6352**
市直单位	Municipal Department	8089	1796	2	268	3685	3467	667
市区	Urban Districts	11479	3221		26	3243	6593	1617
海曙区	Haishu	1459	438		4	346	876	233
江东区	Jiangdong	1273	385		6	390	727	150
江北区	Jiangbei	1593	461		4	460	878	251
镇海区	Zhenhai	1655	442		5	493	917	240
北仑区	Beilun	2205	565		3	601	1367	234
鄞州区	Yinhzou	3294	930		4	953	1828	509
县合计	**Total of County**	**13639**	**3578**		**4**	**169**	**9398**	**4068**
余姚	Yuyao	3212	888		1	36	2200	975
慈溪	Cixi	3426	915		2	38	2360	1026
奉化	Fenghua	2242	593		1	33	1592	616
象山	Xiangshan	2424	601			32	1612	780
宁海	Ninghai	2335	581			30	1634	671

表 13－11 部分年份律师、公证工作基本情况 Basic Statistics on Lawyers and Notarization in Partial Years

指标	Indicators	2009	2010	2011	2012
律师工作情况	**Lawyers**				
律师事务所(个)	Number of Law Offices (unit)	104	113	121	128
个人律师事务所(个)	Personal Law Office(unit)			32	34
合伙制律师事务所(个)	Law Offices in Partnership(unit)	81	83	89	94
律师数(人)	Number of Lawyers (person)	1046	1228	1390	1495
#专职律师(人)	Full－time Lawyers (person)	972	1066	1302	1437
聘请担任常年法律顾问单位(家)	Number of Units with Permanent Legal Advisors (unit)	4202	4368	7079	5265
民事案件代理(件)	Agent of Civil Cases (case)	17304	17934	27819	20492
经济案件代理(件)	Agent of Economic Cases (case)				
#索回赔数 (万元)	Debt and Indemnity Claimed (10000 yuan)				
刑事辩护和代理(件)	Agent of Criminal Defense (case)	2897	3354	6003	3715
非诉讼法律事务(件)	Agent of Non－Litigious Legal Affairs (case)	1570	1614	1761	1495
行政案件代理(件)	Agent of Administrative Action (case)	758	666	731	611
涉外及港澳台法律事务(件)	Legal Affairs With Foreign,HongKong,Macao,Taiwan(case)	39	27	24	
解答法律文书(件)	Legal Advisory Services (case)		22023	5676	22518
代写法律文书(件)	Legal Document Written on Behalf of Clients(case)	2868	3296	4920	2688
公证工作情况	**Notarization**				
公证处(个)	Notary Offices (unit)	11	11	11	11
#办理涉外公证(人)	Registered Foreign Affairs (person)	30	31	31	33
公证人员人数(人)	Notarial Personnel (person)	81	132	90	91
#公证员(人)	Notaries(person)	46	52	53	56
办理公证事项(件)	Notarized Documents (case)	59462	65525	62851	60899
国内经济公证(件)	Domestic Economic Affairs(case)	12891	12941	10308	8567
国内民事公证(件)	Domestic Civil Affairs(case)	28354	32242	32020	27578
涉外及港澳台公证(件)	Documents on Foreign,HongKong,Macao,Taiwan(case)	18217	20342	20523	24664
接待来访 (人次)	Reception (person－times)	41300	42658	75693	5896
处理来信 (件)	Treatment (case)	97	389	230	162

表 13－12 部分年份基层司法工作及人民调解情况 Basic Statistics on Basic－Level Judicial Work and People Mediation in Partial Years

指标	Indicators	2009	2010	2011	2012
基层法律服务	**Basic－Level Service for Legal Advice**				
司法助理员人数（人）	Number of Judicial Assistants (person)	745	790	268	397
专职司法助理员（人）	Full－Time Judicial Assistants(person)	604	527	268	291
兼职司法助理员（人）	Part－Time Judicial Assistants (person)	141	263		106
基层法律服务所（所）	**Basic－Level Service for Legal Advice (unit)**	**76**	**76**	**74**	**74**
配备工作人员（人）	Provide Staff (person)	455	502	497	463
代理讼诉事务（件）	Agent of Litigious Affairs (case)	10384	9460	9380	10763
代理非讼诉事务（件）	Agent of Non－Litigious Legal Affairs (case)	1372	1824	966	1067
调解纠纷（件）	Mediating Disputes (case)	2216	1867	320	3153
协办公证（件）	Handling Document Jointly (case)				
见证（件）	Witness (case)				
担任法律顾问（件）	Taking Legal Advisors (case)	2151	2229	2550	6348
代写法律文书（件）	Legal Document Written on Behalf of Clients (case)			3127	965
解答法律咨询人次（人次）	Legal Advisory Services (person－times)	31913	31817	3350	37307
挽回经济损失（万元）	Economic Loss Avoided and Reclaimed (10000 yuan)	51456	54866	41688	47232
办理法律援助事务（件）	Handling Succorab leLegal Affairs (case)	1734	1311	6038	545
参与司法行政工作（人次）	Participating Judicial Administration (person－times)	640	433	247	124
人民调解工作	**Peoples Mediation**				
人民调解委员会（个）	Peoples Mediation Committees (unit)	5136	5213	4786	4793
调解人员数（人）	Number of Mediators (person)	20760	20701	18379	19251
调解纠纷总件数（件）	Number of Mediating Disputes (case)	95927	106291	127927	126447
调解成功件数（件）	Number of Success (case)	94176	104600	126154	124658
婚姻、继承、赡养抚养（件）	Marrige, Rights of Inheritance, Supporting and Fostering (case)	5198	6159	7722	7010
房屋宅基地（件）	Ground of Building (case)	3539	3729	4240	3542
债务（件）	Debt (case)	2241	2932	2876	3670

注：本表数据来自宁波市司法局。

表 13－12 续表 Continued

指标	Indicators	2009	2010	2011	2012
生产经营（件）	Production & Management (case)	7937	8644	1046	1665
邻里关系（件）	Relation of Neighborhood (case)	16619	18704	21291	18366
赔偿（件）	Compensation (case)	43770	49751	15842	12772
其他调解（件）	Other Mediating (case)	16623	12983	73137	79152
调解纠纷成功率（%）	Rate of Mediating Success (%)	98.2	98.4	98.6	98.6
防止可能发生非正常死亡事件（件）	Avoiding Accident of Abnormal Deaths (case)	10	15	36	29
防止可能发生非正常死亡人次（人次）	Avoiding Accident Times of Abnormal Deaths (person－times)	14	15	55	36
安置帮教工作情况	**Placement and help and Educate**				
刑释人员数(当年)(人)	Number of Ex－Convict Personnel in this Year (person)	1936	1936	2411	2667
刑释人员数(五年内)(人)	Number of Ex－Convict Personnel in Current 5 Years (person)	11128	11128	12296	12889
解教人员数(当年)(人)	Number of Unchain Labor Reeducation in this Year(person)	289	289	170	118
刑释人员安置数(当年)(人)	Number of Placement of Ex－convict in this Year (person)	2051	2051	2441	2662
刑释人员帮教数(当年)(人)	Number of Help&Educate of Ex－convictin this Year(person)	2155	2155	2523	2729
重新犯罪人数(当年)(人)	Number of Re－criminal in this Year(person)	163	163	113	155
重新劳教人数(当年)(人)	Number of Again Labor Reeducation in this Year (person)	17	17	10	11
监狱，劳教工作	**Prison and Labor Reeducation**				
市属监狱（所）	Number of Prison (unit)	2	2	2	2
年内新收押罪犯(人)	Detain Criminal in this Year(person)	2924	5483	3497	337
年内刑满释放(人)	Ex－Convict Personnel in this Year(person)	2815	3139	2693	2755
市属劳教所(所)	Numbet of Labor Reeducation Unit (unit)	1	1	1	1
年内新收容劳教人员(人)	Newly Accept Labor Reeducation Personnel in this Year(person)	691	545	383	393
年内解除劳教(人)	Unchain Labor Reeducation (person)	906	662	541	387
年内新收容收教人员(人)	Newly Accept Take in Reeducation Personnel in this Year(person)	59	59	29	28
年内解除收教(人)	Unchain Labor Reeducation (person)	78	67	32	27

Note: Data in this table are obtained from Bureau of Justice of Ningbo Municipality.

表 13－13　二级人民法院收、结案情况(2012)
Cases Accepted & Settled by People's Court

单位:件(case)

指标	Indicators	上年留案 Retained in Last Year	全年新收案 New Accepted in this Year	办结案件数 Number of Cases Closed	年末未结案件 Retained Caseat Year－end
总计	**Total**	**10154**	**133988**	**133237**	**10905**
一审案件数	Number of First Trial Cases	7567	82062	81750	7879
刑事	Criminal Case	351	13984	13990	345
民商事	Civil & Economic Case	7177	67532	67212	7497
行政	Administrative Case	39	546	548	37
二审案件数	Number of Second Trial Case	381	3826	3857	350
刑事	Criminal Case	28	533	529	32
民事	Civil Case	214	1919	1986	147
经济	Economic Case	124	1173	1139	158
行政	Administrative Case	15	201	203	13
审判监督	Number of Cases Judged and Supervised	44	179	196	27
刑事	Criminal Case	6	19	23	2
民商事	Civil & Economic Case	37	160	172	25
行政	Administrative Case	1		1	
执行	Carry out Case	2132	39367	38883	2616
刑事案件(有财产部分)	Criminal Case (With Property)	76	829	845	60
民事	Civil Case	1888	28570	28130	2328
行政	Administrative Case	1	14	15	
行政非审查与执行	Administration No－examine and Carry Out	88	2658	2670	76
其他案件	Others Case	79	7296	7223	152
申诉申请再审	Appeal and Applying for Review	27	306	314	19
司法赔偿	Juridical Compensation		3	3	
减刑	Commutation		4632	4632	
假释	Parolee		662	662	

表 13—14 人民法院及检察院补充信息(2012)
Added Information of People's Court and Procurator's Offices

指标	单位	Indicators	unit	总计 Total
人民法院		**People's Court**		
办结申诉申请再审案件	件	Appeal and Applying for Review Closed	case	314
处理群众来信	件次	Deal with Letter from People	case—times	2092
群众来访人数	人次	People Come to Appeal for Help	person—times	2599
判决被告人	人	Adjudge defendant	person	20286
判处罪犯		Sentence Criminals	person	20285
宣告无罪	人	Declare Innocent	person	1
五年以上有期徒刑直到无期徒刑	人	Fixed—term Imprisonment of More than 5 years until Life Imprisonment	person	1783
不满五年有期徒刑	人	Fixed—term Imprisonment of Below 5 years	person	9118
缓刑	人	Probation	person	5506
免于刑事处分	人	Avoid Criminal Sanction	person	91
其他处理	人	Others	person	3787
#18—25 周岁罪犯	人	Between 18 until 25 Years Old	person	4408
#少年犯	人	Juvenile Criminal	person	1059
#女性犯罪	人	Female Criminal	person	1755
一审民商案件中解决争议标的	万元	Solve Amount of Disputed Bid for Civil & Economic Case in First Instance	10000 yuan	2720038
执行案件中执结标的	万元	Carry out Amount of Money in Carry out Case	10000 yuan	908510
办结经济犯罪	件	Closed Economic Criminal	case	2193
为国家,集体挽回经济损失	万元	Retrieve Economic Losses for State & Collective	10000 yuan	9756
办结申请公示催告和支付令的案	件	Closed Apply to Show the Demand Commonly & Indemnity	case	1426
标的	万元	Total Amount of Money	10000 yuan	31811
检察机关		**Procurator's Offices**		
立案查处贪污贿赂犯罪	件	Cases Registered for Corruption and Bribery	case	213
立案查处贪污贿赂犯罪	人	Cases Registered for Corruption and Bribery	person	251
立案查处渎职侵权犯罪	件	Cases Registered for Abuse and Dereliction of Duty	case	31
立案查处渎职侵权犯罪	人	Cases Registered for Abuse and Dereliction of Duty	person	56
批捕各类犯罪嫌疑人	人	Approve to Arrest Crime Suspects	person	12759
起诉各类犯罪被告人	人	Accuse Crime Suspects	person	20792
受理群众来信来访	件	Accept Public Report, Accuse Crime and Visit	case	1713
举报	件	Reporting of the Offence	case	604
控告	件	Accuse	case	559
申诉	件	Appeal	case	550
提出民事行政抗诉	件	Submit Civil and Administrative Counterappeal.	case	70

表 13－15 各县(市)火灾情况(2012)
Basic Statistics on Fires by Region

指标	单位	Indicators	Unit	全市 Total
火灾起因情况		**Cause of Fire**		
放火	起	Arson	case	8
电器	起	Electric Appliances	case	219
违章操作	起	Operation Against Rules	case	40
生产作业	起	Production Operations	case	40
吸烟	起	Smoking	case	19
其他原因	起	Others	case	31
重大火灾		**Heavy Fire**		
起火	起	Fire	case	
损失	万元	Losses	10000 yuan	
死亡	人	Deaths	person	
损失情况		**Situation of Losses**		
起数	起	Number	case	416
死亡	人	Deaths	person	9
伤人	人	Injuries	person	20
损失	万元	Losses	10000 yuan	981.40

市区 Urban District	#鄞州 Yinzhou	余姚 Yuyao	慈溪 Cixi	奉化 Fenghua	象山 Xiangshan	宁海 Ninghai
4	2				4	
74	32	15	50	14	27	39
23	3	1	7		4	5
23	3	1		7	4	5
11	4	1	2	1	4	
9	4	3	15	2		1
171	62	25	97	22	52	49
1		2	2	2	2	
13			2		5	
582.97	234.02	116.20	172.30	25.35	30.35	54.23

表 13－16 交通事故情况(2012) Basic Statistics on Traffic Accident

指标	Indicators	合计(Total)			
		事故次数(次) Number of Accident (case)	死亡人数(人) Deaths (person)	受伤人数(人) Injuries (person)	直接损失(万元) Direct Pecunlary Losses (10000 yuan)
总计	**Total**	**3082**	**680**	**3106**	**871.10**
机动车	Motor Vehicles	2742	639	2709	826.60
客运车辆	Passenger Vehicles	102	26	92	40.50
公共汽车	Buses	42	10	37	9.17
一般货运	General Cargos	521	187	443	174.83
企事业单位	Institutions and Enterprises	37	20	21	16.46
军队武警	Armed Forces	7	1	8	3.21
私用轿车	Individuals	965	145	976	314.04
其他	Others	628	146	609	183.66
摩托车	Motorcycles	390	91	482	76.44
拖拉机	Tractors	50	13	41	8.29
非机动车	Non－motor－driven Vehicles	329	35	392	43.05
其他及行人	Others and Pedestrians	11	6	5	1

城市(Urban)				农村(Rural)			
事故次数(次) Number of Accident (case)	死亡人数(人) Deaths (person)	受伤人数(人) Injuries (person)	直接损失(万元) Direct Pecunlary Losses (10000 yuan)	事故次数(次) Number of Accident (case)	死亡人数(人) Deaths (person)	受伤人数(人) Injuries (person)	直接损失(万元) Direct Pecunlary Losses (10000 yuan)
1202	**208**	**1212**	**282.95**	**1880**	**472**	**1894**	**588.15**
1055	190	1046	259.43	1687	449	1663	567.17
47	7	47	7.08	55	19	45	33.42
31	8	25	6.48	11	2	12	2.69
144	42	123	43.25	377	145	320	131.58
9	4	5	2.57	28	16	16	13.58
4		6	1.81	3	1	2	1.40
446	51	454	104.13	519	94	522	209.91
261	52	250	73.41	367	94	359	110.25
108	25	132	20.29	282	66	350	56.15
5	1	4	0.41	45	12	37	7.88
144	17	164	23.39	185	18	228	19.66
3	1	2	0.1	8	5	3	1.32

表 13－17 全市档案人员及馆藏和编研情况（2012） Conditions of Files Stored and Used in the Archives

指标	单位	Indicators	Unit	全市 Total	其中 of Which 市局馆 Municipal	市区合计 Urban District	县市合计 County
机构数	个	**Number of Institutions**	**unit**				
档案行政管理机构（档案馆）	个	Administrative Department of Archives	unit	12	1	6	5
现有工作人员数	人	Number of Staff and Workers	person				
档案行政管理机构（档案馆）	人	Administrative Department of Archives	person	176	39	56	81
馆藏档案		**Archives Stored**					
全宗	个	Whole Volume	unit	2554	421	801	1332
案卷	卷	Files	volume	1331985	224416	385275	722294
以件为保管单位档案	件	Archives Which Regard a Storage Unit by Files	pieces	848907	16824	729176	102907
录音、录象影片档案	盘	Records, Films on Videotape	copy	2462	445	683	1334
照片档案	张	Pictures	pieces	191597	24694	85603	81300
馆藏资料	册	Number of Material Stored	volume	97035	27650	37189	32196
档案馆总建筑面积	平方米	Floor Space of Archives	sq. m	38595	7900	16950	13745
档案库房建筑面积	平方米	Floor Space of Storerooms	sq. m	15302	3500	6954	4848
本年档案资料利用		Use of Material in This Year					
利用人次	人次	Number of Persons Using Material	times	59043	3339	14438	41266
利用档案	卷件次	Number of Archives Used	times	118584	11240	21442	85902
利用资料	册次	Number of Material Used	times	8045	2764	1963	3318
复制	页数	Copies	pages				
本年编研档案资料内部参考	万字	**Compiling and Researching Material Restricted**	**10000 words**	**58**	**5**	**15**	**38**
本年编研档案资料公开出版物	万字	**Public Press Compiling and Researching Material**	**10000 words**	**173.2**	**57.2**	**28**	**88**

注：统计范围：市，县（市）区档案局，国家综合档案馆

Note: Statistical Limits are Archives of Each District and County

主要统计指标解释

【全年供水总量】 指公用自来水厂和自备水源的社会单位全年的供水总量,包括有效供水量及损失水量。

【城市人口用水普及率】 指城市用水的非农业人口数(不包括临时人口和流动人口)与城市非农业人口总数的比例。计算公式:

用水普及率=(城市用水的非农业人口数÷城市非农业人口数)×100%

【公共绿地】 指供游览休息的各种公园﹑动物园、植物园、陵园、以及花园、游园和供旅游休息用的林荫道绿地、广场绿地。不包括一般栽植的行道树及林荫道的面积。

【废水排放总量】 包括生产废水和生活污水。生产废水指企、事业单位在生产、科研过程中向外排放的所有排放口的废水量总和。生活污水指城镇居民区和企、事业单位职工集中居住区排放的污水量。

【工业废水排放量】 指经过企业厂区所有排放口排到企业外部的工业废水量 。包括生产废水、外排的直接冷却水、超标排放的矿井地下水和与工业废水混排的厂区生活污水,不包括外排的间接冷却水(清污不分流的间按冷却水应计算在内)。

【工业废水排放达标量】 指各项指标都达到国家或地方排放标准的外排工业废水量,包括未经处理外排达标的和经过处理后外排达标的和两部分。国家排放标准见 GB8978-88。

【工业废气排放量】 指企业厂区内燃料燃烧和生产工艺过程中产生的各种排入空气的含有污染物的气体的总量,以标准状态(273K,101325Pa)计。

【工业粉尘排放量】 指企业在生产工艺过程中排放的颗粒物重量。如钢铁企业的耐火材料粉尘、焦化企业的筛焦系统粉尘、烧结机的粉尘、石灰窑的粉尘、建材企业的水泥粉尘等。不包括电厂排入大气的烟尘。

【工业粉尘回收量】 指经生产工艺废气净化处理装置处理回收的粉尘和尘泥量(包括干法和湿法)。不包括电厂的烟尘。通常情况下:

工业粉尘产生量=工业粉尘排放量+工业粉尘回收量

【工业固体废物产生量】 指企业在生产过程中产生的固体状、半固体状和高浓度液体状废弃物的总量,包括危险废物、冶炼废渣、粉煤灰、炉渣、煤矸石、尾矿、放射性 废物和其他废物等;不包括矿山开采的剥离废石和掘进废石(煤矸石和呈酸性或碱性的废石 除外)。酸性或碱性废石是指采掘的废石其流经水、雨淋水的 pH 值小于 4 或 pH 值大于 10.5 者 。

【社会福利事业单位】 指集中收养社会孤老,残,幼的机构。包括由民政部门管理的社会福利院、儿童福利院、精神病人福利院和城镇集体办的福利院,以及农村集体举 办的敬老院。

Explanatory Notes on Main Statistical Indicators

【Annual Volume of Water Supply】 refers to the total volume of water supplied by the public water—works and those owned by individual enterprises and institutions during the whole year, including both the effective water supply and loss during the water supply.

【Percentage of Urban Population with Access to Tap Water】 refers to the ratio of urban non—agricultural population (excluding temporary and mobile population) with access to tap water to the total urban non—agricultural population. The formula is: Percentage of Population with Access to Tap Water = (Urban Non—agricultural Population with Access to Tap Water ÷ Urban Non—agricultural Population) 100%

【Public Green Area】 refers to green areas of various parks, zoos, botanical gardens, cemeteries, amusement parks, tree—flanked boulevards, green—land squares for tourism and relaxation. Area with trees planted along—side the streets and boulevards are excluded.

【Total Discharge of Sewage】 includes production sewage and domestic sewage. Production sewage refers to the total discharge by the enterprises and institutions in their production and scientific research. Domestic sewage refers to the discharge by urban and rural residential communities and the residential neighborhoods of the enterprise/institutions staff.

【Volume of Industrial Waste Water Discharged】 refers to the volume of industrial waste water discharged, through all outlets, to the outside of industrial enterprises, including waste water produced, direct cooling water, underground water from mines that does not meet the standard of discharge, and the domestic sewage mixed up with industrial waste water when discharged, but excluding discharged indirect—cooling water.

【Volume of Waste Water up to the Standard for Discharge】 refers to the volume of discharged industrial waste water that, with or without treatment, has come up to the national or local standards for discharge.

【Volume of Waste Gas Emission】 refers to waste gas emitted from burning of fuels and from production process in the area of the factory, and is measured by 10000 standard cubic metres each year under normal condition.

【Industrial Dust Discharged】 refers to the total weight of solid dust discharged by industrial enterprises in the production process, such as dust of refractory materials from iron plants, dust from coke—screening system or from sintering machines of coking plants, dust from lime kilns, cement dust from building material enterprises, etc. but excluding smoke and dust discharged by power plants.

【Volume of Recovery of Industrial Dust】 refers to the volume of dust and dirt recovered by production process purification devices, including both dry process and wet process, not the fly ash emitted into the air by power station. Generally, the formula goes:

Industrial Dust Produced = Industrial Dust Emitted + Industrial Dust Recovered

【Volume of Industrial Solid Wastes Produced】 refers to the total volume of solid, semi-solid or high concentration liquid residue produced by industrial enterprises in their production process, including dangerous wastes, residues from melting, slag, powdered coal ash, gangue, chemical residues, tailings, radioactive residues and other residues, but excluding stripped or dug stones in mining (except gangue and acid or alkali stones which are stones washed or soaked by water with a pH value smaller than 4 or larger than 10. 5.)

【Social Welfare Institutions】 refer to institutions taking care of old people without children, handicapped people and orphans. They include social welfare institutions run by civil affairs departments, children's welfare institutions social welfare institutions for mental patients, and collective-owned old people's homes in tualareas.

NINGBO

Statistical YearBook

第十四篇

企业景气指数

PROSPERITY INDEX ON ENTERPRISES

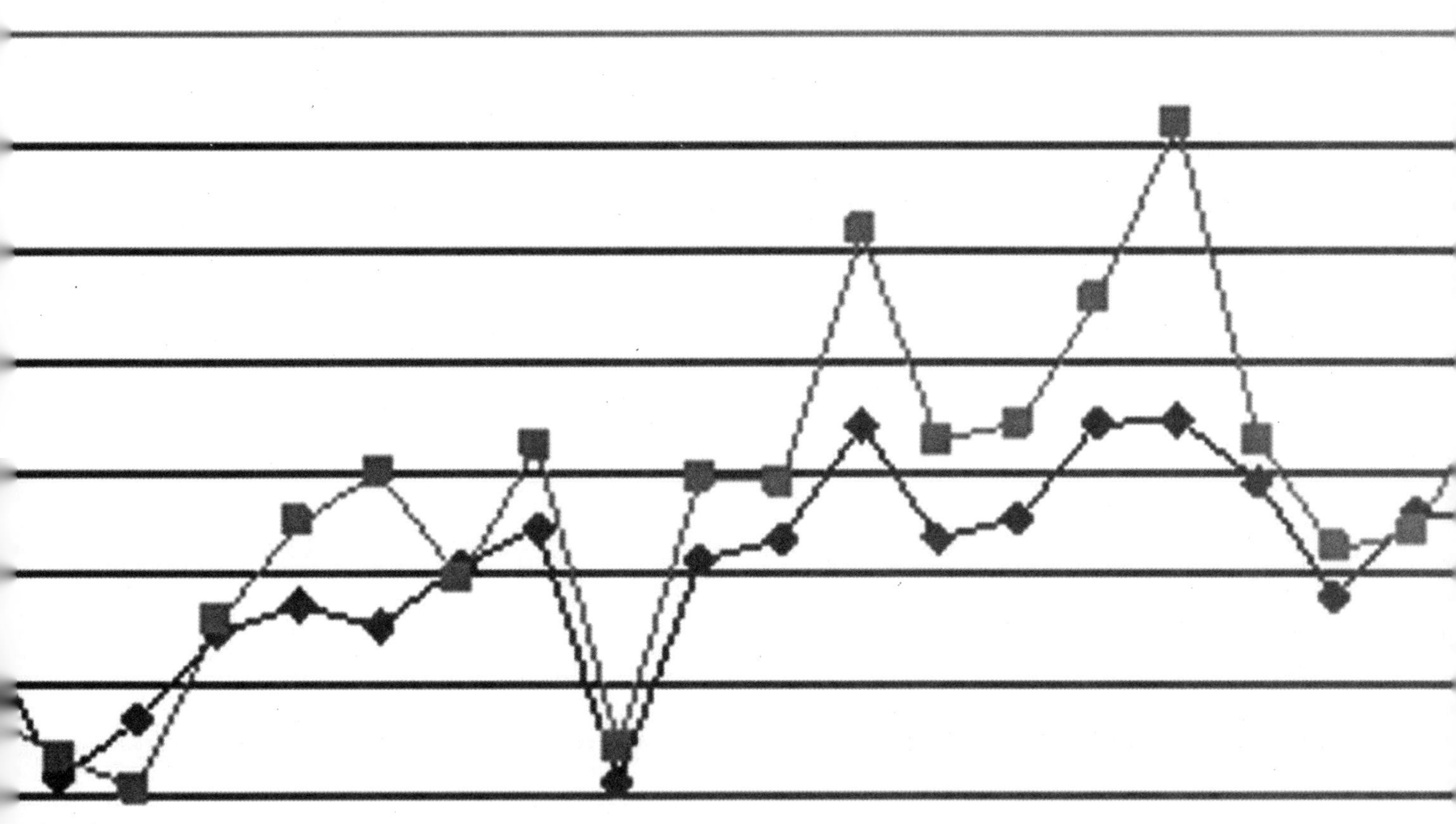

企业景气
Prosperity on Enterprises

主要统计指标
Major Statistics Indicators

		第一季度 1st. Quarter	第二季度 2st. Quarter	第三季度 3st. Quarter	第四季度 4st. Quarter
企业家信心指数	Index of Confidence by Enterprisers				
指数	Index	118.8	115.6	110.1	117.9
即期	Demand	114.1	114.9	109.8	117.7
预期	Expectation	121.9	116.1	110.3	118.0
企业景气指数	Prosperity index of Enterprises				
指数	Index	126.5	126.0	120.6	123.7
即期	Demand	117.0	123.9	116.3	125.9
预期	Expectation	132.8	127.4	123.5	122.1
工业企业	Industrial Enterprises				
指数	Index	123.6	120.2	115.3	116.4
即期	Demand	108.2	119.0	111.3	121.0
预期	Expectation	133.9	121.0	118.0	113.3
建筑业企业	Construction Enterprises				
指数	Index	162.9	166.9	152.6	161.6
即期	Demand	154.3	160.0	145.7	162.9
预期	Expectation	168.6	171.4	157.1	160.0
交通运输、仓储和邮政业企业	Transport. Storage and Post Enterprises				
指数	Index	111.6	126.5	114.8	113.3
即期	Demand	100.0	122.6	112.9	113.3
预期	Expectation	119.4	129.0	116.1	113.3
批发和零售业企业	Wholesale and Retail Sale Enterprises				
指数	Index	130.4	130.8	128.8	131.3
即期	Demand	129.2	127.1	125.0	125.0
预期	Expectation	131.3	133.3	131.3	135.4
住宿和餐饮业企业	Hotels and Catering Trade Enterprises				
指数	Index	118.7	116.0	118.0	118.7
即期	Demand	112.9	120.0	90.0	116.7
预期	Expectation	122.6	113.3	136.7	120.0
房地产企业	Real Estate Enterprises				
指数	Index	84.0	99.4	94.3	108.2
即期	Demand	85.7	94.3	94.3	111.8
预期	Expectation	82.9	102.9	94.3	105.9
社会服务业企业	Social Services Enterprises				
指数	Index	139.4	126.1	122.4	130.9
即期	Demand	139.4	133.3	124.2	136.4
预期	Expectation	139.4	121.2	121.2	127.3
信息传输、计算机服务和软件业企业	Information Transmission, Computer Service and Software Enterprises				
指数	Index	158.8	146.1	141.8	130.9
即期	Demand	151.5	142.4	136.4	145.5
预期	Expectation	163.6	148.5	145.5	121.2

表 14-1 企业景气指数(2012)
Prosperity Index of Enterprises

单位:点(point)

指标	Indicators	一季度 1st. Quarter	二季度 2st. Quarter	三季度 3st. Quarter	四季度 4st. Quarter
企业景气指数	**Prosperity Index of Enterprises**				
指数	**Index**	**126.5**	**126.0**	**120.6**	**123.7**
即期	**Demand**	**117.0**	**123.9**	**116.3**	**125.9**
预期	**Expectation**	**132.8**	**127.4**	**123.5**	**122.1**
按登记注册类型分	**By Registration Status**				
国有企业	State-Owned Enterprises				
指数	Index	152.0	143.7	142.7	146.1
即期	Demand	146.6	124.5	145.0	162.9
预期	Expectation	155.6	156.6	141.1	134.9
有限责任公司	Limited Liability Corporations				
指数	Index	121.9	123.3	122.5	121.3
即期	Demand	113.7	123.3	118.3	120.5
预期	Expectation	127.4	123.4	125.3	121.8
股份有限公司	Share-holding Corporations Ltd.				
指数	Index	127.4	131.6	121.4	122.2
即期	Demand	116.7	125.6	120.0	126.1
预期	Expectation	134.5	135.6	122.4	119.5
私营企业	Private Enterprises				
指数	Index	120.2	127.2	113.5	121.8
即期	Demand	110.6	118.5	100.4	125.2
预期	Expectation	126.6	133.0	122.3	119.5
港、澳、台商投资企业	Hongkong, Macao and Taiwan Funded				
指数	Index	134.5	123.5	118.0	118.5
即期	Demand	123.7	128.8	119.2	117.3
预期	Expectation	141.7	119.9	117.2	119.3
外商投资企业	Enterprises with Foreign Investment				
指数	Index	111.2	99.5	98.7	107.6
即期	Demand	96.2	104.5	88.4	110.7
预期	Expectation	121.2	96.2	105.6	105.6
按行业分	**By Sector**				
工业	Industry				
指数	Index	123.6	120.2	115.3	116.4
即期	Demand	108.2	119.0	111.3	121.0
预期	Expectation	133.9	121.0	118.0	113.3

表 14-1 续表 Continued 单位:点(point)

指标	Indicators	一季度 1st. Quarter	二季度 2st. Quarter	三季度 3st. Quarter	四季度 4st. Quarter
建筑业	Construction				
指数	Index	162.9	166.9	152.6	161.1
即期	Demand	154.3	160.0	145.7	162.9
预期	Expectation	168.6	171.4	157.1	160.0
交通运输、仓储和邮政业	Transport,Storage and Post				
指数	Index	111.6	126.5	114.8	113.3
即期	Demand	100.0	122.6	112.9	113.3
预期	Expectation	119.4	129.0	116.1	113.3
批发和零售业	Wholesale and Retail Sale Trade				
指数	Index	130.4	130.8	128.8	131.3
即期	Demand	129.2	127.1	125.0	125.0
预期	Expectation	131.3	133.3	131.3	135.4
住宿和餐饮业	Hotels and Catering Trade				
指数	Index	118.7	116.0	118.0	118.7
即期	Demand	112.9	120.0	90.0	116.7
预期	Expectation	122.6	113.3	136.7	120.0
房地产业	Real Estate				
指数	Index	84.0	99.4	94.3	108.2
即期	Demand	85.7	94.3	94.3	111.8
预期	Expectation	82.9	102.9	94.3	105.9
社会服务业	Social Services				
指数	Index	139.4	126.1	122.4	130.9
即期	Demand	139.4	133.3	124.2	136.4
预期	Expectation	139.4	121.2	121.2	127.3
信息传输、计算机服务和软件业	Information Transmission,Computer Service and Saftuare				
指数	Index	158.8	146.1	141.8	130.9
即期	Demand	151.5	142.4	136.4	145.5
预期	Expectation	163.6	148.5	145.5	121.2
按观察指标分	**By the Observation Index**				
盈利(亏损)变化	Changes of Profit(Loss)	90.0	92.4	88.7	93.2
企业融资	Corporate Finance	101.2	102.8	105.6	104.5
用工计划	Employment Plan	118.9	107.0	106.3	107.2
固定资产投资	Fixed Asset	112.1	101.4	101.4	94.4

表 14-2　企业家信心指数(2012)
Index of Confidence on Macro Economy of Enterprisers

单位:点(point)

指标	Indicators	一季度 1st. Quarter	二季度 2st. Quarter	三季度 3st. Quarter	四季度 4st. Quarter
企业家信心指数	**Index of Confidence by Enterprisers**				
指数	**Index**	**118.8**	**115.6**	**110.1**	**117.9**
即期	**Demand**	**114.1**	**114.9**	**109.8**	**117.7**
预期	**Expectation**	**121.9**	**116.1**	**110.3**	**118.0**
按登记注册类型分	**By Registration Status**				
国有企业	State-Owned Enterprises				
指数	Index	146.9	131.2	135.2	155.7
即期	Demand	145.1	128.6	128.3	157.4
预期	Expectation	148.0	132.9	139.8	154.6
有限责任公司	Limited Liability Corporations				
指数	Index	119.0	116.4	112.0	118.2
即期	Demand	112.8	116.2	112.0	118.1
预期	Expectation	123.1	116.5	112.0	118.3
股份有限公司	Share-holding Corporations Ltd.				
指数	Index	114.3	111.7	104.3	105.5
即期	Demand	108.9	107.5	102.7	100.7
预期	Expectation	117.9	114.5	105.4	108.8
私营企业	Private Enterprises				
指数	Index	115.6	118.9	111.2	122.5
即期	Demand	113.5	119.0	117.7	119.8
预期	Expectation	117.0	118.9	106.8	124.3
港、澳、台商投资企业	Hongkong, Macao and Taiwan Funded				
指数	Index	117.9	117.1	104.7	108.8
即期	Demand	114.3	116.7	100.1	111.4
预期	Expectation	120.3	117.4	107.8	107.0
外商投资企业	Enterprises with Foreign Investment				
指数	Index	108.6	98.1	96.0	107.2
即期	Demand	102.2	96.2	87.4	105.6
预期	Expectation	112.9	99.4	101.8	108.4

表 14－2 续表 Continued 单位：点(point)

指标	Indicators	一季度 1st. Quarter	二季度 2st. Quarter	三季度 3st. Quarter	四季度 4st. Quarter
按行业分	**By Sector**				
工业	Industry				
指数	Index	119.5	111.9	101.6	111.3
即期	Demand	111.8	111.3	101.0	112.8
预期	Expectation	124.6	112.3	102.1	110.3
建筑业	Construction				
指数	Index	160.0	149.7	143.4	154.3
即期	Demand	160.0	142.9	148.6	154.3
预期	Expectation	160.0	154.3	140.0	154.3
交通运输、仓储和邮政业	Transport,Storage and Post				
指数	Index	101.9	114.8	101.9	112.0
即期	Demand	100.0	112.9	109.7	110.0
预期	Expectation	103.2	116.1	96.8	113.3
批发和零售业	Wholesale and Retail Sale Trade				
指数	Index	122.1	120.4	120.8	124.6
即期	Demand	120.8	122.9	120.8	120.8
预期	Expectation	122.9	118.8	120.8	127.1
住宿和餐饮业	Hotels and Catering Trade				
指数	Index	120.0	122.0	127.3	135.3
即期	Demand	125.8	130.0	103.3	143.3
预期	Expectation	116.1	116.7	143.3	130.0
房地产业	Real Estate				
指数	Index	50.9	77.1	78.9	88.2
即期	Demand	45.7	68.6	77.1	79.4
预期	Expectation	54.3	82.9	80.0	94.1
社会服务业	Social Services				
指数	Index	125.5	118.2	122.4	125.5
即期	Demand	118.2	118.2	124.2	127.3
预期	Expectation	130.3	118.2	121.2	124.2
信息传输、计算机服务和软件业	Information Transmission,Computer Service and Saftuare				
指数	Index	149.7	132.7	141.2	129.7
即期	Demand	151.5	145.5	139.4	133.3
预期	Expectation	148.5	124.2	142.4	127.3

表 14－3 工业企业景气状况(2012) Prosperity Index of Industrial Enterprises

单位:点(point)

指标	Indicators	一季度 1st. Quarter	二季度 2st. Quarter	三季度 3st. Quarter	四季度 4st. Quarter
企业景气指数	Prosperity Index of Enterprises				
总指数	Combined Index	123.6	120.2	115.3	116.4
即期	Demand	108.2	119.0	111.3	121.0
预期	Expectation	133.9	121.0	118.0	113.3
企业家信心指数	Index of Confidence by Enterprisers				
总指数	Combined Index	119.5	111.9	101.6	111.3
即期	Demand	111.8	111.3	101.0	112.8
预期	Expectation	124.6	112.3	102.1	110.3
产品订货量(与上季度比)	Production Order (Compared with the Previous Quarter)				
指数	Index	87.7	107.7	95.9	103.6
增加(%)	Increase(%)	17.4	29.7	23.6	27.2
持平(%)	Flat(%)	52.8	48.2	48.7	49.2
减少(%)	Decrease(%)	29.2	22.1	27.7	23.6
产品订货中的出口订货量	Export Orders				
指数	Index	93.9	109.2	95.4	98.5
增加(%)	Increase(%)	12.3	22.6	15.4	16.4
持平(%)	Flat(%)	69.2	64.1	64.6	65.6
减少(%)	Decrease(%)	18.0	13.3	20.0	17.4
产成品库存(本季度)	Stock of Finished Production				
指数	Index	110.8	112.8	116.9	107.7
增加(%)	Increase(%)	15.9	17.4	18.5	12.3
持平(%)	Flat(%)	79.0	78.0	80.0	83.1
减少(%)	Decrease(%)	5.1	4.6	1.5	4.6
企业融资(本季度)	Corporate Finance				
指数	Index	106.2	110.3	110.8	111.3
增加(%)	Increase(%)	16.4	18.5	20.0	21.0
持平(%)	Flat(%)	73.3	73.3	70.8	69.2
减少(%)	Decrease(%)	10.3	8.2	9.2	9.7
用工计划(下季度比本季度)	Employment Plan (Next Quarter than the Quarter)				
指数	Index	118.5	102.1	99.5	107.7
增加(%)	Increase(%)	28.2	15.9	12.3	17.4
持平(%)	Flat(%)	62.1	70.3	74.9	72.8
减少(%)	Decrease(%)	9.7	13.9	12.8	9.7
固定资产投资(下季度比本季度)	Fixed Asset (Next Quarter than the Quarter)				
指数	Index	111.8	97.4	99.5	92.3
增加(%)	Increase(%)	24.6	14.9	17.4	13.9
持平(%)	Flat(%)	62.6	67.7	64.6	64.6
减少(%)	Decrease(%)	12.8	17.4	18.0	21.5

表 14－4　建筑业企业景气状况(2012)
Prosperity Index of Construction Enterprises

单位:点(point)

指标	Indicators	一季度 1st. Quarter	二季度 2st. Quarter	三季度 3st. Quarter	四季度 4st. Quarter
企业景气指数	Prosperity Index of Enterprises				
总指数	Combined Index	162.9	166.9	152.6	161.1
即期	Demand	154.3	160.0	145.7	162.9
预期	Expectation	168.6	171.4	157.1	160.0
企业家信心指数	Index of Confidence by Enterprisers				
总指数	Combined Index	160.0	149.7	143.4	154.3
即期	Demand	160.0	142.9	148.6	154.3
预期	Expectation	160.0	154.3	140.0	154.3
工程合同(比去年同期)	Project Contract Signed (year－on－year)				
指数	Index	108.6	111.4	105.7	120.0
增加(%)	Increase(%)	37.1	45.7	40.0	45.7
持平(%)	Flat(%)	34.3	20.0	25.7	28.6
减少(%)	Decrease(%)	28.6	34.3	34.3	25.7
建筑工程量(比去年同期)	Project Quantity of Construction (year－on－year)				
指数	Index	111.4	137.1	145.7	142.9
增加(%)	Increase(%)	34.3	54.3	57.1	48.6
持平(%)	Flat(%)	42.9	28.6	31.4	45.7
减少(%)	Decrease(%)	22.9	17.1	11.4	5.7
新开工工程量(比去年同期)	New Construction Projects (year－on－year)				
指数	Index	111.4	120.0	114.3	108.6
增加(%)	Increase(%)	31.4	45.7	34.3	37.1
持平(%)	Flat(%)	48.6	28.6	45.7	34.3
减少(%)	Decrease(%)	20.0	25.7	20.0	28.6
建筑材料购进价格(比上季度)	Purchase Price of Building Materials (Compared with the Previous Quarter)				
指数	Index	74.3	88.6	117.1	97.1
下降(%)	Decline(%)	11.4	8.6	31.4	20.0
持平(%)	Flat(%)	51.4	71.4	54.3	57.1
上升(%)	Rise(%)	37.1	20.0	14.3	22.9

表 14－4 续表 Continued　　　　单位：点(point)

指标	Indicators	一季度 1st. Quarter	二季度 2st. Quarter	三季度 3st. Quarter	四季度 4st. Quarter
盈利(亏损)变化	Changes of Profit(Loss)				
指数	Index	91.4	88.6	85.7	85.7
好于正常水平(%)	Better than Normal Level(%)	0.0	0.0	0.0	2.9
正常水平(%)	Normal Level(%)	91.4	88.6	85.7	80.0
差于正常水平(%)	Worse than Normal Level(%)	8.6	11.4	14.3	17.1
企业融资	Corporate Finance				
指数	Index	94.3	85.7	91.4	88.6
容易(%)	Easy(%)	14.3	8.6	11.4	17.1
一般(%)	General(%)	65.7	68.6	68.6	54.3
困难(%)	Difficulties(%)	20.0	22.9	20.0	28.6
工程款拖欠(比上季度)	Arrears (Compared with the Previous Quarter)				
指数	Index	111.4	111.4	71.4	91.4
减少(%)	Decrease(%)	28.6	22.9	8.6	20.0
持平(%)	Flat(%)	54.3	65.7	54.3	51.4
增加(%)	Increase(%)	17.1	11.4	37.1	28.6
用工计划(下季度比本季度)	Employment Plan (Next Quarter than the Quarter)				
指数	Index	154.3	151.4	134.3	105.7
增加(%)	Increase(%)	60.0	54.3	34.3	22.9
持平(%)	Flat(%)	34.3	42.9	65.7	60.0
减少(%)	Decrease(%)	5.7	2.9	0.0	17.1
固定资产投资(下季度比本季度)	Fixed Asset (Next Quarter than the Quarter)				
指数	Index	120.0	117.1	102.9	97.1
增加(%)	Increase(%)	31.4	31.4	22.9	17.1
持平(%)	Flat(%)	57.1	54.3	57.1	62.9
减少(%)	Decrease(%)	11.4	14.3	20.0	20.0

表 14－5 交通运输、仓储和邮政业企业景气状况(2012)
Prosperity Index of Transport, Storage and Post Enterprises

单位:点(point)

指标	Indicators	一季度 1st. Quarter	二季度 2st. Quarter	三季度 3st. Quarter	四季度 4st. Quarter
企业景气指数	Prosperity Index of Enterprises				
总指数	Combined Index	111.6	116.3	114.8	113.3
即期	Demand	100.0	100.0	112.9	113.3
预期	Expectation	119.4	127.1	116.1	113.3
企业家信心指数	Index of Confidence by Enterprisers				
总指数	Combined Index	101.9	120.4	101.9	112.0
即期	Demand	100.0	122.9	109.7	110.0
预期	Expectation	103.2	118.8	96.8	113.3
业务预订(本季度比上季度)	Business Book (Compared with the Previous Quarter)				
指数	Index	87.1	104.2	103.2	100.0
增加(%)	Increase(%)	19.4	18.8	22.6	16.7
持平(%)	Flat(%)	48.4	66.7	58.1	66.7
减少(%)	Decrease(%)	32.3	14.6	19.4	16.7
业务量(下季度比本季度)	Business Volume (Next Quarter than the Quarter)				
指数	Index	148.4	116.7	96.8	93.3
增加(%)	Increase(%)	54.8	35.4	16.1	13.3
持平(%)	Flat(%)	38.7	45.8	64.5	66.7
减少(%)	Decrease(%)	6.5	18.8	19.4	20.0
盈利(亏损)变化	Changes of Profit(Loss)				
指数	Index	74.2	93.8	61.3	76.7
好于正常水平(%)	Better than Normal Level(%)	3.2	4.2	3.2	3.3
正常水平(%)	Normal Level(%)	67.7	85.4	54.8	70.0
差于正常水平(%)	Worse than Normal Level(%)	29.0	10.4	41.9	26.7
企业融资	Corporate Finance				
指数	Index	103.2	85.4	87.1	83.3
容易(%)	Easy(%)	19.4	10.4	12.9	16.7
一般(%)	General(%)	64.5	64.6	61.3	50.0
困难(%)	Difficulties(%)	16.1	25.0	25.8	33.3
用工计划(下季度比本季度)	Employment Plan (Next Quarter than the Quarter)				
指数	Index	116.1	116.7	106.5	96.7
增加(%)	Increase(%)	25.8	18.8	9.7	6.7
持平(%)	Flat(%)	64.5	79.2	87.1	83.3
减少(%)	Decrease(%)	9.7	2.1	3.2	10.0
固定资产投资(下季度比本季度)	Fixed Asset (Next Quarter than the Quarter)				
指数	Index	125.8	102.1	103.2	90.0
增加(%)	Increase(%)	29.0	8.3	12.9	10.0
持平(%)	Flat(%)	67.7	85.4	77.4	70.0
减少(%)	Decrease(%)	3.2	6.3	9.7	20.0

表 14－6　批发和零售业企业景气状况(2012)
Prosperity Index of Wholesale and Retail Sale Enterprises

单位:点(point)

指标	Indicators	一季度 1st. Quarter	二季度 2st. Quarter	三季度 3st. Quarter	四季度 4st. Quarter
企业景气指数	Prosperity Index of Enterprises				
总指数	Combined Index	130.4	130.8	128.8	131.3
即期	Demand	129.2	127.1	125.0	125.0
预期	Expectation	131.3	133.3	131.3	135.4
企业家信心指数	Index of Confidence by Enterprisers				
总指数	Combined Index	122.1	120.4	120.8	124.6
即期	Demand	120.8	122.9	120.8	120.8
预期	Expectation	122.9	118.8	120.8	127.1
购货合同	Purchase Contract				
指数	Index	97.9	104.2	104.2	112.5
增加(%)	Increase(%)	16.7	18.8	22.9	22.9
持平(%)	Flat(%)	64.6	66.7	58.3	66.7
减少(%)	Decrease(%)	16.7	14.6	18.8	10.4
商品销售(下季度比本季度)	Total Sales of Goods (Next Quarter than the Quarter)				
指数	Index	110.4	116.7	135.4	125.0
较多(%)	More(%)	31.3	35.4	43.8	37.5
一般(%)	General(%)	47.9	45.8	47.9	50.0
较少(%)	Less(%)	20.8	18.8	8.3	12.5
商品库存	Inventory of Goods				
指数	Index	93.8	93.8	85.4	91.7
低于正常水平(%)	Below the Normal Level (%)	2.1	4.2	4.2	6.3
正常水平(%)	Normal Level (%)	89.6	85.4	77.1	79.2
高于正常水平(%)	Higher than Normal Level (%)	8.3	10.4	18.8	14.6
盈利(亏损)变化	Changes of Profit(Loss)				
指数	Index	85.4	85.4	77.1	91.7
好于正常水平(%)	Better than Normal Level(%)	4.2	10.4	6.3	8.3
正常水平(%)	Normal Level(%)	77.1	64.6	64.6	75.0
差于正常水平(%)	Worse than Normal Level(%)	18.8	25.0	29.2	16.7
企业融资	Corporate Finance				
指数	Index	110.4	116.7	122.9	114.6
容易(%)	Easy(%)	16.7	18.8	25.0	20.8
一般(%)	General(%)	77.1	79.2	72.9	72.9
困难(%)	Difficulties(%)	6.3	2.1	2.1	6.3
用工计划(下季度比本季度)	Employment Plan (Next Quarter than the Quarter)				
指数	Index	110.4	102.1	110.4	112.5
增加(%)	Increase(%)	12.5	8.3	16.7	18.8
持平(%)	Flat(%)	85.4	85.4	77.1	75.0
减少(%)	Decrease(%)	2.1	6.3	6.3	6.3
固定资产投资(下季度比本季度)	Fixed Asset (Next Quarter than the Quarter)				
指数	Index	114.6	100.0	97.9	95.8
增加(%)	Increase(%)	18.8	6.3	12.5	8.3
持平(%)	Flat(%)	77.1	87.5	72.9	79.2
减少(%)	Decrease(%)	4.2	6.3	14.6	12.5

表 14－7 住宿和餐饮业企业景气状况(2012)
Prosperity Index of Hotels and Catering Trade Enterprises

单位:点(point)

指标	Indicators	一季度 1st. Quarter	二季度 2st. Quarter	三季度 3st. Quarter	四季度 4st. Quarter
企业景气指数	Prosperity Index of Enterprises				
总指数	Combined Index	118.7	116.0	118.0	118.7
即期	Demand	112.9	120.0	90.0	116.7
预期	Expectation	122.6	113.3	136.7	120.0
企业家信心指数	Index of Confidence by Enterprisers				
总指数	Combined Index	120.0	122.0	127.3	135.3
即期	Demand	125.8	130.0	103.3	143.3
预期	Expectation	116.1	116.7	143.3	130.0
业务预订(比上季度)	Business Book (Compared with the Previous Quarter)				
指数	Index	71.0	76.7	90.0	110.0
增加(%)	Increase(%)	12.9	26.7	33.3	36.7
持平(%)	Flat(%)	45.2	23.3	23.3	36.7
减少(%)	Decrease(%)	41.9	50.0	43.3	26.7
业务量(比上季度)	Business Volume (Compared with the Previous Quarter)				
指数	Index	64.5	86.7	73.3	120.0
增加(%)	Increase(%)	12.9	30.0	23.3	46.7
持平(%)	Flat(%)	38.7	26.7	26.7	26.7
减少(%)	Decrease(%)	48.4	43.3	50.0	26.7
客房出租	Room Occupancy				
指数	Index	77.4	103.3	90.0	90.0
80%以上(%)	More than 80%	9.7	16.7	13.3	10.0
50－80%(%)	50－80%	58.1	70.0	63.3	70.0
50%以下(%)	Below than 50%	32.3	13.3	23.3	20.0
盈利(亏损)变化	Changes of Profit(Loss)				
指数	Index	64.5	73.3	66.7	90.0
好于正常水平(%)	Better than Normal Level(%)	3.2	6.7	6.7	13.3
正常水平(%)	Normal Level(%)	58.1	60.0	53.3	63.3
差于正常水平(%)	Worse than Normal Level(%)	38.7	33.3	40.0	23.3
企业融资	Corporate Finance				
指数	Index	109.7	106.7	113.3	110.0
容易(%)	Easy(%)	19.4	16.7	23.3	23.3
一般(%)	General(%)	71.0	73.3	66.7	63.3
困难(%)	Difficulties(%)	9.7	10.0	10.0	13.3
用工计划(下季度比本季度)	Employment Plan (Next Quarter than the Quarter)				
指数	Index	106.5	103.3	120.0	126.7
增加(%)	Increase(%)	25.8	16.7	26.7	40.0
持平(%)	Flat(%)	54.8	70.0	66.7	46.7
减少(%)	Decrease(%)	19.4	13.3	6.7	13.3
固定资产投资(下季度比本季度)	Fixed Asset (Next Quarter than the Quarter)				
指数	Index	122.6	116.7	126.7	110.0
增加(%)	Increase(%)	32.3	30.0	36.7	20.0
持平(%)	Flat(%)	58.1	56.7	53.3	70.0
减少(%)	Decrease(%)	9.7	13.3	10.0	10.0

表 14－8 表 14－8 房地产业企业景气状况(2012) Prosperity Index of Real Estate Enterprises

单位:点(point)

指标	Indicators	一季度 1st. Quarter	二季度 2st. Quarter	三季度 3st. Quarter	四季度 4st. Quarter
企业景气指数	Prosperity Index of Enterprises				
总指数	Combined Index	84.0	99.4	94.3	108.2
即期	Demand	85.7	94.3	94.3	111.8
预期	Expectation	82.9	102.9	94.3	105.9
企业家信心指数	Index of Confidence by Enterprisers				
总指数	Combined Index	50.9	77.1	78.9	88.2
即期	Demand	45.7	68.6	77.1	79.4
预期	Expectation	54.3	82.9	80.0	94.1
土地购置(比上季度)	Acquisition of Land (Compared with the Previous Quarter)				
指数	Index	80.0	82.9	88.6	88.2
增加(%)	Increase(%)	0.0	0.0	2.9	0.0
持平(%)	Flat(%)	80.0	82.9	82.9	88.2
减少(%)	Decrease(%)	20.0	17.1	14.3	11.8
土地购置(下季度比本季度)	Acquisition of Land (Next Quarter than the Quarter)				
指数	Index	80.0	91.4	88.6	94.1
增加(%)	Increase(%)	0.0	0.0	2.9	5.9
持平(%)	Flat(%)	80.0	91.4	82.9	82.4
减少(%)	Decrease(%)	20.0	8.6	14.3	11.8
新开工情况(比上季度)	Buildings Newly Started (Compared with the Previous Quarter)				
指数	Index	71.4	85.7	88.6	88.2
增加(%)	Increase(%)	2.9	2.9	5.7	8.8
持平(%)	Flat(%)	65.7	80.0	77.1	70.6
减少(%)	Decrease(%)	31.4	17.1	17.1	20.6
商品房预售(比上季度)	Commercial House Advance Sold (Compared with the Previous Quarter)				
指数	Index	68.6	108.6	100.0	111.8
增加(%)	Increase(%)	5.7	20.0	22.9	26.5
持平(%)	Flat(%)	57.1	68.6	54.3	58.8
减少(%)	Decrease(%)	37.1	11.4	22.9	14.7
商品房销售(包括预售)价格(比上季度)	Commercial Housing Sales (including Pre－sale) Price (Compared with the Previous Quarter)				
指数	Index	74.3	82.9	85.7	91.2
上升(%)	Rise(%)	2.9	5.7	5.7	8.8
持平(%)	Flat(%)	68.6	71.4	74.3	73.5
下降(%)	Decline(%)	28.6	22.9	20.0	17.7

表 14—8 续表 Continued　　单位：点(point)

指标	Indicators	一季度 1st. Quarter	二季度 2st. Quarter	三季度 3st. Quarter	四季度 4st. Quarter
商品房销售(包括预售)价格(下季度比本季度)	Commercial Housing Sales (including Pre－sale) Price (Next Quarter than the Quarter)				
指数	Index	80.0	88.6	88.6	105.9
上升(%)	Rise(%)	2.9	2.9	11.4	11.8
持平(%)	Flat(%)	74.3	82.9	65.7	82.4
下降(%)	Decline(%)	22.9	14.3	22.9	5.9
待售商品房(上季度)	Commercial housing for sale (the Previous Quarter)				
指数	Index	117.1	102.9	122.9	123.5
增加(%)	Increase(%)	28.6	20.0	37.1	35.3
持平(%)	Flat(%)	60.0	62.9	48.6	52.9
减少(%)	Decrease(%)	11.4	17.1	14.3	11.8
盈利(亏损)变化	Changes of Profit(Loss)				
指数	Index	57.1	80.0	71.4	73.5
好于正常水平(%)	Better than Normal Level(%)	0.0	2.9	5.7	2.9
正常水平(%)	Normal Level(%)	57.1	74.3	60.0	67.7
差于正常水平(%)	Worse than Normal Level(%)	42.9	22.9	34.3	29.4
企业融资	Corporate Finance				
指数	Index	51.4	51.4	60.0	64.7
容易(%)	Easy(%)	0.0	0.0	2.9	0.0
一般(%)	General(%)	51.4	51.4	54.3	64.7
困难(%)	Difficulties(%)	48.6	48.6	42.9	35.3
用工计划(下季度比本季度)	Employment Plan (Next Quarter than the Quarter)				
指数	Index	100.0	91.4	94.3	91.2
增加(%)	Increase(%)	8.6	5.7	8.6	5.9
持平(%)	Flat(%)	82.9	80.0	77.1	79.4
减少(%)	Decrease(%)	8.6	14.3	14.3	14.7
固定资产投资(下季度比本季度)	Fixed Asset (Next Quarter than the Quarter)				
指数	Index	91.4	97.1	94.3	88.2
增加(%)	Increase(%)	5.7	5.7	5.7	8.8
持平(%)	Flat(%)	80.0	85.7	82.9	70.6
减少(%)	Decrease(%)	14.3	8.6	11.4	20.6

表 14－9 表 14－9 社会服务业企业景气状况(2012) Prosperity Index of Social Services Enterprises

单位：点(point)

指标	Indicators	一季度 1st. Quarter	二季度 2st. Quarter	三季度 3st. Quarter	四季度 4st. Quarter
企业景气指数	Prosperity Index of Enterprises				
总指数	Combined Index	139.4	126.1	122.4	130.9
即期	Demand	139.4	133.3	124.2	136.4
预期	Expectation	139.4	121.2	121.2	127.3
企业家信心指数	Index of Confidence by Enterprisers				
总指数	Combined Index	125.5	118.2	122.4	125.5
即期	Demand	118.2	118.2	124.2	127.3
预期	Expectation	130.3	118.2	121.2	124.2
服务预订(比上季度)	Reservation Services (Compared with the Previous Quarter)				
指数	Index	136.4	103.0	100.0	109.1
增加(%)	Increase(%)	39.4	21.2	18.2	21.2
持平(%)	Flat(%)	57.6	60.6	63.6	66.7
减少(%)	Decrease(%)	3.0	18.2	18.2	12.1
业务量(比去年同期)	Business Volume(year－on－year)				
指数	Index	115.2	106.1	103.0	109.1
增加(%)	Increase(%)	30.3	21.2	15.2	30.3
持平(%)	Flat(%)	54.6	63.6	72.7	48.5
减少(%)	Decrease(%)	15.2	15.2	12.1	21.2
盈利(亏损)变化	Changes of Profit(Loss)				
指数	Index	84.9	84.9	87.9	93.9
好于正常水平(%)	Better than Normal Level(%)	6.1	6.1	3.0	15.2
正常水平(%)	Normal Level(%)	72.7	72.7	81.8	63.6
差于正常水平(%)	Worse than Normal Level(%)	21.2	21.2	15.2	21.2
企业融资	Corporate Finance				
指数	Index	103.0	106.1	109.1	109.1
容易(%)	Easy(%)	21.2	27.3	24.2	24.2
一般(%)	General(%)	60.6	51.5	60.6	60.6
困难(%)	Difficulties(%)	18.2	21.2	15.2	15.2
用工计划(下季度比本季度)	Employment Plan (Next Quarter than the Quarter)				
指数	Index	112.1	97.0	109.1	100.0
增加(%)	Increase(%)	18.2	15.2	18.2	15.2
持平(%)	Flat(%)	75.8	66.7	72.7	69.7
减少(%)	Decrease(%)	6.1	18.2	9.1	15.2
固定资产投资(下季度比本季度)	Fixed Asset (Next Quarter than the Quarter)				
指数	Index	97.0	106.1	112.1	103.0
增加(%)	Increase(%)	6.1	12.1	18.2	9.1
持平(%)	Flat(%)	84.9	81.8	75.8	84.9
减少(%)	Decrease(%)	9.1	6.1	6.1	6.1

表 14－10 信息传输、计算机服务和软件业企业景气状况(2012)
Prosperity Index of Information Transmission, Computer Service and Software Enterprises

单位:点(point)

指标	Indicators	一季度 1st. Quarter	二季度 2st. Quarter	三季度 3st. Quarter	四季度 4st. Quarter
企业景气指数	Prosperity Index of Enterprises				
总指数	Combined Index	158.8	146.1	141.8	130.9
即期	Demand	151.5	142.4	136.4	145.5
预期	Expectation	163.6	148.5	145.5	121.2
企业家信心指数	Index of Confidence by Enterprisers				
总指数	Combined Index	149.7	132.7	141.2	129.7
即期	Demand	151.5	145.5	139.4	133.3
预期	Expectation	148.5	124.2	142.4	127.3
产品订货	Products Order				
指数	Index	100.0	93.9	106.1	115.2
较多(%)	More(%)	27.3	21.2	18.2	36.4
一般(%)	Flat(%)	45.5	51.5	69.7	42.4
较少(%)	Less(%)	27.3	27.3	12.1	21.2
营业收入(比去年同期)	Business Income(year－on－year)				
指数	Index	115.2	93.9	124.2	130.3
增加(%)	Increase(%)	39.4	33.3	48.5	51.5
持平(%)	Flat(%)	36.4	27.3	27.3	27.3
减少(%)	Decrease(%)	24.2	39.4	24.2	21.2
盈利(亏损)变化	Changes of Profit(Loss)				
指数	Index	90.9	90.9	87.9	90.9
好于正常水平(%)	Better than Normal Level(%)	9.1	6.1	6.1	15.2
正常水平(%)	Normal Level(%)	72.7	78.8	75.8	60.6
差于正常水平(%)	Worse than Normal Level(%)	18.2	15.2	18.2	24.2
企业融资	Corporate Finance				
指数	Index	103.0	103.0	97.0	106.1
容易(%)	Easy(%)	18.2	15.2	12.1	18.2
一般(%)	General(%)	66.7	72.7	72.7	69.7
困难(%)	Difficulties(%)	15.2	12.1	15.2	12.1
用工计划(下季度比本季度)	Employment Plan (Next Quarter than the Quarter)				
指数	Index	142.4	130.3	118.2	124.2
增加(%)	Increase(%)	48.5	36.4	24.2	27.3
持平(%)	Flat(%)	45.5	57.6	69.7	69.7
减少(%)	Decrease(%)	6.1	6.1	6.1	3.0
固定资产投资(下季度比本季度)	Fixed Asset (Next Quarter than the Quarter)				
指数	Index	127.3	109.1	121.2	103.0
增加(%)	Increase(%)	33.3	21.2	33.3	21.2
持平(%)	Flat(%)	60.6	66.7	54.6	60.6
减少(%)	Decrease(%)	6.1	12.1	12.1	18.2

表 14－11 部分年份企业家信心指数 Index of Confidence on Macro Economy of Enterprisers in Recent Years

单位：点(point)

年份 year	一季度 1st. Quarter	二季度 2st. Quarter	三季度 3st. Quarter	四季度 4st. Quarter
1999	113.1	109.8	108.2	110.7
2000	131.5	133.7	127.3	133.2
2001	142.2	135.6	133.0	120.9
2002	136.5	138.0	146.0	145.1
2003	145.4	133.7	149.8	148.9
2004	148.3	141.1	139.7	133.4
2005	137.1	132.2	130.4	132.0
2006	138.3	130.7	132.8	139.4
2007	139.0	140.5	137.8	137.1
2008	123.4	109.6	106.7	88.8
2009	89.1	104.6	115.1	123.4
2010	137.3	135.0	138.2	140.1
2011	132.6	126.1	126.1	111.1
2012 指数	118.8	115.6	110.1	117.9
2012 即期	114.1	114.9	109.8	117.7
2012 预期	121.9	116.1	110.3	118.0

表 14－12 部分年份企业景气指数 Prosperity Index of Enterprises in Recent Years

单位：点(point)

年份 year	一季度 1st. Quarter	二季度 2st. Quarter	三季度 3st. Quarter	四季度 4st. Quarter
1999	124.5	119.3	117.3	118.2
2000	122.7	131.8	126.7	125.8
2001	12.9	128.1	124.5	127.3
2002	134.2	144.5	143.1	147.9
2003	144.3	131.8	140.7	153.4
2004	148.7	140.2	138.1	144.4
2005	136.5	135.3	136.1	143.8
2006	130.7	134.6	139.8	146.5
2007	136.9	145.8	137.0	137.5
2008	119.9	122.2	108.1	102.1
2009	98.4	114.1	124.5	126.4
2010	137.9	142.6	140.8	146.3
2011	135.5	134.1	133.8	132.8
2012 指数	126.5	126.0	120.6	123.7
2012 即期	117.0	123.9	116.3	125.9
2012 预期	132.8	127.4	123.5	122.1

主要统计指标解释

【企业家信心指数】 也称宏观经济景气指数。是根据企业决策者对企业外部市场经济环境与宏观政策的认识、看法、判断与预期(对"乐观"、"一般"、"不乐观"的选择)而编制的指数,反映企业决策者对国家宏观经济发展的信心和预期,是企业决策者对当前宏观经济状况及未来走势的一种感受、体验与期望。

【企业景气指数】 也称企业综合生产经营景气指数。是根据企业决策者对本企业当前生产经营情况的判断及未来企业生产经营状况的预期(对"良好"、"一般"、"不佳"的选择)而编制的指数,是企业决策者对企业生产经营现状及未来景气动向的一种综合评价和判断。

【景气指数】 又称景气度,是对企业景气调查中定性指标的定量描述,以直观地反映经济所处的状态。景气指数采用纯正数形式表示,以 100 为临界值,取值范围在 0－200 之间。当景气指数大于 100 点时,表明经济状况趋于上升或改善,处于景气状态;当景气指数小于 100 点时,表明经济状况趋于下降或恶化,处于不景气状态。

2012 年之后改变计算方法:

1. 计算方法改进说明:为更充分体现企业景气调查对经济形势的预判功能,从 2012 年一季度开始,企业景气指数的计算方法,改进为对当前形势的判断和对未来预期的综合,并赋予预期相对更高的权重。

2、指数计算方法:企业景气指数＝0.4×即期企业景气指数＋0.6×预期企业景气指数;即期企业景气指数＝企业负责人对本季度本企业综合经营状况回答良好比重－回答不佳的比重＋100;预期企业景气指数＝企业负责人对预计下季度本企业综合经营状况回答良好比重－回答不佳的比重＋100。

Explanatory Notes on Main Statistical Indicators

【Entrepreneur Confidence Index】 As well as Macroeconomic Business Cycle Index, which is indexed according to the entrepreneurs' opinions, consideration, estimations and expectations (choice of "optimistic", "general" and "miserable") on outer economic environment and macroeconomic policies, to reflect general confidence about the macroeconomic environment of entrepreneurs of the business deciders, and also to reflect the situation and trend of the macroeconomics. **【Enterprise Business Prosperity Index】** As well as Enterprise General Production and Management Business Cycle Index, which is indexed according to estimations and expectations (choice of "good", "general" and "bad") of general management of products at present and in the future, to reflect the enterprisers' evaluation and judgement of the production and management status comprehensively. **【The range of Business Prosperity Index is between 0－200】** As well as Booming Index, which uses the positive to reflect the status of economy directly. 100 is the critical value of Business Cycle Index (ranges from 0 to 200) which shows unobvious change of business cycle. 100－200 is the prosperous space interval, which shows ascending and improving economic status, closer to 200 more prosperous. 0－100 is the unprosperous space interval, which shows descending and deteriorating economic status, closer to 0 more unprosperous.

中国统计出版社最新图书简目

(仅供参考,以最后出书为准)

统计资料

中国统计年鉴-2013
2013 中国发展报告
中国劳动统计年鉴-2013
中国建筑业统计年鉴-2013
中国商品交易市场统计年鉴-2013
中国民政统计年鉴-2013
中国科技统计年鉴-2013
中国高技术产业统计年鉴-2013
全国农产品成本收益资料汇编-2013
大中型批发零售和住宿餐饮企业统计年鉴-2013
第二次全国 R&D 资源清查资料汇编-工业企业卷
第二次全国 R&D 资源清查资料汇编-综合卷
中国统计摘要-2013
中国第三产业统计年鉴-2013
中国社会统计年鉴-2013
中国人口和就业统计年鉴-2013
中国房地产统计年鉴-2013
中国贸易外经统计年鉴-2013
中国农村统计年鉴-2013
中国教育经费统计年鉴-2013
中国科学技术协会统计年鉴-2013
中国住户调查年鉴-2013
中国县域统计年鉴-2013
中国人才资源统计报告-2011
中国民族统计年鉴-2013
国际统计年鉴-2013
中国区域经济统计年鉴-2013
中国城市统计年鉴-2013
中国工业经济统计年鉴-2013
中国能源统计年鉴-2013
2013 中国地区经济监测报告
中国农产品价格调查年鉴-2013
中国农村贫困监测报告-2013
工业企业科技活动资料-2013
中国价格统计年鉴-2013
中国农村全面建设小康监测报告-2013
中国零售和餐饮连锁企业统计年鉴-2013
2010 年中国第六次人口普查公报

2013 年省级综合统计年鉴系列

北京 天津 河北 山西 内蒙古 辽宁 吉林 黑龙江 上海 江苏 浙江 安徽 福建 江西 山东
河南 湖北 湖南 广东 广西 海南 重庆 四川 贵州 云南 西藏 陕西 甘肃 青海 宁夏
新疆 新疆生产建设兵团

2013 年市(县)级综合统计年鉴系列

天津滨海新区 石家庄 唐山 邯郸 太原 大同 长治 阳泉 晋城 朔州 晋中
运城 忻州 临汾 呼和浩特 包头 通辽 沈阳 大连 长春 吉林市 四平 哈尔滨 黑龙江垦区
上海浦东新区 南京 苏州 无锡 常州 徐州 南通 盐城 镇江 宿迁 泰州 连云港 江阴 丹阳
杭州 宁波 绍兴 台州 温州 金华 嘉兴 衢州 舟山 福州 福州经济技术开发区
厦门经济特区 宁德 南昌 上饶 济南 青岛 潍坊 郑州 洛阳 三门峡 南阳 武汉 宜昌
十堰 荆州 咸宁 长沙 广州 东莞 惠州 深圳 桂林 南宁 柳州 来宾 河池 海口 成都 绵阳
贵阳 昆明 庆阳 西安 兰州 银川 乌鲁木齐

2010 年人口普查资料系列

中国 2010 年人口普查资料 北京 天津 河北 山西 内蒙古 辽宁 吉林 黑龙江 上海 江苏
浙江 安徽 福建 江西 山东 河南 湖北 湖南 广东 广西 海南 重庆 四川 贵州 云南
西藏 陕西 甘肃 青海 宁夏 新疆 新疆生产建设兵团 河南省各市 2010 年人口普查资料丛书
中国分县 2010 年人口普查资料
中国分乡镇、街道 2010 年人口普查资料
中国分民族 2010 年人口普查资料

"十一五"规划教材

统计学("十二五"规划,黄良文)
抽样调查理论与实践("十二五"规划,冯士雍)
统计学("十二五"规划,单微)
试验设计("十二五"规划,茆诗松)
贝叶斯统计("十二五"规划,茆诗松)
统计学:从数据到结论(十二五规划,吴喜之)
医学统计学(陆守曾)
非参数统计(吴喜之)
概率论与数理统计(茆诗松)
现代金融投资统计分析(李腊生)
多元统计分析(任雪松)
应用时间序列分析(王振龙)
统计指数理论及应用(徐国祥)
经济计量学教程(贺铿)
质量管理统计方法 (茆诗松)
统计实验系列教材(许涤龙)
社会统计学(蒋萍)
市场调查与预测(蒋志华)
统计学原理(非统计专业用,朱胜)
国民经济核算教程(杨灿)
概率论与数理统计(经济、管理类专业使用,朱胜)

重点图书

挑大学选专业 2013—高考志愿填报指南
挑大学选专业 2013—考研择校指南

中国统计出版社发行部电话:(010)63376907,63376908 同模行书店电话:68783171,68783172
通讯地址:北京市西城区三里河月坛南街 57 号 邮政编码:100826
网址:http://csp.stats.gov.cn